MEDIEVAL ENGLISH VERSE AND PROSE

Medieval English Verse

and Prose

IN MODERNIZED VERSIONS

by

Roger Sherman Loomis

Professor of English
Columbia University

and

Rudolph Willard

Professor of English
University of Texas

APPLETON-CENTURY-CROFTS, Inc.

New York

MANUFACTURED IN THE UNITED STATES OF AMERICA

E-57569

TO

Laura Hibbard Loomis

Preface

I~n~ the opinion of the editors of this book no representative anthology of English verse and prose between 1100 and 1500 has hitherto been available either for the student or the lover of *belles lettres*. There have been readers for the purpose of linguistic study, collections limited to particular periods, samples of verse in somewhat mediocre and inaccurate translation, and good modernized renderings of particular authors such as Chaucer, Langland, Rolle, and Dame Julian of Norwich. But no single book known to us has exhibited the range and the richness of English and Scottish literature in the period from the Norman Conquest to the Renaissance.

The present anthology is an attempt to meet this need. We have had the good fortune to include certain masterpieces of translation such as Wordsworth's version of *The Cuckoo and the Nightingale*, Sophie Jewett's version of *The Pearl*, and Professor Banks' version of *Gawain and the Green Knight;* and some friends and colleagues have generously contributed felicitous renderings of other pieces. Most of the poems reproduce the form, whether alliterative or rimed, of the original; but Mr. Hunt and Sir Theodore Martin in their translations of *Sir Orfeo* and *The Debate of the Body and the Soul* have changed the rime pattern, and *Abraham and Isaac*, as well as the passages from *Havelok*, Mannyng, Barbour, *The Pilgrims at Canterbury*, Hoccleve, and Lydgate, have been turned into prose,—it is hoped without much loss.

We have aimed to provide accurate renderings, intelligible to the contemporary reader, and at least inoffensive to his ear; we have tried (not always with success) to avoid obsolete words and unnatural accents, such as are found in some modernizations. Deliberately, however, we have admitted obsolete words in two situations. If the reader is to feel the quality of Purvey's translation of the New Testament by comparing it with that of 1611, he must have Purvey's own words, not their modern equivalents. Moreover, the English vocabulary of the second half of the fifteenth century is intelligible enough so that we have merely modernized the spelling of Caxton, Malory, *Everyman*, and *The Nut-Brown Maid*, the few obsolete words being glossed in the footnotes.

Any collection will have its shortcomings, and this one is not exempt. Some readers may be surprised at the omission of Chaucer. But many, who would be baffled by the Middle English of Layamon or Henryson,

Preface

are quite capable of reading Chaucer in the original, and others can turn to the superb modernizations of his work, particularly Krapp's version of *Troilus*. The fifteenth-century ballads, too, are easy to read and easy to procure, so that we have limited ourselves to two examples: *St. Stephen and Herod, Robin Hood and the Monk*. We should have liked to include *The Fox and the Wolf, The Tournament of Totenham, Rauf Coilyear, Gamelyn*, extracts from the Troy and Alexander romances, and a fuller representation of Gower, Lydgate, and Henryson. But either from inadequacy to the task or from exigencies of space, we have had to rest content with the selections which follow.

At the end of the book will be found notes on each of the pieces, containing a few essential facts and bibliographical references.

We are indebted to Professor Albert Baugh for enabling us to give references to his recently published *Literary History of England* from the proofsheets. We wish to record our gratitude to Dr. Muriel Bowden, Professor Mabel Van Duzee and Mrs. Laura Hibbard Loomis for making translations for this book; to Mr. Edward Eyre Hunt and Professor Marshall Stearns for allowing us to reprint their work; to Colonel W. Butler-Bowdon and the Early English Text Society for permission to modernize extracts from *The Book of Margery Kempe;* and to Methuen and Co., Thomas Y. Crowell & Co., Constable and Co., and Sheed and Ward, Inc. for permission to use copyright material.

ROGER SHERMAN LOOMIS
Columbia University
RUDOLPH WILLARD
University of Texas

Contents

[ix]

Contents

Contents

Contents

LATE TWELFTH AND EARLY
THIRTEENTH CENTURY

The Brut

Layamon

THE PROLOG

(VSS. 1–67)

There was a priest in the land;   Layamon was he called.
He was Leovenath's son;   the Lord be gracious to him;
He dwelt at Ernley,[1]   at a noble church,
Upon Severn shore,—good there he thought it,—
Quite near to Redstone;   he read there his service book.[2]
   It came to his mind   and into his serious thought,
To relate of the English   their noble deeds,
What they were called,   and whence they had come,
Who first did possess   the land of the English,
After the flood,   which came from the Lord,   10
And did destroy all things   that it found alive,
Except Noah and Shem,   Japhet and Ham,
And their four wives   who were with them in the ark.
Layamon did travel   widely among the people,
And got him those noble books   that he set as his pattern.
He took that English book   that Saint Bede had made;
Another he took, in Latin,   that Saint Albin had made
And the fair Augustine,   who brought baptism hither;
A third book he took,   and laid it alongside,
Which a French cleric had made,   well learned in lore;   20
Wace was his name,[3]   he knew well how to write,
And he then did give it   to the noble Eleanor,
Who was Henry's queen,   that high king's.

---

[1] Now Arley or Areley, north of Worcester.
[2] He read the divine office.
[3] Wace, a Norman cleric, wrote a free translation, in rimed couplets, of Geoffrey of Monmouth's fraudulent *History of the Kings of Britain* (ca. 1136). He dedicated it in 1155 to Eleanor of Aquitaine, who, divorced from the King of France, married the Count of Anjou, destined to rule England as Henry II, 1154-89. Wace's poem was actually the only one of these sources mentioned which Layamon used.

Layamon laid these books out,   and he turned the leaves;
With love he searched them,   the Lord be to him gracious.
He took feathers in his fingers,   and he composed on parchment;
And these most true words   he set then together,
And these three books   he condensed into one.
   Now Layamon prayeth   each noble man,
For the love of Almighty God   and of his gracious heart,   30
Who will read these books   and learn these runes,
That some true words   he will say together
For his father's soul,   who did beget him,
And for his mother's soul,   who bore him as man,
And for his own soul,   that it be the better for them. Amen.

THE PROPHECY OF DIANA

(vss. 1097–1252)

Brutus [4] took Ignogen   and upon the ship led her.
They righted their sails,   they raised their masts,
They wound up the sails;   the wind stood at their will.
Sixteen times twenty ships   took out from the haven,
And four ships, great ones,   that were ground-laden   40
With the very best weapons   that Brutus had then.
They hastened from the strand   out of the Greek land;
They went out on the wide sea;   the wild men were tamed.
Two days and two nights   in the sea were they;
The next day they came sailing   at evening to land.
That island was called Logice; [5]   no people were there,
Neither men nor women,   but waste paths only.
Outlaws had robbed that land,   and all the folk slain,
And so was it all waste   and void of dwellings.
But so many wild beasts were there   that it seemed a wonder to them,   50
And the Trojan men   took after those deer,
And did with those wild things   all of their will;
To the ships they carried   as much as they would.
   They found in that island   a very strong city,
But tottering were the walls,   waste were the halls.
A single temple they found there,   made all out of marble stone,

[4] A figure whose role as the fabulous founder of Britain is largely due to Geoffrey of
Monmouth's invention. He was supposed to be the great-grandson of Aeneas. Being
exiled to Greece, he raised an insurrection among the Trojan captives and their descendants and, equipping a fleet, put out with his people to sea.
[5] Unidentified.

A great one and glorious;   the Worse [6] did rule it.
Therein was a statue   in woman's likeness,
Fair it was and very tall;   in a heathenish name
Diana she was called;   the devil did love her.   60
She was queen of all woodlands   that waxed upon earth;
   In the heathen laws   she was held a great god.
To her would betake them   the wonder-crafty men;
Of things that were to come   she would inform them,
With tokens and with dreams   when they were asleep.
At one time on that island   there were folk dwelling,
Who gave worship to that image;   the devil received it.
   Brutus heard it said   through his seamen,
Who were earlier in that island   and knew of those laws;
Brutus took twelve wizards,   who were of his wisest,   70
And a priest of his laws,   which prevailed in heathen days;
That priest was called Gerion;   he was high in the court.
He went to that place   wherein stood Diana.
Brutus went into that temple,   and the twelve with him,
And he let all his folk   remain there outside.
A dish he bore in his hand,   it was all of red gold;
Milk was in that dish,   and some wine as well;
The milk was from a white hind   that Brutus shot with his own hand.
He made at the altar   a most fair fire;
Nine times that altar   he circled for his needs;   80
He cried out to that lady;   she was dear to his heart;
With gracious words   he besought her power.
Often he kissed that altar   with reverent looks;
He poured that milk in the fire   with devout words;
"Lady Diana, dear Diana,   mighty Diana, help me at need.
Teach me and guide me   through thy wise skill
Whither I may betake me   and guide my people,
To a pleasant land,   where I may dwell.
And if that land I gain me,   and my folk overrun it,
I will erect in thy name   a noble temple,   90
And I will obey thee   with reverent worship."
Thus spoke Brutus.
Then he took the hide   that came from that hind;
Before the altar he spread it,   as if he would lie on a bed;
He kneeled there upon it,   and then he lay down;
So he began to slumber   and after to sleep.
Then it seemed in his dream,   as he lay there asleep,

[6] The Devil.

That his lady Diana   beheld him tenderly
With winsome laughter;   fair she did promise him,
And her hand she graciously   laid on his head,   100
And thus she said to him,   as he lay there asleep:
"Beyond France, in the west,   thou shalt find a fair land;
That land is surrounded by the sea;   therein shalt thou be happy.
There is fowl, there is fish;   there dwell the fair deer;
There is wood, there is water;   there is great wilderness.
Lovely is that land,   fair springs abound there;
There dwell in that land   very strong giants.
Albion is that land called,   but it hath no people.
Thither shalt thou go,   and a new Troy make there;
There shall of thy kindred   kingly sons arise,   110
And thy illustrious kin   shall wield this land,
Throughout the world be exalted;   and thou be hale and sound."

THE BUILDING OF LONDON

(vss. 1985–2060)

Brutus held Britain,   and Corineus, Cornwall.
Brutus took all his friends,   who came in his forces;
Nigh him he settled them,   for they were dear to him.
Corineus then called to him   all his chosen ones;
All of them he settled   where it most pleased them.
Waxed that folk, and well did thrive,   for each had his wish;
Within few years' time   was that folk so many
That there was no end   of people most gracious.   120
Brutus took thought,   and looked over his people;
He beheld the mountains   fair and lofty;
He beheld the meadows   that were full spacious;
He beheld the waters   and the wild deer;
He beheld the fishes;   beheld the fowls;
Beheld the leas   and those lovely woods;
He beheld the wood, how it bloomed;   beheld the corn, how it grew;
He surveyed all in that land   that was dear to his heart.
Then thought he of Troy-town,   where his kin suffered sorrow,
And he went throughout this land,   and looked at the country;   130
He found a pleasant place   upon a water stream;
There he did raise up   a very rich borough,
With bowers and with halls,   and with high stone walls.
When that city was made,   it was most glorious.

The city was very well built,   and he set a name on her;
He gave her a glorious name,   Troy the New,
To remind his kindred   whence they were come.
Since then the people,   a long time after,
Gave up that name,   and Trinovant named it.
Within a few winters   it befell after,   140
There arose from Brutus' kin   one who was a high king,
Lud was he called;   he loved that city greatly;
He had it named Lud   throughout his folk,
Had it called Kaerlud,   after that king.
Since then came a second glory   and a new meaning,
That men called it Lundin   throughout all that people.
Since then came English men   and called it Lundene;
Then came in the French—who with a fight did win it—
With their native customs,   and Lundres they named it.

LEIR AND HIS DAUGHTERS [7]

(vss. 2902–3778)

Bladud had one son,   Leir was he called;   150
After his father's day   he held this noble land
Altogether in his lifetime   sixty winters.
He made him a rich city   through his wise skill,
And he had it named   after himself:
Kaerleir was that city called,   dear was it to the king,
Which we in our own tongue   now do call Leirchester.[8]
Already in the old days   it was a very fine city,
But later there befell it   a very great sorrow,
That it was completely ruined   through the fall of its people.
Sixty winters had Leir   this whole land to rule.   160
The king had three daughters   by his royal queen.
He did not have a son,—for which he was sorrowful,—
To maintain his honor;   only these three daughters.
The eldest was called Gornoille,   the second Regau, the third Cordoille;
She was the youngest,   the fairest of face;
She was as lief to her father   as his own life.
Now the king grew old   and weakened in deeds,
And he bethought him   what he might do
For his kingdom   after his day.

---

[7] The story of Leir is in all probability a pure fabrication of Geoffrey's.
[8] Leicester.

[7]

He said to himself   what turned out to be evil: 170
"I will divide up my kingdom   among all my daughters,
And give them my royal people,   and apportion it to my children.
But first will I find out   which may be my best friend,
And she shall have the best share   of my royal land."
Thus the king thought,   and accordingly he wrought.
He called then Gornoille,   his goodly daughter,
Out of her bower   to her dear father;
And thus spake the old king,   where he sat in state:
"Tell me, Gornoille,   in truthful words;
Very dear art thou to me;   how dear am I to thee?   180
How much worth settest thou on me,   to wield my kingdom?"
Gornoille was right wily,   as are women everywhere,
And she spake a false thing   to her father the king.
"Beloved father dear,   as I hope for God's mercy,
So help me Apollin,   for all my faith is in him,
That dearer thou art to me, e'en,   than this world all clean.
And I tell thee furthermore,   thou art dearer than my life.
And I tell thee this in truth;   thou may'st believe me enough."
And this answer he gave,   he who was the old king:
"To thee, Gornoille, I declare,   beloved daughter dear,   190
Good shall be thy meed   for they good words.
I am, because of my age,   greatly enfeebled.
If thou lovest me greatly,   more than all that is alive,
I will divide my royal land   wholly in three.
Thine is the best share;   thou art my daughter dear,
And shalt have as husband   the best of all my thanes
That I may find   in my royal domain."
   Afterwards spoke the old king   with his second daughter:
"Dear daughter Regau,   what sayest thou after this plan?
Tell me, before my warriors,   how dear I am to thee in heart."   200
Then answered Regau   with prudent words:
"To me all that is alive   is not nearly so dear
As is a single limb of thine,   not even my life."
But she said nothing true,   no more than her sister,
And all her lying   her father believed.
Then answered the king—his daughter had pleased him:
"The third part of my land   I commit to thy hand.
Thou shalt take a husband   where it most pleases thee."
   Even yet would not the folk-king   forsake his folly;
He bade come before him   his daughter Cordoille.   210
She was the youngest of all,   and truly the quickest-witted,

[8]

And the king loved her more   than both the two others.
Cordoille heard that lying   which her sisters told the king.
She made up her honest mind   that she would not lie;
She would tell her father the truth,   were him lief, were him loath.
Then spoke the old king—unwisdom followed him:
"To hear is my will   from thee, Cordoille,
So help thee Apollin,   how dear is this life of mine."
Then answered Cordoille,   loud and no wise still,
With joking and laughter,   to her dear father: 220
"Thou art dear to me as my father,   and I to thee as thy daughter.
I have towards thee true love,   for we are very close kin;
And, as I look for salvation,   I will tell thee more:
Just so much art thou worth   as thou art powerful.
And as much as thou hast   men will love thee;
For soon will be loathed   the man who hath little."
Thus said that maiden Cordoille,   and then sat very still.
  Then the king grew angry,   for he was not pleased,
And he weened in his thought   that it was for discourtesy
That to her he was so worthless   that she would not praise him,   230
As did her two sisters,   who had both told lies.
The king turned very black   as if he had become a black cloth;
His skin and his hue changed,   for he was deeply hurt.
In his wrath he was so stunned   he fell in a swoon.
But at last he sprang up;   the maiden was afraid.
Wholly then out it broke;   it was evil that he spoke:
"Harken, Cordoille;   I will tell thee my will.
Of my daughters thou wert dearest;   now of all thou art loathest.
Nor shalt thou ever hold   a bit of my land.
But to my two daughters   I will divide my kingdom;   240
And thou shalt become a pauper   and dwell in misery.
For never did I suppose   that thou wouldst thus shame me;
Therefore, thou shalt be dead, I ween;   flee from my eye-sight.
Thy sisters shall have my royal domain;   and this to me is pleasing.
The duke of Cornwall   shall have Gornoille,
And the Scottish king   Regau the fair.
And I give them all the wealth   that I am lord over."
And the old king did everything   as he had decreed.
  Oft woe was that maiden,   and never more than then;
Woe was in her heart   because of her father's wrath.   250
She turned to her bower,   where she sat often in sorrow,
Because she would not lie   to her dear father.
That maiden was greatly ashamed   since her father shunned her.

She chose the best course   and abode in her bower,
And there she suffered grief of mind   and mourned greatly,
And thus for a while   it stood in this fashion.
    In France there was a king,   rich and very keen;
Aganippus was he called,   he was the prince of heroes.
He was a young king,   but queen had he none.
He sent his messenger   into this land,   260
To Leir the king,   and affectionately greeted him.
He begged him to do his will,   to give him Cordoille,
And he would hold her   high as a queen,
And then do promptly what to her   will be dearest of all.
For there had travelers   spoken of that maiden,
Of her fairness and courtesy,   before the French king,
Of her very great beauty,   and of her great dignity—
How she was patient,   and of her fair virtues—
That there was in King Leir's land   no woman so gracious.
And the king Aganippus   greeted Leir the king thus: 270
King Leir bethought him,   what he might do.
He had a letter written,   and well did he endite it,
And he sent it by his messenger   into the French land.
Thus spake the king's writ;   widely was it made known:
"The King of Britain,   who is called Leir,
Greeteth Aganippus,   the prince of France:
Worship mayst thou have   of thy good offices,
And of thy fair message,   that thou did'st send me.
But I would have thee wit   herewith by my writ,
That my royal land   I have divided in two,   280
And given it to my daughters,   who are very dear to me.
A daughter I have, a third;   but I care not whether she live;
For she hath derided me,   and she hath held me for base;
And for my old age   she hath dishonored me.
She made me very wroth: the worse shall befall her.
Of all of my land,   and of all of my people,
That ever I obtained,   or yet may obtain,
I tell thee the right truth,   she shall never have aught.
But if thou wilt have her—as a maid she is gracious—
I will take charge of her for thee,   and send her on a ship,   290
With her clothes only: of me shall she have no more.
If thou wilt receive her,   all this will I do.
I have told thee the ground.   Be thou hale and sound!"
This writ came to France,   to that free king.
He let it be read;   dear to him were the runes.

[10]

Then supposed the king   that it was for deceit
That Leir the king, her father,   would dismiss her from him.
And he much the more madly   desired that maiden.
And said to his nobles,   he who was the anxious king:
"I am a man rich enough,   and care not for more.   300
Never shall Leir the king   withhold that maiden from me,
But I will have her   as my high queen.
Let her father have all his land,   all his silver and his gold;
No treasure do I ask,—I have enough myself,—
Except that maiden Cordoille;   then will I have my will."
With writ and with word   he sent again to this land,
And asked Leir the King   to send his daughter who was gracious,
And he would do well,   with much worship receive her.
Then took the old king   this noble maiden,
With her clothes only,   and let her go gladly   310
Over the sea-streams;   her father was stern to her.
    Aganippus, the French king,   received this maiden child;
To all his folk it was pleasing,   and they made her queen.
And thus she remained there,   dear was she to the people.
    And Leir the king, her father,   lived in this country,
And had given his two daughters   all his royal land.
He gave Gornoille, the young,   to Scotland's king
(He was called Maglaunus,   his wealth was great);
To Cornwall's duke   he gave Regau his daughter.
    Then befell it later,   shortly thereafter,   320
That the Scottish king   and the duke spoke together:
With their secret rune   they betook them to counsel,
That they would own all this land   in their own hand,
And feed Leir the King,   the while that he lived,
Days and nights,   with forty knights of his household;
And they would provide him   with hawks and hounds,
That he might ride about   among all the people,
And live in bliss   while he was alive.
Thus they spoke   and afterwards it broke.
And King Leir did it please,   and for him after was it the worse.   330
And Leir did journey   to the Scottish people,
With Maglaunus his son-in-law,   and with the elder daughter.
They received the king   with very great fairness,
And did furnish him well   with forty retainers,
With horses and with hounds,   with all that behoved him.
    Then befell it later,   shortly thereafter,
That Gornoille bethought her   what she might do.

She thought very grievously   of her royal father,
And she began to moan of it   to Maglaunus her lord,
And she told him in bed,   as they lay together: 34
"Tell me, my lord;   of men thou art dearest to me,
It seemeth that my father   is not at all clever;
He doth not know dignity;   he hath lost his wits.
I think that the old man   will be doting forthwith.
He holdeth here forty knights,   by days and by nights;
He hath here these thanes   and all of their swains,
Both hounds and hawks,   from which we suffer harm.
And ever do they spend,   and nowhere do they mend.
All the good that we do them,   they blithely accept,
And show us but ingratitude   for all our good deeds;   350
They show us much scorn;   our men they beat.
My father hath too many   of these idle fellows.
A whole fourth part   let us dismiss quickly;
Enough he hath in thirty   to throng to the board.
We ourselves have cooks   to run to the kitchen,
And we have dish-bearers   and cup-bearers a plenty;
Let some of this great company   go where they will.
As I look ever for salvation,   I will bear it no more."
This heard then Maglaunús,   that his queen discoursed thus;
And he answered her   with a lordly speech: 360
"My lady, thou art very wrong;   hast thou not kingdom enough?
Just keep your father in joy;   he will not live very long.
For, if faraway kings   heard those tidings,
That we so dealt with him,   they would blame us.
But let us let him wield   his folk at his will;
And this is my advice,   for he will be dead soon hereafter.
And also we have in our hand   the good half of his royal land."
   Then said Gornoille,   "My lord, keep thou still.
Let me entirely be,   and I will manage him."
She sent with guile   to the lodgings of the knights;   370
She bade them go their way,   for she would feed them no longer—
Many of those thanes,   many of those swains,
Who had come thither   with Leir the king.
This Leir heard at once;   thereof was he very wroth.
Then spoke forth the old king,   sorrowful in heart:
"Woe worth the man   who owneth land with honor,
And committeth it to his child   the while he may wield it;
For it befalleth often   that later he rueth it.
I will now fare hence   forthwith to Cornwall.

I will seek counsel   of Regau my daughter,   380
Who had Hemeri the duke   and my royal land."
   Forth the king did wend   to the land's southern end,
To Regau his daughter;   for reason failed him.
When he came to Cornwall   he was received fairly,
And all that half year   with his men he stayed there.
Then said Regau his daughter   to her duke Hemeri:
"My lord, harken thou to me;   truly I declare to thee,
We have done folly   in receiving my father,
With thirty knights;   not at all doth it please me.
Let us do away twenty;   a ten will be plenty;   390
They only drink and eat,   and no good do they do."
Then said Hemeri the duke,   who betrayed his old father:
"As I am alive,   he shall have but five;
He would have retinue enough,   for they never do anything.
And, if he will fare hence,   let us hasten him forth at once."
   They accomplished everything,   just as they had spoken;
They took away his retainers   and all his royal folk;
They would not leave him   knights more than five.
This saw Leir the king: woe was him to be alive.
His mood began to be troubled,   and he mourned greatly,   400
And he spoke these words   with sorrowful countenance:
"Alas, O wealth, alas!   how thou betrayest many a man!
When they trust thee most of all,   then thou betrayest them.
It is not long ago,   not fully two years,
That I was a rich king,   and had all my knights.
Now I have come to endure   that I sit quite bare,
Bereaved of delights.   Woe is me that I live!
I was with Gornoille,   my goodly daughter,
Dwelt in her country   with thirty knights.
There might I yet live,   but thence I departed.   410
I meant to do better,   but worse I have received.
I will go again to Scotland,   to the fair one, my daughter,
To ask for her mercy,   which she will not refuse me,
To ask her to receive me   with my five knights.
There will I dwell   and endure these woes
A little while,   for I shall not live long."
   Leir the king went forth   to his daughter in the north;
She, for fully three nights,   harbored him and his knights;
She swore on the fourth day,   by all heavenly powers,
That he should have no more   than a single knight there.   420
And if he would not,   he might fare where he would.

Well oft was Leir woe,   and never more than then.
Then said the old king—sad was he in heart:
"Alas, death! alas, death!   that thou wilt not condemn me.
Cordoille spoke the truth,   which is now known to me,
My youngest daughter,   she was very dear to me,
And afterwards became the loathest,   because she answered me the truest,
That he will be worthless and loathed,   the man that hath little,
And that I was never of more worth   than I had power.
Too truly spoke the young woman;   much wisdom followeth her.   430
While I had my royal land,   my people loved me;
For my land and my fee,   my earls fell at my knee.
Now am I a poor man,   for there loveth me no man.
But my daughter told the truth;   now I believe her well enough.
And both her two sisters   told me falsehoods,
That I was so dear to them,   dearer than their own life;
But Cordoille, my daughter,   said what was dutiful,
That she loved me as fairly   as one should his father.
What more would I ask   of my dear daughter?
Now will I go forth,   and hasten over sea,   440
And hear from Cordoille,   what may be her will;
Her true words I did blame,   for which I now have much shame;
For I must now beseech   what I once forsook.
She will not do me worse   than forbid me her country."
    Leir fared then to sea   with but a single swain,
Into a ship did he come;   there knew him no man.
They sailed over sea,   they soon reached the harbor;
Forth went the king Leir;   he had but one companion.
They asked after the queen,   that they might reach her in haste.
The people pointed out to them   where the land's queen abode.   450
Leir the king went into a field,   and rested him on the earth;
And his swain he sent forth—he was a courtly retainer—
To queen Cordoille;   and he told her very secretly:
"Hail to thee, fair Queen;   I am thy father's swain.
Thy father is come hither,   for all his land is taken from him;
Both of thy sisters   are forsworn towards him.
He cometh in great need   into this country.
Help now with thy might   thy father, as is right."
The queen Cordoille   sat long very still;
She turned red on her bench   as though from a wine-draught.   460
And the swain sat at her feet;   for him was it forthwith the better.
Then out it all broke;   it was good that she spoke:
"Apollin my lord, I thank thee,   that my father is come to me.

Dear tidings do I hear, that my father is alive.
Of me shall he have good counsel, unless I die sooner.
Tell me now, dear swain, and harken my instruction:
To thee will I commit a very rich wallet;
There's money in it, safe and sound; to wit, a hundred pound.
I will give thee a horse as good as the best,
To carry this gift to my dear father, 470
And tell him that I greet him with goodly greeting;
And bid him go quickly to a fair city;
And there find him shelter in some rich house;
And buy him first of all what he most wisheth,
Food and drink and precious clothes,
Hounds and hawks and handsome horses;
Let him hold in his house forty retainers,
Men of rank, and rich, with robes bemantled.
Let him get a good bed, and often bathe him,
And let him have blood let, little and often. 480
When thou wilt have more silver, seek it from myself,
And plenty will I send him from this very place.
Thus need he never speak of his old country,
To knight or swain, or ever to any thane.
When forty days are gone let him make known anon
To my dear husband that Leir is in his land,
Come over the sea-stream to behold his realm;
And let him send thus letters to my lord the king.
And I will pretend that as yet I knew naught of him,
And will haste to meet him with my husband, 490
And be glad of my father and his sudden arrival.
No man must ever know but that he is newly come.
Do thou take these moneys, and look that thou do well,
And, if thou thus spendest them, it shall be to thy good."
    And the swain took those goods and went to his lord,
To Leir the king, and told him this tiding,
Where he lay in the field and rested him on the earth.
At once became the old king joyfully exalted;
And these words he said with a true voice:
"After evil cometh good; well is him that may have it." 500
They went to a lofty city, as the queen commanded.
And they did everything there after her instruction.
When forth were passed the forty days,
Then took Leir the king his dearest knights,
And greeted Aganippus, who was his dear son-in-law.

And told him by his messenger   that he was come to his country,
To speak with his daughter,   who was so dear to him.
   Aganippus was happy   that Leir had come journeying.
He went to meet him   with all of his thanes,
And the queen Cordoille.   Then Leir had his wish.   510
They came together,   and often they kissed.
They turned towards the city;   joy was in their company.
There was the trumpets' song;   there were pipes besides.
Everywhere the halls   were behung with palls.
All the dining boards   were bristling with gold.
Rings all of gold   had each man on his hand.
With fiddles and harps   the courtiers there sang.
The king bade one go to the wall   and cry aloud over all,
And announce that King Leir   had now come to this land:
"Now biddeth Aganippus,   who is highest over us,   520
That ye to Leir the king   shall all be obedient;
And he shall be your lord   within this people,
Just as many a year   as he shall dwell here.
And Aganippus our king   shall be his underling.
And whoever would live,   to him peace must he give;
And if anyone will it break,   he shall punishment take.
Let each inform his liegemen   that they hold to the law."
Then answered the courtiers,   "Do it, we will,
Both loud and still,   all the king's will."
Throughout that same year,   so dwelt they all there,   530
In very great concord,   in very great peace.
   When this year was now gone,   then the king would fare home,
And journey to this land;   and he asked the king's leave.
The king Aganippus   answered him thus:
"Thou shalt never fare thither   without a great army.
But I will lend thee,   from my nation's people,
Five hundred ships   filled full of knights,
And all that behoveth them   to have on a voyage.
And thy daughter Cordoille,   who is this land's queen,
She with a great army   shall go along with thee,   540
And go to that land,   where thou art the people's king;
And if thou shouldst find anyone   who will withstand thee,
Deprive thee thy right   and thy royal kingdom,
Do thou bravely fight,   and fell them to the ground;
And clean out all that land,   and set it in Cordoille's hand,
That she may have it all   after thy days."

Those words spoke Aganippus,   and King Leir did thus;
And everything he wrought   as his friend had him taught.
To this land did he come   with his beloved daughter.
He protected in the best way   those who submitted to him,   550
And all them he felled   who against him rebelled.
And all this royal land   he re-won to his own hand,
And gave it to Cordoille,   who was the Frenchman's queen.
And for a long time   it stood in this wise.
Leir, king in the land,   three years did live;
Then came his end-day,   that the king lay dead.
Within Leirchester   his daughter did lay him,
In Janus's temple,   just as the book tells us.
     And Cordoille held this land   with her firm strength;
Fully five year   queen was she here.   560
While the French king   made a fated journey,
To Cordoille came the word   that she was made a widow.
Then these tidings came   to Scotland's king,
That Aganippus was dead,   Cordoille's lord.
He sent then across Britain,   into Cornwall,
And ordered that strong duke   to harry the south land,
And he would in the north   possess him the land.
For it was an exceeding shame,   as well as great grief,
That a queen should be   king of this country,
And their own sons be left out,   who were her betters,—   570
Those of the older sisters,   who should possess that dignity.
"No more will we suffer it!   All that land we will have!"
They began to make war,   wasted and ravaged,
And the queen's sisters' sons   summoned an army.
Their names were called thus: Morgan and Cunedagius.
Often they led armies,   often they fought;
Often they had the upper hand,   often the lower,
Until there came at last   what was dearest of all.
The Britons they slew,   Cordoille they captured.
They put her in prison   in a torture-house.   580
They stirred up their aunt   more than they should,
So that this woman was so wroth   that to herself she was loath.
She took a long knife   and reft herself of life.
That was an evil thought   that her death she wrought.

THE BIRTH OF ARTHUR

(vss. 19246–69)

There Uther the king   took Ygerne for queen.
Ygerne was with child   by Uther the king,
All through Merlin's wiles,   ere she was wedded.
The time came that was chosen;   then was Arthur born.
As soon as he came on earth   fays took him.[9]
They enchanted the child   with magic right strong: 590
They gave him the might   to be best of all knights;
They gave him another thing,   that he should be a mighty king;
They gave him a third,—his death would long be deferred.
They gave to that royal child   right good virtues,
That he was most liberal   of all living men.
This the fays gave him,   and thus the child thrived.

THE BATTLE OF BATH [10]

(vss. 21111–456)

There came tidings   to Arthur the king,
That his kinsman Howell   lay sick at Clud.[11]
Therefor he was sorry,   but there he left him.
With very great haste   he hied him forth   600
Until beside Bath   he came to a field.
There he alighted   and all his knights,
And the doughty warriors   donned their byrnies,
And he in five parts   divided his army.
When he had arrayed all,   and all seemed ready,
He did on his byrny,   made of linked steel,
Which an elvish smith made   with his noble craft;
It was called Wigar,   and a wizard wrought it.
He hid his shanks   in hose of steel.
Caliburn, his sword,   he swung at his side;   610
It was wrought in Avalon   with cunning craft.

[9] The fàys and their gifts are not mentioned in Wace. Possibly Layamon got this tradition either directly or in some written form from Breton story-tellers who circulated in England.

[10] The Britons actually won a great victory over the Saxons at a place called Mount Badon about 500 A.D., but where Mount Badon was is unknown and Arthur's participation, though probable, is uncertain. All the circumstances are fictitious.

[11] Dumbarton on the Clyde.

[18]

He set on his head   a high helm of steel;
Thereon was many a jewel   all adorned with gold.
It had been Uther's,   the noble king's;
It was called Goose-white;   'twas unlike any other.
He slung from his neck   a precious shield;
Its name in British   was called Pridwen.
Thereon was graven   in red-gold figures
A dear likeness   of the Lord's Mother.
He took in hand his spear,   which was called Ron.   620
When he had all his weeds,   he leapt on his steed.
Then might they behold   who stood there beside him
The fairest knight   who would ever lead host.
Never saw any man   a goodlier knight
Than Arthur was,   the noblest of ancestry.
    Then Arthur called   with a loud voice:
"Lo, here are before us   the heathen hounds
Who killed our chieftains   with their base crafts;
And they on this land   are loathest of all things.
Now let us attack them   and lay on them starkly,   630
And avenge wondrously   our kin and our kingdom,
And wreak the great shame   with which they have shamed us,
That they over the waves   have come to Dartmouth.
They are all forsworn   and they all shall be lorn;
They all are doomed   with the aid of the Lord.
Hasten we forward   fast together,
Even as softly   as if we thought no evil.
And when we come on them,   I myself will attack;
Foremost of all   I will begin the fight.
Now let us ride   and pass over the land,   640
And let no man, on his life,   make any noise,
But fare firmly,   with the help of the Lord."
Then Arthur, the rich man,   to ride forth began,
Went over the weald   and would seek Bath.
    The tidings came to Childric,   the strong and the mighty,
That Arthur came with his army,   all ready to fight.
Childric and his brave men   leapt on their horses,
Gripped their weapons;   they knew themselves fey.[12]
This saw Arthur,   noblest of kings.
He saw a heathen earl   hastening against him,   650
With seven hundred knights   all ready to fight.
The earl himself came   ahead of his troop,

[12] Fated to die.

[19]

And Arthur himself galloped   before all his army.
Arthur, the fierce,   took Ron in his hand;
He couched the strong shaft,   that stern-minded king.
He let his horse run   so that the earth rumbled.
He laid shield to his breast;   the king was bursting with anger.
He smote Borel the earl   right through the breast,
So that his heart was split.   The king cried at once:
"The foremost hath met his fate!   Now the Lord help us   660
And the heavenly Queen,   who gave birth to the Lord!"
Then cried Arthur,   noblest of kings:
"Now at them, now at them!   The foremost is done for!"
The Britons laid on,   as men should do to the wicked.
They gave bitter strokes   with axes and swords.
There fell of Childric's men   fully two thousand,
But Arthur never lost   one of his men.
There were the Saxon men   most wretched of all folk,
And the men of Almain   most miserable of all peoples.
Arthur with his sword   executed doom;   670
All whom he smote   were soon destroyed.
The king was enraged   as is the wild boar
When he in the beechwood   meeteth many swine.
This Childric beheld   and began to turn back,
And bent his way over Avon   to save himself.
Arthur pursued him,   as if he were a lion,
And drove them to the flood;   many there were fey.
There sank to the bottom   five and twenty hundred.
Then was Avon's stream all   bridged over with steel.
Childric fled over the water   with fifteen hundred knights;   680
He thought to journey forth   and pass over sea.
Arthur saw Colgrim   climb to a mount,
Turn to a hill   that standeth over Bath;
And Baldulf followed after   with seven thousand knights.
They thought on that hill   to make a stout stand,
To defend themselves with weapons   and work harm to Arthur.
   When Arthur saw,   noblest of kings,
Where Colgrim withstood   and made a stand,
Then cried the king   keenly and loud:
"My bold thanes,   make for that hill!   690
For yesterday was Colgrim   most daring of all men.
Now he is as sad as a goat,   where he guardeth the hill.
High on a hilltop   he fighteth with horns,
When the wild wolf cometh,   toward him stalking.

Though the wolf be alone,   without any pack,
And there be in the fold   five hundred goats,
The wolf falleth on them   and biteth them all.
So will I now today   destroy Colgrim altogether.
I am a wolf and he is a goat.   The man shall be fey!"
Then still shouted Arthur,   noblest of kings: 700
"Yesterday was Baldulf   of all knights boldest.
Now he standeth on the hill   and beholdeth the Avon,
How there lie in the stream   steel fishes!
Ready with sword,   their health is broken!
Their scales float   like gold-colored shields;
There float their fins   as if they were spears.
These are marvelous things   come to this land,
Such beasts on the hill,   such fish in the stream!
Yesterday was the kaiser   boldest of all kings;
Now hath he become a hunter,   and horns follow him;   710
He flieth over the broad weald;   his hounds bark.
But beside Bath   he hath abandoned his hunting;
He fleeth from his deer   and we shall bring it down,
And bring to naught   his bold threats;
And so we shall revel   in our rights again."
   Even with the words   that the king said,
He raised high his shield   before his breast,
He gripped his long spear   and set spurs to his horse.
Nearly as swiftly   as the bird flieth,
There followed the king   five and twenty thousand   720
Valorous men,   raging under their arms,
Held their way to the hill   with high courage,
And smote at Colgrim   with full smart strokes.
There Colgrim received them   and felled the Britons to earth.
In the foremost attack   there fell five hundred.
Arthur saw that,   noblest of kings,
And wroth he was   with wondrous great wrath,
And Arthur the noble man   to shout thus began:
"Where be ye, Britons,   my warriors bold?
Here stand before us   our foes all chosen.   730
My warriors good,   let us beat them to the ground."
Arthur gripped his sword aright   and smote a Saxon knight,
So that the good sword   stopped at the teeth.
Then he smote another   who was that knight's brother,
So that his helm and his head   fell to the ground.
Soon a third dint he gave   and in two a knight clave.

Then were the Britons   much emboldened
And laid on the Saxons   right sore strokes
With spears that were long   and swords that were strong.
There Saxons fell,   met their fated hour,   740
By hundreds and hundreds   sank to the earth,
By thousands and thousands   dropped there to the ground.
When Colgrim saw   where Arthur came toward him,
He could not, for the slaughter,   flee to any side.
There fought Baldulf   beside his brother.
Then called Arthur   with a loud voice:
"Here I come, Colgrim!   we will gain us a country.
We will so share this land   as will be least to thy liking."
Even with the words   that the king uttered,
He heaved up his broad sword   and brought it down hard,   750
And smote Colgrim's helm   and clove it in the middle,
And the hood of the byrny;   the blade stopped at the breast.
He struck at Baldulf   with his left hand,
And smote off the head   and the helm also.
   Then laughed Arthur,   the noble king,
And began to speak   with gamesome words:
"Lie now there, Colgrim!   Thou didst climb too high!
And Baldulf thy brother   lieth by thy side.
Now all this good land   I place in your hand,
Dales and downs   and all my doughty folk.   760
Thou didst climb on this hill   wondrously high,
As if thou soughtest heaven;   now thou shalt to hell!
There thou mayst ken   many of thy kin!
Greet thou there Hengest,   who of knights was fairest,
Ebissa and Ossa,   Octa and more of thy kin;
And bid them dwell there,   winters and summers.
And we on this land   will live in bliss,
And pray for your souls   that they may never be blessed.
And here shall your bones   lie beside Bath."

THE ROUND TABLE [13]

(vss. 22737-996)

It was on a Yule Day that Arthur in London lay.	770

Then were come to him   from out his whole kingdom,
From Britain, from Scotland,   from Ireland, from Iceland,
And from out every land   that Arthur had in hand,
All the highest thanes   with horses and with swains.
There were seven kings' sons   come with seven hundred knights,
Besides that household   which followed Arthur.
Each one had in his heart   over-proud feelings,
And felt that he was better   than his fellow.
That folk was from many lands;   there was great envy:
When one held him high,   the other held him much higher.   780
   Then men blew upon trumpets   and spread the tables;
Water was brought on the floor   with golden bowls;
And then soft cloths   all of white silk.
Then Arthur sat him down,   and by him Wenhaver; [14]
After him sat the earls,   and after them the nobles;
Afterwards the knights,   even as it was ordained them.
Men of high birth   then bore in the meats,
First to the head of the table,   and then to the knights,
Then towards the thanes,   after that to the swains,
Then to the bearers   forth at the board.   790
The courtiers became angered;   dints there were rife.
First they hurled the loaves [15]   the while that they lasted,
And then the silver bowls   that were filled with wine;
And afterwards fists   sped forth to necks.
Then there leapt forth a young man   who came from Winetland; [16]
He was given to Arthur   to hold as a hostage;
He was the son of Rumaret,   the king of Winet; [16]
The knight thus spoke there   to Arthur the king:
"Lord Arthur, go quickly   into thy bower,
And thy queen with thee,   and thy native-born kinsmen,   800

[13] Geoffrey of Monmouth does not mention the Round Table. Wace gives a short account and says that the Bretons tell many tales about it. Evidently Layamon is retelling one of them.
[14] Guinevere.
[15] Presumably trenchers, slices of bread on which meats were placed.
[16] Gwynedd, northwestern Wales.

And we shall settle this fight   with these foreign-born warriors."
With these very words   he leapt to the board,
Where lay the knives   before the land's king.
Three knives he seized,   and with the one he smote
On the neck of that knight   who first began that fight,
That his head on the floor   fell to the ground.
At once he slew another,   that same thane's brother;
Ere the swords came in,   seven he had cut down.
There was then a great fight;   each man smote the other;
There was much bloodshed;   in the court was disaster.   810
   Then came the king hastening   out from his bower,
With him a hundred warriors   with helms and with byrnies;
Each bore in his hand   a white steel brand.
Then called out Arthur,   the noblest of kings:
"Sit down, sit down at once,   each man on pain of his life!
And whoever will not do that,   condemned shall he be.
Take me that same man   who this fight first began,
And put a withy on his neck   and drag him to a moor,
And throw him in a low-lying fen,   where he shall lie.
And take all his next of kin,   whom ye can find,   820
And smite off their heads   with your broad swords;
And the women that ye can find   nearest him of kin,
Carve off their noses   and ruin their beauty;
And thus will I wholly destroy   that kin that he came from.
And if I evermore   shall hear afterwards
That any in my court,   be he high, be he low,
For this same assault   stir a quarrel later,
No ransom shall be given for him,   neither gold nor any treasure,
Tall horse nor armor,   that he shall not die
Or be drawn asunder with horses,   as beseemeth such traitors.   830
Bring ye holy relics,   and I will swear thereon;
And so shall ye, knights,   who were at this fight,
Both earls and warriors,   that ye will not break it."
First swore Arthur,   the noblest of kings;
Then swore the earls;   after swore the warriors;
Then swore the thanes,   and then swore the swains,
That they would nevermore   stir up that quarrel.
They took all the dead men   and to their grave bore them.
Afterwards they blew trumpets   with exceeding merry sounds.
Were him lief, were him loath,   each took water and cloth;   840
And they afterwards sat down   in peace at the board,
All in fear of Arthur,   the noblest of kings.

Cup bearers then thronged in; minstrels sang there,
Harps aroused melodies; the court was in happiness.
Thus for a full seven nights was that company maintained.
   Afterwards, it says in the tale, the king went to Cornwall;
There came to him anon one who was a skilled craftsman,
And went to meet the king, and courteously greeted him:
"Hail to thee, Arthur, noblest of kings.
I am thine own man; I have traversed many a land.   850
I know in woodwork wondrous many devices.
I heard beyond the sea men telling new tidings,
How thine own knights at thy board did fight
On midwinter's day; many there fell;
For their mighty pride they played the death-game,
And because of his high race each would be on the inside.[17]
Now I will make for thee a work most skillful
That there may sit at it sixteen hundred and more,
All in succession, that none may sit at the end,
But without and within,[18] man beside man.   860
Whenever thou wilt ride, with thee thou mayst take it,
And set it up where thou wilt after thine own will;
And thou needest never dread throughout the wide world
That ever any proud knight at thy board stir a fight;
For there shall the high be equal to the low.
Let me but have timber, and begin that board."
In four weeks' time that work was completed.
On a high day the court was assembled;
And Arthur himself went forthwith to that board,
And summoned every knight to that table forthright.   870
When they were all set, the knights at their meat,
Then spoke each with the other as though it were his brother.
All of them sat round about; none had an end seat;
A knight of every race had there a good place;
They were all side by side, the low and the high;
None might there boast of a better beverage,
Than had his companions who were at that table.
   This was the same board that the Britons [19] boast of,
And tell many kinds of lies about Arthur the king.

[17] End seats were apparently considered degrading.
[18] The table was apparently in the form of a hollow circle, and there were seats both
on the inner and the outer side.
[19] This translates Wace's *Bretons,* and probably means the Continental people, not
the descendants of the ancient Britons in Wales, who were called Welsh in the twelfth
and thirteenth centuries, as now.

[25]

So doth every man   who loveth another;   880
If he is too dear to him,   then will he lie,
And say in his worship   more than he is worth;
Be he never so base,   his friend will wish him well.
Further, if among people   there arise hostility,
At any time so ever,   between two men,
Men can tell of the loathed one   many lies,
Though he were the best man   that ever ate at board.
The man who is loath to him   can find charges against him.
'Tis neither all truth nor all lies   which the people's bards sing.
But this is the truth   about Arthur the king: 890
Was never ere such a king   so valiant in everything,
For the truth stands in writings,   how it came to pass,
From the beginning to the ending,   of Arthur the king,
Neither more nor less,   but as his traits were.
But the Britons loved him greatly,   and oft tell lies of him,
And say many things   about Arthur the king,
That took place never   in this earthly kingdom.
Enough can he say   who will relate the truth
Of wondrous things   about Arthur the king.

ARTHUR'S DREAM [20]

(vss. 27993–28200)

Then there came at that time   a valiant man riding,   900
And brought tidings   to Arthur the king
From Modred, his sister's son;   to Arthur he was welcome,
For he weened that he brought   exceeding good news.
Arthur lay all the long night   and spoke with that young knight;
But he never would tell him   the truth, how it fared.
When it was day, in the morning,   and the court began to stir,
Arthur then rose up   and stretched his arms;
He rose up, and down he sat,   as though he were very sick.
Then asked the young knight,   "Lord, how hast thou fared this night?"
Arthur then answered,   in mood he was uneasy,   910
"This night in my bed,   as I lay in my bower,
I dreamt a dream   for which I am most sorrowful.
I dreamt I was taken   high upon a hall;
That hall I did bestride   as though I would ride;

[20] Most of this section is not found in Wace.

[26]

All the lands that I owned,   all them I looked over;
And Walwain [21] sat before me,   my sword he bore in hand.
Then came Modred faring thither   with numberless folk;
He bore in his hand   a strong battle-ax;
He began to hew   exceeding vigorously,
And all the posts he hewed down   that held up the hall.   920
There I saw Wenhaver [22] also,   the woman dearest to me;
All that mighty hallroof   with her hands she pulled apart.
The hall began to fall,   and I fell to the ground,
So that my right arm broke.   Then said Modred, 'Take that.'
Down fell that hall,   and Walwain began to fall,
And fell to the earth;   both his arms broke.
And I gripped my beloved sword   with my left hand,
And smote off Modred's head   that it rolled to the field.
And the queen I cut to pieces   with my dear sword,
And I then put her down   in a dark pit.   930
And all my royal folk   betook them to flight,
So that I knew not under Christ   where they had gone.
But myself, I did stand   upon a wooded land,
And there I did wander   widely over the moors.
There saw I griffins   and grisly fowl;
Then came a golden lioness   moving over the down,
Of all beasts the most gracious   that our Lord hath made;
The lioness ran towards me,   and by the middle seized me,
And forth she betook her,   and turned towards the sea;
And I saw the waves   driving in the sea,   940
And the lioness into the flood   went bearing me.
When we two were in the sea,   the waves took me from her;
There came a fish gliding,   and ferried me to land;
Then was I all wet and weary,   and sick from sorrow.
When I did awake,   I began greatly to quake,
And I began to quiver   as though I were all afire.
And so I have thought   all the night of my dream,
For I know in certain   that gone is all my bliss;
Forever in my life   I must suffer sorrow;
Woe is me I have not here   Wenhaver my queen!"   950
    Then answered the knight,   "Lord, thou art not right;
Never should a dream   with sorrow distress me.
Thou art the mightiest man   that reigneth on earth,
And the wisest of all   that dwell under heaven.
If it hath befallen—may the Lord forbid it—

---

[21] Gawain.   [22] Guinevere.

That Modred, thy sister's son,   have taken thy queen,
And all thy royal land   have set in his own hand,
Which thou didst entrust him   when thou didst set out for Rome,
And he have done all this   in his treachery,
Even yet thou mightest avenge thee   honorably with weapons,   960
And hold again thy land   and rule thy people,
And fell thy foes   who wish thee evil,
And slay them all wholly,   that none should survive."
   Arthur then answered,   the noblest of kings:
"So long as is ever,   I have weened never
That Modred, my kinsman,   who of men is dearest to me,
Would betray me   for all of my riches,
Or Wenhaver, my queen,   weaken in her thoughts;
She will never begin it   for any man on earth!"
   With those words straightway   then answered the knight: 970
"I tell thee the truth, dear king,   for I am thine underling,
Thus hath Modred now done: thy queen he hath taken,
And thy beautiful land   he hath set in his own hand.
He is king, she is queen;   of thy coming they no longer ween,
For they believe never   that thou wilt return from Rome ever.
I am thine own man,   and I saw this betrayal;
And I am come to thee myself   the truth to tell thee;
I will stake my head,   it is true what I have said,
The truth without lies,   of thy beloved queen,
And of Modred, thy sister's son,   how he hath taken Britain from thee!"
Still sat they all   in Arthur's hall;   981
Then was there great sorrow   for that blessed king.
Then were the British men   much disheartened therefor.
Then after a while   there stirred a sound;
Widely might one hear   the Britons' outcries,
And they began to tell   in various speeches
How they would condemn   Modred and the queen,
And punish all those men   who held with Modred.
   Then called out Arthur,   most gracious of all Britons:
"Sit you down still,   knights in this hall,   990
And I will tell you   news unheard of.
Now tomorrow when it is day,   if the Lord send it,
Forth will I turn me   on towards Britain;
And Modred I will slay   and burn the queen,
And I will destroy all   who favored that treachery.
And here will I leave   the man dearest to me,
Howell, my dear kinsman,   the highest of my race,

And half of my army   I leave in this country,
To hold all this royal land   that I have in my hand.
And when these things are all done   I will go on to Rome,   1000
And entrust my beloved land   to Walwain my kinsman,
And perform my promise [23] afterwards   with my bare life;
All of my enemies   shall make a doomed journey."

ARTHUR'S LAST FIGHT

(vss. 28486–651)

Modred was in Cornwall,   and summoned many knights;
To Ireland he sent   his messenger in haste;
To Saxonland he sent   his messenger in haste;
To Scotland he sent   his messenger in haste;
He bade come all at once,   those who would have land,
Either silver or gold,   either goods or lands;
He in every wise   looked out for himself,
As doth wise man   when need cometh upon him.   1010
Arthur heard that,   the most wrathful of kings,
That Modred was in Cornwall   with a very great host,
And would there abide   till Arthur thither should ride.
Arthur sent messengers   throughout all his kingdom,
And commanded all to come   who were alive in the land,
Who were able to fight,   and could bear weapons;
And whoso should neglect   what the king ordered,
The king would to the ground   burn him alive wholly.
There moved towards the court   countless folk,   1020
Riding and marching,   as the rain falleth down.
Arthur went to Cornwall   with immeasurable army.
Modred heard that,   and held against him
With countless folk—there were many fated.
Upon the Tamar [24]   they met together;
The place called Camelford,[25]   forever will that name endure;
And at Camelford were assembled   sixty thousand,
And more thousands besides;   Modred was their leader.
Now thitherwards did ride   Arthur the royal,
With countless folk,   fated though they were;   1030
Upon the Tamar   they met together,
Raised their battle-standards,   advanced together;

[23] To go to the Holy Land.   [24] River between Cornwall and Devon.
[25] Near Tintagel, not on the Tamar.

Drew their long swords,   laid on upon helms;
Fire sprang out there;   and spears did shiver;
Shields began to break,   shafts to shatter;
There fought together   folk uncounted.
The Tamar was in flood   with immeasurable blood;
No man there in that fight   could know any knight,
Who did worse, or who better,   so closely joined was the conflict.
For each one struck downright,   were he swain, were he knight.   1040
There was Modred slain   and taken from his lifeday,
And all his knights   were slain in that fight.
There too were slain   all the swift men,
Arthur's retainers,   the high and the low,
And all of the Britons   of Arthur's board,
And all his fosterchildren   from many kingdoms.
And Arthur was wounded   with a broad battle-spear;
Fifteen had he,   all ghastly wounds:
Into the least could one   thrust two gloves.
There were none more   left in that fight,   1050
Of two hundred thousand,   who lay hewn in pieces,
Save Arthur the king only,   and two of his knights.
   Arthur was wounded   wondrously sore.
There came to him a boy   who was of his kin;
He was the son of Cador,   the earl of Cornwall;
Constantine was the boy called;   he was dear to the king.
Arthur looked at him   as he lay on the ground,
And these words spoke he   with sorrowful heart:
"Constantine, thou art welcome;   thou wert Cador's son;
Here I commit to thee   all of my kingdom;   1060
Defend my Britons ever   to thy life's end,
And keep all the laws   that have stood in my days,
And all the good laws   that stood in Uther's days.
And I will fare to Avalon,   to the fairest of all maidens,
To Argante [26] the queen,   a fay most fair,
And she will make sound   all my wounds,
And make me all whole   with healing potions;
And afterwards I shall come   again to my kingdom,
And dwell with the Britons   in very great joy."
   At these very words   there came from out the sea   1070
A short boat gliding,   driven by the waves,
And two women therein,   wondrously clad;

[26] A corruption of the name Morgan, that of Arthur's faery sister. Her transporting the king to Avalon is a Breton tradition, not found in Wace.

And they took Arthur anon   and in haste bore him,
And softly laid him down,   and then forth did glide.
Then was it come to pass   what Merlin once said,
There would be very great sorrow   at Arthur's departure;
The Britons believe yet   that he is alive,
And dwelleth in Avalon   with the fairest of fays;
And the Britons still look ever   for Arthur to come.
There was never man born,   of any maiden chosen,   1080
Who knoweth of the truth   more to say of Arthur.
But there was once a prophet,   Merlin by name;
He foretold in words,—his sayings were true,—
That an Arthur must still come   to help the Britons.[27]

[27] The older manuscript reads "Anglen," i.e. English. The later manuscript reads "Bruttes," i.e. Britons, which, of course, makes sense.

The Vision of Paul

from the

Lambeth Homilies

DEARLY beloved brethren, if ye will listen and understand willingly, we shall speak plainly to you of the high worth that pertains to the day which is called Sunday.

Sunday is called the Lord's Day, and also the day of joy and of ease and of rest for all things. In this day the angels of heaven rejoice because the wretched souls have respite from their torments. If any of you would know who first obtained rest for these wretched souls, I shall tell you truly. It was St. Paul and Michael the archangel.

These two once upon a time went into hell, as the Lord commanded
10 them, to see how it was there. Michael went before and Paul followed after, and Michael then showed St. Paul the wretched sinful ones who were dwelling there. Afterwards he showed him the high trees burning horribly before hell gates, and upon those trees he showed him miserable souls hanging, some by the feet, others by the hands; some by the tongue and others by the eyes; some by the head and some by the heart.

Afterwards he showed him an oven in burning fire. It threw out seven flames, each of marvelous hue, which were all horrible to behold, and much harder to endure than any torture. And within there were very many souls suspended.

20 And he showed him a well of fire, and all its streams ran with burning fire. And twelve master devils presided over this well, as if they were kings, to torment therein the wretched souls that had been found guilty. And yet their own torment was not any the less, though they were masters there.

And after he showed him the Sea of Hell, and within that sea were seven bitter waves. The first was snow; the second, ice; the third, fire; the fourth, blood; the fifth, adders; the sixth, smoke; the seventh, foul stench, that is worse to endure than ever any of all the other torments. In that sea were innumerable animals, some four-footed, and others entirely without feet; and their eyes were like fire, and their breath shone like the lightning in
30 the midst of thunder. These never cease, day or night, to break the miserable bodies of those men who in this life did not complete their penance.

Some of the men weep sorely, some cry out like animals; some there sigh with groans, others pitiably gnaw their own tongues. Some there weep, and all their tears, like burning coals, glide down their own faces. And very mournfully at all times they cry out, and earnestly entreat that someone would protect them from these cruel tortures. Of these torments speaketh David, the holy prophet, and thus saith: *Miserere nostri, Domine, quia penas inferni sustinere non possumus.* "Lord, have mercy upon us, for we are not able to endure the pains of hell."

Afterwards he showed him a place in the midst of hell; before that same place there were seven cloisters, near which no living man dare go, because 10 of the noxious vapor. And there within he showed him an old man going about, led by four devils. Then Paul asked Michael who that old man might be. Then said Michael the archangel, "He was a bishop in the other life, who never would observe or keep Christ's laws. Very often he would treat his subjects wrongfully, and oppress them for a long time rather than sing psalms or do any other good deeds."

After that Paul saw where three devils were leading a maiden with very great cruelty. Eagerly he asked Michael why she was so led about. Then said Michael, "She was a maiden in the other life, who kept her body in all purity, but would never do any other good thing. She was never glad to 20 give alms, but was very proud and haughty, and a liar and a cheat, and wrathful and envious, and for that she is now dwelling in these pains."

Now began St. Paul to weep wondrously, and the archangel Michael then wept also with him. Then came our Lord to them from the kingdom of heaven, in the likeness of thunder, and said, "Why weepest thou, Paul?" Paul answered Him, "Lord, I bewail the manifold tortures which I see here in hell." Then said our Lord, "Why did they not keep my laws while they were on earth?" Then said Paul mercifully to Him in reply, "Lord, I now entreat Thee, if it be Thy will, that Thou give them rest, at any rate on Sunday, forever until doomsday come." Then said our Lord to him, "Paul, 30 I know well where I ought to show mercy. I will have mercy upon those who sought my mercy while they were alive." Then was St. Paul very sorrowful, and bowed him quickly to his Lord's feet, and began to adjure Him in these words, which ye may now hear: "Lord," he said then, "now I beseech Thee by Thy kingdom, by Thine angels, and by Thy great mercy, by all Thy works, by all Thy saints, and also by Thine elect, that Thou have mercy upon them, the more so that I have come to them; and do Thou give them respite on Sunday ever until Thy high doomsday come." Then answered him the Lord in a more gentle voice, "Arise now, Paul, arise! I will give them rest, as thou hast asked, from noon on Saturday until 40 Monday's dawn comes, ever from this time forth until doomsday."

Now, dearly beloved brethren, ye have heard who first obtained respite

for the souls of the damned. Now it becometh each Christian man so much the more to hallow and honor that day which is called Sunday, for of that day our Lord Himself said, *Dies dominicus dies letitie et requiei.* "Sunday is a day of bliss and of all rest." *Non faciatur in ea aliquid nisi Deum orare, manducare, et bibere cum pace et letitia.* "Let nothing be done on this day but to go to church and pray to Christ, and to eat and drink in peace and gladness." *Sicut dicitur, pax in terra, pax in celo, pax inter homines.* "For, as it is said, 'Peace on earth, and peace in heaven, and peace among all Christian men.'" Again our Lord Himself said, *Maledictus homo qui non*
10 *custodit sabatum.* "Cursed be the man who will not observe Sunday."

And therefore, dearly beloved brethren, each Sunday is to be observed as Easter Day, for it is the commemoration of His holy resurrection from death to life, and a commemoration of the Holy Ghost, which He sent upon His apostles on that day which is called Whitsunday. Also we understand that on a Sunday the Lord will come to judge all mankind.

We ought to honor Sunday exceedingly well and to observe it in all purity, for it hath in it three worthy virtues, which ye may hear: The first virtue is, that Sunday on earth gives rest to all earth-slaves, men and women, from their servitude. The second virtue is in heaven, because the angels
20 rest themselves more on it than on any other day. The third virtue is, that the wretched souls of hell have respite in hell from their great torment. Let each one then always keep Sunday well, and the other holy days which in church we are commanded to keep like Sunday. Then will they be partakers of the joy of the kingdom of heaven, with the Father and the Son and the Holy Ghost, ever world without end.

The Owl and the Nightingale

I was in a summery dale,
In a very secret vale;
An owl there and a nightingale
I heard at one another rail.
Their argument was stiff and strong,
Now soft at times, now loud in song,
As each one did the other flout,
And let her mood of malice out.
For each said of the other all
The very worst she could recall;　10
But chiefly of each other's song
They held debate intense and long.

　The nightingale began her speech,
Within a corner, out of reach;
Upon a handsome bough she stood
Where blossoms had bedecked the
　　wood,
In a thick solitary hedge,
Mingled with rushes and green sedge;
She greatly in that bough rejoiced,
And cunningly her pleasure voiced.　20
That music rather seemed to rise
From harp and pipe than otherwise.
One would have thought that it did
　　float
From harp and pipe, not out of throat.
　An old stump stood beside those
　　bowers,
Where the owl would sing her hours;
The ivy did it overlace;
There made the owl her dwelling place.

　The nightingale the owl espies,
Does her inspect, and her despise;　30
She thought most evil of the owl,
For she was loathsome held and foul.
"Monster," she said, "away now, flee!
I am the worse for sight of thee.

Right often at thy visage vile
I needs must stop my song a while;
My heart must sink, my tongue grow
　　dumb,
Whenever thou dost near me come.
I had rather spit than sing
At thy dreadful clamoring."　40
　The owl abode till it was eve;
That charge she could no longer leave;
Her heart with wrath was now so
　　tossed,
It seemed that she her breath had lost.
But then she hurled a tirade long:
"How think'st thou now of this my
　　song?
Dost thou suppose I sing but ill
Because I know not how to trill?
Thou very often dost me blame,
And causest me both grief and shame.
If in my feet I thee could trap,　51
What I would give for that to hap!
If thou wert caught out of thy tree,
Then wouldst thou sing most dole-
　　fully!"
　The nightingale at once replied:
"While in this leafage thick I hide
And fly not in the open air,
I pay no heed then to thy dare;
So long as in my hedge I stay,
I need not care what thou dost say.　60
I know how cruel thou canst be
To them that cannot scape from thee.
Thou bulliest and thou treatest ill
All smaller birds when at thy will.
For this thee hate the whole bird race;
They thee attack, and off do chase,
And screech at thee and sharply chide,

Closely pursue and long deride.
The titmouse even will readily
Tear thee asunder utterly.   70
For thou art monstrous to their gaze,
And thou art loathed in many ways;
Thy body is short, thy neck is small.
Thy head is greater than thee all;
Thy eyes are both coal-black and broad,
As though they painted were with woad.
Thou starest as if about to bite
Everything thy talons smite.
Thy bill is stiff and sharp and hooked,
And even like an awl 'tis crooked;   80
Thou clackest with it oft and long,—
A noise that some would call thy song!
How thou threatenest my flesh,
With thy sharp claws me to enmesh!
For thee more fitting is a frog,
That at the mill sits by the cog;
Snails and mice and vermin foul
Are natural feeding for an owl.
Thou sittest by day and fliest at night.
Thou knowest thyself a fearful sight:
For thou art loathly and unclean,   91
And in thy nest is what I mean,
As well as in thy dirty brood;
Thou feedest them on filthy food.
Well knowest thou what they do therein:
They foul it up unto the chin;
There they sit as they were blind;
Thereof do men a proverb find:
'Bad luck that self same beast befall
That fouleth up his nest at all.'   100
A falcon fair one year did breed,
But to his nest gave little heed.
Thou stolest to it on a day,
Thy foul egg therein to lay.
It happened that the eggs did hatch,
And in his nest new birds did scratch.
Then to his birds he brought their meat,
Looked at his nest, and watched them eat.

He noticed there, off on a side,
His nest befouled on the outside.   110
The falcon, irate with his birds,
Screamed aloud with angry words:
'Tell me now, who has done this?
'Tis not your nature to act amiss.
'Twas done in a disgusting way.
Just tell me who, if you can say.'
Then quoth that one and quoth that other,
'Indeed, it was this our own brother,
He yonder, with so great a head:
Woe to him, that he is not dead!   120
Throw him out with the worst of all,
And may his neck break with the fall!'
The falcon then his young believed,
And from their midst the foul bird heaved;
From out that wild bough he it threw,
Where pie and crow apart it drew.
From this can we make an example,
Though not complete, yet fully ample:
Just like, indeed, this creature rude,
One that has come of a foul brood,   130
And joins with those of noble name,
He shows up ever whence he came,
That from an addled-egg he grew,
Though he was laid in free nest, too.
When apple trundles from the tree,
Where it and others likewise be,
Though it away from thence be taken,
It shows up well whence it was shaken."
    Those words spoke forth the nightingale,
And when she ended this long tale,
She sang so loud, so very sharp,   141
As if one touched a well-tuned harp.
This owl, she listened thitherward,
And both her eyes held netherward,
And sat quite swollen and all bellowed,
As if a frog she had just swallowed;
For she knew well, could easily see,
This song was meant in mockery.

Nevertheless she made reply:
"Why not out in the open fly,   150
And show there which one of us two
Has fairer color, brighter hue?"

"Oh, no, for thou art sharp of claw;
I have no wish that thou me claw.
Thou hast talons very strong;
Thou clutchest with them like a tong.
Thou didst intend, as does thy kind,
With fair words to deceive my mind.
I will not do as thou tellest me;
I know it will ill counsel be.   160
Now shame on thee, thy bad advice;
Revealed is thy deception nice.
Shield thy treachery from the light,
And hide the false amid the right.
When to deception thou wilt bend,
See that no one knows the end.
For treachery rouses shame and hate
In those who do it penetrate.
Thy wily tricks will not succeed, 169
For I can dodge thy spite with speed.
A bold front will not serve thy end,
For I with cunning can contend
Better than thou, though thou be
      strong.
And for a castle broad and long,
This my branch may well suffice.
'Who flies well fights well,' say the
      wise.
But let us put away dispute,
For words of this kind never suit;
With right judgment let us begin,
And with fair words and friendly win.
Though we be not of one accord, 181
Fair words are better than a sword.
Without wrangling, and without a
      fight,
Argue we decently and right;
And either one may, as she will,
Speak forth with right as well as skill."

      Then quoth the owl, "Who does it
      seem
Can hear us best and rightly deem?"
"I know well," quoth the nightingale:
"There need of that be no long tale:

Master Nicholas of Guilford, he   191
Is full of wit and subtlety.
In judging he is sharp and nice,
And loath to him is every vice.
Insight he has into each song,
Who sings well, and who sings
      wrong.
He can distinguish wrong from right
And the darkness from the light."
      The owl awhile remained in
      thought;
Then out these words she duly
      brought: 200
"I grant it well, that he us deem;
For, though a while he wild did seem,
And the nightingale to him was dear,
And other gentle creatures here,
I know that now he has much cooled.
He will no longer now be fooled,
That he, because of thy old love,
Would judge me down, and thee
      above;
Nor shalt thou please him so that he
For thee would grant a false de-
      cree.   210
Firm in himself and fair in measure,
No more he takes in folly pleasure,
No longer gives himself to play,
But follows ever the right way."
      The nightingale does her prepare
With lore she gathered everywhere:
"Owl," she said, "now tell me true:
Why dost thou what these monsters
      do?
Thou singest by night and not by day,
And all thy song is 'Wellaway!'   220
Thou often with thy song dost fright
All who hear it in the night.
Thou screechest and hootest to thy
      mate;
It fearful is to hear thee prate!
It seems to both the fools and wise,
Thou singest no song, but only cries.
Thou fliest by night and not by day;
At that I wonder, and well I may:
For every thing that shuns the right

Loves ever darkness and hates the
    light;   230
And every thing that loves misdeeds
Cherishes darkness for its deeds.
A wise word, though it be unclean,
In many a mouth has often been;
Alfred the King [1] once said and wrote,
'We shun them who our vices note.'
Now this applies to thee also,
Since thou by night dost ever go.
Another thing that seems not right:
At night thy eyes are strong and
    bright,   240
Though by day thou art stark-blind,
And seest not bough or bark, we find.
By day thou art so dim of sight,
That men of thee a proverb write:
'It is the bad man's destiny
That goodness he can never see.
He is so full of vile devices
That naught can turn him from his
    vices.
The dark way he so fully knows
That in the bright he never goes.' 250
So all do who are of thy kind;
For the light they have no mind."
    The owl sat listening very long,
Her feelings hurt, both deep and
    strong.
She said, "They call thee nightingale;
It better might be tattle-tale.
Far too many a tale you've sung:
In a splint, now, rest your tongue!
Pray, judge not that this day is thine;
Let me speak, the turn is mine. 260
And as I speak, just quiet be,
For I will be revenged on thee!
Hear me, how I myself defend,
With simple truth the contest end.
Thou sayst I hide myself by day;
To that I say not 'No' or 'Nay';
But listen, and I'll tell thee, therefore,
Just why it is, as well as wherefore:
I have a bill both stiff and strong
And talons that are sharp and long,

As it befits all hawks by right; 271
They are my joy and my delight,
And well become one of my race;
No one can blame my love of chase.
In me this is right fitly seen:
By nature's law I am so keen.
For this the small birds me decry,
By ground and thicket as they fly;
They scream at me in anxious twitter,
Make forays on me, sharp and bitter.
I much prefer to take my rest 281
Within the quiet of my nest;
For I would never be the better,
If I with jawing or with chatter
Should foully scold those little birds,
As herdsmen do, with dirty words;
I do not like to strive with shrews,
So I their company refuse.
Prudent men have often thought,
And they have often said and taught:
'Against the giddy do not chide, 291
Or yawn against an oven wide.'
Once on a time I heard men tell
How Alfred said in counsel well:
'See to it that thou be not where
Debate is, and of strife beware;
Let fools there chide; forth do thou
    go.'
Now I am wise, and do just so.
And Alfred said, another time, 299
A word now widely spread in rime:
'Who with the foul will him demean,
From them can never come out clean.'
Does that hawk sink in thy esteem
If crows scold him by marsh or
    stream,
And go at him with noisy cry,
As if to fight they him defy?
The hawk here follows a good saw:
He flies away, and lets them caw.
Thou chargest me with another thing,
And sayest that I cannot sing, 310
That my whole voice is but a groan,
And is, to hear, a grisly moan.
That is not so: 'tis not the truth;

[1] Many current proverbs were ascribed to King Alfred (d. 899).

My song is glad and loud and smooth.
Thou judgest every song is bitter
That is not like thy feeble twitter.
My voice is bold, no whit forlorn,
But rather like a powerful horn;
And thine is like a little pipe,
Made of wood, slender and unripe.
Better than thou I sing at least;   321
Thou chatterest like an Irish priest.
I sing at eve, at vesper time,
Then later, when it is bed-time;
The third time, at the dead of night;
Again my song I sing with might
When I see rising from afar
The light of dawn or the daystar.
I do much good with this my throat,
I warn men that their needs they
      note.   330
But thou dost sing throughout the
      night,
From eve until it is daylight,
And still repeatest thy one song
As long as ever the night is long,
And still thou crowest thy wretched
      wail,
That neither night nor day does fail.
How with thy piping thou repellest
The ears of them with whom thou
      dwellest!
Thou mak'st thy song so little prized,
That by all men it is despised.   340
Each mirth can merely last so long
Before it cease to please the throng;
For harp and pipe and sound of bird
Displease at length if too long heard;
And be the song never so merry,
It will at last sound most unmerry
If prolonged beyond one's fill.
Thus thy singing suits men ill.
For this is true, as Alfred said,
And it in books is often read: 350
'All good things lose their pleasant-
      ness
With overdoing and excess.'
If thou overstuff on pleasant things,
A surfeit quickly loathing brings.

For every mirth will fade away,
If we enjoy it without stay.
Of God's realm only can we claim,
It ever is sweet and ever the same:
However much thou take away,
That basket heaping full will stay.   360
Wondrous kingdom, where Godhead
      reigns,
Which ever spends, yet full remains.
Thou sayest likewise in derision
That I am feeble in my vision,
And chargest, since I fly by night,
That I cannot see in light.
Thou liest! I can quickly show
I have good sight, and prove it so:
The darkness never is so black
That my vision keen I lack   370
Thou thinkest that I cannot spy
If by day I do not fly.
The hare all day will quiet be,
But, none the less, he well can see.
If towards him the hounds should run,
He will them very nimbly shun.
He hooks about on narrow tracks,
And not a single trick he lacks,
But hops and starts with sudden move,
And seeks out safe paths to the grove;
He could do this in no degree,   381
If it were true he could not see.
I see as well as can the hare,
Though I by day do sit and stare.
When off to war go valiant men,
And near and far deploy them then,
And pass through many forests wide,
And on nocturnal forays ride.
I follow their example right,
I join their troop and fly at night." 390
   The nightingale within her thought
Took all this in, and long time thought
What she thereafter best might say;
For lightly she could not gainsay
What the owl to her did tell,
Because she spoke both right and well.
And she was grieved because her foe
Had gotten an advantage so,
And was afraid lest her reply

Would not come off successfully. 400
However, she spoke boldly out,
For it is wise with courage stout
Firmly thine enemy to face,
And not flee from him in disgrace:
For when thou yieldest, men will fight
Who otherwise would turn in flight.
If thy courage is but big,
From boar thy foe will turn to pig.
And therefore, though the nightingale
Was frightened, boldly she did
    rail: 410
  "Owl," she said, "dost thou not see?
Thou singest in winter, 'Woe is me!'
Thou singest like a hen in snow,
Where all she sings is song of woe.
In winter thy song is sad and rough;
In summer thou art dumb enough,
Because thou dost in envy writhe,
Thou mayest not with us be blithe.
With malice thou art quite consumed,
When we our pleasures have re-
    sumed. 420
Thou actest like a man demented,
Who others' bliss has much resented.
Grumbling and louring, they are sad
If they see others gay and glad.
They look in hope that they can spy
Tears flowing in another's eye;
For tufts of wool they have no care,
Though all mixed in with threads and
    hair.
Just so dost thou, owl, on thy side:
For when the snow lies thick and
    wide, 430
And when all men are vexed with sor-
    row,
Then dost thou sing from eve till
    morrow,
But I, with me all joys I bring;
All men are glad because I sing.
For, when I come, all earth rejoices,
And at my coming raise their voices.
Blossoms begin to spring and spread,
In trees and meadows, white and red;
The lilies with their radiant glow 439

Do welcome me, as thou dost know;
And beg, in their fair hue and dye,
That I to them should straightway fly.
With ruddy tint likewise the rose,
That yearly from the thorn-wood
    grows,
Beseeches me with all her might
To sing a song for her delight.
And so I do, through night and day;
The more I sing the more I may.
I chant to her with my full song,
But none the less, not over long; 450
When I see men are elated,
I take care lest they be sated.
When that is done for which I came.
I go back home, in wisdom's name.
When men are anxious for their
    sheaves,
And yellow turn the once green leaves,
I take my leave and journey back,
And reck not of the winter's wrack.
Hard weather when I see at hand,
I homeward hasten to my land. 460
Their love and thanks with me I take,
That I came thither for their sake.
Then is my errand done this season.
Should I then tarry? For what reason?
He is neither wise nor clever,
Who, where none need him, stays for
    ever."

*   *   *

The owl was most exasperated; 1043
At these words her eyes dilated:
"Thou say'st thou knowest well men's
    bowers,
Where flourish leaves and lovely flow-
    ers,
Where in one bed two lovers lie,
Embracing, safe from prying eye.
Once thou sangest, I know the spot,
Nigh to a bower, and lewdly sought
To lead a lady's heart astray, 1051
And sangest high and low thy lay
And taughtest her the way of shame,
Adultery, and evil fame.

Of this her lord was soon aware,
Spread birdlime, and every sort of
    snare
He set around to catch thee in.
Shortly thou camest to the gin,
And thou wast taken in the trap; 1059
Thy shins did sorely feel the snap.
And sentence was imposed by law
That wild horses should thee draw.
Try again with wife or maid
And see if she will be betrayed!
If thou persist in tuneful jangling,
Again in springe thou may'st be dan-
    gling."
    The nightingale, in furious mood,
If she had been a man, she would
Have snatched up sword and spear to
    fight.   1069
At least she did the best she might:
She fought with her sagacious tongue.
"Who speaks well fights well," says
    the song.
Her speech she pondered in her head.
"Who speaks well fights well," Alfred
    said.
"What! dost thou say this for my
    shame?
That lord himself was much to blame.
He was so jealous of his wife
That he could not, to save his life,
See any man go near and speak
With her, but all his heart would break.
He locked her up within a bower 1081
That was as strong as any tower.
I sorely pitied her distress
And sorrowed for her wretchedness,
And gave her solace with my song,
As early as I could and long.
Therefore the knight with me was
    wroth
And for sheer malice held me loath.
He visited his shame on me,   1089
But all turned out quite differently.
King Henry [2] heard the matter whole;
Jesu have mercy on his soul!

    [2] Probably King Henry II (d. 1189).

He banished that outrageous knight
Who had so meanly wreaked his
    spite,
And in so good a monarch's land
With malice sheer had vengeance
    planned,
Had trapped that bird and sentenced
    him
To the loss of life and limb.
All this brought honor to my kin;
The knight was punished for his
    sin   1100
And fined therefor a hundred pound,
The while my young sat safe and
    sound,
Enjoying bliss and true delight
And happiness, as well they might.
I was so well avenged therefor
I speak more boldly than before,
And since it all turned out that way,
I am the merrier for aye.
Wherever I will I now may sing,
And no objection can one bring. 1110
But thou, thou miserable ghost,
There is no hollow stump, thou
    know'st,
Wherein thyself thou seek'st to hide,
But someone will not bruise thy hide.
For boys and farmers and their hinds
On thy torment put their minds.
If they can but spy thee once,
They fill their pockets full of stones,
And hurl them hard to break thy
    back
And give thy ugly bones a crack. 1120
If they can knock thee to the ground,
Then first thou servest a purpose
    sound.
Upon a pole they set thee high,
Expose thy corpse to every eye,
Which with its wicked claws alarms
The birds and keeps the grain from
    harms.
Thy life is worthless and thy blood,
But as a scarecrow thou art good.
When a man his seeds doth sow,

The sparrow, goldfinch, rook, and
    crow   1130
Dare not ever come anear;
Thy carcase, hanging there, they fear.
Yearly when trees are burgeoning
And tender seeds burst forth and
    spring,
No fowl will dare approach that place,
If over them he sees thy face. . . .
'Tis right that men be wroth with
    thee;   1145
Ever thou sing'st of griefs to be.
Thou sing'st of nothing soon or late,
But only some unhappy fate.
When thou hast cried throughout the
    night,
Justly may men be filled with
    fright.   1150
Thou singest where some man will
    die;
Always thou bodest evil nigh.
Thou foretellest poverty,
Or some friend's adversity.
Or thou foretellest conflagrations,
Battles, or robbers' depredations,
Or cattle smit with plague and dying,
Or farms in wrack and ruin lying,
Or sundering of man and wife,
Or thou bodest war and strife.   1160
Ever thou singest of distress;
Through thee come sorrow and
    wretchedness.
Thou singest not by any chance
Except it be of some mischance.
Therefore it is that men dislike thee,
Pelt thee, belabor thee, and strike thee
With staff and turf and clod and stone;
So place of shelter there is none.
Evil befall the messenger
Who comes but when mishaps oc-
    cur,   1170
And only tales of misery brings,
And always speaks of wretched things.
God almighty be with him wroth,
And with all wearing linen cloth!"[8]

The owl delayed not very long,
But gave an answer stark and strong:
"What," quoth she. "hast thou been
    ordained?
Or dost thou curse though unor-
    dained?
Thou dost the work of priest, I wot;
Whether thou art priest I know
    not.   1180
I know not if thou canst sing masses;
In cursing, though. thy tongue sur-
    passes.
It is thine old malignity
Caused thee to put a curse on me.
But well the carter once replied;
He said, 'Draw over to thy side!'
Why dost thou reproach me so
With all I feel and all I know?
For I a clever bird am rated,
And foresee all things that are fated.
I know of hunger and of war,   1191
Who will live ninety years and more;
I know if woman loves her spouse;
I know when danger nears a house;
I know who the hangman's noose will
    fit,
Or other shameful death will meet.
I know, when men in battle fight,
Which side at last will turn in flight.
I know if plague will strike the herds
And death will take the beasts and
    birds.   1200
I know if trees will blossom out;
I know if seeds of grain will sprout;
I know if house will burn at night,
I know if men will flee or fight;
I know if sea will swallow ship;
I know if snows the land will grip.
And then I know a great deal more:
I have enough of bookish lore.
And I have learned the gospel well,
More than I ever will thee tell.   1210
For to the church I oft repair
And gather much of wisdom there.
Of symbols and their tokenings

[8] The clergy.

I know, and many other things.
Should one be hunted with hue and
    cry,
I know it when the threat is nigh.
Often, because of my great wit,
In sorry mood and sad I sit,
And when I see that grievous harm
Is near a man, I give the alarm.   1220
I bid men sharply to beware
And proper measures to prepare.
Alfred a word of wisdom said,—
Each man should hoard it in his head;
'If thou see woe ere it arrive,
Thou dost it of its strength deprive.'
And heavy blows will hurt thee less
If thou be armed with wariness,
And arrows oft will touch thee not
If thou perceive them when they're
    shot.   1230
For thou mayst dodge them readily
Whene'er thou seest them aimed at
    thee.
If a man should be disgraced,
Why should the blame on me be
    placed?
Although I see his shame before,
I should not bear reproach therefor.
Although I see a blind man stray,
Who does not know the proper way,
And head toward a loathsome pit
And fall and soil himself in it,   1240
Thinkest thou, though I see it all,
Because of me it doth befall? . . .
Now it may clearly be perceived 1281
That thou art thoroughly deceived.
For all thou sayest to my shame
Turns to dishonor on thy name.
Smite as thou canst, yet thou must
    own,
The stroke that fells thee is thine own.
All that thou say'st of scorn and
    slander
But makes my glory seem the grander.
Unless thou find a better strain,   1289
Naught but infamy thou wilt gain."
    The nightingale sat still and sighed,

In doleful state and injured pride,
Because of what the owl had said
And all the telling points she'd made.
She grieved and was exceeding vexed,
And pondered what she might say
    next;
She gathered all the wits she had,
And "What!" she said, "owl, art thou
    mad?
Thou braggest of thy wondrous sense,
And yet thou knowest never whence
It comes except by sorcery.   1301
Thou must be purged right thoroughly
Of that if thou near men wilt stay,
Or thou must quickly flee away.
Because all those who witchcraft
    know
Were by the priest's mouth long ago
Accursed; and of such folk thou art;
Thou from thy craft wilt never part.
I told this not long since to thee,
And thou didst ask if true it be   1310
That I had been ordained in jest.
But every man from east to west,
Knows well that thou art under curse;
There needs no priest to make it
    worse.
For all the children call thee foul,
And all the men, a wretched owl.
It is the truth, I have heard tell,
A man must know the stars full well
If he would know the fates' decree,
As thou sayest it haps with thee.   1320
But, wretch, what know'st thou of a
    star,
Save that thou seest it from afar?
But so does many a man and beast
Who of such things knows not the
    least.
An ape can hold an open book
And turn the pages o'er and look,
But for all that he has no more
Of learning than he had before.
Even so at the stars thou starest,
But never a wiser head thou wear-
    est.   1330

And yet, foul thing, thou chidest me
And blamest me right cruelly,
Saying I sing near many a house
And teach the wife to break her vows.
Vile thing, thou liest in thy throat!
Spouse-breach never did I promote.
'Tis very true I sing roulades
Where ladies dwell and lovely maids;
'Tis also true of love I sing.
For sure it is a better thing   1340
For wife to love her husband pure
Than wanton with a paramour.
Also a maid to love may choose
Where she no honest fame may lose,
And give her heart and plight her
     word
To one whom she may call her lord.
Such is the love I always preach,
And only of such love I teach.
And though some wives are frail of
     nature
(For woman is a tender creature, 1350
So that through some fool's enterprise,
Who strongly pleads and hotly sighs,
She may at some time do amiss),
Shall I be held the cause of this?
And if a woman turn to wrong,
I cannot therefore cease my song.
A woman may sport beneath the sheet
In wedded love or lustful heat;
And she may, listening to my lay,
Be moved to right or reckless
     play.   1360
For nothing in the world God sends
But may be turned to evil ends.
Naught in the world that is of use
But may be twisted to abuse
If men an evil purpose hold.
Silver is good, and so is gold;
Nonetheless thou canst with them buy
Injustice and adultery.
Weapons are useful to maintain
The peace, and yet with them are
     slain   1370
Honest men in many lands

When robbers bear them in their
     hands.
Even so it is with this my song;
Though it be good, men may be
     wrong
And make it an excuse for vice
Or other wanton enterprise.
But, wretch, wilt thou condemn love
     wholly?
Howe'er it be, love is not folly
But right, between man and his mate,
Except outside the married state. 1380
Then is it infamy and shame.
May Holy Cross be wroth with them
Who natural longing use so badly!
It is not strange if they rave madly,
For they are certainly possessed
Who start to brood without a nest."

* * *

The nightingale her pleading ceased,
And sat in that fair place, well
     pleased.   1654
Thereafter she began to trill
And sang so blithely and so shrill
That she was heard both far and near.
At once around her did appear
Throstle and woodpecker and thrush
And divers birds from tree and
     bush.   1660
Because it seemed to them she had
O'ercome the owl, they were right
     glad,
And caroled with so various voice
That all the greenwood did rejoice.
Just so when one has lost a game,
Men jeer at him with cries of shame.
     The owl at all this din exclaimed:
"Hast thou a muster-call proclaimed?
And, wretch, dost thou desire to
     fight?
Nay, nay, thou hast too little might.
What do these birds mean by their
     screams?   1671
Thou summonest a host, it seems!

[44]

Ere ye fly hence, ye shall find out
How powerful is the tribe ye flout.
All those birds whose bills are hooked,
And talons are right sharp and
    crooked,
My kindred are they, one and all,
And will come gladly if I call.
The cock himself, who well can fight,
Must naturally uphold my right. 1680
For both of us have voices bright,
And sit beneath the sky at night.
If I should raise the hue and cry,
I'd lead so strong a company
Against you that your pride would
    fall.
A turd I'd not give for you all!
Nor would I, ere it be full eve,
One wretched feather on you leave!
But when we two came to this spot
It was agreed on, was it not? 1690
That we should take our quarrel
    where
We should receive a verdict fair.
Wilt thou then thy promise break?
Dost thou find judgment hard to
    take?
Judgment thou darest not abide,
And so, wretch, thou wilt fight and
    chide.
And yet if my advice ye try,
Before I raise the hue and cry,
Ye all will think no more of fight
But rather speed away in flight. 1700
For, by these talons that I carry,
If for my clan's attack ye tarry,
Ye'll sing in quite a different key
And curse the day ye fought with me.
For there is none of you so bold
That he my visage dare behold."
The owl spoke thus audaciously,
Because she would not willingly
Have gone to summon up her clan,
But rather wished to try the plan 1710
Of talking down the nightingale.
For many a man is weak and frail

In combat with a spear and shield,
And yet upon the battlefield,
By warlike show and direful threat,
Causes his foe with fear to sweat.
    But then the wren, expert in singing,
Promptly with the dawn came wing-
    ing,
To bring the nightingale her aid.
For though a modest sound she
    made, 1720
She had so good and shrill a voice
Her song caused many to rejoice.
Besides she had a clever head,
For she in woodland was not bred
But was brought up among mankind
And so with wisdom filled her mind.
She anywhere she wished could plead,
Before the King if there were need.
"Listen," she said, "your brawling
    cease.
What! do ye wish to break the
    peace, 1730
And would ye have our good king
    shamed?
But he is neither dead nor maimed,
And ye will both pay sore for it
If ye in his domains commit
A breach of peace. Stop, and agree
Before a judge to make your plea
And let his verdict bring accord,
For ye to this have pledged your
    word."
    The nightingale said: "So be it;
But not to thy plea I submit, 1740
But from the law I seek redress.
I would not that unlawfulness
Should end this quarrel wrongfully,
And judgment does not frighten me.
I have promised—and still advise—
That Master Nicholas, the wise,
Shall serve as judge between us two;
And this I trust that he will do.
But where are we to find him then?"
    Up in a linden sat the wren, 1750
And said, "His dwelling know ye not?

At Portisham, there is the spot;
In Dorsetshire the place would be,
Where the downs open toward the
    sea.
True justice he does there dispense,
And writes much that is full of sense,
So that his influence reaches far;
Even Scottish things the better are.
To find him would be no great bother,
For he has one house and no
    other.   1760
For this the bishops are to blame,
And all those who have heard his
    name
And know his work, the merit of it.
Why will they not, to their own
    profit,
Add him to their establishments
To hear his wisdom and good sense,
And, to secure his company,
Grant him good livings plentifully?"
   The owl said, "Certes, that is true.
These great men know not what they
    do   1770
When they so good a man neglect

And all his many gifts reject,
Grant livings to unworthy clerks,
But wholly disregard his works.
To kinsfolk they are kinder yet
And children may fat livings get.
Can their intelligence let pass
The claims of Master Nicholas?
But let us haste to him away
And hear the judgment he will
    say."   1780
   "Let us do so," said the nightingale.
"But who will go over in detail
Before the judge the points we made?"
   The owl said: "Do not be afraid,
For every word of our debate
I can from first to last relate;
And if in any thing I err,
Do thou but stand up and demur."
Speaking these words, away they
    flew
Without armed force or retinue, 1790
And so at Portisham arrived.
But if ye ask me how they thrived
In their debate, I cannot say.
For the story ends this way.

The Rule of Anchoresses [1]

THE ORDER OF ST. JAMES

IF ANY ignorant person ask of what order ye be, as some do, as ye tell me, who strain out the gnat and swallow the fly, answer and say that ye are of St. James' order, who was God's apostle, and, for his great holiness, was called God's brother. If such an answer seemeth strange to him or unusual, ask him what an order is, and where he may find in holy writ religion more plainly described and made clear than in St. James' canonical epistle. He saith what religion is, and what is a true order: *Religio munda et immaculata apud Deum et Patrem, hec est, visitare pupillos et viduas in tribulatione eorum et immaculatum se custodire ab hoc seculo,* that is, "Pure religion and without blemish is to visit and help widows and fatherless children, 10 and to keep him clean and unspotted from the world." Thus St. James describeth religion and order.

The latter part of his saying pertaineth to recluses, for there are two parts, for two manner of men that are of religion. To each pertaineth his part, as ye may hear.

There are good religious men in the world, some particularly as prelates and true preachers; they have the first part of what St. James said. They are, as he said, they who go to help widows and fatherless children. The soul is a widow that hath lost her spouse, that is, Jesu Christ, through any capital sin. He also is fatherless who hath, through his sin, lost the Father 20 of heaven. To go and visit such, and comfort them, and help with the food of holy teaching, this is true religion, saith St. James.

The latter part of his statement pertaineth to anchoresses, to your religion, as I said before, who keep you from the world, above all other religious, pure and unspotted. Thus the apostle St. James describeth religion and order; neither white nor black [2] doth he name in his order, as do many that strain at the gnat and swallow the fly, that is, make great matter of what is small. Paul, the first anchorite, Antonius, Arsenius, Macarius, and the

---

[1] As monks and nuns are men and women who lead a strict religious life in communities apart from the world, so anchorites and anchoresses are men and women who lead a similar life either alone or in very small groups.

[2] Monastic and mendicant orders (i.e. monks and friars) were often referred to by the color of their habits.

others, were they not religious and of St. James' order? Also St. Sara, St. Sincletica, and many other such men and women, with their coarse mattresses and their hard hair-cloth, were they not of good order? But whether white or black, as the ignorant ask you, who suppose that order lieth in the kirtle or in the cowl, God knoweth; nonetheless, they were both; not, however, as to clothes, but as God's spouse singeth of herself, *Nigra sum sed formosa:* "I am black, and yet white," she said, "unseemly without, and beautiful within." In this wise answer him that asketh you of your order, and whether white or black; say that ye are both, through the grace of
10 God, and of the order of St. James, as he wrote, the latter part, *Immaculatum se custodire ab hoc seculo,* that is, as I said before, "to keep him clean and unspotted from the world." Herein is religion, and not in the wide hood, or in the black, or in the white, or in the gray cowl.

Where many are gathered together, on this account, as a matter of agreement, men make an important matter of oneness of costume, and of other outer things, that the outer conformity may betoken the unanimity of love and will, that they all possess in common, along with their habit, that is, what each hath like the other; and also of other things, so long as they have all together, in one love and one will, each like the other. See to it that they
20 do not lie. Thus it is in a convent.

But wheresoever women or men live by themselves alone, as hermit or anchoress, outer things, whereof no offence may come, are not an important matter. Harken now to Micah, God's prophet: *Indicabo tibi, homo, quid sit bonum et quid Dominus requirat a te, utique facere iudicium et iustitiam, et sollicite anbulare cum Domino Deo tuo.* "I shall show thee, man, what is good, and what is religion, and what is order, and what holiness God asketh of thee. Observe this, understand it, do well, and judge thyself every week, and with fear and love walk with God thy Lord." And there, where these things be, is right religion, and there is true order;
30 and to do all the other things, and to leave this, is but trickery and false guile. All that the good religious do or think according to the outer rule, is altogether to this end; all is merely a tool to build with here, all is but a handmaid, to serve the lady in the rule of her heart.

THE ANCHORESS AND HER WINDOW

Wherefore, my beloved sisters, the least that ever ye may, love your windows; let them all be small, and those of your parlors the smallest and the narrowest. Let the cloth in them be twofold: the cloth black, the cross white, within and without. The black cloth betokeneth that ye are black, and of no worth as respects the world outwardly, in that the true Sun, that is Jesu Christ, hath discolored you on the outside; and so on the outside, as ye are, he hath made you unattractive to look upon, through the gleams of his grace. That white cross belongeth properly to you, for there are three kinds of crosses: red, black, and white. The red belongeth to them that are, for God's love, through the shedding of their blood, reddened and ruddied, as were the martyrs. The black cross is appropriate to those who do their penance in the world for loathsome sins. The white cross belongeth to white maidenhood and to purity, which is very difficult to keep well. Pain is everywhere to be understood by the cross. Thus, a white cross betokeneth the preservation of chastity, which is very difficult to guard well. The black also carrieth a signification, causeth less harm to the eye, and 10 is thicker against the wind, and harder to see through, and holdeth its color better against wind or aught else.

See that the parlors be enclosed on every side, and also carefully shut; and watch well your eyes, lest your heart fly out and wend away, as with David, and your soul turn sick as soon as it be outside. I write largely for others, since nothing of this toucheth you, dear sisters, for ye do not have the name, through the grace of God, of roving-eyed anchoresses, or of having catching looks or expressions, which some, at times, alas, put on contrary to their nature; for contrary to nature is it, and an exceeding great wonder, if the dead do roll their eyes about, and wed with living men 20 of the world, with sin.

"My dear master," some one will say readily enough, "and is it so exceedingly evil to look about outside?" It is, dear sisters, because of the evil that cometh of it, evil above every evil for every anchoress, and particularly for the young, and likewise to the old, since they are to give the young an example and a shield to protect themselves with. For, if anyone reprove one of them, will she not say right away, "My master, that doth she, who is better than I am, and knoweth better than I know, what she should do!" O dear anchoresses, oft a very skillful smith beateth out a very weak knife-blade; and the wise ought to follow wisdom, and not folly; and an old 30 anchoress may well be the cause that thou dost evil. But to look about outside, neither of you may, without evil; and take heed now what evil may befall you from looking around: not one evil, not two, but all the evil, and all the woe, that now is, and was ever yet, and shall ever be, all came from a looking.

That this is true, lo, here is the proof! Lucifer, through the fact that he saw and beheld in himself his own fairness, leaped into pride, and changed from an angel to a terrible devil. And of Eve, our common mother, is recorded, at the very beginning, the fresh entry of sin into her from her eyesight: *Vidit igitur mulier quod bonum est lignum ad vescendum, et* 40 *pulchrum oculis, spectuque delectabile, et tulit de fructu ejus et comedit, deditque viro;* that is, "Eve beheld that forbidden fruit, and saw it fair, and began to delight in that sight, and turned her desire thitherward, and took, and ate thereof, and gave her lord." Lo, how holy writ speaketh, and inwardly explaineth how sin began! Thus, looking went first, and made a way for wicked lust; and there came death thereafter, which all mankind feeleth. This apple, dear sisters, betokeneth all things that desire inclineth toward, and the delight of sin. When thou beholdest the man, thou art in Eve's case: thou lookest upon the apple.

UNSPOTTED FROM THE WORLD

It is not fitting that an anchoress be generous out of other men's alms. Would not one laugh a beggar loudly to scorn who invited a man to a 10 feast? Mary and Martha were both sisters, yet their lives were different. Ye anchoresses have taken you to Mary's part, which our Lord Himself praised: *Maria optimam partem elegit.* "Martha, Martha," said He, "thou art in great turmoil; Mary hath chosen better, and nothing shall take from her her part." Housewifeship is Martha's part, and Mary's part is stillness and rest from all the world's noise, that nothing may hinder her from hearing God's voice. And look what God saith, that nothing shall take from you this part. Martha had her office; let her be, and sit ye with Mary stonestill, at God's feet, and harken to Him alone. Martha's business is to feed and clothe poor men, like as doth a lady of the house; Mary ought not to meddle 20 in this; and if any one blame her, God himself will defend her for this, as holy writ maketh known.

On the other hand, an anchoress ought to take but sparingly that which she needeth. Whereof then may she show herself generous? She shall live by alms as closely as ever she may, and not gather to give it away later. She is not at all a housewife, but is a church anchoress. If she may spare any poor shreds, let her send them all secretly out of her dwelling. Under semblance of good is often concealed sin. And how shall these rich anchoresses, who are farmers or have established rents, give alms to their poor neighbors in secret? Do not desire to have the renown of being a generous 30 anchoress, neither to give much, nor to be the greedier to have the more. If greediness be the root of her bitterness, all the boughs are bitter that spring from her. To ask a thing in order to give it, is not right for an anchoress. Of anchoresses' courtesy and anchoresses' largess often cometh sin, and shame at the end.

Women and children that have worked hard for you, whatsoever ye can spare from yourselves, make them to eat. Let no man eat before you, unless he have need. Do not ye invite any to drink. Do not yearn that people esteem thee a charming anchoress. From a good friend take all that ye have need of, when she asketh you; but, for no bidding, take ye nothing without need, lest ye catch the name of a gathering anchoress. Of a person that ye mistrust, take ye neither more nor less, not so much as might be a root of ginger. Great necessity will drive you to beg outside; however, show your great distress humbly to your dearest friend.

Ye, my dear sisters, shall have no beast except a cat only. An anchoress that hath cattle seemeth more like a housewife, as Martha was, than an anchoress; in no way may she be Mary, in peace of heart. For then must she think of the cow's fodder, and of the herdman's hire, blandish the bailiff, defend her when men impound the cow, and yield therefore any damages. 10 Christ knoweth this is a loathly thing, when a complaint is made in town of an anchoress's cattle. However, if any must needs have a cow, look that she trouble no man, or harm any man, or that the anchoress have her thought fixed on the cow. An anchoress ought not to have anything that draweth her heart outward.

Drive ye no bargains; an anchoress that is a bargainer selleth her soul to the chapman of hell. Keep ye nothing in your house of another man's things, either possessions or clothing; do not at all receive church vestments, or the chalice, unless ye are forced to, for great danger; because from such keeping often times cometh much evil. Within your dwellings, let no man 20 sleep. If great necessity absolutely forceth you to break your rule, the while that it is broken see ye that ye have therein with you a woman of clean life, days and nights.

Since no man seeth you, and ye see no man, well may ye take no regard to your clothes, be they white, be they black; but let them be unadorned and warm, and well made, of skins well dressed, and have as many as ye need, for your bed and also for your back.

Next the flesh wear no linen cloth, unless it be of hards and of great coarseness. Let who will have stamin, and whoever will, let her be without. Ye shall lie in one garment, and girt. Wear ye no iron, or hair-cloth, or por- 30 cupine skins; do not scourge you therewith, or with leathern scourges or leaded, or with holly, or with briars; do not cause yourselves to bleed without the permission of your confessor. Do not take upon you too many disciplines at one time. Let your shoes be large and warm. In summer ye have leave to go and sit barefoot, and to wear hose without vamps, and to sleep in them, if any one wish. . . .

If ye must be wimpleless, be provided with warm capes, and black veils over them. It anyone intendeth to be seen, it is no great wonder if she deck herself out; but to God's sight she is more lovable, that is for the love of Him, without ornament outwardly. 40

THE BIRDS OF HEAVEN

True anchoresses are betokened by birds: for they leave the earth, that is, the love of all earthly things, and, through yearning of heart towards heavenly things, they fly upwards, towards heaven. But, though they fly high, with a life high and holy, they hold their heads low in gentle humility, as a bird flying bendeth its head low; and she considereth all of no worth that she doth, and doth well, and saith as our Lord taught all his own, *Cum omnia bene feceritis, dicite quod servi inutiles estis:* "When ye have done all well," said our Lord, "say that ye are unprofitable servants." Fly high, and yet hold your heads ever low. The wings that bear them upward are
10 good habits, that they must beat into good works, as a bird, when it flieth, beateth its wings. But the true anchoresses, that we liken to birds—not we, however, but God doth—they spread their wings, and make a cross of themselves, as a bird doth when it flieth, that is, in the thoughts of their heart, and in bitterness of mind, they bear God's cross.

Those birds fly well that have little flesh, like the pelican, and many feathers. The stork,[3] because of its great flesh, maketh a semblance to fly, and beateth its wings, but its feet drag ever down to earth. Just so, the anchoress that loveth the lusts of the flesh, and followeth her ease, the heaviness of the flesh and the evil habits of the flesh deprive her of her
20 flight; and though she maketh semblance, and much noise with her wings, that is, she letteth on as though she flew, and were a holy anchoress, yet, whoever beholdeth her laugheth her to scorn, for her feet, as doth the stork's, which are her lusts, draw her to earth. They are not like the lean pelican, and they do not fly high, but are earth-birds, and nest on the earth.

But God calleth the good anchoresses birds of heaven, as I said earlier: *Vulpes foveas habent, et volucres celi nidos:* "Foxes have their holes, and birds of heaven their nests." True anchoresses are rightly birds of heaven, that fly on high, and sit singing merrily on the green boughs; that is, their thoughts are upward, of the bliss of heaven that never fadeth, but is ever
30 green, and they sit on this green, singing very merrily; that is, they rest them in such thoughts, and have mirth of heart, as they that sing. The bird, however, at another time, to seek food for the flesh's need, lighteth down to earth, but the while that it sitteth on the ground, it is never secure, but turneth him often, and looketh ever eagerly about him.

Right so, the good anchoress, fly she never so high, must alight at times down to earth because of her body, eat, drink, sleep, work, speak, hear, as is needed, of earthly things. But then, as the bird doth, she must look well about her, and see on every hand, that she nowhere mistake, lest she be

---

[3] There seems to have been a confusion between the stork and the ostrich, owing to the similarity of Latin *strucio* to stork. See Rolle's *The Bee and the Stork*, p. 114.

caught through some snare of the devil, or be hurt some way, while she sitteth so low. "These birds have nests," said our Lord: *Volucres celi habent nidos.* A nest is hard, of pricking thorns on the outside, but delicate and soft within, and so must the anchoress suffer hard things outwardly in her flesh, and pricking torments; so wisely must she, however, overcome the flesh that she may say with the Psalmist, *Fortitudinem meam ad te custodiam,* that is, "I shall entrust my strength, Lord, to thy service." The nest must be hard without and soft within, and the heart sweet.

THE WHELPS OF PRIDE

The wilderness, that is the solitary life of the dwelling of an anchoress. For even as in a wilderness are all wild beasts, and as they will not permit 10 that a man draw nigh, but flee away when they have seen or heard him, so must all anchoresses, above all other women, be wild in this manner, for then will they, above all others, be dearest to Our Lord, and seem most lovely to Him. For of all flesh, the flesh of the wild deer is choicest and best. In this wilderness journeyed our Lord's people, as Exodus telleth, towards that blessed land of Jerusalem, that He had promised them; and ye, my dear sisters, have turned you by that same way to the high Jerusalem, to the kingdom that He hath promised His chosen ones. Go forth, however, very warily; for in this wilderness are many evil beasts: the lion of pride, the adder of poisonous envy, the unicorn of wrath, the bear of deadly 20 sloth, the fox of covetousness, the swine of greediness, the scorpion with the tail of stinking lechery, that is, lust. Here now are listed in order the seven capital sins.

The Lion of Pride hath very many whelps; and I will name some of them. *Vana Gloria,*[4] is called the first: that is, whoso thinketh highly of any thing that she doth, and is well pleased if she is praised, and is displeased if she is not esteemed as highly as she would like. The second whelp is called *Indignatio:* [5] that is, if one is scornful of anything that she seeth in another, or heareth, or if she despiseth chastisement or instruction from one lower. The third whelp is *Hypocrisis:* [6] that is one who maketh herself seem better 30 than she is. The fourth is *Presumptio:* [7] that is, she who undertaketh more than she can accomplish, or meddleth in things that do not fall to her. The fifth whelp is called Disobedience: that is, that child which doth not obey his parents; the underling, his prelate; the parishioner, his priest; the maid, her mistress; every inferior, his superior. The sixth whelp is *Loquacitas:* [8] she who feedeth this whelp, that is of much speaking, boasteth, and judgeth others; she lieth at times; she gabbeth, upbraideth, chideth, flattereth, stir-

---

[4] Vain Glory.   [5] Disdain.   [6] Hypocrisy.   [7] Presumption.
[8] Loquacity.

reth laughter. The seventh whelp is Blasphemy: this whelp's nurse is she who sweareth great oaths, or curseth bitterly, or speaketh evil of God or of His saints, because of any thing that she suffereth, seeth, or heareth. The eighth whelp is Impatience: this whelp he feedeth who is not patient under all wrongs and in all evils. The ninth whelp is Contumacy: and this whelp feedeth one who is head-strong in any thing that she hath undertaken to do, be it good, be it evil, so that no wiser counsel can bring her out of her unrestrained action. Many others there are that come of wealth, and of prosperity, of high family, of handsome clothes, of wit, of beauty, of
10 strength; of high living there waxeth pride, and of holy habits. Many more whelps than I have named the Lion of Pride hath whelped, but of these, think and give heed very greatly, for I do but go over them lightly, and but name them.

THE SEVEN DEADLY SINS

The proud are [the devil's] trumpeters; they draw in the wind of worldly praise, and then, with idle boasting, puff it out again, as doth the trumpeter, to make a noise, a loud blast of music, to show their vain glory. But, if they thought well upon God's trumpeters, and upon the trumpets of the angels of heaven, which must blow terribly in the four quarters of the world, before the dread Judgment, "Arise, ye dead, arise! come to the Lord's judg-
20 ment, to be judged," where no proud trumpeter may be saved,—if they thought rightly of this, they would readily enough sound in a lower strain in the devil's service. Of those trumpeters saith Jeremiah, *Onager solitarius in desiderio anime sue, attraxit ventum amoris.*[9] Of those who draw in wind for love of praise, Jeremiah saith thus, as I said before.

There are some jugglers who can be funny by no means but to make wry faces, and wrench their mouths out of shape, and scowl with their eyes. This art the unhappy, envious man practiseth in the devil's court, to arouse the laughter of their envious lord. For, if any one speaketh well or doth well, they cannot, by any means, look that way with the direct eye
30 of a good heart; but wink on one side, and look aloft, and squint; and if there is anything to blame or dislike, at that they scowl with both eyes; and when they hear anything good, they hang down both their ears; but their joy in what is evil is ever wide open. Then they distort their mouth, when they turn good to evil; and if there is somewhat evil, they make it worse through greater detraction. These are their own prophets, foretelling what is to come. They show, beforehand, how the hateful fiend shall terrify them with his hideous grinning; and how they shall themselves gnash their teeth, and beat their breasts, and show true expressions of their great anguish

9 The solitary wild ass in the desire of its heart snuffs up the wind of love.

in the pains of hell. But they are the less to be pitied, because they have learned beforehand the art of making grim cheer.

The wrathful man playeth before the devil with swords, and he is his knife-thrower, and playeth with swords, and beareth them by the sharp point upon his tongue. Sword and knife are both sharp and cutting words, which he casteth forth from him, and throweth towards others. But they forebode how the devils will play with them, with their sharp awls, and skirmish about them, and toss them like a woolen clout, each one towards the other, and pierce them through with hell-swords, which are keen, cutting, and horrible pains.   10

The slothful man lieth and sleepeth in the devil's bosom, as his dear darling; and the devil layeth his snout to his ears, and telleth him whatever he will. This is certainly true of him who is not busied in anything good; the devil eagerly talketh, and idle men lovingly receive his lessons. He that is idle and careless is the devil's bosom-sleeper; but he shall on Doomsday be fearfully awakened with the dreadful sound of the angels' trumpets, and shall awaken in terrible amazement in hell. *Surgite, mortui qui jacetis in sepulchris; surgite, et venite ad judicium Salvatoris.*[10]

The covetous man is the devil's ashman, and lieth always in the ashes, and goeth about the ashes, and busily bestirreth himself to heap up much, 20 and to rake many together, and bloweth therein, and blindeth himself, poketh, and maketh figures therein of Arabic numerals, as those reckoners do who have much to reckon up. This is the whole joy of this foolish man, and the devil beholdeth this whole game, and laugheth so that he bursteth. Every wise man will understand this well, that gold and silver both, and all earthly goods, are but earth and ashes, which blind every man that bloweth upon them, that is, who vexeth himself with them, and through them is proud of heart; and all that he heapeth up and gathereth together, and possesseth more than is necessary, is nothing but ashes, and it shall all become toads and adders for him in hell; and both his kirtle and his covering, as 30 Isaiah saith, shall be of worms for him who would not feed or clothe the needy: *Subter te sternetur tinea, et operimentum tuum vermis.*[11]

The greedy glutton is the devil's manciple, for he sticketh ever in the cellar or in the kitchen. His heart is in the dishes, his thought is all in the table-cloth; his life is in the tun, his soul in the pitcher. He cometh into the presence of his lord besmutted and besmeared, with a dish in one hand, and a bowl in the other. He talketh much with words, and staggereth like a drunken man who seemeth about to fall; he beholdeth his great belly, and the fiend laugheth so that he bursteth. God threateneth these men through Isaiah: *Servi mei comedunt, et vos esurietis,* etc.; "My men," he saith, "shall 40

---

[10] Arise, ye dead, who lie in graves; arise and come to the Savior's judgment.
[11] The worm will be spread under thee, and worms will be thy covering.

eat, and ye shall hunger forever," and ye shall be food for fiends, world without end. *Quantum glorificavit se et in deliciis fuit, tantum date ei luctum et tormentum.*[12] In Apocalypse: *Contra unum poculum quod miscuit, miscete ei duo;* "Give the toss-pot boiling brass to drink, and pour it into his wide throat, that he may perish inwardly. For one cup, give him two." Lo! such is God's judgment towards the glutton and towards drinkers, in the Apocalypse.

The lechers in the devil's court have rightly their own name. For, in these great courts, they are called lechers who have so lost shame that they are ashamed of nothing, but they seek out those with whom they may work most villainy. The lecher in the devil's court defileth himself foully, and all his fellows, and stinketh of that filth, and pleaseth well his lord with that same stinking breath, better than he would with any sweet incense. In *Vitae Patrum*[13] it relateth how he stinketh before God. The angel showed it truly and openly, who held his nose when the lecher came riding by, and not on account of the rotted body which he had helped the hermit bury. Of all others, then, they have the foulest office in the fiend's court, who so conduct themselves; and he shall thus treat them and torment them with eternal stench in the pains of hell.

Now have ye heard one part, my beloved sisters, concerning what are called the Seven Mother Sins, and of their offspring, and as to what office those men hold in the devil's court, who have wived with these seven hags, and why they are greatly to be hated and shunned.

OF SPEECH

Speech and taste both lie in the mouth, as sight in the eyes. But we must leave tasting until the time that we speak of your food, and speak now of speech, and after that of hearing, and sometimes of both in common, as they go together.

First of all, when ye must go to your parlor window, learn from your maid who it is that hath come, for it may be someone from whom ye must excuse yourself. And when ye must absolutely go out, cross most earnestly your mouth, ears, and eyes, and your breast also, and go forth, in the fear of God, to the priest. First say, *Confiteor,* and after that, *Benedicite.*

Harken to his words which he ought to say, and sit very still, that when he parteth from you he may not know of you either good or ill, and may not be able either to praise or to blame you. Some anchoress is so well learned, or so wisely worded, that she would have him know who it is that

[12] As much as she glorified herself and lived in pleasure, so much sorrow and torment give ye to her.

[13] The lives of the hermit saints of the Egyptian desert.

sitteth and speaketh with him, and replieth word against word, and becometh master when she should be anchoress, and teacheth him who is come to teach her. She wisheth, on her own account, to be recognized and known among the wise. Known is she well, for through the same things whereby she supposeth that she will be held to be wise, he understandeth that she is a fool, because she hunteth after renown and catcheth but blame. For, at the last, when he hath gone away, he will say, "This anchoress is of much speech!"

Eve held in Paradise a long talk with the adder, and told it all the lesson that God had taught her and Adam with regard to the apple. Thus the fiend through her own words understood right off her weakness, and found a way towards her, to effect her fall. Our Lady, St. Mary, did all in another wise: she did not tell the angel any tale, but briefly asked him something that she did not understand. Do ye, my dear sisters, follow our Lady, and not that cackler Eve. Wherefore, an anchoress, whatsoever she may be, as much as ever she can and may, let her keep still. Let her in no wise have a hen's nature. The hen, when she hath laid, can do nothing but cackle. And what doth she get from it? The stealthy man cometh right away, and taketh from her her eggs, and eateth up all that from which she was to bring forth her live birds. Right so that treacherous stealthy one, the devil, beareth away from the cackling anchoress, and swalloweth up all the good that she hath gained, which should, like birds, bear them up to heaven, had there not been cackling. The wretched peddler maketh more noise to cry up his soap than doth a rich mercer about all his precious merchandise.

Of some spiritual man that ye can trust in, as may be, it is good that ye ask counsel and remedy, that he may instruct you against temptations. Show him in your shrift, if he will hear it, your greatest and your loathliest sins, that he may have pity on you, and through that pity inwardly cry mercy of Christ for you. *Sed multi veniunt ad vos in vestimentis ovium, intrinsecus autem sunt lupi voraces:* "But know you and beware," saith our Lord, "for many will come to you shrouded with lamb's fleece, and are mad wolves." Believe worldly men little, the religious yet less; desire ye not too much their acquaintance. Eve without fear spoke with the adder; our Lady was adread of Gabriel's speech.

Without witness of a man or a woman that can hear you, do ye speak with no man often or long; and though it be of shrift, in the same house, or where he can look towards you, let there sit a third person, unless such a third person must some time be lacking. This is not said in particular on your account, dear sisters, nor of any like you, but because the truth is often misbelieved, and the innocent are often belied for lack of witness. Men believe straightway what is evil, and the evil blithely tell lies against the good. Some unhappy soul, when she hath said that she shrove her, hath shriven her all too wondrously. Wherefore, ought the good ever to have witness for two reasons: namely, one is, that if the envious tell lies against them, the witness may prove them false; that second is, in order to give others an example, and take away from the evil anchoress that same unhappy guile that I spoke of.

Out of a church window hold ye no conversation with no man, but bear honor thereto because of the holy sacrament that ye may see through it. At other times take your women to the house window. Let other men and women speak at the parlor window only for necessity; ye ought not to 10 speak but at these two windows.

Let there be silence ever at meals, for if other religious practise it, as ye well know, ye ought before all others. And if any hath a dear guest, let her maid, in her stead, gladden her companion; and she shall have leave to open her window once or twice, and make signs toward her of glad cheer. The courtesy of some, nevertheless, is turned her to evil; under semblance of good is oft concealed sin. An anchoress and a lady of the house ought to differ much from each other.

Every Friday of the year hold silence, unless it be a double feast, and then hold it some other day in the week: in the Advent, and on the Ember-20 days, hold silence Wednesdays and Fridays; in Lent three days, and all the Silent Week before the nones of Easter Eve. To your maid ye may, however, speak a few words, whatsoever ye will; and if any good man is come from afar, harken to his speech, and answer with few words to his asking.

A great fool would he be who might, at his own choice, grind whichever he would, chaff or wheat, and were to grind the chaff, and leave the wheat. "Wheat is holy speech," as St. Anselm saith. She grindeth chaff who chattereth. The two cheeks are the two grindstones; the tongue is the clapper. Look to it, beloved sisters, that your cheeks grind never but soul's food, and that your ears harken never but to soul's health, and that ye close not 30 only your ears, but the windows of your eyes as well, against idle speech, and that to you come no tale or tiding of the world.

BACKBITERS

Backbiters, who bite other men from behind, are of two kinds, but the latter sort is the worse. The former cometh quite openly, and speaketh evil of another, and speweth out his poison, as much as ever cometh to his mouth, and throweth out together all that the poisonous heart sent up to the tongue. But the latter cometh forward all in another wise, and is a worse enemy than the other, though under the cloak of a friend. He casteth down his head, and beginneth to sigh ere he may say anything, and maketh a drooping cheer, and moralizeth long in general that he may be the better believed. But when it cometh forth wholly, then is it but yellow poison.

"Alas and alack!" she saith, "woe is me, that he, or she, hath caught such a reputation! Busy enough was I about it, but it availed me nothing, to bring her to amendment. Long is it that I knew of it, but yet it would never have been exposed through me; but now it is so widely known, thanks to others, that I cannot deny it. They say that it is evil, and it is even worse. So grieved and sorry am I that I must admit it, but, in truth, it is so; and that is great sorrow. For many things he, or she, is truly to be praised, but not for this; and grieved am I therefor. No man can defend them." 10

These are the devil's serpents that Solomon speaketh of. Our Lord, by His grace, keep your ears from their venomous tongues, and permit you never to smell the foul pit that they uncover. Let those uncover it whom it befitteth, and let them hide it from others. That is a great service, and not to those only who hate that filth as soon as they smell it.

Now, my dear sisters, keep your ears from all evil speech, which is thus three-fold: idle, foul, and poisonous. People say of anchoresses, that almost every one hath an old woman to feed her ears; a prating gossip, who relateth to her all the tales of the land; a magpie, that chattereth of all that she seeth or heareth, so that it is a common saying, "From mill and market, 20 from smithy and from a house of anchoresses, tidings are brought." Christ knoweth, this is a sorry tale, and a house of anchoresses, which should be the most enclosed place of all, should be likened to the same three places in which is most idle chatter. But as free as ye be of all this, dear sisters, would that all others were likewise; which may our Lord grant.

THE KINGLY WOOER

There was a lady who was beset by her foes on all sides, and her land was all laid waste, and she became very poor, within an earthen castle. The love of a mighty king, however, was turned towards her, so immeasurably great that he, to court her, sent her his messengers, one after the other, and often many at a time, and sent her beautiful jewels, both many and fair, 30 and means of sustenance, and help from his high household to hold her castle. She accepted all this like a heedless thing, who was so hard-hearted that to her love he might be never the nearer. What wilt thou more? He came at last himself, and showed her his fair face, as he that was of all men fairest to behold, and he spoke exceeding sweetly, and words so merry, they could raise the dead from death to life; and he wrought many wonders, and performed many miracles before her sight, and showed her his might; and told her of his kingdom, and promised to make her queen of all that he owned. All this helped nothing. Is this not wondrous scorn? For she was never worthy to be his scullion. But so greatly, through his debonairness, had love overcome him that he declared at length:

"My Lady, thou art warred upon, and thy foes are so strong that thou mayst no wise, without succor of men, escape their hands, that they put thee not to shameful death. I will, for love of thee, take this fight upon me, and save thee from them that seek thy death. I know, however, in truth, that I shall receive in their midst a death-wound, and I will accept it heartily, to win thy heart. Now then I beseech thee, for the love that I have made
10 known to thee, that thou love me, at least after that same death, whom thou wouldst not when I was alive."

This king did all this, he rescued her from all her foes, and was himself grievously mistreated, and slain upon earth. Through a miracle, however, he arose from death to life. Would not this lady be of a race of evil nature if she, after all these things, did not love him hereafter?

This king is Jesu Christ, God's Son, who all in this wise wooed our soul, which the devils had beset. And He, as a noble wooer, after many messengers and many good deeds, came to prove His love, and showed through knightly prowess that He was worthy of love, even as sometimes knights
20 were wont to do. He entered a tournament, and for His lady's love, He, like a bold knight, had His shield pierced in every part in the fight.

THIRTEENTH CENTURY

· 5 ·

𝔄 𝔏𝔬𝔳𝔢-𝔖𝔬𝔫𝔤

Thomas of Hales

A maid of Christ entreateth me
That I for her a love-song write
By which most plainly she may see
The way to choose a faithful knight;
One that to her shall loyal be
And guard and keep her by his might.
Never will I deny her plea,
To teach her this be my delight.

Maiden, thou mayest well behold
How this world's love is but a race   10
Beset with perils manifold,
Fickle and ugly, weak and base.
Those noble knights that once were
    bold
As breath of wind pass from their
    place,
Under the mold now lie they cold,
Wither like grass and leave no
    trace. . . .

There's none so rich, nor none so free,
But that he soon shall hence away.   26
Nothing may ever his warrant be,
Gold, nor silver, nor ermine gay.
Though swift, his end he may not flee,
Nor shield his life for a single day.   30
Thus is this world, as thou may'st see,
Like to the shadow that glides away.

This world all passes as the wind.
When one thing comes, another flies;
What was before, is now behind;
What was held dear, we now despise.

Therefore he does as doth the blind
That in this world would claim his
    prize.
This world decays, as ye may find;
Truth is put down and wrong doth
    rise.   40

The love that may not here abide,
Thou dost great wrong to trust to
    now;
E'en so it soon shall from thee glide,
'Tis false, and brittle, and slight, I
    trow,
Changing and passing with every tide,
While it lasts it is sorrow enow;
At end, man wears not robe so wide
But he shall fall as leaf from
    bough. . . .

Paris and Helen, where are they   65
That were so bright and fair of face?
Amadas, Tristram, did they stay,
Or Iseult with her winsome grace?
Could mighty Hector death delay,
Or Caesar, high in pride of place?   70
They from this earth have slipped
    away
As sheaf from field, and left no trace.

They are as though they never were,
Of them are many wonders said,
And it is pity for to hear
How these were slain with tortures
    dread,

And how alive they suffered here;
Their heat is turned to cold instead,
Thus doth the world but false appear,
The foolish trust it,—lo! 'tis sped. 80

For though a mighty man he were
As Henry,[1] England's king by birth,
Though he as Absalom were fair,
Whose peer lived not in all the earth,
Yet of his pride he's soon stripped
    bare,
At last he'll fetch not a herring's
    worth.
Maid, if thou mak'st true love thy
    care,
I'll show thee a love more true than
    earth.

Ah! maiden sweet, if thou but knew
All the high virtues of this knight! 90
He is fair and bright of hue,
Mild, with face of shining light,
Meet to be loved and trusted too,
Gracious, and wise beyond man's
    sight,
Nor through him wilt thou ever rue,
If thou but trust in his great might.

He is the strongest in the land;
As far as man can tell with mouth,
All men lie beneath his hand,
East, and West, and North, and South;
Henry, King of Engellánd,   101
He holds of him and to him boweth.
His messenger, at his command,
His love declares, his truth avow'th.

Speak'st thou of buildings raised of
    old,   113
Wrought by the wise king Solomon,
Of jasper, sapphire, and fine gold,
And of many another stone?
His home is fairer by many fold
Than I can tell to any one;
'Tis promised, maid, to thee of old,

If thou wilt take him for thine
    own.   120

It stands upon foundations sound,
So built that they shall never fall;
Nor miner sap them underground,
Nor shock e'er shake the eternal wall;
Cure for each wound therein is
    found,
Bliss, joy, and song, fill all that hall.
The joys that do therein abound
Are thine, thou may'st possess them
    all.

There friend from friend shall never
    part,
There every man shall have his right;
No hate is there, no angry heart,   131
Nor any envy, pride or spite;
But all shall with the angels play
In peace and love in heavenly light.
Are they not, maid, in a good way,
Who love and serve our Lord aright?

No man may Him ever see
As He is in all His might,
And without pure bliss may be
When he knows the Lord of light. 140
With Him all is joy and glee,
He is day without a night.
Will he not most happy be
Who may bide with such a
    knight? . . .

This writing, maiden, that I send, 193
Open it, break seal and read;
Wide unroll, its words attend,
Learn without book each part with
    speed.
Then straight to other maidens wend
And teach it them to meet their need;
Whoso shall learn it to the end
In sooth 'twill stand him in good
    stead.   200

5: A Love-Song

And when thou sittest sorrowing,
Draw forth the scroll I send thee here,
And with sweet voice its message sing,
And do its bidding with good cheer.
To thee this does His greeting bring;
Almighty God would have thee near;
He bids thee come to His wedding,
There where he sits in Heaven's high
    sphere.

HENRY S. PANCOAST

· 6 ·

Three Sorrowful Things

When I think upon things three,
Never may I happy be.
The one is that I must away;

Another, I know not the day;
The third one is my greatest care,
I know not whither I must fare.

MABEL VAN DUZEE

· 7 ·

When the Turf Is Thy Tower

When the turf is thy tower,
And the grave is thy bower,
Thy skin and throat so white

Will the worms invite.
Can all the world's bliss
Save thee from this?

MABEL VAN DUZEE

· 8 ·

Look on Me with Thy Sweet Eyes

Lady, I thank thee
  With heart very mild
For the good thou hast done me
  With thy sweet Child.

Thou art good, sweet, and bright,
  Chosen above all other;
Thou wert of that sweet wight
  That was Jesu, the mother.

Gentle Maiden, I pray thee
  With thy sweet Child
That thou shelter me
  In God's mercy mild.

Mother, look on me
  With thine eyes sweet;
Rest and bliss give thou me,
  When I die, Lady meet.

MABEL VAN DUZEE

· 9 ·

𝕿ell 𝕸e, 𝖂ight in the 𝕭room

"Tell me, wight in the broom,
Teach me what I must do
So that my husband
Will love me true."

"Hold thy tongue still,
And thou'lt have all thy will."

MABEL VAN DUZEE

· 10 ·

𝕹ow 𝕾prings the 𝕾pray

Now springs the spray;
All for love I am so sick
That sleep I never may.

As I rode the other day
  In my playíng,
Saw I where a little maid
  Began to sing:
  "May the clod to him cling!
Woe is him who in love-longing
  Shall live for aye!   10
  Now springs the spray, etc."

When I heard that merry note,
  Thither I drew;
I found her in an arbor sweet
  Under a bough
  With joy enow.
Soon I asked, "Thou merry maid,
  Why sing'st thou aye,
  '*Now springs the spray*, etc.'"

Then answered me that maiden sweet
  With words so few: 21
"My sweetheart, he has promised me
  His love so true;
  But he changes for new.
If I may, he shall it rue,
  By this day!
  Now springs the spray, etc."

MABEL VAN DUZEE

[67]

· II ·

Alisoun

———

When March doth into April merge,
And slender shoots first spring,
The little birds obey the urge
Their several songs to sing.
For one I live in love-longing,
The comeliest above everything;
She delight to me may bring,
To her my heart I tune.
   By happy chance my life is blessed,
   Of all heaven's gifts this is the best;   10
   My love is turned from all the rest,
   And lights on Alisoun.

In hue her hair is fair to see,
Her eyes are black, her brows are brown.
With lovesome face she laughed on me—
So small of waist, so slender grown.
Unless she take me for her own,
I will cut short this life alone—
A fate that I would sore bemoan—
And death will be a boon.   20
   By happy chance etc.

When at night I turn and wake,
And in my cheeks the color dies,
Lady, all for thy sweet sake,
Only my longing with me lies.
In all the world no man so wise,
Her graciousness to realize;
Whiter than swan her neck doth rise,
Fairest maid under moon.
   By happy chance, etc.   30

Longing and spent, at night I wake,
Weary as water in a weir.
Lest one my sweetheart from me take,
I've yearned with love sincere.
Rather than mourn for many a year,
Most patiently I'll bid her hear.
Graceful one and dear,
Hearken to my rune.
   By happy chance, etc.

MABEL VAN DUZEE

The Bestiary

THE LION'S NATURE

The lion standeth on a hill; if he hear a man hunting,
Or through his sense of smell scent that he draweth nigh,
By whatever way that he will, to the dale he descendeth;
All of his footsteps he after him filleth,
He draweth dust with his tail, where he walketh down,
Either dust or dew, that man may not find him;
He hasteneth down to his den where he may shelter him.
    Another trait he hath: when he is just born,
The lion lieth still, he stirreth not from his sleep,
Until the sun hath shone three times about him;   10
Then his father arouseth him with the roar that he maketh.
    The third law hath the lion: when he lieth down to sleep,
He must never lock the lids of his eyes.

Signification

    Most high is that hill, which is heaven's kingdom.
Our Lord is that lion, who liveth there above;
When it did please Him to alight here on earth,
The devil might never find out, though he hunted with cunning,
How He came down, nor how He took His dwelling,
In that gentle maiden, Mary by name,
Who bore Him for man's salvation.   20
    When our Lord was dead, and buried, as His will was,
In a stone He lay still, till it came the third day;
His Father so strengthened Him that He rose from the dead then,
To bring us to life.
He watcheth, as His will is, like a shepherd over his fold;
He is the Shepherd, we are the sheep; shield us He will,
If we harken to His word, that we go nowhere astray.

THE EAGLE'S NATURE

I will explain the eagle's nature,
As I in books have read it:
How he reneweth his youth,[1]
How he cometh out of old age.
When his limbs are unwieldy,
When his beak is quite awry,
When his flight is very feeble,
And his eye-sight dim,
Hear how he reneweth him.
A well he seeketh, that springeth ever,   10
Both by night and by day;
Over that he flieth and upwards soareth,
Until the heaven he seeth,
Through the skies, six and seven,
Until he cometh to heaven.[2]
And as straight as ever he may,
Into the sun he maketh his way;
The sun strengtheneth his whole flight;
Likewise it maketh his eyes be bright; [3]
His feathers fall off from the heat,   20
And straight down, into the wet,
He falleth to the well's ground,[4]
Where he becometh hale and sound.[5]
Out he cometh, wholly new,
Except his bill is still untrue;
His upper bill is somewhat wrong,
Though his limbs are strong.
He cannot get him any food
That will do him any good.
Then he goeth to a stone,   30
And rubbeth his bill thereon,
Whetteth till his upper beak
All its crookedness hath lost;

---

[1] Psalm 103:5 (Vulgate 102:5). Compare Milton's passage in the *Areopagitica* on the eagle's newing (often misprinted "mewing") her mighty youth.

[2] A reference to the Ptolemaic astronomy, which taught that the earth is at the centre of nine spheres, eight of them occupied by the planets and the stars. The author has erred in placing the sun in the eighth, instead of the fourth, sphere.

[3] Cf. *3 Henry VI*, II, i: "Nay, if thou be that princely eagle's bird, Show thy descent by gazing 'gainst the sun."

[4] Bottom.

[5] Cf. *1 Henry IV*, IV, i: "Bated like eagles having lately bathed."

After, with his straightened bill,
He eateth such food as he will.

Signification

Like as man, so is the eagle,
   If ye would but listen;
Old in those his secret sins,
   Before the priest him christen.
And thus reneweth him this man,   40
   When he is brought to kirk;
Ere he could take thought of it,
   His eyes were dark with murk.
He there forsaketh Satanas
   And each sinful deed;
He taketh him to Jesu Christ,
   For He shall help his need,
Believeth on Lord Jesu Christ,
   And learneth the priest's teaching;
Removeth from his eyes the mist,   50
   As he tarrieth there beseeching.
All his hope is placed in God,
   And he on His love intendeth,
That is the sun, assuredly,
   Which thus his eye-sight mendeth.
Naked he falleth in baptismal font,
   And cometh out quite new,
All but a little: what is that?
   His mouth is still untrue.
His mouth is yet somewhat unskilled,   60
   In *paternoster* and creed;
Fare he north; or fare he south,
   Learn he must his need,
Beg his boon of his God,
   And thus his mouth make right,
Take to him thus the soul's food,
   Through our Lord's own might.

THE SERPENT'S NATURE

There is a worm [6] in the world,   well man knoweth him;
Adder is its name,   and thus he reneweth him.

[6] Serpent.

When he is crippled and twisted,   and weakened with age,
He fasteth until his skin slacketh,   ten days fully,
So that he is lean and feeble,   and with difficulty moveth;
He creepeth forth like a cripple,   his craft thus revealing,
Seeketh out a stone   that hath a hole in it,
Narrow, but he forceth him   with great hardship through it;
For his fell [7] he there leaveth,   his flesh forth creepeth.
He walketh towards the water   where he will drink deep;   10
But he speweth out first   all of the venom
That in his breast is bred   since his birth-time;
He drinketh afterwards deeply,   and thus he reneweth him.

Signification

Know, Christian man,   what thou Christ didst promise,
At the kirk door,   where thou wert christened.
Thou didst promise to believe on Him   and to love His laws,
To hold in thine heart   the commands of Holy Church.
If thou hast broken this,   then hast thou harmed all;
Thou perishest and witherest   in attaining life eternal.
Made aged art thou, out of all bliss,   like the snake in this world.   20
Renew thyself, therefore,   as doth the adder;
It is thy need.
Confirm thee in fasting,   and fill thee with virtues,
And help those poor men   that are living about thee.
Deem not thyself worthy   to look upon the door
That leadeth heavenwards,   but walk upon earth,
Merciful among men.   No pride feel thou,
Pride nor men's vices,   but cease thou from sinning.
Pray grace for thee ever,   both by night and by day,
That thou mayst find mercy   for thy misdeeds.   30
This life betokeneth the path   that the adder passeth over,
And this is the hole in the stone   that thou must go through;
Leave thy foulness behind thee,   as the adder doth his skin;
Go thou then to God's house,   the gospel to hear there,
Which is the soul's drink   for the quenching of sins.
But first say thou in shrift   thy sins to the priest,
Free thyself of thy breast-filth,   and confirm thy covenant,
Make fast in thy heart   what thou first didst promise.
Thus art thou young and new;   henceforth be thou true.
The devil need not compel thee,   for he may not harm thee,   40

[7] Skin.

But he fleeth from thee,   as the adder from the naked.
Against the clothed is the adder courageous,   and the devil clever in sins;
Ever the sinful man   he will beset,
And against all mankind   he holdeth war and strife.
What if he have leave   from the Lord of heaven
To harm us, as once he did   our elders now dead?
Let our body be afflicted,   but shelter we the soul,
Which is like to our head;   let us protect it worthily.

THE WHALE'S NATURE

The great whale is a fish,
The greatest that in the water is;
Thou wouldest say, indeed,
If thou were to see it when it floated,
That it was an island
Stationed on the sea-sand.
  This fish, which is enormous,
When he is hungry, gapeth wide;
Out of his throat there rusheth a breath,
The sweetest thing that is on land;   10
For this, other fishes draw to him;
When they smell it, they are delighted;
They come and hover in his mouth;
Of his trap they are unwary.
The whale his jaws then locketh,
All these fishes in he sucketh;
The small he will thus entrap; [8]
The great he may in no wise catch.
  This fish dwelleth on the sea bottom,
And liveth ever hale and sound,   20
Till there cometh the time
When the storm stirreth all the sea,
When summer and winter contend.
He cannot dwell therein,
So troubled is the sea's bottom
That he cannot remain there that time,
But he cometh up and floateth still,
Whilst that weather is so ill.
The ships that are storm-driven on the sea,—

---

[8] Cf. *All's Well That Ends Well*, IV, iii: "Who is a whale to virginity and devours up all the fry it finds."

Death is loath to them, to live is dear,— 30
They look about them, and see this fish;
An island they suppose it is.
For that they are deeply grateful,
And with all their might thereto they draw
The ships to anchor,
And they all go ashore.
From stone and steel in the tinder
They kindle a fire on this monster;
They warm them well and eat and drink.
The fire he feeleth and maketh them sink; [9] 40
At once he diveth to the ground,
And destroyeth them all without a wound.

Signification

   The devil is great in will and might,
As witches are in their craft;
He causeth men hunger and thirst,
And many another sinful lust;
He draweth men to him with his savor;
Who followeth him, findeth shame.
Those are the little ones in the faith's law,
The great to him he cannot draw; 50
By the great I mean the steadfast,
In true belief, in flesh and spirit.
Who listeneth to the devil's lore,
At length he shall rue it sore;
Whoso fasteneth hope on him
Shall follow him to hell so dim.

[9] Cf. *Paradise Lost*, I, 200–8.

Havelok

(ABRIDGED FROM VSS. 338–1384)

Now there was in Denmark in those days a rich and powerful king, named Birkabeyn, who had a son and two fair daughters whom he loved as his own life. And it came to pass that death, which will not forbear for rich or poor, for king or emperor, seized upon him. Then Earl Godard, his friend, who was chosen by his knights to care for the children, took Havelok, the heir, and his sisters, Swanborow and Helfled, and put them in a castle where they wept bitterly for hunger and cold. When he had presently brought all the land into his power, he planned against them a very great treachery. He went to their tower where Havelok, who was brave enough, greeted
10 him fairly.

"We hunger," he said. "We have naught to eat, nor knight nor knave to serve us. Woe for us that we were born! Alas, is there no grain that men could make bread? We are very near to death."

But Godard cared nothing for their woe and, as if in sport, took the maidens—wan and green they were for hunger—and cut their throats. In their blood they lay by the wall, and Havelok, in terror, saw the knife at his own heart. Little as he was, he kneeled down before that Judas and said:

"Lord, have pity. My homage and all Denmark will I give you if you will let me live. On the book will I swear never to bear shield nor spear
20 to harm you, and today will I flee from Denmark and never come again."

Now when this devil heard that, somewhat did he begin to soften. He drew back the knife, still warm with the children's blood, and a fair miracle it was, that for pity he went his way. But though he would not kill the boy himself, he grieved that Havelok was not dead. Staring as if he were mad, he mused alone and then he sent for a fisherman, who he knew would do his will.

"Grim, my thrall," he said, "thou knowest that all I bid thee thou must do. To-morrow I will make thee free and rich if thou wilt take a child when thou seest the moon to-night, and cast him in the sea. The sin of it
30 will I take for mine own."

Then Grim took the child, and bound him fast; he wrapped him in an old cloth, gagged him with foul rags, so that he could not speak nor breathe, and cast him in a black bag. Lifting him on his back, he bore him to his cottage and gave him over to Dame Leve, whom he told what his lord commanded. When she heard that, she started up and threw the boy down so hard that his head cracked against a great stone. Then might Havelok well say: "Alas, that ever I was born a king's son!"

In this fashion did the child lie until midnight, when Grim bade Leve bring a light that he might put on his clothes. As she was handling them, she saw a light very clear and bright shining about the child. From his mouth came a ray like a sunbeam. It was as light as though wax candles burned within the house.

"Jesu Christ!" quoth Dame Leve: "what light is this in our dwelling? 10 Rise up, Grim, and see what it means."

Both of them hastened to the boy and unbound him, and shortly, as they turned over his shirt, they found on his right shoulder a king's mark, very bright and fair.

"God knows, this is the heir who will be Lord of Denmark," cried Grim, and he fell down and sorely grieved. "O lord, have pity on me and on Leve here! Both of us are thy churls, thy hinds. Well will we feed thee till thou canst ride and bear helmet and shield and spear, and never shall Godard know, that vile traitor! Through no other man than thee, lord, will I have my freedom." 20

Then was Havelok a blithe lad, and he sat up and asked hungrily for bread. Dame Leve said: "Well is it for me that thou canst eat. I will fetch thee bread and cheese, butter and milk, pasties and cheese cakes, and with all such, lord, will we feed thee in this great need. Oh, true it is as men swear, 'Where God will help, nothing shall harm.'"

Then Havelok ate ravenously, and when he was fed, Grim made a fair bed, undressed him and laid him therein. "Sleep fast," he said, "and do not fear the night, for from sorrow thou art brought to joy."

Now as soon as it was daybreak, Grim took his way to Godard, that wicked steward of Denmark, and telling him the boy was dead, asked for 30 his reward and freedom.

Godard looked at him grimly. "So thou wilt be an earl now, wilt thou?" he said. "Get thee gone, thou foul churl of the dirt, and be forever thrall, as thou hast been before. For but a little more I will give thee to the gallows."

Overlate Grim thought how he should escape from that traitor. "What shall I do?" he pondered. "Should Godard know that Havelok lives, he will hang us both. Better is it for us to flee the land and save our lives."

Then Grim sold all his corn, his woolly sheep, his horned cow, the horse, swine, and bearded goat, the geese and farmyard hens; everything that he 40 could, he sold, and drew out the last penny. He tarred his ship and put in a mast, strong, firm cables, good oars, and a sail. When he had made all ready, he took young Havelok, himself and his wife, his three sons, and his two pretty daughters, and pulled out to the high sea. When he was about a mile from land the north wind came, which men call "bise," and drove them into England, that afterward was to be Havelok's.

Now Grim landed at the north end of Lindsey in the Humber and, drawing up his ship on the sand, he made there a little earth house. Because he owned it, the place there took the name of Grim, and men call it Grimsby and shall until Doomsday.

Grim was a wise fisherman, and with net and hook he caught many a
10 good fish; sturgeon, whale, turbot, salmon, seal, and cod he took, and porpoise, herring, mackerel, flounder, plaice and thornback. He made panniers for himself and his three sons, for carrying the fish they sold in the upland. To town and grange he went, and never did he come home with empty hand. He knew well the Lincoln road, and often he went from end to end of that good city till he had sold everything and counted his pennies. When he came home he brought with him wastels [1] and horn-shaped cakes, and his bags full of corn and meat. Hemp, too, he would have, and strong ropes for the nets he cast in the sea.

Thus did Grim live, and for twelve years or more he fed his family well.
20 But Havelok came to know that while he lay at home, Grim was sorely toiling for his food, and he thought: "No longer am I a child, but well grown, and easily can I eat more than Grim can ever get. God knows I will go now and learn to labor for my meat. Work is no shame! Gladly will I bear the panniers, and it shall not grieve me though the burden be great."

On the morrow when it was day, Havelok sprang up, cast on his back a pannier stacked high with fish, and alone carried as much as four men. He sold every bit and brought home each piece of silver, keeping back not a farthing. And never, thereafter, did he lie at home, but went forth each day so that he would learn his trade.

30 Now it chanced that there came a great dearth of bread and grain, and Grim knew not how he should feed his family. Great fear did he have because of Havelok, who was so strong and could eat so heartily. Then Grim said to him: "Havelok, I think we will soon die of hunger, for our meat is long since gone, and the famine lasts. For myself I care not, but it is better that thou go hence, ere it be too late. Thou knowest the way to Lincoln, and therein is many a good man from whom thou canst win thy food. But alas for thy nakedness! I will make thee a coat from my sail, so thou shalt take no cold."

Taking down the shears from the peg, Grim made the coat, and Havelok
40 put it on. With no other kind of dress, and barefoot, he went to Lincoln. He had no friend there, and he knew not what to do. For two days he

---

[1] Cakes made with fine flour.

fasted, but on the next he heard one calling: "Porters, porters, come hither!" Like a flash all the poor folk sprang forward and Havelok was in their midst. Leaping to the earl's cook, who was buying meat at the bridge, he bore the food to the castle, and for this service he got a farthing cake. On yet another day when the cook called the porters, Havelok knocked down sixteen good lads who stood in his way, and ran with his fish basket and began snatching up the fish. He lifted up a whole cartload of cuttle fish, of salmon and plaices, great lampreys, and eels, and he spared not his heels nor his toes, till he came to the castle and men took the burden from his head. The cook looked at him and, thinking he was a strong fellow, asked: "Wilt thou 10 be with me? I will feed thee gladly."

"God knows I ask no other hire, dear sir. Give me enough to eat and I will make the fire burn clear, crack sticks for eel-skinning, and wash your dishes fairly."

When the cook had said, "I ask no more," and told him to sit down, Havelok was still as a stone till he had eaten enough. Then he went to the well and, filling a great tub, bore it alone to the kitchen. He would let no one fetch water, nor bear meat from the bridge; he alone bore the peat, the sedges and the wood, and drew all the water that was needed. He took no more rest than as if he were a beast, and of all men was he meekest. He 20 was always laughing and blithe of speech, for his griefs he could well conceal. No child was so little that Havelok would not sport with him, and young or old, knights or children, gentle or bold, all who saw, loved him. His fame went far, how he was meek and strong and fair, and how he had nothing to wear save one clumsy wretched coat. Then the cook took pity on him and bought him new clothes, stockings and shoes, and he put them on quickly. When he was clothed, no one on earth was fairer, nor did any in the kingdom seem more fit to be king. When all the earl's men were together at the Lincoln games, Havelok stood like a mast shoulders taller than any. At wrestling he overthrew every one, and yet for all his strength 30 he was gentle, and despite a man's misdeeds to him, he never laid hand on him for ill. Virgin he was, and would no more lie with a whore than with an old witch.

It came to pass then, that Earl Godrich made barons and earls and all the men of England come to Lincoln to be at the Parliament. With them came many a champion, and some nine or ten began to sport, while grooms and husbandmen with their goads, just as they had come from the plow, gathered to watch. A bar lay at their feet and the strong young men began mightily to put the stone. Strong was he who could lift it to his knee, and a champion was he reckoned who could put it one inch beyond another. 40

Now as the crowd stood and stared, making a great noise over the best throw, Havelok looked on. Never before had he seen stone putting and of it

[79]

he was very ignorant. His master bade him try what he could do, and half afraid he started, caught the heavy stone, and hurled it the first time twelve feet beyond all other throws. The champions that saw it shouldered each other and laughed. "We stay here too long," they said, and would play no more. Now the wonder could not be hid, and very shortly through all England went the tale of how Havelok had put the stone. In castle and hall, the knights told of it and how he was strong and fair, till Godrich,[2] hearing them, thought to himself: "Through this knave shall I and my son win England. On the mass-gear King Æthelwold made me swear that I 10 would give his daughter to the tallest, strongest, fairest man alive. Though I went to India, where could I find one so tall and cunning as Havelok? It is he who shall have Goldborough."

Planning this wicked treason, for he believed Havelok a churl's son, God-rich sent quickly for Goldborough and told her, though she vowed she would wed none save a king or a king's son, that on the morrow she would wed his cook's knave. When the day came, that Judas called to him Have-lok and asked him if he would marry.

"Nay, by my life!" quoth Havelok. "What should I do with a wife? I could not feed nor clothe her, and where would I take a woman? No kine 20 have I, no house nor cot, no stick nor blade of grass, no food nor clothes, but one old white coat. These clothes I wear are the cook's, and I am his servant."

Godrich started up and struck him: "Save thou take her whom I give thee for wife, I will hang or blind thee." Then Havelok was afraid and granted that which was asked, and Goldborough too, though she liked it but little, dared not hinder the marriage. She thought it was the will of God who makes the growing grain and who had made her a woman. So they were married and pennies were thick on the book, and all was done fair and well at the mass. The good cleric who married them was the Archbishop of 30 York, whom God had sent to that Parliament.

When the marriage was done, then Havelok knew not what to do, where to stay, nor where to go, for plainly he saw that Godrich hated them. Be-cause Havelok knew full well that shame would come to his wife, he de-cided that they should flee to Grim and his three sons, since there they could best hope to be fed and clothed. On foot they went, since they knew no help for it, and held the right way till they came to Grimsby. Now Grim had died, but his five children were still alive and they made great joy to welcome Havelok. They fell on their knees and cried: "O welcome dear lord, and welcome thy fair companion. Blessed be the time when in 40 God's law thou didst take her. Well is it for us who see thee alive. We have goods and horses, nets and ships in the sea, gold, silver, and many things

[2] Regent of England, guardian of Princess Goldborough.

which our father Grim charged us to give to thee. Stay here, and all is thine. Thou shalt be our lord and we will serve thee and her. Our sisters will wash and wring her clothes, and bring water for her hands, and they will make her bed and thine."

Joyously then they broke sticks and set the fire ablaze. So that there should be no lack of meat, they spared neither goose nor hen nor duck, and also they fetched wine and ale. But at nightfall with sad heart, Goldborough lay down, for all unfittingly had she been wed. A light, fair and bright like flame, suddenly filled the room, and she saw that it came from the mouth of him who slept beside her. "He is dead," she thought, "or else most nobly born." Then she saw on his shoulder a red gold cross, and the voice of an angel said:

"Goldborough, let be thy sorrow. That fair cross shows that he who hath wedded thee is a king's son, and that thou shalt be a queen. Of Denmark and of England he shall be king."

When she had heard these words of the heavenly angel, she was too blithe to hide her joy, and she kissed Havelok as he slept unknowing. He started up from his sleep.

"Lady," he said, "hear a dream most wonderful. I thought I was in Denmark on a hill so high that I could see all the world. And as I sat there, my arms were so long that I could hold all Denmark. But when I would draw my arms to me, all things that ever were there cleaved to them, and the keys of strong castles fell at my feet. And again I dreamed that I flew over the salt sea to England. I closed it in my hand and, Goldborough, I gave it to thee."

"May Christ turn thy dreams to joy," she answered. "As though I saw it, I believe that within a year thou shalt wear England's crown, and be king of Denmark too. But delay not thy going. Take with thee Grim's sons, for they are eager and love thee heartily."

Now when the day came, Havelok rose and went ere he did any other deed to the church, there to kneel and call on Christ and the cross.

"O Thou who dost rule the wind and water, the wood and field," he cried, "of Thy mercy pity me, Lord. Give me vengeance on the foe who killed my sisters and bade Grim drown me in the sea. With wicked wrong he holds my land who has made me a beggar, though I never did him harm. Let me pass safely across the sea, O Lord, and bring me to that land which Godard holds."

LAURA HIBBARD LOOMIS

The Debate of the Body and the Soul

Once as I lay upon a winter night,
    And chid the laggard coming of the day,
Before my eyes there came a dismal sight,
    That settled there, and would not pass away:
    All on a bier a clay-cold Body lay;
A Knight's it was, who, in the o'erblown pride
    Of youth and lustihead, cared not to pay
God's service, but his gracious hests defied;
And now the parting Ghost stood by the Body's side.

But, ere it parted on its flight, it turned   10
    Back to the Body, as 'twere loath to leave
The home wherein it whilom had sojourned,
    But to its haunt familiar fain would cleave;
    And, looking sadly on it, seemed to grieve,
And thus it said—"Alas, and well-a-wo!
    What could thee now of all thy sense bereave,
Thou fickle flesh—why liest thou rotting so,
That erst so high of heart and bearing wont to go?

"Thou, that wert ever wont on prancing steed
    To ride abroad, by country or by town;   20
Thou, that wert known for many a shining deed
    Of high emprise, a knight of fair renown:
    How are thy swelling honors stricken down,
Thy heart of lion-daring lowly bowed!
    Where now is thy imperious voice, thy frown
Of withering hate? Thou, that wert once so proud,
What dost thou lying here, wrapt in a vulgar shroud?

"Where is thy arras stiffening with gold,
    Thy couches all with gorgeous hangings strewed,
Thy ambling jennets, and thy destrier ¹ bold,   30

---

¹ War-horse.

[82]

Thy hawks and hounds, that came to thee for food?
Where now the troops of friends that round thee stood?
Where thy swollen treasure-heaps, the jewels worn
    About the proud brows of thine altitude?
Ah! thou, whose banner once, in field upborne,
Shook terror, now liest low, of all thy lustre shorn!

"Where are thy cooks, whose curious skill did whet
    Thy glutton lust, made thy lewd flesh to swell,
That now with worms in rottenness must fret,
    While I must bide the bitter pangs of hell?   40
    Thy towers that look so fair o'er wood and dell,
Thy chambers with sweet flowers all garlanded,
    Thy vestments rare of pall and purple—tell,
What shall they all thy wretched corse bestead,
That in the dull dark grave to-morrow shall be laid?

"Where be thy gleemen, that did crown thy cheer
    With minstrel song and merry jargoning
Of viol, tabor, and the trumpet clear,
    Whilst to them aye rich largess thou wouldst fling
    Of robes or the red gold, and bid them sing   50
Thy praises wide by cottage, bower, or hall?
    Thou, who brought'st ever wail and sorrowing
On poor men's hearths, that cursed thy tyrant thrall,
Who is there at this hour to sorrow o'er thy fall?

"The morsel won by the o'ertoilèd brow
    Of poverty thou took'st to feed the state
Of revelers, that fattened were enow.
    The rich were ever welcome at thy gate,
    But blows and spurns did still the poor await.
Wretch, who now thanks or blesses thee? Ere morn   60
    From the high palace where thou ruledst late,
From wealth, and rank, and kin, thou shalt be borne,
To make thy bed with worms, in loathsome pit forlorn.

"Thou, for whose wild ambition's sateless grasp
    The world's dominion seemèd scarce too wide,
A few poor feet of earth shall soon enclasp
    Thy wretched limbs, and to thee nought beside
    Of all thou'st won so dearly shall abide.
There others now shall play the ruler's part.
    All's lost to thee, that erewhile was thy pride;   70

Gone is all vaunting joyaunce from thy heart:
Oh! I could weep to see how fallen and poor thou art!

"A joyful day to thy false heir is this,
   This day to us so woeful-sad and drear;
He would not yield one rood of thine, ywis,[2]
   To bring us out of bale to blissful cheer.
   No more shall weep for thee thy wedded fere,[3]—
Her eye courts a new mate; nor may she sleep
   This night for thinking him her side anear.
Soon shall that new lord to her bosom creep,   80
To revel there, when thou in clay art buried deep.

"Now may thy neighbours live secure from ill,
   And all the wrongs thy vengeful malice wrought:
Hunted were those that stooped not to thy will,
   Till they to meagre penury were brought.
   The thousand curses on thy head besought
By day and night shall cling thee now!" With this
   Down fell the Soul, and cried, as sore distraught,
"Woe's me! that I, who ne'er did aught amiss,
Should be for thy foul deeds for aye thrust out from bliss!"   90

When thus the Soul had spoke with rueful cheer,
   The Body, ghastly thing! lift up anon
Its head, there as it lay upon the bier,
   And heaving, as 'twere sick, a piteous groan,
   "Art thou my ancient mate, that mak'st this moan?"
It cried. "Oh, why upbraid me thus, my Soul,
   With this my sore mishap? Am I alone,
Of all men, doomed to dree [4] death's bitter dole?
No! e'en the haughtiest brows must bend to its control.

"Full well I know that I must rot, for thus   100
   Did Alexander and great Caesar fare,
Nor was there left of wights so glorious
   One jot to tell of that which once they were.
   The very mother, too, which did them bear,
Worms fed upon her throat so marble white;
   So shall they feed on mine, I know, for ne'er,
Where once the biting shaft of death did smite,
Came cheer or pleasaunce more to heart of mortal wight.

[2] Surely.   [3] Mate.   [4] Endure.

[84]

"My youth was hot within me, and I sped
    With mirth and revelry the flying hours,   110
Nor deemed life's summer-time would e'er have fled,
    And torn me from my halls and pleasant bowers.
    Woods, waters, lands I bought, and stately towers,
And lived as life were all a holiday,
    When death, that lays in dust the bravest powers,
Stole on my joys, and hurried me away
From all my fair domains, which others now shall sway.

"Soul, chide me not, that thou art brought to shame,
    And that in torments drear we both must bide!
Thou, and thou only, art for this to blame: 120
    Wisdom and wit did God to thee confide,
    And set thee up my keeper and my guide;
I was no more but bond-slave to thy will,
    Working its bidding morn and eventide;
In all I did thou wert my tutor still,
Then blame thyself alone that thou art brought to ill."

"Peace, Body!" cried the Soul; "who hath thee taught
    To heap on me reproaches most unfit?
What! think'st thou, wretch, though thou art come to naught,
    And thy foul flesh must rot in noisome pit,   130
    That therefore thou so lightly shalt go quit
Of thy misdeeds? No! Though aneath men's feet
    Thy dust be trod, and wild winds scatter it,
Yet we again, as once we were, shall meet
To abide our woeful doom, before God's judgment-seat.

"For I was given thee, but to do thy hest: [5]
    Thou shook'st my counsel from thee with disdain,
Spurning the curb that would have tamed thy crest,
    And in thy wicked track dashed on amain
    To shame and sorrow. When I've been full fain   140
To bid thee think of thy Soul's needs, at mass,
    Matin, or even-song—'Let fools go sain [5a]
Their souls, so go not I!' thine answer was,
And forth with shout to field or greenwood thou wouldst pass.

"The winding horn, that rang the struck stag's knell,
    More pleased thine ear than chant of holy men;
More dear the dance, and music's gladsome swell,

[5] Command.   [5a] Heal.

And smiles to bright eyes that smiled back again.
Well dost thou know, my rede thou reck'dst not when
I told thee, 'twould not evermore be so: 150
    I gave up all to do thee pleasure then,
Yet now thou'dst purchase thine own ease, although
I should be doomed to pine in everlasting woe.

"No more or beast or bird shall fly thy mark,
    No more thy horn through merry greenwood ring:
Thy heart is cleft in twain, thine eyes are dark,
    And thou liest there, mute, moveless, festering.
    What lady bright, of those that used to cling
To thee, would lay her by thy side to-night,
    Or press her sweet lips to so foul a thing?   160
Go out into the street, and in affright
Thy friends will fly from thee, thou'rt so abhorred a sight."

"Soul! Soul! thou wrong'st me," cried the Body, "so
    To charge thy fall from heaven's delights on me!
Whate'er I did or said, for weal or woe,
    Thou know'st full well was ever seen by thee.
    Where'er I went, I bore thee with me; we
Were loving co-mates then, blithe was my cheer,
    I lacked for nought, and time went merrily.
O woeful time! since thou hast left me here,   170
A dull unmoving clod, upon my joyless bier."

" 'Tis true, that thou didst bear me," said the Soul,
    "With thee at all times, as thou wert my steed.
So was I helpless bound in thy control,—
    I could not else but stoop to thee, as need
    Must he whose fate is to his hand decreed.
I loved thee! We had grown from infancy
    Together, and I durst not cross thy rede,
Afeared of losing thee, for where by me
Might a new home be found, if once thrown off by thee?   180

"I saw thee fair and goodly to the view,
    And on thee all my love I cast. Methought
Thou couldst not err; and so thy passions grew
    Headstrong and fierce, nor would not e'er be taught.
    It had been vain, that with thee I had fought.
Greed, envy, hatred, pride, that did defy
    E'en God, possessed thy heart; thou didst besot

[86]

Thyself in lust and gluttony: and I
Must fast in fires for this. Well may I wait and cry!

"Oft were we threatened with the coming doom,   190
    Yet little heed took'st thou of that, when thou
Saw'st dead men laid to moulder in the tomb.
    The world and its temptations held thee now,
    And to thy lusts I servilely must bow.
Thou say'st I made thee bond-slave to my will,—
    Thee, the untamed, the imperious! Well I trow,
Of all thy wasteful crimes the thought was still
Thine own. Betide what may, I ne'er did aught of ill.

"Oh! hadst thou by Christ's favor, on me thrown
    The griping pangs of hunger, frost, and cold,   200
Purged me, and brought my vaulting spirit down!
    But what I learned when young I did when old,
    Chained to a will impure and overbold.
Thou knew'st me prone to sin, as men are all,
    And shouldst my erring wishes have controlled—
Have bound me fast, nor left me to their thrall;
But when blind lead the blind, both in the ditch must fall."

Then 'gan the Soul to weep, and cried, "Alas!
    Alas; that ever, Body, I did see
Thee, who hast brought me to this woeful pass,   210
    That wrought in love thy pleasure cheerfully.
    But thou wert ever a false churl to me:
When I bade shrive thee, and in dust and tears
    Turn from thy sins, the foul Fiend whispered thee,
'So young, to quit thy joys for gloom and fears!
Be merry, take thine ease—thou'rt sure of many years.'

"And when I bade thee with the dawn arise,
    And care for thy Soul's health, then thou wouldst say,
'Leave me to dream, with half-unclosèd eyes,
    Of joys to be upon the morrow-day.'   220
    And when I bade thee fling thy pride away,
'Bear,' said the Fiend, 'a fierce and haughty mien,
    Robe thee in purple and all rich array,
Not, beggar-like, in russet gaberdine,
And on fair-harnessed steed of fire abroad be seen.'

[87]

"Oh! had I been a beast, that ranged at will,
   Ate, drank, and utterly was slain at last,
Then had I never known or good or ill,
   Or for the sins which thou, thou only, hast
   Wrought in thy body, into hell been cast.   230
And though all men beneath the moon should try
   To ease the pains that on us shall be passed,
Nor power nor wile our least release shall buy;—
Hell's hounds will soon be here, nor may I from them fly."

And when it saw the Soul thus wail its doom,
   The Body cried, "Oh that my heart had burst,
When I was taken from my mother's womb,
   And I been cast to snakes in pit accursed!
   Then had I ne'er in worldly sins been nursed,
Nor now been borne away to torments dire.   240
   Is there no saint, to call on Him who erst
Did for our sakes on bloody cross expire,
To free us by His grace from hell's consuming fire?"

"Nay, Body, nay, to pray is now too late,
   Thy tongue is mute, reft utterly of speech;
And even now the wain is at the gate.
   Our pains are past remede of mortal leech;
   That woeful pit of doom we both must reach.
Oh! hadst thou, whilst life yet remained, but lent
   Thine ear to Heaven, and turned thee to beseech   250
Kind Jesu's grace, and so the Fiend yshent,[6]
Though thou wert dyed in guilt, He would us help have sent.

"But though all living men were priests to sing
   Masses for thee, and wives and widows all
Their hands for thee in agony should wring,
   They could not our lost happiness recall.
   But I must leave thee in thy dusky pall:
I hear the hell-hounds bark, and through the gloom
   Come countless fiends, prepared on me to fall,
And bear me off to hell. But thou shalt come   260
To speak again with me upon the day of doom."

Scarce had it spoken, and in wild dismay
   Turned as 'twould flee, but knew not where to go,
When on it sprang a thousand fiends, and they

   [6] Harmed.

Grasped it with hooks and tugged it to and fro.
O Heaven! their eyes shot out a fiery glow.
Rough were their limbs, plague-spotted, and long-nailed
 Their talons were; and, till it howled with woe,
Their quivering prey they limb by limb assailed.
"Oh mercy, God!" it cried, but nought its cry availed.   270

Some thrust its jaws apart, and cried, "Drink, drink!"
 While molten lead was poured adown its throat.
Then came there one, the master-fiend, I think,
 And with a burning spear its heart he smote.
 Then through sides, back, and breast, they plunged red-hot
Falchions of steel, till all their points did meet
 In the heart's core; and they did cry, and gloat
Upon its pangs—"This heart, that once did beat
So hot with pride, ho! feels it now another heat?"

"Oh, thou wert fain in robes of costly woof   280
 To vaunt thyself," they said, and straightway flung
A shirt of mail upon it, massy proof,
 And all aglow, with clasps that firmly clung
 To back and breast. Then forth a charger sprung,
Breathing out flames from throat and nostrils wide,
 And loud and fearfully its neighings rung.
Its back a saddle bore, for him to ride,
With spikes of burning steel stuck o'er on every side.

Into it he was flung, the fiendish rout
 Pursuing close behind with blow and yell;   290
As from a blazing brand the sparks flew out,
 Whilst on him blow on blow redoubling fell.
 Then they let slip the baying hounds of hell;
On, on they hunted him, and did not slack,
 And, as they flew, they tore him flesh and fell.
Behind them ran a long blood-stainèd track,
Till to hell's throat they came, grim, sulphurous, and black.

The earth did split, and there came roaring out
 Fierce sulphurous flames in many a whirling wreath
That blasted all the air for miles about.   300
 Oh! woe is them, that toss in fires beneath!
 And when the Soul saw the wild flashes seethe,
"O Jesu Lord!" it cried, "look from on high,

And mercy on Thy wretched creature breathe;
Thine own hand's work, like other men, am I,
Whom Thou hast ta'en to bliss, and set Thyself anigh.

"Thou God, that knewest all things from the first,
    Why mad'st Thou me for wrath, and to be torn
By bloody fiends, a creature all accursed?
    Well may I wail that ever I was born,   310
    For I am here unfriended and forlorn,
Left without hope in sore distressful case!"
    Then cried the fiends, and laughed loud laughs of scorn,
"It boots not thee to call on Jesu's grace,
Thou art for ever shut out from before His face.

"For thou our servant wert in times of yore,
    And of thy labor thou shalt reap the fruit,
As others do that love our master's lore!"
    Ended was now the demons' mad pursuit,
    And catching up their victim head and foot   320
They hurled him headlong down that murky pit,
    Where never sun its blessed rays can shoot.
And downwards straight they all sank after it;
The earth closed up again, as though it ne'er had split.

And now drew on apace the welcome day—
    Cold drops of sweat stood on each several hair,
And nigh distraught with agony I lay.
    Then did I call on Jesu blest in prayer,
    And thanked His grace that our afflictions bare,
And saved me from the fiend and fires of bale.   330
    Now sinners quit your sins, and shrive you ere
Too late, and your past guilt with tears bewail!
No sin so great, but Christ's dear love shall more prevail.
                                    SIR THEODORE MARTIN

The Land of Cockayne

Far in the sea and west of Spain
There is a country called Cockayne.
No other land beneath the skies
So many kinds of joy supplies.
Though Paradise be merry and bright,
Cockayne is yet a fairer sight.
What is there in Paradise to see
But grass and flowers and greenery?
Though doubtless there the joy is great,
There is naught but fruit to eat.　10
There is no hall nor bower nor bench,
And only water thirst to quench.
But two men live there, I've heard say,
Enoch and Elijah they.
It is a doleful place to be,
With so little company.
　In Cockayne there's ample fare
Without trouble, toil, or care.
The food is choice, the drink is bright
At noon, late afternoon, and night.　20
I say in sooth—ye need not fear—
There is no land on earth its peer.
There is no land beneath the sun
Where there is so much joy and fun.
There is many a pleasant sight;
All is day, there is no night.
There is no quarreling or strife;
There is no death but ever life.
There is no lack of meat or cloth;
There is no man or woman wroth.　30
There is no serpent, wolf, or fox,
No horse or nag or cow or ox;
There is no sheep, no swine, no goat.
There is no filthiness, God wot!
No cattle breeding and no studs.
The land is full of other goods.

There is no fly or flea or louse
In clothing, farmyard, bed, or house.
There is no thunder, sleet, or hail,
No vile worm crawls, or any snail.　40
No tempest rages, rain or wind.
No man or woman there is blind.
But all is mirth and joy and glee.
Well he fares who there may be!
There are rivers great and fine
Of oil and honey, milk and wine.
Water is never used at all,
Save to look at or wash withal.
There is fruit of every sort,
And all is frolic and disport.　50
　There is an abbey fair and gay,
Where white monks dwell and also gray.
There are chambers good and halls;
All of pasties are the walls,
Of flesh and fish and tender meat,
The most delicious man may eat.
Flour-cakes are the shingles all
Of cloister, chamber, church, and hall.
The pinnacles are puddings fat,
No prince or king could cavil at.　60
One may eat thereof his fill,
And yet be guilty of no ill.
All is common to young and old,
To stern and haughty, meek and bold.
There is a cloister fair and bright,
Broad and long, a noble sight.
The pillars of the fine arcade
Are every one of crystal made;
Each base and capital, 'tis said,
Of jasper and of coral red.　70
　In the meadow stands a tree,
A great delight it is to see.

The root is ginger and galingale;
The shoots are all of zedewale;
The flower is the choicest spice,
The bark, cinnamon smelling nice,
The fruit is cloves of pleasant smack,
And of cubebs there is no lack.
There are roses red of hue,
And many lovely lilies too.   80
They wither never, day or night;
They are indeed a joyous sight.
   Four springs within that abbey run,
One of treacle,[1] of cordial one,
One balm, and one of spicèd wine;
Ever they flow, they ne'er decline,
Welling upward from the earth.
   Gold and jewels of great worth,
Pearl and sapphire, all are there,
Carbuncle and astrion rare,   90
Emerald, ligure, chrysoprase,
Beryl, onyx, and topase,
Amethyst and chrysolite,
Chalcedony and hepatite.
   There are birds in every bush,
Throstle, nightingale, and thrush,
The lark and the green woodpecker,—
Hard to name them all it were.
Never ceasing, with all their might
They gaily sing both day and night.
There are other birds, to wit: 101
Geese ready roasted on the spit
Fly to that abbey—God it wot—
And cry out, "Geese, all hot! all hot!"
They bring too garlick plenteously,
The best dressing that one could see.
The larks, it is a well known truth,
Light adown in a man's mouth,
Stewed daintily and right well done,
Sprinkled with cloves and cinnamon.
For drink there is no need to ask;
To take it is the only task.   112

[1] Medicinal syrup.

When the monks proceed to mass,
All the windows made of glass
Are turnèd into crystal bright,
To give the monks the greater light.
When the masses are all said
And the books aside are laid,
The crystal turns to glass once more,
Into the state it was before.   120
The younger monks go every day
After meat to have their play.
There is no hawk or bird that flies
With greater swiftness through the skies
Than these young monks in sportive mood
With their long sleeves and their hood.
When the abbot sees their flight,
In it he takes great delight,
Nevertheless with charges strong
Bids them alight at evensong.   130
The monks, however, will not obey
And in a covey soar away. . .
The monk who'd be a stallion good
And knows how to adjust his hood,
He can have the use each year
Of twelve wenches, never fear,   170
Not by grace but all by right,
To furnish him his due delight.
And the monk who slumbers best
And gives his body ample rest,
There is a goodly certainty
That he'll be abbot speedily.
Whoso will come that land unto,
Full great penance he must do.
For seven years, as it is said,
Through dung of swine he must needs wade,   180
Sunk up to the very chin.
Thus he may to that land win.

FOURTEENTH CENTURY

Sir Orfeo[1]

We often read with new delight
  The lays that clerks would have us
    know,
For lays there are that sing aright
  Each wondrous thing of long ago:
Some are of weal, and some of woe,
And some of joy and gentle mirth,
  And some of guile and treacherous
    foe,
And some the strangest haps of earth;

Some are of jests and ribaldry,
  And some there are of fairy lore;   10
But most of all, as men may see,
  They sing of love and trials sore.
  In Brittany in days of yore
The harpers writ that men should
    praise
  The gallant deeds that were be-
    fore—
Of such the Bretons made their lays.

And that we all should featly hold
  In heart the mirth of elder days,
Some took their harps and gaily told
  Of olden loves in tender lays.   20
  I know not all their subtle ways;
I tell the little that I know;
  So hearken, lords, your poet prays,
And I will sing of Orfeo.

Sir Orfeo, a king was he,
  And in his time a mighty man,

Stalwart and strong and masterly,
  A kind and courteous Christian.
  To King Pluto his lineage ran,
His mother from King Juno sprang; 30
  Men called them gods when time
    began
For lofty deeds they did and sang.

Orfeo most of any king
  Loved a harper and his lay;
Every harper there might sing,
  Honored if he chose to stay.
  And the king himself would play,
Singing with a merry mind.
  And, as all the gleemen say,
A better harper none could find.   40

None before him was, I trow,
  Or in after days will be
Held the peer of Orfeo
  When he struck his harp. And he
  Who could hear that minstrelsy
Would have deemed his spirit were
  Housed in Heaven, such melody
Was it, and such joy to hear.

Thrace they named his stout demesne,
  Then the strongest of cities; [2]   50
With him dwelt his gracious queen,
  Called the Lady Heurodis,
  Fairest of all fair ladíes;
Naught surpassed her gentleness,
  Full of love and courtesies;
None can tell her loveliness.

[1] From *Sir Orfeo*, adapted from the Middle English by Edward Eyre Hunt (Cambridge, Mass., 1909). Reprinted by permission of the author.

[2] Two lines are omitted here from the translation which state that Traciens (Thrace) was the ancient name of Winchester!

And in the merry month of May,
 When day is fraught with happy
  hours,
When wintry storms have passed
  away,
 And every field is full of flowers, 60
When clustered blossoms deck the
  bowers,
And morn is made to spend in sport,
 Sweet Heurodis went from her
  towers
With two fair maidens of the court,

And out into the air of spring,
 To revel in a grove, and see
The lovely blossoms bourgeoning,
 And linnets piping cheerily.
At last, beneath a grafted tree,
They sat them down in grasses
  deep, 70
 And soon—the maids watched at
  her knee—
The queen was lying fast asleep.

They feared to waken her too soon,
 So let her lie in sweet repose.
She slept till it was afternoon,
 And morn had gone, as morning
  goes;
 Then sudden with a cry she rose
And burst in tears of wild despair,
 And wrung her hands, and show-
  ered blows
Upon her breast, and tore her hair. 80

Her jeweled robe she seized and rent,
 For she was frantic in her pain.
The maids in their bewilderment
 No longer dared with her remain,
 But to the palace ran again
And summoned every squire and
  knight,
 And bade them haste with might
  and main
To aid their mistress in her plight.

Knights, pages, squires, and ladies too,
 And damsels hasten from the wall;
Into the orchard quick they go, 91
 And, fearful of what may befall,
 They lift and bear her to the hall
And moaning on her pillows lay;
 Yet wild and heedless still of all
Ever she strove to flee away.

Sir Orfeo, when he was told,
 Was as he ne'er before had been;
With all his knights he entered bold
 Into the chamber of the queen, 100
 But when he saw, he cried in teen,
"Ah, dearest wife, what aileth thee?
 Thee joyless I have never seen,
Yet now thou wailest dreadfully.

"Thy lovely body, once so bright,
 Is bruised as if thou wished thee
  dead.
Alas! alas! how wan and white
 Thy little mouth that was so red!
 And dark with blood thy nails have
  shed 109
Thy fingers that were erst as snow!
 Thy lovely eyes are full of dread
And gaze as if I were thy foe!

"Cease, Dearest, I implore thee now
 These cries that all the palace fill,
And tell me what hath been, and how,
 Or who hath done thee aught of ill."
 At last she ceased and lay full still,
And weeping bitter tears of woe,
 She answered at his royal will,
"Alas! my lord, Sir Orfeo, 120

"Since we were first together, naught
 Hath marred our life; no smallest
  sign;
But we have loved as love we ought;
 Thou art my life, and I am thine.
 Now do thy best and do not pine,
For we must part, and I to doom!"
 "Alas!" he cried, and "woe is mine!

Where dost thou go, Love, and to
  whom?

"Whither thou goest I will go   129
  And where I go thou too shalt fare!"
"Nay, nay, my lord; thou dost not
  know:
My doom no mortal man may share.
This morn, as I was lying there
Asleep beneath an orchard-tree,
  Two gallant horsemen, young and
    fair,
Rode to my feet, and bent the knee,

"And bade me come with haste and
    speed
To parley with their lord the king.
But I replied I durst not heed,
  Nor would I come for any thing.
Then they departed galloping,   141
And came the king with all his court:
  Knights and fair damsels in a ring,
All clothed in white of wondrous
    sort.

"I never in my life before
  Have seen such creatures as they
    were.
Upon his head the monarch wore
  A crown, but nought of gold was
    there:
It was a precious jewel rare,
And blazed as brightly as the sun; 150
  And when he came, he spoke me
    fair,
And though I wept, he placed me on

"A steed. And so I rode away
  Upon a palfrey by his side.
He brought me to his palace gay;
  More beautiful I never spied.
He showed me castles, rivers wide,
Towers, and vast forests, mead and
    plain.
  Again to horse, again we ride,
And so he brought me home again. 160

"And hither to our orchard borne
  He let me down and said to me,
'See, lady, that to-morrow morn
  Thou art beneath this grafted tree;
  Then thou shalt go with us and be
For aye with us in fairy land;
  And if thou failest, woe to thee,
For thou shalt feel the fairies' hand!

"'Where'er thou art thy limbs shall
    fail,
  No man shalt thou find piteous; 170
Thou shalt be torn with tooth and
    nail,
  And would thou hadst returned
    with us!'"
When Orfeo had heard, he was
Distraught, and moaned, "Alas! my
    life,
  Dearer than life, and must I thus
Lose thee, my queen, my love, my
    wife?"

He sought for counsel: all were dumb,
  For none could proffer words of
    good.
At last the morrow morn had come,
  And Orfeo in armour stood   180
With hundreds of his knightlihood,
Each armed and harnessed, stout and
    grim;
  They sallied forth into the wood
And girt about the queen and him.

In close array they stood at guard
  And swore upon their weapons keen
They each should die upon the sward
  Ere aught should come and take the
    queen.
  Yet from their circle, and unseen,
The woeful Heurodis was won.   190
  Alas! naught was where she had
    been,
  And none could tell where she had
    gone.

Then there was wailing wild and
    dread;
The king into his chamber went,
And oft he swooned upon her bed,
    And made such dole and such lament
His very life was wellnigh spent
    Ere he could find a space for words;
Then woefully he rose, and sent
For all his barons, earls, and lords. 200

When they had come in solemn train,
    "My lords," he said, "all ye have
        seen;
Hear now: my steward I ordain
    To rule throughout my broad
        demesne.
He shall be lord as I have been,
And I must wander hence forlorn,
    For I have lost the fairest queen
And sweetest lady ever born.

"No other lady shall I see;   209
    Forth must I fare on woeful quest
To dwell where never man may be,
    Of beasts and birds to be the guest.
    And when ye know my soul has rest,
Call then yourselves a parliament,
    And choose a king as seems you best.
Do all as this my testament."

Then there was wailing in the hall;
    Men wept as there were no surcease,
And not a man among them all
    Might speak for tears. Upon their
        knees   220
    They knelt and made their woeful
        pleas,
Beseeching him he would not go,
    Else were they desolate. But,
        "Cease,"
Answered the king; "it shall be so!"

And so his kingdom he forsook;
    He had no kirtle and no hood;
A simple palmer's cloak he took;
    No shoes he had, no store of food.

But with his harp he sadly strode
Barefooted from the castle gate, 230
    Alone to wander where he would.
Alas! how woeful was his state!

Alas! the wailing in the hall,
    When he that had been king with
        crown
Went like a beggar from them all.
    In poverty he left the town;
    Through wood and waste and
        dreary down
And towards the wilds he set his face;
    Now found he deserts bleak and
        brown
And naught to ease his woeful
    case.   240

He that had worn but garments gay
    And slumbered in a purple bed,
Now on the barren heather lay,
    His couch with leaves and grasses
        spread.
He that had castles turreted,
Rivers, and forests, fields, and flowers,
    Now had the snow and sleet in-
        stead,
And passed in woe his weary hours.

He that had scores of gentle knights
    And ladies at his beck and call,   250
Now saw but dread unhappy sights,
    Serpents and beasts that creep and
        crawl.
    He that had supped in bower and
        hall
On dainty dishes and sweet fruits,
    Now must he dig to find a small
Repast of herbs and bitter roots.

In summer, fruits of every kind
    He had, and berries from the bough;
In winter, nothing could he find
    But roots and leaves beneath the
        snow.   260

His form was bent, his pace was
  slow,
And he was worn by tempests sore.
Ah, who can tell the pain and woe
This king endured ten years and more!

His beard, that once was black and
  trim,
  Was white, and lengthened to his
    knee;
His harp that ever solaced him,
  He hid within a hollow tree;
  And when the day was clear and
    free
He took it forth, and musing played,
  And when the gentle melody   271
Was echoed far through gorse and
  glade,

The wildest creatures hidden there
  For very joy about him played,
And all the birds from everywhere
  Came forth and heard; for all obeyed
  The witching music that he made,
Such perfect melody it was;
  And when he ceased, they fled
    afraid
And hid them, wild and timorous. 280

And oft on dewy summer morns
  Sir Orfeo beheld at hand
The fairy king, and heard the horns
  Of hunting, and his shouting band
  A-ranging wide across the land
With barking hounds; yet never game
  He saw them take, nor heard a
    stand,—
Nor never knew he whence they came.

He saw across the hazy heights
  A mighty host another day: 290
A thousand well-accoutred knights
  Went riding ready for the fray.
  Bright were their ranks, with large
    display

Of gorgeous banners gaily blent;
  Each brandished sword in that
    array,—
Yet never knew he where they went.

Again, he saw a wondrous rout
  Of knights and ladies dancing free,
In quaint attire, and in and out   299
  They wove and wandered daintily,
  To sound of pipes and minstrelsy
And every kind of music sweet.
  One day he saw a galaxy
Of ladies ride by his retreat;

Gentle and sweet they were, he wist,
  And not a man rode in their train;
Each had a falcon on her wrist,
  And to the river in the plain
  They passed. The prey rose up
    amain,
Cormorants, herons, mallards flew; 310
  The falcons soared with proud dis-
    dain,
Stooped, and each hawk his quarry
  slew.

"Ho!" laughed the king, "there is fair
  game!
I too will see their gay intent,
For I was wont to do the same."
  He rose in haste and thither went,
  And to a beauteous lady bent
His steps, when lo! he starts, he sees
  Dumb with a like astonishment,
His stolen queen, sweet Heurodis. 320

For when she saw that it was he
  She neither spoke nor uttered cry,
He was so spent with misery
  That once had been so rich and
    high.
  And then she wept as if to die,
But quick the others caught her rein,
  And closed about, and made her fly,
And would not let her there remain

"Alas! alas!" he gan to cry,
  "Why will not death dispel my
    pain? 330
Alas! alas! would I could die
Now I have seen my love again.
  Alas, that I must live, who fain
Would perish! for I dared not speak
To her, nor she to me. Ah, vain
Is life; alas! my heart will break!"

"But nay," he cried at last, "not so:
  I too shall wend, tide what betide,
Whither these gentle ladies go,
  And learn the spot where they
    abide!" 340
He took his cloak and harp, and hied
Him forth, his harp upon his back,
  Nor stock nor stone could turn
    aside
His footsteps from that beaten track.

In at a rock the ladies rode,
  And fearlessly he followed fast.
When far into the rock he strode,
  It grew more bright, and so at last
Into a far countree he passed,
Bright as the fairest summer sun: 350
  All smooth and plain and green and
    vast,
For hills and valleys were there none.

Amid the land a castle tall
  And rich and proud and wondrous
    high
Uprose, and all the outmost wall
  Shone as a crystal to the eye.
A hundred towers lit up the sky,
With battlements so strange and stout;
  And buttresses rose up near by,
Arched with red gold and broad
    about. 360

The vaulting was all carved in stone
  With every beast and every wight,
And all within the castle shone
  And sparkled with unearthly light.

The meanest pillars to the sight
Seemed every whit of burnished gold.
  And all that land was warm and
    bright,
For when our earth is dark and cold,

The jeweled stones shed forth a light
  Like sunbeams on a summer's
    day. 370
None may describe that wondrous
    sight
  Or sculptured work so proud and
    gay;
But one would think that rich array
Were of the courts of Paradise.
  Therein the ladies led the way;
He followed fast in sweet surprise.

When at the gate, Sir Orfeo
  Knocked, and the porter came anear
And asked what he would have him
    do.
  "Parfay, I am a minstrel here," 380
He said, "to please thy lord with
    cheer,
If he will deign to summon me."
  The porter lent a willing ear
And led him in the castle free.

There, as he gazed, his glances fell
  On many marvels all around;
Folk long thought dead were by a
    spell
  Brought hither, and as living found:
  Some headless stood upon the
    ground,
Some had no arms, and some were
    torn 390
  With dreadful wounds, and some
    lay bound
Fast to the earth in hap forlorn.

And some full-armed on horses sat,
  And some were strangled as at
    meat,
And some were drowned as in a vat,

And some were burned with fiery
  heat,
Wives lay in child-bed, maidens
  sweet
Were there, and other marvels more;
  Each wondrous wight was at his
  feet
As each had slumbered long before.   400

Each thus was stolen out of life,
  For such the fairies seize and keep.
And there he saw his darling wife,
  Sweet Heurodis, as one asleep
Beneath a tree in grasses deep,
  For by her garb he knew it all;
And when he saw, he fain would
  weep,
But entered bold into the hall.

And there he saw a seemly thing,
  A tabernacle fair and light,   410
Whereunder sat the fairy king,
  Near him his queen, a lovely wight.
Their crowns, their garments, glis-
  tened bright;
He could not gaze, so hot they shone;
  And when he saw that noble sight,
He knelt him down before the throne,

And said, "Lord, if thou wilt allow,
  My melody shall pleasure thee."
The king replied, "What man art thou
  That hither comes? and for what
  plea?   420
I did not send, nor none with me
Hath bid thee come to fairy lond.
  My faith, I never yet did see
Since I was crowned, a man so fond

"As thou who durst us so defy,
  And comest lacking summons true."
"Lord," answered he, "know this;
  that I
As a poor simple minstrel sue.
  And, sir, it is our custom to
Seek out the hall of many a lord; 430

Though we be welcome to but few,
Sweet is the music we afford."

He sat him down before the king
  And all the court in rich array;
He took his merry harp to sing,
  And when he gan that blissful lay,
  All crowded to his feet, and they
That were without the palace, lo!
  They came to hear the minstrel play,
To hear the lay of Orfeo.   440

The king was pleased and sat full still,
  Right gladly did he hear the glee;
The lovely queen with right good will
  Joyed in the lovely melody.
  And when it ceased at last, "Thy
  fee,"
The king exclaimed, "for, harper
  mine,
I love thy tender minstrelsy:
Ask what thou wilt, and it is thine;

"Largess I proffer for thy task;
  Speak now, what shall I give to
  thee?"   450
"Sir," answered he, "one thing I ask;
  This—that thou wilt bestow on me
The lady 'neath the grafted tree
A-slumbering in grasses deep."
  "Nay," quoth the king, "that cannot
  be;
A sorry couple ye would keep.

"For thou art rough, and foul, and
  lean,
  But lovely as a rose is she.
'T were lothly thing to let a queen
  Be partner of thy company."   460
  "Oh, sir," he cried, "thy courtesy,
But surely, 't were a fouler thing
  To hear thy lips lie thus to me!
So, sir, my boon, as thou art king!

"I have but asked of thee my due,
  And thou must needs requite me
  so."

The king replied, "Ay, it is true;
  Then take her by the hand and go.
Joy have of her and never woe!"
He thanked him sweet, and by the
  hand   470
He led his wife; thus Orfeo
And Heurodis left fairy land.

They wandered from that woeful
  place
  That wrought them so much misery,
Along the way that led to Thrace,
  His high demesne, his own city;
  And no man knew that it was he.
Then paused they at the city's end;
  For fear of fraud and treachery
That day no further would they
  wend.   480

In at a beggar's, poor and old,
  Who dwelt a space beyond the
  wall,
He and his lady turned, and told
  How he was but a minstrel-thrall;
  He asked the beggar news of all
That had befallen: who was king,
  Or who the ruler in the hall:
The beggar told him everything.

How the fair queen was rapt away
Ten years agone, by fairy spell; 490
And how the king the self-same day
  Had gone; none knew where he
  might dwell;
  And how the steward ruled full
  well;
And many other things he told.
  Then Orfeo left the beggar's cell
And Heurodis with the beggar old.

Straightway the beggar's rags he took;
  He took his merry harp, and went
Into the town, where all might look
  Upon his body soiled and bent. 500
  Men laughed aloud in merriment;
The ladies, earls, and barons said,

"Lo, see the man! his hair is sprent
Like moss about his shaggy head;

"His beard is fallen to his feet
  Like weathered ivy tumbling
  down!"
There as he went, he chanced to meet
  His steward coming through the
  town.
  Then loud he cried, and plucked his
  gown,
"Sir steward, hearken, pity me! 510
  I am a harper of renown;
Ah, help me in my misery!"

The steward straightway answered,
  "Come!
  Thou shalt share aught I can bestow.
Every good harper is welcome
  For my lord's sake Sir Orfeo."
  Straight to the castle then they go,
And all the lords sit down to meat;
  Tabours are beat and trumpets
  blow;
Harpers and fiddlers play full
  sweet.   520

And much of melody they had,
  But Orfeo heard it silently.
When all was still, the steward bade
  Him take his harp and sing his glee.
  He touched it soft, and melody
Sweeter than ever tongue can tell
  Delighted all that company.
The steward heard and marked it well.

He knew the harp, and said, "Say now,
  Minstrel, as thou hast fear of
  Hell,   530
Where gottest thou thy harp, and
  how?
  I pray thee haste and quickly tell!"
"Lord," quoth he, "in a desert fell
As I was wandering one morn,
  I found within a dismal dell
A corse by angry lions torn.

"The wolves had gnawed him flesh
    and bone;
  His harp was lying in the snow.
'Tis full ten weary years agone."
    "Oh," cried the steward, "dost thou
      know   540
That was my lord, Sir Orfeo!
Alas! now am I all forlorn.
  My lord is lost! ah, me is woe!
Ah, would that I had ne'er been born!"

He fell a-swooning to the ground;
  His barons caught him up again,
And sought to heal his woeful wound,
  And give him comfort in his pain,
  But still he mourned, for all was
    vain.
And when Sir Orfeo well knew   550
  His steward's love had not a stain,
He rose, and spake, and nearer drew.

"Sir steward, hearken now and hear:
  If I were Orfeo the king,
And had sore suffered many a year,
  Enduring every cruel thing,
  And by my lays at last could bring
My queen from fairy land again,
  And now had left her sorrowing
In a poor hovel in the plain,   560

"Sheltered with but a beggar poor,
  And all alone had come to thee
In poverty to try thy door,
  To test thy faith and loyalty,
  And found thee constant still to
    me,—
Sure thou shouldst never rue the day!
  But for thy fealty, thou shouldst be
The king when I had passed away."

Then all who sat within the hall
  Knew that it was the king aright.

The steward o'erthrew the table
  all,   571
  Fell at his feet in dumb delight,
  And all his lordings at the sight
Crowded about his feet, to cling
  And shout for joy with all their
    might,
"Thou art our lord, sir, and our king!"

Sure all were glad when they had
  heard;
  Quickly they led him in with glee,
And bathed his face and shaved his
  beard
  And tired him as a king should be;
  And then with mirth and jollity 581
They brought the queen into the
  town,
  With every sort of minstrelsy!
Lord, how the tale went up and down!

For very joy the people wept
  That he was come so safe and sound;
For very joy they danced and leapt;
  His soul was healed of every wound;
  Again Sir Orfeo was crowned;
Again sweet Heurodis was queen; 590
  In love they lived, till death they
    found;
Then the steward ruled their wide
  demesne.

In Brittany, after many a day,
  The harpers learned this wondrous
    thing,
And made thereof this pleasant lay,
  And named it for the harper-king.
  And so of Orfeo I sing:
Good is the lay, and sweet the air;
  Thus cometh mirth from sorrow-
    ing,—
God grant us all as well to fare. 600
        EDWARD EYRE HUNT

Handling Sin

Robert Mannyng

PROLOG

(vss. 41–146)

I am emboldened to tell you what may well be told in English; for laymen I undertook to write this book in the English tongue. For there are many men who will blithely harken to tales and rimes; at sports and feasts, and at the alehouse men love to listen to tittle-tattle, which often leads to boorishness, deadly sin or other folly. For such men I have made this rime that they may spend their time well, hear what will lead them from all such vile ways, and learn to know what is sinful, though they deem it to be innocent. All Christian men under the sun and good men of Brunne [1] and specially the brotherhood of Sempringham, each by name, Robert of Brunne greeteth
10 you in the name of all that is good and profitable. At Brunnewake in Kesteven, six miles from Sempringham, I dwelt in the priory fifteen years. I was there ten years, in the time of good Dan John of Camelton, who now is gone, and I knew and heard of his good manners. Then I was five winters under Dan John of Clinton. Dan Philip was novice master when I began this English rime. It was the year of grace one thousand three hundred and three.

At that time I turned this into the English tongue from a French book called "Handling Sin." When a scholar sees it in French, he calls it *Manuel de Péchés. Manuel* means "handling with the hand"; *péché* is sin I under-
20 stand. Put these two words together, and that is "Handling Sin." Well is this book so named, as I will show you. We handle sin every day; in word and deed, little or much, we sin, as the fiend and our flesh incite us. . . . There should also be another handling,—to cleanse thyself by oral confession. . . . Handle thy sins so that thou mayst rise from them all and none may cause thee to fall again; handle them with confession of mouth and will of heart, and some of them with sore penance. For this reason this book may be called "Handling Sin" in many ways. . . .

Herein thou shalt find tales of misfortunes that came about through sin

---

[1] Bourne in Lincolnshire.

and of marvels, some of which I found written down and others which have been observed and reported. There are none, long or short, but what I have found in writing or heard from witnesses. Therefore and for good reason may it be called "Handling Sin" openly, for it toucheth no secret sin but what may be called open sin.

Begin we then at once in the name of the Father, Son, and Holy Ghost and in worship of Our Lady and all the saints that dwell with them. May they give us grace and judgment, to our profit and God's pleasure.

ON WITCHCRAFT AND SUPERSTITIONS

(vss. 147–50, 339–606)

The first commandment of all is "Thou shalt have no god but one," and thou shalt believe in but one God and do naught to grieve Him. . . .   10

If through folly thou hast ever practised necromancy or done sacrifice to the devil through witchcraft or paid any man to raise the devil in order that he may reveal a thing stolen from thee; if thou hast done any of these things, thou hast sinned and done amiss, and thou art worthy to be damned because of this commandment. If thou hast caused any child to gaze at a sword-blade or in a basin or on a thumb or a crystal, all this is called witchcraft. Believe not in the chattering of a magpie; it is not truth but falsehood. Many believe in the magpie; when she cometh chattering low or loud and will not be quiet, then they say, "We shall have a guest." Many trust in her wiles and many times the magpie deceiveth them. Also if thou 20 meetest anyone in the morning when thou goest to town or borough, and if thine errand speed not, then wilt thou curse him thou didst meet. This is an incitement of the devil, to curse him who meant thee no harm.

Believe not much in dreams, for many are but glittering illusions. Learned men say they are vain and signify naught that is or shall be. Oft thou mayst find that what thou hast dreamed by night cometh to pass, but to put much trust in it may sooner bring thee mischance. In six ways a man may dream; some are to be believed, some to be put aside. Some men who eat and drink beyond measure dream because of surfeit, and some dream of vain things because of severe fasting. Some dreams are the fiend's temptation, which is 30 a false betrayal of truth. Some come of overmuch thinking on what one desireth to happen. Some are God's secrets that He showeth to warn thee. Some come through great meditation and reveal things to thee clearly. Of these six kinds a learned man, St. Gregory, who hath written a long discourse, telleth us. . . .

Since there are so many kinds of dreams, it is doubtful and very difficult to know whence the dreams come which we by custom dream every night.

There are so many vain dreams that no one knoweth any certainly save those men who are privy with God, and to whom it is granted to see such things. Such men the devil doth not deceive; they have grace to perceive his wicked intent. But otherwise dreams are so deceptive that no man may find them stable. . .

If thou believest that there are three fatal sisters who come where a child is born and shape its fate beforehand, whether good or ill, and according to thy wicked belief they cause the child to fall into sin, thou shouldst not hold such belief since it is against the faith of Holy Church. There is 10 no fate but God Almighty, who alighted in the Virgin Mary. He is the Shaper of all things; He knoweth the end of all that is. He is both God and man; He hath all knowledge and all power. The other shapers of which men speak, let us commend them to the fiend of hell.

If thou thinkest that sin shall be forgiven without repentance and absolution, as some of these stupid fellows say, "God of heaven is so courteous that at Doomsday he will certainly forgive the sin of lechery. Lechery is but a light sin, and He will have mercy on all in that regard," . . . if thou wilt learn the truth, thou must be forgiven here.[2] In the other world where we shall come, there is naught but just judgment; there is full and 20 final justice. Ask mercy ere thou go thither, else thou getest no forgiveness, here or there, more or less. God give us grace, ere we go, to keep this first commandment.

SACRILEGE

(vss. 8583–92, 8669–716)

The seven deadly sins with which we anger the God of Heaven we have duly touched on, as holy men have written and spoken. But we will not do well if we forget Holy Church, our dear Mother. We shall now tell you here how and in what wise men sin against her privileges. . . .

In Norfolk there dwelt in a village a knight beside a parson. It happed that the knight's manor was not far from the church, and as often befalleth, the churchyard walls were broken down. The lord's herdsmen often let his 30 beasts into the churchyard to graze, and the beasts, as they needs must, fouled every place they went. A bondman saw that and was filled with woe. He came to the lord and said to him:

"Lord," said he, "your beasts have strayed. Your herdsman and your servants do wrong who let your beasts defile these graves. Where men's bones are to lie beasts should not commit a nuisance."

The lord's answer was a mockery which ill becometh a nobleman. "It

[2] In this world.

[106]

would be well done to honor such churls' bones! Why should men do honor to the black bodies of churls?"

The bondman answered and spoke words that were well composed: "The Lord who made earls of the earth made churls of the same earth. Power of earls and pride of lords shall be buried in the earth even as churls. Earls and churls, no man shall know your bones from ours."

The lord listened to these words and retained them in his mind, every one. He said no more to the bondman but let him go his way. He commanded that his cattle no more, by his will, go into the churchyard and closed it so that no beast could enter to feed or to defile it. For it seemed 10 to him sinful.

There are but few lords now who will turn a word to their profit. But whosoever saith any wise word to them they foully abuse. Lords—of them there are enough, of gentlemen there are but few.

DANCING IN THE CHURCHYARD

(vss. 8987–9252)

Caroles, wrestlings, or summer games, whosoever frequenteth such shameful sports in church or churchyard, he should dread lest he do sacrilege. Interludes or singing or drumming or piping, all such things are forbidden while the priest standeth at mass. All such are loathsome to every good priest and he will be wroth sooner than one who hath no wit and understandeth not holy scripture. And specially at sacred seasons to sing 20 caroles and read rimes in holy places, which might disturb the priest's prayers, if he were at his orisons or any other devotion, it is reckoned sacrilege many times over.

In order that ye may avoid dancing in church I will tell you, a great misfortune, and most of what befell is I believe as true as the gospel. It happened in this land of England, as I understand; in the time of a King called Edward this hard calamity befell. It was on a Christmas night that twelve fools danced a carole. They had come in their madness to a village called Colbek.[8] The church of that village was dedicated to St. Magnus, who suffered martyrdom, and also to St. Bukchester, St. Magnus' sister. 30 I found the names of these folk written in a book, and now ye shall know them. The leader, who made them mirth, was named Gerlew, as it is written. Two maidens were in their company, Merswinde and Wibessine. All came to this place because of the village priest's daughter. The priest was called

---

[8] Mannyng is badly confused. The miracle took place not in England, but at Kölbigk in Germany.

Robert, and his son was Azone by name. His daughter, whom these men desired, it is written that she was clept Ave. They all agreed who should go to fetch Ave out, and were of one consent to send both Wibessine and Merswinde. These women went and brought her out to dance with them around the church. Bevo arranged their dancing; Gerlew composed their song. This is the carole they sang, as it is told in Latin:

> *"Equitabat Bevo per silvam frondosam,*
> *Ducebat secum Merswinden formosam.*
> *Quid stamus? cur non imus?"*

> "By the leafy wood rode Bevoline;
> With him he led the fair Merswine.
> Why stand we still? why go we not?"

This is the carole that Gerlew composed; this is the song they sang in the churchyard (they were nowise afraid of folly) until matins were all done and mass was about to begin. The priest put on his vestments to sing mass,
10 but they did not cease and danced on as they had begun, and in spite of the mass they would not stop. The priest, as he stood at the altar, heard their noise and riotous behavior, went down from the altar, came to the church porch, and said:

"In God's name, I forbid you longer to do this. But come in decorously to hear God's service, and observe the law of Christian men. Carole no more for dread of Christ, and worship with all your might Him who was born of a Virgin this very night."

For all his forbidding they would not cease but danced on. Therefore this priest was sorely vexed. He prayed to God, in whom he believed, and
20 to St. Magnus, to whom the church was built, that such a vengeance should be sent down on them before they left that place that they might ever go on so until the end of a twelvemonth. (In the Latin I found that he said not a "twelvemonth" but "evermore.") He cursed them all as they caroled in their sport.

As soon as the priest had so spoken, every hand was locked in the other so fast that no man by any miracle could part them for a twelvemonth. The priest went in when this was done and commanded his son Azone to go quickly and bring Ave out of that carole. But all too late the word was spoken, for the vengeance had fallen on them all. Azone thought he would
30 not fail and went at once to the carole. He caught his sister by the arm, and the arm parted from the body. All who were there wondered, and ye may hear a greater marvel, for when he had seized the arm, the body continued dancing, and neither body nor arm shed blood, cold or warm, but it was as dry at the shoulder as if a branch were torn from a tree. Azone went to his father and brought him a sorry present.

"Look, father," he said, "have here the arm of thy dear daughter, my own sister Ave, whom I thought to save. Now thy cursing hath brought open vengeance on thine own flesh. Thou didst curse in anger and in haste. Thou didst ask vengeance and thou hast thy boon."

Ye need not ask if the priest and many more were woe. The priest who cursed because of that dance, on his own child a calamity fell. He took the arm his daughter had lost and buried it in the morning. The next day he found the arm of Ave lying above the grave. He buried it once more and again it lay above the grave. He buried it a third time and again it was cast out of the pit. The priest would bury it no more, for he sorely dreaded vengeance. He bore it into church, and through fear of more harm he ordained it to be put where every man could see it with his eyes.

These folk who continued to carole thus all that year, hand in hand, never went from that place nor could anyone bring them away. Where the curse first began, there they ran around and never felt such weariness as many do for walking. They ate no meat and drank no drink and slept not a moment. They were aware of neither night nor day, when it came, when it was gone. Frost and snow, hail and rain, cold and heat caused them no distress. Their hair and nails never grew; their clothes did not soil or change color. Thunder and lightning hurt them not, for God's mercy protected them. But they still sang that song which wrought them that woe, "Why stand we still? Why go we not?"

The time of grace came through Christ's power at the year's end on Yule night; at the same hour that the priest banned them, they were separated; at the same hour that he cursed them they were released. And in the twinkling of an eye they flew to the church and fell down on the pavement as if they had been dead or fallen in a swoon. Three days they lay still and none stirred, flesh or bone; and at the three days' end God granted them to go. They stood up and said openly to the parish priest, Sir Robert:

"Thou art the cause of our long confounding; thou art the maker of our travail, which has been a marvel to many. And thine own travail thou shalt soon end and go to thy long home."

They all rose then but Ave; she lay dead beside them. Her father and brother had great sorrow, and all others had marvel and dread. I trow it was no fear in her soul, but bodily suffering which brought about her death. The arm of Ave which no one might lay in grave, the emperor had a vessel wrought to put it in and hung in the church, so that all men could see it and think on that mischance.

These men who had been dancing thus the whole year, hand in hand, though they were parted now, still all the world would speak of them with wonder. They went through many lands and peoples hopping with the same step they had used. And as they could not then be unbound, so later they could never be seen together nor could they assemble in one place.

Four went to the court of Rome and always continued to hop. With sundry leaps they came thither, but they never came together again. Their clothes did not rot; their nails and hair did not grow, nor did their color grow sallow. They never were helped at any saint's shrine that we know of, but at that of the virgin, St. Edith. There Theodoric was cured on Our Lady's day in Lent, as he slept beside the tomb of St. Edith, the holy virgin; there he received his cure. . .

10 Some hold this tale naught but idle chatter; in other places it is cherished and heard as a great marvel. It is a goodly and instructive example to teach the fear of cursing. I have told it you to make you dread dancing in church or churchyard, specially against the priest's will. Desist when he biddeth you be still.

BAPTISM

(vss. 9493–651)

The first sacrament is holy baptism, the sprinkling with water, and anointing with chrism. It is in English, our speech, "christendom" or "christening." Christendom belongeth to Christ and to all who accept Christendom. This is the first and principal sacrament through which we are all saved from the chief sin of Adam, in whose sin all mankind was, is, and shall be born. Adam's sin was so grievous that there was no man so 20 dear to God but he should go to hell unless he was washed in the font and baptized with water, as Jesu Christ hath prescribed.

If thou believe that anyone is saved without christening, I say forsooth that thou hast gone contrary to this holy sacrament. Often we hear ignorant men, who go far astray, saying that they know not whether Jews be saved or not. But it is an even greater mischief that some priests think likewise of the Jews. Surely these men are all mistaken and confused in the faith, for never shall a Jew who dieth a Jew have part or profit in heaven's bliss, unless he be christened in the Holy Ghost and be steadfast in the sacrament. . .

30 I shall teach you what I heard a friar Minor [4] once say: "If thou see a child in such peril that no one can save it, then say thou thus in all haste: 'I christen thee in the name of the Father and Son and Holy Ghost,' and give it what name thou wilt, and cast on water. Then it is saved. And if thou give it no name, neither Robert, William, nor John, look that these words at least be properly said, and water be applied, and that there be no wasted

---

[4] A Franciscan.

words but 'in the Father and Son and Holy Ghost.' Forget not these words nor the water, whatsoever else be done."

Midwives who attend women ought to know all the points. Priests should teach them the ordinance, what they should say and do in case of need, and examine them as to what they know, what they should do and utter with mouth.

I will tell you of a midwife who lost a child, both soul and body. The friar told it in his sermon and often gave her his curse. When the child was born, the midwife held it on her lap and, when she saw that it would die, she began to cry loudly, "God and St. John christen thee, child, both 10 flesh and bone." The midwife said naught else. They would have laid it in the churchyard as another child would have been who had received the solemnity. The priest asked the midwife if it had been christened when it was alive, who had christened it, in what manner, and what was said that one could hear. The midwife said to the priest:

"Those who stood nearest me heard this: 'God Almighty and St. John give the child christendom in flesh and bone.'"

Then said the priest: "God and St. James give thee both sorrow and shame, and have thou and all others who were with thee Christ's malison! In evil time wert thou born, for by thy fault a soul is lost." 20

She was commanded that she should no more go again where children were born. Midwives, I told this tale for you so that, if ye can, ye may learn how to save what God redeemed full dearly.

THE SACRAMENT OF THE EUCHARIST

(VSS. 9999–10074)

There was a monk who had great renown for his alms, but because the fiend would destroy him, he would not believe in this sacrament and said that it was not Jesu who was conceived through the power of the Holy Ghost; Jesu was not the wafer that was raised at the mass, and that they who worshiped it did wrong. He told this to two abbots, and they wrote this tale to be preserved. It ought to be told to everyone who is against Christendom till it is proved by learning whether it is faith or heresy. 30

These abbots showed the monk the right way with all the examples that they could tell, and he said that it was false unless he could see it with his eyes. "Let me see it. Then will I believe that it can be so."

These abbots prayed a full sennight that God, through His might, would show Himself in flesh and blood on the altar to confirm the monk's belief. And he too prayed specially that God would show Himself in the body.

"Lord," he said, "not that Thou shouldst be grieved with me for lack of faith, but to show the very truth that Thou art the Sacrament of the mass, so that I may make others certain when I have seen it with my eyes."

The abbots lay in their orisons till the sennight was done. On the seventh day they came to the church and brought the other with them. A seat was prepared for the three to behold the privity of the sacrament that was shown in their presence. . . . When the wafer was laid on the altar and the priest had said the words, all thought verily that a living Child lay before the priest in the fair form of flesh and blood. This all three saw where they
10 were.

When the priest was about to break the sacramental wafer, an angel was sent down from Heaven and sacrificed the Child right there. As the priest broke it, the angel cut it. Into the chalice ran the blood of that Child, both God and man.

This monk went to the highest step to receive the sacrament as was proper. It seemed to him that the priest brought on the paten morsels of the Child newly slain, and offered him a bit of the flesh with the blood fresh upon it. Then he cried with a loud voice: "Mercy, Son of the God of Heaven! The bread I saw lying on the altar is Thy body; I saw it with
20 mine eyes. The bread through sacrament has all turned to flesh and blood. This I believe and ever shall, for verily we all saw it."

When he and they were all assured, it turned again into bread. He received the eucharist as did the others, and was a good man ever afterward. And all others who hear this tale or read it will be the better.

The Bee and the Stork

Richard Rolle

THE bee has three traits. One is, that she is never idle, and she is not with them that will not work, but casts them out and puts them away. Another is, that, when she flies, she takes earth in her feet, that she be not lightly carried over-high in the air by the wind. The third is, that she keeps clean and bright her wings. Thus, righteous men that love God are never in idleness; for either they are in travail, praying, or thinking, or reading, or doing other good work, or reproving idle men and showing them worthy to be put out from the rest of heaven, because they will not travail here. They take earth; that is, they hold themselves vile and earthly, that they be not blown with the winds of vanity and of pride. They keep their wings 10 clean; that is, the two commandments of charity they fulfill in good conscience; and they have other virtues unblended with the filth of sin and unclean lust.

Aristotle says that the bees are fighting against him that will draw their honey from them. So should we do against devils that strive to steal from us the honey of a life of poverty and of grace. For many there are that never can hold the commandment of love regarding their friends, whether kinsfolk or unrelated, but either they love them overmuch, setting their thoughts unrighteously on them, or they love them over little, if they do not all as they would to them. Such cannot fight for their honey, wherefore 20 the devil turns it to wormwood, and makes their souls oftentimes full bitter in anguish and vexation, and business of vain thoughts, and other wretchedness; for they are so heavy in earthly friendship that they may not fly into the love of Jesu Christ, in the which they might well forgo the love of all creatures living on earth.

Wherefore, accordingly, Aristotle says that some fowls are of good flying, that pass from one land to another. Some are of ill flying, for heaviness of body, and because their nest is not far from the earth. Thus is it of them that turn themselves to God's service: some are of good flight, for they fly from earth to heaven, and rest them there in thought, and are fed in 30 delight of God's love, and have thought of no love of the world; some are, that cannot fly from this land, but on the way let their heart rest, and delight them in various loves of men and women, as they come and go, now one and now another, and in Jesu Christ they can find no sweetness, or if they any time feel aught, it is so little and so short, for other thoughts that are in them, that it brings them to no stableness. For they are like to a fowl that is called *strucio,* or stork,[1] that has wings, and it may not fly for weight of body. So they have understanding, and fast and watch and seem holy in men's sight; but they may not fly to love and contemplation of God, they are so charged with other affections and other vanities.

[1] *Strucio* really is the Latin for ostrich. Note the same confusion in the *Rule of Anchoresses.*

Meditations on the Passion

Richard Rolle

SWEET Jesu, I thank Thee and yield Thee thankings for the pains and agonies, the shames and felonies, that men did to Thee all with treason. Men bound Thee as a thief, without mercy and pity. Lord, I thank Thee for those sweet and piteous paces that Thou didst go, for our love, towards Thine own pain and Thine own death. I pray Thee, Lord, and beseech Thee that Thou unbind us from the bonds of all our sins, as Thou didst suffer Thyself to be bound for our love. *Adoramus. Pater. Ave.*

I thank Thee, sweet Lord Jesu Christ, for the pains and shames that Thou didst suffer before the bishops and masters of the law, and for Thine enemies, for the buffets and neck-blows, and the many other shames that 10 Thou didst suffer; and among other things I thank Thee, Lord, for the looking that Thou didst look at the disciple who Thee had forsaken, Saint Peter. Thou didst look at him a look of mercy, when Thou wert in Thine utmost anguish, and in Thine utmost pain. Openly Thou didst show there the love and the charity that Thou didst have for us, that no shame or pain, nor anything may draw Thy heart from us in as much as it is in Thee. Sweet Lord, full of mercy and of pity, may we, through Thy blessed looking there, turn to Thy grace and repent us of our trespass and of our misdoing, so that we may come with Saint Peter to Thy mercy. . . .

Alas, that I should live and see my gracious Lord, so suffering and so 20 meek, who never trespassed, so shamefully bedight! The murmur and the moaning, the sorrow and the sighing, the pity of His aspect, I would were my death. He, the crown of all bliss, who crowns all the blessed, who is king of all kings and lord of all lords, by hell-hounds He is crowned with thorns; He, the worship of heaven, is despised and defouled; He who shaped the sun and all that is good on earth, that is wholly His gift, He had not wherein His head he might hide. So poor has He become, us to make rich. that all naked He goeth in sight of all the folk.

Ah, Lord, Thy sorrow, why is it not my death? Now they lead Thee forth naked as a worm, the tormentors about Thee, and the armed knights. 30

The press of the people was terribly strong; they hurled Thee and harried Thee so shamefully, they spurned Thee with their feet, as if Thou hadst been a dog. I see in my soul how pitifully Thou goest: Thy body is so bloody, made so raw and blistered; Thy crown is so sharp that sitteth on Thy head; Thy hair moveth with the wind, clotted with blood; Thy lovely face so wan and so swollen with buffeting and with beating, with spitting and spouting. Therewith the blood ran, grisly to my sight; so loathly and so loathsome the Jews have made Thee, that more like a leper art Thou than a clean man. The cross is so heavy, so high and so strong, that they
10 hung on Thy bare back, trussed so hard.

Ah, Lord, the groaning that Thou didst make, so sore and so hard sat the cross to the bone. Thy body is so sick, so feeble and weary, what with the great fasting before Thou wast taken, and all night awake without any rest; with beating and buffeting so far it is crushed that all stooping Thou goest, and dreadful is Thy look. The flesh, where the cross sitteth, is all raw; the blisters and blains are wan and blue; the pain of that burden costs Thee so sorely that each foot that Thou goest, it stingeth Thee to Thy heart. Thus, in this groaning, and in this great pain, Thou goest out of Jerusalem towards Thy death. The city is so noble, the people so many!
20 The folk come running out of every street. Then the folk standeth up and there is a great press, that men may wonder that think thereon. With such a procession of worldly wonderers was never any thief led to his death. Some there were among the common people who sighed sorely and grieved for Thy woe, who knew that it was for envy Thou wast tormented. For the princes and the bishops, who led the law, they did Thee to death for Thy true sayings, when Thou of their errors wouldst reprove them. They knew it was outrage and wrong that Thou didst suffer, and they followed Thee, weeping and sighing full sore. Thou didst then say a thing that afterwards befell: Thou didst bid them weep for themselves and for the great
30 vengeance that for Thy death should fall on them, and upon their children, and upon the city, that afterwards was destroyed. For vengeance on their own guilt they were chased out of their place.

Ah, Lord, what sorrow fell on Thy heart, when Thou on Thy mother didst cast Thine eyes. Thou didst see her following after among the great crowd. Like a woman beside herself, her hands she wrung; weeping and sighing she cast out her arms; the water from her eyes dropped at her feet. She fell in a dead swoon, more than once, through sorrow for the pains that smote to her heart. The sorrow that she made and the great grief aggravated many fold all Thine other pains; when she knew that it was so,
40 then was it worse for her, and Thou also for her didst weep. Such was your sorrow, each for the other, waxing manifold with heaping sorrows. The love of your hearts, that over all other loves was without mate, burning

sharply, made you to burn, either for other, with sorrow unlike to any other woe. As the love was without mate, so the sorrow was without peer; it stuck in your hearts as if it were death.

Ah, Lady, mercy, why wert thou so bold, among so many fierce foes to follow so close? How was it that the timidity of womanhood, the modesty of a maiden, had not withdrawn thee? For it was not seemly for thee to follow such a rout, so vile and shameful, so horrible to see. But thou hadst no regard for fear of any man nor for aught else that should hinder thee, but, as if beside thyself, for dole and for sorrow for thy Son's passion, all thine heart was set. Your love was so sharp, each for the other, and so 10 burning hot, thy sighings were so deep, the grief of your look was deadly woe. The love and the sorrow, that stuck in thy breast, reft from thee the reckoning of bodily fear and of worldly shame and every kind of restraint, for thy sorrow had made thee as if beside thyself.

Ah, Lady, for the sorrow that thou didst suffer for thy Son's passion—it should have been mine own, for I had deserved it and much worse, because I was the cause thereof, and He was guiltless, so the dear wounds were mine own of right—get for me, of thy mercy, one of them all, a prick at my heart of that same pain, a drop of that pity with which to follow Him. If all that woe is my right, get me some of mine own, and be not so wrong- 20 ful as to withhold it all. Though all thy woe be dear to thee, art thou not very generous? Share it with the poor, who hath little or nothing. Give to me of thy sighings, who sighest so sorely, so that I may sigh with thee who began that woe. I ask not, dear Lady, castles, or towers, or other worldly weal, the sun, the moon, the bright stars. But all my desire is for the wounds of pity, pain and compassion for my Lord Jesu Christ. Worst and unworthiest of all men's holding, I have appetite for pain, to beseech my Lord for a drop of His red blood to make bloody my soul, a drop of that water to wash it with.

Ah, Lady, for that mercy, who art mother of mercy, succor of all sorrow, 30 and help of all harm, mother made of all wretched and woeful, hearken to this wretch, and visit thy child. Sow in my heart, that is hard as a stone, a spark of compassion for that dear passion, with a wound of that pity to make it pliant.

LAURA HIBBARD LOOMIS

The Form of Living

Richard Rolle

CHAPTER II

THE state that thou art in, that is solitude, is fittest of all others for revelation of the Holy Ghost. For when St. John was in the isle of Patmos, then God showed him His secrets. The goodness of God it is that He comforts them wonderfully who have no comfort of the world, if they give their heart entirely to Him, and covet not, nor seek, but Him. Then He gives Himself to them in sweetness and delight, in burning of love, and in joy and melody, and dwells always with them in their soul, so that the comfort of Him departs never from them. And if they at any time begin to err, through ignorance or frailty, soon He shows them the right way and all that they
10 have need of, He teaches them. No man to such revelation and grace on the first day may come, but through long travail and effort to love Jesu Christ, as hereafter thou shalt hear.

Nevertheless He suffers them to be tempted in various ways, both waking and sleeping. For always the more temptations and the more grievous that they stand against and overcome, the more shall they rejoice in His love when these are passed. Waking they are sometimes tempted with foul thoughts, vile lusts, wicked delights, with pride, ire, envy, despair, presumption, and many others. But their remedy shall be prayer, weeping, fasting, waking. These things, if they be done with discretion, put away
20 sin and filth from the soul, and make it clean to receive the love of Jesu Christ, who may not be loved but in cleanness.

Also sometimes the fiend tempts men and women, who are alone by themselves, in a wily and subtle way. He transfigures himself into the likeness of an angel of light, and appears to them, and says that he is one of God's angels come to comfort them; and so does he deceive fools. But they that are wise, and will not quickly believe in all spirits, but ask counsel of learned men, he may not beguile them. Thus I find it written of a recluse, who was a good woman, to whom the bad angel ofttimes appeared in the form of a good angel, and said that he was come to bring her joy of heaven.
30 Wherefore she was right glad and joyful. But nevertheless she told it to her shrift-father;.and he, as a wise man and wary, gave her this counsel. "When

[118]

he comes," he said, "bid him show thee Our Lady, Saint Mary. When he has done so, say *Ave Maria*." She did so. The fiend said: "Thou hast no need to see her; let my presence suffice thee." And she said, despite all she must see her. He saw that it behooved him either to do her will or she would despise him. So quickly he brought forth the fairest woman that might be, as to her look, and showed her to the recluse. And she fell down on her knees and said, "*Ave Maria*." And straightway all vanished away, and for shame never after came he to her. This I say, not because I expect that he will have leave to tempt thee in this way, but because I wish that thou beware, if any such temptations befall thee, sleeping or waking, that thou shouldst not believe over quickly, until thou knowest the truth.

More secretly he transfigures himself in the form of an angel of light, by which commonly all men are tempted, when he hides ill under the likeness of good; and that is done in two ways. One is, when he eggs us on to too much ease and rest of body and softness for our flesh, because of necessity to sustain our nature. For such thoughts he puts into us: unless we eat well, and drink well, and sleep well, and lie softly, and sit warmly, we may not serve God, nor may we last in the work we have begun. But he thinks to bring us to overmuch lust. Another way it is, when under the likeness of spiritual good, he entices us to sharp and over-great penance, to destroy ourselves, and thus he says: "Thou dost know well, that he who suffers most penance for God's love, he shall have the greatest reward. Therefore eat little and feeble meat, and drink less; the thinnest drink is good enough for thee. Care nothing for sleep. Wear the hairshirt and the habergeon.[1] Everything that is affliction for thy flesh, do it, so that none may surpass thee in penance." He that says thus to thee is about to slay thee with overmuch abstinence, as he that said the other thing, to slay thee with overlittle. Therefore, if we will be rightly disposed, it behooves us to set ourselves in a good mean, in order that we may destroy our vices and hold under our flesh, and nevertheless be stalwart in the service of Jesu Christ.

CHAPTER IX

If thou wilt be well with God, and have grace to rule thy life, and come to the joy of love, this name Jesu, fasten it so fast in thy heart, that never should it come out of thy thought. And when thou speakest to Him and sayest "Jesu," through custom it shall be in thy ear joy, in thy mouth honey, and in thy heart melody. For it shall seem joy to thee to hear that name be named, sweetness to speak it, mirth and song to think it. If thou dost think Jesu continually and hold it steadfastly, it purges thy sin and kindles thy

---

[1] A sort of jacket of steel links, worn by knights for protection, but here prescribed to mortify the flesh.

heart; it clarifies thy soul; it removes anger and does away with sloth; it wounds in love and fulfills with charity; it chases the devil and puts out dread; it opens heaven and makes a contemplative man. Have in mind Jesu; for all vices and phantoms it puts away from the lover. And hail often Mary, both day and night. Great love and joy shalt thou feel, if thou wilt do according to this teaching. Thou needst not covet greatly many books; hold love in heart and in work, and thou hast everything that we may say or write. For the fullness of the law is charity; on that hangs everything.

CHAPTER XII

Two lives there are that Christian men live. One is called Active Life, 10 for it is in more bodily work. Another is Contemplative Life, for it is in more spiritual sweetness. Active life is largely outward, and in more travail and more peril because of the temptations that are in the world. Contemplative life is largely inward, and for that it is more lasting and certain, more restful and delectable, lovelier and more rewarding. For it has joy in God's love and savor of the life that lasts forever, if in this present time it be rightly led. And that feeling of joy in the love of Jesu passes all other merits on earth. For it is so hard to come to, through the frailty of our flesh and the many temptations with which we are beset that hinder us night and day. All other things are lightly come at in comparison with that, for that may 20 no man deserve, but it is given only of God's goodness to those that truly give themselves to contemplation and to quiet for Christ's love.

To men or women that take to active life, two things fall. One is to ordain their household in fear and in the love of God, and to find for them their necessaries, and for themselves to keep entirely the commandments of God, doing unto their neighbor as they wish to have done unto them. Another thing is, that they do, according to their power, the seven works of mercy: that is, to feed the hungry, to give to the thirsty drink, to clothe the naked, to harbor him who has no housing, to visit the sick, to comfort those that are in prison, and put dead men in the grave. All who can and 30 have the means, they may not be quit with one or two of these, but it behooves them to do them all, if they will have on Doomsday the blessing that Jesu will give to all who have done them. Otherwise they may fear the malison which all men have who will not do them, when they had goods to do them with.

Contemplative life has two parts, a lower and a higher. The lower is meditation on holy writings, God's words, and in other good thoughts and sweet, which men have by the grace of God about the love of Jesu Christ, and also in loving God through psalms and hymns, or through prayers. The higher part of contemplation is beholding and desire of the things of heaven, and joy in the Holy Ghost, which men often have. And if it be so that they are not praying with the mouth, but only thinking of God and the fairness of angels and holy souls, then I may say that contemplation is a wonderful joy of God's love, which is a joy, the loving of God, that can not be told. And that wonderful loving is in the soul, and for abundance of joy and sweetness it ascendeth into the mouth, so that the heart and the tongue are in one accord, and body and soul rejoice, living in God.

A man or woman who is ordained to contemplative life first God inspires to forsake this world and all the vanity and the covetousness and the vile lust thereof. Afterwards He leads them by themselves, and speaks to their 10 heart, and as the prophet says, "He gives them to suck the sweetness of the beginning of love." And then He sets them in the will to give them wholly to prayers and meditations and tears. Afterwards, when they have suffered many temptations, and the foul annoyance of idle thoughts and vanities, which will encumber those who cannot destroy them, are passing away, He makes them gather up their heart, and fasten it only on Him. He opens to the eye of their souls the gates of heaven, so that the same eye looks into heaven. And then the fire of love verily lies in their heart and burns therein, and makes it clean of all earthly filth. And from then on they are contemplative men, and ravished in love. For contemplation is a seeing, 20 and they see into heaven with their spiritual eye. But thou shalt know that no man has perfect sight of heaven whilst living in the body here. But as soon as they die, they are brought before God and see Him face to face and eye to eye, and dwell with Him without end. For Him they sought, and Him they coveted, and Him they loved with all their might.

Lo, Margaret, I have said shortly for thee the form of living, and how thou mayst come to perfection, and to love Him to whom thou hast betaken thee. If it do thee good and profit thee, thank God, and pray for me. The grace of Jesu Christ be with thee and keep thee. Amen.

LAURA HIBBARD LOOMIS

Revelations of Divine Love[1]

Dame Julian of Norwich

CHAPTER III

AND when I was thirty years old and a half, God sent me a bodily sickness, in which I lay three days and three nights; and on the fourth night I took all my rites of Holy Church, and weened not to have lived till day. And after this I languored forth two days and two nights, and on the third night I weened oftentimes to have passed; and so weened they that were with me.

And being in youth as yet, I thought it great sorrow to die;—but for nothing that was in earth that me liked to live for, nor for no pain that I had fear of: for I trusted in God of His mercy. But it was to have lived that I might have loved God better, and longer time, that I might have the more 10 knowing and loving of God in bliss of Heaven. For methought all the time that I had lived here so little and so short in regard of that endless bliss,— I thought it was as nothing. Wherefore I thought: *Good Lord, may my living no longer be to Thy worship!* And I understood by my reason and by my feeling of my pains that I should die; and I assented fully with all the will of my heart to be at God's will.

Thus I dured till day, and by then my body was dead from the middle downwards, as to my feeling. Then was I minded to be set upright, backward leaning, with help,—for to have more freedom of my heart to be at God's will, and thinking on God while my life would last.

20 My curate was sent for to be at my ending, and by that time when he came I had set my eyes, and might not speak. He set the Cross before my face and said: *I have brought thee the Image of thy Maker and Savior: look thereupon and comfort thee therewith.*

Methought I was well as it was, for my eyes were set uprightward unto Heaven, where I trusted to come by the mercy of God; but nevertheless I assented to set my eyes on the face of the Crucifix, if I might; and so I did. For methought I might longer dure to look evenforth than right up.

---

[1] From Dame Juliana of Norwich, *Revelations of Divine Love*, ed. by Grace Warrack (London, 1901). Reprinted by permission of Methuen and Co.

After this my sight began to fail, and it was all dark about me in the chamber, as if it had been night, save in the Image of the Cross, whereon I beheld a common light; and I wist not how. All that was away from the Cross was of horror to me, as if it had been greatly occupied by the fiends.

After this the upper part of my body began to die, so far forth that scarcely I had any feeling;—with shortness of breath. And then I weened in sooth to have passed.

And in this moment suddenly all my pain was taken from me, and I was as whole (and specially in the upper part of my body) as ever I was afore.

I marveled at this sudden change; for methought it was a privy working 10 of God, and not of nature. And yet by the feeling of this ease I trusted never the more to live; nor was the feeling of this ease any full ease unto me: for methought I had liefer have been delivered from this world.

Then came suddenly to my mind that I should desire the second wound of our Lord's gracious gift: that my body might be fulfilled with mind and feeling of His blessed Passion. For I would that his pains were my pains, with compassion and afterward longing to God. But in this I desired never bodily sight nor showing of God, but compassion such as a kind soul might have with our Lord Jesu, that for love would be a mortal man: and therefore I desired to suffer with Him. 20

CHAPTER IV

In this moment suddenly I saw the red blood trickle down from under the Garland hot and freshly and right plenteously, as it were in the time of His Passion when the Garland of thorns was pressed on His blessed head who was both God and Man, the same that suffered thus for me. I conceived truly and mightily that it was Himself showed it me, without any mean.

And in the same Showing suddenly the Trinity fulfilled my heart most of joy. And so I understood it shall be in heaven without end to all that shall come there. For the Trinity is God: God is the Trinity; the Trinity is our Maker and Keeper, the Trinity is our everlasting love and everlasting 30 joy and bliss, by our Lord Jesu Christ. And this was showed in the First Showing and in all: for where Jesu appeareth, the blessed Trinity is understood, as to my sight.

And I said: *Benedicite Domine!* This I said for reverence in my meaning, with mighty voice; and full greatly was astonied for wonder and marvel that I had, that He that is so reverend and dreadful will be so homely with a sinful creature living in wretched flesh.

This Showing I took for the time of my temptation,—for methought by the sufferance of God I should be tempted of fiends ere I died. Through this sight of the blessed Passion, with the Godhead that I saw in mine understanding, I knew well that *It* was strength enough for me, yea, and for all creatures living, against all the fiends of hell and spiritual temptation.

In this Showing He brought our blessed Lady to my understanding. I saw her spiritually, in bodily likeness: a simple maid and a meek, young of age and little waxen above a child, in the stature that she was when she conceived. Also God showed in part the wisdom and the truth of her soul: wherein I understood the reverent beholding in which she beheld her God and Maker, marveling with great reverence that He would be born of her

10 that was a simple creature of His making. And this wisdom and truth: knowing the greatness of her Maker and the littleness of herself that was made,—caused her to say full meekly to Gabriel: *Lo me, God's handmaid!* In this sight I understood soothly that she is more than all that God made beneath her in worthiness and grace; for above her is nothing that is made but the blessed Manhood of Christ, as to my sight.

CHAPTER XXVII

After this the Lord brought to my mind the longing that I had to Him afore. And I saw that nothing hindered me but sin. And so I looked, generally, upon us all, and methought: *If sin had not been, we should all have been clean and like to our Lord, as He made us.*

20 And thus, in my folly, afore this time often I wondered why by the great foreseeing wisdom of God the beginning of sin was not prevented: for then, methought, all should have been well. This stirring of mind was much to be forsaken, but nevertheless mourning and sorrow I made therefor, without reason and discretion.

But Jesu, who in this Vision informed me of all that is needful to me, answered by this word and said: *It behoved that there should be sin; but all shall be well, and all shall be well, and all manner of thing shall be well.*

In this naked word *sin*, our Lord brought to my mind all that is not good, and the shameful despite and the utter scorning that He bare for us in this

30 life, and His dying; and all the pains and passions of all His creatures, spiritual and bodily; (for we be all partly scorned, and we shall be scorned following our Master, Jesu, till we be fully purged, that is to say, till we be fully mortified of our deadly flesh and of all our inward affections which are not truly good;) and the beholding of this, with all pains that ever were or ever shall be—and with all these I understand the Passion of Christ as the most pain, and overpassing. All this was showed in a touch and quickly passed over into comfort: for our good Lord would not that the soul were affeared of this terrible sight.

But I saw not sin: for I believe it hath no manner of substance nor no part of being, nor could it be known but by the pain it is cause of.

And this pain, *it* is something, as to my sight, for a time; for it purgeth, and maketh us to know ourselves and to ask mercy. For the Passion of our Lord is comfort to us against all this, and so is His blessed will. And for the tender love that our good Lord hath to all that shall be saved, He comforteth readily and sweetly, signifying thus: *It is sooth that sin is cause of all this pain; but all shall be well, and all shall be well, and all manner of thing shall be well.*

These words were said full tenderly, showing no manner of blame to me nor to any that shall be saved. Then were it a great unkindness to blame or wonder on God for my sin, since He blameth not me for sin.

And in these words I saw a marvelous high mystery hid in God, which mystery He shall openly make known to us in Heaven: in which knowing we shall verily see the cause why He suffered sin to come. In which sight we shall endlessly joy in our Lord God.

CHAPTER XXXII

One time our good Lord said: *All things shall be well;* and another time he said: *Thou shalt see thyself that all manner of things shall be well;* and in these two sayings the soul took sundry understandings.

One was that He willeth we know that not only He taketh heed to noble things and to great, but also to little and to small, to low and to simple, to one and to other. And so meaneth He in that He saith: *All manner of things shall be well.* For He willeth we know that the least things shall not be forgotten.

Another understanding is this, that there be deeds evil done in our sight, and so great harms taken, that it seemeth to us that it were impossible that ever it should come to good end. And upon this we look, sorrowing and mourning therefor, so that we cannot resign us unto the blissful beholding of God as we should do. And the cause of this is that the use of our reason is now so blind, so low, and so simple, that we cannot know that high marvelous Wisdom, the Might and the Goodness of the blissful Trinity. And thus signifieth He when He saith: *Thou shalt thyself see if all manner of things shall be well.* As if He said: *Take now heed faithfully and trustingly, and at the last end thou shalt verily see it in fulness of joy.*

And thus in these same five words aforesaid: *I may make all things well,* etc., I understand a mighty comfort of all the works of our Lord God that are yet to come. There is a Deed which the blessed Trinity shall do in the last Day, as to my sight, and when the Deed shall be, and how it shall be done, is unknown of all creatures that are beneath Christ, and shall be till when it is done. . . .

And in this sight I marveled greatly and beheld our Faith, marveling thus: Our Faith is grounded in God's word, and it belongeth to our Faith that we believe that God's word shall be saved in all things; and one point of our Faith is that many creatures shall be condemned: as angels that fell out of Heaven for pride, which be now fiends; and many in earth that die out of the Faith of Holy Church: that is to say, they that be heathen men; and also many that have received christendom and live unchristian life and
10 so die out of charity: all these shall be condemned to hell without end, as Holy Church teacheth me to believe. And all this so standing, methought it was impossible that all manner of things should be well, as our Lord showed in the same time.

And as to this I had no other answer in Showing of our Lord God but this: *That which is impossible to thee is not impossible to me: I shall save my word in all things and I shall make all things well.* Thus I was taught, by the grace of God, that I should steadfastly hold me in Faith as I had aforehand understood, and therewith that I should firmly believe that all things shall be well, as our Lord shewed in the same time.

20 For this is the Great Deed that our Lord shall do, in which Deed He shall save His word and He shall make all well that is not well. How it shall be done there is no creature beneath Christ that knoweth it, nor shall know it till it is done; according to the understanding that I took of our Lord's meaning in this time.

CHAPTER XLIX

For this was a high marvel to the soul which was continually showed in all the Revelations, and was with great diligence beholden, that our Lord God, as for Himself, may not forgive, for He may not be wroth: it were impossible. For this was showed: that our life is all grounded and rooted in love, and without love we may not live; and therefore to the soul that of His
30 special grace seeth so far into the high, marvelous Goodness of God, and seeth that we are endlessly united to Him in love, it is the most impossible that may be, that God should be wroth. For wrath and friendship be two contraries. For He that wasteth and destroyeth our wrath and maketh us meek and mild, it must needs be that He himself be ever one in love, meek and mild: which is contrary to wrath.

For I saw full surely that where our Lord appeareth, peace is brought and wrath hath no place. For I saw no manner of wrath in God, neither for short time nor for long;—for in sooth, as to my sight, if God might be wroth for an instant, we should never have life nor place nor being. For as verily as we have our being of the endless Might of God and of the endless Wisdom and of the endless Goodness, so verily we have our keeping in the endless Might of God, in the endless Wisdom, and in the endless Goodness. For though we feel in ourselves,—frail wretches,—debates and strifes, yet are we in all ways enclosed in the mildness of God and in His meekness, in His benignity and in His graciousness. For I saw full surely that all our endless friendship, our place, our life and our being, is in God.

For that same endless Goodness that keepeth us when we sin, that we perish not, the same endless Goodness continually treateth in us a peace against our wrath and our contrarious falling, and maketh us to see our 10 need with a true dread, and mightily to seek unto God to have forgiveness, with a gracious desire of our salvation. And though we, by the wrath and the contrariness that is in us, be now in tribulation, distress, and woe, as falleth to our blindness and frailty, yet are we surely safe by the merciful keeping of God, that we perish not. But we are not blissfully safe, in having of our endless joy, till we be all in peace and in love: that is to say, full pleased with God and with all His works, and with all His judgments, and loving and peaceable with ourselves and with our fellow Christians and with all that God loveth, as love beseemeth. And this doeth God's Goodness in us. 20

Thus saw I that God is our very Peace, and He is our sure Keeper when we are ourselves in unpeace, and He continually worketh to bring us into endless peace. And thus when we, by the working of mercy and grace, be made meek and mild, we are fully safe; suddenly is the soul united to God when it is truly at peace in itself: for in Him is found no wrath. And thus I saw when we are all in peace and in love, we find no contrariness, nor no manner of hindrance through that contrariness which is now in us; nay, our Lord of His Goodness maketh it to us full profitable. For that contrariness is cause of our tribulations and all our woe, and our Lord Jesu taketh them and sendeth them up to Heaven, and there are they made more sweet 30 and delectable than heart may think or tongue may tell. And when we come thither we shall find them ready, all turned into very fair and endless worships. Thus is God our steadfast Ground: and He shall be our full bliss and make us unchangeable, as He is, when we are there.

GRACE WARRACK

The Alliterative Morte Arthur

Arthur turns into Tuscany   when the time is favorable,
Takes towns very quickly,   with towers of height;
Walls he cast down,   and knights he wounded;
Made many fair widows   woefully sing,
Be weary often, and weep,   and wring their hands.
He wastes all with war   wherever he rides past;
Their wealth and their dwellings   he turns to destruction.
Thus they [1] spring forth and spread far,   and spare but little,
They spoil without pity,   and lay waste their vines;
Spend without sparing   what long was saved up;   3160
Speed then to Spoleto,   with spears in plenty.
From Spain into Spruysland [2]   the report of him springs,
The tale of his destruction;   despair is full huge.
    Towards Viterbo this valiant man   turns his reins.
Wisely in that vale   he victuals his warriors,
With vernage [3] and other wines,   and venison baked.
And with the viscount of that land   he decides to tarry.
Quickly the vanguard   dismount from their horses,
In the vale of Vertennon   among the vineyards;
There sojourns this sovereign   with solace of heart,   3170
To see when the senators   should send any word;
He revels with rich wine,   rejoices himself,
This king with his royal men   of the Round Table,
With mirth and melody,   and manifold games;
Were never merrier men   made on this earth.
    But on a Saturday, at noon,   a seven-night thereafter,
The cunningest cardinal   that to the court belonged,
Kneels to the conqueror   and utters these words:
Prays him for peace   and proffers full largely,
To have pity on the pope,   who thus was put down;   3180
Besought him assurance,   for the sake of our Lord,

---

[1] Arthur's forces; Arthur has undertaken to conquer Rome.
[2] Prussia.   [3] Vernacchia, a strong, sweet Italian wine.

But a seven-night's day,   when they would all be assembled,
And they would surely see him   the Sunday thereafter
In the city of Rome   as sovereign and lord,
And crown him properly   with chrismed [4] hands,
With his scepter and his sword,   as sovereign and lord.
For this undertaking   hostages are come thither,
Of heirs most comely   eight score children,
In togas of Tars [5]   most richly attired,
And commit themselves to the king   and his renowned knights.   3190
   When they had treated their truce,   with trumpet blasts after,
They turn unto a tent   where tables are set up;
The king himself is seated   and certain lords
Under a ceiling of silk,   in peace at the table;
All the senators are set   apart by themselves,
And are solemnly served   with seldom-known dishes.
The king, mighty of mirth,   with his mild words
Heartens the Romans   at his rich table,
Comforts the cardinal   in knightly wise himself;
And this royal ruler,   as the romance tells us,   3200
The Romans did reverence   at his rich table.
The trained men and knowing,   when time it seemed them,
Took their leave of the king,   and turned them again;
To the city that night   they made way the quickest.
And thus the hostage of Rome   is left with Arthur.
   Then this royal king   rehearses these words:
"Now may we revel and rest,   for Rome is our own;
Make our hostages at ease,   these comely young nobles,
And look ye hold them all,   who linger in my host;
The Emperor of Almain [6]   and all these east marches,   3210
We shall be overlord of all   that dwell upon earth.
We will by Holy Cross Day [7]   acquire these lands,
And at Christmas Day   be crowned accordingly;
Reign in my royalty   and hold my Round Table
With the rents [8] from Rome,   as it right pleases me.
Then go over the Great Sea   with good men of arms,
To avenge that Warrior   that died on the Rood."
   Then this comely king,   as chronicles tell us,
Turns bravely to bed   with a blithe heart;
He slings off with sleight   and slackens his girdle,   3220
And for sloth of slumber   falls then asleep.

[4] Anointed.   [5] Silk of Tartary.   [6] Germany.   [7] September 14.
[8] Income.

But at one after midnight   all his mood changed;
He dreamt in the morning hour   most marvelous dreams.
And when his dreadful dream   was driven to its end,
The king stares in dismay,   as though he should die,
Sends after philosophers,   and his affright tells them.
   "Since I was formed in faith,   so frightened was I never!
Wherefore ransack [9] readily   and reveal me my dreams,
And I shall fully and rightly   rehearse the truth.
Me thought I was in a wood   at mine own will,   3230
Since I knew no way,   whither I should wend,
Because of wolves and wild swine   and wicked beasts.
I walked in that wasteland   to seek out dangers.
There lions full loathly   licked their tushes,
As they lapped up the blood   of my loyal knights.
Through that forest I fled,   where flowers grew tall,
For the great fear that I had   of those foul creatures.
I made way to a meadow,   with mountains closed in,
The merriest of middle-earth   that men might behold.
The enclosure was encompassed   and closed all about,   3240
With clover and with cleve-wort   clad evenly all over;
The vale was environed   with vines of silver,
All with grapes of gold—   greater grew never,
Surrounded with shrubs   and all kinds of trees,
Arbors most handsome   and herdsmen thereunder.
All fruits were produced   that flourished on earth,
Fairly sheltered in hedges   upon the tree boughs.
There was no dankness of dew   that could harm aught;
With the drying of daytime   wholly dry were the flowers.
   "There descends in the dale,   down from the clouds,   3250
A duchess preciously dight   in diapered garments,
In a surcoat of silk   most rarely hued,
Wholly with ermine overlaid   low to the hems,
And with lady-like lappets   the length of a yard,
And all readily reversed   with ribbons of gold,
With brooches and bezants [10]   and other bright stones
Her back and her breast   were bedecked all over;
With a caul [11] and a coronal [12]   she was neatly arrayed,
And that so comely of color   none was known ever.
   "About she whirled a wheel   with her white hands,   3260
Turned most skilfully   the wheel as she would.

---

[9] Examine.   [10] A coin struck at Byzantium.
[11] A close-fitting cap or headdress.   [12] Circlet for the head.

The rim was of red gold   with royal stones,
Arrayed in richness   and rubies in plenty;
The spokes were resplendent   with splinters of silver,
The space of a spear-length   springing most fairly;
Thereon was a chair   of chalk-white silver,
And checkered with carbuncle,[13]   changing in hues;
To the circumference there clung   kings in a row,
With crowns of clear gold   that were cracked asunder;
Six from that seat   were suddenly fallen,   3270
Each man by himself,   and said these words:
   " 'That ever I reigned on this wheel,   it rues me ever.
Was never king so rich,   that reigned upon earth!
When I rode on my route,   I wrought nothing else
But hawk and revel   and tax the people.
And thus I drive forth my days,   while I can endure it;
And therefore in agony   am I condemned forever.'
   "The last [14] was a little man   that was laid beneath,
His loins lay very lean   and loathly to look on,
The locks gray and long   the length of a yard,   3280
His flesh and his body   were lamed quite sorely;
The one eye of the man   was brighter than silver,
The other was yellower   than the yolk of an egg.
'I was lord,' quoth the man,   'of lands aplenty,
And all people louted to me,   who lived upon earth;
And now is left me no flap   to cover my body,
But lightly am I lost;   let all men believe it.'
   "The second sir, forsooth,   that followed him after,
Was surer in my sight,   and more serious in arms;
Oft he sighed heavily,   and spoke these words: 3290
'On yonder seat have I sat   as sovereign and lord,
And ladies loved me,   to embrace in their arms:
And now is my lordship lost   and laid by forever!'
   "The third man was massive   and thick in the shoulders,
A stout man to threaten   where thirty were gathered;
His diadem had dropped down,   bedecked with stones,
Indented all with diamonds,   and richly adorned.
'I was dreaded in my days,' he said,   'in divers realms,
And now am damned among the dead,   and my dole is the more.'
   "The fourth was a fair man   and forceful in arms,   3300

---

[13] Brilliant gem of deep red color.
[14] i.e., the one lowest down, at the bottom of the heap.

The fairest in figure   that ever was formed.
'I was fierce in my faith,' he said,   'whilst I on earth reigned,
Famous in far lands,   and flower of all kings;
Now my face is faded,   and foul hap has befallen me,
For I am fallen from afar,   and friendless am left.'
   "The fifth was a fairer man   than many of these others,
A forceful man and fierce,   with foaming lips;
He hung fast to the felly   and clasped his arms,
But still he failed and fell   a full fifty feet;
But still he sprang up and leapt   and spread his arms,   3310
And on the spear-length spokes   he speaks these words:
'I was a sire in Syria,   and set by myself
As sovereign and seigneur   of several kings' lands;
Now from my solace am I   full suddenly fallen,
And for sake of my sin   yonder throne is lost to me.'
   "The sixth had a psalter   most seemly bound,
And a surplice of silk,   sewn very fairly,
A harp and a hand-sling,   with hard flint stones;
What harms he has had   he declares straightway:
'I was deemed in my days,' he said,   'for deeds of arms   3320
One of the doughtiest   that dwelt upon earth;
But I was marred on earth   in my greatest strength,
By this maiden [15] so mild   that moves us all.'
   "Two kings were climbing   and clambering on high,
The crest of the compass   they covet most eagerly.
'This chair of carbuncle,' they said,   'we claim hereafter,[16]
As two of the chiefest   chosen upon earth.'
The young nobles were chalk-white,   both cheeks and faces,
But the chair above them   achieved they never.
The furthermost was handsome,   with a broad forehead,   3330
The fairest of physiognomy   that ever was formed;
And he was clad in a coat   of noble blue,
With fleurs-de-lys of gold   flourished all over;
The other was clad in a coat   all of pure silver,
With a comely cross   carved out of fine gold;
Four skillful crosslets   by that cross rest them,
And thereby I knew the king,   that christened he seemed.
   "Then went I to that fair one,   and affectionately greeted her,
And she said, 'Welcome, in truth,   well art thou found now;
Thou oughtest worship my will,   and thou well knowest,   3340
Of all the valiant men   that were ever in the world;

[15] Lady Fortune.   [16] They will be born, and famous, after Arthur's time.

For, all thy worship in war,   by me hast thou won it;
I have been friendly, man,   and helped against others;
That hast thou found in faith,   and many of thy warriors,
For I felled down Sir Frolle   with froward knights,
Wherefore the fruits of France   are freely thine own.
Thou shalt achieve the chair,   I choose thee myself,
Before all the chieftains   chosen in this earth.'
   "She lifted me up lightly   with her slim hands,
And set me softly in that seat;   the scepter she reached me;   3350
Carefully with a comb   she combed my head,
That the crisping curl   reached my crown;
Dressed me in a diadem   beauteously bedecked;
Then she proffers me an apple   set full of fair stones,
Enameled with azure,   the earth thereon painted,
Encircled with the salt sea   upon every side,
In sign that I surely   was sovereign on earth.
Then she brought me a brand   with very bright hilts,
And bade me brandish the blade: 'The brand is mine own;
Many a swain with the swing   has left his blood; [17]   3360
For, while thou didst work with the sword,   it failed thee never.'
   "Then she departed in peace,   and in quiet, when it pleased her,
To the trees of the forest,   a richer was never;
No orchard is so ordained   by princes on earth,
No appointments so proud,   but paradise only.
She bade the boughs bend down   and bring to my hands
Of the best that they bore   on branches so high;
Then they inclined to her command   all wholly at once,
The highest of every holt: [18]   I tell thee the truth.
She bade me spare not the fruit,   but take whilst it pleased me: 3370
'Take of the finest,   thou noble warrior,
And reach towards the ripest,   and refresh thyself;
Rest, thou royal king,   for Rome is thine own,
And I shall readily bring thee   rest most quickly,
And reach thee the rich wine   in well-rinsed cups.'
   Then she went to the well   by the wood-border,
That bubbled up with wine   and wondrously runs,
Caught up a cupful,   and covered it carefully;
She bade me deeply draw   and drink to herself,
And thus she led me about   the length of an hour,   3380
With all the liking and love   that any man should have.
   "But just at midday exactly   all her mood changed,

---

[17] i.e., died.   [18] Woodland, forest.

And she made me great menace   with marvelous words.
When I cried upon her,   she lowered her brows:
'King, thou speakest for naught,   by Christ that made me!
For thou shalt lose this game   and thy life after;
Thou hast lived in delight   and lordship enough.'
  "About she whirls the wheel,   and whirls me under,
Till all my quarters that time   were crushed all to pieces,
And my backbone with that chair   was chopped asunder;   3390
And I have shivered with chill   since this chance happened.
Then I awakened, indeed,   all weary and dreamt out,
And now thou knowest my woe;   word it as it please thee."
  "Friend," said the philosopher,   "thy fortune has passed,
For thou shalt find her thy foe,   ask when thou likest.
Thou art at the highest,   I declare to thee truly;
Complain now when thou wilt,   thou achievest no more.
Thou hast shed much blood   and fighters destroyed
Guiltless,[19] in thy pride,   in many kings' lands;
Shrive thee of thy shame,   and shape thee for thine end.   3400
Thou hast a foreshowing, Sir King,   take keep if thou like.
For fiercely shalt thou fall   within five winters.
Found abbeys in France,   the fruits are thine own,
For Frolle and for Feraunt,[20]   and for their fierce knights,
Whom thou hostilely in France   didst leave as dead.
Take thought now of the other kings,   and cast in thy heart,
Who were conquerors renowned,   and crowned upon earth.
  "The eldest was Alexander,   that all the earth louted to;
The second was Hector of Troy,   the chivalrous man;
The third was Julius Caesar,   who held was a giant,   3410
On each famous campaign,   accompanied with lords.
The fourth was Sir Judas,[21]   a jouster most noble,
The masterful Maccabee,   the mightiest in strength;
The fifth was Joshua,   that jolly man of arms,
To whom in a Jerusalem inn [22]   great joy befell once;
The sixth was David the valiant,   deemed among kings
One of the doughtiest   that dubbed was ever,
For he slew with a sling,   by the sleight of his hands,
Goliath the great giant,   grimmest on earth.

---

[19] It is those whom Arthur destroyed who were guiltless.
[20] Killed earlier on Arthur's campaign.
[21] Judas Macchabeus, a Jewish patriot of the second century B.C.
[22] See Joshua 6:17-25. According to some commentators, Rahab was an innkeeper.

He endited in his days   all the dear psalms,   3420
That in the psalter are set forth   in peerless words.
  "The one climbing king,   I know it in truth,
Shall Charles be called,   the king's son of France;
He shall be cruel and keen   and held a conqueror,
Recover by conquests   countries many;
He shall acquire the crown   that Christ Himself bore; [23]
And that beloved lance   that leapt to His heart,
When He was crucified on the cross,   and all the keen nails
As a knight he shall conquer   for Christian men's hands.
  "The second shall be Godfrey,   who God shall revenge   3430
For that Good Friday,   with gallant knights;
He shall be lord of Lorraine   by leave of his father;
And after in Jerusalem   much joy shall befall him,
For he shall recover the cross [24]   by craft of arms,
And then be crowned king   with chrism anointed.
  "There shall no duke in his day   attain such destiny,[25]
Nor suffer so great misfortune,   when truth shall be measured.
For thy fortune will fetch thee   to fill up the number
As ninth of the noblest   named upon earth;
This shall be read in romances   by noble knights,   3440
Be reckoned and renowned   by reveling kings,
And deemed [26] on Doomsday,   for deeds of arms,
As the doughtiest ever   that dwelt upon earth.
Thus, many clerks [27] and kings   shall proclaim your deeds,
And keep your conquests   in chronicles for ever.
But the wolves in the wood,   and the wild beasts,
Are certain wicked men   that war on thy realms,
Are entered in thine absence   to attack thy people,
And aliens and hosts   from barbarous lands.
Thou gettest tidings, I trow,   within ten days,   3450
That some trouble is betid   since thou didst turn from home;
I urge thee recall and reckon   unreasonable deeds,
Or repent thee most quickly   of all thy wrongful works.
Man, amend thy heart   ere mishap befall thee,
And meekly ask mercy   for meed of thy soul."
  Then rises the king,   and arrayed him in clothing,

[23] Charlemagne acquired the relics of the Crucifixion.
[24] It was the Holy Sepulchre that Godfrey recovered.
[25] As did Arthur, the ninth and last of the Nine Worthies.
[26] Held.   [27] Scholars, writers.

A red jacket of rose,   the richest of flowers,
A pisan [28] and a paunch-cover,[29]   and a precious girdle;
And he slips on a hood   of very rich hue,
A shield-like pillion-hat,[30]   that set was most richly   3460
With pearls of Orient   and precious stones;
His gloves gaily gilt   and embroidered at the hems,
Sprinkled with rubies,   full seemly to look on;
His greedy greyhound and his brand,   and no man with him,
He walks over a broad meadow   with woe at his heart;
He stalks over a path   by the still wood-edge,
Stops at a high street,   in his deep study.
At the rising of the sun   he sees there coming,
Hastening Rome-wards,   by the shortest way,
A man in a round cloak   with right full clothes.   3470
With hat and high shoes,   homely and round;
With flat farthings the man   was flourished all over;
Many shreds and tatters   at his skirts hang,
With scrip and with mantle,   and scallops [31] aplenty,
With pike and with palm,   such as pilgrims should have.
   The man hastily greeted him,   and bade him good-morning;
The king himself, lordly,   in the language of Rome,
In Latin quite corrupt,   speaks to him courteously:
"Whither wilt thou, wight,   walking by thyself?
Whilst this world is at war,   a peril I hold it;   3480
Here is an enemy with a host   under yon vines;
If they see thee, in truth,   sorrow betides thee,
Unless thou hast conduct   from the king himself,
Knaves will kill thee,   and keep what thou hast;
And if thou holdest the highway,   they will seize thee also,
Unless thou hastily have help   from his friendly knights."
   Then replies Sir Craddock   to the king himself:
"I shall forgive him my death,   so God help me,
Any groom under God,   that walks on this ground
Let the keenest one come,   that to the king belongs,   3490
I shall encounter him as a knight,   so Christ have my soul!
For thou canst not reach me   nor arrest me thyself,
Though thou be richly arrayed   in very rich weeds;
I shall not shrink for any war,   to wend where it please me,
Nor for any wight of this world   that is wrought on earth.

[28] Armor to protect the upper chest and neck.
[29] Armor for the lower part of the trunk.   [30] A round cap.
[31] Pilgrimage badges, suggesting that the wearer had been to Compostella.

But I shall pass in pilgrimage   this path unto Rome,
To procure me pardon   of the pope himself,
And from the pains of Purgatory   be plenarily absolved.
Then shall I seek surely   my sovereign lord,
Sir Arthur of England,   that adventurous warrior.   3500
For he is in this empire,   as valiant men tell me,
Campaigning in this Orient   with awesome knights."
   "From whence comest thou, keen man,"   quoth the king then,
"Who knowest King Arthur,   and his knights also?
Wast thou ever in his court   whilst he dwelt at home?
Thou speakest so familiarly   it comforts my heart;
Full well hast thou come,   and wisely thou seekest,
For thou art a British warrior,   by thy broad speech."
   "I ought to know the king,   he is my avowed lord,
And I was called in his court   a knight of his chamber;   3510
Sir Craddock was I called   in his royal court,
Keeper of Caerleon   under the king himself.
Now am I chased out of the country   with care at my heart,
And that castle is captured   by uncouth people."
   Then the comely king   caught him in his arms,
Cast off his kettle-hat,[32]   and kissed him at once;
Said, "Welcome, Sir Craddock,   so may Christ help me!
Dear cousin in kin,   thou makest cold my heart.
How fares it in Britain   with all my bold men?
Are they beat down or burnt   or brought out of life?   3520
Make me know quickly   what chance has befallen;
I need crave no assurance,   I know thee a true man."
   "Sir, thy warden is wicked   and wild of his deeds,
For he has caused sorrow   since thou wentest away.
He has captured castles   and crowned himself,
Taken in all the rent   of the Round Table;
He has divided the realm,   and dealt as it pleased him;
Dubbed them of Denmark   dukes and earls,
Sent them out diversely,   and destroyed cities;
Of Saracens and Saxons,   upon many sides,   3530
He has assembled an army   of strange warriors,
Sovereigns of Surgenale,[33]   and mercenaries many,
Of Picts [34] and of Paynims,   and proved knights
Of Ireland and of Argyle,[35]   outlawed fighters;
All those lads are knights   who belong to the mountains,

---

[32] A helmet.   [33] South Wales?
[34] Ancient people of northern Britain.   [35] Western Scotland.

And lead and have lordship   as it pleases them.
And there is Sir Childeric [36]   held as a chieftain;
That same chivalrous man,   he afflicts thy people.
They rob thy religious   and ravish thy nuns;
And he rides ready with his rout   to ransack the poor.   3540
From Humber to Hawick [37]   he holds as his own,
And all the country of Kent,   by covenant entailed,
The comely castles   that belonged to the crown,
The holts and hoar-wood   and the hard banks,
All that Hengist and Horsa [38]   held in their time.
At Southampton on the sea   are seven score ships,
Freighted full of fierce folk   out of far lands,
To fight with thy forces,   when thou assailest them.
But yet a word, truly;   thou knowest not the worst:
He has wedded Waynor [39]   and as wife holds her,   3550
And dwells in the wild bounds   of the west marches,
And has got her with child,   as witnesses tell us.
Of all men of this world,   may woe befall him,
As the warden unworthy   to look after women!
Thus has Sir Modred   marred us all!
Wherefore I marched over these mountains to report thee the truth."
    Then the burly king,   for anger at his heart,
And for this bootless bale,[40]   quite changed all his hue.
"By the Rood," said the king,   "I shall revenge it;
He shall repent full quickly   all his wicked works!"   3560
    Weeping deeply for woe   he went to his tents;
Without joy this wise king   awakens his warriors,
Called in by a clarion   kings and others,
Calls them to council,   and tells of this case:
"I am betrayed through treason   for all my true deeds!
And all my labor is lost;   it befalls me no better;
Woe shall betide him   who wrought this treason,
If I can surely take him,   and I am a true lord!
This is Modred, the man,   whom I most trusted;
He has captured my castles,   and crowned himself   3570
With the rents and riches   of the Round Table.
He has made his whole retinue   of renegade wretches,
And dealt out my kingdom   to divers lords,
To soldiers and to Saracens   out of several lands.

[36] King of Saxony.   [37] A town in southern Scotland.
[38] Two famous fifth century Germanic leaders of the invasion of Britain.
[39] Guinevere.   [40] Cureless sorrow or injury.

He has wedded Waynor,   and holds her as wife;
And a child is begotten,   the luck is no better.
They have assembled on the sea   seven score ships,
Full of fierce folk   to fight with mine own.
Wherefore, to Britain the Broad [41]   to return it behoves us,
To break down the warrior   that has begun all this injury.   3580
No fierce man shall fare thither   except on fresh horses,
That [42] are tested in fight,   and flower of my knights.
Sir Howell and Sir Hardolf   here shall remain
To be lords of these people   that belong here to me;
They shall look into Lombardy,   that there no man change,
And tenderly to Tuscany   take charge as I bid them;
Receive the rents of Rome,   when they are reckoned;
Take seizin [43] the same day   that last was assigned,
Or else all the hostages,   without the walls,
Shall be hanged high aloft   all wholly at once."   3590
   Now prepares the bold king   with his best knights,
Bids sound trumpet and truss, [44]   and goes forth after;
Turns through Tuscany,   tarries but little,
Alights not in Lombardy,   except when the light failed;
Marches over the mountains   many marvelous ways.
Journeys through Germany   even at the quickest;
Fares into Flanders   with his fierce knights.
Within fifteen days   his fleet is assembled,
And then he shaped him to ship,   and shuns no longer;
Steers with the sharp wind   over the sheer waters;   3600
By the rocks with ropes   he rides at anchor.
   There the false men floated   and on the flood lingered,
With strong cargo chains   linked together,
Charged even cheekful   with chivalrous knights;
And in the hind part on high   were helms and crests,
Hatches with heathen men covered were thereunder.
Proudly portrayed   upon painted cloths, [45]
Each, piece by piece,   fastened to the other,
Dubbed with dagswain, [46]   they seemed to be doubled;
And thus had the sharp Danes   dressed all their ships,   3610
That no dint from any dart   might damage them ever.

[41] Great Britain, as distinct from Brittany.
[42] It was the knights who were tested in battle.
[43] Taking possession of the land on the day agreed on in the truce.
[44] Pack the baggage.
[45] Apparently a combination of camouflage and protection against showers of arrows.
[46] Trimmed or lined with coarse shaggy material.

Then the king and the knights   of the Round Table
All royally in red   array his ships.
That day he dealt out duchies   and dubbed knights;
Dressed dromons [47] and drags,[48]   and they draw up stones;
The top-castles he stuffed   with tools as it pleased him,
Bent bows [49] with screws   swiftly afterwards;
Toolmen attentively   their tackle do righten,
Brazen heads very broad   they mount upon arrows;
Make ready to defend them,   draw up their men,   3620
With grim gads of steel,   gyves [50] of iron;
Station strong men on the stern,   with stiff men of arms;
Many a fair lance   stands up aloft;
Men upon lee-board,   lords and others,
Place pavises on the port,   painted shields;
On the hinder hurdace [51] on high   stood helmed knights.
Thus they make way with their shots   toward those sheer strands,
Each man in his mantle,   resplendent were their weeds.

   The bold king is in a barge,   and he rows about,
Quite bareheaded and busy,   with beaver-brown locks—   3630
And a warrior bears his brand   and an inlaid helmet,
Attached to a mantle   of silver mail—
Crowned with a coronet,   and covered very richly,
He keeps his way to each cog,[52]   to comfort his knights.
To Cleges and to Cleremond   he cries aloud:
"O Gawain! O Galyron!   these good men's bodies!"
To Lot and to Lionel   he lovingly calls out,
And to Sir Launcelot of the Lake,   in lordly words:
"Let us recover the country,   the coast is our own,
And make them hastily blench,   all yonder bloodhounds.   3640
Break them down aboard,   and burn them afterwards;
Hew down heartily   yonder heathen tikes:
They are on the rascal's side,   I wager my hand."

   Then regains he his cog,   and catches an anchor,
Caught up his comely helm   with the shining mail;
Runs up banners abroad,   embroidered with gules,[53]
With crowns of clear gold   carefully arrayed.
But there was seen in the top   a chalk-white Maiden,
And a Child in her arms,   that is Chief of heaven;
Without change thereafter,   these were the chief arms   3650

---

[47] Medieval sailboats using both oars and sails.   [48] A raft or lighter.
[49] Crossbows.   [50] Fetters.   [51] Palisades or hurdles of wicker-work.
[52] A freight ship, also used as a war vessel.   [53] Red, as a color in heraldry.

Of Arthur the adventurous   whilst he lingered on earth.
  Then the mariners call forth,   and masters of ships,
Merrily each mate   shouts to the other;
In their jargon they jangle,   how it befell them:
They tow trussel [54] on treats,[55]   and truss [56] up sails,
Beat bonnets [57] abroad,   battened down [58] hatches;
Brandished brown steel,   bragged on trumpets;
Stand stiffly on the stem,   and steer thereafter;
Streak over the stream,   where the striving begins
From the time the raging wind   out of the west rises,   3660
And fiercely sweeps with the blast   into the warriors' sails;
With her bring on board   the heavy cogs,
Whilst the bilge [59] and the beam   burst asunder;
So stoutly the fore-stern   on the stem hits,
The stocks of the steerboard   strike in pieces.
At that, cog upon cog,   one craft and another,
Cast creepers [60] across,   as to the craft is fitting.
Then were the head-ropes hewn,   that held up the masts;
There was conflict most keen,   and crashing of ships;
Great ships of battle   dashed asunder;   3670
Many a cabin was cleaved,   cables destroyed;
Knights and keen men   killed the fighters,
Splendid castles [61] were carved   with all their keen weapons,
Castles most comely,   beautifully painted.
With upward glances   they cut in afterwards,
With the swinge of the sword   the mast sways;
At the first moment fall over   fighters and others,
Many a bold man in the foreship   is found to be fated.
Then sternly they turn about   with savage tackle;
There brush boldly aboard   byrnied [62] knights;   3680
Out of boats on decks   they attack with stones,
Beat down the best ones,   burst the hatches;
Some men are gored through   with gads of iron.
Men gaily clad   bebloody the weapons.
Archers of Ireland   shoot full eagerly,
They hit through the hard steel   many mortal dints.
Soon stagger in the hull   the heathen knights,

[54] A furled sail.   [55] At full length?   [56] Make fast.
[57] Spread abroad an additional canvas, laced to the foot of a sail to catch more wind.
[58] Perhaps, improved the hatches.   [59] Rounded part of ship's bottom.
[60] Apparently, grappling irons.   [61] Elevated structures on ships.
[62] The byrnie is a coat of mail.

Hurt through the hard steel;   heal will they never.
Then they fall to the fight,   foin with spears,
All the fiercest of front,   as befits that fighting;   3690
And each one freshly   puts forth his strength,
To fight the war in the fleet   with their fell weapons.
Thus they dealt that day,   these dubbed knights,
Till all the Danes were dead   and into the deep thrown.
    Then Britons breathing wrath   hew with their brands,
There leap up aloft   lordly fighters;
When men from foreign lands   lept into the waters,
All our lords aloud   laughed together.
At that spears were sprung,   ships splintered,
Spaniards speedily   sprinted overboard;   3700
All the keen men of war,   knights and others,
Are killed cold dead,   and cast overboard.
Their squires swiftly   shed their life-blood,
Heave up hence on the hatches,   arise on the hedged place,
Sinking into the salt sea   seven hundred at once.
Then Sir Gawain the good   has gained his desire,
And all the great cogs   he gave to his knights.
Sir Geryn and Sir Griswold,   and other great lords,
Caused Galuth, a good knight,   to strike off their heads.
Thus to the false fleet   it befell on the flood,   3710
And thus the foreign folk   are left there as fated.
    Yet is the traitor on land   with his trusted knights,
And with trumpets they trip   on their trapped steeds,
Show themselves under shields   upon the sheer banks.
He shuns not for any shame,   but shows himself on high.
Sir Arthur and Gawain   made way, both of them,
To sixty thousand men   that in their sight hovered.
But when the folk was felled,   then was the tide out;
It was much like a mire   in mud-banks most huge,
That hindered the king from landing   in the low water;   3720
Wherefore he lingered a while,   lest he lose his horses,
To look over his liegemen   and his loyal knights.
If any were lamed or lost,   and whether they should live.
    Then Sir Gawain the good,   a galley he takes him,
And glides up an inlet   with good men of arms;
When he grounded, in grief   he springs into the water,
That to the girdle he goes,   in all his gilt weeds;
He shoots up upon the sand   in sight of the lords,
Singly with his band—   my sorrow is the greater!

With banners of his emblems, the best of his arms,[63] 3730
He twists up upon the bank in his bright clothing.
He bids his banner-man, "Betake thee quickly
To yonder broad battalion that stands on yon bank;
And I assure you, truly, I shall follow after you.
Look that ye blench for no brand, nor for any bright weapon,
But bear down on the best, and bring them out of day.
Be not abashed of their boast; abide on the earth;
Ye have borne my banners in very great battles;
We shall fell yon false ones— the fiend have their souls!
Fight fast with that phalanx, the field shall be ours. 3740
If I overtake that traitor, misfortune betide him,
Who has timbered this treason against my true lord;
Of such an engendrure full little joy happens,
And that shall this day be judged most justly."
   Now they seek over the sand this band at the best point,
Meet with the soldiers, and deal them their dints;
Through the shields so radiant the men they touch,
With the short-shivered shafts of those bright lances;
Dreadful dints they dealt with dagging [64] spears;
In the dank of the dew many a dead man lies; 3750
Dukes and douzepers,[65] and dubbed knights,
The doughtiest of Denmark are undone for ever.
Thus these men in misery rip their byrnies,
And receive from the strongest unreckoned blows;
There they throng in the thick and thrust to the earth
Of the sturdiest men three hundred at once.
   But Sir Gawain in grief could not resist:
He grips him a spear and runs toward a man,
Who bore gules most gay with gouts [66] of silver;
He thrusts him in at the throat with his grim lance, 3760
So that the ground glaive breaks asunder;
With that massive blow he puts him to death.
The king of Gothland it was, a good man of arms.
Their advance guard then all retreat after this,
As vanquished verily by valiant warriors;
They meet with the middle guard that Modred is leading.
Our men make towards them, as it misfalls them;
For had Sir Gawain had grace the green hill to hold,

[63] Coat of arms.   [64] Cutting.
[65] Nobles; originally the twelve peers of Charlemagne.
[66] Heraldic elements indicating tears or drops.

He had won him indeed   worship for ever.
But Sir Gawain in truth   watches full well   3770
To avenge him on this traitor   who this war had started;
And makes way to Sir Modred   among all his fighters,
With the Montagues lightly,   and other great lords.
Then Sir Gawain was grieved,   and with a great will
Fixes a fair spear   and freshly challenges:
"False fostered fellow,   the fiend have thy bones!
Fie on thee, felon,   and thy false works!
Thou shalt be dead and undone   for thy deeds so violent,
Or I shall die this day,   if it be my destiny."
Then his enemy with a host   of outlawed barons   3780
Wholly engulfs   our excellent knights,
As the traitor in his treason   had devised himself;
Dukes of Denmark   he draws up most quickly,
And leaders of Lettow   with legions in plenty,
Surrounded our men   with very keen lances.
Mercenaries and Saracens   out of many lands,
Sixty thousand men,   seemlily arrayed.
Surely there assail   seven score knights
Suddenly by stratagem   near those salt strands.
Then Sir Gawain wept   with his gray eyes   3790
For grief of his good men,   whom he must guide;
For he knew they were wounded,   weary and fought out;
And what for wonder and woe,   all his wit failed him.
Then said he sighing,   with sliding tears,
"We are with Saracens beset   upon several sides!
I sigh not for myself,   so save me our Lord;
But to see us surprised,   my sorrow is the more.
Be doughty today,   yon dukes shall be yours!
For our dear Lord today,   dread no weapons.
We shall end this day   as peerless knights,   3800
Go to endless joy   with the spotless angels.
Though we have unwittingly   wasted ourselves,
We shall work all well   in the worship of Christ.
We shall for yon Saracens,   I plight you my troth,
Sup with our Savior   solemnly in heaven,
In the presence of that precious One,   Prince of all others,
With prophets and patriarchs,   and apostles most noble,
Before His gracious face,   who formed us all!
Now to yon jades' sons,   he who yields him ever,
Whilst he is quick and in health,   unkilled by hands,   3810

Be he never more saved,   nor succored by Christ,
But may Satan his soul   sink into hell!"
   Then grimly Sir Gawain   grips his weapon,
Against that great battalion   he addresses him forthwith;
Hastily rightens the chains   of his rich sword;
He brandishes his shield;   he holds back no longer,
But quite unwisely and madly   the quickest way charges.
The wounds of those adversaries,   for the vengeful dints,
All well full of blood   where he passes by;
And though he were in great woe,   he wanders but little,   3820
But wreaks, to his worship,   the wrath of his lord.
He strikes steeds in the onset   and stern-faced knights,
That strong men in their stirrups   stone-dead lie there.
He rives the stout steel,   he rips the coats of mail,
There can no man stop him,   his reason was gone.
He fell in a frenzy   through fierceness of heart;
He fights and fells down   him who stands before him.
There befell never a doomed man   such fortune on earth.
In the whole battle   headlong he runs him,
And hurts the hardiest of men   that move upon earth;   3830
Raging like a lion   he lunges throughout them,
These lords and leaders   who wait on the land.
Still Sir Gawain in his woe   wavers but little,
But wounds his opponents   with wonderful dints,
As one who wilfully   would waste himself;
And through his pain and his will   all his wits failed him,
That mad as a wild beast   he charged at the nearest;
All wallowed in blood   where he had passed by;
Each man could be wary   at the vengeance on the others.
   Then he moved towards Sir Modred   among all his knights,   3840
And met him in the midshield,   and hammers him through it;
But the man at the sharpness   shunts [67] him a little,
He [68] shore him in the shortribs   about a hand-breadth wide.
The shaft shuddered and shot   onto the bright warrior,
That the blood as it shed   over his shanks ran down,
And showed on the shin-plates,   that were brightly burnished.
And as they shifted and shoved,   he [69] shot to the earth;
With the lunge of the lance   he lighted on his shoulders,
Full length on the lawn,   with loathly wounds.
Then Gawain struck at the man,   and fell groveling;   3850
Although his anger was roused,   his luck was no better.

[67] Modred shrinks aside a little.   [68] Gawain.   [69] Modred.

He pulled out a short knife, sheathed with silver,
And would have stuck his throat, but no slit followed;
His hand slipped and slid aslant on the mail,
And the other man slyly slipped him under;
With a trenchant knife the traitor hit him
Through the helm and the head high up in the brain;
And thus Sir Gawain is gone, the good man of arms,
Unrescued by any man, and more is the pity;
Thus Sir Gawain is gone, that guided many others! 3860
From Gower to Guernsey all the great lords
Of Glamorgan and of Wales, these gallant knights,
From assaults of sadness they may never be glad.
    King Frederick of Friesland carefully after that
Asks of the false man about our fierce knight:
"Knewest thou ever this knight in thy rich kingdom?
Of what kind was he come, reveal now the truth.
What man was he, this with the gay arms,
With his griffon [70] of gold, who is fallen face downward?
He has greatly grieved us, so may God help me! 3870
Struck down our good men, and grieved us sorely.
He was the sternest in stress that ever wore steel,
For he has stunned our host, and destroyed it for ever!"
    Then Sir Modred with his mouth speaks most fairly:
"He was matchless on earth, man, by my truth;
This was Sir Gawain the good, the gladdest of others,
The graciousest man that under God lived,
A man the hardiest of hand, happiest in arms,
And most courteous in the court under heaven's kingdom;
The lordliest of leaders, whilst he might live. 3880
For he was renowned as a lion in many lands;
Hadst thou known him, Sir King, in the land he belonged to,
His knowledge, his knighthood, and his kindly works,
His doings, his doughtiness, his deeds of arms,
Thou wouldst have dole for his death the days of thy life."
    Yet that traitor as quickly tears does let fall,
Turns him forth quickly, and talks no more,
Went weeping away, and curses the hour
That his wierd was wrought to work such destruction;
When he thought on this thing, it pierced his heart. 3890
For the sake of his kinsman's blood, sighing he rides off;
When that renegade wretch remembered within him

---

[70] Fabulous animal, half eagle, half lion.

The reverence and revelry   of the Round Table,
He cried out and repented him   of all his cruel works,
Rode away with his rout,   rests there no longer,
For fear of our rich king,   who should arrive.
Then turns he to Cornwall,   full of care at heart,
Because of his kinsman   who lies on the coast;
He tarries trembling ever   to harken after tidings.
   Then the traitor crept forth   the Tuesday after that,   3900
Went with a trick   treason to work,
And by the Tamar [71] that time   his tents he raises,
And then in a short time   a messenger he sends,
And wrote unto Waynor   how the world was changed,
And at what convenient coast   the king had arrived,
On the flood fought with his fleet,   and felled them alive;
Bade her go far away,   and flee with her children.
Whilst he might slip away,   and get to speak with her,
Withdraw into Ireland,   into those outer mountains,
And live there in the wilderness   within the waste lands.   3910
   Then she weeps and she cries   at York in her chamber,
Groans most grievously   with dropping tears,
Passes out of the palace   with all her peerless maidens;
Towards Chester in a chariot   they choose their way,
Made her ready to die   for dole at her heart.
She goes to Caerleon,   and caught her a veil,
Asks there for a habit   in the honor of Christ,
And all for falsehood and fraud,   and for fear of her lord.
   But when the wise king knew   that Gawain had landed,
He quite writhes for woe,   and, wringing his hands,   3920
Has them launch his boats   upon the low water,
Lands like a lion   with lordly knights,
Slips into the sloppy water   aslant to the girdle,
Sweeps up swiftly   with his sword drawn,
Makes ready his battalion   and his banners displays,
Moves over the broad sands   with anger at his heart.
Fares fiercely afield,   where the dead men lie.
Of the traitor's men   on trapped steeds,
Ten thousand were lost,   the truth to declare,
And certain on our side,   seven score knights,   3930
In suit with their sovereign   unsound [72] are left there.
   The king glanced proudly   over knights and others,
Earls of Africa   and Austrian warriors,

[71] A river between Devon and Cornwall.   [72] Wounded, perhaps lifeless.

From Argyle and from Orkney,   the Irish kings,
The noblest of Norway,   numbers full huge,
Dukes of Denmark   and dubbed knights;
And the king of Gothland   in the gay armor
Lies groaning on the ground,   pierced through and through.
The rich king searches about   with sorrow at heart,
And seeks out the men   of all the Round Table;   3940
Sees them all in a band   together by themselves,
With the Saracens unsound   encircled about,
And Sir Gawain the good,   in his gay armor,
Clutching the grass,   and fallen face downward,
His banners cast down,   adorned with gules,
His brand and his broad shield   with blood overrun.
Was never our fair king   so sorrowful in heart,
Nor did aught touch him so sadly   as that sight alone.
    Then stares the good king   and grieves in his heart,
Groans most grievously   with falling tears,   3950
Kneels down by the corpse,   and caught him in his arms,
Casts up his visor,   and kisses him forthwith,
Looks upon his eyelids,   that closely were shut,
His lips like to lead,   and his cheeks now fallowed.
    Then the crowned king   cries out aloud,
"Dear cousin in kinship,   in care am I left here,
For now my worship has turned   and my war ended;
Here is the health of my welfare,   my success in arms;
My heart and my hardiness   lay wholly in him,
My counsel, my comfort,   that kept up my heart!   3960
Of all knights the king,   who lived under Christ,
Thou wert worthy to be king,   though I wore the crown.
My weal and my worship   in this rich world
Were won through Sir Gawain,   and through his wisdom only.
Alas!" said Sir Arthur,   "now my sorrow increases!
I am utterly undone   within mine own lands;
O, doubtful dread death,   thou dwellest too long!
Why drawest thou on so slowly?   thou drownest my heart!"
    Then faints the sweet king,   and aswoon falls down,
Staggers up swiftly,   and lovingly kisses him,   3970
Until his burly beard   was berun with blood,
As though beasts he had quartered   and brought out of life.
Had not Sir Ewain come,   and other great lords,
His bold heart had burst   for sorrow at that moment.
"Cease," said this bold man,   "thou harmest thyself;

This is bootless bale, for better it grows never.
This is no worship, truly, to wring thy hands;
To weep like a woman is held to be no wit.
Be knightly of countenance, as a king should be,
And leave off such clamor, for Christ's love of heaven!" 3980
"For blood," said the bold king, "cease will I never,
Ere my brain burst in two, or my breast either;
Was never sorrow so soft that sank to my heart,
He is close kin to myself, my sorrow is the more;
So sorrowful a sight was never seen with mine eyes.
In his innocence was he surprised for a sin of mine own."

Down kneels the king, and cries out aloud;
With sorrowful countenance he utters these words:
"O righteous, almighty God, behold Thou this sorrow!
This royal red blood run upon earth, 3990
It were worthy to be taken up and enshrined in gold,
For it is guiltless of sin, so save me our Lord!"
Down knelt the king, with care at his heart,
Caught it [73] up reverently with his clean hands,
Stored it in a kettle-hat, and covered it fairly,
And went forth with the corpse toward the land where he dwells.
"Here make I mine avow," quoth the king then,
"To Messiah and to Mary, the mild Queen of heaven,
I shall never go hunting or hunting dogs uncouple,
At roe or at reindeer, that run upon earth, 4000
Never greyhound let glide, or goshawk let fly,
And never see fowl felled that flies upon wing;
Falcon nor formel upon my fist handle,
Nor yet with gerfalcon rejoice me on earth;
Nor reign in my royalty, nor hold my Round Table,
Till thy death, my dear one, be duly revenged;
But ever droop and mourn, while my day lasts out,
Till the Lord and grim death have done what pleases them."

* * *

Then draws he to Dorset and delays no longer, 4052
Doleful, dreadless, with dropping tears;
Comes into Cornwall with care at his heart.
The trace of the traitor he tracks ever steadily,
And turns in by the Treyntis to seek the betrayer,
Finds him in a forest the Friday thereafter.

[73] Gawain's blood.

The King alights on foot   and freshly observes,
And with his bold folk   he has taken the field.
   Now issues the enemy   from under the wood-eaves,   4060
With hosts of aliens,   most horrible to look at.
Sir Modred the Malebranch,   with his many people,
Advances from the forest   upon many sides,
In seven great battalions   seemlily arrayed,
Sixty thousand men;   the sight was full huge.
All fighting folk   from faraway lands,
They formed one front   by those fresh strands.
And all Arthur's host   was made up of knights
But eighteen hundred in all,   entered in the rolls.
This was a match unmeet,   but for the might of Christ,   4070
To meddle with that multitude   in those main lands.

*   *   *

   Sir Ewain and Sir Errake,   these excellent warriors,   4161
Enter against the host   and eagerly strike;
The giants of Orkney   and Irish kings
They hack in grimmest wise   with their ground swords;
They hew on those hulks   with their hard weapons,
Laid down those men   with loathly dints;
Shoulders and shields   they shred to the haunches,
And their middles through mail-coats   they strike asunder.
Such honor had never   any earthly kings
At their ending day,   save Arthur himself.   4170
The drought of the day   so dried up their hearts
That drinkless they die,   the more was the pity!
Now moves in our main force,   and mingles in with them.
   Sir Modred the Malebranch,   with his many people,
Had hid himself behind   within the wood-eaves,
With a whole battalion on the heath,   the harm was the greater.
He had seen all the conflict   clean to the end,
How our chivalry had achieved   through chances of arms;
He knew our folk were fought out,   who fated were left there;
To encounter with the king   he decides promptly.   4180
But the churlish chicken   had changed his arms;
He had indeed forsaken   the saltire engrailed,[74]
And caught up three lions   all of light silver,
Passant [75] on purple,   with rich precious stones,

[74] Bands drawn diagonally across a shield, marked with wavy lines.
[75] Walking and looking to one side, with the paw raised.

That the king should not know   the crafty wretch.
   Because of his cowardice   he cast off his attire,
But the comely king   knew him right well,
Calls to Sir Cador   these keen words:
"I see the traitor come yonder   moving most eagerly;
Yon lad with the lions   is like to himself.   4190
Misfortune shall betide him,   if I may once touch him,
For all his treason and treachery,   as I am true lord!
Today Clarent and Caliburn   shall contest together,
Which is keener in carving   or harder of edge;
We shall test fine steel   upon fair weeds.
It was my dainty darling,   and held most dear,
Kept for the coronation   of kings anointed;
On days when I dubbed   dukes and earls,
It was gravely borne   by the bright hilts.
I durst never draw it   in deeds of arms,   4200
But ever kept it clean   for mine own cause.
Since I see Clarent unclad,   that is crown of swords,
My wardrobe [76] at Wallingford   I know is destroyed;
There knew no man of its place   but Waynor herself;
She had the keeping herself   of that choice weapon,
Of coffers enclosed,   that belonged to the crown,
With rings and relics   and the regalia of France,
That was found on Sir Frolle,   when he was left dead."
   Then Sir Marroke in melancholy   meets with Sir Modred,
With a hammered mace   mightily strikes him;   4210
The border of his basinet [77]   he bursts asunder,
That the sheer red blood   runs over the byrnie.
The man blenches for pain,   and all his hue changes,
But still he waits like a boar,   and savagely strikes back.
He brings out a brand,   bright as ever any silver,
Which was Sir Arthur's own,   and Uther's, his father's;
In the wardrobe at Wallingford   it was wont to be kept;
Therewith the doughty dog   dealt him such blows,
That the other withdrew aside,   and durst do no other,
For Sir Marroke was a man   marred by old age,   4220
And Sir Modred was mighty   and in his greatest strength;
Came none within the compass,   knight or other man,
Within the swing of that sword,   who lost not his life.
   That perceives our prince,   and presses fast towards him,
Strikes into the struggle   by strength of his hands,

---

[76] Dressing room, closet.   [77] Small, steel headpiece or helmet.

[151]

Meets with Sir Modred, cries out sternly,
"Turn, traitor untrue, it betides thee no better;
By great God, thou shalt die with dint of my hands,
No man shall rescue thee, nor reach thee on earth!"

    The king with Caliburn like a knight strikes him,   4230
The cantle of the bright shield he carves asunder,
In the shoulder of the man, a hand's-breadth large,
That the sheer red blood showed on his mail.
He shudders and flinches and shrinks a little,
But shoves in sharply in his fair weeds;
The felon with the fine sword fiercely strikes at him,
The flesh on the far side he flashes asunder,
Through jupon [78] and jesseraunt [79] of noble mail.
The man cut out in the flesh a half-foot in breadth,
That the grievous blow was his [80] death, and the dole was the greater 4240
That ever the doughty one should die, but at the Lord's will!
Yet with Caliburn his sword in knightly wise he strikes,
Casts up his shining shield, and covers himself well;
Swaps off the sword hand, as he glances by,
An inch from the elbow he hacked it asunder,
That he [81] swoons down on the sward and falls in a faint,
Through bracer [82] of brown steel and the bright mail,
That the hilt and the hand lie upon the heath.
Then fiercely that man [80] raises up the shield,
Bears him in with the brand to the bright hilts,   4250
So that he [81] cries out at the sword, and droops to die.

    "In faith," said the fey king, "much it grieves me,
That such a false thief have so fair an end."

    When they had finished this fight, then was the field won,
And the false folk in the field are left as fated.
To a forest they fled, and fall in the tangle,
And the fierce fighting folk follow after them;
They hunt out and hew down the heathen tikes,
Murder in the mountains Sir Modred's knights;
There escaped never noble youth, chieftain or other,   4260
But they chopped them down in the chase, it cost them but little.

    But when Sir Arthur forthwith does find Sir Ewain,
And Errake the affable, and other great lords,
He caught up Sir Cador with care at his heart,

---

[78] Close-fitting tunic.
[79] Jacket-like armor, with small metal plates sewn into the fabric.
[80] Arthur.   [81] Modred.   [82] Armor protecting arm or wrist.

Sir Cleges, Sir Cleremonde, these famed men of arms,
Sir Loth and Sir Lionel, Sir Launcelot and Lowes,
Marroke and Meneduke, who mighty were ever;
With pain on the heath he lays them together;
Looked on their bodies, and with a loud voice,
As man that might not live and had lost his mirth;   4270
Then he staggers like one mad, and all his strength fails him,
He looks up aloft, and his whole faces changes;
Down he sways heavily, and falls in a swoon,
Recovers him up on his knees, and cries very often:
"O King, comely with crown, in care am I left here;
All my lordship is laid low on the land,
They who gave me guerdons of their own grace,
Maintained my manhood by might of their hands,
Made me manly in the world, and master on earth.
In a sorrowful time this misfortune has arisen,   4280
Which has lost through a traitor all my true lords.
Here rests the rich blood of the Round Table,
Struck down by a scoundrel, the more is the pity!
I must, helpless on the heath, house by myself.
Like a woeful widow, that wants her lord,
I must be weary and weep, and wring my hands,
For my wit and my worship are gone from me for ever.
Of all lordship I take leave now at my ending.
Here is the Britons' blood brought out of life,
And now in this day's work all my joy ends!"   4290
    Then rally the men of all the Round Table;
To that lordly king they all ride up together;
There assemble straightway seven score knights.
In the sight of their sovereign, who was left wounded.
    Then kneels the crowned king, and cries out aloud:
"I thank Thee, God, for Thy grace, with a good will,
That gavest us virtue and wit to vanquish these warriors,
And hast granted us the victory over these great lords!
He sent us never any shame, or disgrace upon earth,
But ever yet the upper hand of all other kings!   4300
We have no leisure now those lords to seek out,
For yon loathly lad has lamed me so sorely.
Let us make our way to Glastonbury, nought else will avail us;
There may we rest us in peace, and ransack our wounds.
For this dear day's work the Lord be praised,
Who has destined and adjudged us to die among our own."

Then they hold to his behest   wholly at once,
And go towards Glastonbury   by the quickest way;
They enter the Isle of Avalon,[83]   and Arthur alights,
Makes way there to a manor,   for he might go no further.   4310
A surgeon from Salerno   searches his wounds;
The king sees by testing   that he will never be sound,
And at once to his faithful men   he utters these words:
   "Call me a confessor,   with Christ [84] in his arms;
I shall be houseled [85] in haste,   whatso may betide me.
Constantine my cousin   shall bear the crown,
As becomes him by nature,   if Christ will permit him.
Man,[86] for my blessing,   do thou bury yon lords,
Who in battle with brands   are brought out of life;
And after make thy way manfully   to Modred's children,   4320
That they be duly slain   and slung into the waters;
Let no wicked weed wax   or bloom on this earth;
I warn thee, for thy worship;   do as I bid thee!
I forgive all the grief,   for God's love of heaven,
If Waynor have wrought well,   well may it betide her!"
   He said "*In manus tuas*" [87] on the earth where he lies,
And thus passes his spirit,   and he speaks no more.
The baronage of Britain then,   bishops and others,
Go to Glastonbury   with grieving hearts,
To bury their bold king,   and bring him to earth,   4330
With all honor and richness   that any man should have.
Sadly they toll the bells,   and sing requiem,
Say masses and matins,   with mourning notes;
The religious vest them   in their rich copes,
Pontiffs and prelates   in precious vestments;
Dukes and douzepers   in their coats of mourning;
Countesses kneeling,   and clasping their hands,
Ladies languishing,   and sorrowful in appearance.
All were clad in black,   brides and others,
Who were seen at the burial   with streaming tears.   4340
Was never so sorrowful a sight   seen in their time!
   Thus ends King Arthur,   as authors declare it,

---

[83] The faery isle of Avalon, purely imaginary, was mistakenly identified with Glastonbury in the marshlands of Somersetshire. Arthur's bones were supposed to have been found there in 1191.
[84] The Host.   [85] Given the Sacrament.   [86] Constantine.
[87] Luke 23:46: "Into thy hands I commend my spirit."

Who was of Hector's kin,   the king's son of Troy,
And of Sir Priam the prince,   praised upon earth;
From thence brought the Britons   all their bold elders,
Into Britain the broad,   as the *Brut* tells us.

Sir Gawain and the Green Knight[1]

When the siege and assault   ceased at Troy, and the city
Was broken, and burned   all to brands and to ashes,
The warrior who wove there   the web of his treachery
Tried was for treason,   the truest on earth.
'Twas Æneas, who later   with lords of his lineage
Provinces quelled,   and became the possessors
Of well-nigh the whole   of the wealth of the West Isles.
Then swiftly to Rome   rich Romulus journeyed,
And soon with great splendor   builded that city,
Named with his own name,   as now we still know it.   10
Ticius to Tuscany   turns for his dwellings;
In Lombardy Langobard   lifts up his homes;
And far o'er the French flood   fortunate Brutus
With happiness Britain   on hillsides full broad
       Doth found.
    War, waste, and wonder there
    Have dwelt within its bound;
    And bliss has changed to care
    In quick and shifting round.

And after this famous knight   founded his Britain,   20
Bold lords were bred there,   delighting in battle,
Who many times dealt   in destruction. More marvels
Befell in those fields   since the days of their finding
Than anywhere else   upon earth that I know of.
Yet of all kings who came there   was Arthur most comely;
My intention is, therefore,   to tell an adventure
Strange and surprising,   as some men consider,
A strange thing among   all the marvels of Arthur.
And if you will list   to the lay for a little,
Forthwith I shall tell it,   as I in the town   30

Heard it told
As it doth fast endure
In story brave and bold,
Whose words are fixed and sure,
Known in the land of old.

In Camelot [2] Arthur the King lay at Christmas,
With many a peerless lord princely companioned,
The whole noble number of knights of the Round Table;
Here right royally held his high revels,
Care-free and mirthful. Now much of the company, 40
Knightly born gentlemen, joyously jousted,
Now came to the court to make caroles; [3] so kept they
For full fifteen days this fashion of feasting,
All meat and all mirth that a man might devise.
Glorious to hear was the glad-hearted gaiety,
Dancing at night, merry din in the daytime;
So found in the courts and the chambers the fortunate
Ladies and lords the delights they best loved.
In greatest well-being abode they together:
The knights whose renown was next to the Savior's, 50
The loveliest ladies who ever were living,
And he who held court, the most comely of kings.
For these fine folk were yet in their first flush of youth
Seated there,
The happiest of their kind,
With a king beyond compare.
It would be hard to find
A company so fair.

And now while the New Year was young were the nobles
Doubly served as they sat on the dais, 60
When Arthur had come to the hall with his court,
In the chapel had ceased the singing of mass;
Loud shouts were there uttered by priests and by others,
Anew praising Noel, naming it often.
Then hastened the lords to give handsel, cried loudly
These gifts of the New Year, and gave them in person;
Debated about them busily, briskly.

[2] A corrupt name-form, due to the confusion of Carlion (Caerleon in Wales) with
Cavalon (a corruption of Avalon), both of which places were associated with Arthur.
[3] Ring-dances.

Even though they were losers,   the ladies laughed loudly,
Nor wroth was the winner,   as well ye may know.
All this manner of mirth   they made till meattime,   70
Then when they had washed,   they went to be seated,
Were placed in the way   that appeared most proper,
The best men above.   And Guinevere, beautiful,
Was in the midst   of the merriment seated
Upon the rich dais,   adorned all about:
Fine silks on all sides,   and spread as a canopy
Tapestries treasured   of Tars [4] and Toulouse,
Embroidered and set   with stones most splendid—
They'd prove of great price   if ye pence gave to buy them
              Some day.   80
       The comeliest was the Queen,
       With dancing eyes of grey.
       That a fairer he had seen
       No man might truly say.

But Arthur would eat not   till all were attended;
Youthfully mirthful   and merry in manner,
He loved well his life,   and little it pleased him
Or long to be seated,   or long to lie down,
His young blood and wild brain   were so busy and brisk.
Moreover, the King   was moved by a custom   90
He once had assumed   in a spirit of splendor:
Never to fall   to his feast on a festival
Till a strange story   of something eventful
Was told him, some marvel   that merited credence
Of kings, or of arms,   or all kinds of adventures;
Or some one besought him   to send a true knight
To join him in proving   the perils of jousting,
Life against life,   each leaving the other
To have, as fortune would help him,   the fairer lot.
This, when the King   held his court, was his custom   100
At every fine feast   'mid his followers, freemen,
              In hall.
       And so with countenance clear
       He stands there strong and tall,
       Alert on that New Year,
       And makes much mirth with all.

[4] Tartary.

At his place the strong King   stands in person, full courtly
Talking of trifles   before the high table.
There sat the good Gawain   by Guinevere's side,
And Sir Agravain, he   of the Hard Hand, also,   110
True knights, and sons   of the sister of Arthur.
At the top, Bishop Baldwin   the table begins,
And Ywain beside him ate,   Urien's son.
On the dais these sat,   and were served with distinction;
Then many a staunch, trusty man   at the side tables.
The first course was served   to the sharp sound of trumpets,
With numerous banners   beneath hanging brightly.
Then newly the kettledrums sounded   and noble pipes;
Wild and loud warbles   awakened such echoes
That many a heart leaped   on high at their melody.   120
Came then the choice meats,   cates rare and costly,
Of fair and fresh food   such profusion of dishes
'Twas hard to find place   to put by the people
The silver that carried   the various stews
                              On the cloth.
              Each to his best loved fare
              Himself helps, nothing loth;
              Each two, twelve dishes share,
              Good beer and bright wine both.

And now I will say nothing   more of their service,   130
For well one may know   that naught there was wanted.
Now another new noise   drew nigh of a sudden,
To let all the folk   take their fill of the feast.
And scarcely the music   had ceased for a moment,
The first course been suitably   served in the court,
When a being most dreadful   burst through the hall-door,
Among the most mighty   of men in his measure.
From his throat to his thighs   so thick were his sinews,
His loins and his limbs   so large and so long,
That I hold him half-giant,   the hugest of men,   140
And the handsomest, too,   in his height, upon horseback.
Though stalwart in breast   and in back was his body,
His waist and his belly   were worthily small;
Fashioned fairly he was   in his form, and in features
                              Cut clean.
              Men wondered at the hue

That in his face was seen.
A splendid man to view
He came, entirely green.

All green was the man,   and green were his garments: 150
A coat, straight and close,   that clung to his sides,
A bright mantle on top of this,   trimmed on the inside
With closely-cut fur,   right fair, that showed clearly,
The lining with white fur   most lovely, and hood too,
Caught back from his locks,   and laid on his shoulders,
Neat stockings that clung   to his calves, tightly stretched,
Of the same green, and under them   spurs of gold shining
Brightly on bands   of fine silk, richly barred;
And under his legs,   where he rides, guards of leather.
His vesture was verily   color of verdure: 160
Both bars of his belt   and other stones, beautiful,
Richly arranged   in his splendid array
On himself and his saddle,   on silken designs.
'Twould be truly too hard   to tell half the trifles
Embroidered about it   with birds and with flies
In gay, verdant green   with gold in the middle;
The bit-studs, the crupper,   the breast-trappings' pendants,
And everything metal   enamelled in emerald.
The stirrups he stood on   the same way were colored,
His saddle-bows too,   and the studded nails splendid,   170
That all with green gems   ever glimmered and glinted.
The horse he bestrode   was in hue still the same,
                              Indeed;
        Green, thick, and of great height,
        And hard to curb, a steed
        In broidered bridle bright
        That such a man would need.

This hero in green   was habited gaily,
And likewise the hair   on the head of his good horse;
Fair, flowing tresses   enfolded his shoulders,   180
And big as a bush   a beard hung on his breast.
This, and the hair   from his head hanging splendid,
Was clipped off evenly   over his elbows,
In cut like a king's hood,   covering the neck,
So that half of his arms   were held underneath it.
The mane of the mighty horse   much this resembled,

[160]

Well curled and combed, and with many knots covered,
Braided with gold threads about the fair green,
Now a strand made of hair, now a second of gold.
The forelock and tail were twined in this fashion,   190
And both of them bound with a band of bright green.
For the dock's length the tail was decked with stones dearly,
And then was tied with a thong in a tight knot,
Where many bright bells of burnished gold rang.
In the hall not one single man's seen before this
Such a horse here on earth, such a hero as on him
                              Goes.
          That his look was lightning bright
          Right certain were all those
          Who saw. It seemed none might   200
          Endure beneath his blows.

Yet the hero carried nor helmet nor hauberk,
But bare was of armor, breastplate or gorget,
Spear-shaft or shield, to thrust or to smite.
But in one hand he bore a bough of bright holly,
That grows most greenly when bare are the groves,
In the other an axe, gigantic, awful,
A terrible weapon, wondrous to tell of.
Large was the head, in length a whole ell-yard,
The blade of green steel and beaten gold both;   210
The bit had a broad edge, and brightly was burnished,
As suitably shaped as sharp razors for shearing.
This steel by its strong shaft the stern hero gripped:
With iron it was wound to the end of the wood,
And in work green and graceful was everywhere graven.
About it a fair thong was folded, made fast
At the head, and oft looped down the length of the handle.
To this were attached many splendid tassels,
On buttons of bright green richly embroidered.
Thus into the hall came the hero, and hastened   220
Direct to the dais, fearing no danger.
He gave no one greeting, but haughtily gazed,
And his first words were, "Where can I find him who governs
This goodly assemblage? for gladly that man
I would see and have speech with." So saying, from toe
                          To crown
          On the knights his look he threw,

And rolled it up and down;
He stopped to take note who
Had there the most renown.   230

There sat all the lords,   looking long at the stranger,
Each man of them marvelling   what it might mean
For a horse and a hero   to have such a hue.
It seemed to them green   as the grown grass, or greener,
Gleaming more bright   than on gold green enamel.
The nobles who stood there,   astonished, drew nearer,
And deeply they wondered   what deed he would do.
Since never a marvel   they'd met with like this one,
The folk all felt   it was magic or phantasy.
Many great lords then   were loth to give answer,   240
And sat stone-still,   at his speaking astounded,
In swooning silence   that spread through the hall.
As their speech on a sudden   was stilled, fast asleep
                              They did seem.
                    They felt not only fright
                    But courtesy, I deem.
                    Let him address the knight,
                    Him whom they all esteem.

This happening the King,   ever keen and courageous,
Saw from on high,   and saluted the stranger   250
Suitably, saying,   "Sir, you are welcome.
I, the head   of this household, am Arthur;
In courtesy light,   and linger, I pray you,
And later, my lord,   we shall learn your desire."
"Nay, so help me He seated   on high," quoth the hero,
"My mission was not   to remain here a moment;
But, sir, since thy name   is so nobly renowned,
Since thy city the best   is considered, thy barons
The stoutest in steel gear   that ride upon steeds,
Of all men in the world   the most worthy and brave,   260
Right valiant to play with   in other pure pastimes,
Since here, I have heard,   is the highest of courtesy—
Truly, all these things   have brought me at this time.
Sure ye may be   by this branch that I bear
That I pass as in peace,   proposing no fight.
If I'd come with comrades,   equipped for a quarrel,
I have at my home   both hauberk and helmet,

[162]

Shield and sharp spear, brightly shining, and other
Weapons to wield, full well I know also.
Yet softer my weeds are, since warfare I wished not; 270
But art thou as bold as is bruited by all,
Thou wilt graciously grant me the game that I ask for
By right."

Arthur good answer gave,
And said, "Sir courteous knight,
If battle here you crave,
You shall not lack a fight."

"Nay, I ask for no fight; in faith, now I tell thee
But beardless babes are about on this bench.
Were I hasped in my armor, and high on a horse, 280
Here is no man to match me, your might is so feeble.
So I crave but a Christmas game in this court;
Yule and New Year are come, and here men have courage;
If one in this house himself holds so hardy,
So bold in his blood, in his brain so unbalanced
To dare stiffly strike one stroke for another,
I give this gisarme, this rich axe, as a gift to him,
Heavy enough, to handle as pleases him;
Bare as I sit, I shall bide the first blow.
If a knight be so tough as to try what I tell, 290
Let him leap to me lightly; I leave him this weapon,
Quitclaim it forever, to keep as his own;
And his stroke here, firm on this floor, I shall suffer,
This boon if thou grant'st me, the blow with another
To pay;

Yet let his respite be
A twelvemonth and a day.
Come, let us quickly see
If one here aught dare say."

If at first he had startled them, stiller then sat there 300
The whole of the court, low and high, in the hall.
The knight on his steed turned himself in his saddle,
And fiercely his red eyes he rolled all around,
Bent his bristling brows, with green gleaming brightly,
And waved his beard, waiting for one there to rise.
And when none of the knights spoke, he coughed right noisily,
Straightened up proudly, and started to speak:

[163]

"What!" quoth the hero, "Is this Arthur's household,
The fame of whose fellowship fills many kingdoms?
Now where is your vainglory? Where are your victories? 310
Where is your grimness, your great words, your anger?
For now the Round Table's renown and its revel
Is worsted by one word of one person's speech,
For all shiver with fear before a stroke's shown."
Then so loudly he laughed that the lord was grieved greatly,
And into his fair face his blood shot up fiercely
                              For shame.
          As wroth as wind he grew,
          And all there did the same.
          The King that no fear knew 320
          Then to that stout man came.

And said, "Sir, by heaven, strange thy request is;
As folly thou soughtest, so shouldest thou find it.
I know that not one of the knights is aghast
Of thy great words. Give me thy weapon, for God's sake,
And gladly the boon thou hast begged I shall grant thee."
He leaped to him quickly, caught at his hand,
And fiercely the other lord lights on his feet.
Now Arthur lays hold of the axe by the handle,
As if he would strike with it, swings it round sternly. 330
Before him the strong man stood, in stature
A head and more higher than all in the house.
Stroking his beard, he stood with stern bearing,
And with a calm countenance drew down his coat,
No more frightened or stunned by the axe Arthur flourished
Than if on the bench some one brought him a flagon
                              Of wine.
          Gawain by Guinevere
          Did to the King incline:
          "I pray in accents clear 340
          To let this fray be mine."

"If you now, honored lord," said this knight to King Arthur,
"Would bid me to step from this bench, and to stand there
Beside you—so could I with courtesy quit then
The table, unless my liege lady disliked it—
I'd come to your aid before all your great court.
For truly I think it a thing most unseemly

So boldly to beg   such a boon in your hall here,
Though you in person   are pleased to fulfil it,
While here on the benches   such brave ones are seated,   350
Than whom under heaven,   I think, none are higher
In spirit, none better   in body for battle.
I am weakest and feeblest   in wit, I know well,
And my life, to say truth,   would be least loss of any.
I only since you   are my uncle have honor;
Your blood the sole virtue   I bear in my body.
Unfit is this foolish   affair for you. Give it
To me who soonest   have sought it, and let
All this court if my speech   is not seemly, decide
                    Without blame."   360
        The nobles gather round,
        And all advise the same:
        To free the King that's crowned,
        And Gawain give the game.

The King then commanded   his kinsman to rise,
And quickly he rose up   and came to him courteously,
Kneeled by the King,   and caught the weapon,
He left it graciously,   lifted his hand,
And gave him God's blessing,   and gladly bade him
Be sure that his heart   and his hand both were hardy.   370
"Take care," quoth the King,   "how you start, coz, your cutting,
And truly, I think,   if rightly you treat him,
That blow you'll endure   that he deals you after."
Weapon in hand,   Gawain goes to the hero,
Who boldly remains there,   dismayed none the more.
Then the knight in the green   thus greeted Sir Gawain,
"Let us state our agreement   again ere proceeding.
And now first, sir knight,   what your name is I beg
That you truly will tell,   so in that I may trust."
"In truth," said the good knight,   "I'm called Sir Gawain,   380
Who fetch you this blow,   whatsoever befalls,
And another will take   in return, this time twelvemonth,
From you, with what weapon   you will; with no other
                I'll go."
        The other made reply:
        "By my life here below,
        Gawain, right glad am I
        To have you strike this blow.

By God," said the Green Knight,   "Sir Gawain, it pleases me—
Here, at thy hand,   I shall have what I sought.   390
Thou hast rightly rehearsed to me,   truly and readily,
All of the covenant   asked of King Arthur;
Except that thou shalt,   by thy troth, sir, assure me
Thyself and none other   shalt seek me, wherever
Thou thinkest to find me,   and fetch thee what wages
Are due for the stroke   that to-day thou dost deal me
Before all this splendid   assembly." "Where should I,"
Said Gawain, "go look   for the land where thou livest?
The realm where thy home is,   by Him who hath wrought me,
I know not, nor thee, sir,   thy court nor thy name.   400
Truly tell me thy title,   and teach me the road,
And I'll use all my wit   to win my way thither.
And so by my sure word   truly I swear."
" 'T is enough. No more now   at New Year is needed,"
The knight in the green   said to Gawain the courteous:
"If truly I tell   when I've taken your tap
And softly you've struck me,   if swiftly I tell you
My name and my house   and my home, you may then
Of my conduct make trial,   and your covenant keep;
And if no speech I speak,   you speed all the better: 410
No longer need look,   but may stay in your land.
                                    But ho!
                Take your grim tool with speed,
                And let us see your blow."
                Stroking his axe, "Indeed,"
                Said Gawain, "gladly so."

With speed then the Green Knight   took up his stand,
Inclined his head forward,   uncovering the flesh,
And laid o'er his crown   his locks long and lovely,
And bare left the nape   of his neck for the business.   420
His axe Gawain seized,   and swung it on high;
On the floor his left foot   he planted before him,
And swiftly the naked flesh   smote with his weapon.
The sharp edge severed   the bones of the stranger,
Cut through the clear flesh   and cleft it in twain,
So the blade of the brown steel   bit the ground deeply.
The fair head fell   from the neck to the floor,
So that where it rolled forth   with their feet many spurned it.
The blood on the green glistened,   burst from the body;

And yet neither fell   nor faltered the hero,   430
But stoutly he started forth,   strong in his stride;
Fiercely he rushed   'mid the ranks of the Round Table,
Seized and uplifted   his lovely head straightway;
Then back to his horse went,   laid hold of the bridle,
Stepped into the stirrup   and strode up aloft,
His head holding fast   in his hand by the hair.
And the man as soberly   sat in his saddle
As if he unharmed were,   although now headless,
                                        Instead.
        His trunk around he spun,   440
        That ugly body that bled.
        Frightened was many a one
        When he his words had said.

For upright he holds   the head in his hand,
And confronts with the face   the fine folk on the dais.
It lifted its lids,   and looked forth directly,
Speaking this much   with its mouth, as ye hear:
"Gawain, look that to go   as agreed you are ready,
And seek for me faithfully,   sir, till you find me,
As, heard by these heroes,   you vowed in this hall.   450
To the Green Chapel go you,   I charge you, to get
Such a stroke as you struck.   You are surely deserving,
Sir knight, to be promptly   repaid at the New Year.
As Knight of the Green Chapel   many men know me;
If therefore to find me   you try, you will fail not;
Then come, or be recreant   called as befits thee."
With furious wrench   of the reins he turned round,
And rushed from the hall-door,   his head in his hands,
So the fire of the flint   flew out from the foal's hoofs.
Not one of the lords   knew the land where he went to,   460
No more than the realm   whence he rushed in among them.
                                        What then?
        The King and Gawain there
        At the Green Knight laughed again;
        Yet this the name did bear
        Of wonder among men.

Though much in his mind   did the courtly King marvel,
He let not a semblance   be seen, but said loudly
With courteous speech   to the Queen, most comely:

"To-day, my dear lady,   be never alarmed;   470
Such affairs are for Christmas   well fitted to sing of
And gaily to laugh at   when giving an interlude,[5]
'Mid all the company's   caroles, most courtly.
None the less I may go now   to get my meat;
For I needs must admit   I have met with a marvel."
He glanced at Sir Gawain,   and gladsomely said:
"Now sir, hang up thine axe;   enough it has hewn."
O'er the dais 't was placed,   to hang on the dosser,
That men might remark it   there as a marvel,
And truly describing,   might tell of the wonder.   480
Together these two   then turned to the table,
The sovereign and good knight,   and swiftly men served them
With dainties twofold,   as indeed was most fitting,
All manner of meat   and of minstrelsy both.
So the whole day in pleasure   they passed till night fell
                              O'er the land.
            Now take heed, Gawain, lest,
            Fearing the Green Knight's brand,
            Thou shrinkest from the quest
            That thou hast ta'en in hand.   490

II

This sample had Arthur   of strange things right early,
When young was the year,   for he yearned to hear boasts.
Though such words when they went   to be seated were wanting,
Yet stocked are they now   with hand-fulls of stern work.
In the hall glad was Gawain   those games to begin,
But not strange it would seem   if sad were the ending;
For though men having drunk much   are merry in mind,
Full swift flies a year,   never yielding the same,
The start and the close   very seldom according.
So past went this Yule,   and the year followed after,   500
Each season in turn   succeeding the other.
There came after Christmas   the crabbed Lenten,
With fish and with plainer food   trying the flesh;
But then the world's weather   with winter contends;
Down to earth shrinks the cold,   the clouds are uplifted;
In showers full warm   descends the bright rain,
And falls on the fair fields.   Flowers unfold;

---

[5] A short play given between the courses of a banquet.

The ground and the groves   are green in their garments;
Birds hasten to build,   blithesomely singing
For soft summer's solace   ensuing on slopes   510
                    Everywhere.
          The blossoms swell and blow,
          In hedge-rows rich and rare,
          And notes most lovely flow
          From out the forest fair.

After this comes the season   of soft winds of summer,
When Zephyrus sighs   on the seeds and the green plants.
The herb that then grows   in the ground is right happy,
When down from the leaves   drops the dampening dew
To abide the bright sun   that is blissfully shining.   520
But autumn comes speeding,   soon grows severe,
And warns it to wax   full ripe for the winter.
With drought then the dust   is driven to rise,
From the face of the fields   to fly to the heaven.
With the sun the wild wind   of the welkin is struggling;
The leaves from the limbs drop,   and light on the ground;
And withers the grass   that grew once so greenly.
Then all ripens that formerly   flourished, and rots;
And thus passes the year   in yesterdays many,
And winter, in truth,   as the way of the world is,   530
                    Draws near,
          Till comes the Michaelmas moon
          With pledge of winter sere.
          Then thinks Sir Gawain soon
          Of his dread voyage drear.

Till the tide of Allhallows   with Arthur he tarried;
The King made ado   on that day for his sake
With rich and rare revel   of all of the Round Table,
Knights most courteous,   comely ladies,
All of them heavy   at heart for the hero.   540
Yet nothing but mirth   was uttered, though many
Joyless made jests   for that gentleman's sake.
After meat, with sorrow   he speaks to his uncle,
And openly talks   of his travel, saying:
"Liege lord of my life,   now I ask of you leave.
You know my case   and condition, nor care I
To tell of its troubles   even a trifle.

I must, for the blow   I am bound to, to-morrow
Go seek as God guides me   the man in the green."
Then came there together   the best in the castle: 550
Ywain, Eric,   and others full many,
Sir Dodinel le Sauvage,   the Duke of Clarence,
Lancelot, Lyonel,   Lucan the good,
Sir Bors and Sir Bedevere,   both of them big men,
Mador de la Port,   and many more nobles.
All these knights of the court   came near to the King
With care in their hearts   to counsel the hero;
Heavy and deep   was the dole in the hall
That one worthy as Gawain   should go on that errand,
To suffer an onerous stroke,   and his own sword   560
                       To stay.
        The knight was of good cheer:
        "Why should I shrink away
        From a fate stern and drear?
        A man can but essay."

He remained there that day;   in the morning made ready.
Early he asked   for his arms; all were brought him.
And first a fine carpet   was laid on the floor,
And much was the gilt gear   that glittered upon it.
Thereon stepped the strong man,   and handled the steel,   570
Dressed in a doublet   of Tars that cost dearly,
A hood made craftily,   closed at the top,
And about on the lining   bound with a bright fur.
Then they set on his feet   shoes fashioned of steel,
And with fine greaves of steel   encircled his legs.
Knee-pieces to these   were connected, well polished,
Secured round his knees   with knots of gold.
Then came goodly cuisses,   with cunning enclosing
His thick, brawny thighs;   with thongs they attached them.
Then the man was encased   in a coat of fine mail,   580
With rings of bright steel   on a rich stuff woven,
Braces well burnished   on both of his arms,
Elbow-pieces gay, good,   and gloves of plate,
All the goodliest gear   that would give him most succor
                      That tide:
        Coat armor richly made,
        His gold spurs fixed with pride,

Girt his unfailing blade
By a silk sash to his side.

When in arms he was clasped,   his costume was costly;   590
The least of the lacings   or loops gleamed with gold.
And armed in this manner,   the man heard mass,
At the altar adored   and made offering, and afterward
Came to the King   and all of his courtiers,
Gently took leave   of the ladies and lords;
Him they kissed and escorted,   to Christ him commending.
Then was Gringolet [6] ready,   girt with a saddle
That gaily with many   a gold fringe was gleaming,
With nails studded newly,   prepared for the nonce.
The bridle was bound about,   barred with bright gold;   600
With the bow of the saddle,   the breastplate, the splendid skirts,
Crupper, and cloth   in adornment accorded,
With gold nails arrayed   on a groundwork of red,
That glittered and glinted   like gleams of the sun.
Then he caught up his helm,   and hastily kissed it;
It stoutly was stapled   and stuffed well within,
High on his head,   and hasped well behind,
With a light linen veil   laid over the visor,
Embroidered and bound   with the brightest of gems
On a silken border;   with birds on the seams   610
Like painted parroquets   preening; true love-knots
As thickly with turtle doves   tangled as though
Many women had been   at the work seven winters
                              In town.
          Great was the circle's price
          Encompassing his crown;
          Of diamonds its device,
          That were both bright and brown.

Then they showed him his shield,   sheer gules, whereon shone
The pentangle [7] painted   in pure golden hue.   620
On his baldric he caught,   and about his neck cast it;
And fairly the hero's   form it befitted.
And why that great prince   the pentangle suited
Intend I to tell,   in my tale though I tarry.

[6] Gawain's horse.
[7] A five pointed star, made by interlacing lines.

'T is a sign that Solomon   formerly set
As a token, for so   it doth symbol, of truth.
A figure it is   that with five points is furnished;
Each line overlaps   and locks in another,
Nor comes to an end;   and Englishmen call it
Everywhere, hear I,   the endless knot.   630
It became then the knight   and his noble arms also,
In five ways, and five times   each way still faithful.
Sir Gawain was known   as the good, refined gold,
Graced with virtues of castle,   of villainy void,
                        Made clean.
            So the pentangle new
            On shield and coat was seen,
            As man of speech most true,
            And gentlest knight of mien.

First, in his five wits   he faultless was found;   640
In his five fingers too   the man never failed;
And on earth all his faith   was fixed on the five wounds
That Christ, as the creed tells,   endured on the cross.
Wheresoever this man   was midmost in battle,
His thought above everything   else was in this,
To draw all his fire   from the fivefold joys
That the fair Queen of Heaven   felt in her child.
And because of this fitly   he carried her image
Displayed on his shield,   on its larger part,
That whenever he saw it   his spirit should sink not.   650
The fifth five the hero   made use of, I find,
More than all were his liberalness,   love of his fellows,
His courtesy, chastity,   unchangeable ever,
And pity, all further traits   passing. These five
In this hero more surely   were set than in any.
In truth now, fivefold   they were fixed in the knight,
Linked each to the other   without any end,
And all of them fastened   on five points unfailing;
Each side they neither   united nor sundered,
Evermore endless   at every angle,   660
Where equally either   they ended or started.
And so his fair shield   was adorned with this symbol,
Thus richly with red gold   wrought on red gules,
So by people the pentangle   perfect 't was called,

As it ought.
Gawain in arms is gay;
Right there his lance he caught,
And gave them all good-day
For ever, as he thought.

He set spurs to his steed, and sprang on his way   670
So swiftly that sparks from the stone flew behind him.
All who saw him, so seemly, sighed, sad at heart;
The same thing, in sooth, each said to the other,
Concerned for that comely man: "Christ, 't is a shame
Thou, sir knight, must be lost whose life is so noble!
To find, faith! his equal on earth is not easy.
'T would wiser have been to have acted more warily,
Dubbed yonder dear one a duke. He seems clearly
To be in the land here a brilliant leader:
So better had been than brought thus to naught,   680
By an elf-man beheaded for haughty boasting.
Who e'er knew any king such counsel to take,
As foolish as one in a Christmas frolic?"
Much was the warm water welling from eyes
When the seemly hero set out from the city
           That day.
       Nowhere he abode,
       But swiftly went his way;
       By devious paths he rode,
       As I the book heard say.   690

Through the realm of Logres [8] now rides this lord,
Sir Gawain, for God's sake, no game though he thought it.
Oft alone, uncompanioned he lodges at night
Where he finds not the fare that he likes set before him.
Save his foal, he 'd no fellow by forests and hills;
On the way, no soul but the Savior to speak to.
At length he drew nigh unto North Wales, and leaving
To left of him all of the islands of Anglesey,
Fared by the forelands and over the fords
Near the Holy Head; hastening hence to the mainland,   700
In Wyral he went through the wilderness. There,
Lived but few who loved God or their fellows with good heart.

[8] England south of the Humber River.

And always he asked   of any he met,
As he journeyed, if nearby   a giant they knew of,
A green knight, known   as the Knight of the Green Chapel.
All denied it with nay,   in their lives they had never
Once seen any hero   who had such a hue

Of green.

The knight takes roadways strange
In many a wild terrene;
Often his feelings change
Before that chapel 's seen.

710

Over many cliffs climbed he   in foreign countries;
From friends far sundered,   he fared as a stranger;
And wondrous it were,   at each water or shore
That he passed, if he found not   before him a foe,
So foul too and fell   that to fight he could fail not.
The marvels he met with   amount to so many
Too tedious were it   to tell of the tenth part.
For sometimes with serpents   he struggled and wolves too,
With wood-trolls sometimes   in stony steeps dwelling,
And sometimes with bulls   and with bears and with boars;
And giants from high fells   hunted and harassed him.
If he'd been not enduring   and doughty, and served God,
These doubtless would often   have done him to death.
Though warfare was grievous,   worse was the winter,
When cold, clear water   was shed from the clouds
That froze ere it fell   to the earth, all faded.
With sleet nearly slain,   he slept in his armor
More nights than enough   on the naked rocks,
Where splashing the cold stream   sprang from the summit,
And hung in hard icicles   high o'er his head.
Thus in peril and pain   and desperate plights,
Till Christmas Eve wanders   this wight through the country

Alone.

Truly the knight that tide
To Mary made his moan,
That she direct his ride
To where some hearth-fire shone.

720

730

By a mount on the morn   he merrily rides
To a wood dense and deep   that was wondrously wild;
High hills on each hand,   with forests of hoar oaks

740

[174]

Beneath them most huge,   a hundred together.
Thickly the hazel   and hawthorn were tangled,
Everywhere mantled   with moss rough and ragged,
With many a bird   on the bare twigs, mournful,
That piteously piped   for pain of the cold.
Sir Gawain on Gringolet   goes underneath them
Through many a marsh   and many a mire,
Unfriended, fearing   to fail in devotion,   750
And see not His service,   that Sire's, on that very night
Born of a Virgin   to vanquish our pain.
And so sighing he said: "Lord, I beseech Thee,
And Mary, the mildest   mother so dear,
For some lodging wherein   to hear mass full lowly,
And matins, meekly   I ask it, to-morrow;
So promptly I pray   my pater and ave
                    And creed."
            Thus rode he as he prayed,
            Lamenting each misdeed;   760
            Often the sign he made,
            And said, "Christ's cross me speed."

He scarcely had signed himself   thrice, ere he saw
In the wood on a mound   a moated mansion,
Above a fair field,   enfolded in branches
Of many a huge tree   hard by the ditches:
The comeliest castle   that knight ever kept.
In a meadow 't was placed,   with a park all about,
And a palisade, spiked   and pointed, set stoutly
Round many a tree   for more than two miles,   770
The lord on that one side   looked at the stronghold
That shimmered and shone   through the shapely oak trees;
Then duly his helm doffed,   and gave his thanks humbly
To Jesus and Julian,[9]   both of them gentle,
For showing him courtesy,   hearing his cry.
"Now good lodging," quoth Gawain,   "I beg you to grant me."
Then with spurs in his gilt heels   he Gringolet strikes,
Who chooses the chief path   by chance that conducted
The man to the bridge-end   ere many a minute
                    Had passed.   780
            The bridge secure was made,
            Upraised; the gates shut fast;

[9] The patron saint of hospitality.

[175]

> The walls were well arrayed.
> It feared no tempest's blast.

The hero abode   on his horse by the bank
Of the deep, double ditch   that surrounded the dwelling.
The wall stood wonderfully   deep in the water,
And again to a huge height   sprang overhead;
Of hard, hewn rock   that reached to the cornices,
Built up with outworks   under the battlements   790
Finely; at intervals,   turrets fair fashioned,
With many good loopholes   that shut tight; this lord
Had ne'er looked at a barbican   better than this one.
Further in he beheld   the high hall; here and there
Towers were stationed   set thickly with spires,
With finials wondrously   long and fair fitting,
Whose points were cunningly   carven, and craftily.
There numerous chalk-white   chimneys he noticed
That bright from the tops   of the towers were gleaming.
Such pinnacles painted,   so placed about everywhere,   800
Clustering so thick   'mid the crenels, the castle
Surely appeared   to be cut out of paper.
The knight on his foal   it fair enough fancies
If into the court   he may manage to come,
In that lodging to live   while the holiday lasts
                                   With delight.
> A porter came at call,
> His mission learned, and right
> Civilly from the wall
> Greeted the errant knight.   810

Quoth Gawain: "Good sir,   will you go on my errand,
Harbor to crave   of this house's high lord?"
"Yea, by Peter. I know well,   sir knight," said the porter,
"You're welcome as long   as you list here to tarry."
Then went the man quickly,   and with him, to welcome
The knight to the castle,   a courteous company.
Down the great drawbridge   they dropped, and went eagerly
Forth; on the frozen earth   fell on their knees
To welcome this knight   in the way they thought worthy;
Threw wide the great gate   for Gawain to enter.   820
He bade them rise promptly,   and rode o'er the bridge.
His saddle several   seized as he lighted,

[176]

And stout men in plenty   stabled his steed.
And next there descended   knights and esquires
To lead to the hall   with delight this hero.
When he raised his helmet,   many made haste
From his hand to catch it,   to care for the courtly man.
Some of them took then   his sword and his shield both.
Then Gawain graciously   greeted each knight;
Many proud men pressing   to honor that prince,   830
To the hall they led him,   all hasped in his harness,
Where fiercely a fair fire   flamed on the hearth.
Then came the lord   of this land from his chamber
To fittingly meet   the man on the floor,
And said: "You are welcome   to do what your will is;
To hold as your own,   you have all that is here
               In this place."
        "Thank you," said Gawain then,
        "May Christ reward this grace."
        The two like joyful men   840
        Each other then embrace.

Gawain gazed at the man   who so graciously greeted him;
Doughty he looked,   the lord of that dwelling,
A hero indeed huge,   hale, in his prime;
His beard broad and bright,   its hue all of beaver;
Stern, and on stalwart shanks   steadily standing;
Fell faced as the fire,   in speech fair and free.
In sooth, well suited   he seemed, thought Gawain,
To govern as prince   of a goodly people.
To his steward the lord turned,   and strictly commanded   850
To send men to Gawain   to give him good service;
And prompt at his bidding   were people in plenty.
To a bright room they brought him,   the bed nobly decked
With hangings of pure silk   with clear golden hems.
And curious coverings   with comely panels,
Embroidered with bright fur   above at the edges;
On cords curtains running   with rings of red gold;
From Tars and Toulouse   were the tapestries covering
The walls; under foot   on the floor more to match.
There he soon, with mirthful   speeches, was stripped   860
Of his coat of linked mail   and his armor; and quickly
Men ran, and brought him   rich robes, that the best
He might pick out and choose   as his change of apparel.

When lapped was the lord   in the one he selected,
That fitted him fairly   with flowing skirts,
The fur by his face,   in faith it seemed made,
To the company there,   entirely of colors,
Glowing and lovely;   beneath all his limbs were.
That never made Christ   a comelier knight
                              They thought.   870
        On earth, or far or near,
        It seemed as if he ought
        To be a prince sans peer
        In fields where fierce men fought.

A chair by the chimney   where charcoal was burning
For Gawain was fitted   most finely with cloths,
Both cushions and coverlets,   cunningly made.
Then a comely mantle   was cast on the man,
Of a brown, silken fabric   bravely embroidered,
Within fairly furred   with the finest of skins,   880
Made lovely with ermine,   his hood fashioned likewise.
He sat on that settle   in clothes rich and seemly;
His mood, when well   he was warmed, quickly mended.
Soon was set up a table   on trestles most fair;
With a clean cloth that showed   a clear white it was covered,
With top-cloth and salt-cellar,   spoons too of silver.
When he would the man washed,   and went to his meat,
And seemly enough men   served him with several
Excellent stews   in the best manner seasoned,
Twofold as was fitting,   and various fishes;   890
In bread some were baked,   some broiled on the coals,
Some seethed, some in stews   that were savored with spices;
And ever such subtly made   sauces as pleased him.
He freely and frequently   called it a feast,
Most courtly; the company   there all acclaimed him
                              Well-bred.
        "But now this penance take,
        And soon 't will mend," they said.
        That man much mirth did make,
        As wine went to his head.   900

They enquired then and queried   in guarded questions
Tactfully put   to the prince himself,
Till he courteously owned   he came of the court

The lord Arthur, gracious   and goodly, alone holds,
Who rich is and royal,   the Round Table's King;
And that Gawain himself   in that dwelling was seated,
For Christmas come,   as the case had befallen.
When he learned that he had   that hero, the lord
Laughed loudly thereat   so delightful he thought it.
Much merriment made   all the men in that castle   910
By promptly appearing   then in his presence;
For all prowess and worth   and pure polished manners
Pertain to his person.   He ever is praised;
Of all heroes on earth   his fame is the highest.
Each knight full softly   said to his neighbor,
"We now shall see, happily,   knightly behavior,
And faultless terms   of talking most noble;
What profit 's in speech   we may learn without seeking,
For nurture's fine father   has found here a welcome;
In truth God has graciously   given His grace   920
Who grants us to have   such a guest as Gawain
When men for His birth's sake   sit merry and sing.
                              To each
            Of us this hero now
            Will noble manners teach;
            Who hear him will learn how
            To utter loving speech."

When at length the dinner   was done, and the lords
Had risen, the night-time   nearly was come.
The chaplains went   their way to the chapels   930
And rang right joyfully,   just as they should do,
For evensong solemn   this festival season.
To this goes the lord,   and the lady likewise;
She comes in with grace   to the pew closed and comely,
And straightway Gawain   goes thither right gaily;
The lord by his robe   took him, led to a seat,
Acknowledged him kindly   and called him by name,
Saying none in the world   was as welcome as he was.
He heartily thanked him;   the heroes embraced,
And together they soberly   sat through the service.   940
Then longed the lady   to look on the knight,
And emerged from her pew   with many fair maidens;
In face she was fairest   of all, and in figure,
In skin and in color,   all bodily qualities;

Lovelier, Gawain thought,   even than Guinevere.
He goes through the chancel   to greet her, so gracious.
By the left hand another   was leading her, older
Than she, a lady   who looked as if aged,
By heroes around her   reverenced highly.
The ladies, however,   unlike were to look on: 950
If fresh was the younger,   the other was yellow;
Rich red on the one   was rioting everywhere,
Rough wrinkled cheeks   hung in rolls on the other;
One's kerchiefs, with clear pearls   covered and many,
Displayed both her breast   and her bright throat all bare,
Shining fairer than snow   on the hillsides falling;
The second her neck   in a neck-cloth enswathed,
That enveloped in chalk-white   veils her black chin;
Her forehead in silk   was wrapped and enfolded
Adorned and tricked   with trifles about it   960
Till nothing was bare   but the lady's black brows,
Her two eyes, her nose,   and her lips, all naked,
And those were bleared strangely,   and ugly to see.
A goodly lady,   so men before God
                    Might decide!
          Her body thick and short,
          Her hips were round and wide;
          One of more pleasant sort
          She led there by her side.

When Gawain had gazed on   that gay one so gracious   970
In look, he took leave   of the lord and went toward them,
Saluted the elder,   bowing full lowly,
The lovelier lapped   in his two arms a little,
And knightly and comely   greeted and kissed her.
They craved his acquaintance,   and quickly he asked
To be truly their servant   if so they desired it.
They took him between them,   and led him with talk
To the sitting-room's hearth;   then straightway for spices
They called, which men sped   to unsparingly bring,
And with them as well   pleasant wine at each coming.   980
Up leaped right often   the courteous lord,
Urged many a time   that the men should make merry,
Snatched off his hood,   on a spear gaily hung it,
And waved it, that one   for a prize might win it
Who caused the most mirth   on that Christmas season.

"I shall try, by my faith, to contend with the finest
Ere hoodless I find myself, helped by my friends."
Thus with laughing speeches the lord makes merry
That night, to gladden Sir Gawain with games.

So they spent   990
The evening in the hall.
The king for lights then sent,
And taking leave of all
To bed Sir Gawain went.

On the morn when the Lord, as men all remember,
Was born, who would die for our doom, in each dwelling
On earth grows happiness greater for His sake;
So it did on that day there with many a dainty:
With dishes cunningly cooked at meal-times,
With doughty men dressed in their best on the dais.   1000
The old lady was seated the highest; beside her
Politely the lord took his place, I believe;
The gay lady and Gawain together sat, mid-most,
Where fitly the food came, and afterward fairly
Was served through the hall as beseemed them the best,
Of the company each in accord with his station.
There was meat and mirth, there was much joy, too troublous
To tell, though I tried in detail to describe it;
Yet I know both the lovely lady and Gawain
So sweet found each other's society (pleasant   1010
And polished their converse, courtly and private;
Unfailing their courtesy, free from offence)
That surpassing, in truth, any play of a prince was

Their game.
There trumpets, drums and airs
Of piping loudly came.
Each minded his affairs,
And those two did the same.

Much mirth was that day and the day after made,
And the third followed fast, as full of delight.   1020
Sweet was the joy of St. John's day to hear of,
The last, as the folk there believed, of the festival.
Guests were to go in the grey dawn, and therefore
They wondrously late were awake with their wine,
And danced delightful, long lasting caroles.

[181]

At length when 't was late   they took their leave,
Each strong man among them   to start on his way.
Gawain gave him good-day;   then the good man laid hold of him,
Led to the hearth   in his own room the hero;
There took him aside,   and gave suitable thanks   1030
For the gracious distinction   that Gawain had given
In honoring his house   that holiday season,
And gracing his castle   with courteous company.
"I'll truly as long   as I live be the better
That Gawain at God's   own feast was my guest."
"Gramercy," said Gawain,   "by God, sir, not mine
Is the worth, but your own;   may the high King reward you.
I am here at your will   to work your behest,
As in high and low   it behooves me to do
                    By right."   1040
          The lord intently tries
          Longer to hold the knight;
          Gawain to him replies
          That he in no way might.

Then the man with courteous   question enquired
What dark deed that feast time   had driven him forth,
From the King's court to journey   alone with such courage,
Ere fully in homes   was the festival finished.
"In sooth," said the knight,   "sir, ye say but the truth;
From these hearths a high   and a hasty task took me.   1050
Myself, I am summoned   to seek such a place
As to find it I know not   whither to fare.
I'd not fail to have reached it   the first of the New Year,
So help me our Lord,   for the whole land of Logres;
And therefore, I beg   this boon of you here, sir;
Tell me, in truth,   if you ever heard tale
Of the Chapel of Green,   of the ground where it stands,
And the knight, green colored,   who keeps it. By solemn
Agreement a tryst   was established between us,
That man at that landmark   to meet if I lived.   1060
And now there lacks   of New Year but little;
I'd look at that lord,   if God would but let me,
More gladly than own   any good thing, by God's Son.
And hence, by your leave,   it behooves me to go;
I now have but barely   three days to be busy.
As fain would I fall dead   as fail of my mission."

[182]

Then laughing the lord said: "You longer must stay,
For I'll point out the way   to that place ere the time's end,
The ground of the Green Chapel.   Grieve no further;
For, sir, you shall be   in your bed at your ease   1070
Until late, and fare forth   the first of the year,
To your meeting place come   by mid-morning, to do there
                                        Your pleasure.
                        Tarry till New Year's day,
                        Then rise and go at leisure.
                        I'll set you on your way;
                        Not two miles is the measure."

Then was Gawain right glad,   and gleefully laughed.
"Now for this more than anything   else, sir, I thank you.
I have come to the end   of my quest; at your will   1080
I shall bide, and in all things   act as you bid me."
The lord then seized him,   and set him beside him,
And sent for the ladies   to better delight him.
Seemly the pleasure   among them in private.
So gay were the speeches   he spoke, and so friendly,
The host seemed a man   well-nigh mad in behavior.
He called to the knight there,   crying aloud:
"Ye have bound you to do   the deed that I bid you.
Here, and at once,   will you hold to your word sir?"
"Yes, certainly sir,"   the true hero said;   1090
"While I bide in your house   I obey your behest."
"You have toiled," said the lord;   "from afar have travelled,
And here have caroused,   nor are wholly recovered
In sleep or in nourishment,   know I for certain.
In your room you shall linger,   and lie at your ease
To-morrow till mass-time,   and go to your meat
When you will, and with you   my wife to amuse you
With company, till   to the court I return.
                                        You stay
                        And I shall early rise,   1100
                        And hunting go my way."
                        Bowing in courteous wise,
                        Gawain grants all this play.

"And more," said the man   "let us make an agreement:
Whatever I win   in the wood shall be yours;
And what chance you shall meet   shall be mine in exchange.

Sir, let's so strike our bargain   and swear to tell truly
Whate'er fortune brings,   whether bad, sir, or better."
Quoth Gawain the good: "By God, I do grant it.
What pastime you please   appears to me pleasant."   1110
"On the beverage brought us   the bargain is made,"
So the lord of the land said.   All of them laughed,
And drank, and light-heartedly   revelled and dallied,
Those ladies and lords,   as long as they liked.
Then they rose with elaborate   politeness, and lingered,
With many fair speeches   spoke softly together,
Right lovingly kissed,   and took leave of each other.
Gay troops of attendants   with glimmering torches
In comfort escorted   each man to his couch
                              To rest.   1120
                     Yet ere they left the board
                     Their promise they professed
                     Often. That people's lord
                     Could well maintain a jest.

III

Betimes rose the folk   ere the first of the day;
The guests that were going   then summoned their grooms,
Who hastily sprang up   to saddle their horses,
Packed their bags   and prepared all their gear.
The nobles made ready,   to ride all arrayed;
And quickly they leaped   and caught up their bridles,   1130
And started, each wight   on the way that well pleased him.
The land's beloved lord   not last was equipped
For riding, with many   a man too. A morsel
He hurriedly ate   when mass he had heard,
And promptly with horn   to the hunting field hastened.
And ere any daylight   had dawned upon earth,
Both he and his knights   were high on their horses.
The dog-grooms, accomplished,   the hounds then coupled,
The door of the kennel   unclosed, called them out,
On the bugle mightily   blew three single notes;   1140
Whereupon bayed   with a wild noise the brachets,
And some they turned back   that went straying, and punished.
The hunters, I heard,   were a hundred. To station
                            They go,
            The keepers of the hounds,

And off the leashes throw.
With noise the wood resounds
From the good blasts they blow.

At the first sound of questing,[10] the wild creatures quaked;
The deer fled, foolish   from fright, in the dale,   1150
To the high ground hastened,   but quickly were halted
By beaters, loud shouting,   stationed about
In a circle. The harts   were let pass with their high heads,
And also the bucks,   broad-antlered and bold;
For the generous lord   by law had forbidden
All men with the male deer   to meddle in close season.
The hinds were hemmed in   with hey! and ware!
The does to the deep valleys   driven with great din.
You might see as they loosed them   the shafts swiftly soar—
At each turn of the forest   their feathers went flying—   1160
That deep into brown hides   bit with their broad heads;
Lo! they brayed on the hill-sides,   bled there, and died,
And hounds, fleet-footed,   followed them headlong.
And hunters after them   hastened with horns
So loud in their sharp burst   of sound as to sunder
The cliffs. What creatures   escaped from the shooters,
Hunted and harried   from heights to the waters,
Were pulled down and rent   at the places there ready;
Such skill the men showed   at these low-lying stations,
So great were the greyhounds   that quickly they got them   1170
And dragged them down, fast   as the folk there might look
                                        At the sight.
                         Carried with bliss away,
                         The lord did oft alight,
                         Oft gallop; so that day
                         He passed till the dark night.

Thus frolicked the lord   on the fringe of the forest,
And Gawain the good   in his gay bed reposed,
Lying snugly, till sunlight   shone on the walls,
'Neath a coverlet bright   with curtains about it.   1180
As softly he slumbered,   a slight sound he heard
At his door, made with caution,   and quickly it opened.
The hero heaved up   his head from the clothes;
By a corner he caught up   the curtain a little,

[10] Baying.

[185]

And glanced out with heed   to behold what had happened.
The lady it was,   most lovely to look at,
Who shut the door after her   stealthily, slyly,
And turned toward the bed.   Then the brave man, embarrassed,
Lay down again subtly   to seem as if sleeping;
And stilly she stepped,   and stole to his bed,   1190
There cast up the curtain,   and creeping within it,
Seated herself   on the bedside right softly,
And waited a long while   to watch when he woke.
And the lord too, lurking,   lay there a long while,
Wondering at heart   what might come of this happening,
Or what it might mean—   a marvel he thought it.
Yet he said to himself,   " 'T would be surely more seemly
By speaking at once   to see what she wishes."
Then roused he from sleep,   and stretching turned toward her,
His eyelids unlocked,   made believe that he wondered,   1200
And signed himself so   by his prayers to be safer
                              From fall.
          Right sweet in chin and cheek,
          Both white and red withal,
          Full fairly she did speak
          With laughing lips and small.

"Good morrow, Sir Gawain,"   that gay lady said,
"You're a sleeper unwary,   since so one may steal in.
In a trice you are ta'en!   If we make not a truce,
In your bed, be you certain   of this, I shall bind you."   1210
All laughing, the lady   delivered those jests.
"Good morrow, fair lady,"   said Gawain the merry,
"You may do what you will,   and well it doth please me,
For quickly I yield me,   crying for mercy;
This method to me   seems the best—for I must!"
So the lord in turn jested   with laughter right joyous.
"But if, lovely lady,   you would, give me leave,
Your prisoner release   and pray him to rise,
And I'd come from this bed   and clothe myself better;
So could I converse with you   then with more comfort."   1220
"Indeed no, fair sir,"   that sweet lady said,
"You'll not move from your bed;   I shall manage you better;
For here—and on that side   too—I shall hold you,
And next I shall talk   with the knight I have taken.
For well do I know   that your name is Sir Gawain,

By everyone honored   wherever you ride;
Most highly acclaimed   is your courtly behavior
With lords and ladies   and all who are living.
And now you're here, truly,   and none but we two;
My lord and his followers   far off have fared;   1230
Other men remain   in their beds, and my maidens;
The door is closed,   and secured with a strong hasp;
Since him who delights all   I have in my house,
My time, as long   as it lasts, I with talking
     Shall fill.
   My body's gladly yours;
   Upon me work your will.
   Your servant I, perforce,
   Am now, and shall be still."

"In faith," quoth Sir Gawain,   "a favor I think it,   1240
Although I am now   not the knight you speak of;
To reach to such fame   as here you set forth,
I am one, as I well know   myself, most unworthy.
By God, should you think   it were good, I'd be glad
If I could or in word   or action accomplish
Your ladyship's pleasure—   a pure joy 't would prove."
"In good faith, Sir Gawain,"   the gay lady said,
"Ill-bred I should be   if I blamed or belittled
The worth and prowess   that please all others.
There are ladies enough   who'd be now more delighted   1250
To have you in thraldom,   as here, sir, I have you,
To trifle gaily   in talk most engaging,
To give themselves comfort   and quiet their cares,
Than have much of the gold   and the goods they command.
But to Him I give praise   that ruleth the heavens,
That wholly I have   in my hand what all wish."
     So she
   Gave him good cheer that day,
   She who was fair to see.
   To what she chanced to say   1260
   With pure speech answered he.

Quoth the merry man, "Madam,   Mary reward you,
For noble, in faith,   I've found you, and generous.
People by others   pattern their actions,
But more than I merit   to me they give praise;
    [187]

'T is your courteous self who can show naught but kindness."
"By Mary," said she, "to me it seems other!
Were I worth all the host of women now living,
And had I the wealth of the world in my hands,
Should I chaffer and choose to get me a champion, 1270
Sir, from the signs I've seen in you here
Of courtesy, merry demeanor, and beauty,
From what I have heard, and hold to be true,
Before you no lord now alive would be chosen."
"A better choice, madam, you truly have made;
Yet I'm proud of the value you put now upon me.
Your servant as seemly, I hold you my sovereign,
Become your knight, and Christ give you quittance."
Thus of much they talked till mid-morning was past.
The lady behaved as if greatly she loved him, 1280
But Gawain, on guard, right gracefully acted.
"Though I were the most lovely of ladies," she thought,
"The less would he take with him love." He was seeking,
With speed,
Grief that must be: the stroke
That him should stun indeed.
She then of leaving spoke,
And promptly he agreed.

Then she gave him good-day, and glanced at him, laughing,
And startled him, speaking sharp words as she stood: 1290
"He who blesses all words reward this reception!
I doubt if indeed I may dub you Gawain."
"Wherefore?" he queried, quickly enquiring,
Afraid that he'd failed in his fashion of speech.
But the fair lady blessed him, speaking as follows:
"One as good as is Gawain the gracious considered,
(And courtly behavior's found wholly in him)
Not lightly so long could remain with a lady
Without, in courtesy, craving a kiss
At some slight subtle hint at the end of a story." 1300
"Let it be as you like, lovely lady," said Gawain;
"As a knight is so bound, I'll kiss at your bidding,
And lest he displease you, so plead no longer."
Then closer she comes, and catches the knight
In her arms, and salutes him, leaning down affably.

Kindly each other   to Christ they commend.
She goes forth at the door   without further ado,
And he quickly makes ready   to rise, and hastens,
Calls to his chamberlain,   chooses his clothes,
And merrily marches,   when ready, to mass.   1310
Then he fared to his meat,   and fitly he feasted,
Made merry all day   with amusements till moonrise.

> None knew
> A knight to better fare
> With dames so worthy, two:
> One old, one younger. There
> Much mirth did then ensue.

Still was absent the lord   of that land on his pleasure,
To hunt barren hinds   in wood and in heath.
By the set of the sun   he had slain such a number   1320
Of does and different   deer that 't was wondrous.
Eagerly flocked in   the folk at the finish,
And quickly made   of the killed deer a quarry;
To this went the nobles   with numerous men;
The game whose flesh   was the fattest they gathered;
With care, as the case   required, cut them open.
And some the deer searched   at the spot of assay,
And two fingers of fat   they found in the poorest.
They slit at the base   of the throat, seized the stomach,
Scraped it away   with a sharp knife and sewed it;   1330
Next slit the four limbs   and stripped off the hide;
Then opened the belly   and took out the bowels
And flesh of the knot,   quickly flinging them out.
They laid hold of the throat,   made haste to divide, then,
The windpipe and gullet,   and tossed out the guts;
With their sharp knives carved out   the shoulders and carried them
Held through a small hole   to have the sides perfect.
The breast they sliced,   and split it in two;
And then they began   once again at the throat,
And quickly as far   as its fork they cut it;   1340
Pulled out the pluck,   and promptly thereafter
Beside the ribs   swiftly severed the fillets,
Cleared them off readily   right by the backbone,
Straight down to the haunch,   all hanging together.
They heaved it up whole,   and hewed it off there,

And the rest by the name   of the numbles—and rightly—
                            They knew.
                    Then where divide the thighs,
                    The folds behind they hew,
                    Hasten to cut the prize   1350
                    Along the spine in two.

And next both the head   and the neck off they hewed;
The sides from the backbone   swiftly they sundered;
The fee of the ravens   they flung in the branches.
They ran through each thick side   a hole by the ribs,
And hung up both   by the hocks of the haunches,
Each fellow to have   the fee that was fitting.
On the fair beast's hide,   they fed their hounds
With the liver and lights   and the paunch's lining,
Among which bread   steeped in blood was mingled.   1360
They blew boldly the blast   for the prize; the hounds barked.
Then the venison took they   and turned toward home,
And stoutly many   a shrill note they sounded.
Ere close of the daylight,   the company came
To the comely castle   where Gawain in comfort
                            Sojourned.
                    And when he met the knight
                    As thither he returned,
                    Joy had they and delight,
                    Where the fire brightly burned.   1370

In the hall the lord bade   all his household to gather,
And both of the dames   to come down with their damsels.
In the room there before   all the folk he ordered
His followers, truly,   to fetch him his venison.
Gawain he called   with courteous gaiety,
Asked him to notice   the number of nimble beasts,
Showed him the fairness   of flesh on the ribs.
"Are you pleased with this play?   Have I won your praise?
Have I thoroughly earned   your thanks through my cunning?"
"In faith," said Sir Gawain,   "this game is the fairest   1380
I've seen in the season   of winter these seven years."
"The whole of it, Gawain,   I give you," the host said;
"Because of our compact,   as yours you may claim it."
"That is true," the knight said,   "and I tell you the same:

[190]

That this I have worthily   won within doors,
And surely to you   with as good will I yield it."
With both of his arms   his fair neck he embraced,
And the hero as courteously   kissed as he could.
"I give you my gains.   I got nothing further;
I freely would grant it,   although it were greater."   1390
"It is good," said the good man;   "I give you my thanks.
Yet things so may be   that you'd think it better
To tell where you won   this same wealth by your wit."
" 'T was no part of our pact," said he;   "press me no more;
For trust entirely   in this, that you've taken
                              Your due."
                   With laughing merriment
                   And knightly speech and true,
                   To supper soon they went
                   With store of dainties new.   1400

In a chamber they sat,   by the side of the chimney,
Where men right frequently   fetched them mulled wine.
In their jesting, again   they agreed on the morrow
To keep the same compact   they came to before:
That whatever should chance,   they'd exchange at evening,
When greeting again,   the new things they had gotten.
Before all the court   they agreed to the covenant;
Then was the beverage   brought forth in jest.
At last they politely   took leave of each other,
And quickly each hero   made haste to his couch.   1410
When the cock but three times   had crowed and cackled,
The lord and his men   had leaped from their beds.
So that duly their meal   was dealt with, and mass,
And ere daylight they'd fared   toward the forest, on hunting
                              Intent.
                   The huntsmen with loud horns
                   Through level fields soon went,
                   Uncoupling 'mid the thorns
                   The hounds swift on the scent.

Soon they cry for a search   by the side of a swamp.   1420
The huntsmen encourage   the hounds that first catch there
The scent, and sharp words   they shout at them loudly;
And thither the hounds   that heard them hastened,

And fast to the trail fell,　forty at once.
Then such clamor and din　from the dogs that had come there
Arose that the rocks　all around them rang.
With horn and with mouth　the hunters heartened them;
They gathered together then,　all in a group,
'Twixt a pool in that copse　and a crag most forbidding.
At a stone-heap, beside　the swamp, by a cliff,　　　　　　1430
Where the rough rock had fallen　in rugged confusion,
They fared to the finding,　the folk coming after.
Around both the crag　and the rubble-heap searched
The hunters, sure　that within them was hidden
The beast whose presence　was bayed by the bloodhounds.
Then they beat on the bushes,　and bade him rise up,
And wildly he made　for the men in his way,
Rushing suddenly forth,　of swine the most splendid.
Apart from the herd　he'd grown hoary with age,
For fierce was the beast,　the biggest of boars.　　　　　　1440
Then many men grieved,　full grim when he grunted,
For three at his first thrust　he threw to the earth,
And then hurtled forth swiftly,　no harm doing further.
They shrilly cried hi!　and shouted hey! hey!
Put bugles to mouth,　loudly blew the recall.
The men and dogs merry　in voice were and many;
With outcry they all　hurry after this boar
　　　　　　　　　　　　　　　To slay.
　　　　　　　He maims the pack when, fell,
　　　　　　　He often stands at bay.　　　　　　　　1450
　　　　　　　Loudly they howl and yell,
　　　　　　　Sore wounded in the fray.

Then to shoot at him came up　the company quickly.
Arrows that hit him　right often they aimed,
But their sharp points failed　that fell on his shoulders'
Tough skin, and the barbs　would not bite in his flesh;
But the smooth-shaven shafts　were shivered in pieces,
The heads wherever　they hit him rebounding.
But when hurt by the strength　of the strokes they struck,
Then mad for the fray　he falls on the men,　　　　　　1460
And deeply he wounds them　as forward he dashes.
Then many were frightened,　and drew back in fear;
But the lord galloped off　on a light horse after him,

Blew like a huntsman   right bold the recall
On his bugle, and rode   through the thick of the bushes,
Pursuing this swine   till the sun shone clearly.
Thus the day they passed   in doing these deeds,
While bides our gracious knight   Gawain in bed,
With bed-clothes in color   right rich, at the castle
                          Behind.   1470
        The dame did not forget
        To give him greetings kind.
        She soon upon him set,
        To make him change his mind.

Approaching the curtain,   she peeps at the prince,
And at once Sir Gawain   welcomes her worthily.
Promptly the lady   makes her reply.
By his side she seats herself   softly, heartily
Laughs, and with lovely look   these words delivers:
"If you, sir, are Gawain,   greatly I wonder   1480
That one so given   at all times to goodness
Should be not well versed   in social conventions,
Or, made once to know,   should dismiss them from mind.
You have promptly forgotten   what I in the plainest
Of talk that I knew of   yesterday taught you."
"What is that?" said the knight.   "For truly I know not;
If it be as you say,   I am surely to blame."
"Yet I taught you," quoth   the fair lady, "of kissing;
When clearly he's favored,   quickly to claim one
Becomes each knight   who practices courtesy."   1490
"Cease, dear lady,   such speech," said the strong man;
"I dare not for fear   of refusal do that.
'T would be wrong to proffer   and then be repulsed."
"In faith, you may not   be refused," said the fair one;
"Sir, if you pleased,   you have strength to compel it,
Should one be so rude   as to wish to deny you."
"By God, yes," said Gawain,   "good is your speech;
But unlucky is force   in the land I live in,
And every gift   that with good will's not given.
Your word I await   to embrace when you wish;   1500
You may start when you please,   and stop at your pleasure."
                            With grace
        The lady, bending low,

Most sweetly kissed his face.
Of joy in love and woe
They talked for a long space.

"I should like," said the lady, "from you, sir, to learn,
If I roused not your anger   by asking, the reason
Why you, who are now   so young and valiant,
So known far and wide   as knightly and courteous   1510
(And principally, picked   from all knighthood, is praised
The sport of true love   and the science of arms;
For to tell of these true   knights' toil, it is surely
The title inscribed   and the text of their deeds,
How men their lives   for their leal love adventured,
Endured for their passion   doleful days,
Then themselves with valor   avenged, and their sorrow
Cast off, and brought bliss   into bowers by their virtues),
Why you, thought the noblest   knight of your time,
Whose renown and honor   are everywhere noted,   1520
Have so let me sit   on two separate occasions
Beside you, and hear   proceed from your head
Not one word relating   to love, less or more.
You so goodly in vowing   your service and gracious
Ought gladly to give   to a young thing your guidance,
And show me some sign   of the sleights of true love.
What! know you nothing,   and have all renown?
Or else do you deem me   too dull, for your talking
                          Unfit?
             For shame! Alone I come;   1530
             To learn some sport I sit;
             My lord is far from home;
             Now, teach me by your wit."

"In good faith," said Gawain,   "God you reward;
For great is the happiness,   huge the gladness
That one so worthy   should want to come hither,
And pains for so poor a man   take, as in play
With your knight with looks   of regard; it delights me.
But to take up the task   of telling of true love,
To touch on those themes,   and on tales of arms   1540
To you who've more skill   in that art, I am certain,
By half than a hundred men   have such as I,
Or ever shall have   while here upon earth,

[194]

By my faith, 't would be, madam, a manifold folly.
Your bidding I'll do, as in duty bound,
To the height of my power, and will hold myself ever
Your ladyship's servant, so save me the Lord."
Thus the fair lady tempted and tested him often
To make the man sin— whate'er more she'd in mind;
But so fair his defence was, no fault was apparent, 1550
Nor evil on either side; each knew but joy
> On that day.
>> At last she kissed him lightly,
>> After long mirth and play,
>> And took her leave politely,
>> And went upon her way.

The man bestirs himself, springs up for mass.
Then made ready and splendidly served was their dinner;
In sport with the ladies he spent all the day.
But the lord through fields oft dashed as he followed 1560
The savage swine, that sped o'er the slopes,
And in two bit the backs of the best of his hounds
Where he stood at bay; till 'twas broken by bowmen,
Who made him, despite himself, move to the open,
The shafts flew so thick when the throng had assembled.
Yet sometimes he forced the stoutest to flinch,
Till at last too weary he was to run longer,
But came with such haste as he could to a hole
In a mound, by a rock whence the rivulet runs out.
He started to scrape the soil, backed by the slope, 1570
While froth from his mouth's ugly corners came foaming.
White were the tushes he whetted. The bold men
Who stood round grew tired of trying from far
To annoy him, but dared not for danger draw nearer.
> Before,
>> So many he did pierce
>> That all were loth a boar
>> So frenzied and so fierce
>> Should tear with tusks once more,

Till the hero himself came, spurring his horse, 1580
Saw him standing at bay, the hunters beside him.
He leaped down right lordly, leaving his courser,
Unsheathed a bright sword and strode forth stoutly,

Made haste through the ford   where that fierce one was waiting.
Aware of the hero   with weapon in hand,
So savagely, bristling   his back up, he snorted
All feared for the wight   lest the worst befall him.
Then rushed out the boar   directly upon him,
And man was mingled   with beast in the midst
Of the wildest water.   The boar had the worse,   1590
For the man aimed a blow   at the beast as he met him,
And surely with sharp blade   struck o'er his breast bone,
That smote to the hilt,   and his heart cleft asunder.
He squealing gave way,   and swift through the water
                                        Went back.
                    By a hundred hounds he's caught,
                    Who fiercely him attack;
                    To open ground he's brought,
                    And killed there by the pack.

The blast for the beast's death   was blown on sharp horns,   1600
And the lords there loudly   and clearly hallooed.
At the beast bayed the brachets,   as bid by their masters,
The chief, in that hard,   long chase, of the hunters.
Then one who was wise   in woodcraft began
To slice up this swine   in the seemliest manner.
First he hews off his head,   and sets it on high;
Then along the back roughly   rends him apart.
He hales out the bowels,   and broils them on hot coals,
With these mixed with bread,   rewarding his brachets.
Then slices the flesh   in fine, broad slabs,   1610
And pulls out the edible   entrails properly.
Whole, though, he gathers   the halves together,
And proudly upon   a stout pole he places them.
Homeward they now   with this very swine hasten,
Bearing in front   of the hero the boar's head,
Since him at the ford   by the force of his strong hand
                                        He slew.
                    It seemed long till he met
                    In hall Sir Gawain, who
                    Hastened, when called, to get   1620
                    The payment that was due.

The lord called out loudly,   merrily laughed
When Gawain he saw,   and gladsomely spoke.

The good ladies were sent for, the household assembled;
He shows them the slices of flesh, and the story
He tells of his largeness and length, and how fierce
Was the war in the woods where the wild swine had fled.
Sir Gawain commended his deeds right graciously,
Praised them as giving a proof of great prowess.
Such brawn on a beast, the bold man declared,   1630
And such sides on a swine he had ne'er before seen.
Then they handled the huge head; the courteous hero
Praised it, horror-struck, honoring his host.
Quoth the good man, "Now, Gawain, yours is this game
By our covenant, fast and firm, you know truly."
"It is so," said the knight; "and as certain and sure
All I get I'll give you again as I pledged you."
He about the neck caught, with courtesy kissed him,
And soon a second time served him the same way.
Said Gawain, "We've fairly fulfilled the agreement   1640
This evening we entered on, each to the other
                    Most true."
              "I, by Saint Giles, have met
              None," said the lord, "like you.
              Riches you soon will get,
              If you such business do."

And then the tables they raised upon trestles,
And laid on them cloths; the light leaped up clearly
Along by the walls, where the waxen torches
Were set by the henchmen who served in the hall.   1650
A great sound of sport and merriment sprang up
Close by the fire, and on frequent occasions
At supper and afterward, many a splendid song,
Conduits of Christmas, new carols, all kinds
Of mannerly mirth that a man may tell of.
Our seemly knight ever sat at the side
Of the lady, who made so agreeable her manner,
With sly, secret glances to glad him, so stalwart,
That greatly astonished was Gawain, and wroth
With himself; he in courtesy could not refuse her,   1660
But acted becomingly, courtly, whatever
The end, good or bad, of his action might be.
                    When quite
              Done was their play at last,

The host called to the knight,
And to his room they passed
To where the fire burned bright.

The men there make merry   and drink, and once more
The same pact for New Year's   Eve is proposed;
But the knight craved permission   to mount on the morrow: 1670
The appointment approached   where he had to appear.
But the lord him persuaded   to stay and linger,
And said, "On my word   as a knight I assure you
You'll get to the Green Chapel,   Gawain, on New Year's,
And far before prime,   to finish your business.
Remain in your room then,   and take your rest.
I shall hunt in the wood   and exchange with you winnings,
As bound by our bargain,   when back I return,
For twice I've found you   were faithful when tried:
In the morning 'best   be the third time,' remember.   1680
Let's be mindful of mirth   while we may, and make merry,
For care when one wants it   is quickly encountered."
At once this was granted,   and Gawain is stayed;
Drink blithely was brought him;   to bed they were lighted.

                    The guest
          In quiet and comfort spent
          The night, and took his rest.
          On his affairs intent,
          The host was early dressed.

After mass a morsel   he took with his men.   1690
The morning was merry;   his mount he demanded.
The knights who'd ride   in his train were in readiness,
Dressed and horsed   at the door of the hall.
Wondrous fair were the fields,   for the frost was clinging;
Bright red in the cloud-rack   rises the sun,
And full clear sails close   past the clouds in the sky.
The hunters unleashed   all the hounds by a woodside:
The rocks with the blast   of their bugles were ringing.
Some dogs there fall   on the scent where the fox is,
And trail oft a traitoress   using her tricks.   1700
A hound gives tongue at it;   huntsmen call to him;
Hastens the pack   to the hound sniffing hard,
And right on his track   run off in a rabble,

He scampering before them. They started the fox soon;
When finally they saw him, they followed fast,
Denouncing him clearly with clamorous anger.
Through many a dense grove he dodges and twists,
Doubling back and harkening at hedges right often;
At last by a little ditch leaps o'er a thorn-hedge,   1710
Steals out stealthily, skirting a thicket,
In thought from the wood to escape by his wiles
From the hounds; then, unknowing, drew near to a hunting-stand.
There hurled themselves, three at once, on him strong hounds,
                              All gray.
                    With quick swerve he doth start
                    Afresh without dismay.
                    With great grief in his heart
                    To the wood he goes away.

Huge was the joy then to hark to the hounds.
When the pack all met him, mingled together,   1720
Such curses they heaped on his head at the sight
That the clustering cliffs seemed to clatter down round them
In heaps. The men, when they met him, hailed him,
And loudly with chiding speeches hallooed him;
Threats were oft thrown at him, thief he was called;
At his tail were the greyhounds, that tarry he might not.
They rushed at him oft when he raced for the open,
And ran to the wood again, reynard the wily.
Thus he led them, all muddied, the lord and his men,
In this manner along through the hills until midday.   1730
At home, the noble knight wholesomely slept
In the cold of the morn within comely curtains.
But the lady, for love, did not let herself sleep,
Or fail in the purpose fixed in her heart;
But quickly she roused herself, came there quickly,
Arrayed in a gay robe that reached to the ground,
The skins of the splendid fur skillfully trimmed close.
On her head no colors save jewels, well-cut,
That were twined in her hair-fret in clusters of twenty.
Her fair face was completely exposed, and her throat;   1740
In front her breast too was bare, and her back.
She comes through the chamber-door, closes it after her,
Swings wide a window, speaks to the wight,

And rallies him soon   in speech full of sport
                  And good cheer.
        "Ah! man, how can you sleep?
        The morning is so clear."
        He was in sorrow deep,
        Yet her he then did hear.

In a dream muttered Gawain,   deep in its gloom,   1750
Like a man by a throng   of sad thoughts sorely moved
Of how fate was to deal   out his destiny to him
That morn, when he met   the man at the Green Chapel,
Bound to abide   his blow, unresisting.
But as soon as that comely one   came to his senses,
Started from slumber   and speedily answered,
The lovely lady came near,   sweetly laughing,
Bent down o'er his fair face   and daintily kissed him.
And well, in a worthy   manner, he welcomed her.
Seeing her glorious,   gaily attired,   1760
Without fault in her features,   most fine in her color,
Deep joy came welling up,   warming his heart.
With sweet, gentle smiling   they straightway grew merry;
So passed naught between them   but pleasure, joy,
                  And delight.
        Goodly was their debate,
        Nor was their gladness slight.
        Their peril had been great
        Had Mary quit her knight.

For that noble princess   pressed him so closely,   1770
Brought him so near   the last bound, that her love
He was forced to accept,   or, offending, refuse her:
Concerned for his courtesy   not to prove caitiff,
And more for his ruin   if wrong he committed,
Betraying the hero,   the head of that house.
"God forbid," said the knight;   "that never shall be";
And lovingly laughing   a little, he parried
The words of fondness   that fell from her mouth.
She said to him, "Sir,   you are surely to blame
If you love not the lady   beside whom you're lying,   1780
Of all the world's women   most wounded in heart,
Unless you've one dearer,   a lover you like more,
Your faith to her plighted,   so firmly made fast

You desire not to loosen it— so I believe.
Now tell me truly   I pray you; the truth,
By all of the loves   that in life are, conceal not
                    Through guile."
          The knight said, "By Saint John,"
          And pleasantly to smile
          Began, "In faith I've none,   1790
          Nor will have for a while."

"Such words," said the lady,   "the worst are of all;
But in sooth I am answered,   and sad it seems to me.
Kiss me now kindly,   and quickly I'll go;
I on earth may but mourn,   as a much loving mortal."
Sighing she stoops down,   and kisses him seemly;
Then starting away from him,   says as she stands,
"Now, my dear, at parting,   do me this pleasure:
Give me some gift,   thy glove if it might be,
To bring you to mind, sir,   my mourning to lessen."   1800
"On my word," quoth the hero,   "I would that I had here,
For thy sake, the thing   that I think the dearest
I own, for in sooth   you've deserved very often
A greater reward   than one I could give.
But a pledge of love   would profit but little;
'T would help not your honor   to have at this time
For a keepsake a glove,   as a gift of Gawain.
I've come on a mission   to countries most strange;
I've no servants with splendid things   filling their sacks:
That displeases me, lady,   for love's sake, at present;   1810
Yet each man without murmur   must do what he may
                    Nor repine."
          "Nay, lord of honors high,
          Though I have naught of thine,"
          Quoth the lovely lady, "I
          Shall give you gift of mine."

She offered a rich ring,   wrought in red gold,
With a blazing stone   that stood out above it,
And shot forth brilliant rays   bright as the sun;
Wit you well that wealth   right huge it was worth.   1820
But promptly the hero   replied, refusing it,
"Madam, I care not   for gifts now to keep;
I have none to tender   and naught will I take."
          [201]

Thus he ever declined   her offer right earnest,
And swore on his word   that he would not accept it;
And, sad he declined,   she thereupon said,
"If my ring you refuse,   since it seems too rich,
If you would not so highly   to me be beholden,
My girdle, that profits you   less, I'll give you."
She swiftly removed the belt   circling her sides,   1830
Round her tunic knotted,   beneath her bright mantle;
'T was fashioned of green silk,   and fair made with gold,
With gold, too, the borders   embellished and beautiful.
To Gawain she gave it,   and gaily besought him
To take it, although   he thought it but trifling.
He swore by no manner   of means he'd accept
Either gold or treasure   ere God gave him grace
To attain the adventure   he'd there undertaken.
"And, therefore, I pray,   let it prove not displeasing,
But give up your suit,   for to grant it I'll never   1840
                         Agree.
              I'm deeply in your debt
              For your kind ways to me.
              In hot and cold I yet
              Will your true servant be."

"Refuse ye this silk,"   the lady then said,
"As slight in itself?   Truly it seems so.
Lo! it is little,   and less is its worth;
But one knowing the nature   knit up within it,
Would give it a value   more great, peradventure;   1850
For no man girt   with this girdle of green,
And bearing it fairly   made fast about him,
Might ever be cut down   by any on earth,
For his life in no way   in the world could be taken."
Then mused the man,   and it came to his mind
In the peril appointed him   precious 'twould prove,
When he'd found the chapel,   to face there his fortune.
The device, might he slaying   evade, would be splendid.
Her suit then he suffered,   and let her speak;
And the belt she offered him,   earnestly urging it   1860
(And Gawain consented),   and gave it with good will,
And prayed him for her sake   ne'er to display it,
But, true, from her husband   to hide it. The hero
Agreed that no one   should know of it ever.

Then he
Thanked her with all his might
Of heart and thought; and she
By then to this stout knight
Had given kisses three.

Then the lady departs,   there leaving the lord,   1870
For more pleasure she could not   procure from that prince.
When she's gone, then quickly   Sir Gawain clothes himself,
Rises and dresses   in noble array,
Lays by the love-lace   the lady had left him,
Faithfully hides it   where later he'd find it.
At once then went   on his way to the chapel,
Approached in private   a priest, and prayed him
To make his life purer,   more plainly him teach
How his soul, when he had   to go hence, should be saved.
He declared his faults,   confessing them fully,   1880
The more and the less,   and mercy besought,
And then of the priest   implored absolution.
He surely absolved him,   and made him as spotless,
Indeed, as if doomsday   were due on the morrow.
Then among the fair ladies   he made more merry
With lovely caroles,   all kinds of delights,
That day than before,   until darkness fell.

All there
Were treated courteously,
"And never," they declare,   1890
"Has Gawain shown such glee
Since hither he did fare."

In that nook where his lot   may be love let him linger!
The lord's in the meadow still,   leading his men.
He has slain this fox   that he followed so long;
As he vaulted a hedge   to get view of the villain,
Hearing the hounds   that hastened hard after him,
Reynard from out   a rough thicket came running,
And right at his heels   in a rush all the rabble.
He, seeing that wild thing,   wary, awaits him,   1900
Unsheaths his bright brand   and strikes at the beast.
And he swerved from its sharpness   and back would have started;
A hound, ere he could,   came hurrying up to him;
All of them fell on him   fast by the horse's feet,

Worried that sly one   with wrathful sound.
And quickly the lord   alights, and catches him,
Takes him in haste   from the teeth of the hounds,
And over his head holds him   high, loudly shouting,
Where brachets, many   and fierce, at him barked.
Thither huntsmen made haste   with many a horn,   1910
The recall, till they saw him,   sounding right clearly.
As soon as his splendid   troop had assembled,
All bearing a bugle   blew them together,
The others having   no horns all hallooed.
'T was the merriest baying   that man ever heard
That was raised for the soul   of reynard with sounding
                                                Din.
                    They fondle each dog's head
                    Who his reward did win.
                    Then take they reynard dead   1920
                    And strip him of his skin.

And now, since near   was the night, they turned homeward,
Strongly and sturdily   sounding their horns.
At last at his loved home   the lord alighted,
A fire on the hearth found,   the hero beside it,
Sir Gawain the good,   who glad was withal,
For he had 'mong the ladies   in love much delight.
A blue robe that fell   to the floor he was wearing;
His surcoat, that softly   was furred, well beseemed him;
A hood of the same hue   hung on his shoulders,   1930
And both were bordered   with white all about.
He, mid-most, met   the good man in the hall,
And greeted him gladly,   graciously saying:
"Now shall I first   fulfil our agreement
We struck to good purpose,   when drink was not spared."
Then Gawain embraced him,   gave him three kisses,
The sweetest and soundest   a man could bestow.
"By Christ, you'd great happiness," quoth then the host,
"In getting these wares,   if good were your bargains."
"Take no care for the cost,"   the other said quickly,   1940
"Since plainly the debt   that is due I have paid."
Said the other, "By Mary,   mine's of less worth.
The whole of the day   I have hunted, and gotten
The skin of this fox—   the fiend take its foulness!—
Right poor to pay   for things of such price

[204]

As you've pressed on me here   so heartily, kisses
                  So good."
          "Say no more," Gawain saith;
          "I thank you, by the rood!"
          How the fox met his death   1950
          He told him as they stood.

With mirth and minstrelsy,   meat at their pleasure
They made as merry   as any men might
(With ladies' laughter,   and launching of jests
Right glad were they both,   the good man and Gawain)
Unless they had doted   or else had been drunken.
Both the man and the company   make many jokes,
Till the time is come   when the two must be parted,
When finally the knights   are forced to go bedward.
And first of the lord   his respectful leave   1960
This goodly man took,   and graciously thanked him:
"May God you reward   for the welcome you gave me
This high feast, the splendid   sojourn I've had here.
I give you myself,   if you'd like it, to serve you.
I must, as you know,   on the morrow move on;
Give me some one to show me   the path, as you said,
To the Green Chapel, there,   as God will allow me,
On New Year the fate   that is fixed to perform."
"With a good will, indeed,"   said the good man; "whatever
I promised to do   I deem myself ready."   1970
He a servant assigns   on his way to set him,
To take him by hills   that no trouble he'd have,
And through grove and wood   by the way most direct
                  Might repair.
          The lord he thanked again
          For the honor done him there.
          The knight his farewell then
          Took of those ladies fair.

To them with sorrow   and kissing he spoke,
And besought them his thanks   most sincere to accept;   1980
And they, replying,   promptly returned them,
With sighings full sore   to the Savior commended him.
Then he with courtesy   quitted the company,
Giving each man   that he met his thanks
For kindness, for trouble   he'd taken, for care

Whereby each had sought   to serve him right eagerly.
Pained was each person   to part with him then,
As if long they in honor   had lived with that noble.
With people and lights   he was led to his chamber,
To bed gaily brought there   to be at his rest;   1990
Yet I dare not say   whether soundly he slept,
For much, if he would,   on the morn to remember
                                        Had he.
                        Let him lie stilly there
                        Near what he sought to see.
                        What happened I'll declare,
                        If you will silent be.

IV

The New Year draws near,   and the nighttime now passes;
The day, as the Lord bids,   drives away darkness.
Outside, there sprang up   wild storms in the world;   2000
The clouds cast keenly   the cold to the earth
With enough of the north sting   to trouble the naked;
Down shivered the snow,   nipping sharply the wild beasts;
The wind from the heights,   shrilly howling, came rushing,
And heaped up each dale   full of drifts right huge.
Full well the man listened   who lay in his bed.
Though he shut tight his lids,   he slept but a little;
He knew by each cock   that crowed 'twas the tryst time,
And swiftly ere dawn   of the day he arose,
For there shone then the light   of a lamp in his room;   2010
To his chamberlain called,   who answered him quickly,
And bade him his saddle   to bring and his mailshirt.
The other man roused up   and fetched him his raiment,
Arrayed then that knight   in a fashion right noble.
First he clad him in clothes   to ward off the cold,
Then his other equipment,   carefully kept:
His pieces of plate armor,   polished right cleanly,
The rings of his rich mail   burnished from rust.
All was fresh as at first;   he was fain to give thanks
                                        To the men.   2020
                        He had on every piece
                        Full brightly burnished then.
                        He, gayest from here to Greece,
                        Ordered his steed again.
                        [206]

He garbed himself there   in the loveliest garments
(His coat had its blazon   of beautiful needlework
Stitched upon velvet   for show, its rich stones
Set about it and studded,   its seams all embroidered,
Its lovely fur   in the fairest of linings),
Yet he left not the lace,   the gift of the lady: 2030
That, Gawain did not,   for his own sake, forget.
When the brand on his rounded   thighs he had belted,
He twisted his love-token   two times about him.
That lord round his waist   with delight quickly wound
The girdle of green silk,   that seemed very gay
Upon royal red cloth   that was rich to behold.
But Gawain the girdle   wore not for its great price,
Or pride in its pendants   although they were polished,
Though glittering gold   there gleamed on the ends,
But himself to save   when he needs must suffer   2040
The death, nor could stroke then   of sword or of knife
                              Him defend.
                    Then was the bold man dressed;
                    Quickly his way did wend;
                    To all the court expressed
                    His great thanks without end.

Then was Gringolet ready   that great was and huge,
Who had safely, as seemed to him   pleasant, been stabled;
That proud horse pranced,   in the pink of condition.
The lord then comes to him,   looks at his coat,   2050
And soberly says,   and swears on his word,
"In this castle's a company   mindful of courtesy,
Led by this hero.   Delight may they have;
And may love the dear lady   betide all her lifetime.
If they for charity   cherish a guest,
And gives so great welcome,   may God reward them,
Who rules the heaven   on high, and the rest of you.
Might I for long   live my life on the earth,
Some repayment with pleasure   I'd make, if 't were possible."
He steps in the stirrup,   strides into the saddle,   2060
Receives on his shoulder   the shield his man brings him,
And spurs into Gringolet   strikes with his gilt heels;
Who leaps on the stones   and lingers no longer
                              To prance.
                    The knight on his horse sits,
                    [207]

Who bears his spear and lance,
The house to Christ commits,
And wishes it good chance.

Then down the drawbridge   they dropped, the broad gates
Unbarred, and on both sides   bore them wide open.   2070
He blessed them quickly,   and crossed o'er the planks there
(He praises the porter,   who knelt by the prince
Begging God to save Gawain,   and gave him goodday),
And went on his way   with but one man attended
To show him the turns   to that sorrowful spot
Where he must to that onerous   onset submit.
By hillsides where branches   were bare they both journeyed;
They climbed over cliffs   where the cold was clinging.
The clouds hung aloft,   but 'twas lowering beneath them.
On the moor dripped the mist,   on the mountains melted;   2080
Each hill had a hat,   a mist-cloak right huge.
The brooks foamed and bubbled   on hillsides about them,
And brightly broke   on their banks as they rushed down.
Full wandering the way was   they went through the wood,
Until soon it was time   for the sun to be springing.
                              Then they
            Were on a hill full high;
            White snow beside them lay.
            The servant who rode nigh
            Then bade his master stay.   2090

"I have led you hither,   my lord, at this time,
And not far are you now   from that famous place
You have sought for, and asked   so especially after.
Yet, sir, to you surely   I'll say, since I know you,
A man in this world   whom I love right well,
If you'd follow my judgment,   the better you'd fare.
You make haste to a place   that is held full of peril;
One dwells, the worst   in the world, in that waste,
For he's strong and stern,   and takes pleasure in striking.
No man on the earth   can equal his might;   2100
He is bigger in body   than four of the best men
In Arthur's own household,   Hestor or others.
And thus he brings it   about at the chapel:
That place no one passes   so proud in his arms
That he smites him not dead   with a stroke of his hand.
                    [208]

He's a man most immoderate,   showing no mercy;
Be it chaplain or churl   that rides by the chapel,
Monk or priest,   any manner of man,
Him to slay seems as sweet   as to still live himself.
So I say, as sure   as you sit in your saddle   2110
You're killed, should the knight   so choose, if you come here;
That take as the truth,   though you twenty lives had
                              To spend.
               He's lived in this place long
               In battles without end.
               Against his strokes right strong
               You cannot you defend.

"So let him alone,   good Sir Gawain, and leave
By a different road,   for God's sake, and ride
To some other country   where Christ may reward you.   2120
And homeward again   I will hie me, and promise
To swear by the Lord   and all his good saints
(So help me the oaths   on God's halidom sworn)
That I'll guard well your secret,   and give out no story
You hastened to flee   any hero I've heard of."
"Thank you," said Gawain,   and grudgingly added,
"Good fortune go with you   for wishing me well.
And truly I think   you'd not tell; yet though never
So surely you hid it,   if hence I should hasten,
Fearful, to fly   in the fashion you tell of,   2130
A coward I'd prove,   and could not be pardoned.
The chapel I'll find   whatsoever befalls,
And talk with that wight   the way that I want to,
Let weal or woe follow   as fate may wish.
                    Though the knave,
               Hard to subdue and fell,
               Should stand there with a stave,
               Yet still the Lord knows well
               His servants how to save."

Quoth the man, "By Mary,   you've said now this much: 2140
That you wish to bring down   your own doom on your head.
Since you'd lose your life,   I will stay you no longer.
Put your helm on your head,   take your spear in your hand,
And ride down this road   by the side of that rock
Till it brings you down   to the dale's rugged bottom;

Then look at the glade   on the left hand a little:
You'll see in the valley   that self-same chapel,
And near it the great-limbed   knight who is guarding it.
Gawain the noble,   farewell now, in God's name!
I would not go with thee   for all the world's wealth,   2150
Nor in fellowship ride   one more foot through the forest."
The man in the trees there   then turns his bridle,
As hard as he can   hits his horse with his heels,
And across the fields gallops,   there leaving Sir Gawain
                                                Alone.
            "By God," the knight said, "now
            I'll neither weep nor groan.
            Unto God's will I bow,
            And make myself His own."

He strikes spurs into Gringolet,   starts on the path;   2160
By a bank at the side   of a small wood he pushes in,
Rides down the rugged slope   right to the dale.
Then about him he looks,   and the land seems wild,
And nowhere he sees   any sign of a shelter,
But slopes on each side of him,   high and steep,
And rocks, gnarled and rough,   and stones right rugged.
The clouds there seemed to him   scraped by the crags.
Then he halted and held back   his horse at that time,
And spied on all sides   in search of the chapel;
Such nowhere he saw,   but soon, what seemed strange,   2170
In the midst of a glade   a mound, as it might be,
A smooth, swelling knoll   by the side of the water,
The falls of a rivulet   running close by;
In its banks the brook bubbled   as though it were boiling.
The knight urged on Gringolet,   came to the glade,
There leaped down lightly   and tied to the limb
Of a tree, right rugged,   the reins of his noble steed,
Went to the mound,   and walked all about it,
Debating what manner   of thing it might be:
On the end and on each side   an opening; everywhere   2180
Over it grass   was growing in patches,
All hollow inside,   it seemed an old cave
Or a crag's old cleft: which, he could not decide.
                                Said the knight,
            "Is this the chapel here?
            Alas, dear Lord! here might
                    [210]

The fiend, when midnight's near,
His matin prayers recite.

"Of a truth," said Gawain,   "the glade here is gloomy;
The Green Chapel's ugly,   with herbs overgrown.   2190
It greatly becomes here   that hero, green-clad,
To perform in the devil's   own fashion his worship.
I feel in my five senses   this is the fiend
Who has made me come   to this meeting to kill me.
Destruction fall   on this church of ill-fortune!
The cursedest chapel   that ever I came to!"
With helm on his head   and lance in his hand
He went right to the rock   of that rugged abode.
From that high hill he heard,   from a hard rock over
The stream, on the hillside,   a sound wondrous loud.   2200
Lo! it clattered on cliffs   fit to cleave them, as though
A scythe on a grindstone   some one were grinding.
It whirred, lo! and whizzed   like a water-mill's wheel;
Lo! it ground and it grated,   grievous to hear.
"By God, this thing,   as I think," then said Gawain,
"Is done now for me,   since my due turn to meet it
                        Is near.
        God's will be done! 'Ah woe!'
        No whit doth aid me here.
        Though I my life forego   2210
        No sound shall make me fear."

And then the man there   commenced to call loudly,
"Who here is the master,   with me to hold tryst?
For Gawain the good   now is going right near.
He who craves aught of me   let him come hither quickly;
'T is now or never;   he needs to make haste."
Said somebody, "Stop,"   from the slope up above him,
"And promptly you'll get   what I promised to give you."
Yet he kept up the whirring noise   quickly a while,
Turned to finish his sharpening   before he'd descend.   2220
Then he came by a crag,   from a cavern emerging,
Whirled out of a den   with a dreadful weapon,
A new Danish axe   to answer the blow with:
Its blade right heavy,   curved back to the handle,
Sharp filed with the filing tool,   four feet in length,
'Twas no less, by the reach   of that lace gleaming brightly.

The fellow in green   was garbed as at first,
Both his face and his legs,   his locks and his beard,
Save that fast o'er the earth   on his feet he went fairly,
The shaft on the stone set,   and stalked on beside it.   2230
On reaching the water,   he would not wade it;
On his axe he hopped over,   and hastily strode,
Very fierce, through the broad field   filled all about him
                                   With snow.
                    Sir Gawain met the man,
                    And bowed by no means low,
                    Who said, "Good sir, men can
                    Trust you to tryst to go."

Said the green man, "Gawain,   may God you guard!
You are welcome indeed,   sir knight, at my dwelling.   2240
Your travel you've timed   as a true man should,
And you know the compact   we came to between us;
A twelvemonth ago   you took what chance gave,
And I promptly at New Year   was pledged to repay you.
In truth, we are down   in this dale all alone;
Though we fight as we please,   here there's no one to part us.
Put your helm from your head,   and have here your payment;
Debate no further   than I did before,
When you slashed off my head   with a single stroke."
"Nay," quoth Gawain, "by God,   who gave me my spirit,   2250
I'll harbor no grudge   whatever harm happens.
Exceed not one stroke   and still I shall stand;
You may do as you please,   I'll in no way oppose
                                   The blow."
                    He left the flesh all bare,
                    Bending his neck down low
                    As if he feared naught there,
                    For fear he would not show.

Then the man in green raiment   quickly made ready,
Uplifted his grim tool   Sir Gawain to smite;   2260
With the whole of his strength   he heaved it on high,
As threateningly swung it   as though he would slay him.
Had it fallen again   with the force he intended
That lord, ever-brave,   from the blow had been lifeless.
But Gawain a side glance   gave at the weapon

As down it came gliding   to do him to death;
With his shoulders shrank   from the sharp iron a little.
The other with sudden jerk   stayed the bright axe,
And reproved then that prince   with proud words in plenty:
"Not Gawain thou art   who so good is considered,   2270
Ne'er daunted by host   in hill or in dale;
Now in fear, ere thou feelest   a hurt, thou art flinching;
Such cowardice never   I knew of that knight.
When you swung at me, sir,   I fled not nor started;
No cavil I offered   in King Arthur's castle.
My head at my feet fell,   yet never I flinched,
And thy heart is afraid   ere a hurt thou feelest,
And therefore thy better   I'm bound to be thought
                    On that score."
          "I shrank once," Gawain said,   2280
          "And I will shrink no more;
          Yet cannot I my head,
          If it fall down, restore.

"But make ready, sir, quickly,   and come to the point;
My destiny deal me,   and do it forthwith;
For a stroke I will suffer,   and start no further
Till hit with thy weapon;   have here my pledged word."
Quoth the other, heaving it   high, "Have at thee!"
As fierce in his manner   as if he were mad,
He mightily swung   but struck not the man,   2290
Withheld on a sudden   his hand ere it hurt him.
And firmly he waited   and flinched in no member,
But stood there as still   as a stone or a stump
In rocky ground held   by a hundred roots.
Then the Green Knight again   began to speak gaily:
"It behooves me to hit,   now that whole is thy heart.
Thy high hood that Arthur   once gave you now hold back,
Take care that your neck   at this cut may recover."
And Gawain full fiercely   said in a fury,
"Come! lay on, thou dread man;   too long thou art threatening.   2300
I think that afraid   of your own self you feel."
"In sooth," said the other,   "thy speech is so savage
No more will I hinder   thy mission nor have it
                  Delayed."
          With puckered lips and brow

He stands with ready blade.
Not strange 't is hateful now
To him past hope of aid.

He lifts his axe lightly,   and lets it down deftly,
The blade's edge next   to the naked neck.   2310
Though he mightily hammered   he hurt him no more
Than to give him a slight nick   that severed the skin there.
Through fair skin the keen axe   so cut to the flesh
That shining blood shot   to the earth o'er his shoulders.
As soon as he saw   his blood gleam on the snow
He sprang forth in one leap,   for more than a spear length;
His helm fiercely caught up   and clapped on his head;
With his shoulders his fair shield   shot round in front of him,
Pulled out his bright sword,   and said in a passion
(And since he was mortal man   born of his mother   2320
The hero was never   so happy by half),
"Cease thy violence, man;   no more to me offer,
For here I've received,   unresisting, a stroke.
If a second thou strikest   I soon will requite thee,
And swiftly and fiercely,   be certain of that,
                                        Will repay.
            One stroke on me might fall
            By bargain struck that way,
            Arranged in Arthur's hall;
            Therefore, sir knight, now stay!"   2330

The man turned away,   on his weapon rested,
The shaft on the ground set,   leaned on the sharp edge,
And gazed at Sir Gawain   there in the glade;
Saw that bold man, unblenching,   standing right bravely,
Full-harnessed and gallant;   at heart he was glad.
Then gaily the Green Knight   spoke in a great voice,
And said to the man   in speech that resounded,
"Now be not so savage,   bold sir, for towards you
None here has acted   unhandsomely, save
In accord with the compact   arranged in the King's court.   2340
I promised the stroke   you've received, so hold you
Well payed. I free you   from all duties further.
If brisk I had been,   peradventure a buffet
I'd harshly have dealt   that harm would have done you.
In mirth, with a feint   I menaced you first,

With no direful wound rent you;   right was my deed,
By the bargain that bound us   both on the first night,
When, faithful and true,   you fulfilled our agreement,
And gave me your gain   as a good man ought to.
The second I struck at you,   sir, for the morning   2350
You kissed my fair wife   and the kisses accorded me.
Two mere feints for both times   I made at you, man,
Without woe.
True men restore by right,
One fears no danger so;
You failed the third time, knight,
And therefore took that blow.

" 'Tis my garment you're wearing,   that woven girdle,
Bestowed by my wife,   as in truth I know well.
I know also your kisses   and all of your acts   2360
And my wife's advances;   myself, I devised them.
I sent her to try you,   and truly you seem
The most faultless of men   that e'er fared on his feet.
As a pearl compared   to white peas is more precious,
So next to the other   gay knights is Sir Gawain.
But a little you lacked,   and loyalty wanted,
Yet truly 't was not   for intrigue or for wooing,
But love of your life;   the less do I blame you."
Sir Gawain stood   in a study a great while,
So sunk in disgrace   that in spirit he groaned;   2370
To his face all the blood   in his body was flowing;
For shame, as the other   was talking, he shrank.
And these were the first words   that fell from his lips:
"Be cowardice cursed,   and coveting! In you
Are vice and villainy,   virtue destroying."
The lace he then seized,   and loosened the strands,
And fiercely the girdle   flung at the Green Knight.
"Lo! there is faith-breaking!   evil befall it.
To coveting came I,   for cowardice caused me
From fear of your stroke   to forsake in myself   2380
What belongs to a knight: munificence, loyalty.
I'm faulty and false,   who've been ever afraid
Of untruth and treachery;   sorrow betide both
And care!
Here I confess my sin;
All faulty did I fare.

[215]

> Your good will let me win,
> And then I will beware."

Then the Green Knight laughed,   and right graciously said,
"I am sure that the harm   is healed that I suffered.   2390
So clean you're confessed,   so cleared of your faults,
Having had the point   of my weapon's plain penance,
I hold you now purged   of offence, and as perfectly
Spotless as though   you'd ne'er sinned in your life.
And I give to you, sir,   the golden-hemmed girdle,
As green as my gown.   Sir Gawain, when going
Forth on your way   among famous princes,
Think still of our strife   and this token right splendid,
'Mid chivalrous knights,   of the chapel's adventure.
This New Year you'll come   to my castle again,   2400
And the rest of this feast   in revel most pleasant
> > > Will go."
> > Then pressed him hard the lord:
> > "My wife and you, I know
> > We surely will accord,
> > Who was your bitter foe."

"No indeed," quoth the hero,   his helm seized and doffed it
Graciously, thanking   the Green Knight; "I've stayed
Long enough. May good fortune   befall you; may He
Who all fame doth confer   give it fully to you, sir.   2410
To your lady, gracious   and lovely, commend me,
To her and that other,   my honored ladies,
That so with their sleights   deceived their knight subtly.
But no marvel it is   for a fool to act madly,
Through woman's wiles   to be brought to woe.
So for certain was Adam   deceived by some woman,
By several Solomon,   Samson besides;
Delilah dealt him   his doom; and David
Was duped by Bath-sheba,   enduring much sorrow.
Since these were grieved by their guile,   't would be great gain   2420
To love them yet never   believe them, if knights could.
For formerly these   were most noble and fortunate,
More than all others   who lived on the earth;
> > > And these few
> > By women's wiles were caught
> > With whom they had to do.

Though I'm beguiled, I ought
To be excused now too.

"But your girdle," said Gawain,   "may God you reward!
With a good will I'll use it,   yet not for the gold,   2430
The sash or the silk,   or the sweeping pendants,
Or fame, or its workmanship   wondrous, or cost,
But in sign of my sin   I shall see it oft.
When in glory I move,   with remorse I'll remember
The frailty and fault   of the stubborn flesh,
How soon 't is infected   with stains of defilement;
And thus when I'm proud   of my prowess in arms,
The sight of this sash   shall humble my spirit.
But one thing I pray,   if it prove not displeasing;
Because you are lord   of the land where I stayed   2440
In your house with great worship   (may He now reward you
Who sitteth on high   and upholdeth the heavens),
What name do you bear?   No more would I know."
And then "That truly   I'll tell," said the other;
"Bercilak de Hautdesert   here am I called.
Through her might who lives with me,   Morgan le Fay,
Well-versed in the crafts   and cunning of magic
(Many of Merlin's   arts she has mastered,
For long since she dealt   in the dalliance of love
With him whom your heroes   at home know, that sage   2450
                                Without blame.
                    'Morgan the goddess,' so
                    She's rightly known by name.
                    No one so proud doth go
                    That him she cannot tame),

"I was sent in this way   to your splendid hall
To make trial of your pride,   and to see if the people's
Tales were true   of the Table's great glory.
This wonder she sent   to unsettle your wits,
And to daunt so the Queen   as to cause her to die   2460
From fear at the sight   of that phantom speaker
Holding his head in his hand   at the high table.
Lives she at home there,   that ancient lady;
She's even thine aunt,   King Arthur's half-sister,
Tyntagel's duchess's   daughter, whom Uther
Made later the mother   of mighty Lord Arthur.

I beg thee, sir, therefore,   come back to thine aunt;
In my castle make merry.   My company love thee,
And I, sir, wish thee   as well, on my word,
As any on earth   for thy high sense of honor."   2470
He said to him, nay,   this he'd never consent to.
The men kiss, embrace,   and each other commend
To the Prince of Paradise;   there they part
                    In the cold.
      Gawain on his fair horse
      To Arthur hastens bold;
      The bright Green Knight his course
      Doth at his pleasure hold.

Through the wood now goes   Sir Gawain by wild ways
On Gringolet, given   by God's grace his life.   2480
Oft in houses, and oft   in the open he lodged,
Met many adventures,   won many a victory:
These I intend not   to tell in this tale.
Now whole was the hurt   he had in his neck,
And about it the glimmering   belt he was bearing,
Bound to his side   like a baldric obliquely,
Tied under his left arm,   that lace, with a knot
As a sign that with stain   of sin he'd been found.
And thus to the court   he comes all securely.
Delight in that dwelling   arose when its lord knew   2490
That Gawain had come;   a good thing he thought it.
The King kissed the lord,   and the Queen did likewise,
And next many knights   drew near him to greet him
And ask how he'd fared;   and he wondrously answerc
Confessed all the hardships   that him had befallen,
The happenings at chapel,   the hero's behavior,
The lady's love,   and lastly the lace.
He showed them the nick   in his neck all naked
The blow that the Green Knight   gave for deceit
                    Him to blame.   2500
      In torment this he owned;
      Blood in his face did flame;
      With wrath and grief he groaned,
      When showing it with shame.

Laying hold of the lace,   quoth the hero, "Lo! lord!
The band of this fault   I bear on my neck;

[218]

And this is the scathe   and damage I've suffered,
For cowardice caught there,   and coveting also,
The badge of untruth   in which I was taken.
And this for as long   as I live I must wear,   2510
For his fault none may hide   without meeting misfortune,
For once it is fixed,   it can ne'er be unfastened."
To the knight then the King   gave comfort; the court too
Laughed greatly, and made   this gracious agreement:
That ladies and lords   to the Table belonging,
All of the brotherhood,   baldrics should bear
Obliquely about them,   bands of bright green,
Thus following suit   for the sake of the hero.
For the Round Table's glory   was granted that lace,
And he held himself honored   who had it thereafter,   2520
As told in the book,   the best of romances.
In the days of King Arthur   this deed was done
Whereof witness is borne   by Brutus's book.
Since Brutus, that bold man,   first came here to Britain,
When ceased, indeed,   had the siege and assault
                              At Troy's wall,
          Full many feats ere now
          Like this one did befall.
          May He with thorn-crowned brow
          To His bliss bring us all. Amen.   2530

THEODORE HOWARD BANKS, JR.

The Pearl [1]

Pearl that the Prince full well might
    prize,
So surely set in shining gold!
No pearl of Orient with her vies;
To prove her peerless I make bold:
So round, so radiant to mine eyes,
So smooth she seemed, so small to
    hold,
Among all jewels judges wise
Would count her best an hundred
    fold.
Alas! I lost my pearl of old!
I pine with heart-pain unforgot;   10
Down through my arbour grass it
    rolled,
My own pearl, precious, without spot.

Since in that spot it slipped from me
I wait, and wish, and oft complain;
Once it would bid my sorrow flee,
And my fair fortune turn again;
It wounds my heart now ceaselessly,
And burns my breast with bitter pain.
Yet never so sweet a song may be
As, this still hour, steals through my
    brain,   20
While verily I muse in vain
How clay should her bright beauty
    clot;
O Earth! a brave gem thou dost stain,
My own pearl, precious, without spot!

Needs must that spot with spices
    spread,
Where such wealth falleth to decay;

Fair flowers, golden and blue and red,
Shine in the sunlight day by day;
Nor flower nor fruit have witheréd
On turf wherein such treasure lay;   30
The blade grows where the grain lies
    dead,
Else were no ripe wheat stored away;
Of good come good things, so we say;
Then surely such seed faileth not,
But spices spring in sweet array
From my pearl, precious, without spot.

Once, to that spot of which I rime,
I entered, in the arbour green,
In August, the high summer-time
When corn is cut with sickles keen;   40
Upon the mound where my pearl fell,
Tall, shadowing herbs grew bright and
    sheen,
Gilliflower, ginger and gromwell,
With peonies powdered all between.
As it was lovely to be seen,
So sweet the fragrance there, I wot,
Worthy her dwelling who hath been
My own pearl, precious, without spot.

Upon that spot my hands I crossed
In prayer, for cold at my heart
    caught,   50
And sudden sorrow surged and tossed,
Though reason reconcilement sought.
I mourned my pearl, dear beyond cost,
And strange fears with my fancy
    fought;
My will in wretchedness was lost,

[1] From Sophie Jewett, *The Pearl* (Thomas Y. Crowell, New York, 1908). Reprinted by permission of the publisher.

And yet Christ comforted my thought.
Such odours to my sense were brought,
I fell upon that flowery plot,
Sleeping,—a sleep with dreams in-
   wrought   59
Of my pearl, precious, without spot.

From the spot my spirit springs into
   space,
The while my body sleeping lies;
My ghost is gone in God's good grace,
Adventuring mid mysteries;
I know not what might be the place,
But I looked where tall cliffs cleave the
   skies,
Toward a forest I turned my face,
Where ranks of radiant rocks arise.
A man might scarce believe his eyes,
Such gleaming glory was from them
   sent;   70
No woven web may men devise
Of half such wondrous beauties blent.

In beauty shone each fair hillside
With crystal cliffs in shining row,
While bright woods everywhere
   abide,
Their boles as blue as indigo;
Like silver clear the leaves spread
   wide,
That on each spray thick-quivering
   grow;
If a flash of light across them glide
With shimmering sheen they gleam
   and glow;   80
The gravel on the ground below
Seemed precious pearls of Orient;
The sunbeams did but darkling show
So gloriously those beauties blent.

The beauty of the hills so fair
Made me forget my sufferings;
I breathed fruit fragrance fine and
   rare,
As if I fed on unseen things;

Brave birds fly through the woodland
   there,
Of flaming hues, and each one
   sings;   90
With their mad mirth may not com-
   pare
Cithern nor gayest citole-strings;
For when those bright birds beat their
   wings,
They sing together, all content;
Keen joy to any man it brings
To hear and see such beauties blent.

So beautiful was all the wood
Where, guided forth by Chance, I
   strayed,
There is no tongue that fully could
Describe it, though all men es-
   sayed.   100
Onward I walked in merriest mood
Nor any highest hill delayed
My feet. Far through the forest stood
The plain with fairest trees arrayed,
Hedges and slopes and rivers wide,
Like gold thread their banks' garnish-
   ment;
And when I won the waterside,
Dear Lord! what wondrous beauties
   blent!

The beauties of that stream were steep,
All-radiant banks of beryl bright; 110
Sweet-sighing did the water sweep,
With murmuring music running light;
Within its bed fair stones lay deep;
As if through glass they glowed, as
   white
As streaming stars when tired men
   sleep
Shine in the sky on a winter night.
Pure emerald even the pebbles seemed,
Sapphire, or other gems that lent
Luster, till all the water gleamed
With the glory of such beauties
   blent.   120

For the beauteousness of downs and
    dales,
Of wood and water and proud plains,
My joy springs up and my grief quails,
My anguish ends, and all my pains.
A swift stream down the valley hales
My feet along. Bliss brims my brains;
The farther I follow those watery
    vales,
The stronger joy my heart constrains.
While Fortune fares as her proud will
    deigns,
Sending solace or sending sore,   130
When a man her fickle favour gains,
He looketh to have aye more and
    more.

There was more of marvel and of
    grace
Than I could tell, howe'er I tried;
The human heart that could embrace
A tenth part were well satisfied;
For Paradise, the very place,
Must be upon that farther side;
The water by a narrow space
Pleasance from pleasance did divide.
Beyond, on some slope undescried 141
The City stood, I thought, wherefore
I strove to cross the river's tide,
And ever I longed, yet more and more.

More, and still more wistfully,
The banks beyond the brook I
    scanned;
If, where I stood, 'twas fair to see,
Still lovelier lay that farther land.
I sought if any ford might be
Found, up or down, by rock or sand;
But perils plainer appeared to me, 151
The farther I strode along the strand;
I thought I ought not thus to stand
Timid, with such bright bliss before;
Then a new matter came to hand
That moved my heart yet more and
    more.

Marvels more and more amaze
My mind beyond that water fair:
From a cliff of crystal, splendid rays,
Reflected, quiver in the air.   160
At the cliff's foot a vision stays
My glance, a maiden debonair,
All glimmering white before my gaze;
And I know her,—have seen her other-
    where.
Like fine gold leaf one cuts with care,
Shone the maiden on the farther shore.
Long time I looked upon her there,
And ever I knew her more and more.

As more and more I scanned her face
And form, when I had found her so,
A glory of gladness filled the place 171
Beyond all it was wont to show.
My joy would call her and give chase,
But wonder struck my courage low;
I saw her in so strange a place,
The shock turned my heart dull and
    slow.
But now she lifts that brow aglow,
Like ivory smooth, even as of yore,
It made my senses straying go,
It stung my heart aye more and
    more.   180

More than I liked did my fear rise.
Stock still I stood and dared not call;
With lips close shut and watchful
    eyes,
I stood as quiet as hawk in hall.
I thought her a spirit from the skies;
I doubted what thing might befall;
If to escape me now she tries,
How shall my voice her flight fore-
    stall?
Then graciously and gay withal,
In royal robes, so sweet, so slight, 190
She rose, so modest and so small,
That precious one in pearls bedight.

Pearl bedight full royally,
Adown the bank with merry mien,

Came the maiden, fresh as fleur-de-lys.
Her surcoat linen must have been
Shining in whitest purity,
Slashed at the sides and caught between
With the fairest pearls, it seemed to me,
That ever yet mine eyes had seen; 200
With large folds falling loose, I ween,
Arrayed with double pearls, her white
Kirtle, of the same linen sheen,
With precious pearls all round was dight.

A crown with pearls bedight, the girl
Was wearing, and no other stone;
High pinnacled of clear white pearl,
Wrought as if pearls to flowers were grown.
No band nor fillet else did furl
The long locks all about her thrown.
Her air demure as duke or earl, 211
Her hue more white than walrus-bone;
Like sheer gold thread the bright hair strown
Loose on her shoulders lying light.
Her color took a deeper tone
With bordering pearls so fair bedight.

Bedight was every hem, and bound,
At wrists, sides, and each aperture,
With pearls the whitest ever found,—
White all her brave investiture; 220
But a wondrous pearl, a flawless round,
Upon her breast was set full sure;
A man's mind it might well astound,
And all his wits to madness lure.
I thought that no tongue might endure
Fully to tell of that sweet sight,
So was it perfect, clear and pure,
That precious pearl with pearls bedight.

Bedight in pearls, lest my joy cease,
That lovely one came down the shore; 230
The gladdest man from here to Greece,
The eagerest, was I, therefore;
She was nearer kin than aunt or niece,
And thus my joy was much the more.
She spoke to me for my soul's peace,
Courtesied with her quaint woman's lore,
Caught off the shining crown she wore,
And greeted me with glance alight.
I blessed my birth; my bliss brimmed o'er
To answer her in pearls bedight. 240

"O pearl," I said, "in pearls bedight,
Art thou my pearl for which I mourn,
Lamenting all alone at night?
With hidden grief my heart is worn.
Since thou through grass didst slip from sight,
Pensive and pained, I pass forlorn,
And thou livest in a life of light,
A world where enters nor sin nor scorn.
What fate has hither my jewel borne,
And left me in earth's strife and stir? 250
Oh, sweet, since we in twain were torn,
I have been a joyless jeweler."

That Jewel then with gems besprent
Glanced up at me with eyes of grey,
Put on her pearl crown orient,
And soberly began to say:
"You tell your tale with wrong intent,
Thinking your pearl gone quite away.
Like a jewel within a coffer pent,
In this gracious garden bright and gay, 260
Your pearl may ever dwell at play,

Where sin nor mourning come to
    her;
It were a joy to thee alway
Wert thou a gentle jeweler.

"But, Jeweler, if thou dost lose
Thy joy for a gem once dear to thee,
Methinks thou dost thy mind abuse,
Bewildered by a fantasy;
Thou hast lost nothing save a rose
That flowered and failed by life's de-
    cree: 270
Because the coffer did round it close,
A precious pearl it came to be.
A thief thou hast dubbed thy destiny
That something for nothing gives thee,
    sir;
Thou blamest thy sorrow's remedy,
Thou art no grateful jeweler."

Like jewels did her story fall,
A jewel, every gentle clause;
"Truly," I said, "thou best of all!
My great distress thy voice with-
    draws.   280
I thought my pearl lost past recall,
My jewel shut within earth's jaws;
But now I shall keep festival,
And dwell with it in bright wood-
    shaws;
And love my Lord and all His laws,
Who hath brought this bliss. Ah! if I
    were
Beyond these waves, I should have
    cause
To be a joyful jeweler."

"Jeweler," said that Gem so dear,
"Why jest ye men, so mad ye be?   290
Three sayings thou hast spoken clear,
And unconsidered were all three;
Their meaning thou canst not come
    near,
Thy word before thy thought doth
    flee.
First, thou believest me truly here,

Because with eyes thou mayst me see;
Second, with me in this countrý
Thou wilt dwell, whatever may deter;
Third, that to cross here thou art free;
That may no joyful jeweler.   300

"The jeweler merits little praise,
Who loves but what he sees with eye,
And it were a discourteous phrase
To say our Lord would make a lie,
Who surely pledged thy soul to raise,
Though fate should cause thy flesh to
    die.
Thou dost twist His words in crooked
    ways
Believing only what is nigh;
This is but pride and bigotry,
That a good man may ill assume,   310
To hold no matter trustworthy
Till like a judge he hear and doom.

"Whate'er thy doom, dost thou com-
    plain
As man should speak to God most
    high?
Thou wouldst gladly dwell in this do-
    main;
'Twere best, methinks, for leave to
    apply.
Even so, perchance, thou pleadest in
    vain.
Across this water thou wouldst fly,—
To other end thou must attain.
Thy corpse to clay comes verily,—
In Paradise 'twas ruined by   321
Our forefather. Now in the womb
Of dreary death each man must lie,
Ere God on this bank gives his doom."

"Doom me not, sweet, to my old fears
And pain again wherein I pine.
My pearl that, long, long lost, appears,
Shall I again forego, in fine?
Meet it, and miss it through more
    years?

Thou hast hurt me with that threat of
    thine.   330
For what serves treasure but for tears,
One must so soon his bliss resign?
I reck not how my days decline,
Though far from earth my soul seek
    room,
Parted from that dear pearl of mine.
Save endless dole what is man's
    doom?"

"No doom save pain and soul's dis-
    tress?"
She answered: "Wherefore thinkst
    thou so?
For pain of parting with the less,
Man often lets the greater go.   340
'Twere better thou thy fate shouldst
    bless,
And love thy God, through weal and
    woe;
For anger wins not happiness;
Who must, shall bear; bend thy pride
    low;
For though thou mayst dance to and
    fro,
Struggle and shriek, and fret and fume,
When thou canst stir not, swift nor
    slow,
At last, thou must endure His doom.

"Let God doom as He doth ordain;
He will not turn one foot aside;   350
Thy good deeds mount up but in vain,
Thou must in sorrow ever bide;
Stint of thy strife, cease to complain,
Seek His compassion safe and wide,
Thy prayer His pity may obtain,
Till Mercy all her might have tried.
Thy anguish He will heal and hide,
And lightly lift away thy gloom;
For, be thou sore or satisfied,
All is for Him to deal and doom."   360

"Doom me not, dearest damosel;
'Tis not for wrath nor bitterness,
If rash and raving thoughts I tell.
For sin my heart seethed in distress,
Like bubbling water in a well.
I cry God mercy, and confess.
Rebuke me not with words so fell;
I have lost all that my life did bless;
Comfort my sorrow and redress,
Piteously thinking upon this: 370
Grief and my soul thou hast made ex-
    press
One music,—thou who wert my bliss.

"My bliss and bale, thou hast been
    both,
But joy by great grief was undone;
When thou didst vanish, by my troth,
I knew not where my Pearl was gone.
To lose thee now I were most loth.
Dear, when we parted we were one;
Now God forbid that we be wroth,
We meet beneath the moon or sun 380
So seldom. Gently thy words run,
But I am dust, my deeds amiss;
The mercy of Christ and Mary and
    John
Is root and ground of all my bliss.

"A blissful life I see thee lead,
The while that I am sorrow's mate;
Haply thou givest little heed
What might my burning hurt abate.
Since I may in thy presence plead,
I do beseech thee thou narrate,   390
Soberly, surely, word and deed,
What life is thine, early and late?
I am fain of thy most fair estate;
The high road of my joy is this,
That thou hast happiness so great;
It is the ground of all my bliss."

She said, "May bliss to thee betide,"
Her face with beauty beaming clear;
"Welcome thou art here to abide,
For now thy speech is to me dear. 400
Masterful mood and haughty pride,
I warn thee win but hatred here;

For my Lord loveth not to chide
And meek are all that to Him come
    near.
When in His place thou shalt appear,
To kneel devout be not remiss,
My Lord the Lamb loveth such cheer,
Who is the ground of all my bliss.

"Thou sayest a blissful life I know,
And thou wouldst learn of its de-
    gree.   410
Thou rememberest when thy pearl fell
    low
In earth, I was but young to see;
But my Lord the Lamb, as if to show
His grace, took me His bride to be,
Crowned me a queen in bliss to go
Through length of days eternally;
And dowered with all His wealth is
    she
Who is His love, and I am His;
His worthiness and royalty
Are root and ground of all my
    bliss."   420

"My blissful one, may this be true.
Pardon if I speak ill," I prayed:
"Art thou the queen o' the heaven's
    blue,
To whom earth's honor shall be paid?
We believe in Mary, of grace who
    grew,
A mother, yet a blameless maid;
To wear her crown were only due
To one who purer worth displayed.
For perfectness by none gainsaid,
We call her the Phoenix of Araby,   430
That flies in faultless charm arrayed,
Like to the Queen of courtesy."

"Courteous Queen," that bright one
    said,
And, kneeling, lifted up her face:
"Matchless Mother and merriest Maid,
Blessed Beginner of every grace."
Then she arose, and softly stayed,

And spoke to me across that space:
"Sir, many seek gain here, and are paid,
But defrauders are none within this
    place;   440
That Empress may all heaven embrace,
And earth and hell in her empery;
Her from her heritage none will chase,
For she is Queen of courtesy.

"The court of the kingdom of God
    doth thrive
Only because of this wondrous thing:
Each one who therein may arrive,
Of the realm is either queen or king;
And no one the other doth deprive,
But is fain of his fellow's guerdon-
    ing,   450
And would wish each crown might be
    worth five,
If possible were their bettering.
But my Lady, from whom our Lord
    did spring,
Rules over all our company,
And for that we all rejoice and sing,
Since she is Queen of courtesy.

"Of courtesy, as says St. Paul,
Members of Christ we may be seen.
As head and arm and leg, and all, 459
Bound to the body close have been,
Each Christian soul himself may call
A living limb of his Lord, I ween.
And see how neither hate nor gall
'Twixt limb and limb may intervene;
The head shows neither spite nor
    spleen,
Though arm and finger jeweled be,
So fare we all in love serene,
As kings and queens by courtesy."

"Courtesy flowers thy folk among,
And charity, I well believe.   470
If foolish words flow from my tongue,
Let not my speech thy spirit grieve.
A queen in heaven while yet so young,
Too high thou dost thyself upheave.

Then what reward from strife were
  wrung?
What worship more might he achieve
Who lived in penance morn and eve,
Through bodily pain in bliss to be?
Honor more high might he receive,
Than be crowned king by courtesy?

"That courtesy rewards no deed 481
If all be true that thou dost say;
Our life not two years didst thou lead
Nor learned to please God, nor to
  pray,
No Paternoster knew nor creed;
And made a queen on the first day!
I may not think, so God me speed!
That God from right would swerve
  away;
As a countess, damsel, by my fay!
To live in heaven were a fair boon, 490
Or like a lady of less array,
But a queen! Ah, no! it is too soon."

"With Him there is no soon nor late,"
Replied to me that worthy wight;
"True always is His high mandáte;
He doth no evil, day nor night.
Hear Matthew [2] in the mass narrate,
In the Gospel of the God of might;
His parable portrays the state
Of the Kingdom of Heaven, clear as
  light: 500
'My servants,' saith He, 'I requite
As a lord who will his vineyard prune;
The season of the year is right,
And laborers must be hired soon.'

"Right soon the hirelings all may see
How the master with the dawn arose;
To hire his laborers forth went he,
And workmen stout and strong he
  chose.
For a penny a day they all agree,
Even as the master doth propose, 510
They toil and travail lustily,

Prune, bind, and with a ditch enclose.
Then to the market-place he goes,
And finds men idle at high noon;
'How can a man stand here who
  knows
The vineyards should be tilled so
  soon?'

" 'Soon as day dawned we hither won,
And no man hath our labor sought;
We have been standing since rose the
  sun
And no one bids us to do aught.' 520
'Enter my vineyard every one,'
The master answered quick as
  thought:
'The work that each by night has done
I will truly pay, withholding naught.'
Among the vines they went and
  wrought,
While morning, noon and afternoon,
More laborers the master brought,
Until the night must gather soon.

"Soon fell the time of evensong.
An hour before the sun was set, 530
He saw more idlers, young and
  strong;
His voice was sober with regret:
'Why stand ye idle all day long?'
'No man,' they said, 'hath hired us yet.'
'Go to my vineyard, fear no wrong;
Each man an honest wage shall get.'
The day grew dark and darker yet,
Before the rising of the moon;
The master who would pay his debt,
Bade summon all the hirelings
  soon. 540

"The lord soon called his steward: 'Go,
Bring in the men quick as ye may;
Give them the wages that I owe,
And, lest they aught against me say,
Range them along here in a row,

[2] Matthew 20: 1–16.

To each alike his penny pay;
Start with the last who standeth low,
And to the first proceed straightway.'
And then the first began to pray,
Complaining they had travailed
    sore: 550
'These wrought but one hour of the
    day,
We think we should receive the more.

"'More have we served,' they mut-
    tered low,
'Who have endured the long day's
    heat,
Than these who not two hours toiled
    so;
Why should their claim with ours
    compete?'
Said the master: 'I pay all I owe;
Friend, no injustice shalt thou meet;
Take that which is thine own and go.
For a penny we settled in the street;
Why dost thou now for more entreat?
Thou wast well satisfied before.   562
Once made, a bargain is complete;
Why shouldst thou, threatening, ask
    for more?

"'What can be more within my gift
Than what I will with mine to do?
Let not thine eyes to evil shift,
Because I trusty am, and true.'
'Thus I,' said Christ, 'all men shall sift.
The last shall be the first of you;   570
And the first last, however swift,
For many are called, but chosen, few.'
And thus poor men may have their
    due,
That late and little burden bore;
Their work may vanish like the dew,
The mercy of God is much the more.

"More gladness have I, herewithin,
Of flower of life, and noble name,
Than all men in the world might win,

Who thought their righteous deeds to
    name.   580
Nathless even now did I begin;
To the vineyard as night fell I came,
But my Lord would not account it sin;
He paid my wages without blame.
Yet others did not fare the same,
Who toiled and travailed there before,
And of their hire might nothing claim,
Perchance shall not for a year more."

Then more, and openly, I spake:
"From thy tale no reason can I
    wring;   590
God's righteousness doth ever wake,
Else Holy Writ is a fabled thing.
From the Psalter one verse let us take,
That may to a point this teaching
    bring:
'Thou requitest each for his deed's
    sake,
Thou high and all-foreknowing King.'
If one man to his work did cling
All day, and thou wert paid before,
Most wage falls to least laboring,
And ever the less receives the
    more."   600

"Of more or less where God doth
    reign,
There is no chance," she gently said,
"For, whether large or small his gain,
Here every man alike is paid.
No niggard churl our High Chieftain,
But lavishly His gifts are made,
Like streams from a moat that flow
    amain,
Or rushing waves that rise unstayed.
Free were his pardon whoever prayed
Him who to save man's soul did
    vow;   610
Unstinted his bliss, and undelayed,
For the grace of God is great enow.

"But now thou wouldst my wit check-
    mate,

Making my wage as wrong appear;
Thou say'st that I am come too late,
Of so large hire to be worthy here;
Yet sawest thou ever small or great,
Living in prayer and holy fear,
Who did not forfeit at some date   619
The meed of heaven to merit clear?
Nay much the rather, year by year,
All bend from right and to evil bow;
Mercy and grace their way must steer,
For the grace of God is great enow.

"But enow of grace have the innocent
New-born, before the sacred shrine,
They are sealed with water in sacra-
    ment,
And thus are brought into the vine.
Anon the day with darkness blent,
Death by its might makes to de-
    cline;   630
Who wrought no wrong ere hence
    they went,
The gentle Lord receives, in fine;
They obeyed His will, they bore His
    sign,
Why should He not their claim allow?
Yea, and reward them, I opine,
For the grace of God is great enow.

" 'Tis known enow that all mankind
At first were formed for perfect bliss;
Our forefather that boon resigned,
All for an apple's sake, ywis;   640
We fell condemned, for folly blind,
To suffer sore in hell's abyss;
But One a remedy did find
Lest we our hope of heaven should
    miss.
He suffered on the cross for this,
Red blood ran from His crownèd
    brow;
He saved us by that pain of His,
For the grace of God is great enow.

"Enow there flowed from out that
    well,

Blood and water from His broad
    wound: 650
The blood bought us from bale of hell,
And from second death deliverance
    found.
The water is baptism, truth to tell,
That followed the spear so sharply
    ground,
And washes away the guilt most fell
Of those that Adam in death had
    drowned.
Now is there nothing in earth's great
    round,
To bar from the bliss wherewith God
    did endow
Mankind,—restored to us safe and
    sound,
For the grace of God is great
    enow.   660

"Grace enow a man may get
By penitence, though he sin again;
But with long sorrow and regret,
He must bear punishment and pain;
But righteous reason will not let
The innocent be hurt in vain;
God never gave His judgment yet,
That they should suffer who show no
    stain.
The sinful soul of mercy fain
Finds pardon if he will repent,   670
But he who sinless doth remain
Is surely saved, being innocent.

"Two men are saved of God's good
    grace,
Who severally have done His will:
The righteous man shall see His face,
The innocent dwells with Him still.
In the Psalter thou may'st find a case:
'Lord, who shall climb to Thy high
    hill,
Or rest within Thy Holy Place?'
The psalmist doth the sense fulfill: 680
'Who with his hands did never ill,
His heart to evil never lent,

There to ascend he shall have skill;'
So surely saved is the innocent.

"That the righteous is saved I hold
    certain;
Before God's palace he shall stand
Who never took man's life in vain,
Who never to flatter his fellow
    planned.
Of the righteous, the Wise Man
    writeth plain
How kindly our King doth him com-
    mand;   690
In ways full strait he doth restrain,
Yet shows him the kingdom great and
    grand,
As who saith: 'Behold! yon lovely
    land!
Thou may'st win it, if so thy will be
    bent.'
But with never peril on either hand,
Surely saved is the innocent.

"Of the righteous saved, hear one man
    say—
David, who in the Psalter cried:
'O Lord, call never Thy servant to
    pay,
For no man living is justified.'   700
So thou, if thou shalt come one day
To the court that each cause must de-
    cide,
For mercy with justice thou may'st
    pray
Through this same text that I espied.
But may He on the bloody cross that
    died,
His holy hands with hard nails rent,
Give thee to pass when thou art tried,
Saved, not as righteous, but innocent.

"Of the sinless saved the tale is told,—
Read in the Book where it is said: 710
When Jesus walked among men of
    old,

The people a passage to Him made;
Bringing their bairns for Him to hold,
For the blessing of His hand they
    prayed.
The twelve reproved them: 'Over-
    bold
To seek the Master;' and sternly
    stayed.
But Jesus said: 'Be ye not afraid;
Suffer the children, nor prevent;
God's kingdom is for such arrayed.'
Surely saved are the innocent.   720

"Christ called to Him the innocents
    mild,
And said His kingdom no man might
    win,
Unless he came thither as a child,—
Not otherwise might he enter in,
Harmless, faithful, undefiled,
With never a spot of soiling sin,—
For these whom the world has not be-
    guiled
Gladly shall one the gate unpin.
There shall that endless bliss begin
Which the merchant sought, and
    straight was led   730
To barter all stuffs men weave and
    spin,
To buy him a pearl unblemishéd.

" 'This pearl unblemished, bought so
    dear,
For which the merchant his riches
    gave,
Is like the kingdom of heaven clear;'
So said the Father of world and wave.
It is a flawless, perfect sphere,
Polished and pure, and bright and
    brave;
As on my heart it doth appear,
It is common to all who to virtue
    clave.   740
My Lord, the Lamb Who died to save,
Here set it in token of His blood shed

For peace. Then let the wild world
rave,
But buy thee this pearl unblemishéd."

"O Pearl unblemished, in pure pearls
dressed,
That beareth," said I, "the pearl of
price,
Who formed thy figure and thy vest?
Truly he wrought with cunning nice;
For thy beauty, above nature's best,
Passeth Pygmalion's artifice;   750
Nor Aristotle the lore possessed
To depict in words so fair device.
Than fleur-de-lys thou art fairer
thrice,
Angel-mannered and courtly bred,—
Tell to me truly: in Paradise
What meaneth the pearl unblem-
ishéd?"

"My spotless Lamb, who all doth
heal,"
She answered, "my dear Destiny,
Chose me in marriage bond to seal;
Unfit, He graced me regally,   760
From your world's woe come into
weal.
He called me of His courtesy:
'Come hither to me, my lover leal,
For mote nor spot is none in thee.'
He gave me my might and great
beauty;
He washed my weeds in His blood so
red,
And crowned me, forever clean to be,
And clothed me in pearls unblem-
ishéd."

"Unblemished bride, bright to behold,
That royalty hath so rich and rare, 770
What is this Lamb, that thou hast told
How for wedded wife He called thee
there?

Above all others dost thou make bold,
As His chosen lady His life to share?
So many, comely in combs of gold,
For Christ have lived in strife and
care,
Must these to a lower place repair,
That never any with Him may wed,
Save only thyself, so proud and fair,
Peerless Queen, and unblemishéd?"

"Unblemished," answered she again,
"Without a spot of black or gray, 782
With honor may I this maintain;
But 'peerless Queen' I did not say.
Brides of the Lamb in bliss we reign,
An hundred and forty thousand gay,
As in the Apocalypse [3] is made plain,
Saint John beheld them on a day;
On the hill of Zion he saw them stay,
In vision his spirit looked on them, 790
For the wedding clad in bright array,
At the city of New Jerusalem.

"Of Jerusalem in speech I tell;
And what He is if thou wouldst see—
My Lamb, my Lord, my dear Jewél,
My Joy, my Love, my Bliss so free,—
The prophet Isaiah writeth well
Of His most mild humility:
'Guiltless, when men upon Him fell
For never a fault nor felony,   800
As a sheep to the slaughter led was
He;
Quiet, the while the crowd contemn,
As a lamb in the shearer's hands
might be,
He was judged by Jews in Jerusalem.'

"In Jerusalem was my Lover slain,
Rent on the rood by ruffians bold;
To bear our ills He was full fain,
To suffer our sorrows manifold;
Buffeted until blood did stain

[3] Revelation 14:1-5.

That face so lovely to behold; 810
He took upon Him all sin and pain,
Even He of Whom not one sin is told;
On the rude cross stretched faint and
cold,
He let men deride him and condemn;
Meek as a lamb, betrayed and sold,
He died for us in Jerusalem.

"At Jerusalem, Jordan and Galilee,
Wherever Saint John came to baptize,
His words with Isaiah's words agree.[4]
On Jesus he lifted up his eyes, 820
Speaking of Him this prophecy:
'Behold the Lamb of God!' he cries:
'Who bears the world's sins, this is
He!
The guilt of all upon Him lies,
Though He wrought evil in no wise.
The branches springing from that
stem
Who can recount? 'Tis He who dies
For our sake in Jerusalem.'

"In Jerusalem my Lover sweet
Twice as a lamb did thus appear, 830
Even as the prophets both repeat,
So meek the mien that He did wear;
The third time also, as is meet,
In the Revelation [5] is written clear.
Reading a book on His high seat
Midmost the throne that saints en-
sphere,
The Apostle John beheld Him near;
That book seven sacred seals begem;
And at that sight all folk felt fear
In hell, in earth and Jerusalem. 840

"This Jerusalem Lamb had never stain
Of other hue than perfect white,
That showeth neither streak nor strain
Of soil, but is like wool to sight;
And souls that free of sin remain
The Lamb receiveth with delight;
And, though each day a group we
gain,

There comes no strife for room nor
right,
Nor rivalry our bliss to blight.
The more the merrier, I profess. 850
In company our love grows bright,
In honor more and never less.

"Lessening of bliss no comer brings
To us who bear this pearl at breast;
Nor show they flaws nor tarnishings
Who wear such pure pearls like a
crest.
Though round our corpses the clay
clings,
And though ye mourn us without rest,
Knowledge have we of goodly things.
Through the first death our hope we
test; 860
Grief goes; at each mass we are blest
By the Lamb Who gives us happiness;
The bliss of each is bright and best,
And no one's honor is the less.

"That thou my tale the less may
doubt,
In the Revelation 'tis told, and more:
'I saw,' says John, 'a goodly rout
The hill of Zion covering o'er,
The Lamb, with maidens round about,
An hundred thousand and forty and
four, 870
And each brow, fairly written out,
The Lamb's name and His Father's
bore.
Then a sound from heaven I heard
outpour,
As streams, full laden, foam and press,
Or as thunders among dark crags
roar,
The tumult was, and nothing less.

" 'Nathless, though high that shout
might ring,
And loud the voices sounding near,
A strain full new I heard them sing,

[4] John 1:28-36.
[5] Revelation 5:1-14.

[232]

And sweet and strange it was to
    hear. 880
Like harper's hands upon the string
Was that new song they sang so clear;
The noble notes went vibrating,
And gentle words came to my ear.
Close by God's throne, without one
    fear,
Where the four beasts His power con-
    fess,
And the elders stand so grave of cheer,
They sang their new song, none the
    less. 888

" 'Nathless is none with skill so fine,
·For all the crafts that ever he knew,
That if that song might sing a line,
Save these that hold the Lamb in view;
From earth brought to that land
    divine,
As first fruits that to God are due,
They serve the Lamb and bear His
    sign,
As like Himself in face and hue;
For never lying nor tale untrue
Defiled their lips in life's distress;'
Whatever might move them, they but
    drew
Nearer the Master, none the less." 900

"Nevertheless, speak out I must,
My Pearl, though queries rude I pose.
To try thy fair wit were unjust
Whom Christ to His own chamber
    chose.
Behold, I am but dung and dust,
And thou a rare and radiant rose,
Abiding here in life, and lust
Of loveliness that ever grows.
A hind that no least cunning knows,
I needs must my one doubt ex-
    press; 910
Though boisterous as the wind that
    blows,

Let my prayer move thee none the
    less.

"Yet, none the less, on thee I call,
If thou wilt listen verily,
As thou art glorious over all,
Hearken the while I question thee.
Within some splendid castle wall,
Have ye not dwellings fair to see?
Of David's city, rich, royál,
Jerusalem, thou tellest me. 920
In Palestine its place must be;
In wildwood such none ever saw.
Since spotless is your purity,
Your dwellings should be free from
    flaw.

"Now this most fair and flawless rout,
Thronging thousands, as thou dost
    tell,
They must possess, beyond a doubt,
A sightly city wherein to dwell.
'Twere strange that they should live
    without;
For so bright a band it were not
    well; 930
Yet I see no building hereabout.
Dost thou linger as in a woodland cell,
Alone and hidden, for the spell
Of rushing stream and shining shaw?
If thou hast a dwelling beyond this
    dell,
Now show me that city free from
    flaw."

"Not flawless the city in Juda's land,"
That gentle one gently to me spake,
"But the Lamb did bless it when He
    planned
To suffer there sorely for man's
    sake. 940
That is the old city we understand,
And there the bonds of old guilt did
    break;
But the new, alighted from God's
    hand,

The Apostle John for his theme did
take.
The Lamb Who is white with never a
flake
Of black, did thither His fair folk
draw;
For His flock no fenced fold need He
make,
Nor moat for His city free from flaw.

"To figure flawlessly what may mean
Jerusalems twain: the first of those 950
Was 'the Sight of Peace' as it is seen
In the word of God, for the gospel
shows
How there our peace made sure hath
been,
Since to suffer therein the Savior
chose;
In the other is always peace to glean,
Peace that never an ending knows.
To that city bright the spirit goes
When the flesh hath fallen beneath
death's law;
There glorious gladness forever grows
For His fair folk that are free from
flaw." 960

"Flawless maid so mild and meek,"
Then said I to that lovely flower:
"Let me that stately city seek,
And let me see thy blissful bower."
That bright one said, "Thou art too
weak,
Thou may'st not enter to its tower;
Yet of the Lamb I did bespeak
This goodly gift, that He would
dower
Thine eyes with the sight for one short
hour,—
From without,—within none ever
saw; 970
To step in that street thou hast no
power,
Unless thy soul were free from flaw.

⁶ Revelation 21:1–22:5.

"This flawless sight I will not hide;
Up toward the brook's head thou must
go,
While I will follow on this side,
Till yonder hill the city show."
And then I would no longer bide,
But stole through branches, bending
low,
Till from the summit I espied,
Through green boughs swaying to
and fro, 980
Afar, the city, all aglow,
That brighter than bright sunbeams
shone.
In writing it is pictured so,
In the Revelation of St. John.

As John the Apostle saw the sight,⁶
I saw that city, standing near
Jerusalem, so royal dight,
As if from Heaven alighted here.
The city all of gold burned bright,
Like gleaming glass that glistens
clear. 990
With precious stones beneath set
right:
Foundations twelve of gems most dear,
Wrought wondrous richly, tier on
tier.
Each base was of a separate stone
As, perfectly, it doth appear
In the Revelation of St. John.

John named the stones that he had
seen,
I knew the order that he made;
The first a jasper must have been,
That on the lowest base was laid, 1000
Beneath the rest it glinted green;
A sapphire in the second grade;
Chalcedony, from blemish clean,
In the third course was fair arrayed;
Fourth, emerald, of greenest shade,
Fifth, sardonyx, was raised thereon;

The sixth a ruby, as is said
In the Revelation of St. John.

John joined to these the chrysolite,
The seventh gem in that base-
 mént;   1010
The eighth, a beryl, clear and white;
The topaz, ninth, its luster lent;
Tenth, chrysoprase, both soft and
bright;
Eleventh, the jacinth, translucent;
And twelfth, and noblest to recite,
Amethyst, blue with purple blent.
The wall above those basements went
Jasper, like glass that glistening shone;
I saw, as the story doth present,—
The Revelation of St. John.   1020

I saw, as John doth clear devise:
The great stones rose like a broad
stair;
Above, the city, to my eyes,
In height, length, breadth appeared
four-square;
The jasper wall shone amber-wise,
The golden streets as glass gleamed
fair;
The dwellings glowed in glorious
guise
With every stone most rich and rare.
Each length of bright wall builded
there
For full twelve furlongs' space
stretched on,   1030
And height, length, breadth all equal
were:
"I saw one mete it," writeth John.

As John doth write more met mine
eye:
Within each wall were set three gates;
Twelve in succession I could spy,
Portals adorned with bright gold
plates;
Each gate a single pearl saw I,
A perfect pearl, as John relates.

On each a name was written high
Of Israel's sons after their dates, 1040
The oldest first, as the story states.
Within those streets by night or noon,
Light beams that not one hour abates;
They needed neither sun nor moon.

Of sun or moon they had no need;
For God Himself was their lamp light,
The Lamb their lantern was indeed;
From Him the city shone all bright.
Through wall and dwelling my looks
might speed,
Such clearness could not hinder
sight.   1050
Of the high throne ye might take
heed,
With draperies of radiant white,
As John the Apostle doth endite;
High God Himself did sit thereon.
From the throne a river welled out-
right
Was brighter than both sun and moon.

Sun nor moon shone never so sweet
As the full flood of that bright stream;
Swiftly it swept through every street,
Untainted did the water gleam. 1060
Chapel nor church mine eyes did
meet;
There is no temple as I deem;
The Almighty is their minster meet,
The Lamb their sacrifice supreme.
The gates with neither bolt nor beam,
Wide open stand at night and noon;
To enter there let no man dream
Whom sin hath stained beneath the
moon.

The moon may there win no least
might,
She is too spotty, grey and grim; 1070
Therein, moreover, is never night.
Why should the moon fill full her rim
To rival the all-glorious light
That beams upon the river's brim?

The planets are in poorest plight;
The sun itself is far too dim.
Beside the stream trees tall and trim
Bear living fruits that none doth
    prune;
Twelve times a year bends low each
    limb,   1079
Renewed with fruitage every moon.

Beneath the moon full well might fail
The heart of mortal to endure
The marvel that did mine eyes assail,
Fashioned the fancy to allure.
I stood as still as a startled quail,
For wonder of its fair figure,
I felt no rest and no travail,
Ravished before such radiance pure.
I say, and with conviction sure,
Had the eyes of man received that
    boon,   1090
Though wisest clerks sought for his
    cure,
His life were lost beneath the moon.

Now, even as the full moon might rise
Ere daylight doth to darkness fall,
Sudden I saw with still surprise
Within that shining city-wall,
The streets full-thronged in wondrous
    wise,
Silent, with never a herald's call,
With virgins in the selfsame guise
As my beloved, sweet and small.   1100
Each head was crowned with coronal,
Pearl-wrought, and every robe was
    white;
On each breast bound, imperial,
The Pearl of Price with great delight.

With great delight together going
On glassy golden streets they tread;
To a hundred thousand swiftly grow-
    ing,
And all alike were they garmented:
The gladdest face who could be
    knowing?   1109
The Lamb did proudly pass ahead,
His seven horns of clear red gold
    glowing,
His robes like pearls high valuéd.
On toward the throne their way they
    thread,
None crowded in that band so bright,
But mild as maidens when mass is said,
So fared they forth with great de-
    light.[7]

The great delight His coming gave,
It were too much for me to tell.
When He approached the Elders
    grave,
Prone there before His feet they
    fell;   1120
Legions of summoned angels brave
Swayed censers of the sweetest smell;
With music like a mighty wave,
All sang in praise of that gay Jewél.
The hymn might strike through earth
    to hell
That with joy those hosts of heaven
    recite;
To praise the Lamb I liked full well,
Amid the group in great delight.

Delighted, I would fain devise
His loveliness, with mind intent;   1130
First was He, blithest, best to prize,
Of all on whom man's speech is spent;
So nobly white His draperies,
Such grace His simple glances lent;
But a wide, wet wound my gaze
    descries

   [7] For illustrations of the Adoration of the Lamb and the procession of maidens in the altar-piece by the Brothers Van Eyck cf. L. van Puyvelde, *Van Eyck: The Holy Lamb* (1947).

Beneath His heart, through His skin
   rent;
Down His white side the blood was
   sent.
Alas! I thought, what scorn or spite
Could any human heart have bent
In such a deed to take delight?   1140

The Lamb's delight might no man
   doubt,
Though that wide wound His hurt
   displayed,
From His fair face looked lovely out
Glad glances, glorious, unafraid.
I looked upon His shining rout,
With fullest life so bright arrayed,
My little queen there moved about,
I had thought beside me in the glade.
Ah Lord! how much of mirth she
   made!   1149
Among her peers she was so white!
The stream I surely needs must wade,
For longing love, in great delight.

Delight that flooded eye and ear
My mortal mind beatified;
When I saw her, I must reach my dear,
Though she beyond the brook abide.
Nothing, I thought, could keep me
   here,
No crippling blow hold my strength
   tied;
I would plunge, whatever interfere,
And swim the stream, though there I
   died.   1160
But ere the water I had tried,
Even as I would my vow fulfill,
From my purpose I was turned aside;
It was not to my Prince's will.

My wilful purpose pleased not Him,
That I with headlong zeal essayed;
Though I was rash of thought and
   limb,
Yet suddenly my deed was stayed.

As I sprang forward to the brim,
The action in my dreaming made   1170
Me waken in my arbour trim.
My head upon the mound was laid
Where my pearl to the grass once
   strayed.
I stretched my body, frightened, chill,
And, sighing, to myself I said:
"Now all be to the Prince's will."

Against my will was I exiled
From that bright region, fair and fain,
From that life, glad and undefiled,
And longing dulled my sense again;
I swooned in sorrow for the child,
Needs must my heart cry and com-
   plain: 1182
"O Pearl, dear was thy counsel mild,
In this true vision of my brain!
If very truth divide us twain;
If thou goest crowned, secure from ill,
Well for me in my prison-pain
That thou art to the Prince's will."

To the Prince's will had my heart
   bent,
And sought but what to me was
   given,   1190
Held fast to that, with true intent,
As my Pearl prayed me out of heaven;
Did I to God my thoughts present,
More in His mysteries had I thriven.
But a man will seek more than is sent,
Till from his hand his hope be riven.
Thus from my joy was I forth driven,
From the life upon that holy hill.
Oh, fools, that with the Lord have
   striven,   1199
Or proffered gifts against his will!

The Prince's will to serve aright
The Christian may full well divine;
For I have found Him, day and night,
A God, a Lord, a Friend in fine.

[237]

Upon this mound my soul hath sight,
Where I for piteous sorrow pine;
My Pearl to God I pledge and plight,
With Christ's dear blessing and with
    mine,—   1208
His, who, in form of bread and wine,

The priest doth daily show us still.
His servants may we be, or shine,
Pure pearls, according to his will.
    Amen. Amen.
    SOPHIE JEWETT

Saint Erkenwald

At London in England,   not a very long time
Since Christ suffered on the cross   and established Christendom,
There was a bishop in that borough,   blessèd and saintly,
Saint Erkenwald, I understand,   that holy man was called.

In his time in that town   the greatest temple of all
Was pulled down, one part of it,   to dedicate it anew;
For it had been heathen   in Hengist's [1] days,
Whom the savage Saxons   had sent hither.

They beat out the Britons   and drove them into Wales,
And perverted all the people   who dwelt in that place.   10
Then was this realm apostate   many proud years,
Till Saint Augustine to Sandwich   was sent by the Pope. [2]

Then he preached here the pure faith   and planted the truth,
And converted all the communities   to Christendom anew;
He changed temples that belonged   at that time to the devil,
And cleansed them in Christ's name   and called them churches.

He hurled out the idols   and had saints brought in,
And promptly changed their patrons   and improved their observance;
What had been of Apollo   was now of Saint Peter;
Mahomet gave place to Saint Margaret   or to Mary Magdalen.   20

The synagogue of the Sun   was assigned to Our Lady;
Jupiter and Juno yielded   to Jesu or James.
So he dedicated and devoted   all to dear saints
That once was sacred to Satan   in the Saxons' time.

Now that which London is named   was called the New Troy; [3]
The metropolis and master-town   it has been ever since.

---

[1] A Germanic leader, who became king of Kent in second half of fifth century.
[2] 597 A.D.   [3] By Brutus, great-grandson of Aeneas, 1126 B.C.

The great minster therein a mighty devil once owned,
And the title of the temple had been given his name.

For he had been lord most dearly praised of idols,
And the solemnest in his sacrifices in Saxon lands. 30
It was held the third temple of the triapolitans; [4]
By all Britain's banks there were but two others.

Now in this Augustine's province Erkenwald is bishop [5]
At beloved London town, and the law he teaches.
He takes his seat on the throne of Saint Paul's minster,
Which was the temple triapolitan, as I told earlier.

Then it was razed and torn down, and reared up anew,
A noble work of that time, and it was named the "New Work."
Many a merry mason was called there to labor,
To hew out hard stones with sharp-edged tools. 40

Many grubbed in the ground to seek a firm base,
That the foundation from the first should hold its footing;
And as they shoveled and mined, a marvel they found there,
As yet in careful chronicles is recorded the memory.

For as they dug and delved so deep in the earth,
They found built on a floor a wondrous fair tomb;
It was a coffin of thick stone, skillfully hewn,
Garnished about with gargoyles, all of gray marble.

Three bolts of the coffin that barred it aloft
Were fitly made of marble and carefully planed. 50
The border was embellished with bright gold letters;
But runic [6] were the writings that in a row stood there.

Clear cut were the carvings, as many beheld them,
But all were puzzled to express what they should mean.
Many clerics in that cathedral, with very broad tonsures,
Busied themselves vainly to put them into words.

[4] Name given by Geoffrey of Monmouth to the three chief centers of British pre-Christian religion, which later became centers of British Christianity.
[5] 675–693 A.D.
[6] In runic characters; perhaps merely strange and unintelligible.

25: Saint Erkenwald

When tidings reached the town   of that tomb-wonder,
Many hundred high-born men   hied thither forthwith.
Burgesses betook themselves there,   beadles and others,
And many craftsmen   of different kinds.   60

Laborers left their work   and leaped thitherwards,
Ran rapidly in a rout   with uproarious noises.
There came thither so quickly   many of all kinds,
As if the whole world was gathered   there in an instant.

The mayor with his retinue   looked on that marvel;
With the assent of the sacristan   they observed the sanctuary.[7]
He bade them unlock the lid   and lay it alongside;
They would look in that coffin,   what lay there within.

Then workmen strong   went to the task,
Put levers in place   and pried underneath,   70
Caught it by the corners   with crowbars of iron,
And, were the lid never so large,   they laid it by quickly.

But then was great wonder   among them who stood there,
Who could not understand   a marvel so strange,
So gay was that bright space within,   with gold wholly painted,
And a blessed body   on the bottom was lying,

Arrayed in rich manner,   in royal weeds.
All with glistening gold   his gown was hemmed,
With many precious pearls   mounted thereon;
And a girdle of gold   encircled his middle.   80

A large mantle was over them,   furred with miniver,
The cloth of finest camel's hair,   with comely borders;
And on his coif was placed   a very rich crown,
And a splendid sceptre   was set in his hand.

As spotless were his weeds,   without any blemish,
Whether of mould or of stains   or of moth-eaten holes,
And as bright in their beauty   of glowing hues
As if recently in that close   they had been made yesterday.

---

7 Kept the place holy.

[241]

And as fresh was his face   and the bare flesh
That by his ears and his hands   openly showed,   90
With rich ruddiness like the rose,   and two red lips,
As if in sound health suddenly   he had slipped into sleep.

It was a profitless task   to inquire of each other
What body it might be   that was buried there,
How long he had lain there,   his lineaments so unchanged,
And his clothing unspotted.   Thus each man pondered:

"It cannot be but such a man   remained long in memory.
He has been king of this country,   as clearly it seems.
He lies delved thus deep.   'Twould be a rare wonder
If some soul could not say   that he had seen him."   100

But that notion went for naught,   for no one could announce,
Either by title or by token   or by any tradition
That was recorded in the city   or read of in books,
Any mention of such a man,   either more or less.[8]

The news to the bishop   was brought in short time,
All the awesome wonder   of that buried body.
The pontiff with his prelates   had departed from home;
In Essex was Sir Erkenwald   to visit an abbey.

Men told him the tale   and of the turmoil among the people,
How such a cry about a corpse   continued ever to rumble.   110
The bishop sent word to quiet them,   by beadles and letters,
And hied thither at once   on his white horse.

When he came to the church   consecrated to Saint Paul,
Many met him on that mare,   the marvel to tell.
He passed on to his palace   and peace he enjoined,[9]
And avoided the dead man   and barred the door after.

The dark night drove over   and the day-bell rang;
And Sir Erkenwald was up   in the dawn even earlier;
Wellnigh all the night   he had recited his hours,
To beseech his Sovereign,   of His sweet grace,   120
To vouchsafe to reveal this thing   by avision[10] or otherwise.

[8] Great or small.   [9] The usual greeting is "Peace be with you."
[10] Special revelation to a person of importance.

"Though I be unworthy," while weeping he said,
In his deep humility, "grant it, my Lord;
In confirming Thy Christian faith help me to know
The mystery of this miracle that men wonder upon."

So long he pled for grace that it was granted him,
An answer from the Holy Ghost; and thereafter it dawned.
Minster doors were thrown open when matins were sung;
The bishop prepared solemnly to sing the high mass.

The prelate in pontificals was promptly attired,   130
Solemnly with his ministers the mass he begins
Of *Spiritus Domini* [11] sagely, beseeching success,
With sweet questings [12] of the choir and many skilled notes.

Many a gay lord and great was gathered to hear it,
Since the choicest of that realm repair thither often,
Till the service ceased and was said to the end.
Then forth from the altar went all the high company.

The prelate passed down to the level, where lords bowed to him;
Richly vested as he was, he made his way to the tomb;
Men unclosed for him the enclosure with clustered keys,   140
But it was painful for the great press that passed in after him.

The bishop came to the burial-place, with barons beside him,
The mayor with his mighty men and mace-bearers before him.
The dean of that dear place described all at first;
The finding of that wonder with finger he pointed.

"Lo, lords," said the dean, "a body is here
That has lain locked below,— how long is unknown.
Yet his color and his cloth have caught no defect,
Neither his visage nor the vessel that he is laid in.

"There is no man now alive who has lived so long   150
Who can remember in his mind that such a man reigned,
Either his name or his renown report in speech.
Yet many poorer in this place have been put in their graves,
Whose memorial in our martyrology is recorded forever.

[11] A mass of the Holy Spirit, appropriate when seeking illumination.
[12] A cheerful figure from the baying of hounds, suggestive either of the antiphonal
singing or of the harmony of the choir.

"We have looked in our library   these seven long days,
But one chronicle of this king   can we never find.
He has not lain here so long,—   to look at it naturally,—
To melt so out of memory,   unless it be a miracle."

"Thou sayest sooth," said the man   who was consecrated bishop.
"It is a marvel to men,   but it amounts to little   160
Beside the providence of the Prince   who rules over Paradise,
When it pleased Him to unlock   the least of His powers.

"But when man's might is checkmated   and his mind surpassed,
And all his reasoning shattered,   and resourceless he stands,
Then right little hinders God   from loosing with a finger
What all the hands under heaven   can never hold fast.

"Where the creature's craft   swerves away from wisdom,
The Creator's comfort   must be taken as cure.

"So let us do now our deed   and conjecture no further;
To seek the sooth of ourselves,   ye see is no remedy.   170
But call we all upon God   and ask His grace,
Who is boundless of counsel,   His comfort to send.

"Therefore, to confirm your faith   and fine belief,
I will teach you so truly   of those His virtues
That ye may believe at length   that He is a Lord of might,
And fain to fulfill your desire,   if ye trust Him as friend."

Then he turns to the tomb   and talks to the corpse;
Lifting his eyelids,   he loosed these words:
"Now, body that thus liest,   conceal thou no longer,
Since Jesu has judged this day   His joy to be shown.   180

"Be obedient to His bidding;   I bid on His behalf.
As He was bound on a beam [18]   when He shed His blood,
As thou knowest it truly   and we well believe it,
Answer here my query;   conceal thou no truth.

"Since we know not who thou art,   inform us thyself,
What wight thou wert in the world,   and why thou thus liest,

[18] Tree, cross.

How long thou hast lain here,   and what law thou didst follow,
Whether thou art joined to joy   or judged to torment."

When the man had thus spoken   and sighed thereafter,
The bright body in the burial-place   budged a little,   190
And with a dreary sound   he drove out words
Through some spirit of life   lent by Him who rules all things.

"Bishop," quoth this body,   "thy bidding is dear to me;
I may not but yield to thy prayer,   I vow by mine eyes.
The Name thou hast named   and invoked in my presence
All heaven and hell bow to,   and the earth between.

"First, to tell the truth   as to who I was:
The most hapless of men   that was ever on earth;
Never king nor kaiser   nor yet a knight either,
But a man of the law   that this land then followed.   200

"I was commissioned and made   a magistrate here,
To sit on serious cases.   This city I governed
Under a high-born prince   of the paynims' belief,
And each man who followed him   held the same faith.

"The length of my lying here,   that is a difficult date,
Too much for any man   to make out the number.
After Brutus had built   this borough first,[14]
Naught of eight hundred years   but eighteen there wanted,[15]

"Before your Christ was born,   by Christian account,
Three hundred years and thirty   and yet thrice eight,[16]   210
I was on the circuit of an oyer [17]   in the New Troy,
In the reign of the rich king   who ruled us then.

"The bold Briton, Sir Belin,   and Sir Bering his brother,[18]—
Many were the insults   exchanged between them,
Because of their ruinous war   while their wrath lasted.
Then was I a judge here,   in gentile law appointed."

[14] 1136 B.C.   [15] 782 years later.   [16] 354 B.C.
[17] Court to hear and determine indictments.
[18] The brothers Belinus and Brennius, according to Geoffrey of Monmouth kings
of Britain 354 years after the founding of Rome.

While he spake thus in the coffin,   there sprang among the people
In all this world not a word,   nor awoke any noise,
But just as still as the stone   stood they and listened,
Worried with great wonder;   there was weeping of many.   220

The bishop bids that body: "Reveal thou the cause,
Since thou wast known for no king,   why thou wearest the crown.
Why holdest thou so high   in hand the sceptre?
And yet hadst no land of liegemen,   nor hadst power of life and limb."

"Dear sir," quoth the dead body,   "I desire to explain to thee,
Though it was never my will   that it was thus wrought.
I was deputy and doomsman [19]   under a noble duke,
And this place was put   in my power altogether.

"I did justice in this jolly town   in gentle wise,
And ever in faithful form   more than forty winters.   230
The folk was fierce and false   and froward to rule;
I suffered harms very often   to hold them to right.

"But for no danger nor wealth   nor wrath nor dread,
Nor for mastery nor for meed   nor for any man's goods
I recoiled never from right,   as my reason showed it,
To render a wrong doom [20]   any day of my life.

"My conscience never strayed,   for covetousness on earth,
Through devious decisions   to do any wrongs,
Out of reverence for riches,   however rich a man was,
Nor for any man's menace   nor for mischief nor pity.   240

"No one got me from the highroad   to go from the right,
As far as my faith   conformed to my heart.
Though it had been my father's murderer,   I judged him fairly,
Nor would I falsely favor my father   though it befell him to be hanged.

"Because I was righteous and upright   and ready in the law,
When I died, with dole   resounded all Troy.
All lamented my death,   the low and the high,
And as guerdon they buried   my body in gold.

"They clad me as the courtliest   who then did hold court,
In a mantle as the meekest   and most humane on the bench,   250

[19] Judge.   [20] Decision.

Girdled me like a governor,   the most gifted in Troy,
Furred me as the finest   for the good faith within me.

"For the honor of my honesty   of highest renown
They crowned me the famed king   of keen-witted justices
Who were ever throned in Troy   or were hoped for in future;
And since I rewarded ever right,   they reached me the sceptre."

The bishop asks him again,   with bale at his heart,
Though men reverenced him so,   how might it be
That his clothes were so clean;   "in clouts, methinks,
They ought to have rotted and been rent   in rags long since.   260

"Thy body may be embalmed;   so it abashes me not
That neither rot has riven it,   nor rank worms.
But thy color and thy cloth,   I can no wise conceive
How they might lie and last so long,   after the learning of men."

"Nay, bishop," quoth the body,   "embalmed was I never;
By no man's counsel my cloth   has kept thus unspotted.
But the rich King of Reason,   who regards ever right
And loves all the laws loyally   that belong unto truth,

"He most honors men   for being mindful of justice,
Rather than for all works of merit   that men use on earth.   270
And if the folk rightfully   have arrayed me thus,
He who loves right best   has allowed me to last."

"Yea, but speak of thy soul,"   then said the bishop.
"Where is it stablished and placed   if so strictly thou wroughtest?
He who rewards every man   as he has served right
Could ill forbear to give thee   some branch of His grace.

"For, as He says in soothfastness   in His book of Psalms:
'The righteous and the innocent   ascend ever to Me.'
Wherefore tell me of thy soul,   where in bliss it dwells,
And of the rich restitution   that Our Lord rendered it."   280

Then hummed he who lay there   and wagged his head,
Gave a groan full great,   and to God he said:
"Mighty Maker of men,   Thy mights are great!
How could Thy mercy extend   unto me any time?

"Was I not a paynim without knowledge, who knew never Thy cove-
     nant
Nor the measure of Thy mercy nor Thy miraculous power;
But aye a faithless fellow who failed Thy laws
That Thou, Lord, wast ever loved in? Alas, the hard hours!

"I was not of the number whom Thou with pain boughtest,
With the blood of Thy body upon the dark cross.   290
When Thou didst harrow hell and hale from thence
Thy remnant out of Limbo, Thou leftest me there.

"There sits my soul and may see no further,
Pining in the dark death which our father gained us,—
Adam, our ancestor, who ate of that apple
Which many pledgeless people has poisoned forever.

"Ye were poisoned by his teeth and taken with the venom;
But, amended with a medicine, ye are made to live;
That is baptism in the font, added to faithful belief.
And that we have missed without mercy, myself and my soul.   300

"What won we with our well-doing who wrought ever right
When we were damned dolefully into the deep lake
And exiled from that supper, that solemn feast,
Where richly are refreshed they who hungered after righteousness?

"My soul may sit there in sorrow and sigh full wretchedly,
Dimly in that dark death where dawns never morrow,
Hungry in hell-hole, and hanker for meals
Long ere it may see that supper or any man to invite it."

Thus dolefully this dead body declared its sorrow,
So that all wept there for woe who heard those words.   310
And the bishop for dolor cast down his eyes,
And had no space to speak, so steadily he sobbed;

Till he left off a moment and, with laving tears,
Looked at the tomb and the body that lay there.
"Our Lord grant," quoth that man, "that thou mayest have life
Long enough, by God's leave, that I may fetch water,

"And sprinkle it on thy fair body and speak these words:
'I baptize thee in the Father's name and His bounteous Child's

And of the gracious Holy Ghost's,'   and not one whit longer.
Then, though thou shouldst drop down dead,   it would endanger me
    less."   320

With that word that he uttered,   the wet from his eyes,
The tears, trickled down   and on the tomb lighted,
And one fell on the face   and the man sighed.
Then he said with a solemn sound: "Our Savior be praised.

"Now blessed be Thou, high God,   and Thy gracious Mother,
And blessed be that hour   that she bore Thee in!
And blessed be thou, bishop,   who abatest my sorrow
And relievest the loathly losses   that my soul has lived in!

"For the words thou hast spoken   and the water thou didst shed,
The bright stream from thine eyes,   have become my baptism.   330
The first sprinkle that fell on me   slaked all my woe;
Right now to supper my soul   is set at the table.

"For with the words and the water   that wash us from pain
Lightly flashed there a light   low into the abyss,
And my spirit sprang speedily   with unspared mirth
Solemnly into the cenacle [21]   where sup all who are true.

"And there met her a marshal   with mien most kindly,
And with reverence he gave her   a room forever.
I praise therefor my high God   and also thee, bishop;
From bale hast thou brought us to bliss,   blessed be thou!"   340

With this he ceased his sound;   he spoke no more;
But suddenly his sweet cheer   failed and vanished,
And all the hue of his body   was black as the earth,
As rotten as the rotted thing   that rises in powder.

For, as soon as the soul   was stablished in bliss,
Corrupted was that other creation   that covered the bones;
For the everlasting life   that hath no end
Makes void each vainglory   that avails so little.

Then there was praising of Our Lord,   with lauds upraised;
Much mourning and mirth   were mingled together.   350
They passed forth in procession,   and all the people followed;
And all the bells in the city   boomed out at once.

[21] Supper room.

Abraham and Isaac

from the

Brome Manuscript

[*On the upper stage God with His angels; on the lower stage Abraham and his son Isaac. Abraham kneels in prayer.*]

ABRAHAM: Omnipotent Father of Heaven, with all my heart I call on Thee. Thou hast given me both land and revenue, and sent me my livelihood. I thank Thee highly evermore for all. First Thou madest Adam of the earth, and Eve also to be his wife, and all other men came from those two. And now Thou hast granted to me, Abraham, to lead my life in this land. In my old age Thou hast granted that this young child should dwell with me. I love nothing so much indeed, except Thine own self, dear Father of Bliss,
10 as Isaac, my own sweet son. I have divers other children whom I love not half so well. This fair sweet child cheers me so in every place I go that nothing may distress me. Therefore, Father of Heaven, I pray Thee for his health and his grace. Keep him now, Lord, both day and night, so that never may harm or fear come to my child in any place. [*Rises.*] Now come on, Isaac, my own sweet child, go we home and take our rest.

ISAAC: Abraham, my own gentle father, I am full ready to follow you both early and late.

ABRAHAM: Come on, sweet child. I love thee best of all the children I ever begat.

20 [*They cross to another place. God speaks above.*]

GOD: Mine angel, hie thee fast on thy way, and go at once to middle-earth. I will now assay Abraham's heart, whether he be steadfast or not. Say that I command him to take Isaac, his young son, whom he loves so well, and make sacrifice with his blood, if he will enjoy any of My friendship. Show him the way to the hill where his sacrifice shall be made. I will assay now his good will, whether he loves best his child or Me. All men shall find an example in him, how they shall keep My commandments.

[*The angel descends. Abraham, returning, kneels in prayer.*]

ABRAHAM: Now, Father of Heaven, who formed all things, I make my
30 prayers to Thee again, for this day, surely, I must give Thee here my burnt

offering. Ah, Lord God, Almighty King, what manner of beast will please Thee most? If I knew of a surety, it should be done with all my power at once. It is my desire, verily, to do Thy pleasure on this hill, dear Father, God in Trinity.

ANGEL: Abraham! Abraham! stay. Our Lord commands thee to take Isaac, thy young son whom thou lovest best, and make sacrifice with his blood. Go thou into the Land of Vision, and offer thy child unto the Lord. I will lead and show thee. Submit, Abraham, to God's behest, and follow me on this green.

ABRAHAM: Welcome be to me my Lord's messenger, and I will not with- 10 stand His behest. Yet Isaac, my young son, has been a full dear child to me. I had rather, if God were pleased, lose all the goods I have than that Isaac, my son, should be harmed, so may God in Heaven save my soul! I have never loved anything on earth so much, and now I must go kill the child. Ah, Lord, my conscience is strongly stirred! And yet, my dear Lord, I am sore afraid to begrudge anything against Thy will. I love my child as my life, but yet I love my Lord much more; for though my heart resist, yet will I not spare child or wife, but do after my Lord's bidding. Though I love my son never so well, yet I will promptly smite off his head. Ah, Father of Heaven, I kneel to Thee! A hard death my son shall meet, to 20 honor Thee with, O Lord.

ANGEL: Abraham, Abraham, this is well said, and see that thou keep all these commands. But in thy heart be no whit dismayed.

ABRAHAM: Nay, nay, forsooth, I am well content to please my God with the best that I have. For though my heart be heavy to see the blood of my own dear son, yet for all this I will not pause, but I will go fetch my son Isaac and return as fast as we can. [*Abraham crosses to the other side of the stage, where Isaac is kneeling in prayer.*] Now Isaac, my own dear son, where art thou, child? Speak to me.

ISAAC: My father, sweet father, I am here, and make my prayers to the 30 Trinity.

ABRAHAM: Rise up, my child, and come hither fast, my gentle son, who art so wise; for we two must go together and make sacrifice unto my Lord.

ISAAC: Lo, I am right ready, my father. I stand here even by your side, and whatsoever ye bid me do, it shall be done with glad cheer.

ABRAHAM: Ah, Isaac, my own son so dear, I give thee God's blessing and mine. Put this faggot on thy back, and I myself will bring fire.

ISAAC: Father, I will take all this burden; I am right glad to do your bidding.

ABRAHAM: [*Aside.*] Ah, Lord of Heaven! I wring my hands; the words of 40 this child deeply wound my heart. [*To Isaac.*] Now, Isaac, son, go we our way to yonder hill with all our strength.

ISAAC: Go we, dear father, as fast as I may. I am full fain to follow you although I am weak.

ABRAHAM: [*Aside.*] Ah, Lord, my heart breaks in twain, so tender are the words of this child! [*They arrive at the mount.*] Ah, Isaac, son, lay down thy load and bear it no longer on thy back, for I must make ready quickly to honor my Lord as I should.

ISAAC: Lo, my dear father, here it is. I always strive to cheer you by my
10 presence. But, father, I marvel sore why ye seem so mournful; and I too am in dread. Where is the live beast that ye would kill? Both fire and wood we have ready, but we have no live beast on this mount. I know well a live beast must be slaughtered to make your sacrifice.

ABRAHAM: Dread not, my child, I tell thee; our Lord will send me by His sweet messenger some manner of beast in this place.

ISAAC: Yea, father, but my heart begins to quake, to see that sharp sword in your hand. Why bear ye your sword drawn so? I wonder much at your countenance.

ABRAHAM: [*Aside.*] Ah, Father of Heaven, woe is me! This child here
20 breaks my heart asunder.

ISAAC: Tell me, dear father, bear ye your sword drawn for me?

ABRAHAM: Ah, Isaac, sweet son, peace, peace! For indeed thou breakest my heart in three.

ISAAC: Now truly, father, ye have some thought, that ye mourn thus more and more.

ABRAHAM: [*Aside.*] Ah, dear Lord of Heaven, send down thy grace, for my heart was never half so heavy!

ISAAC: I pray you, father, to tell me whether I shall have any harm or not.

ABRAHAM: Surely, sweet son, I may not tell thee yet, my heart is now so
30 full of woe.

ISAAC: Dear father, I pray you, hide it not from me, but tell me some of your thought.

ABRAHAM: Ah, Isaac, Isaac, I must kill thee!

ISAAC: Kill me, father? Alas, what have I done? If I have trespassed against you in aught, ye may make me full meek with a rod. And with your sharp sword kill me not, for indeed, father, I am but a child.

ABRAHAM: I am full sorry, son, to spill thy blood, but truly, my child, I cannot choose.

ISAAC: Now I would to God my mother were here on this hill! She would kneel for me on her knees to save my life. And since my mother is not here, I pray you, father, change your mind and kill me not with your knife.

ABRAHAM: In sooth, son, unless I kill thee, I should grieve God right sore, I fear. It is His commandment and His will that I should do this deed. He commanded me, son, certainly to make my sacrifice with thy blood.

ISAAC: And is it God's will that I should be slain?

ABRAHAM: Yea, truly, Isaac, my good son; therefore my hands I wring.

ISAAC: Now, father, I will never complain, aloud or silently, against my Lord's will. But He might have sent me a better destiny if it had been His pleasure.   10

ABRAHAM: Forsooth, son, if I do not this deed, our Lord will be grievously displeased.

ISAAC: Nay, nay, father, God forbid that ever ye should grieve Him for me. Ye have other children whom ye love well by nature. I pray you, father, be not woeful, for, when I am once dead and gone from you, I shall soon be out of your mind. Therefore, do our Lord's bidding, and when I am dead, pray for me. But, good father, tell my mother nothing. Say that I am dwelling in another country.

ABRAHAM: Ah, Isaac, Isaac, blessed mayst thou be! My heart begins strongly to rise, to see the blood of thy blessed body!   20

ISAAC: Father, since it may not be otherwise, be reconciled to it as well as I. But ere I go to my death, I pray you bless me with your hand. [*Kneels.*]

ABRAHAM: Now, Isaac, with all my breath I give thee my blessing and God's also. Isaac, Isaac, son, stand up that I may kiss thy fair sweet mouth.

ISAAC: Now farewell, my own good father; and greet well my mother. But I pray you, hide my eyes that I may not see the stroke of your sharp sword bite my flesh.

ABRAHAM: Son, thy words make me weep full bitterly. Now, my dear son Isaac, speak no more.   30

ISAAC: Ah, my own dear father, why so? We shall speak together here but a while. And since I must needs be dead, yet my dear father, I pray you, smite but few strokes at my head; make an end as soon as ye may and tarry not too long.

ABRAHAM: Thy meek words, child, frighten me. "Welladay!" would be my song, were it not God's will. Ah, Isaac, my own sweet child, kiss me yet again on this hill. In all this world there is none so meek.

ISAAC: Now truly, father, all this delay only doth my heart harm. I pray you make an end.

ABRAHAM: Come, sweet son, into my arms. [*Starts to bind him.*] I must bind thy two hands, though thou be never so meek.

ISAAC: Ah, mercy, father, why do ye so?

ABRAHAM: That thou shouldst not hinder me, my child.

ISAAC: Nay, surely, father, I will not hinder you. Do your will with me, and perform the purpose, for God's love, on which ye are set. I am full sorry this day to die, but yet I would not grieve my God. Resolutely do your pleasure with me; my fair sweet father, I give you leave. But, father, I pray you, never tell my mother a word. If she wist it, she would weep full sore, for in truth she loved me right well. God's blessing may she have! Now farewell, my mother so sweet, we two are likely to meet never more!

ABRAHAM: Ah, Isaac, Isaac, son, thou makest me weep, and grievest me with thy words.

ISAAC: Indeed, sweet father, I am sorry to distress you. I cry you mercy for what I have done and for all the wrong that ever I did you. Now, dear father, forgive me for what I have done. God of Heaven, be with me!

ABRAHAM: Ah, dear child, leave off thy moans! In all thy life thou hast never grieved me once. Blessed be thou, body and soul, that ever thou wert born and bred! Thou hast been a right good child to me. But, though I mourn never so deeply, yet I must needs at last shed thy blood in this place. Therefore, my dear son, here shalt thou lie. [*Places him on the altar.*] I must set myself to my task. In sooth, I had as lief die myself and offer my own body if God will be pleased with my deed.

ISAAC: Ah, mercy, father, mourn ye no more! Your weeping wounds my heart, even as the death that I shall suffer. Your kerchief, wind it about my eyes.

ABRAHAM: So I will, my sweetest child on earth.

ISAAC: Once more, good father, remember and smite me not often with your sharp sword, but work swiftly.

Here Abraham lays a cloth on Isaac's face, saying:

ABRAHAM: Now farewell, my child so full of grace!

ISAAC: Ah, father, father! turn my face downward, for of your sword I am still in dread.

ABRAHAM: [*Aside.*] I am full sorry to do this deed, but, Lord, I will not withstand Thy behest.

ISAAC: Ah, Father of Heaven, to Thee I cry. Lord, receive me into Thy hand!

ABRAHAM: [*Aside.*] Lo, now the time is surely come that my sword must bite into his neck. Ah, Lord, my heart rebels against it; I may not find it in my heart to strike; my heart will not consent thereto. Yet I would fain do my Lord's will. But this young innocent lies so quietly, I may not find it in my heart to kill him. O, Father of Heaven, what shall I do?

ISAAC: Ah, mercy, father, why tarry ye so, and let me lie thus long on this heath? I would to God the stroke were done! Father, I pray you heartily, shorten my woe and let me not wait for my death!

ABRAHAM: Now, heart, why wouldst thou not break in three? Yet thou shalt not make me disobedient to my God. I will no longer delay for thy sake, for my God would be wroth. Now receive the stroke, my own dear child!

Here Abraham struck, and the angel took the sword in his hand suddenly.   10

ANGEL: I am an angel, thou mayst gladly see, who is sent to thee from heaven. Our Lord thanks thee a hundred times for keeping his commandment. He knows thy will and also thy heart, that thou fearest Him above all things. And to dispel some of thy sorrow I have brought a fair ram yonder; lo, he stands tied among the briars. Now, Abraham, mend thy cheer, for Isaac, thy young son, shall not shed his blood this day. Go, make thy sacrifice with yonder ram. Farewell, blessed Abraham, for now I go home to heaven; right short is the way. Take up thy noble son. [*Exit.*]

ABRAHAM: Ah, Lord, I thank thee for thy great favor! Now am I comforted in many ways. Arise up, Isaac, my dear son, arise! Arise up, sweet 20 child, and come to me!

ISAAC: Ah, mercy, father, why smite ye not? Smite, father, but once with your knife.

ABRAHAM: Peace, my sweet son, and have no fear, for our Lord of Heaven hath now granted thy life by His angel now, and thou shalt not die this day, son, in very truth.

ISAAC: Ah, father, I should be full glad surely, father,—surely, I say,—if this tale were true.

ABRAHAM: A hundred times, my fair son, I will now kiss thy mouth for joy.   30

ISAAC: Ah, my dear father Abraham, will not God be angered that we do this?

ABRAHAM: No, in truth no, my sweet son, for He hath sent yonder ram down to us. That beast shall die here in thy stead, in worship of our Lord. Go, fetch him hither, my child.

ISAAC: Father, I will go catch him by the head and quickly bring the beast with me. [*Untying the ram.*] Ah, sheep, sheep, blessed be thou, that thou wast sent down hither! Thou shalt die for me this day in worship of the Holy Trinity. Now come fast and go we together to my father. Though thou be never so gentle and good, yet I had rather thou shedest thy blood, 40 sheep, than I, in faith! [*Leads ram to Abraham.*] Lo, father, I have brought here speedily this gentle sheep, and to you I give him. But, Lord God, I thank Thee with all my heart, for I am glad that I shall live and kiss again my dear mother.

ABRAHAM: Now be right merry, my sweet child, for I will sacrifice here this living beast, that is so meek.

ISAAC: And I will begin to blow the fire at once, and it will burn speedily. But, father, while I am stooping low, ye will not kill me with your sword, I trust?

10 ABRAHAM: No, verily, sweet son, have no dread. My grief is past.

ISAAC: Yea, but I would that sword were thrown in a fire, for surely, father, it filled me with terror.

Here Abraham made his offering, kneeling and saying thus:

ABRAHAM: Now, Lord God of Heaven in Trinity, almighty, omnipotent God, I make my offering in worship of Thee, and present Thee with this live beast. Lord, as Thou art God and the ground of our grace, receive Thou mine intent.

GOD: [*Speaking above.*] Abraham, Abraham, well mayst thou flourish, and Isaac, thy young son beside thee. Truly, Abraham, for this thy deed

20 I will multiply the seed of you both as thick as the stars in the sky and as thick as the gravel in the sea. This I grant you for your goodness. From you shall spring numerous fruit, and ye shall enjoy bliss without end, for ye dread Me alone as God and keep each of My commandments. My blessing I give you wherever ye go.

ABRAHAM: Lo, Isaac, what thinkest thou of this that we have done? Full glad and blithe we may be that on this fair heath we murmured not against the will of God.

ISAAC: Ah, father, I thank our Lord utterly that I had the wisdom to fear God more than my death.

30 ABRAHAM: What, precious son, wert thou afraid? Boldly tell me, child, thy thought.

ISAAC: Yea, by my faith, father, I was never so afraid before as I was on yonder hill. And by my faith, I swear I will never go there but it be against my will.

ABRAHAM: Yea, come on with me, my own sweet son, and let us go homeward fast.

ISAAC: By my faith, father, I am willing. Never had I such good will to go home and to speak with my dear mother.

ABRAHAM: Ah, Lord of Heaven, I thank Thee, for now I may lead home

40 with me Isaac, my noble young son, the gentlest child above all others, this I well avow. Now let us set forth, my blessed son.

ISAAC: I assent, father, let us go; for, by my troth, if I were home again, I would never go out on such an errand. I pray God to give grace evermore to us and all those to whom we are beholden. [*Exeunt.*]

[*Enter Doctor of Theology.*]

DOCTOR: Lo, sovereigns and sirs, we have now shown this solemn story to great and small. It is good doctrine for the layman and the learned and even the wisest of all, barring none. For this story shows you how we should keep God's commands to the utmost of our ability without murmuring. Believe ye, sirs, if God sent an angel and commanded you to slay your child, by your troth, is there any of you who would murmur or strive 10 against it? What think ye now, sirs? I believe there are three or four or more. And these women, who weep so sorrowfully when their children die in the course of nature, it is but folly, I avow, to murmur against God or to grieve. For ye will never see Him harmed by land or water; keep this in mind. Murmur not against Our Lord God, whether He send you weal or woe, though ye be never so sore oppressed, for when He will, He may amend it if ye truly keep His commandments with a good heart, as this story has now shown you, and faithfully serve Him in safety. So ye may please God both evening and morning. Now may Jesu, who wore the crown of thorns, bring us all to heaven's bliss! 20

The Bruce

John Barbour

FREEDOM

(BK. I, VSS. 179–274)

WHEN Sir Edward, the mighty king, had done his pleasure in this wise with John Baliol, who was so quickly degraded and undone, he went in haste to Scotland and occupied all the land so completely that both castle and town were in his possession from Wick opposite the Orkney Isles to the Mull of Galloway, and filled it all with Englishmen. He then made sheriffs and bailiffs; and all other officers he made of Englishmen, to govern the land's affairs. They became so outrageous, wicked and covetous, so haughty and ruthless that Scottish men could do nothing to please them. Often the English would lie with their wives and daughters without pity. . . .

10   Alas that folk who were always free and wont to live in freedom, through their own mischance and folly were treated so wickedly that their foes became their judges! What greater wretchedness may a man have? Ah, freedom is a noble thing! Freedom makes a man rejoice. Freedom gives a man all solace. He lives at ease who freely lives. A noble heart may have no ease nor aught else that may please him if freedom fail; for free delight is craved above all other things. He that hath always lived free cannot know the nature, the anguish, the wretched fate that is coupled to foul thraldom. But if he had tried it, then would he know it in his heart and would think freedom more to prize than all the gold in the world. Thus evermore things 20 are revealed by their opposites. A thrall hath nothing; all that he hath is abandoned to his lord, whoever he may be. . . .

   Thraldom is well worse than death; for, so long as a thrall has his life, it irks him in body and bone, but death strikes him but once. In short, there is none can tell the whole condition of a thrall.

27: The Bruce

THE CROSSING OF LOCH LOMOND

(BK. III, VSS. 405–66)

The king [1] took his way to Loch Lomond, and came there on the third day. But they found no boat thereabout to bear them over the water. Then were they right woeful, for it was far to go around it, and they were afraid also of meeting their foes who were spread wide. Therefore they sought busily and fast along the loch's side, till James of Douglas at last found a little sunken boat and drew it, hot-foot, to the shore. But it was so little that it could carry but three at a time. They sent word thereof to the king, who was joyful of that discovery. He first went into the boat and Douglas with him; the third was one who rowed them over speedily, and set them dry on land, and rowed so often to and fro, fetching always two and two, that in a night and a day all had crossed the loch. For some of them could swim full well and bear a burden on their backs. Thus with swimming and with rowing they brought themselves over and their things.

The king meanwhile merrily read to those who were with him the romance of valiant Ferumbras, who was worthily overcome by the right doughty Oliver; and how the twelve peers were besieged in Aigremont, where King Lavine lay before them with more thousands than I can say. And only eleven men were they within, and one woman. They were so bestead that they had no food but such as they won from their foes. Yet they so bore themselves that they held the tower manfully till Richard of Normandy, despite his foes, informed the king,[2] who was joyful of these tidings, for he thought they had all been slain. Therefore he returned in haste, won Mantrible, passed Flagot, then mercilessly discomfited Lavine and all his host, and delivered all his men. He won the nails, the spear, and the crown that Jesu wore, and through his chivalry won a large part of the cross. In this manner the good king comforted them that were near him and made them sport and solace till his folk had all passed over.

THE DEATH OF EDWARD I AND THE DECEITS OF SATAN

(BK. IV, VSS. 184–311)

When King Edward heard how Neill Bruce held Kildrummy so stalwartly against his son, he gathered a great chivalry and went in haste toward Scotland. And as he was riding with his great host in Northumberland, a sickness took him on the way and oppressed him so hard that he could neither walk nor ride. Despite all he could do, he was forced to abide

[1] Of Scotland, Robert Bruce (d. 1329). [2] Charlemagne.

in a hamlet near by, a little and unworthy village. With great pain they brought him thither. He was so hard bestead that he could not draw his breath save with great pain, nor speak except very low. He bade them tell him what town it was in which he lay.

"Sir," they said, "Burgh-on-the-Sand this town is called in this country."

"Call they it Burgh? Alas!" said he," my hope is destroyed. For I thought never to endure the pain of death till by my strength I had taken the borough of Jerusalem. There I weened my life should end. I knew well that in a borough I should die, but I was neither wise nor cunning enough to
10 give heed to other boroughs. Now I may go no farther."

Thus he bemoaned his folly, as he surely had reason to do since he thought he knew the certainty of what no man may be certain. Some men say he had a spirit imprisoned who gave answers to whatever he would inquire. But he was a fool, without doubt, who trusted that creature. Fiends are of such nature that they envy mankind; for they wot well that men who live rightly here shall win the seats from which they were hurled down through their great pride. Therefore it will often betide that when fiends are constrained through force of conjuration to appear and answer, they are so false and treacherous that they always make their answers have a
20 double meaning to deceive those who believe them.

I will set down here an example which I heard concerning a war which befell between France and the Flemings. The mother of Earl Ferrand [3] was a necromancer and raised Satan and asked him what would be the outcome of the fighting betwixt the French king and her son. And Satan, as he was always wont to do, made his answer deceptive, and said to her these verses:

> *"Rex ruet in bello tumulique carebit honore*
> *Ferrandus, comitissa, tuus, mea cara Minerva,*
> *Parisius veniet, magna comitante caterva."*

This was the speech he made, in faith; that is to say in English: "The
30 King will fall in the fight and will lack the honor of burial; and thy Ferrand, my dear Minerva, will go to Paris, without doubt, followed by a great company of noble and worthy men."

This is the meaning of the answer that he made to her in Latin. He called her his dear Minerva because Minerva was always ready to serve him fully, and since the Countess gave him the same service, he called her his dear Minerva. And also through his great subtlety he called her "dear," the sooner to deceive, so that she would more quickly take the meaning of his speech which was most to her liking. His double speech so deceived her that many through her met their death. For she was glad of his answer,
40 and speedily told it to her son, and bade him hasten to the battle, for he

3 Of Flanders.

would have the victory without fear. And when he had heard her discourse, he hastened to the fight, where he was discomfited and captured and sent to Paris. Nevertheless through his valor the King was brought to earth during the battle and lamed also; but his men quickly mounted him again. When Ferrand's mother heard how her son had fared in the battle and that he was so discomfited, she raised the evil spirit at once and asked why he had mocked her with the answer he had given. And he replied that he had told only the truth:

"I said to thee that the King would fall in the battle, and so he did; he lacked burial too, as may be seen. And I said that thy son would go to Paris, 10 and he did right so, followed by such a retinue as he never had led in his lifetime. Now thou seest that I did not mock thee."

The woman was confounded and durst say no more to him. Thus through a double meaning that bargain ended in the deception of one party. Even so it befell in the case of King Edward. He believed that he would be buried in the borough of Jerusalem, but in fact he was buried at Burgh-on-the-Sand in his own country.

BRUCE MEETS THREE TRAITORS

(BK. VII, VSS. 400–87)

It so happened on a day that the king went to hunt, to find what game there was in that country. It so happened that he went to sit by a woodside alone with his two hounds, but he ever bore his sword with him. He had 20 sat there but a short while when he saw coming from the wood three men with bows in their hands, who approached him speedily; and he perceived at once by their bearing that they loved him not a whit. He rose, drew his leash toward him and let his hounds go free. God in His might help the King now! For unless he be now wary and strong, he will be in a sore plight; for the three men, in truth, were utterly his foes, and had watched so busily to see when they might take vengeance on the King for John Comyn's sake that they thought they had now the opportunity. And since he was alone, they thought they would quickly slay him, and if they could achieve this, as soon as they had slain the King, they could reach the wood again 30 without dread of his men.

Swiftly they came toward the King, and bent their bows when they were near. And he greatly feared their arrows since he wore no armor, loudly spoke to them and said:

"Ye ought, by God, to be ashamed to shoot at me from afar since I am one, and ye are three! If ye are brave, come near with your swords to attack me. Overcome me so, if ye can; ye shall be prized all the more."

"By God," said one of the three, "no man shall say we dread thee so that we shall slay thee with arrows."

Thereupon they cast away their bows and came on fast without delay. The King met them full hardily, and smote the first so vigorously that he fell down dead on the green. When the King's hound saw those men assail his master so, he leapt at one and took him by the neck full fiercely till he threw him down, top over tail. And the King, who had raised his sword, when he saw the hound had given him such fair succor, before the man who had fallen could rise, assailed him so that he clove his back in two. The third, when he saw his fellows thus slain without recovery, took his way to the wood again. But the King followed speedily, and also the hound that was with him, when he saw the man flee away shot after him at once, took him by the neck and pulled him down. The King, as he drew near, gave him such a blow in his rising that stone dead he dropped to the earth. The King's company approached and when they saw the King attacked in this manner so suddenly, sped toward him in haste, and asked how the adventure had gone. He told them fully how all three had assailed him.

"In faith," quoth they, "we can see that it is a hard task to meddle with you, who have so adroitly slain these three without suffering hurt."

"In faith," said he, "I slew but one and no more. God and my hound killed the two. Their treason encumbered them, in faith, for right strong men were they, all three."

THE VICTORY OF BANNOCKBURN [4]

(BK. XII, VSS. 152–381, 631–50)

There the battle was well fought. There was such a din of strokes as weapons clashed on armor, and so great a shattering of spears, and such flinging and thrusting, such shouting and groaning, so great a noise as men battered each other, war cries were raised on every side and wide wounds were given and taken, that it was hideous to hear all the four mighty divisions fighting on one front. Almighty God! full doughtily Sir Edward Bruce [5] and his men bore themselves among their foes. They fought with such skill, hardihood and valor, that the English vanguard was pressed back and in spite of all they could do, gave ground, and retreated for support to the main army, which was in such straits that they were afraid. For the Scots assailed them so stoutly that they were all in one mass. Whoever happened to fall in that fight, I trow he would not rise again. There one could see hardihood displayed in many ways, and many a man that was strong and

[4] Won by the Scots under King Robert over the English under Edward II, 1314.
[5] King Robert's brother.

bold lying dead underfoot where all the field was red with blood. The arms and heraldic devices which they bore were so fouled with blood that they could not be distinguished. Ah, mighty God! he who could see Walter Stewart and his army and the good stout Douglas fighting in that stalwart stour, would say that they were worthy of all honor, for in that battle they pressed their powerful foes so fast that, wherever they went, they drove them back. There many a steed which had no master could be seen fleeing astray. Ah, Lord! he who took heed could see the good Earl of Murray and his men giving such blows, fighting so fast in that battle, enduring such pain and hardship that wherever they came, they made a path for them- 10 selves. One could hear war cries and the Scots shouting boldly, "At them! At them! At them! They falter!" Then they attacked fiercely and slew all whom they could overtake; the Scottish archers, too, shot among the enemy so sturdily, grieving them so greatly, that what with those who fought with them, dealing them great blows, and what with the arrows that dealt them many great wounds and killed their horses fast, they retreated a little. They dreaded so greatly to die that their courage was worse than before; for their opponents in the fight gave hardihood, strength, will, heart, and all their might and main to put them shamefully to flight.

At this time that I tell of, while the battle was going thus and both sides 20 were fighting right manfully, the yeomen, swains, and poor men, who had been left in the park to guard the provisions, learned in truth that their lords were engaged in fierce fighting with their enemies; and they made one of themselves captain of them all. They fastened, instead of banners, somewhat broad sheets on long poles and spears, and said they would see the battle and help their lords as far as they had power. When all had assented to this and were assembled in a throng they were fifteen thousand and more. Then in great haste they went with all their banners in a host, as if they had been stout and stalwart men. All that assembly came where they could see the battle, and all at once they gave a shout: "At them! At 30 them boldly!" And therewith they advanced. But they were still far away, and when the English men, who were yielding ground through the pressure of the fight, as I have already said, saw such a company coming toward them with such a cry that they thought there were as many whom they had not seen before as those who were fighting with them already, then, wit ye well, they were so grievously disheartened that the best and bravest in the host that day would gladly, without loss of honor, have been away.

King Robert perceived by their wavering that they were near defeat, and loudly shouted his battle-cry. Then with those of his company he pressed his foes so fast that they in great terror yielded ground more and 40 more. All the Scots who were there, when they saw them withdraw from the fight, battered them with all their might so that they were split into groups and were near discomfiture, and some fled outright. But the strong and bold, who were hindered by shame from taking flight, continued the battle with great loss and stood firm.

When the King of England saw his men fleeing in sundry places, and saw his enemy's army which had become so bold and strong that all his folk were wholly confused and had no power to halt their foes, he was so grievously disheartened that he and all his company, five hundred well armed, all took to flight in a sudden rush, and held their way to the castle.[6]

Yet I have heard some men say that Sir Aymer de Valence, when he saw
10 the field near lost, led the King by the rein away from the fight, against his will. When Sir Giles de Argentine saw the King and his retinue thus prepare to flee so suddenly, he came in haste to the King and said:

"Sir, since ye thus will go your way, good day to you! For back will I turn. Never yet have I fled indeed, and I choose rather to abide here and die than to live and shamefully flee."

He turned his bridle without more tarrying, and against Sir Edward Bruce's army, which was steadfast and firm, he rode, crying "Argente!" as if he feared nothing. They met him with spears and fixed so many in him that he and his horse were overburdened and both sank to the earth, and
20 he was slain in that place. It was great pity of his death, for he was known, in faith, as the third best knight living in his day. He did many a feat of arms. He made three campaigns against the Saracens, and in each he vanquished two Saracens. There his great glory came to an end.

When Sir Aymer had fled with the King, none durst stay but all fled, scattered on every side. Their foes pressed close after them; and they, to tell the truth, were all in a panic and fled so fearfully that a great number of them sought the River Forth and there most of them were drowned. And Bannockburn was so filled with drowned horses and men between the banks that one could cross dryshod over the corpses. Lads, swains, and
30 the rabble, when they saw the battle won, ran among the folk who could offer no defense and slew them so that it was a pity to see. I have never heard of folk in any country who were in such a grievous plight. On one side they had their foes who cut them down without mercy, and on the other they had Bannockburn, which was so miry and deep that no one could ride across it. Perforce they must abide so that some were slain and some were drowned; none who came there could escape. Yet many who had fled elsewhere, as I have heard, got away. The King and those he had with him rode in a body to the castle and would have entered, for they knew not by what way to escape. But Sir Philip Mowbray said to him:
40 "The castle, sir, is at your will, but if ye come in, ye shall see that ye shall at once be besieged, and there is no one in all England to undertake your

[6] Of Stirling, near Bannockburn.

rescue, and without rescue no castle may be held long, ye wot well. There-fore take heart, rally your men closely about you, and go around the park. Link up as solidly as ye can, for I think no pursuers will be strong enough to fight so many."

They did as he counseled. They went their way at once beneath the castle walls right by the Round Table, and then encircled the park, and he hastened toward Linlithgow. . . .

In this wise the King escaped. Lo, how fickle is Fortune. Awhile she will smile upon a man, and then wound him. At no time will she remain stable. This mighty King of England she had set high on her wheel when with a 10 marvelous force of men-at-arms, archers, foot soldiers, and light horsemen he came riding out of his land, as I have related. And then in a night and a day she put him in such hard straits that he was fain to return home with seventeen men in a boat. But King Robert should not mourn at the turning of this wheel, for his side, through the rising of the wheel, vanquished their foes and proved their great might.

Thomas of Erceldoune

As I did roam the other day,
  Full fast in mind making my moan,
In the merry month of May,
  By Huntly banks, myself alone,

I heard the jay and throstle cock;
  The song-thrush moaned to herself
    and sang;
The wood-lark rang out like a bell,
  That all the wood about me rang.

Alone in longing thus I lay,
  Underneath a seemly tree;   10
Saw I where a lady gay
  Came riding over a lovely lea.

If I should sit until Doomsday,
  With my tongue, I avow to thee,
In certainty that lady gay
  Never could be described by me.

Her palfrey was of dapple gray,
  Such as I have never known;
As does the sun on a summer's day,
  That lady fair, herself she shone. 20

Her saddle was of ruel-bone,[1]
  Most seemly was that sight to see,
Stiffly set with precious stone,
  And encompassed all with crapotee,[2]

Stones of Orient, in great plentý;
  Her hair about her head did hang.
She rode over that lovely lea;

One while she whistled, another
  sang.

Her girths of noble silk they were,
  The buckles were of beryl stone; 30
Her stirrups were of crystal clear,
  And all with pearls in beauty shone.

Her poitrel [3] was of coral fine,
  Her crupper was of orphery; [4]
Her bridle was of gold most fine,
  On either side did hang bells three.

She led three greyhounds in a leash,
  And seven raches [5] by her raced;
She bore a horn about her neck,
  And arrows in her belt were
    placed.   40

Thomas lay and saw that sight,
  Underneath a seemly tree;
He said: "Yonder is Mary, most of
  might,
  That bore that Child that died for
  me.

"Unless I speak with yon lady bright,
  I fear my heart will break in three;
Now must I go with all my might,
  Her to meet at Eildon tree."

Thomas himself did quickly raise,
  And ran over that mountain lea; 50

---

[1] Ivory.
[2] Toadstone, a precious stone fabled to be found in the head of a toad.
[3] Her horses's breastplate.   [4] Gold embroidery.   [5] Hunting dogs.

If it be as the story says,
  He met her at the Eildon tree.

He kneelèd down upon his knee,
  Underneath the greenwood spray;
"Lovely lady, have mercy on me,
  Queen of Heaven, as thou well
    may."

Then spoke that lady mild of thought,
  "Thomas. such words do thou let
    be;
The Queen of Heaven am I not,
  For I took on me never so high de-
    gree.   60

"But I am of another land,
  Though appareled now in greatest
    price;
I ride after these wild deer;
  My raches run at my device."

"If thou be appareled in greatest price,
  And here dost ride in folly free,
Dear lady, as thou in love art wise,
  Grant me then leave to lie by thee."

She said, "Thou man, that would be
    folly;
  I pray thee, Thomas, let me be; 70
For I do here assure thee wholly,
  That sin would end all my beautee."

"Lovely lady, have mercy on me.
  And I evermore will with thee
    dwell;
Here my troth I plight to thee,
  Whether thou wilt, in heaven or
    hell."

"Man of clay, thou wilt me mar,
  But yet thou shalt have all thy will;
But know thou well, thou achievest
  ·the worst,
  For all my beauty thou wilt
    spill."   80

Down then did light that lady bright,
  Underneath the greenwood spray;
And, as the story tells aright,
  Seven times by her he lay.

She said, "Man, thou likest thy play;
  What maid in bower may deal with
    thee?
Thou harriest me all this long day;
  I pray thee, Thomas, let me be."

Thomas then stood up in that stead,
  And he beheld that lady gay; 90
Her hair it hung all over her head;
  Her eyes seemed out, they were so
    gray;

And all that rich clothing was away
  That he before saw in that stead;
Her one shank black, her other gray,
  And all her body was like lead.

Then said Thomas, "Alas, alas!
  In faith, this is a doleful sight!
How art thou faded in the face,
  That shone before like the sun so
    bright!"   100

She said, "Thomas, take now leave of
    sun and moon,
  And of the leaf that grows on tree;
This twelvemonth must thou with me
    go,
  And middle-earth shalt thou not
    see."

"Alas," he said, "and woe is me!
  I trow my deeds will work me care.
My soul, Jesu, entrust I thee,
  Whithersoever my bones may fare."

She led him in at Eildon Hill,
  Underneath a secret lea; 110
Here it was dark as midnight murk,
  And ever the water to his knee.

For the space of days full three,
 He heard but the soughing of the
  flood;
At last he said, "O woe is me!
 Almost I die for want of food."

She led him into an arbor fair,
 Where fruit was growing plente-
  ously;
Pear and apple, both ripe they were;
 The date and damson plum on
  tree,   120

The fig and the wineberry too.
 The nightingales there built their
  nest;
The popinjays about fast flew;
 And throstles sang and would have
  no rest.

He pressed forth to pull fruit with his
  hand,
 As one who for lack of food was
  faint;
She said, "Thomas, do thou let them
  stand,
 Or else the fiend will thee attaint.

"If thou do pluck it, the truth to say,
 Thy soul will go to the fire of
  hell;   130
It will never come out before Dooms-
  day,
 But there in pain forever dwell.

"Thomas, truly I do thee implore,
 Come, lay thy head down on my
  knee,
And thou shalt see the fairest sight
 That ever man of thy land did see."

He did in haste as she him bade;
 Upon her knee his head he laid,

For, her to please, he was full glad,
 And then that lady to him said: 140

"Seest thou now yon pleasant way
 That lies over yon high mountain?
Yonder is the way to heaven for aye,
 When sinful souls have passed their
  pain.[6]

"Seest thou now yon other way,
 That low beneath yon branches
  lies?
That is the way, the truth to say,
 Unto the joy of Paradise.

"Seest thou yet yonder third way,
 That lies underneath yon green
  plain?   150
That is the way, with teen and tray,[7]
 Where sinful souls do suffer their
  pain.[8]

"But seest thou now yonder fourth
  way,
 That lies there over yon deep dell?
Yon is the way, O wellaway!
 Unto the burning fires of hell.

"Seest thou yet that castle fair,
 That over yon high hill does sit?
Of town and tower there's no com-
  pare;
 On earth is none is like to it.[9] 160

"My lord is served at every course
 By thirty knights, so fair and free.
I shall say, sitting at the dais,
 I took thy speech beyond the
  sea.

"When thou comest to yon castle gay,
 I pray thee a courteous man to be;
And whatso any man to thee say,

---

[6] That is, the road from purgatory to heaven.   [7] Sorrow and affliction.
[8] Purgatory.   [9] Her own country of fairyland.

Look that thou answer none but
  me."

Thomas as still as stone he stood,
  And beheld that lady gay;   170
She was again as fair and good,
  And just as rich on her palfréy.

Her greyhounds were filled with
  blood of deer;
  Her raches were coupled,[10] by my
  fay;
She blew her horn full loud and clear,
  And to the castle she took her way.

She went in sooth, into the hall,
  And Thomas followed at her hand;
Then ladies came, fair were they all,—
  And knelt to her in courtly
  band.   180

Harp and fiddle there they found,
  The gittern and the psaltery,
Lute and rebeck both did sound,
  And all manner of minstrelsy.

The greatest marvel, Thomas thought,
  Was when he stood upon the floor;
Fifty harts were therein brought,
  Bigger than he had ever seen before.

Raches lay lapping up the blood;
  Cooks came in with dressing-
  knife;   190
They cut up the deer as well they
  could;
  Revel amongst them was full rife.

Knights did dance by three and three,
  There was revel, game, and play;
Lovely ladies, fair and free,
  Sat and sang in rich array.

[10] Her dogs stand leashed together.

Thomas dwelt in that joyous place
  Longer than I can say, pardee;
Till on a day, as I hope for grace,
  My lovely lady said to me: 200

"Prepare thee, Thomas, thou must be
  gone,
  For here thou may no longer be;
Hie thee fast with might and main,
  I shall thee bring to Eildon tree."

Thomas said then with heavy cheer,
  "Lovely lady, now let me be;
For certainly I have been here
  The space of days no more than
  three."

"Forsooth, Thomas, as I thee tell,
  Thou hast been here three years and
  more;   210
And longer here thou must not dwell;
  And why? I shall thee tell where-
  fore:

'Tomorrow the foul fiend of hell
  Among this folk will fetch his fee;
And thou art a large man, shapen well;
  I know full well he will choose thee.

"For all the gold that ever may be,
  From hence unto this world's end,
Thou shalt be never betrayed by me;
  Therefore with me I urge thee
  wend."   220

She brought him again to Eildon tree,
  Underneath that greenwood spray.
On Huntly banks it is merry to be,
  Where birds do sing both night and
  day.

The Travels of Sir John Mandeville

THE PROLOG

I, John Mandeville, Knight, albeit I be not worthy, . . . was born in England, in the town of St. Albans, and passed the sea in the year of Our Lord Jesu Christ 1322, on the day of St. Michael, and hitherto have been long time over the sea, and have seen and gone through many divers lands and many provinces and kingdoms and isles; and have passed throughout Turkey, Armenia the Little and the Great, through Tartary, Persia, Syria, Arabia, Egypt the High and the Low, through Lybia, Chaldea, and a great part of Ethiopia, through Amazonia, India the Less and the More, and throughout many other isles that are about India, where dwell many divers
10 folk of divers manners and laws and of divers shapes of men; of which lands and isles I shall speak more plainly hereafter. And I shall describe to you some part of the things that are there when it shall be time and as it may best come to my mind, and specially for them who intend and are purposed to visit the holy city of Jerusalem and the holy places that are thereabout. And I shall tell the way that they shall take thither, for I have oftentimes passed and ridden that way with a good company of many lords, God be thanked! And ye shall understand that I have put this book out of Latin into French and translated it again out of French into English, that every man of my nation may understand it. But lords and knights and other noble
20 and worthy men who know Latin but little and have been beyond the sea know and understand if I say truth or not.

THE RELICS OF THE PASSION

(CHAP. II)

At Constantinople is the Cross of Our Lord Jesu Christ and His coat without seams, which is called *Tunica Inconsutilis*, and the sponge and the reed with which the Jews gave Our Lord vinegar and gall on the cross. And there is one of the nails that Christ was nailed with on the cross. And some men trow that half the cross that Christ was put on is in Cyprus in an abbey of monks that men call the Hill of the Holy Cross, but it is not so. For that cross that is in Cyprus is the cross on which Dismas, the good thief, was hanged, but all men know it not; and that is ill done, for because of the profit from the offering they say that it is the cross of Our Lord Jesu Christ. And ye shall understand that the cross of Our Lord was made of four manner of trees, as it is contained in this verse: *"In cruce fit palma, cedrus, cypressus, olyva."* For that piece that went upright from the earth to the head was of cypress, and the piece that went overthwart to which his hands were nailed was of palm. And the stock that stood within the earth, in which was made the mortise, was of cedar, and the tablet above his head, that was 10 a foot and a half long, on which the title was written in Hebrew, Greek, and Latin, that was of olive. . .

And the Christian men who dwell beyond the sea in Greece say that the tree of the cross that we call cypress was of that tree of which Adam ate the apple, and so they find it written. And they say also that their scripture saith that Adam was sick and said to his son Seth that he should go to the angel who kept Paradise that he would send him the oil of mercy to anoint his members with so that he might have healing. And Seth went, but the angel would not let him come in and said to him that he might not have of the oil of mercy. But he gave him three grains of the same tree that his 20 father ate the apple of, and bade him as soon as his father was dead that he should put these three grains under his tongue and bury him so. And so he did, and of these three grains sprang a tree as the angel said that it would and bear a fruit, through which fruit Adam should be saved. And when Seth came back, he found his father near dead, and when he was dead, Seth did with the grains as the angel bade him, from which sprang the three trees, of which the cross was made, which bore good fruit and blessed, Our Lord Jesu Christ, through whom Adam and all that come of him should be saved and delivered from dread of death without end, unless it be their own fault. 30

This holy cross the Jews hid in the earth under a rock of the Mount of Calvary, and it lay there two hundred years and more until the time of St. Helena, who was mother to Constantine, the emperor of Rome. And she was daughter of King Cole, born in Colchester, who was king of England, which was then called Britain the More. The emperor Constantius wedded her as his wife for her beauty and begat on her Constantine, who was afterwards emperor of Rome and king of England. And ye shall understand that the cross of Our Lord was eight cubits long, and the overthwart piece was three and a half cubits in length.

And one part of the crown of Our Lord wherewith he was crowned 40 and one of the nails and the spearhead and many other relics are in France in the king's chapel, and the crown lieth in a vessel of crystal richly dight.

For a king of France bought these relics at some time from the Jews to whom the emperor had given them as security for a great sum of silver. And if it be as men say that this crown is of thorns, ye shall understand that it was of rushes of the sea, which prick as sharply as thorns. For I have seen and beheld many times the one of Paris and the one of Constantinople, for they were both made of rushes of the sea. But men have parted them in two parts, of which one part is at Paris and the other part is at Constantinople. And I have one of the precious thorns, which seems like a white thorn, and that was given to me for a great specialty. For there are many of them 10 broken and fallen into the vessel that the crown lieth in. For they break for dryness when men move them to show them to great lords who come thither. And ye shall understand that Our Lord Jesu, in that night that He was taken, was led into a garden, and there He was examined right sharply, and there the Jews scorned Him and made Him a crown of the branches of white thorn that grew in that same garden, and set it on His head so fast and so sore that the blood ran down many places of His visage and of His neck and of His shoulders. And therefore hath the white thorn many virtues; for he that beareth a branch thereof on him, no thunder nor any manner of tempest may harm him, nor in the house that it is in may any 20 evil ghost enter nor come unto the place that it is in. And in that same garden St. Peter denied Our Lord thrice. Afterward was Our Lord led forth before the bishops and the masters of the law into another garden of Annas. And there also He was examined, reproved, and scorned, and crowned again with a sweet thorn that men call barberry, which grew in that garden and which hath also many virtues. And afterwards He was led into a garden of Caiaphas, and there He was crowned with sweet-briar. And afterwards He was led into the chamber of Pilate, and there He was examined and crowned. And the Jews set Him in a chair and clad Him in a mantle, and there they made the crown of rushes of the sea. And there they 30 kneeled to Him and scorned Him saying: "*Ave rex Judeorum,*" that is to say, "Hail, King of the Jews!" And of this crown half is at Paris and the other half at Constantinople. And this crown Christ had on his head when he was put upon the cross, and therefore ought men to worship it and hold it more worthy than any of the others. And the spear shaft the emperor of Almain [1] hath, but the head is at Paris. And nevertheless the emperor of Constantinople saith that he hath the spear head, and I have oftentimes seen it, but it is greater than that at Paris.

[1] Germany.

HIPPOCRATES' DAUGHTER

(CHAP. IV)

And some men say that in the isle of Lango [2] is still the daughter of Hippocrates in the form and likeness of a great dragon, which is a hundred fathoms in length as men say, for I have not seen her. And they of the isles call her Lady of the Land, and she lieth in an old castle in a cave and showeth herself twice or thrice in the year, and doth harm to no man unless men do her harm. And she was thus changed and transformed from a fair damsel into the likeness of a dragon by a goddess who was called Diana. And men say that she shall so endure in the form of a dragon until a knight come who is so hardy that he dare come to her and kiss her on the mouth, and then shall she turn again to her own kind and be a woman again, but after that she shall not live long. And it is not long since that a knight of the Hospital of Rhodes, who was hardy and doughty in arms, said that he would kiss her. And when he was upon his courser and went to the castle and entered into the cave, the dragon lifted up her head against him. And when the knight saw her in that form so hideous and so horrible, he fled away, and the dragon bore the knight upon a rock in spite of all he could do, and from that rock she cast him into the sea, and so were lost both horse and man.

And also a young man who knew not of the dragon went out of a ship and went through the isle till he came to the castle and came into the cave and went so long till he found a chamber, and there he saw a damsel who combed her head and looked in a mirror. And she had much treasure about her, and he thought that she was a common woman who dwelt there to receive men to folly. And he abode till the damsel saw the shadow of him in the mirror, and she turned toward him and asked him what he would. And he said he would be her leman or paramour, and she asked him if he were a knight, and he said nay. And then she said that he might not be her leman, but she bade him go again unto his fellows and cause himself to be knighted and come again on the morrow, and she would come out of the cave before him, and then let him come and kiss her on the mouth. "And have no dread, for I shall do thee no manner of harm, albeit thou see me in the likeness of a dragon. For though thou see me hideous and horrible to look on, I assure thee that it is made by enchantment. For without doubt I am none other than thou seest now, a woman, and therefore dread thee not. And if thou kiss me, thou shalt have all this treasure and be my lord and lord also of all that isle."

[2] Cos, near the island of Rhodes. On this legend cf. *Studi Medievali*, nuova serie XVII, 104-113.

And he departed from her and went to his fellows to the ship, and caused him to be made knight and came again on the morrow for to kiss this damsel. And when he saw her come out of the cave in the form of a dragon so hideous and so horrible, he had so great dread that he fled again to the ship and she followed him. And when she saw that he turned not again, she began to cry as a thing that had much sorrow, and then she turned again into her cave. And anon the knight died, and since then no knight might see her but that he died anon. But when a knight cometh who is so hardy as to kiss her, he shall not die but he shall turn the damsel into her right form and
10 natural shape, and he shall be lord of all the countries and isles abovesaid.

THE HOLY SEPULCHRE

(CHAP. XI)

And ye shall understand that when men come to Jerusalem, their first pilgrimage is to the church of the Holy Sepulchre, where Our Lord was buried, which is without the city on the north side, but it is now enclosed within the town wall. And there is a full fair church, all around and open above and covered with lead; and on the west side is a fair tower and an high for bells, strongly made. And in the midst of the church is a tabernacle, as it were a little house, made with a low little door. And that tabernacle is made in manner of half a circle, right curiously and richly made of gold and azure and other rich colors full nobly; and in the right side of that
20 tabernacle is the sepulchre of Our Lord. And the tabernacle is eight feet long and five feet wide and eleven feet in height. And it was not long since that sepulchre was all open that men might kiss it and touch it. But because pilgrims who came thither tried to break the stone in pieces or into powder, therefore the Sultan hath had a wall made about the sepulchre so that no man may touch it. But in the left side of the wall of the tabernacle, at about the height of a man, there is a great stone of the size of a man's head which was part of the Holy Sepulchre, and that stone the pilgrims who come thither kiss. In that tabernacle are no windows, but it is all made light with lamps that hang before the sepulchre; and there is a lamp that hangeth be-
30 fore the sepulchre that burneth bright, and on Good Friday it goeth out by itself, and on Easter Day it lights again by itself at the hour Our Lord rose from death to life.

THE SULTAN OF EGYPT

(CHAPS. VI AND XVI)

At Babylon [3] there is a fair church of Our Lady, where she dwelt seven years when she fled out of the land of Judea for dread of King Herod. And there lieth the body of St. Barbara, the virgin and martyr, and there dwelt Joseph when he was sold by his brethren. And there Nebuchadnezar, the king, had the three children put in the furnace of fire because they were in the right truth of belief, which children men called Hananiah, Azariah, and Mishael as the psalm of *Benedicite* saith; but Nebuchadnezar called them otherwise, Shadrach, Meshach, and Abednego, that is to say, God glorious, God victorious, and God over all things and realms, and that was by reason of the miracle that he saw God's Son go with the children 10 through the fire, as he said. There dwelleth the Sultan in his Calahelyk, for there is commonly his seat in a fair castle, strong and great and well set upon a rock. In that castle dwell always, to keep it and to serve well the Sultan, more than six thousand persons who receive all their necessities from the Sultan's court. I ought right well to know it, for I dwelt with him a great while as a mercenary in his wars against the Bedouins. And he would have married me full highly to a great prince's daughter if I would have forsaken my religion and my belief. But I thank God I had no will to do it for anything that he promised me.

* * * * *

I shall tell you what the Sultan told me upon a day in his chamber. He 20 sent out of his chamber all manner of men, lords and others, for he would speak with me in secret. And there he asked me how Christian men conducted themselves in our country, and I said to him, "Right well, thanked be God." And he said to me: "Truly nay, for ye Christian men reck not at all how untruly ye serve God. Ye should give example to do well, and ye give them example to do evil. For the common folk on festival days, when they should go to church to serve God, then go to taverns and bide there in gluttony all the day and all night, and eat and drink like beasts that have no reason and know not when they have enough. And also Christian men strive in all manners that they can 30 to fight and to deceive one another, and therewith they are so proud that they know not how to be clothed, now long, now short, now tight, now wide, now sworded, now daggered, and in all manner of guises. They should be simple, meek, and true, and full of almsdeeds, as Jesu was, in whom they believe, but they are all the contrary and ever inclined to evil

[3] Not the ancient Babylon, but a town near Cairo.

[275]

and to do evil. And they are so covetous that for a little silver they sell their daughters, their sisters, and their own wives to put them in lechery; and one draweth away the wife of another, and none of them holdeth faith to another, but they violate their law that Jesu Christ gave them to keep for their salvation. And thus for their sins have they lost all this land that we hold. For because of their sins God hath given them into our hands, not only through our strength but for their sins. For we know well in very sooth that when ye serve God, God will help you, and when He is with you, no man may be against you. And that know ye well by our prophecies, 10 that Christian men shall win again this land out of our hands when they serve God more devoutly. But as long as they be of foul and unclean living, as they are now, we have no kind of dread of them, for their God will help them in no wise." . . .

Alas, it is a great disgrace to our faith and our religion when folk who are without religion reprove us and charge us with our sins. And they who should be converted to Christ and to the law of Jesu by our good examples and by our living acceptably to God, and so be converted to the law of Jesu Christ, are through our wickedness and evil living far from us. And strangers to the holy and true belief thus accuse us and hold us for wicked 20 livers and cursed. And truly they say sooth, for the Saracens are good and faithful, for they keep entirely the commandment of the holy book, Alkoran, which God sent them by his messenger Mohammed, to whom, as they say, St. Gabriel, the angel, oftentimes told the will of God.

POLOMBE

(CHAP. XIX)

Toward the head of that forest is the city of Polombe,[4] and above the city is a great mountain that is also called Polombe, and from that mount the city hath its name. And at the foot of that mount is a fair well and a great, which hath the odor of all spices, and at every hour of the day it changeth its odor and its savor diversely. And whoso drinketh three times fasting of the water of that well is whole of all manner of sickness that he 30 hath, and they that dwell there and drink often of that well never have sickness and they seem always young. I have drunk thereof three or four times, and methinketh I fare the better still. Some men call it the Well of Youth, for they that often drink thereof seem always young and live without sickness, and men say that that well cometh out of Paradise, and therefore it is so virtuous. . . .

And when any man dieth in that country, they burn his body in the

---

[4] Koulam, on the coast of India.

name of penance, to the intent that he suffer no pain in the earth to be eaten of worms. And if his wife have no child, they burn her with him and say that it is reason that she make him company in that other world as she did in this. But if she have children by him, they let her live with them to bring them up if she will. And if she love more to live with her children than to die with her husband, men hold her to be false and cursed, and she shall never be loved or trusted by the people.

THE EARTH IS ROUND

(CHAP. XXI)

In that land and in many others beyond that, no man may see the star Transmontane, which is called the star of the sea, which is immovable and which is toward the north, which we call the lodestar. But men see another 10 star opposite to it, which is toward the south, which is called Antarctic. And just as shipmen here take their direction and guide themselves by the lodestar, right so do shipmen beyond those parts by the star of the south, which star appeareth not to us. And this star that is toward the north, which we call the lodestar, appeareth not to them. For which cause men may well perceive that the land and the sea are of a round shape and form, for the part of the firmament showeth in one country which showeth not in another country. And men may well prove by experience and subtle exercise of mind that if a man find passage by ships that would go to search the world, men might go by ship all about the world, above and be- 20 neath. . . .

And therefore hath it befallen many times as I have heard recounted when I was young, how a worthy man departed once from our countries to go search the world, and so he passed India and the isles beyond India, where there are more than five thousand isles. And so long he went by sea and land and so encircled the world for many seasons that he found an isle where he heard speak his own language, calling oxen at the plow with such words as men speak to beasts in his own country, whereof he had great marvel, for he knew not how it might be. But I say that he had gone so long by land and by sea that he had encircled all the earth, so that by en- 30 circling, that is to say, going around, he had come again unto his own frontiers. And if he had passed further, he would have found his own country and recognized it. . .

But it seemeth to simple men, unlearned, that men may not go under the earth and also that men would fall toward the heaven from under. But that may not be unless we may fall toward heaven from the earth where we are. For in whatever part of the earth that men dwell, either above or beneath, it seemeth always to them that dwell that they walk more right than any other folk; and just as it seemeth to us that they are under us, so it seemeth to them that we are under them. For if a man might fall from the earth to the firmament, by greater reason the earth and the sea, which are so great and so heavy, should fall to the firmament; but that may not be. And therefore saith Our Lord God: *"Non timeas me qui suspendi terram ex nihilo."* [5]

ANTHROPOPHAGI AND MEN WHOSE HEADS DO GROW BENEATH THEIR SHOULDERS

(CHAP. XXIII)

From that isle in going by sea toward the south is another great isle that is called Dondun. In that isle are folk of divers kinds, so that the father
10 eateth the son, the son the father, the husband the wife, and the wife the husband. And if it so befall that the father or mother or any of their friends are sick, anon the son goeth to the priest of their religion and prayeth him to ask the idol if his father or mother or friend shall die of that illness or not. And then the priest and the son go together before the idol and kneel full devoutly and ask of the idol their question. And if the devil that is within answer that he shall live, they keep him well; and if he say he shall die, then the priest goeth with the son and the wife of him that is sick, and they put their hands upon his mouth and stop his breath and so they slay him. And after that they chop all the body in small pieces and pray all his
20 friends to come and eat of him that is dead, and they send for all the minstrels of the country and make a solemn feast. . .

In one of these isles are folk of great stature like giants, and they are hideous to look upon, and they have but one eye and that is in the middle of the forehead, and they eat nothing but raw flesh and raw fish. And in another isle toward the south dwell folk of foul stature and of cursed nature, that have no heads and their eyes are in their shoulders, and their mouth is crooked as a horse shoe, and that is in the midst of their breast.
. . . And in another isle are folk of foul fashion and shape, that have the lip above the mouth so great that when they sleep in the sun, they cover all
30 the face with that lip.

[5] "Fear Me not, who hung the earth from nothing."

THE OLD MAN OF THE MOUNTAIN [6]

(CHAP. XXXI)

Beside the isle of Pentexoire, which is the land of Prester John, is a great isle, long and broad, that men call Milstorak, and it is in the lordship of Prester John. In that isle is great plenty of goods. There was dwelling once a rich man, and it is not long since, and men called him Gatholonabes, and he was full of wiles and subtle deceits. And he had a full fair castle and a strong in a mountain, so strong and so noble that no man could devise a fairer or a stronger. And he had caused all the mountain to be enclosed with a strong wall and a fair, and within those walls he had the fairest garden that any man might behold, and therein were trees bearing all manner of fruits that any man could devise. And therein were also all 10 manner of potent herbs of good smell and all other herbs also that bear fair flowers. And he had also in that garden many fair wells, and beside those wells he caused to be made fair halls and fair chambers, painted all with gold and azure. And there were in that place many divers things and many divers [painted] stories, and beasts and birds that sang full delectably and moved by contrivances so that it seemed that they were alive. And he had also in his garden all manner of fowls and beasts that any man might think of, for to have play and disport to behold them. And he had also in that place the fairest damsels that might be found under the age of fifteen years, and the fairest young striplings that men might get of that same age; and 20 they were all clothed in cloths of gold full richly, and he said that those were angels. And he had also had made three wells, fair and noble and all surrounded with stone of jasper and crystal sprinkled with gold and set with precious stones and great orient pearls. And he had made a conduit under the earth so that at his desire one of the three wells should run milk, another wine, and another honey; and that place he called Paradise.

And when any good knight who was hardy and noble came to see this royalty, he would lead him into his Paradise and show him these wonderful things for his disport, and the marvelous and delicious song of divers birds, and the fair damsels, and the fair wells of milk, wine, and honey, 30 plenteously running. And he would cause divers instruments of music to sound in a high tower so merrily that it was joy to hear, and no man could see the craft thereof. And those, he said, were angels of God, and that place was Paradise, which God had promised to his friends saying: "*Dabo vobis terram fluentem lacte et melle.*" [7] And then would he make them drink of a certain drink with which anon they would be drunk, and then would it

---

[6] On this legend cf. *Speculum*, XXII (1947), 497–519.
[7] "I will give you a land flowing with milk and honey."

seem to them a greater delight than they had before. And then would he say to them that if they would die for him and his love, after death they should come to his Paradise, and they should be of the age of those damsels, and they should play with them and yet be maidens. And after that he would put them in a still fairer Paradise, where they should see the God of nature visibly in his majesty and in his bliss. And then would he show them his intent, and say to them that if they would go slay such a lord or such a man who was his enemy or opposed to his will, they should not dread to do it and be slain therefor themselves, for after their death he would 10 put them into another Paradise that was a hundred fold fairer than any of the others, and there they should dwell with the fairest damsels that might be and play with them evermore. And thus went many divers lusty young knights to slay great lords in divers countries who were his enemies, and caused themselves to be slain in hope to have that Paradise. And thus oftentimes he was revenged on his enemies by his subtle deceits and false wiles.

And when the worthy men of the country had perceived this subtle falsehood of this Gatholonabes, they assembled with force and assailed his castle and slew him and destroyed all the fair places and all the nobilities 20 of that Paradise. The place of the wells and of the walls and of many other things are yet openly seen, but the richness is clean vanished.

THE GYMNOSOPHISTS

(CHAP. XXXIII)

Another isle there is that men called Oxidrate and another isle that men called Gynosophe, where there is also a good folk and full of good faith. And they hold for the most part the good conditions and customs and good manners as do men of the country abovesaid, but they go all naked. Into that isle entered King Alexander [the Great] to see their manner, and when he saw their great faith and the truth that was among them, he said that he would not grieve them and bade them ask of him what they would have of him, riches or anything else, and they should have it with good 30 will. And they answered that he that had meat and drink to sustain the body with was rich enough, for the riches of this world which is transitory are not of value. But if it was in his power to make them immortal, thereof they would pray him and thank him. And Alexander answered that it was not in his power to do it because he was mortal as they were. And then they asked him why he was so proud and so fierce and so busy to put all the world under his subjection, "even as thou wert a god and had no end of thy life, neither day nor hour, and willest to have at thy commandment all the world, which shall leave thee without fail, or thou shalt leave it. And even as it hath been to other men before thee, right so it shall be to others after thee, and from hence shalt thou bear nothing. But as thou wert born all naked, right so all naked shall thy body be turned into the earth that thou wert made of. Wherefore thou shouldst think and impress it on thy mind that nothing is immortal, but only God, who made all things."

By which answer Alexander was greatly astonished, and, abashed and all confounded, he departed from them. And albeit that these folk have not the articles of our faith as we have, nevertheless, for their good natural faith and for their good intent I trow fully that God loveth them and that 10 God accepteth their service gladly, as he did of Job, who was a pagan, and held him for his true servant. And therefore, albeit that there are many divers religions in the world, yet I trow that God loveth always them that love him and serve him meekly in truth, and specially them that despise the vain glory of this world, as these folk do and as Job did.

CONFIRMATION BY THE POPE [8]

(CHAP. XXXV)

And ye shall understand, if it please you, that at my home coming I came to Rome and showed my life to our holy father, the Pope, and was absolved of all that lay on my conscience of many a grievous point, as men must needs be who have dwelt in company with so many divers folk of divers sects and beliefs as I have been. And among all I showed him this treatise 20 that I had made after the information of men that knew of things that I had not seen myself, and also of marvels and customs that I had seen myself, as far as God would give me grace; and I besought his holy fatherhood that my book might be examined and corrected by the advice of his wise and discreet council. And our holy father of his special grace transmitted my book to be examined and proved by the advice of his said council, by which my book was proved as true, inasmuch as they showed me a book that my book was examined by, which comprehended much more by a hundred parts, and in accordance with which the Mappa Mundi was made. And so my book, albeit that many men will not give credence to anything 30 but what they see with their eye, though the author or person be ever so true, is affirmed and approved by our holy father in manner and form as I have said.

[8] This confirmation is not in the original French work.

The General Prolog to the

Translation of the Old Testament

John Purvey

THOUGH covetous clerics are mad by reason of simony, heresy, and many other sins, and despise and stop Holy Writ as much as they can, yet the unlearned people cry after Holy Writ, to know it and keep it, with great cost and peril of their life. For these reasons and others, with common charity to save all men in our realm whom God would have saved, a simple creature hath translated the Bible out of Latin into English.

First, this simple creature had much travail, with divers companions and helpers, to gather many old Bibles and other doctors and common glosses, and to make one somewhat accurate Latin Bible text; and then to study 10 it anew, the text with the gloss and other doctors, such as he could obtain, and especially Lyra on the Old Testament,[1] which helped full much in this work; in the third place, to take counsel with old grammarians and old divines concerning hard words and hard meanings, how they might best be understood and translated; in the fourth place, to translate as clearly as he could according to the meaning, and to have many good and wise companions correct the translation.

First, it is to be understood that the best translating out of Latin into English is to translate according to the meaning and not only according to the words, so that the meaning may be as open (or more open) in Eng- 20 lish as in Latin, and to depart not far from the letter; and if the letter may not be followed in the translating, let the meaning ever be complete and open, for the words ought to bring out the intent and meaning, and otherwise the words are superfluous or false.

In translating into English many renderings may make the meaning open, as an ablative absolute case may be resolved into these three words, with appropriate verb, *while, for, if*—as grammarians say. As thus: *the master reading, I stand* may be resolved thus: *While the master readeth, I*

---

[1] Nicholas of Lyra (d. 1340), a Norman Franciscan Friar, was a good Hebraist and wrote famous glosses on the Bible.

stand, or *If the master readeth,* or *For the master* etc. And sometimes it would accord well with the meaning to be resolved into *when* or into *after.* Thus: *When the master read, I stood,* or *After the master read, I stood.* And sometimes it may well be resolved into a verb of the same tense as others in the same sentence, and into the word *et,* that is, *and,* in English. And thus: *Arescentibus hominibus prae timore:* that is, *And men shall wax dry for dread.*

Also a participle of the present tense or preterite, of active voice or passive, may be resolved into a verb of the same tense and a copulative conjunction. As thus: *dicens,* that is, *saying,* may be resolved thus, *and saith,* or *that saith.* And this will in many places make the meaning open where to English it according to the word would be dark and doubtful. . .

At the beginning I purposed with God's help to make the meaning as true and open in English as it is in Latin, or more true and more open than it is in Latin. And I pray, for the sake of charity and the general profit of Christian souls, that if any wise man find any fault in the truth of the translation, let him insert the true and open meaning of Holy Writ; but let him examine truly his Latin Bible, for no doubt he will find many Bibles in Latin full false if he look at many, especially new ones. And the common Latin Bibles, as many as I have seen in my life, have more need to be corrected than hath the English Bible late translated. And where the Hebrew, by the witness of Jerome, Lyra, and other expositors, is out of accord with our Latin Bibles, I have set in the margin by way of a gloss, what the Hebrew hath and how it is understood in some place. And I did this most in the Psalter, which of all our books departeth most from Hebrew. . .

Lord God! since at the beginning of the faith so many men translated into Latin, and to the great profit of Latin men, let one simple creature of God translate into English for the profit of English men. For if worldly clerics consult well their chronicles and books, they will find that Bede translated the Bible and expounded it much in Saxon,[2] that was the English or the common language of this land in his time. And not only Bede, but also King Alfred, who founded Oxford,[3] translated in his last days the beginning of the Psalter into Saxon, and would have done more if he had lived longer.

Also Frenchmen, Bohemians, and Bretons (?)[4] have the Bible and other

[2] This is an error. Though there is good testimony that Bede finished dictating a translation of the Gospel of St. John on his deathbed, he left no other work in Anglo-Saxon except a traditional deathsong.

[3] The foundation of Oxford by Alfred is mere legend, and his translation of the Psalter is first reported over two hundred years after his death.

[4] Purvey has "Britons;" Wynn suggested that this means the Welsh, but in the fourteenth century it would refer rather to the Continental Bretons. Neither in Welsh nor in Breton has any medieval translation of the Bible survived.

books of devotion and exposition translated into their mother language. Why Englishmen should not have the same in their mother language, I cannot understand, unless for falseness and negligence of clerics, or because our people is not worthy to have so great grace and gift of God in punishment of their old sins.

But in the translating of equivocal words, that is, those that have many significations under one letter, there may easily be peril. For Augustine saith in the second book of *Christian Doctrine* that if equivocal words be not translated according to the sense or understanding of the author, it is
10 error; as in that place of the Psalm: "The feet of them be swift to shed out blood." The Greek word is equivocal, meaning *sharp* and *swift;* and he who translated *sharp feet* erred; and a book that hath *sharp feet* is false and must be emended; as that sentence "Unnatural young trees will not give deep roots," ought to be thus: "Plantings of adultery will not give deep roots." Augustine saith this here.

Therefore a translator hath great need to study well the meaning both before and after, and see that such equivocal words accord with the meaning. And he hath need to live a clean life and be full devout in prayers and not to have his mind occupied with worldly things, so that the Holy Spirit,
20 author of wisdom and cunning and truth, direct him in his work and suffer him not to err.

Also this word *ex* signifieth sometimes *of* and sometimes it signifieth *by,* as Jerome saith. And this word *enim* signifieth commonly *in sooth,* and, as Jerome saith, it signifieth *for this reason, because.* And this word *secundum* is taken for *after,*[5] as is commonly said and by many; but it signifieth well *by* or *upon;* thus *by your word* or *upon your word.* Many such adverbs, conjunctions, and prepositions are often set one for another and sometimes at the free choice of authors; and now those ought to be interpreted as it accordeth best with the meaning.
30 In this manner, with good living and great travail, men may arrive at true and clear translating and a true understanding of Holy Writ, seem it never so hard at the beginning. God grant to us all grace to know well and keep well Holy Writ, and suffer joyfully some penalty for it at the last! Amen.

[5] According to.

Translations from the Bible

John Purvey

JOHN, 13:12–50. But on the morrow a much people that came together to the feast day, when they had heard that Jesus came to Jerusalem, took branches of palms and came forth against Him,[1] and cried: "Osanna, blessed is the King of Israel, that cometh in the name of the Lord!" And Jesus found a young ass and sat on him, as it is written: "The daughter of Sion, nill thou dread;[2] lo, thy king cometh sitting on an ass's foal." His disciples knew not first these things, but when Jesus was glorified, then they had mind,[3] for these things were written of Him and these things they did to Him. Therefore the people bare witnessing that was with Him when He cleped[4] Lazarus from the grave and raised him from death. And therefore 10 the people came and met with Him, for they heard that He had done this sign. Therefore the Pharisees said to themselves: "Ye see that we profit nothing; lo, all the world went after Him." And there were some heathen men of them that had come up to worship in the feast day. And these came to Philip, that was of Bethsaida of Galilee, and prayed him and said: "Sir, we will see Jesus." Philip cometh and saith to Andrew; eft[5] Andrew and Philip said to Jesus. And Jesus answered to them and said: "The hour cometh that Man's Son be clarified.[6] Truly, truly, I say to you, but a corn of wheat fall into the earth and be dead, it dwelleth alone; but if it be dead, it bringeth much fruit. He that loveth his life shall lose it; and he that hateth 20 his life in this world keepeth it into everlasting life. If any man serve Me, sue he Me;[7] and where I am, there my minister[8] shall be. If any man serve Me, My Father shall worship[9] him. Now My soul is troubled, and what shall I say? Father, save Me from this hour; but therefore I came into this hour; Father, clarify Thy name." And a voice came from heaven and said: "And I have clarified, and eft[10] I shall clarify." Therefore the people that stood and heard said that thunder was made; other men said: "An angel spake to Him." Jesus answered and said: "This voice came not for Me but for you. Now is the doom of the world; now the prince of this world shall be cast out. And if I shall be enhanced[11] from the earth, I shall draw all 30

[1] To meet Him.	[2] Dread thou not.	[3] Remembered.
[4] Called.	[5] In turn.	[6] Glorified.
[7] Let him follow Me.	[8] Servant.	[9] Honor.
[10] Again.	[11] Exalted.	

things to Myself." And He said this thing, signifying by what death He was to die.

I CORINTHIANS, 13:1–13. If I speak with tongues of men and of angels, and I have not charity, I am made as brass sounding or a cymbal tinking. And if I have prophecy and know all mysteries and all cunning, and if I have all faith so that I move hills from their place, and I have not charity, I am naught. And if I depart [12] all my goods into the meats [13] of poor men, and if I bitake [14] my body so that I burn, and if I have not charity, it profiteth me nothing. Charity is patient, it is benign; charity envieth not, it doth
10 not wickedly, it is not blown,[15] it is not covetous, it seeketh not those things that be his own, it is not stirred to wrath, it thinketh not evil, it joyeth not on wickedness, but it joyeth together to truth; it suffereth all things, it believeth all things, it hopeth all things, it sustaineth all things. Charity falleth never down, whether prophecies shall be voided, either [16] languages shall cease, either [16] science shall be destroyed. For a party [17] we know, and a party we prophesy; but when that shall come that is perfect, that thing that is of party shall be avoided.[18] When I was a little child, I spake as a little child, I understood as a little child; but when I was made a man, I avoided [19] those things that were of a little child. And we see now
20 by a mirror in darkness, but then face to face; now I know of party,[20] but then I shall know as I am known. And now dwell [21] faith, hope, and charity; but the most of these is charity.

APOCALYPSE, 14:1–5. And I saw, and lo! a Lamb stood on the mount of Sion, and with Him an hundred thousand and four and forty thousand, having His name and the name of His Father written in their foreheads. And I heard a voice from heaven, as the voice of many waters and as the voice of a great thunder; and the voice which is heard was a voice of many harpers harping in their harps. And they sang as a new song before the seat of God, and before the four beasts and seniors.[22] And no man might say the
30 song, but they an hundred thousand and four and forty thousand that be bought [28] from the earth. These it be that be not defouled [24] with women, for they be virgins. These sue [25] the Lamb, whither ever He shall go; these be bought of all men, the first fruits of God and to the Lamb; and in the mouth of them leesing [26] is not found; for they be without wem [27] before the throne of God.

APOCALYPSE, 21:1–22:6. And I saw new heaven and new earth; for the first heaven and the first earth went away, and the sea is not now. And I,

[12] Divide.	[13] Food.	[14] Give up.	[15] Puffed.
[16] Or.	[17] Part.	[18] Done away.	[19] Put away.
[20] In part.	[21] Remain.	[22] Elders.	[28] Redeemed.
[24] Defiled.	[25] Follow.	[26] Lying.	[27] Blemish.

John, saw the holy city Jerusalem, new coming down from heaven, made
ready of God, as a wife orned [28] to her husband. And I heard a great voice
from the throne saying: "Lo! the tabernacle of God is with men, and He
shall dwell with them; and they shall be His people, and He, God, with
them shall be their God. And God shall wipe away each tear from the eyes
of them; and death shall no more be, neither mourning, neither crying,
neither sorrow shall be ever, which first things went away." And He said
that sat on the throne: "Lo! I make all things new." And He said to me:
"Write thou, for these words be most faithful and true." And He said to
me: "It is done; I am alpha and O, the beginning and the end. I shall give 10
freely of the well of quick [29] water to him that thirsteth. He that shall overcome shall wield [30] these things; and I shall be God to him, and he shall be
son to me. But to fearful men and unbelieveful and cursed and man-
quellers [31] and fornicators, and to witches and worshipers of idols, and to
all liars, the part of them shall be in the pool burning with fire and brim-
stone, that is the second death." And one came of the seven angels, having
vials full of seven the last vengeances. And he spake with me and said:
"Come thou, and I shall show to thee the spouse, the wife of the Lamb."
And he took me up in spirit into a great hill and high; and he showed to me
the holy city Jerusalem, coming down from heaven of God, having the 20
clarity [32] of God; and the light of it like a precious stone, as the stone jasper,
as crystal. And it had a wall great and high, having twelve gates, and in the
gates of it twelve angels, and names written in, that be the names of twelve
lineages of the sons of Israel; from the east three gates, and from the north
three gates, and from the south three gates, and from the west three gates.
And the wall of the city had twelve fundaments, and in them the twelve
names of twelve apostles and of the Lamb. And he that spake with me had
a golden measure of a reed, that he should mete [33] the city and the gates
of it and the wall. And the city was set in square, and the length of it is so
much, as much as is the breadth. And he meted the city with the reed, 30
by furlongs twelve thousands. And the height and the length and breadth
of it be even.[34] And he meted the walls of it, of an hundred and four and
forty cubits by measure of man, that is, of an angel. And the building of
the wall thereof was of the stone jasper. And the city itself was clean gold,
like clean glass. And the fundaments of the wall of the city were orned
with all precious stones. The first fundament, jasper; the second, sapphire;
the third, chalcedony; the fourth, smaragdus; [35] the fifth, sardonyx; the
sixth, sardius; the seventh, chrysolite; the eighth, beryl; the ninth, topaz; the
tenth, chrysoprase; the eleventh, jacynth; the twelfth, amethyst. And
twelve gates be twelve margarets [36] by each; and each gate was of each 40

28 Adorned.   29 Living.   30 Possess.   31 Murderers.
32 Splendor.   33 Measure.   34 Equal.   35 Emerald.
36 Pearls.

margaret. And the streets of the city were clean gold, as of glass full shining. And I saw no temple in it, for the Lord God Almighty and the Lamb is temple of it. And the city hath no need of sun neither moon, that they shine in it; for the clarity [37] of God shall lighten it; and the Lamb is the lantern of it. And folks shall walk in light of it; and the kings of the earth shall bring their glory and honor into it. And the gates of it shall not be closed by day; and night shall not be there. And they shall bring the glory and honor of folks into it. Neither any man defouled and doing abomination and leesing [38] shall enter into it; but they that be written in the book of life and of the Lamb.

And he showed to me a flood of quick [39] water, shining as crystal, coming forth of the seat of God and of the Lamb, in the middle of the street of it. And on each side of the flood the tree of life, bringing forth twelve fruits, yielding his fruit by each month; and the leaves of the tree be health of folks. And each cursed thing shall no more be; but the seats of God and of the Lamb shall be in it. And the servants of Him shall serve to Him. And they shall see His face, and His name in their foreheads. And night shall no more be, and they shall not have need to the light of lantern neither to light of sun; for the Lord God shall lighten them, and they shall reign into worlds of worlds. And he said to me: "These words be most faithful and true."

[37] Splendor.   [39] Living.   [38] Lying.

A Treatise Against Miracle Plays

Kɴᴏᴡ ye, Christian men, that, as Christ, who is both God and man, is likewise the way, the truth, and the life, as says the gospel of John: the way to
the erring, truth to the ignorant and doubting; and life to those who climb
to heaven and are growing weary, so Christ did nothing for us that was in-
effectual in the way of mercy, in the truth of righteousness, and in a life
yielding everlasting joy in return for our continued mourning and sorrowing in this vale of tears. The miracles, therefore, that Christ did here on
earth, either in Himself or in His saints, were so effectual and done in such
earnest, that, to sinful men who err, they brought forgiveness of sin, setting
them again on the path to true faith; to doubting men, who were not stead- 10
fast, they brought knowledge of how to please God better, and true hope
in God, to be steadfast in Him; and to those weary in God's way, because
of the great penance and suffering arising from the tribulation that men
have therein, they brought the love of burning charity, because of which
everything is light (even if a man were to suffer death, the which men most
dread) in comparison with the everlasting life and joy that men most love
and desire, the true hope of which does away all weariness here on the way
to God.

Then, since the miracles of Christ and of His saints were thus effectual,
as by our religion we are assured, no man should take in jest and play the 20
miracles and works that Christ so earnestly wrought for our salvation. For,
whosoever so doth, errs in the faith, reverses Christ, and scorns God. He
errs in the faith, in that he takes the most precious works of God in play
and jest; he taketh His name in vain, and so misuses our faith. Ah, Lord,
since an earthly servant dare not take in play and jest that which his earthly
lord takes seriously, so much the more should we not make our play and
jest of those miracles and works that God so earnestly wrought for us; for,
truly, when we so do, the dread of sin is removed—as a servant, when he
jokes about his master, loses his dread of offending him, particularly when
he jests about that which his master takes seriously. . . .   30

Now then, since these players of miracles take in jest the serious works
of God, there is no doubt that they scorn God, as did the Jews who mocked
Christ; for they laughed at His passion, as these laugh and poke fun at the

miracles of God. Therefore, as they scorned Christ, so do these scorn God;
and even as Pharaoh, who was wroth to do that which God bade him,
displeased God, so with these miracle-players, and those who support them,
when they cease with pleasure to do what God bade them, they displease
God. He indeed has commanded us to hallow His name, showing fear and
reverence at every remembrance of His works, without any playing or
joking, according as all holiness lies in very earnest men; then, playing on
the name of God's miracles, thus for the fun of it, they as willingly leave
off doing what God commands them; so scorn they His name, and so scorn
10 Him.

But in reply to these things they say that they play the miracles to the
worship of God, as did not those Jews that mocked Christ. Also, often
times by such miracle playing men are converted to good living, as when
men and women, seeing in miracle plays that the devil, through those acts
by which they incite each other to lechery and pride, makes them his
servants, to bring them themselves and many others to hell, and observing
that they have far more suffering hereafter, because of their proud conduct
here, than they have honor here; and seeing, furthermore, that all these
worldly things are but vanity, and that for but a short while—as is the
20 playing of a miracle—they will leave their pride, and take for themselves
afterwards the meek conversation of Christ and of His saints; and so miracle
playing turns men to the faith, and does not turn them aside.

Likewise, often times by such miracle playing men and women, seeing
the passion of Christ and of His saints, are moved to compassion and devotion, weeping bitter tears; then are they not scornful of God, but reverent. Also profitable to men and to the worship of God is it, to present fully
and to seek out all the means by which men flee sin and draw them to
virtue. And, since there are men who only by earnestful action will be
converted to God, so there are other men that will be turned to God only
30 by game and play; and nowadays men are not turned by the serious actions
of either God or man. Therefore it is timely and reasonable to try to turn
the people by play and game, as by miracle playing, and other manner of
entertainment.

Also, men must have some recreation, and it is better, or less evil, that
they have their recreation in the playing of miracles than by the playing
of other jokes. Also, since it is permissible to make paintings representing
the miracles of God, why is it not also permissible to have the miracles of
God played? since men may the better explain the will of God and His
marvelous works, in the acting of them than in painting them, and they
40 are better held in mind, and rehearsed the more often by the acting of them
than by representing them in painting, since the latter is a dead book, the
other a living.

To the first argument we answer, saying that such miracle playing is not to the worship of God, for they are performed more to be seen of the world, and to please the world, than to be seen of God, or to please Him, as Christ never taught their use by example, but only heathen men, who evermore dishonor God, declaring that to be to the worship of God which tends to the greatest debasing of Him. Therefore, as the wickedness of the misbelief of heathen men deceives them, when they say that the worshiping of idols is conducive to the worship of God, so men's lechery nowadays, to the having of their own lusts, deceives them, when they say that such miracle playing is to the worship of God. . . . 10

In the same manner, miracle playing, although it be sin, is at times occasion for converting men; but as it is sin, it is far more an occasion of perverting men, not only one individual person, but a whole community, as it makes a whole people to be occupied in vain, contrary to the behest of the Psalter Book, that says to all men, and especially to priests, who read it each day in their services, "Turn away mine eyes from beholding vanities," and again, "Lord, thou hatest all ensnaring vanities." How then may a priest play in interludes, or give himself to the sight of them? . . .

Miracle playing, since it is against the commandment of God, which forbids that we take God's name in vain, is contrary to our faith, and so 20 it cannot offer an occasion of turning men to the faith, but of turning them aside; and, therefore, many men suppose that there is no hell of everlasting pain, but God does threaten us, and will not actually carry it out, as in the playing of miracles, symbolically and not actually.

A priest of the New Testament, who has passed the age of childhood, and who should maintain not only chastity but all the other virtues, administers not only the sacrament of matrimony, but all other sacraments, and, particularly, since he must administer to all people the precious body of Christ, ought to abstain from all idle play, both of miracles and otherwise. . . . 30

These men that say, "Let us play a play of Antichrist and of the Day of Doom, that some man may be converted thereby," fall into the heresy of them that, reversing the Apostle, said, "Let us do evil that good may come," "of whom," as saith the Apostle, "damnation is just."

By this do we answer the third argument, saying that such acting of miracles gives no occasion of true and profitable weeping; but the weeping that befalls men and women at the sight of such acting of plays, as it is not principally for their own sins, nor inwardly, of their own good faith, but more because of their beholding that which is without, is not acceptable before God, but the more reprehensible; for, since Christ Himself reproved 40 the women who wept for him at His passion, much more are they to be reproved who weep because of a play on Christ's passion, failing to weep for their own sins and those of their children, as Christ bade the women who wept for him.

And by this do we answer the fourth argument, replying that no man can be converted to God except by the earnest working on God's part, and by no empty acting; for that which the word of God and His sacraments cannot effect, how should acting bring about, which is of no virtue, but only of error? . . . The weeping that men weep often in such a play is commonly false, witnessing that they love more the affections of their body and the welfare of this world than affection for God and the welfare of
10 the soul; and, therefore, having more consciousness of pain than of sin, they falsely weep for the lack of bodily welfare rather than for the loss of spiritual. . . .

And hereby do we answer the fifth argument, saying that true recreation is the lawful occupying of oneself in lesser works, to perform more ardently the greater. Therefore, neither the playing of miracles nor the watching of them is true recreation, but false and worldly, as prove the deeds of those who attend such plays. . . . And if one were to ask what recreation men should have for the holiday, after their holy contemplation in Church, we say to them two things: the one, that if he had verily busied
20 himself before in contemplation, he would neither ask that question nor desire to behold vanity; the other, that his recreation should be in works of mercy towards his neighbor, and in delighting him in all good communication with his neighbor, as before he delighted in God, and in all other needful works that are reasonable and natural.

And to the last argument we reply that painting, if it be true, without admixture of falsehood, and not too ingenious, to the great feeding of men's wits, and not an occasion of idolatry for the people, they are but as naked letters for a clerk to read the truth; but so are not many miracle plays, which are made more to delight men bodily than to be books for unedu-
30 cated men, and, therefore, if they are living books, they are living books of wickedness more than of goodness. Good men, therefore, seeing their time too short to occupy them in good earnest works, and seeing the day of their reckoning draw quickly near, and not knowing when they must go hence, flee all such idleness, hastening that they might be with their spouse, Christ, in the bliss of heaven. . .

If thou hadst had a father, who had suffered a spiteful death to get thee thine heritage, and if after that thou wouldst so lightly consider him as to make play out of it, for thyself and for all people, no doubt all good men would judge thee unnatural. Much more, God and all His Saints would
40 judge all those Christian men unnatural who play or favor the acting of the death or of the miracles of their most kind Father, Christ, who died and wrought miracles to bring men to the everlasting heritage of heaven.

But, possibly, here thou mayst say that, if the acting of miracles be sin, nevertheless it is but a little sin. But on this point, dear friend, know ye that each sin, be it never so little, if it be continued and preached as good and profitable, is deadly sin. And on this saith the prophet, "Woe to them that call good evil and evil good:" and therefore the wise man condemneth them that rejoice when they do evil. And therefore all saints say that it is human to fall, but devilish is it to abide still therein. Therefore, since this performance of miracles is sin, as thou dost acknowledge, and it is steadfastly supported, and also men delight them therein, there is no doubt that it is mortal sin, damnable, devilish, not human. . . .   10

As this is a very lie, to say that, for the love of God, one will be a good fellow with the devil, so is it a true lie, to say that, for the love of God, one will act His miracles, for in neither is the love of God shown, but His commandments are broken. And since the ceremonies of the Old Law, albeit they were given by God, because they were fleshly cannot be held equal with the New Testament, because it is spiritual, much more, acting, for it is carnal, and never commanded of God, should never be applied to the marvelous works of God, since they are spiritual. For, as the playing of Ishmael with Isaac would have deprived Isaac of his heritage, so the keeping of the ceremonies of the Old Law in the New Testament would 20 have taken from men their belief in Christ, and have made men go backwards, that is to say, from the spiritual life of the New Testament to the carnal life of the Old Testament. . . .

This acting of miracles is true witness to men's avarice, and covetousness before, which is idolatry, as saith the Apostle; for that which they should spend upon the needs of their neighbors, they spend upon plays; and to pay their rent and their debt, they will complain; but to spend twice as much upon the play, they make no complaint. Furthermore, to gather men together, so as to buy their victuals at higher cost, and to stir men to gluttony and to pride and boast, they perform these miracles; and also, to 30 have money to spend on these miracles, and to hold fellowship with gluttony and lechery on such days of the giving of plays, they busy themselves beforehand, more greedily to beguile their neighbors, in buying and selling; and so this performing of miracles nowadays is true evidence of hideous covetousness, which is idolatry.

The Vision Concerning Piers Plowman

William Langland

THE FIELD FULL OF FOLK

(A, PROLOG)

In a summer season, when soft was the sun,
I clad myself humbly, clothed like a shepherd,
In habit like a hermit unholy of works,
And went wide in this world, wonders to hear.
And on a May morning on Malvern Hills [1]
There befell me a marvel of magic, methought.
I was weary from wandering and went to rest me
Under a broad bank by the side of a brook,
And as I lay and leaned and looked on the waters,
I slipped off to sleep, so sweetly they murmured.　　　　10
Then began I to dream a marvelous dream,
That I was in a wilderness, I wist never where.
As I looked to the east, aloft to the sun,
I saw a tower on a hilltop, handsomely builded;
A deep dale beneath, and a dungeon-keep in it,
With deep ditches and dark and dreadful to see.
A fair field full of folk I found there between,
Of all manner of men, the mean and the rich,
Working and wandering as the world requireth.
Some put themselves to the plow, played full seldom,　　　　20
In planting and sowing sweated full hard,
And produced what wastrels with gluttony waste.
Some gave themselves to pride and wore such apparel
That they seemed to be mummers or masquers at least.
To prayers and to penance many applied them;
All for love of Our Lord, they lived full strictly,

[1] On the borders of Worcestershire and Herefordshire; pronounced Mawlvern.

In the hope of having heavenly bliss.
As anchorites and hermits they held close to their cells,
And sought not afield to saunter about,
To pamper their bodies with bawdy living.   30
Some chose to be merchants and prospered the more,
For it seemeth to our sight that such men thrive.
Some chose to give mirth as minstrels are wont,
And to get gold with their glee, without guilt methinketh.
But jesters and babblers, Judas's children,
Invent absurd fantasies and behave like fools,
And yet are clever enough to work if compelled to.
What Paul saith of them, I will not cite here;
Qui turpiloquium loquitur, he is Lucifer's servant.
Wheedlers and beggars went about whining,   40
Till their bellies and bags were crammed to the brim,
Dissembled for their food and fought at the ale-house;
In gluttony, God knoweth, they go to their beds,
And rise up with ribaldry, those Robert's knaves! [2]
Sleep and sloth pursue them ever.
Pilgrims and palmers pledged themselves together
To seek the shrine of St. James [3] and saints at Rome.
They went forth on their way with many wise tales,
And took leave to lie all their lives after.
Hermits in a crowd, with hooked staves in their hands,   50
Went to Walsingham, and their wenches after them;
Big lubbers and tall, who were loth to toil,
Did on copes to be distinguished from others,
And clad themselves as hermits to have their ease.
I found there friars of all the four orders,
Who preached to the people for their own profit,
Expounded the gospel as seemed to them good,
Construed it as they would, they so coveted copes.
Many of these master-friars may dress as they please,
For their money and their trading march forward together.   60
For since love hath turned pedlar and sold shrift to lords,
Many strange things have befallen in a few years.
Unless Holy Church and the friars hold together in harmony,
The greatest mischief on earth will mount full fast.
There a pardoner preached as if he were a priest,
Brought forth a bull [4] with seals from the bishop,

---

[2] A common term for rascals.
[3] Santiago da Compostela, in northwestern Spain.   [4] A papal proclamation.

And said he had power to absolve them all
From breaking of fasts and broken vows.
The lay folk believed him and liked his words,
Came up and kneeled to kiss his bulls.   70
With his brevet of pardon he banged them and blinded their eyes,
And got with his bull rings and brooches.
Thus they give their gold to support gluttons
And yield it to lechers who live in debauchery.
If the bishop were holy and were worth both his ears,
His seal should not be sent to deceive the people.
But 'tis not only the bishop's fault that the fellow preaches,
For the parish priest and the pardoner part between them the silver
That, but for them, the poor of the parish would have.
Parsons and parish priests complained to the bishop   80
That their parishes were poor since the pestilence came,
And asked license and leave to live in London
And sing there for simony, for silver is sweet.
There stood about a hundred in coifs of silk;
They seemed sergeants of law who served at the bar,
And pleaded causes for pence and pounds,
But ne'er for love of Our Lord loosed their lips once.
Thou might'st better measure the mist on Malvern Hills
Than get a mumble from their mouths unless money were shown.
I saw brazen bishops and bachelors of divinity   90
Become clerks of account in the king's service.
Archdeacons and deacons, who claim the dignity
To preach to the people and poor men to feed,
Have leapt up to London by leave of their bishops
To be clerks of the King's Bench, to the country's damage.
Barons and burgesses and bondsmen also
I saw in that assembly, as ye shall hear later;
Bakers and butchers and brewsters many,
Women who wove wool and weavers of linen,
Tailors and tanners and fullers too,   100
Masons, miners, and many other craftsmen,
Diggers and delvers who do their work ill,
And spend all the long day, singing *"Dieu vous save, Dame Emme!"*
Cooks and their servant-boys cried "Hot pies, hot!
Good pigs and geese! Let us go and dine!"
Tavern-keepers too touted their wares:
"White wine of Alsace and red wine of Gascony,

Rhenish and Rochelle, to digest the roast!"
All this I saw sleeping and seven times more.

HOLY CHURCH

(B, PASSUS I)

What this mountain meaneth and the murky dale
And the field full of folk, I shall fairly show you.
A lady lovely of visage, in linen clothed,
Came down from the castle and called me fairly,
And said: "Son, sleep'st thou? Seest thou these people,
How busy they be, buzzing round in a maze?
Most of these people who pass on this earth,
So they have honor in this world, wish for naught better.
Of other heaven than here they hold no account."
I was afraid of her face, though fair she looked,   10
And said: "Mercy, madam; what doth this mean?"
"The tower on the hilltop," quoth she, "there Truth abideth,
And willeth that ye do as His word teacheth;
For He is the Father of Faith who formed you all,
Both with skin and with face, and gave you five senses
To worship Him with while ye are here.
Therefore He bade the earth at all times to serve you
With woolen and linen and food needful for life,
In a moderate manner to make you at ease;
And commanded of His courtesy three things common to all men.   20
None are necessary but these, and name them I will,
And by rule and reason rehearse them as follows.
One of them is clothing, to save thee from cold;
Another, meat at mealtime lest a malady take thee;
The third, drink when thou art dry, but do it not beyond reason,
That thou be not the worse when work is required. . .
Then I questioned her fairly, for the Creator's sake: 58
"That dungeon-keep in the dale that is dreadful to see,
What may it mean, madam, I you beseech?"   60
"That is the Castle of Sorrow," quoth she. "Whoso cometh therein
May curse the day he was born, in body and soul.
There dwelleth a wight, Wrong is his name;
The father of falsehood, he founded it himself.
Adam and Eve he egged on to do evil,

And counseled Cain   to kill his brother;
Made a mock of Judas   with the Jews' silver,
And afterward hanged him   on an elder-tree.
He is destroyer of love   and lieth to all
Who trust in their treasure,   wherein truth doth not dwell."   70
Then I wondered in my mind   what woman it was
Who set forth so wisely   words of Holy Scripture,
And I asked her in the High Name,   ere she went thence,
Who she was truly   that taught me so well.
"Holy Church am I," quoth she;   "thou oughtest to know me.
I took thee first at baptism   and taught thee thy creed.
Thou broughtest me sureties   my bidding to do
And to love me loyally   while thy life endured."
Then I fell on my knees   and favor besought,
And prayed her piteously   to pray for my sins;   80
Also to teach me kindly   on Christ to believe,
That I might work His will   who created me man.
"Guide me to no treasure,   but tell me but this,
How I may save my soul,   thou saintly maiden."
"When all treasure is tested,   truth is the best.
I appeal to 'God is love,'   to judge thereof;
It is as precious a love-gift   as the Lord God Himself.
For whosoever is true of his tongue   and telleth no falsehood,
Doth his work with truth   and doth no man ill,
He is held a god by the gospel,   here below and above,   90
And eke likened to Our Lord   in St. Luke's words. . ."

(A, PASSUS I)

"Yet I have no natural knowledge," quoth I;   "thou must teach me bet-
    ter,   127
By what power in my body   truth beginneth and where."
"Thou art daft and a dotard,"   quoth she; "dull are thy wits!
There is a natural knowledge   that maketh known in thy heart,   130
Thou should'st love thy Lord   liefer than thyself. . .
Here thou may'st see an example   in Himself alone,   146
How He was mighty and meek   and mercy did grant
To them who hung Him on high   and pierced His heart.
Therefore I recommend to the rich   to have ruth on the poor;
Though ye be mighty in the court-room,   be meek of your works.   150
Eadem mensura qua mensi fueritis,   remetietur vobis.
For by the same measure that ye mete,   amiss or otherwise,
Ye shall be weighed therewith   when ye wend hence.

For though ye be true of tongue   and toil honestly,
And be as chaste as a child   who weepeth in church,
Unless ye live truly   and love the poor,
And faithfully share the goods   that God hath sent,
Ye have no more merit   in mass nor in hours
Than Malkin hath in her maidenhood,   whom no man desireth.
For James, the gentle,   judged in his book
That faith without works   is feebler than nothing,   160
And dead as a doornail   unless deeds do accord.
Chastity without charity [5]   (wit thou the truth)
Is as senseless as a lamp   that no light is in. . .
Love is the dearest thing   that Our Lord asketh,   180
And eke the straight path   that passeth to heaven.
Therefore I say as I said,   citing these texts,
When all treasures are tested,   truth is the best.
Now have I told thee what truth is,   that no treasure is better.
I may linger no longer;   Our Lord look upon thee!"

LANGLAND'S LIFE

(C, PASSUS VI)

Thus I woke, God wot,   when I dwelt on Cornhill,
With Kit in a cottage,   clothed as an idler
And little esteemed,   believe me truly,
Among loungers of London   and unlettered hermits.
For I judged those men   as Reason taught me.
For when I had come unto Conscience,   I encountered Reason.
During a hot harvest,   when I had good health
And limbs to labor with,   and I loved my ease
And to do no deed   but to drink and to sleep,
In such health and quietude   came one to question me.   10
Roaming in memory,   thus Reason rebuked me:
"Canst thou serve," he said,   "or sing in a church,
Or cock hay for my harvesters   or pitch it on the cart,
Mow grass or stack it   or bind up sheaves,
Be reaper or overseer   and arise early,
Or have a horn and be a cattle-ward   and lie out at night,
And guard my grain in my field   from pickers and thieves?
Or shape shoes or clothes,   or keep sheep or kine,
Cut hedges or harrow   or drive swine or geese,

[5] Love.

Or pursue any craft   that the common need serveth   20
And that supplieth sustenance   to such as are bed-ridden?"
"Certes," I said,   "and, so help me God,
I am too weak to work   with sickle or with scythe,
And too long, believe me,   to stoop down low,
Or to work like a laborer   any length of time."
"Then hast thou lands to live by," quoth Reason,   "or lineage rich,
Who provide thee with victuals?   An idle varlet thou seemest,
A spendthrift fellow   or a spiller of time,
Or thou beggest thy bread   at buttery doors,
Or feignest poverty on Fridays   or feast-days in churches,—   30
Which is a lounger's life   and earneth little praise
There where Righteousness rewardeth   as each man rightly deserveth:
Reddit unicuique juxta opera sua.[6]
Or thou art broken, it may be,   in body or in member,
Or maimed through some mishap   and thus may be excused."
"When I was young," quoth I,   "many years ago,
My father and my friends   furnished my schooling
Till I had understanding   of what Holy Writ meant,
And what is best for the body   as the Book telleth,
And surest for the soul;   so will I continue.
But I never found, by my faith,   since my friends died,   40
Any life that I liked,   save in these long garments.
If I should live by labor   and earn my livelihood,
By that labor I should live   that I learned the best:
In eadem vocatione in qua vocati estis manete.[7]
And I live *in* London   and *on* London both;
The tools that I toil with   and gain my living
Are *paternoster* and primer,   *placebo* and *dirige*,
And sometimes my psalter   and my seven psalms.[8]
Thus I sing for the souls   of such folk as help me,
And they who provide me with victuals   vouchsafe me, I trow,
A welcome when I come,   one month and another,   50
Now with him, now with her;   and thus-wise I beg
Without bag or bottle   but with my belly only. . .
Therefore rebuke me not,   Reason, I pray you;   82
For in my conscience I ken   what Christ would that I wrought.
The prayers of a perfect man   and proper penance
Are the labors that please   Our Lord most dearly.

[6] "He rendereth unto each according to his works."
[7] "Remain in the same vocation in which ye are called."
[8] Langland made a living by saying prayers for those who supported him.

Non de solo," I said, "forsooth *vivit homo,*
Nec in pane et pabulo,[9] the *paternoster* witnesseth.
'*Fiat voluntas tua*'[10] furnisheth us with all things."
Quoth Conscience, "By Christ, I cannot agree to this.
It seemeth not perfection in cities to beg,   90
Unless thou be subject to prior or monastery."
"That is sooth," I said, "and so I acknowledge;
I have wasted time and spent time amiss,
And yet I hope as he who hath often bargained,
And aye lost and lost, but at last happened
To win such a boon he was the better forever,
And rated his losses as a leaf in the end,
So great was his gain through God's gracious words:
Simile est regnum caelorum thesauro abscondito in agro, etc.[11]
Mulier quae invenit dragmam unam, etc.[12]
So hope I to have from Him who is almighty
A morsel of His mercy and to commence a time   100
That will turn all times of my time to profit."
"I counsel thee," quoth Reason, "quickly to begin
The life that is laudable and lawful to the soul."
"Yea, and continue," quoth Conscience; and I went to the church.
To the church did I go to do God honor,
Before the cross on my knees I knocked my breast,
Sighing for my sins, saying my *paternoster,*
Weeping and wailing till I went to sleep.
Then I dreamed much more than I have mentioned before
Of the matter that I dreamed first on Malvern Hills.   110

THE CONFESSION OF THE DEADLY SINS

(A, PASSUS V)

For I saw the field full of folk that before I described   10
And Conscience with a cross came to preach.
He prayed the people to have pity on themselves,
And proved that these pestilences were purely for sin,
And that this southwest wind on Saturday at evening [13]

---

[9] "Man doth not live by bread alone."   [10] "Thy will be done."
[11] "The kingdom of heaven is likened unto a treasure hid in a field."
[12] "A woman who found a shilling."
[13] References to visits of the Black Death (bubonic plague) in 1362 and 1369, and to
a great windstorm in 1362.

Was plainly a punishment   for pride and naught else.
Pear-trees and plum-trees   were pushed to the ground,
As a lesson to men   that they should mend their ways.
Beeches and broad oaks   were blown to the earth,
And turned tail-upward   as a terrible token
That deadly sin ere Doomsday   would destroy them all.   20
Of this matter I might   mumble too long,
But I say what I saw   (so help me God!)
How Conscience with a cross   commenced to preach.
He bade wasters go to work   at what they best could,
And earn what they wasted   by some manner of craft.
He prayed Peronelle   to leave her fur-trimming,
And keep it in her coffer   in case of need.
He taught Thomas   to take two staves
And fetch home Felice   from the cucking stool.
He warned Wat   that his wife was to blame   30
That her head-dress was worth a mark   and his hood but a groat.
He charged pedlars   to chasten their children;
Let them lack no respect   to their elders when young.
He prayed priests   and prelates together
That what they preach to the people   they display in themselves,
"And live as ye teach us;   we will love you the better."
Then he counseled religious orders   to keep their rule,
"Lest the King and his council   cut short your supplies,
And be stewards in your stead   till ye be stablished better.
And ye that seek the shrine of St. James   and saints at Rome,   40
Seek St. Truth,   for he may save you all.
Qui cum Patre et Filio,   fare ye well!"
Then ran Repentance   and rehearsed this theme,
And made William to weep   water with his eyes.
Peronelle Proud-heart   fell prostrate on the earth,[14]
And lay long ere she looked up   and on Our Lady cried,
And promised Him   who made us all
She would unsew her smock   and stitch in a haircloth
To tame her flesh   that was frail to sin.
"Never shall haughtiness rule me,   but I will be lowly   50
And suffer slander of my neighbors,   as I never have done.
Now I will practise meekness   and mercy beseech
Of all whom I have envied   ever in my heart."

---

[14] Here follows the confession of the Seven Deadly Sins: Pride, Lechery, Envy, Covetousness, Gluttony. Anger was omitted in the A version. Compare the plan of Gower's *Confessio Amantis.*

Lecher said, "Alas!"   and to Our Lady cried
To gain for him mercy   for his misdeeds
Between God Almighty   and his poor soul,
Vowing that on Saturday   for seven years after
He would drink but with the duck   and dine but once.
Envy with a heavy heart   asked after shrift,
And began to confess   fully his guilt. . .   60
Then came Covetousness;   I could not describe him,   107
So hungry and so hollow   Sir Harvey looked.
He was beetle-browed,   with two bleary eyes,
And his cheeks hung loose   like a leather purse.   110
He wore a torn tabard   twelve winters old;
Unless a louse could leap,   I do not believe
It could cross that cloth,   so threadbare it was.
"I have been covetous," quoth this caitiff,   "I acknowledge it here.
For some time I was in service   to Sim at the oak,
And was his pledged prentice,   to look after his profit.
First I learned to lie   in a lesson or two,
And then to weigh wickedly   was another lesson.
To Winchester and Weyhill   I went to the fair
With many sorts of merchandise,   as my master bade.   120
If the grace of guile   had not been given to my wares,
They would have gone unsold for seven years,   so help me God!
Then I passed over to the drapers,   my primer to learn,
How to stretch out the selvage   so that it seemed longer;
Among these striped cloths   I learned a lesson,
Pierced them with a pack-needle   and pleated them together,
Put them in a press   and fastened them therein,
Till ten yards or twelve   turned into thirteen.
And my wife at Westminster,   who wove woolen cloth,
Spoke to the spinning women   to spin it soft.   130
The pound that she weighed with   weighed a quarter more
Than my balance did   when I weighed truly.
I bought her barley   and she brewed it to sell;
Penny-ale and pudding-ale   she poured from the same cask
For laborers and low folk   who live by their toil.
The best by the wall   in the bedchamber lay;
Whoever guzzled thereof   gave a good price,
A gallon for a groat,   God wot, and no less,
When it came in cups;   such craft my wife used.
Rose the retailer   is her right name;   140
She hath peddled ale   these eleven winters.

But I swear now soothly   that I will sin no longer,
And never weigh wickedly   nor use false wiles,
But I will wend to Walsingham   and my wife also,
And pray the cross of Bromholm   to forgive my shortcomings." [15]
Now beginneth Glutton   to go to be shriven,
And fareth churchward   his confession to make.
But Beton, the brew-wife,   bade him good morrow,
And then she asked him   whither he would.
"To holy church," quoth he,   "to hear mass sung,   150
And then I shall be shriven   and sin no more."
"I have good ale, gossip," quoth she;   "Glutton, wilt thou try it?"
"What hast thou?" quoth he;   "any hot spices?"
"Yea, Glutton, gossip," quoth she,   "God wot, full good.
I have pepper and peony-seeds   and a pound of garlick,
A farthing's worth of fennel-seed   for these fasting days."
Then goeth Glutton in   and great oaths follow him.
Cis, the cobbler's wife,   sat on the bench,
Wat, who kept the rabbit-warren,   and his wife beside him,
Tomkin, the tinker,   and two of his prentices,   160
Hick, the horse-dealer,   and Hodge, the needle-seller,
Clarice of Cock's Lane   and the clerk of the church,
Sir Piers of Pridy   and Pernel of Flanders,
Daw, the ditch-digger,   and a dozen others.
A fiddler, a rat-catcher,   a street-sweeper of Cheapside,
A rope-maker, a retainer,   and Rose, the dish-maker,
Godfrey of Garlickhithe,   and Griffin the Welshman,
And an assortment of second-hand dealers,   thus soon in the morning,
All treated Glutton   to good ale gladly.
Then Clement, the cobbler,   cast off his cloak,   170
And offered it for barter   at the game of New Fair.
Hick, the horse-dealer,   put up his hood,
And bade Bette, the butcher,   bargain for him.
Then were chapmen chosen   to appraise the garments;
Whoever got the hood   should have something besides
To make up the difference   and match the cloak's value.
Two rose up in haste   and whispered together
And appraised the pennyworths   apart by themselves.
There was a heap of oaths   for anyone who harkened,
But they could not on their conscience   reach an accord;   180

[15] Walsingham and Bromholm were famous shrines in Norfolk, where miracles were
alleged to occur. The former possessed a famous image of Our Lady, and the latter
claimed to possess the true Cross.

Till Robin, the rope-maker, was requested to rise
And named as an umpire to end the dispute
And to set values on the things, as seemed to him good.
Then Hick, the horse-dealer, had the cloak awarded him,
On condition that Clement had a cup filled full
And Hick's hood to boot, and would hold himself satisfied;
And whoever went back on this bargain, behoved him to rise
And treat Sir Glutton to a gallon of ale.
There was laughing and louring and "Let the cup pass!"
And they sat till even-song and sang at times   190
Till Glutton had guzzled a gallon and a gill.
He piddled two quarts while a paternoster might be said,
And blew the round bugle at his backbone's end,
So that all who heard the horn held their noses
And wished it were wiped with a wisp of briars.
He had no strength to stand till he took his staff;
Then he began to walk like a blind minstrel's bitch,
Sometimes to the side, sometimes to the rear,
Like a man who spreads nets to snare birds with.
When he drew near his door, dim grew his eyes,   200
He stumbled at the threshold and was thrown to the ground.
Clement, the cobbler, caught him by the middle,
And to lift him aloft laid him on his knees.
Glutton was a great churl and a grim one to lift,
And he coughed up a caudle in Clement's lap,
Such that the hungriest hound in all Hertfordshire
Would not lap up those leavings, so unlovely they smelt.
With all the woe of this world his wife and his daughter
Bore him home to his bed and laid him therein.
And after this surfeit he suffered a sickness   210
And slept Saturday and Sunday till the sun went to rest.
Then he woke from his napping and wiped his eyes;
The first word that he spoke was, "Where is the cup?"
His wife then warned him of wickedness and sin.
Then he repented, that rascal! and rubbed his ears,
And began to groan grimly and make great dole
For the wicked life that he had been leading.
"For neither hunger nor thirst I vow that never
Shall fish on Friday be found in my belly
Until Abstinence, my aunt, hath given me leave;   220
And yet I have loathed her all my lifetime!"

(B, PASSUS V)

Then came Sloth all beslobbered,   with two slimy eyes,   392
"I must sit," said he,   "or else I should nap.
I cannot stand or stoop   or kneel without a stool.
If I were lying in bed,   unless my backside forced me,
No ringing would make me rise   till I was ripe to dine."
He began *benedicite* with a belch   and beat his breast,
Stretched himself and groaned   and snored at last.
"What, awake!" quoth Repentance,   "and hasten to shrift."
"Should I die this day," said Sloth,   "I won't open my eyes.   400
I know not perfectly my *paternoster*,   as the priest singeth it,
But I know rimes of Robin Hood   and Randolf, Earl of Chester,
But none of Our Lord or Our Lady,   the least ever made.
I have made forty vows   and forgot them in the morning;
I never performed penance   as the priest charged me,
Nor was I ever contrite   for the sins I committed.
If I offer any prayers,   unless it be in anger,
What I tell with my tongue   is two miles from my heart.
I am occupied every day,   holy days and others,
With idle tales in the ale-house   or else in churches.   410
God's pain and His passion   I ponder on seldom.
I never visit feeble men   or fettered folk in dungeons.
I would sooner hear a shady tale   or a summer-game of shoemakers
Or lies to laugh at,   that belie my neighbor,
Than all that ever Mark wrote,   and Matthew, John, and Luke.
Vigils and fast-days,   I forget all these,
And lie abed in Lent   with my leman in my arms,
Till matins and mass be done;   then I make for the friars' church,
And if I arrive for '*Ite missa est*,' [16]   I think my duty done.
I am not shriven sometimes   (unless sickness compel me)   420
Even twice in two years,   and then my confession is guesswork.
I have been priest and parson   these past thirty winters,
Yet can neither sol-fa nor sing   nor read saints' lives;
But I can find a hare   in a field or a furrow,
Better than read '*Beatus vir*'   or '*Beati omnes*,'
Construe well one clause   and teach it to my parishioners.
I can arbitrate disputes   and hear a steward's reckoning,
But in canon law or decretals   not a line can I read.
Anything I borrow,   if it be not entered on a tally,
I let slip from my memory,   and if men remind me   430

[16] The last words of the mass.

Six times or seven,   I swear I never had it. . .
I ran hither and yon in youth   and heeded not learning,   446
And ever since have been a beggar   because of foul sloth.
Heu mihi! quod sterilem vitam duxi juvenilem!" [17]
"Repentest thou not?" quoth Repentance,   and right then Sloth swooned,
Till Vigilate, the waker,   dashed water on his eyes,   450
Flung it on his face,   and firmly exclaimed;
"Ware thee of despair,   which will betray thee.
Say to thyself,   'I am sorry for my sins';
Beat thyself on thy breast   and beg God's grace,
For no guilt is so great   that His goodness is not more."
Then Sloth sat up   and signed himself with the cross
And made a vow before God   for his foul sloth:
"There shall be no Sunday these seven years,   unless sickness prevent me,
That I shall not before daybreak   go to the dear church,
And hear matins and mass   as if I were a monk.   460
No ale after meat   shall hold me thence
Till I have heard evensong,   I swear by the Rood.
And I will give back again,   if I have the goods,
All I have wickedly won   since I had any wit;
Though my style of living suffer   I will not cease
Till each man has his own again   ere I go hence.
And with the remnant and residue,   by the rood of Chester,
I will seek St. Truth   ere I see Rome."

THE SEARCH FOR ST. TRUTH

(A, PASSUS V)

Then a thousand men   thronged together,   260
Weeping and wailing   for their wicked deeds,
Crying upward to Christ   and His clean Mother
To have grace to seek St. Truth,   God grant that they might! . . .

(A, PASSUS VI)

Now ride these folk   and walk on foot
To seek that saint   in strange lands.
But few men were wise enough   to know the way thither,
But they bustled forth like beasts,   over valleys and hills,
For while they followed their own will,   they went all astray.
When it was late and long,   they met a man

[17] "Woe is me, that I led a sterile life in youth!"

Appareled like a palmer   in pilgrim's weeds.
He bore a staff,   with a broad band
Bound like bind-weed   round about it.
A bag and a bowl   he bore by his side;   10
A hundred ampuls   on his hat were stuck,
Signs of Sinai   and shells of Santiago,
Many crosses on his cloak   and keys of Rome,
Veronica's veil in front,   to advertise to men
And show by his signs   what shrines he had sought.
The folk asked him fairly   from whence he came.
"From Sinai," he said,   "and from the Sepulchre;
From Bethlehem and Babylon,[18]   I have been in both,
In India and Asia   and in many other places.
Ye may see by my signs   that sit on my hat   20
That I have walked full widely   in wet and in dry,
And sought good saints   for my soul's health."
"Knowest thou aught of a saint   men call St. Truth?
Canst thou tell us the way   to where he dwelleth?"
"Nay, so God save me!"   said the man then.
"I have ne'er met a palmer,   with pikestaff or scrip,
Who sought such a saint,   save now in this place."
"Peter!" quoth a plowman,   and put forth his head,
"I know him as naturally   as a scholar knoweth his books.
Conscience and Common Sense   sent me to his place,   30
And pledged me to serve him   since then for ever,
Both to sow and to plant   so long as I might.
I have been his fellow   these fifteen winters,
Have both sowed his seed   and kept safe his cattle,
And eke cared for his corn   and carried it to house,
Dug ditches and delved,   and done what he bade me,
Indoors and out   have advanced his profit.
There is no laborer in this land   whom he loveth more,
For though I say it myself,   my service pleaseth him.
He payeth me good wages   and at times giveth more;   40
He is the promptest in payment   that poor men have;
From no hind he witholdeth his hire,   but he hath it each evening.
He is lowly as a lamb   and lovesome of speech,
And if ye will wit   the place where he dwelleth,
I will show you well   the way to his home."
"Yea, dear Piers," said these palmers,   and proffered him hire.
"Nay, by the peril of my soul,"   quoth Piers, and began to swear:

[18] Not the biblical city of that name, but a town near Cairo.

"I would not touch a farthing   for St. Thomas' shrine!
Truth would love me the less   a great while after.
But ye that wend to him,   this is the way thither: 50
Ye must go through Meekness,   both man and wife,
Till ye come unto Conscience,   that Christ may know the sooth,
That ye love Him dearer   than the life in your hearts,
And your neighbors next,   and in no wise harm them,
Otherwise than thou wouldest   men should do to thyself. . . ."

(A, PASSUS VII)

"This would be a wicked way   if we had not a guide
Who might follow us each foot,"   the folk thus murmured.
Quoth Perkin, the plowman,   "By Peter, the apostle,
I have a half-acre to plow,   hard by the highway;
Were it well plowed,   then would I wend with you,
And guide you aright   till ye reached St. Truth."
"That would be a long delay,"   quoth a lady in a wimple.
"What should we women   work at the while?"
"Some shall sew sacks   to save spilling of wheat,
And, ye wives who have wool,   work it fast,   10
Spin it speedily   and spare not your fingers,
Unless it be holy day   or else holy eve.
Seek out your linen   and labor on it fast;
The needy and the naked,   take note how they lie,
And clothe them against cold,   for so Truth willeth.
For I will find them food,   unless the land fail,
As long as I live   for Our Heavenly Lord's love.
And ye, lovely ladies,   with your long fingers,
Who have silk and sendal,   sew, when ye have time,
Chasubles for chaplains   and to the church's honor.   20
And all manner of men   who need meat to live,
Help ye him to work well   who winneth your food."
"By Christ," quoth a knight then,   "thou canst teach us best!
I never was taught thus,   truly save one time!
But give me a lesson,   and I shall learn to plow;
I will help thee to labor   while my life lasteth."
"By St. Peter," quoth Piers,   "since thou profferest so humbly,
I will toil and sweat   and sow for us both,
And for love of thee labor   all my lifetime,
On condition thou keep   Holy Church and myself   30
From wasters and wicked men   that would destroy us.

[309]

And go thou, hunt hardily   hares and foxes,
Bears and bucks   that break men's hedges,
And bring home falcons,   wild fowl to kill,
For they come into my croft   and crop my wheat."
Full courteously the knight   acknowledged those words:
"By my power, Piers,   I plight thee my troth
To hold this covenant   while I can stand."
"Another point," quoth Piers,   "and I will pray thee no more.
See that thou trouble no tenant,   unless Truth will assent,   40
And if poor men proffer you   presents or gifts,
Take them not; peradventure,   none may ye deserve;
For if ye do, ye shall yield them   when the year endeth
In a right perilous place   that Purgatory is called.
Mistreat not thy bondman,   and the better thou shalt speed.

(B, PASSUS VI)

Though he be thine underling here,   in heaven perchance
He may be sooner received   and more reverently seated.
At church in the charnel   churls are hard to distinguish,   50
Or a knight from a knave,   know this in thy heart.
Be true of thy tongue   and hate all tales,
Save they be of wisdom or sense   to instruct thy workmen.
Hold with no ribalds   and hear not their talk,
And specially at meals   such men eschew,
For they are the devil's tatlers,   I do thee to wit."
"I assent, by St. James,"   said the knight then,
"To work by thy word   while my life lasteth."

(A, PASSUS VII)

"I will apparel myself," quoth Perkin,   "in a pilgrim's garb,   53
And wend with you the right way   till ye find Truth."
He put on his clothes,   that were patched and mended,
His gaiters and his gloves   to guard his nails from the cold.
He hung a basket on his back   instead of a scrip,
And brought a bushel   of bread-grain therein.
"For I will sow it myself   and then go with you.
Whoso helpeth me to plow   or taketh part in any labor,   60
He shall have, by Our Lord,   the more hire in harvest,
And make him merry with the meal,   whosoever may begrudge it.
And all kinds of craftsmen   who can live with truth,

I shall provide with their food, if they faithfully live,
But not Jack the juggler, and Janet of the brothel,
And Robert the ribald for his rusty words.
Truth taught it me once and bade me tell it abroad,
'Deleantur de libro';[19] I should not deal with them.
Holy Church is held strictly to have none of their tithes;
'Et cum justis non scribantur.'[20]
They have escaped by good luck; may God amend them!"   70

THE CRUCIFIXION AND THE HARROWING OF HELL

(B, PASSUS XVIII; C, PASSUS, XXI)

Weary and wet-shod I went forth afterwards,
As a feckless fellow who feeleth not sorrow,
And wandered on lazily all my lifetime,
Till I waxed weary of this world and would slumber again,
And lounged until Lent and long time I slept.
Of children who chanted "*Gloria, laus*" greatly I dreamed,
And how old folk sang Hosanna to the sound of the organ.
One who resembled the Samaritan and somewhat Piers Plowman,
Barefoot on an ass's back, bootless came riding,
Without spurs or a spear, and high-spirited he looked,   10
As is the nature of a knight who cometh to be dubbed,
To get his gilt spurs and shoes cut in a pattern.
Faith stood at a window and cried, "*O fili David!*"[21]
As doth a herald of arms when adventurous knights come to joust.
Old Jews of Jerusalem, joyously they sang:
"*Benedictus qui venit in nomine Domini!*"[22]
Then I asked of Faith what all that fare meant,
And who would joust in Jerusalem. "Jesus," he said;
"He will fetch from the Fiend the fruit of Piers Plowman."
"Is Piers in this place?" quoth I; and he turned and peered at me: 20
"This Jesus in generosity will joust in Piers' armor,
In his helm and habergeon, which is human nature,
So that Christ be not known as consummate God.
In Piers' armor of plate this knight will ride,
For no dint will harm him in the deity of the Father."
"Who will joust with Jesus?" quoth I, "Jews or scribes?"

[19] "Let them be blotted out from the book."
[20] "And let them not be inscribed with the just."   [21] "O Son of David!"
[22] "Blessed is He that cometh in the name of the Lord!"

"Nay," quoth he, "the foul Fiend and Falsehood and Death.
Death saith he will undo and bring to destruction
All living things on land or in water.
Life saith that he lieth and layeth his life in pledge   30
That, for all that Death can do, within three days
He will fetch from the Fiend the fruit of Piers Plowman,
And bring it where he liketh and bind Lucifer,
And beat and bring down bale and death forever.
O mors, ero mors tua! [23]
Then came Pilate with much people, *sedens pro tribunali,*[24]
To see how doughtily Death would do and decide the rights of both.
The Jews and the justices against Jesus raged,
And all the court cried "Crucify Him" loudly.
An accuser put him forth before Pilate and said: 40
"This Jesus made a jest of our Jews' temple,
To destroy it in one day and in three days after
Erect it anew— here he standeth who said it—
And build it again as big as it was,
Both as long and as large, aloft and aground."
"Crucify Him!" quoth a catchpoll; "I warrant Him a wizard."
"*Tolle, tolle*," [25] quoth another, and took keen thorns
And began with green thorn a garland to make,
And set it sorely on His head and spoke in hate:
"Hail, rabbi!" quoth that ribald and threw reeds at Him,   50
And nailed Him with three nails naked on the cross,
And poison on a pole they put up to His lips,
And bade Him drink His death-drink; His days were done.
"If thou be so subtle, save now thyself;
If thou be Christ and a king's son, come down from the rood.
Then shall we believe that Life loveth thee and will not let thee die!"
"*Consummatum est!*" [26] quoth Christ, and commenced to swoon,
Piteous and pale as a prisoner who dieth.
The Lord of Life and Light laid His eyelids together.
The day for dread withdrew and dark became the sun;   60
The wall wavered and clove and all the world quaked.
At that din dead men came out of deep graves
And told why that tempest so long time endured.
"The battle is bitter," a dead body said:
"Life and Death in this darkness destroy each the other.
No wight may know surely who will have the mastery
Till Sunday about sunrise"; and it sank then to earth. . . .

[23] "O Death, I will be thy death!"   [24] "Seated as for a tribunal."
[25] "Take him, take him."   [26] "It is finished!"

For fear of this wonder   and of the false Jews,   110
I drew away in that darkness   to *"descendit ad inferna."* [27]
There I saw soothly,   as say the Scriptures,
A woman who came   out of the west as I thought,
Walking on her way,   and hell-ward she looked.
Mercy was that maid's name,   a meek thing withal,
Benign in behavior   and humble of speech.
Her sister, as it seemed,   came softly walking
Even out of the east,   and westward she looked.
A full comely creature,   she was called Truth;
The virtue that followed her   caused her never to fear.   120
When these maidens were met,   Mercy and Truth,
Either asked the other   of this great marvel,
Of the din and the darkness   and how the day dawned,
And what a luminous light   lay before hell. . .
"Stay we," said Truth,   "I see and hear also   257
A spirit speak to hell   and bid unspar the gates:
'Attollite portas, principes, vestras; et elevamini, portae eternales.' " [28]
A loud voice in that light   to Lucifer cried: 260
"Princes of this place,   unbar and unlock!
For here cometh with crown   he that King is of Glory."
Then sighed Satan   and said to them all:
"Such a light without our leave   took Lazarus from us.
Coldest calamity   has come to us all.
If this king come in,   he will carry away mankind
And lead them where he liketh,   and lightly bind me.
Patriarchs and prophets   have prophesied this long,
That such a lord and such a light   should lead them all hence." . . .
Again the light bade unlock,   and Lucifer answered: 313
"What lord art thou?" quoth Lucifer;   *"quis es iste?"*
"The King of Glory,"   the light soon said,
"And lord of might and of main   and all manner of virtues.
Dukes of this dim place,   haste, undo these gates,
That Christ may come in,   the King's Son of Heaven."
With that breath hell broke,   and the bars of Belial;
Despite watch and ward,   wide opened the gates.   320
Patriarchs and prophets,   *populus in tenebris,* [29]
Sang St. John's song,   *"Ecce Agnus Dei!"* [30]
Lucifer could not look,   the light so blinded him,
And those whom Our Lord loved   He led into His light.

[27] "Descended into hell."
[28] "Lift up your gates, O ye princes, and be ye lifted up, ye everlasting doors."
[29] "The people in darkness."   [30] "Behold the Lamb of God!"

Piers the Plowman's Creed

May the Cross and courteous Christ   aid this beginning,
For the Father's friendship   who formed heaven,
And through the special Spirit   who sprang of those twain,
And all in one godhead,   endless do dwell!
The letter A and my A B C   entire I have learned,
And pattered my *paternoster*,   each point after the other,
And, after that, mine *Ave Mary*   almost to the end;
But all my care is to come,   for I know not my creed.
When I confess my shortcoming,   shamed must I be;
The priest will punish me   and penance enjoin me;   10
The length of a Lent   must I leave off meat
After Easter is come,   and that is hard fare;
And Wednesdays each week   go without flesh.
And Jesu Himself   to the Jews said also,
"He that believeth not on Me   he loseth bliss."
Therefore, to learn the belief   I long sorely
If any worldly wight   will inform me,
Either layman or learned,   who liveth accordingly,
And fully followeth the faith,   and feigneth no other,
Who no worldly weal   willeth at any time,   20
But liveth in the love of God   and holdeth His law,
And for the gain of any goods   never grieveth his God,
But followeth Him the full way,   as He taught the people.
But to many manner of men   when this matter is broached,
Both to learned and laymen,   who say they believe
Wholly on the great God,   and hold all His commandments,
On inquiry therein   many there fail.
But first I questioned the friars,   and they told me fully,
That all the fruit of the faith   was in their four orders,
And the coffers of Christendom   and the keys likewise;   30
And the lock of belief   lieth locked in their hands.
   Then I went forth to learn,   and a wight I met with,
A Minorite,[1] one morning,   and to this man I said:

---

[1] The Minorites, called also Franciscans and Gray Friars, founded in 1209 by St. Francis of Assisi.

"Sir, for great God's love, the plain truth do thou tell me:
Of what man of mid-earth might I best learn
My creed? For I know it not: my care is the more;
And therefore, for Christ's love, thy counsel I ask.
A Carmelite [2] hath covenanted the creed to teach me,
But as thou knowest Carmelites well, thy counsel I crave."

   This Minorite looked at me, and laughing he said: 40
"Beloved Christian man, I believe thou art mad!
How should they teach thee God, who know not themselves?
They are but jugglers and jesters by nature,
Loose-livers and lechers, and lemans they keep.
Neither in orders nor out, uneasily they live,
And bejape the people with gests of Rome.
They are but a feeble folk, founded on fables.
They make them Mary's men, so they tell others,
And tell lies about Our Lady, many a long tale.
And those wicked wretches betray women,   50
Beguile them of their goods with flattering words,
And therewith keep their convent in unclean works.
And, so save me God, I hold it great sin
To give them any goods to feed such gluttons,
To maintain such men that consume much goods.
Yet they say in their subtlety to sots in the towns,
That they are come out of Carmel Christ to follow,
And feign them holiness, that fitteth them ill.
They would rather live in lechery, and lie in their tales,
Than pursue any good life; but they lurk in their cells,   60
And win worldly goods and waste them in sin.
For, if they knew their creed, or in Christ believed,
They would not be so hardy to practice such harlotry.
Surely, I cannot find out who first founded them;
But the fools founded themselves, friars of the Magpie! [3]
They go about as mendicants, and beguile the people.
If any of those gluttons may get any good thing,
He will keep it to himself, and coffer it fast;
And though his fellows are in need, as for him they may die.
Their wealth they may leave by will and bequest;   70
They observe no obedience, but do as they please.

[2] The Carmelites or White Friars were converted from an order of hermits to an order of mendicants and preachers in 1247.

[3] The habit of the Carmelites combined white and black, like the plumage of a magpie.

And, right as Robert's men,⁴   they roister about
At fairs and at full ales,   and they fill up the cup,
And preach about pardon,   to please the people.
Their patience is all past   and put out to farm;
Their pride is in their poverty,   which is little to praise.
At the lullaby of Our Lady,   to please the women,
And at miracle plays of midwives,   they make women believe
That the cord of Our Lady's smock   lightens them of children.
They preach naught of Paul   or penance for sin,   80
But all of mercy and mildness,   that Mary may help.
With stern staves and strong   they stride over the land,
Thither where their wenches lie   and lurk in the towns,
(Queans with great head-dresses   and goldwork by their eyes),
And say they are their sisters   who sojourn about;
Thus they go gadding   and God's folk betray.
These are the people that Paul   preached of in his time.
He wrote of such folk   who roamed hither and thither:
'Weeping, I warn you   of walkers about,
They are enemies of the cross   that Christ suffered upon.   90
Of such slumberers in sleep   sloth is their end,
And gluttony is their god,   and gulping of drink,
And making great mirth   and merry songs.
At the shaming of such   shall many folk laugh.'
Therefore, friend, by thy faith,   find ways to do better!
Believe not in these loose men,   but let them alone,
For they are false in their faith   and many more matters."

    "Alas, friar," quoth I then,   "my purpose hath failed me;
Now is my comfort cast out.   Knowest thou no cure,
Where I may meet with a man   who might teach me   100
How to learn my creed,   so that Christ I can follow?"

    "Certainly, fellow," quoth the friar,   "without any fail:
Of all men upon earth,   we Minors most show forth
The pure apostles' life,   with penance on earth,
Follow them in sanctity   and suffer most hardship.
We never haunt taverns   or hobble about;
At markets and at miracle plays   we meddle never;
We handle no money;   but meanly we fare,
Are hungry at meal time,—   at each meal once.
We have forsaken the world,   and in woe do we live,   110
In penitence and in poverty,   and preach to the people,
By example of our lives   their souls to help;

⁴ Lawless vagabonds.

And in poverty pray we   for all our partners
Who give us any good things,   to the honor of God,
Either bell or book,   or bread for our food,
Either goods or cloth,   to cover up our bones,
Money or money's worth,—   their meed is in heaven.
We are building a convent,   a broad and a large one,
A church and a chapel,   with chambers aloft,
Wrought with wide windows   and very high walls,   120
That must be covered with paintings   and polished full clean,
With gay glittering glass,   glowing as the sun;
And if thou mightest amend us   with money of thine own,
Thou shouldst kneel before Christ   in a circle of gold,
In the wide window westward,   quite near to the middle,
And Saint Francis himself   shall fold thee in his cope,
And present thee to the Trinity,   and pray for thy sins;
Thy name shall be written   and wrought in nobly,
And, in remembrance of thee,   be read there for ever.
And, brother, be not afraid;   bethink in thy heart;   130
Though thou know not thy creed,   care thou no more;
I shall absolve thee, sir,   and set it upon my soul,
If thou do this good deed;   think thou not otherwise."
   "Sir," I said, "certainly,   I shall go and try."
And he set his hand upon me,   and absolved me clean;
And there I parted from him,   without any penance;
In covenant that I come again,   to Christ he commended me.
   Then thought I to question the first   of these four orders,   153
And pressed on to the Preachers,[5]   to prove their will.
I hied me to their house   to harken after more;
And when I came to that court,   I gaped about me.
Such a bold building,   built upon a height,
I had not seen, for certain,   since a long time.
I gazed upon that house,   and eagerly looked there,
How the pillars were painted   and polished full clean,   160
And cunningly were carved   with curious bosses,
With windows well wrought,   wide up aloft.
Then I entered in   and went ever forward.
Fully walled was that dwelling,   though it was wide,
With posterns in private,   to pass through when it pleased one,
Orchards and arbors,   edged very neatly,
And a curious cross   craftily carved,

[5] The Dominicans, called also Friars Preachers and Black Friars, founded by St. Dominic in 1206.

Tricked out with tabernacles   to peep through all about.
The price of a plowland,   in pennies so round,
To provide for that pillar   were all too little.   170
   Then I meandered forth   to look over the minster,
And was aware of a building   wondrously built,
With arches on every side,   artfully carved,
With crockets at the corners,   with bosses of gold.
Wide windows were set in,   thick with inscriptions;
They shine with shapely shields   to show all about,
With badges of merchants   mixed in between,
More than twenty and two   twice numbered;
There is no herald that hath   half such a roll,
Just as if a catalogue   had reckoned them newly.   180
Tombs upon tabernacles   towered high aloft,
Housed in the corners,   set closely about,
Of armed alabaster,   arrayed for the occasion,
Made out of marble   in many a manner,
Knights in their cognizances   clad for the nonce;
All looked like saints   made holy on earth.
And lovely wrought ladies   lay by their sides,
In many gay garments,   that were gold-embroidered.
Though the tax of ten years   should truly be gathered,
It would not make half   of that house, I believe.   190
   Then came I to the cloister,   and gaped about;
It was pillared and painted   with pictures most neatly,
All covered with lead,   low to the stones,
And paved with painted tiles,   each piece after other;
With conduits of pure tin   enclosed all about,
With lavers of bronze   beautifully appointed.
I suppose the produce of the ground   in a great shire
Would not apparel that place   one whit toward the other end.
Then was the chapter house   wrought like a great church,
Carved and covered over   and quaintly sculptured,   200
With a seemly ceiling   set high aloft,
Like a Parliament House   bepainted about.
   Then fared I into the refectory,   and found there another,
A hall for a high king   that could hold a household,
With broad boards all about   benched most fitly;
With windows of glass   wrought like a church.
   Then walked I further,   and went all about,
And saw halls very high,   and houses most noble,
Chambers with chimneys,   and chapels gay,

And kitchens for a high king   to have in his castles,   210
And their dormitory fitted   with doors very strong,
Infirmary and refectory,   with many more houses,
And all with strong stone walls   stern in their height,
With gay garrets and great,   and every hole glazed in;
And other houses enough   to harbor the queen:
And yet these builders will beg   a bagful of wheat
Of a very poor man,   who can scarcely pay
Half his rent in a year,   and be half in arrears.
    Then turned I again,   when I had seen all,
And found in the refectory   a friar on a bench,   220
A great churl and grim,   grown like a tun,
With a face as fat   as a full bladder
Blown brimful of breath,   and like a bag it hung
On both cheeks; and his chin   lolled with a jowl,
As great as a goose-egg   grown full of grease,
That all his flesh quivered   like a quick-mire.
His cope that enfolded him   very neatly was draped;
Of double worsted was it made,   down to the heel:
His kirtle of clean white   carefully was sewn;
It was good enough of texture   to take a dye.   230
    I greeted that pastor   and politely I spoke:
"Good sir, for God's love,   canst thou readily send me
To a trustworthy person,   able to teach me
How I should learn my creed,   that Christ I might follow;
One who believed truly himself,   and lived accordingly,
That feigned not falsehood,   but followed Christ fully?
Such a reliable man   surely I would trust
That he would tell me the truth,   and turn me to none other.
Now an Augustinian [6] the other day   urged me strongly;
That he would teach me well,   he pledged me his truth,   240
And said to me, 'Certainly,   since Christ died,
Our order hath been faultless,   and it was first founded.' "
    " 'First,' fellow?" quoth he,   "Fie on his furs!
He is but an abortion,   eked out with rags!
He upholdeth his order   with whores and thieves,
And purchaseth them privileges   with pennies so round.
It is purely a pardoner's trick;   prove it by testing.
For if he once have thy money,   a month later
If thou come back to him,   recognize thee he will not.

[6] The Augustinians, claiming descent from St. Augustine of Hippo, were first organized in 1256.

But, fellow, our foundation   is first of them all,   250
And we are formally founded,   without feigning I say it.
And we are celebrated scholars,   subtle in the schools,
Proved in procession   by process of law.
Of our order we boast   bishops a plenty,
Saints in sundry places,   who suffered severely;
We have been proved the greatest   of the popes at Rome,
And of highest degree,   as the gospels say."
   "Ah, sir," quoth I then,   "thou say'st a great wonder,
Since Christ said Himself   to all His disciples,
'He that is greatest among you,   greatest be his labor,   260
And he that leadeth,   let him be first to serve.'
Christ said He saw Satan   sitting full high
And then laid full low;   this in parable he told.
And said that in poverty of spirit   is the speediest salvation
And that haughty hearts   work harm to the soul.
Therefore, friar, farewell,   I find here but pride.
I appraise thy preaching   at the price of a mite."

[The poet has the same experience with the
Augustinian and the Carmelite friars.]

   And as I went by the way,   weeping for sorrow,   420
I saw a simple man near me,   hanging upon the plow.
His coat was of a coarse cloth   that was called "cary,"
His hood was full of holes,   and his hair was out;
With his knobbed shoes,   patched most thickly;
His toes peeped out   as he trod over the land;
His hose overhung his heels   on every side,
All bedaubed in the mire   as he followed the plow.
Two mittens, most mean,   made all out of rags,
His fingers were run through,   and hung full of mud.
This wight wallowed in the muck   almost to the ankle;   430
Four oxen before him,   that had grown feeble:
Men might reckon every rib,   so wretched were they.
His wife walked along with him,   with a long goad,
In a short-cut coat,   cut very high,
Wrapped in a winnowing sheet,   to keep her from the weather,
Barefoot on the bare ice,   that the blood flowed forth.
And at the strip's end lay   a little crumb-bowl,
And therein lay a little child,   wrapped up in rags,

[320]

And two of two years' old,   upon the other side;
And they all sang one song,   that was sorrowful to hear;   440
They all cried one cry,   a note full of misery.
The poor man sighed sorely, and said,   "Children, be still."
   This man looked upon me   and let the plow stand,
And said, "Simple man,   why sighest thou so hard?
If thou lack what is needful   to life, I will lend thee
Such goods as God hath sent.   Go we, dear brother."
   I said then, "Nay, sir,   my sorrow is much more;
Because I know not my creed   I am overcome with grief,
For I can find no man   who fully believeth
To teach me the highway,   and therefore I weep.   450
I have tried the friars   of the four orders,
For I thought they would teach me,   but nothing I learned,
And all my hope was in them   and my heart also.
But they are fully faithless   and follow the fiend."
   "Ah brother," quoth he,   "beware of those fools!
For Christ said Himself,   'Of such I warn you,'
And prophets false to the faith   He frankly called them;
'They come in sheep's clothing,   but under this cover
They are wild werewolves   whose will is to rob men.'
The fiend founded them first,   the faith to destroy;   460
By his craft they came in   to encumber the church,
And by his heinous avarice   to help parish priests.
But now they have a hold   and harm full many;
They do not after Dominic,   but bedevil the people,
Nor follow after Francis,   but falsely live,
And Augustine's rule   they reckon but a fable.
But they purchase privileges   from popes at Rome.
They covet confessions   to catch a fee,
And some of them solicit   sepulchres of the rich.
But other service to Christians   they seek not at all,   470
Save only where profit   and pelf may be gained."
   "What name dost thou bear,   that thy neighbors call thee?"
"Piers," quoth the poor man,   "the plowman I am called."
"Ah, Piers," quoth I then,   "I pray thee tell me
More of these traitors   and their treacherous living,
For each one hath told me   a tale of the others,
Of the wicked life   they lead in the world.
I reckon some wicked wight   wrought these orders
By means of the birdlime   that men call Golias;
Or else Satan himself   sent them from hell   480

To rack men with their ruses and to ruin Christendom."
"Dear brother," quoth Piers, "the devil is right subtle;
He contriveth full keenly to cumber Holy Church,
And worketh his wiles in various ways.
And layeth plans long before to destroy the people.
Of the kindred of Cain he created the friars,
And patterned them after Pharisees, who feign to be good. . . .
Look, beloved man, are not these men like   546
Those selfsame Pharisees in many of these points?
All their broad buildings are built with sin,
And in worship of the world, their winning they hold.
They shape their scapulars and stretch them broadly,   550
And fling high their hems while babbling in the streets;
They are sewn up with white silk, with seams most curious,
Shot through with stitches that shine like silver.
And unless friars be set first at the suppers and at festivals,
They will be wondrously wroth, in truth, as I know;
Unless they be at the lord's board, lour they will.
These beggars must begin the board, bad luck to them!
And sit first in the seats of their synagogues,
Which are their high hell-houses of Cain's kind;
For, though a man in their minster would hear a mass,   560
His sight shall so be set on sundry works,
The pennons and the pinnacles, and the points of the shields,
As to distract his devotion and darken his heart;
I liken it to a limed twig, to draw men to hell."

*   *   *   *   *

"Dear Piers," quoth I, "I pray that thou tell me   791
How I may learn my creed and the Christian faith."
"Dear brother," quoth he, "hold what I say;
I will teach thee the truth and tell thee the sooth.
Believe on Our Lord God, who made all the world;
Holy heaven on high wholly He formed,
And is almighty Himself over all His works,
And wrought by His will the world and the heaven;
And on gentle Jesu Christ, engendered by Himself,
His own only Son, known as Lord over all,   800
Who was clearly conceived, according to the truth,
Of the high Holy Ghost— this is the holy belief;
And of the Maiden Mary He was born man
Without sinful seed— this fully believe.

Crowned with thorns and crucified,   He died on the cross,
And then His blessed body   was buried in a rock,
And descended down   to the dark hell,
And fetched out our forefathers;   full fain were they.
The third day readily   He rose from the dead,
And from a stone where He stood   He ascended to heaven,   810
And on His Father's right hand   readily He sitteth,
As Almighty God,   over all other creatures.
And Christ is to come   hereafter Himself,
To judge the quick and the dead,   without any doubt.
And in the high Holy Ghost   wholly believe,
And the universal Church—   hold this in thy mind; . . .
And in the sacrament also,   in which is very God,   822
His flesh and blood fully,   who for our sakes died.
And though these flattering friars   will, in their pride,
Dispute of this deity,   as dunces would do,
The more the matter is argued,   the more mazed they become.
Therefore study not thereon,   nor stir thy wits.
It is His blessed body,   so He bade us believe." . . .

 All that I have ever said   seemeth to me truth,   841
And all that I have written   is truth, I believe,
And to amend these men   is most that I write.
God grant they regard it   and better their works!
But since I am no churchman,   perchance I might
Go somewhat astray   or in some point err.
I will not as a master   vouch for this matter.
But if I have missaid,   mercy I ask,
And pray all manner of men   to amend this matter,
Each word by itself,   and all if it need be.   850

Confessio Amantis

(THE CONFESSION OF A LOVER)

John Gower

PROLOG

(CONDENSED FROM VSS. 1–92)

The books composed before our day
Remain with us to show the way
That men have lived and wisely sown.
Therefore we also should make known
What we have found, whilst dwelling here,
That makes the path of life more clear,
Example taking from the wise
Who light have given our own eyes.
But as we oft in truth indite,
If one of wisdom only write,   10
Then those who deeply con his work
May find the author does but irk,
Or fails in what he would achieve.
So for that reason, by your leave,
My book will take the middle way
Between the serious and the gay:
For profit and for pleasure too,
I write the words which now ensue.
In English 'tis my wish to make
A book for our King Richard's sake.   20
To him belongs my fealty
With all my heart's strong constancy,
As loyal man in everything
I can or may do for my king:
Thus I commend myself to him
Whose servant I am, life and limb,
Beseeching God, who reigns on high

And earthly kings does sanctify,
To keep him and his government.
Now I believe that an event   30
That happened as by chance to me,
Was one that had been shaped to be,—
Beside the town we call New Troy,
Which took from Brutus its first joy,
Upon the Thames when it was flowing,
As I by boat came idly rowing,
'Twas then that Fortune her time set,
For I just then my liege lord met;
And as my boat to his came nigh,
He could my features well descry.   40
He bade me come into his barge,
Where soon he laid on me a charge,
As he so very graciously
In freest speech did talk with me.
He said that I should now record
In his true honor as my lord,
Some untried matter, and that he
Himself the form would oversee
Of what I'd write at his request.
And thus upon his kind behest   50
To write, indeed, I'm more than glad.
The book shall be as he me bade;
And thus my task has lighter grown,
Since no man's envy can be shown
In falsifying what I write,
In blaming me in unjust light:

My words come forth by king's command,
As every man shall understand.
And so, though sickness dwells with me,
And long my woe has proved to be, 60
Yet will I write my feeble best
For him who honors through behest;
I will include some counsel sage,

For those who seek it on my page,
And mirth for him who would be gay.
Now in the proverb, I've heard say,
That he who well his work begins,
The better ending so he wins:
Thus with my prolog I proceed,
To this monition giving heed; 70
Somewhat of past things I will say,
And somewhat of the present day.

THE POET MEETS VENUS AND HER PRIEST

(CONDENSED FROM BK. I, VSS. 1–302)

My hand cannot reach heaven's height
To set the earthly course aright:
So great a task exceeds my skill,
And therefore it must be my will
To pass it by, and then to treat
Of other matters which are meet.
Thus I will change my style of writing,
Devote my words to love's reciting:
For all this world knows Love full well,
About no strangeness shall I tell; 10
For every man is but Love's fool,
And Love himself knows no man's rule.
No measure and no remedy
Can mortal find and thus be free.
Cupid is blind and kin to chance,
Capricious in his dominance:
Who games with Love but casts the dice,
Oft loses all at highest price.
    And now to prove that this is so
I here relate what all should know, 20
To take example from the day
That I encountered Love one May.
The time was when each little bird
Has found his mate, by love bestirred,
And thus his joy is well achieved;
But I so, then, was not relieved,

For I was farther from my love
Than Earth is from the heaven above.
So to the wood I sadly went
To make in woe my lone lament; 30
And there I found a grassy plot
Where I bewailed my sorry lot:
I well-nigh swooned, and with faint breath
I sighed in anguish, wished for death.
Then I awoke from out my pain,
And to the heavens did complain:
"O Cupid and O Venus bright,
O god and goddess of delight,
That I no more in madness rave,
Send me your grace, I humbly crave!" 40
At once I saw before me there
The king and queen of love so fair:
Alas, the king, with wrathful eye,
Did turn from me and pass me by—
Though first, it seemed, with flaming dart
In cruelty he pierced my heart.
But she, of love the Source and Well,
Remained, and sternly bade me tell
The reason for my malady
And who I was and what degree. 50
I said: "A mournful wretch lies here.
What would ye with him, Lady dear?
Shall he be healed, or must he die?"

"Thy words say naught," she made reply.
"What ill calls forth such deep complaining?
Hide nothing, for if thou be feigning
No cure can I then give to thee."
"Madame," I said, "your liegeman see,
Who in your Court full long has served,
Yet ne'er received what he deserved: 60
I ask my rightful due but now."
A doubtful frown then creased her brow.
She said: "Among my men are some
Who false pretenders have become.
Art thou, perhaps, but one of these,
Who mock when they most claim to please?
I bid thee tell me solemn truth!"
"Madame," I said, "but show me ruth,
And I'll recount my story true,
If so my life will last thereto." 70
She pondered, then did me address:
"My will is first that thou confess
Thyself, thy life to purify,
To my own priest, who now comes nigh.
O Genius, priest of Love, be swift
To listen to this mortal's shrift!"
And looking up, I did behold
The very priest of whom she'd told.
This worthy man then said to me
That I should speak most openly 80
Of what I'd felt of woes and joys
In service that fair Love employs.
I fell devoutly on my knees,
And begged him with most earnest pleas

That he'd demand what I should state,
Lest I forget some matter great,
For anguished heart made me unfit
To capably direct my wit.
Then he began at once to preach,
And thus he said in gentlest speech: 90
"My son, to hear thy words and ask
Thee questions is my given task.
I'm priest of Love, but not alone
On love I'll touch, for priests must own
That to their office appertains
The setting forth of all the banes
Which spring from deadliest of sin.
Therefore with love I'll not begin,
But that my duty best be done
I'll treat the vices one by one, 100
Though more I know of love's sweet teaching,
And sin is seldom in my preaching;
But as I may I will relate
Each vice to love, thus vindicate
My office as the Priest of Love
As well as of high God above.
To thee all errors must be clear,
If so thou would be shriven here."
    I knew not if I lived or died,
But heard Love's priest, and then replied 110
That he to me his will should say,
And I would gladly him obey,
As he instructed me to do.
He then decreed that I speak true
Of sins that touched my senses five,
Which are the gates through which arrive
All matters lying in the heart,
Thus forming of man's soul great part.

(The author now begins the poem proper. He writes that the Priest of Venus, as Confessor, preaches of the sins of sight and hearing; the author in the person of Amans, the lover, confesses his guilt. The Confessor then preaches of the Seven Deadly Sins, including in each of his homilies on each division an exemplum in the form of a tale. The following tale illustrates Murmuring and Complaint, one of the subdivisions of the sin of Pride.)

FLORENT AND THE LOATHLY HAG

(BK. I, VSS. 1407–864)

There once did live in days of old
A worthy knight: he was, 'tis told,
The nephew of the emperor,
Whose court he nobly served there-
    fore.   1410
Florent his name, no wife had he,
His might befitted chivalry:
In feats of arms he did succeed,
In love and knighthood lay his meed,
And for the sake of world renown,
He sought strange perils up and down
The borderlands, far leagues away.
When thus he rode in quest one day,
Cold Fortune, who may break life's
    skein
Or knit the threads, did now or-
    dain   1420
That overcome this knight should be
As through a pass he rode so free.
He then was to a castle taken,
Imprisoned fast, by friends forsaken:
For so it chanced that in the fight
Florent had with his deadly might
Himself slain Branchus, son and heir
To Captain of that castle there.
The father and the mother both
In woe and wrath took vengeful
    oath,   1430
For Branchus was the bravest knight
Of whom that land could boast aright.
They vowed Florent with life should
    pay,
But second thoughts advised a stay;
Florent, of chivalry the flower,
Was also kin to mighty power,
Nephew to emperor indeed:
Esteem of virtue and a need
For prudence served to check the
    sword,
They feared swift vengeance from
    their lord;   1440

They argued long what course was fit.
A lady then of artful wit,
Most cunning mind in all that place,
So old she scarce could move a pace,—
In truth, a grandame of the dead,—
Gave subtle counsel, for she said
She'd bring Florent out to the hall,
And there his death before them all
Should settled be by his own grant,
Through strength of very cove-
    nant: 1450
Thus they themselves would guiltless
    be.
Florent was summoned instantly,
The charge made that he'd killed the
    son,
The dame's command was thus be-
    gun:
"Florent, because thou bear'st the
    blame
For death of Branchus, we here claim
That thou shalt our revenge endure:
Thou shalt upon condition sure
The answer to a question find,
A question that will be designed   1460
By me, with one reply that's true.
Thou shalt take oath, as is our due,
That if thou fail in this thy test
Thou wilt no other means request
To shun the fate thou shouldst receive.
No trick is this, for thou may'st leave
To seek advice, to wander wide;
The day and time we will decide,
And conduct safe thou shalt obtain
If so thou pledge to come again   1470
At time that's set, thy life to save."
    This knight, who prudent was and
    brave,
Besought the lady to reveal
The question, which should under
    seal

Be written with formality:
For that put him in jeopardy,
His life depended on success.
The lady then feigned friendliness,
And said: "Florent, on love it turns,
For that my asking e'er concerns:
What do all women most desire? 1481
This will I ask, and in th' empire,
Where thou canst find best knowl-
        edge, go,
Seek counsel for thy answer so."
  Florent agreed to pay the debt,
The limit of his time was set;
Under the seal he wrote his vow,
And forth he went, full promised now,
Home to his uncle's court again,
Where he th'adventure told all
        plain,   1490
Kept nothing back that him befell.
And that he might be counseled well,
The wisest in the land were sought.
Alas, these had no single thought!
For when they talked of women's
        bliss,
The one said that, the other this;
The dispositions, which do range
With natural complexion, change
The pleasures that one woman sees
To others' pain or miseries.   1500
So what could charm in special case,
Yet also with them all find grace?
For that the riddle did require.
To "what do women most desire?"
The wise men thus no answer saw
By help of stars or nature's law.
And so Florent, without their aid,
On chance alone his hopes he laid,
And for his loss he was prepared
If wrong the answer were de-
        clared.   1510
This knight would have preferred to
        die
Than break his word or tell a lie
When he had taken solemn vow:
So his return he planned for now.
The day arrived to go again,

No longer would he there remain,
Begged that his uncle have no ire,
Indeed, his oath did this require:
That no one for his death should pay,
Since afterwards some man might
        say   1520
He died because of daring feat.
The good Florent went forth to meet
His fate alone, as knight on quest,
But in his thoughts he found no rest
For thinking what was best to say.
Now as alone he rode his way
And came near where he'd sworn to
        be,
In forest dark, beneath a tree,
He spied a creature so uncouth
She scarce a woman seemed in
        truth: 1530
Of flesh and bone he'd ne'er seen one
Who could in foulness this outrun.
He glanced and turned away his eye,
And would in haste have passed her
        by,
But she cried out and bade him stay;
He turned his charger from the way,
And to her rode in courtesy
To seek out what her wish might be.
He paused beside the beldame grim,
Who then began to speak to him: 1540
"Note well, Florent—that is thy
        name—
Thou hast on hand a sorry game;
Unless thou better aid procure,
Thy death awaits thee very sure;
There's nought on earth can save thee
        now
Except thy will to mine thou bow."
  Her meaning could not be denied,
And to the hag the knight replied
And prayed she'd give him counsel
        true.
Again she spoke, thus asked her
        due: 1550
"Florent, if I thy fate so shape
That thou through me thy death es-
        cape,

[328]

And I have honor for that deed,
What then from thee shall be my
    meed?"
"Whate'er," he said, "that thou wilt
    ask."
"I'll find great joy in such a task,"
The crone replied; "before thou goest
Thy pledge I'll have—for that thou
    owest—
Thy promised word upon thy life
That thou wilt take me as thy
    wife."   1560
"Nay," said Florent, "that shall not
    be!"
"Then ride away!" retorted she.
"But if thou thus my counsel spurn,
'Tis certain death that thou wilt earn."
Florent did not a promise spare
Of wealth and land, a manor fair,
But all these gifts she set at nought;
The knight, in truth, was sore dis-
    traught,
He rode his charger to and fro,
In heavy thought as he paced so: 1570
He knew not what was best to say,
The choice was evil either way—
To wed the hag and live in sorrow,
Or meet his death upon the morrow.
But reason helped the choice to
    gauge:
The hag was of so great an age
She might live but a little while,
Or might be banished to an isle
Where no one would her see or know
Until with death she had to go.   1580
And so the young and pleasant knight
Addressed this creature foul to sight:
"If so there be no other chance
To give me my deliverance
Except the answer thou alone
Wilt for thy price to me make known,
Take here my hand, I will thee wed."
And thus his oath was fixed as said.
A thoughtful frown then creased her
    brow:
"This covenant I will allow,"   1590

She said, "and if by any other way
Than mine thou haply find to pay
Thy debt of life and so be free,
Thou may'st forget thy pledge to me;
But only in that one event.
Now listen to my words, Florent:
When thou wilt come unto that place
Where lies the menace thou must
    face,
At once thy foes will thee surround,
Demanding that thou shouldst ex-
    pound   1600
The answer thou didst strive to find;
I know that thou wilt search thy mind
In frantic haste for best reply,
And if thou thus canst qualify,
'Tis well, and I do waste my speech—
If not, then mark here what I teach.
For then thou'lt say that on this earth
All women hold of greatest worth
To have in love the sovereignty:
For if they thus the rulers be,   1610
All fancies may be satisfied—
Without this boon, they are denied
Whatever joys they would obtain.
Therefore no other words will gain
Thy health and life, on them depend;
And when thou so hast made an end,
Come here again where I shall be,
Forget not aught I've told to thee."
    He then went forth with heavy
        heart,
As one who takes of joy no part, 1620
He still was sore perplexed in mind,
For if he'd die, then pain he'd find,
And if he'd live, then he'd be yoked
To foulest being e'er invoked
In this world or, indeed, the next.
He knew not what he'd take for text,
But were he pleased or were he loath,
Onward he went as was his oath,
Unto the castle for to give   1629
Answer by which he'd die or live.
Then forth the lord and Council came,
They bore the documents of blame,
They summoned soon the lady old;

[329]

And when she came she quickly told,
In presence of the company,
The terms which might Florent make
    free,
And so they all did understand.
Then to Florent she gave command
To speak the answer in a trice,
As he who knows what is the
    price.   1640
Florent strove for his own reply,
But no words came that he might try,
That freely or by a behest
Could any way his death arrest.
And thus he tarried long and late,
Until the lady did dictate
That he now with no more ado
Should give the answer solely true,
To question that she'd set him first.
And then he understood the worst:
For of his own he'd nought to boast,
The one hope left he dreaded most—
The words the beldame had him
    taught,   1653
He must pronounce them, or be
    caught
By very death, and so with pain
The hag's reply he spoke out plain.
And when the lady heard the knight
Say words which gave him pardon's
    right,
She cried out: "Treason! Woe to thee
Who hast to secrets found the
    key,   1660
Who know'st what women all desire—
I would that thou may burn in fire!"
But none the less by beldame's aid
Florent was freed, his debt now paid;
Though next his sorrow new began,
For he must go, as gentleman,
To keep the pledge he'd made the
    crone,
But which for shame he scarce could
    own.
Thence to the tryst he made advance
To take the fortune of his chance, 1670

As he was truly obligated.
    The loathsome creature him a-
    waited
In place where first he had her seen:
Florent looked up with woeful mien,
And saw the crone beneath the tree;
She seemed the foulest hag to be
On whom a man could cast his eye:
Her nose was low, her brows too high,
Her eyes were small and deeply set,
Her horrid cheeks with tears were
    wet   1680
And wrinkled as an empty skin,
They loosely hung down to her chin,
Her lips so shrunk they scarce were
    seen,
The forehead narrow, hair unclean.
She was unkempt as is a Moor,
She had no saving grace, 'tis sure;
Her neck was short, her shoulders
    bent,
All charms of youth long since were
    spent,   1688
Her body great, in no part small,
And—shortly to describe her all—
She nowhere did foul blemish lack.
As if she were some monstrous sack
Her loathsome self she offered now.
She bade Florent recall his vow,
Since she for him had warrant borne.
Now he must act as he had sworn;
She seized the bridle him to keep,
God only knows his anguish deep:
When on this hag he looked anew,
He thought his heart would break in
    two   1700
For sorrow that he might not flee
Unless he wished untrue to be.
    Just as the sick their health have
    won
By gentian mixed with cinnamon,
Compounding sugar with their myrrh,
In such a way Florent must stir
The bitter potion with the sweet,
With satisfaction sorrow eat

To gain his health, as one may say,
His life with death must interplay:
His youth and beauty he must knit
With age and foulness all unfit,   1712
Thus greet his woe, bid joy farewell;
But so one must whom Fates compel.
He would hold to his promise true,
As all good knights are bound to do
What'er should them befall thereby.
Though she was loathsome to the eye,
She also woman was, indeed—
It seemed to him he must her heed.
And thus in purest chivalry,   1721
Florent set her as best could be,
In ragged garb as she was dressed,
Upon his horse, and much distressed
He slowly rode out on his way.
No wonder that he felt dismay,
Or, like an owl which flies by night
So other birds may not it sight,
That he should spend the days in hid-
ing,
And thus be sure that all his rid-
ing   1730
Took place in blackest night until
He reached his very domicile.
Without a noise, in secrecy,
He brought the crone where she
would be
Within the castle yet unseen
By all who dwelt in his demesne,
Until he led her to the room
Where sat the trusted men from
whom
He counsel took in time of need;
To them his tale he told in speed,   1740
How he must make this hag his wife
Because he owed to her his life.
    The women who could secrets hold
Were summoned next, his oath them
told.
They took the beldame's rags away,
As law demanded in that day,
She then was bathed and given rest
And soon arrayed in all the best,

Though no comb could by any art
Be forced her shaggy locks to
part—   1750
But she no shearing would permit,
And they did not insist on it.
'Twas so they dressed her as they
might,
Ordaining that her choice was right,
And hid themselves so craftily
That no one could them leaving see.
But oh, alas, the garments bright
Did make the hag a monstrous sight,
For she was fouler than before,
A creature all must now abhor.   1760
Yet they were wed without delay,
Thus sad Florent his debt did pay
With anguish he could scarce support.
And she began to play and sport
As one who thinks she's fair enough,
But he could only her rebuff.
Then merrily, with horrid cheer,
She called Florent her husband dear,
And said, "My lord, let us to bed,
For that is why I have thee wed,   1770
So thou shalt be my world's sure
bliss."
And then she tried the knight to kiss
As if she were a lady fair.
Florent in body, true, was there,
Though as to thought and memory,
In purgatory he might be;
But youth brings strength, in spite of
hate,
The marriage must he consummate,
No weakness could excuse him, so
To nuptial bed he had to go.   1780
But when he lay beside the crone,
Awake he stayed, his heart a stone;
He turned his back upon his bride,
Hoping thereby that he might hide
Her age and foulness from his sight—
The chamber was so full of light,
The curtains were of silken gauze.
Then this new wife to plead her cause,
Though it was not with his accord,

[331]

In eager arms embraced her lord 1790
And begged that he would turn to
    her,
For wed they'd been he must concur:
"Lo, now," she said, "we two are one."
But he lay still, made answer none.
Yet ceaselessly she spoke and pled,
Reminding him of what he'd said
When he had given her his hand.

   He heard, the bond did understand,
Knew all his vow's significance,
And like a man who's in a trance, 1800
He turned towards her all unaware,
And saw a lady lying there,
Her age but eighteen winters sure,
Her countenance of fair allure,
In all the world to sight most dear.
But when he would have drawn her
    near,
With gentle hand she gave him token
That he should wait until she'd
    spoken,   1808
And said that would he win or lose
He had one of two things to choose:
Would he have her thus fair by night,
Or when the day had turned to light?
Alas, he could not have the two.
Florent knew not what he should do,
He sorrowed much in troubled
    thought;
The more the better choice he sought,
The less he felt he could decide.
And she, who was his heart's own
    bride,
Entreated him his choice to state,
Until at last, when time was late, 1820
He said: "O ye, my life's true ease,
In this my cause say what you please,
I know not what reply to give;
But long as ever that I live
I'd never you as mistress lose,
For by myself I cannot choose
The course which is the best to take;

Thus you my rule shall always make.
Choose for us both I humbly pray,
And whatsoever that you say   1830
Is your desire that is mine, too."
   "My lord," she said, "great thanks
    to you
For these good words which set me
    free,
Since giving me the sovereignty,
My destined fate you do suppress.
Now never will again grow less
My beauty which you here descry,
Until it is my lot to die;
So fair I'll be both night and day.
Now you have ta'en the spell away.
Daughter of king of Sicily   1841
I am, and woe did come to me
When I was with my father late.
Then my stepmother, for the hate
She feels for me, did change my shape
To that from which I'd no escape
Till I should win the sovereignty
Of that knight who in chivalry
All others leads in noble name,
And by report you are the same: 1850
Your deeds have proved that this is
    true,
Thus always I'll be bound to you."
Then both rejoiced that they were
    one,
Their happy mirth was now begun,
And long they lived in fortune bright.
Then clerks who heard of this good
    knight
In evidence wrote down his tale,
To prove submission will avail
In love, and give advantage sure
To him who would true joy se-
    cure,   1860
As was the lot of brave Florent.
   And all men now will be content
If so they will their love obey,
And follow straight her chosen way.

(In Book VIII, Venus re-appears before Amans, learns that his name is John
Gower, and half jestingly says that his age will prevent his having any real suc-

cess in love; and a great company of youthful lovers, appearing before Amans, prove to him by ignoring him that that is so. Cupid, who accompanies the youthful lovers, then withdraws the fiery arrow from the heart of Amans, and Venus heals the wound. Amans is given absolution, and is allowed to retire in honour from the Court of Love. Venus gives him a string of beads, on which is written in gold *Por reposer;* she bids him go where moral virtue dwells, and addresses him in farewell as she departs.)

CONCLUSION

(CONDENSED FROM BK. VIII, VSS. 2940–70)

"Adieu, for now I've made an end,
And so my way I can but wend.
When Chaucer, poet mine, you meet,
As my disciple do him greet:
For in the flower of his time
He wrote for me in gladsome rime
The songs that this day fill our lands—
In Love's own Court full high he
    stands.
Take surely to him this my praise
For comfort in his latter days,   10

As fitting tribute all should mark,
For Chaucer is my own dear clerk.
And bid him make his testament
Of love, as you love's sins repent."
    And then the goddess suddenly
In starry cloud took leave of me.
And beads in hand, I homeward
    turned,
My thoughts all filled with wisdom
    learned.

MURIEL BOWDEN

The Cuckoo and the Nightingale

Thomas Clanvowe

The God of Love—ah, *benedicite!*
How mighty and how great a Lord is he!
For he of low hearts can make high, of high
He can make low, and unto death bring nigh;
And hard hearts he can make them kind and free.

Within a little time, as hath been found,
He can make sick folk whole and fresh and sound;
Them who are whole in body and in mind,
He can make sick,—bind can he and unbind
All that he will have bound, or have unbound.   10

To tell his might my wit may not suffice;
Foolish men he can make them out of wise;—
For he may do all that he will devise;
Loose livers he can make abate their vice,
And proud hearts can make tremble in a trice.

In brief, the whole of what he will, he may;
Against him dare not any wight say nay;
To humble or afflict whome'er he will,
To gladden or to grieve, he hath like skill;
But most his might he sheds on the eve of May.   20

For every true heart, gentle heart and free,
That with him is, or thinketh so to be,
Now against May shall have some stirring—whether
To joy, or be it to some mourning; never
At other time, methinks, in like degree.

For now when they may hear the small birds' song,
And see the budding leaves the branches throng,
This unto their rememberance doth bring

All kinds of pleasure mix'd with sorrowing;
And longing of sweet thoughts that ever long.   **30**

And of that longing heaviness doth come,
Whence oft great sickness grows of heart and home;
Sick are they all for lack of their desire;
And thus in May their hearts are set on fire,
So that they burn forth in great martyrdom.

In sooth, I speak from feeling, what though now
Old am I, and to genial pleasure slow;
Yet have I felt of sickness through the May,
Both hot and cold, and heart-aches every day,—
How hard, alas! to bear, I only know.   **40**

Such shaking doth the fever in me keep
Through all this May that I have little sleep;
And also 'tis not likely unto me,
That any living heart should sleepy be
In which Love's dart its fiery point doth steep.

But tossing lately on a sleepless bed,
I of a token thought which Lovers heed;
How among them it was a common tale,
That it was good to hear the Nightingale,
Ere the vile Cuckoo's note be utteréd.   **50**

And then I thought anon as it was day,
I gladly would go somewhere to essay
If I perchance a Nightingale might hear,
For yet had I heard none, of all that year,
And it was then the third night of the May.

And soon as I a glimpse of day espied,
No longer would I in my bed abide,
But straightway to a wood that was hard by,
Forth did I go, alone and fearlessly,
And held the pathway down by a brookside;   **60**

Till to a lawn I came all white and green,
I in so fair a one had never been.
The ground was green, with daisy powdered over;

Tall were the flowers, the grove a lofty cover,
All green and white; and nothing else was seen.

There sat I down among the fair fresh flowers,
And saw the birds come tripping from their bowers,
Where they had rested them all night; and they,
Who were so joyful at the light of day,
Began to honour May with all their powers.   70

Well did they know that service all by rote,
And there was many and many a lovely note,
Some, singing loud, as if they had complained;
Some with their notes another manner feigned;
And some did sing all out with the full throat.

They preened themselves, and made themselves right gay,
Dancing and leaping light upon the spray;
And ever two and two together were,
The same as they had chosen for the year,
Upon Saint Valentine's returning day.   80

Meanwhile the stream, whose bank I sat upon,
Was making such a noise as it ran on
Accordant to the sweet Birds' harmony;
Methought that it was the best melody
Which ever to man's ear a passage won.

And for delight, but how I never wot,
I in a slumber and a swoon was caught,
Not all asleep and yet not waking wholly;
And as I lay, the Cuckoo, bird unholy,
Broke silence, or I heard him in my thought.   90

And that was right upon a tree fast by,
And who was then ill satisfied but I?
"Now, God," quoth I, "that died upon the rood,
From thee and thy base throat, keep all that's good,
Full little joy have I now of thy cry."

And, as I with the Cuckoo thus 'gan chide,
In the next bush that was me fast beside,
I heard the lusty Nightingale so sing,

That her clear voice made a loud rioting,
Echoing through all the green wood wide.　　　　　　100

"Ah! good sweet Nightingale! for my heart's cheer,
Hence hast thou stayed a little while too long;
For we have had the sorry Cuckoo here,
And she hath been before thee with her song;
Evil light on her! she hath done me wrong."

But hear you now a wondrous thing, I pray;
As long as in that swooning-fit I lay,
Methought I wist right well what these birds meant,
And had good knowing both of their intent,
And of their speech, and all that they would say.　　　110

The Nightingale thus in my hearing spake:—
"Good Cuckoo, seek some other bush or brake,
And, prithee, let us that can sing dwell here;
For every wight eschews thy song to hear,
Such uncouth singing verily dost thou make."

"What!" quoth she then, "what is't that ails thee now?
It seems to me I sing as well as thou;
For mine's a song that is both true and plain,—
Although I cannot quaver so in vain
As thou dost in thy throat, I wot not how.　　　　　120

"All men may understanding have of me,
But, Nightingale, so may they not of thee;
For thou hast many a foolish and quaint cry:—
Thou say'st OSEE, OSEE, then how may I
Have knowledge, I thee pray, what this may be?"

"Ah, fool!" quoth she, "wist thou not what it is?
Oft as I say OSEE, OSEE, ywis,
Then mean I, that I should be wondrous fain
That shamefully they one and all were slain,
Whoever against Love mean aught amiss.　　　　　130

"And also would I that they all were dead,
Who do not think in love their life to lead;
For who is loth the God of Love to obey,

Is only fit to die, I dare well say,
And for that cause Osee I cry; take heed!"

"Ay," quoth the Cuckoo, "that is a quaint law,
That all must love or die; but I withdraw,
And take my leave of all such company,
For mine intent it neither is to die,
Nor ever while I live Love's yoke to draw.   140

"For lovers, of all folk that be alive,
The most disquiet have and least do thrive;
Most feeling have of sorrow, woe and care,
And the least welfare cometh to their share;
What need is there against the truth to strive?"

"What!" quoth she, "thou art all out of thy mind,
That in thy churlishness a cause canst find
To speak of Love's true Servants in this mood;
For in this world no service is so good
To every wight that gentle is of kind.   150

"For thereof comes all goodness and all worth;
All gentiless and honor thence come forth;
Thence worship comes, content and true heart's pleasure,
And full-assurèd trust, joy without measure,
And jollity, fresh cheerfulness, and mirth;

"And bounty, lowliness, and courtesy,
And seemliness, and faithful company,
And dread of shame that will not do amiss;
For he that faithfully Love's servant is,
Rather than be disgraced, would choose to die.   160

"And that the very truth it is which I
Now say—in such belief I'll live and die;
And Cuckoo, do thou so, by my advice."
"Then," quoth she, "let me never hope for bliss,
If with that counsel I do e'er comply.

"Good Nightingale! thou speakest wondrous fair,
Yet for all that, the truth is found elsewhere;
For Love in young folk is but rage, ywis;

And Love in old folk a great dotage is;
Who most it useth, him 'twill most impair.   170

"For thereof come all contraries to gladness;
Thence sickness comes, and overwhelming sadness,
Mistrust and jealousy, despite, debate,
Dishonor, shame, envy importunate,
Pride, anger, mischief, poverty, and madness.

"Loving is aye an office of despair,
And one thing is therein which is not fair;
For whoso gets of love a little bliss,
Unless it alway stay with him, ywis
He may full soon go with an old man's hair.   180

"And, therefore, Nightingale! do thou keep nigh,
For trust me well, in spite of thy quaint cry,
If long time from thy mate thou be, or far,
Thou'lt be as others that forsaken are;
Then shalt thou raise a clamor as do I."

"Fie," quoth she, "on thy name, Bird ill beseen!
The God of Love afflict thee with all teen,
For thou art worse than mad a thousand fold;
For many a one hath virtues manifold,
Who had been nought, if Love had never been.   190

"For evermore his servants Love amendeth,
And he from every blemish them defendeth;
And maketh them to burn, as in a fire,
In loyalty, and worshipful desire,
And, when it likes him, joy enough them sendeth."

"Thou Nightingale!" the Cuckoo said, "be still,
For Love no reason hath but his own will;—
For to th' untrue he oft gives ease and joy;
True lovers doth so bitterly annoy,
He lets them perish through that grievous ill.   200

"With such a master would I never be;
For he, in sooth, is blind, and may not see,
And knows not when he hurts and when he heals;

Within this court full seldom Truth avails,
So diverse in his wilfulness is he."

Then of the Nightingale did I take note,
How from her inmost heart a sigh she brought,
And said, "Alas! that ever I was born,
Not one word have I now, I am so forlorn,—"
And with that word she into tears burst out. 210

"Alas, alas! my very heart will break,"
Quoth she, "to hear this churlish bird thus speak
Of Love, and of his holy services;
Now, God of Love! thou help me in some wise,
That vengeance on this Cuckoo I may wreak."

And so methought I started up anon,
And to the brook I ran and got a stone,
Which at the Cuckoo hardily I cast,
And he for dread did fly away full fast;
And glad, in sooth, was I when he was gone. 220

And as he flew, the Cuckoo, ever and aye,
Kept crying, "Farewell!—farewell, Popinjay!"
As if in scornful mockery of me;
And on I hunted him from tree to tree,
Till he was far, all out of sight, away.

Then straightway came the Nightingale to me,
And said, "Forsooth, my friend, do I thank thee,
That thou wert near to rescue me; and now,
Unto the God of Love I make a vow,
That all this May I will thy songstress be." 230

Well satisfied, I thanked her, and she said,
"By this mishap no longer be dismayed,
Though thou the Cuckoo heard, ere thou heard'st me;
Yet if I live it shall amended be,
When next May comes, if I am not afraid.

"And one thing will I counsel thee also,
The Cuckoo trust not thou, nor his Love's saw;
All that she said is an outrageous lie."

[340]

"Nay, nothing shall me bring thereto," quoth I,
"For Love, and it hath done me mighty woe."   240

"Yea, hath it? use," quoth she, "this medicine;
This May-time, every day before thou dine,
Go look on the fresh daisy; then say I,
Although for pain thou may'st be like to die,
Thou wilt be eased, and less wilt droop and pine.

"And mind always that thou be good and true,
And I will sing one song, of many new,
For love of thee, as loud as I may cry;"
And then did she begin this song full high,
"Beshrew all them that are in love untrue."   250

And soon as she had sung it to the end,
"Now farewell," quoth she, "for I hence must wend;
And, God of Love, that can right well and may,
Send unto thee as mickle joy this day,
As ever he to Lover yet did send."

Thus takes the Nightingale her leave of me;
I pray to God with her always to be,
And joy of love to send her evermore;
And shield us from the Cuckoo and her lore,
For there is not so false a bird as she.   260

Forth then she flew, the gentle Nightingale,
To all the Birds that lodged within that dale,
And gathered each and all into one place;
And them besought to hear her doleful case,
And thus it was that she began her tale.

"The Cuckoo—'tis not well that I should hide
How she and I did each the other chide,
And without ceasing, since it was daylight;
And now I pray you all to do me right
Of that false Bird whom Love cannot abide."   270

Then spake one Bird, and full assent all gave;
"This matter asketh counsel good as grave,
For birds we are—all here together brought;

And, in good sooth, the Cuckoo here is not;
And therefore we a Parliament will have.

"And thereat shall the Eagle be our Lord,
And other Peers whose names are on recórd;
A summons to the Cuckoo shall be sent,
And judgment there be given; or that intent
Failing, we finally shall make accord.   280

"And all this shall be done, without a nay,
The morrow after Saint Valentine's day,
Under a maple that is well beseen,
Before the chamber-window of the Queen,
At Woodstock, on the meadow green and gay."

She thanked them; and then her leave she took,
And flew into a hawthorn by that brook;
And there she sat and sung—upon that tree—
"For term of life Love shall have hold of me"—
So loudly, that I with that song awoke.   290

Ballade

Unlearned Book and rude, as well I know,
For beauty thou hast none, nor eloquence,
Who did on thee the hardiness bestow
To appear before my Lady? but a sense
Thou surely hast of her benevolence,
Whereof her hourly bearing proof doth give;
For of all good she is the best alive.

Alas, poor Book! for thy unworthiness,
To show to her some pleasant meanings writ
In winning words, since through her gentiless,   300
Thee she accepts as for her service fit!
Oh! it repents me I have neither wit
Nor leisure unto thee more worth to give;
For of all good she is the best alive.

Beseech her meekly with all lowliness,
Though I be far from her I reverence,
To think upon my truth and steadfastness,

And to abridge my sorrow's violence,
Caused by the wish, as knows your sapience,
She of her liking proof to me would give;   310
For of all good she is the best alive.

L'Envoy

Pleasure's Aurora, Day of gladsomeness!
Luna by night, with heavenly influence
Illumined! root of beauty and goodnésse,
Write, and allay by your beneficence,
My sighs breathed forth in silence,—comfort give!
Since of all good you are the best alive.

                          WILLIAM WORDSWORTH

FIFTEENTH CENTURY

La Male Regle

Thomas Hoccleve

ILL-REGULATED YOUTH

(VSS. 121–424)

THE outward sign of Bacchus,[1] and his lure [2] which hangeth day after day
at his door, excite us to taste so often of his liquor that a man cannot well
say "nay." As for me, I was ever inclined without compulsion thither to hie
me, except when such a burden lay on my back that I was forced to abstain
for a time, or when I was rendered naked by the penniless malady; for then
I could not be glad of heart and had no desire to hie to Bacchus' house. Fie!
Lack of coin parteth good company; but a heavy purse, together with a
liberal heart, quencheth the thirsty heat of dry hearts, whereas a niggardly
heart hath little enjoyment.

I dare not tell how the lively society of Venus' dear joyous female chil- 10
dren, who were so goodly, shapely, fair, and pleasant of bearing and manner, and could feed all a world with cheer, and were in their attire so passing
well arrayed, often made me repair to Paul's Head, to talk of mirth and
sport and play. There was sweet wine enough throughout the house, and
thick cakes, for this company that I spake of was somewhat gluttonous.
Where they might espy a draught of wine, sweet and, in its effect, exceeding hot to warm a stomach with, they drank thereof. To suffer them to pay
would have been no courtesy; so that charge I took, to win their love and
thanks.

As yet I touched none of love's art. I knew it not, and also there was 20
no need. Had I a kiss, I was full well content, better than I would have
been with the deed. Of that I know but little, there is no doubt. When men
speak of it in my presence, I wax as red for shame as a live coal. Now will
I return to my subject.

Of him who haunteth taverns by custom, in brief words the profit is this:
it hath the double effect of emptying his wallet and of making his tongue

---

[1] A bush was the sign of a wine-shop.

[2] Hoccleve uses the metaphor of a piece of leather covered with feathers, used by
falconers to lure a falcon back.

speak of folk amiss. For it is seldom found that in his cups any wight commendeth his neighbor. Behold and see what advantage is his who offendeth God, his friend, and eke himself!

But one advantage I have in this matter: I was so afraid to fight with any man that I kept quiet. I durst not disparage any man except in a whisper; I said nothing aloud. But yet I had the will, if I had not been restrained by my manly cowardice, which always impressed on me how heavy were strokes, so that I durst not meddle in any wise.

Where was a greater master eke than I, or one better acquainted at West-
10 minster Gate, especially among the tavern-keepers and cooks, when I came early or late? I did not haggle with them in my purchasing, but paid them what they would ask. Wherefore I was always the more welcome and was regarded as a very man of birth. And if it happened on a summer's day that I had been thus at the tavern, when I was about to depart and go my way home to the office of the Privy Seal, heat and surfeit and reluctance so tempted me to walk to the bridge and take a boat that I durst not oppose them all three, but did as they prompted me, God wot!

And in the winter, because the road was deep [in mud], I betook myself also to the bridge, and there the boatmen gave me their attention, for
20 they knew my extravagance from of old. Between them I was tugged to and fro, so fortunate was he with whom I would fare; for extravagance always payeth generously; he never stinteth till his purse is bare. I was never called other than "Master" in my hearing among this retinue. Methought I was made a man forever; that stupid reverence so tickled me that it made me freer in spending than I had thought to be. O Flattery! the way of thy treacherous diligence is to hasten and hurry folk to misfortune. . . .

Whoso list read in the Book of Nature concerning beasts, may see therein, if he take heed to the scripture, where it speaketh of mermaids in the sea,
30 how she singeth so very merrily that the shipman therewith falleth asleep, and after is devoured by her. From all such song it is good that men keep themselves. . . .

Men set no store by truth nowadays; men love it not; men will not cherish it. And yet truth is best in all trials. When false Favel,[3] sustainer of vice, shall not know how to succeed, full boldly shall Truth lift up her head. Lords, lest Favel draw you away from your good, suffer her no longer to nestle in your ear. . .

Lo, my noble lord, who now art Treasurer, I pray thee let my lord

[3] The *Roman de Fauvel* (1310–14) depicts a horse named Fauvel as a symbol of falsehood. Hence the modern expression "to curry favor" (substituted for Favel) still means to flatter.

Fournival [4] have a token or two from thy Highness to pay me what is due for this year from my yearly ten pounds in the Exchequer, only for the last Michaelmas term. I dare not speak a word of last year, my spirit is so simple and sore aghast.

[4] Thomas Nevil, lord Fournival, appointed subtreasurer in 1405.

The Regement of Princes

Thomas Hoccleve

BADBY'S HERESY

THERE are some men who, for lack of occupation, cogitate further than their minds will stretch, and, at the fiend's prompting, hold damnable errors, and cannot turn away from them for any counsel or advice, as did a wretch not long ago, who was convicted of heresy and burned to dry ashes.[1] He believed not at all in the precious body of Our Lord Jesu in the form of bread. He was no wise abashed nor did he shrink from saying that it was but material bread. He said a priest's power was as little as a street-sweeper's or some other such fellow's, and had no greater efficacy to make it.[2]

10   My lord the prince [3]—God save and bless him!—was present at his fatal punishment, and had great tenderness for his soul, thirsting sorely for his salvation. Great was his piteous lament when this renegade would not relinquish the stinking error that he was in. This good lord promised him to be such a mediator with his father, our sovereign liege lord, if he would cleanly renounce his error and return to our good belief, that he would be secure and certain of his life and would also have a sufficient livelihood till the day he was clad in his grave. Also this noble prince and worthy knight —may God requite him for his charitable deed!—before any stick was kindled or lighted, caused the sacrament, our blessed Savior, to be fetched

20 with great reverence and high honor, in order to convert this wretch and make our faith sink into his heart. But all for naught; it would not come to pass. He held to his damnable opinion and cast our holy Christian faith aside, as one who was acceptable to the fiend by every outward reasonable token. Whether he had any inward repentance, that knoweth He who hath no doubt of anything.

Let divines speak of him and speculate where his soul is, or whither it has gone. My ignorance will excuse me from judging in a matter of which I have no knowledge. But would to God that those foes of Christ who be-

---

[1] John Badby was burned at Smithfield in 1410.
[2] To convert bread into the body of Christ.
[3] Prince Henry or Hal, later Henry V.

lieved as he did should be served, each one, like him, for I am sure that there are many more.

TRIBUTES TO CHAUCER AND GOWER

O MASTER dear and reverend father, my master Chaucer, flower of eloquence, mirror of fruitful wisdom, O universal father of knowledge! Alas, that on thy mortal bed thou mightest not bequeath thine excellent prudence! What aileth Death? Alas, why would he slay thee? O Death! thou didst no private harm in slaying him, but it grieveth all this land. But nevertheless, thou hast no power to slay his name; his high genius escapeth unslain from thee,—and this doth greatly hearten us,—through the books of his ornate enditing which illumine all this land.   10

Hast thou not also slain my master Gower, whose genius I am insufficient to describe? I wot well surely that thou hast intended to slay all this world. But since Our Lord Christ was obedient to thee, I cannot, in faith, say more; His creatures must obey thee. . .

My dear master and father Chaucer—God reward his soul!—fain would have taught me, but I was dull and learned little or naught. Alas, my worthy honorable master, this land's true treasure and wealth, Death by thy death hath done us irreparable harm; her vengeful cruelty hath despoiled this land of the sweetness of rhetoric; for never man among us was so like unto Tullius. Also, who in our tongue was heir to Aristotle in philosophy but 20 thou? Thou also didst follow the steps of Virgil in poetry, men wot well enough. I would that that cumber-earth who slew thee, my master, were slain. Death was too hasty to run at thee and rob thee of thy life! . . .

Alas, my father from the world is gone,—my worthy master Chaucer I mean. Be thou his advocate, Queen of Heaven! As thou well knowest, O blessed Virgin, he wrote with loving heart and high devotion many a line in thine honor. Oh grant now thy help and thy advocacy! To God, thy Son, make mention how he was thy servant, Maiden Mary, and let his love flower and bear fruit.

Though his life be quenched, his likeness hath in me such fresh liveliness 30 that, to put other men in remembrance of his person, I have here caused his portrait to be made, to this end indeed that they who have him least in thought and memory may find him again by this painting.[1]

[1] Manuscripts of the *Regement of Princes* contain in the margin at this point portraits of Chaucer, which are regarded as the most faithful likenesses we possess.

The Temple of Glass

John Lydgate

(VSS. 1–314)

OVERCOME by thought, constraint, grievous melancholy, pensiveness, and high distress, I went to bed the other night, when Lucina with her pale light was last joined with Phoebus in Aquarius, in mid-December, when the calends of January of the new year begin, and when horned Diana, dark and nowise clear, had hid her beams under a misty cloud. For sorrow I covered myself in my bed, desolate and oppressed with woe, turning to and fro through the long night, till at last, ere I was aware, a sudden, deadly sleep came over me.

It seemed that I was ravished in spirit, I knew not how, to a temple of 10 glass, far in a wilderness; which temple was founded apparently, not upon steel, but on a craggy rock like frozen ice. As I approached, it shone against the sun methought as brightly as any crystal, and ever as I came nearer and nearer to this grisly, dreadful place, I grew dazed. The light began to smite so in my face, piercing in every part where I was going, that I could not, as I would, look about me and behold the wondrous interior rooms because of the sun's brightness. Till at last certain dark clouds, chased by the wind, took their course before the rays of Titan and blinded them, so that wherever I walked, within and without, I could look about me and report the fashion of this place, which was circular and round in shape. When I had 20 walked and sought long, I found a wicket and entered quickly and cast my eyes on every side, now low and now aloft.

Presently, as I walked softly, if I shall report the truth, I saw painted on every wall from east to west many a fair image of sundry lovers, arranged according to their age as if they were real, with lifelike colors, wondrous fresh of hue. And methought I saw some sitting and standing, and some kneeling with petitions in their hands, and some with woeful and piteous complaints to lay with doleful cheer before Venus as she sat floating in the sea, beseeching her to have pity on their woe. First of all I saw there Dido, the queen of Carthage, goodly of countenance, who complained her 30 fate, how she was deceived by Aeneas in spite of his promises and sworn oaths, and who said, "Alas that ever she was born," when she saw that she must die.

Next I saw the complaint of Medea, how she was deceived by Jason.

Near Venus I saw Adonis sitting, and all the manner in which the boar slew him, for whom she wept and had pain enough. There I saw also how Penelope, because she could not see her lord for so long a time, waxed often pale and green of color.

Next was the bright queen, Alcestis I mean, the noble, true wife, and how she lost her life for Admetus, and how, if I shall not lie, she was turned for her truth into a daisy. There was also Griselda's innocence and her meekness and her patience. There too was Isolt (and many another) and all the torment and all the cruel woe which she endured for Tristram all her life; and how Thisbe pierced her heart with the sword of Pyramus; and 10 how Theseus, when he was imprisoned in Crete, slew the Minotaur amidst the house which was built as a maze by the craft of Daedalus; and how Phyllis felt a great fire of love for Demophoön, alas, and one might see painted on the walls how, for his falsehood and treachery, she was hanged on a filbert tree.

And many a story—more than I can reckon—were in the temple; how Paris won fair Helen, the joyous, fresh queen, and how Achilles was slain unawares for Polyxena in Troy town. All this I saw, walking up and down. There saw I written also the whole story, how Philomena was turned into a nightingale, and Procne into a swallow; and how the Sabines in their man- 20 ner still keep holy the feast of Lucrece in Rome town.

There saw I also the sorrow and smart of Palamon which he felt in prison, and how he was hurt unawares through his heart by casting an eye on the fair, fresh, young Emily; and all the strife between him and his brother, and how they fought together in the grove till they were accorded by Theseus, as Chaucer telleth us. Furthermore, as I beheld, I saw how Phoebus was wounded with an arrow of gold through his side, only because of the envy of the god Cupid; and how Daphne was turned into a laurel tree when she fled; and how Jove changed his cope for love of fair Europa, and was pleased to transmute his godhead into a bull, when he pursued her; and how 30 by transmutation he took the shape of Amphitryon for the sake of Alcmena, peerless in beauty, so hurt was he by love's dart, for all his deity, that he could not escape it. There saw I too how Mars was caught by Vulcan and found with Venus and bound with invisible chains.

There was also the poem of Mercury and Philology, and how she, for the sake of her wisdom, was wedded to the god of eloquence; and how the Muses in lowly obedience conveyed this lady up into heaven, and how with her song she was magnified and stellified by Jupiter. Uppermost one might see depicted how goodly Canace could understand by means of her ring the language and the song of every bird as she walked among them; 40 and how her brother was helped so often in his misfortune by the steed of brass.

Furthermore there were in the temple many thousands of lovers, here and there, ready to complain in various ways to the goddess of their woe and pain; how they were hindered, some out of envy, and how the serpent of false jealousy hath set many a lover back and without cause charged them with a fault. And some there were who complained of absence, being exiled and removed from the presence of their loves through wicked tongues and false suspicions, without mercy or pardon. And others spent their service in vain through cruel arrogance and scorn. Some also, truth to tell, loved but were not loved again by their ladies; and others by reason 10 of poverty durst in no wise disclose or reveal their great adversity lest they should be refused; and some were charged with a defect; and others loved secretly and durst not ask mercy of their lady lest she should despise them; and some put heavy blame on hypocritical lovers who love novelty and through whose falsehood true lovers are hindered. There were some, as often happens, who for their lady had endured many a bloody wound in many a region, while another possessed his lady and bore away the fruit of all his labor and his wooing.

Others complained of Riches, who with his treasure contriveth to win the victory contrary to nature and right, whereas true lovers are power-20 less. And there were some, young maidens, who complained sorely with furious wailing that they were coupled, in defiance of nature, with crooked age, which cannot long continue to play the game of love. For it suiteth not fresh May to be coupled to old January, they are so different that they must conflict; for age is grudging and melancholy, ever full of ire and suspicion, while youth tendeth to joy, pleasure, mirth, play, and all gladness. "Alas that ever it should hap that sweet sugar be coupled with gall!" cried these young folk full oft, and prayed Venus to show forth her power to remedy this wrong.

Presently I heard others cry, with sobbing tears and piteous sound, and 30 lament before the goddess that they were constrained in their tender youth, and, as is well known, had entered the monastic life in childhood, before they had reached years of discretion, so that all their lives they could not but lament, feigning perfection in their wide copes to cover up covertly all their grief, and show outwardly the contrary of their hearts. Thus I saw many a fair maid weeping, who placed all the blame on her friends, and I saw next others in great anguish, who had been married in their tender age without freedom of choice, where love seldom hath domination. For love, left at liberty, would freely choose and not be subject to bargaining.

Others I saw frequently weeping and wringing their hands because they 40 found such changefulness in men, who love a season while beauty flowereth, and then, with ugly louring, disdain her whom once they had called their lady dear and who had been so gracious and loyal to them. But lust departeth with beauty, so that in their hearts no truth abideth. Some also I saw raining tears and piteously complaining against God and Nature that they would ever bestow on any woman so much beauty, surpassing measure, as to cause a man to love to his destruction, especially when he shall win no favor. For, as he passeth by, it often befalleth that with a look and the glance of an eye a man is wounded so that he must needs die, even though peradventure he may never see her again. Why will God do so great a cruelty to any man, and make him endure so much woe for her whom perchance he will never rejoice, and make him lead his life thenceforth in torment until he is buried? For he dare not crave her mercy, or, 10 if he dare and would, peradventure he cannot learn where he may find her. I saw there also—and it roused my pity—that some were hindered by avarice and sloth, some by their hastiness, and others by their carelessness.

At last, as I walked, I beheld, at the side of Pallas with her crystal shield and before the statue of Venus set on high, a lady kneeling before the goddess. Just as the sun surpasseth the stars and dimmeth their beams; as Lucifer, to drive away the night's sorrow, early in the morning passeth in brilliance; as May hath the sovranty over every month for fairness and beauty; as the rose excelleth other flowers in sweetness and odor, and balm is held in highest esteem of all liquors, and the bright ruby is known to have the king- 20 ship of all stones in beauty; right so this lady, with her kindly eyes and the bright rays of her look, surpasseth all in beauty to my seeming. To tell her great loveliness, her womanhood, her bearing, and her fairness, it was a marvel how Nature could ever in her works make so angelic a creature, so goodly to see, so feminine and excellent in beauty, whose sunny hair, brighter than gold wire, shone like the beams of Phoebus in his sphere. The goodliness, too, of her fresh countenance was so filled with beauty and grace, so well renewed and painted by Nature, and roses and lilies were mingled in such equal proportions that, as I gazed, I marveled how God or work of Nature might discover such a treasury of beauty to give her such 30 surpassing excellence. For, in good faith, the temple was illumined all around by her high presence.

And to speak of her qualities, she was the best that could ever live. For there was none who could contend with her in bounty, nobility, womanliness, humility, courtesy, goodliness, speech, manner, propriety, grace, benign bearing, conversation, and she was the best taught. Besides she was the well-spring of pleasure, the exemplar of honor, the mirror of secrecy, truth, and fidelity, and the lady and mistress of all others in the pursuit of virtue, whoever would desire to learn.

Thus I saw this lady, benign and humble of cheer, all clad in green and 40 white, kneeling before Venus, goddess of all pleasure, her dress embroidered with stones and jewels so richly that it was a joy to see, and also with sundry scrolls to express the truth of her intent and show fully that, by reason of her humility, virtue, and steadfastness, she was the root of womanly pleasure. Therefore her motto, without variation, was embroidered with jewels as one might see,—"*De mieulx en mieulx.*" That is to say, that she, this benign lady, from better to better commendeth her heart and all her will to the goddess Venus when it should please to relieve her distress.

The King's Quair[1]

James I of Scotland

I

High in the heaven's azure hemisphere
The ruddy stars were twinkling as the fire,
And in Aquarius Cynthia the clear
Rinsèd her tresses like the golden wire,
Who late before, in fair and fresh attire,
Through Capricorn her horns had lifted bright,
And north-north-west she approachèd the midnight.

II

When in my bed I lay considering,
Waked out of sleep a little time before,
My mind was filled with many a diverse thing
Of this and that. I cannot say wherefor,
But by no craft on earth could I sleep more;
For which, since then I knew no better wile,
I took a book to read upon a while;

III

Of which the name is callèd properly
Boethius, who was its compilour,
Showing the counsel of Philosophy,
Compilèd by that noble senatour
Of Rome, who of the world was then the flower,
And from a high estate was for a while
Condemned to poverty and durance vile.

VIII

The livelong night aye reading, as I said,
My eyes began to smart with studying;

[1] Book.

My book I shut, and laid it at my head,
And down I lay without more tarrying,
This matter new in my mind pondering,
How Fortune doth determine each estate,
And, as she wills, bring low or elevate. . .

XI

Tossing about and wakeful, wondering,
I weary lay and listened. Suddenly
And soon I heard the bell to matins ring,
And up I rose, no longer would I lie.
And now, what think ye? Such a fantasy
Fell to my mind that aye methought the bell
Said to me, "Tell on, man, what thee befell." . . .

XXII

Not far beyond the age of innocence,
But near about the number of years three,
Whether 'twere caused by heavenly influence
Of God's intent or some fatality,
I cannot say; but out of my countree,
By their advice who had of me the care,
Across the sea it was my lot to fare.

XXIII

And furnished well with all things necessary,
With wind at will, up early on the morrow,
Straight into ship,—no longer would we tarry,—
The way we took, foreseeing naught of sorrow,
With "Farewells" many and "St. John to borrow"
From fellow and from friend, with one assent
We pulled up sail and on our way we went.

XXIV

Upon the waves we weltered to and fro,
Unfortunate on that unhappy day;
In spite of us, whether we would or no,
With strong hand, as by force, in short to say,
We all were captured and conveyed away
By enemies, and brought unto their land.
Thus and no otherwise had Fortune planned.

XXV

There then in strict ward and in prison strong,
No comfort left me nor of hope a sign,
My thread of life, thus wearily and long,
The second sister set about to twine
Through wellnigh all the space of years twice nine;
Till Jupiter to mercy turned his heart
And sent me comfort to relieve my smart. . .

XXVIII

Then would I say: "If God had me devised
To live my life in thraldom thus and pine,
What is the cause that me he more despised
And more than other people did confine?
I stand alone among the figures nine,
A woeful zero, who no wight may aid,
And yet of others' help I stand in need." . . .

XXX

Bewailing in my chamber thus alone,
Despairing of all joy and remedy,
A-weary of my thoughts and woe-begone,
Unto the window did I walk to spy
The world and all its people passing by.
For at that time, though I of cheering food
Might have naught else, to look it did me good.

XXXI

Now there was made fast by the tower wall
A garden fair, and, in the corners set,
Flourished green herbs, with wattles long and small
Railed all about; and so the place was set
With trees, and so with hawthorn hedges knit,
That nobody, though he were walking nigh,
Might there within scarce any wight descry.

XXXIII

And on the slender green-leaved branches sate
The little joyous nightingales, and sang
So loud and clear the hymns that consecrate

Are to Love's use; now soft their tune, now strong,
That all the walls and all the garden rang
Right of their song, and in the stanza next
Of their sweet harmony, lo! is the text:

XXXIV

"Come worship, ye that lovers are this May,
For of your bliss the calends are begun,
And sing with us, 'Away, Winter, away!
Come, Summer, come, the sweet time, and the sun!'
Awake, for shame, ye who your heavens have won,
And amorously in joy your heads lift all;
Thank Love, who doth you to his mercy call." . . .

XXXVI

This was the clear plain ditty of their note,
And therewithal unto myself I thought:
"What life is this that maketh birds to dote?
What may this be, how cometh it of aught?
What needeth it to be so dearly bought?
It is, I trow, nothing but feignèd cheer,
That men pretend and counterfeit as cheer."

XXXVII

And then I'd think: "Whatever may this be,
That Love is of so noble might and kind,
Loving his folk, and such prosperity
Is due to him as we in books do find?
May he affection fasten and unbind?
Hath he upon our heart such mastery?
Or is all this but feignèd fantasy? . . .

XXXIX

"I can naught else conclude, except that he
Is lord and as a god may live and reign,
To bind and loose and set the captives free.
Then would I pray his blissful grace benign
To give me leave to join his train divine,
And evermore to make me one of those
Who serve him faithfully in joys and woes."

XL

And therewith cast I down my eyes to earth,
And there I saw, walking beneath the tower
Full secretly, new coming to make mirth,
The fairest and the freshest youthful flower
That e'er I saw, methought, before that hour;
For which surprise, all suddenly did start
The blood of all my body to my heart. . .

XLVI

If I the form of her array should write,
To wit her golden hair and rich attire,
It was bedecked and set with pearls so white
And balas rubies sparkling as the fire,
With many an emerald and fair sapphire;
And on her head a chaplet fresh of hue,
Of feathers colored red and white and blue. . .

XLVIII

About her neck, white as enamel clear,
A goodly chain of slender goldsmithry,
Whereat there hung a ruby, without peer.
Like to a heart it shaped was verily,
That as a spark of flame so wantonly
Seemed burning bright upon her snowy throat.
Now if that was a good match, God it wot!

XLIX

And for to walk, that merry morn of May,
A mantle she had o'er her kirtle white;
No goodlier had been seen before that day,
As I suppose. Her girdle was not tight,
But partly loose for haste. Lo, such delight
It was to see her youth in goodlihead,
Lest I be rude, to speak thereof I dread.

L

In her were beauty, youth, and humble port,
Virtue and wealth and maiden shapeliness,—

[361]

God better wot than pen of mine report,—
Wisdom, estate, discretion, and largess.
She was so perfect, neither more nor less,
In word, in deed, in form, in countenance,
That Nature could no more her child advance. . .

LXVII

When she had walked a little to and fro
Under the shady sweet green branches bent,
Her fair fresh face as white as any snow,
She turned about and forth her way she went.
And then began my fever and tormént
To see her go where follow not I might;
Methought the day converted into night.

LXVIII

Then said I thus: "Whereunto live I longer?
Woefullest wight and subject unto pain!
Pain? Yea, God knows; for never anguish stronger,
I dare well say, may any wight constrain.
How may this be that death and life, the twain,
Should both at once in any mortal creature
Together dwell, and thus torment his nature? . . ."

LXXIII

So until eve, for lack of might and mind,
I sore complained and wept right piteously.
By sorrow so distraught were heart and mind,
That to the chilly stone my head awry
I laid and leaned, perplexèd verily,
Half sleeping and half swooning in such wise;
And what I dreamt I will you now advise.

LXXIV

Methought that thus all suddenly a light
In at the window came whereat I leant,
With which the chamber window shone full bright,
And all my body so it over-went
That all the virtue of my sight was spent.
And therewithal a voice unto me said:
"I bring thee joy and health, be not afraid."

LXXV

And forth anon the light passed suddenly
Where it had entered, the same way again;
And I forth through the door right hastily
Went on my way; me nothing did restrain.
And all at once, by both of my arms twain,
I was high lifted up into the air,
Caught in a cloud of crystal clear and fair,

LXXVI

Ascending upward aye from sphere to sphere,
Through air, through water, then through flaming fire,
Until I came unto that circle clear,
The zodiac, where shone in bright attire
The signs, and thence into the glad empíre
Of blissful Venus, where one shouted now
So suddenly I wist not almost how.

LXXVII

Of which the palace, when I came anigh,
Was all methought of precious crystals wrought,
And to the door I lifted was on high,
When suddenly and swiftly as a thought
It opened wide, and through it I was brought
Within a chamber, fair and wide and long,
And there I found of folk a mighty throng.

LXXVIII

That is to say, that present in that place
Methought I saw of every earthly nation
Millions of lovers who their mortal race
Had in love's service brought to termination;
But of their fortunes whoso hath occasion
May well in divers books the story see,
And therefore here their names I will let be. . .

XCIV

And sitting in a chair of state near by,
With shining wings, all plumed except his face,
The blind god Cupido I did descry,

With bow in hand, that bent and ready was;
And by him hung three arrows in a case,
Of which the heads were ground full sharp and right,
Of various metals forgèd fair and bright.

XCV

And with the first, that headed was with gold,
He softly smites, and that has easy cure;
The second was of silver, many fold
Worse than the first and harder to endure;
The third of steel, its shot is without cure.
And on his yellow locks so long and sheen
He had a chaplet, all of leaves so green.

XCVI

In a retreat that was of compass narrow,
Painted around with sighs exceeding sad,—
These were not sighs which hearts with anguish harrow,
But such as make true lovers to be glad,—
Venus I found upon her bed, who had
A mantle cast across her shoulders white;
Thus clothèd was the goddess of delight. . .

XCVIII

With quaking heart, astonished at that sight,
Then scarcely wist I what I ought to say;
But at the last and feebly as I might,
I both my hands upon my knees did lay,
And of my cares began I to complain;
With humble air and lamentable cheer
Saluted I that goddess bright and clear.

XCIX

"High Queen of Love! star of benevolence!
Princess of pity, planet merciful!
Appeaser of ill will and violence
By virtue of your aspects powerful!
Unto your grace be now acceptable
My pure request, for I to none can sue
And seek for help, but only unto you. . .

CII

"And though I was to all your statutes strange,
By ignorance and not by felony,
And if your grace be willing now to change
My pliant heart to serve you constantly,
Forgive all this, and shape a remedy
To gain my cause through your benignant grace,
Or give me death forthwith in this same place.

CIII

"And with the radiance of your piercing light
Convoy my heart, that is so woe-begone,
Again unto that sweet and heavenly sight,
That I, within the walls as cold as stone,
So sweetly saw this morning walk alone
Down in the garden, right before mine eye.
Now mercy, Queen! allow me not to die!"

CIV

These words expressed, my spirit in despair,
I ceased awhile and waited for her grace;
And thereupon her crystal eyes so fair
She bent aside, and after that a space
Benignantly she turnèd has her face
Toward myself, that pleasantly conveyed
Her kind intent, and in this wise she said:

CV

"Young man, the cause of all thy sorrow sore
Is not unknown unto my deity,
And thy request, both now and eke before
When thou first mad'st profession unto me;
Since of my grace I have inspirèd thee
To know my law, continue forth, for oft
There where I aimed full sore, I smite but soft. . .

CIX

"And yet considering the nakedness
Both of thy wit, thy person, and thy might,

[365]

They are no match, in their unworthiness,
To her high birth, estate, and beauty bright.
As like ye be as day is to the night,
Or sackcloth is unto fine crimson mesh,
Or ugly dock unto the daisy fresh. . .

CXII

"But that thou mayst discern that I intend
To help thee on, thy welfare to preserve,
Immediately thy spirit will I send
On to the goddess who is called Minerve,
And see that her behests thou well conserve,
For in this case she may be thine ally,
And put thy heart at rest as well as I.

CXIII

"And since the way unknown is unto thee
And where her dwelling is and her sojourn,
I will that Good-hope servant be to thee,
The friend of all, who will not let thee mourn.
He shall thee lead and guide till thou return;
And pray Minerva that she in thy need
Her counsel give for welfare and for speed. . ."

CXXIV

With humble thanks and all the reverence
My feeble wit and wisdom could attain,
I took my leave; from Venus' high presénce
Good-hope and I in company, we twain,
Departure took, and, in few words and plain,
He led me ways that ready were and right
Unto Minerva's palace fair and bright. . .

CXXVI

And straight into the presence suddenly
Of Dame Minerva, patient under stress,
Good-hope, my guide, has led me readily;
To whom anon with proper humbleness
My visit and its cause I did express,
And all the matter whole, unto the end,
Of Venus' charge, as pleasèd her to send.

CXXVII

To which Minerva's answer was in brief:
"My son, I have well heard and understood,
As thou hast told, the nature of thy grief.
Thou would'st attain thy quest and comfort good
And some relief to thy unhappy mood,
As Venus counseled thee, thy lady bright,
That I may be thy helper in this plight. . .

CXXX

"Take Him the first in all thy governance,
Who in His hand the fate has of you all,
And pray that His directing providence
Thy love may guide, and on Him trust and call,
Who corner-stone and base is of the wall
That never fails, and trust Him without dread,
And to thy purpose soon He will thee lead. . .

CXXXIV

"But there be many of so brittle sort
That feign the truth in love a little while,
And set their wits and make it their disport
The weak confiding woman to beguile
And so to win their purpose with a wile;
Such feignèd truth is naught but treachery
Under the cover of hypocrisy. . .

CL

"But for the sake and in the reverence due
Of Venus clear, as I have said before,
I have for thee both sympathy and rue,
And in relief and comfort of thy sore
I herewith give thee my advice therefor.
Ask Fortune's help, for most unlikely things
Full oft and suddenly about she brings.

CLI

"Now go thy way, and set thy mind upon
What I have said, thy conduct to define."
"Madam, I will," quoth I; and right anon
[367]

I took my leave. As straight as any line,
Following a beam which from that land divine
Minerva, piercing through the sky, extended,
To earth again my spirit is descended.

CLII

There, in a pleasant plain, I took my way,
Along a river joyous to behold,
Which bordered was with flowers fresh and gay;
And o'er the gravel, bright as any gold,
The crystal water rippled clear and cold
And in mine ear it made unceasingly
A pleasing sound of sweetest harmony.

CLIII

And little fishes sported by the brim;
Now here, now there, with backs as blue as lead,
They leaped and played, and in a shoal did swim
So prettily, and dressed themselves to spread
Their coral fins, like to the ruby red,
That in the sun their scales so clear and bright
Like coats of mail aye glittered in my sight.

CLIV

And near to this same riverside below
I found a highway running, as I ween,
On which, on every side, a lengthened row
Of trees I saw, all clad in leafage green,
And full of fruit delightful to be seen.
And also, as it came into my mind,
Beasts I beheld of many a diverse kind:

CLV

The lion king, his mate the lioness;
The panther, like unto the smaragdine;
The little squirrel, full of business;
The lazy ass, the drudging beast of pine;
The foolish ape; the bristling porcupine;
The sharp-eyed lynx; the lover unicorn,
That drives out poison with his ivory horn; . . .

CLVIII

With many other beasts diverse and strange,
That do not come at present to my mind.
Now to my purpose; straight on through the range
I held my way, revolving in my mind
Whence I had come and where I hoped to find
The goddess Fortune; then to that deity
Good-hope, my guide, did lead me suddenly.

CLIX

And so at last, turning my glance aside,
A circular and wallèd space I found,
And in the midst thereof I soon espied
The goddess Fortune, standing on the ground,
And right before her feet, of compass round,
A wheel, and on it clinging did descry
A multitude of folk before mine eye. . .

CLXII

And underneath the wheel I saw right there
An ugly pit as deep as any hell,
That to behold thereon I quaked for fear;
But one thing heard I that who therein fell
Came no more up again, tidings to tell;
Of which, astonished at that fearful sight,
I wist not what to do, so great my fright. . .

CLXV

I also saw that, whereas some were slung
By whirling of that wheel unto the ground,
Full suddenly she hath it upward flung
And set them on again right safe and sound,
And I saw ever a new swarm abound
That sought to upward climb upon that wheel
Instead of them that might no longer reel.

CLXVI

And at the last, in presence of them all
That stood about, she summoned me by name;

[369]

And therewith on my knees I down did fall
Right suddenly, somewhat abashed for shame;
And, smiling, thus she said to me in game:
"What dost thou here? Who has thee hither sent?
Say on at once, and tell me thine intent.

CLXVII

"I see well by thy look and countenance
There is some matter lies upon thy heart.
Things stand not with thee as thou would'st, perchance."
"Madam," quoth I, "since love is all the smart
That I feel ever, endlong and athwart,
Help, of your grace, me, woeful wretched wight,
Because to cure me ye have power and might."

CLXVIII

"What help," quoth she, "would'st thou that I ordain
To bring thee to thy longing heart's desire?"
"Madam," quoth I, "just that your grace may deign
Of your great might my weak wits to inspire
To win the well that slacken may the fire
In which I burn. Ah, goddess fortunate!
Help now my game, for I am near checkmate." . . .

CLXXI

And therewithal she quickly did me lead
Unto the wheel and bade me learn to climb,
And I thereon did mount with sudden speed.
"Now hold thy grip," quoth she, "because thy time
An hour and more it has run over prime.
Counting the whole, the half is near away;
Spend therefore well the remnant of the day.

CLXXII

"Example take," quoth she, "of those before,
That from my wheel have tumbled like a ball.
The nature of it is forevermore
After a rise to sink and low to fall;
Thus, as I wish, they mount or downward sprawl.
Farewell," quoth she; and by the ear me took
So earnestly that therewith I awoke. . .

CLXXV

I presently addressed myself to rise,
Quite full of thought, pain, and adversity,
And to myself I said upon this wise:
"Ah, mercy, Lord! what will ye do with me?
What life is this? Where could my spirit be?
Can this be of my hope a mere impression?
Or is it in good sooth a heavenly vision? . . ."

CLXXVII

In haste unto the window did I walk,
Musing within my spirit on this sight,
When quick a turtle-dove, as white as chalk,
So evenly upon my hand did light,
And unto me she turned herself full right;
Her birdlike cheer did chase away my grief
And brought my heart the calends of relief.

CLXXVIII

This beauteous bird right in her bill did hold
Of red carnations with their stalks so green
A goodly branch, where written was with gold
On every edge with letters bright and sheen,
Proportioned fair, full pleasant to be seen,
A sentence plain, which, as I can devise
And bring to mind, said right upon this wise:

CLXXIX

"Awake! awake! I bring, lover, I bring
Glad news to thee, which blissful are, and sure
To comfort thee. Now laugh and play and sing,
Thou art so near a happy adventúre;
For in the heaven appointed is thy cure."
The bird to me the flowers did present,
And with spread wings her way forthwith she went. . .

CLXXXVII

To reckon every single circumstance
That happened me, when lessen gan the sore
Of my heart-sickness and my woeful chance,

Would be too long; I let it be therefore.
And thus this Flower (I cannot tell you more)
So heartily has to my help attended
That against death she has her man defended. . .

CXCIV

Go, little treatise, bare of eloquence,
Devoid of art and poor in subtle wit,
And pray the reader to accept the sense,
Bear with thy weakness, gently speak of it,
And thy fragility with kindness knit;
Let him his tongue so manage and control
That all thy blemishes may be made whole. . .

CXCVII

Unto the poems of my masters dear,
Gower and Chaucer, who on the high steps sate
Of rhetoric while they were living here,
Superlative as poets laureate,
In morals and in eloquence ornate,
I recommend my book in verses seven,[1]
And eke their souls unto the bliss of heaven! Amen.

[1] Stanzas of seven lines.

The Pilgrims at Canterbury

from

The Tale of Beryn

(PROLOG, VSS. 1–308)

WHEN all this fresh fellowship were come to Canterbury, . . . they sought their inn and lodged themselves in the midmorning at the Chessboard of the Hoop, which many a man knoweth. Their Host of Southwark, who went with them, as ye have heard before, and who was ruler of them all, both high and low, ordered their dinner, ere they went to the church, from such victuals as he found at hand and sent out for no others. The Pardoner beheld the bustle, seeing how the people of rank were served while he himself was quietly ignored and avoided, and how the innkeeper was called from one place to another; so he went, staff in hand, to the barmaid.

"Welcome, my own brother," quoth she with a friendly look, all ready 10 for a kiss; and he, like a man learned in such kindness, embraced her by the middle as if he had known her all the past year. She led him into the taproom, where her bed was made. "Lo, here I lie naked all night," quoth she, "without any man's company since my love was dead, Jenkin Harper, if ye remember him. From top to toe, there was not a livelier person to dance or to leap than he was, though I say it myself."

Therewith she made as if to weep, and with her apron, washed fair and white, she wiped her eyes softly for the tears that she shed. As big as any millstone they gushed out for the love of her sweeting, which lay so near her heart. She wept and wailed and wrung her hands and made much to-do, 20 for they that love overmuch suffer such throes. She sniffled, sighed, shook her head, and made rueful cheer.

"Benedicite!" quoth the Pardoner, and clasped her round the neck; "ye make as much sorrow as if ye would lose your life."

"It is no wonder," quoth she, and therewith began to sneeze.

"Aha! all's well again!" quoth the Pardoner; "your pain hath somewhat passed."

"God forbid it were not somewhat lessened," quoth she. "I might not live, thou knowest, an it should last long."

"Now blest be God for amendment, health, and cure!" quoth the Pardoner anon, and seized her by the chin, and said to her these words: "Alas, that love is sin! Ye are so kind a lover and so true of heart! For, by my true conscience, I smart for you still, and shall for a month after, for your sudden distress. Lucky would be the man ye loved, so long as he could please you! I dare swear on a book that he would find you true, for he that's long dead is still fresh in your mind. Ye made me an anxious man; I feared ye were dying."

"Gramercy, gentle sir!" quoth she. "But ye haven't been served! Ye are
10 a noble man, blest may ye be! Sit down, ye shall drink."

"Nay, nay," quoth he, "I haven't broken my fast yet, my own heart's root!"

"Not broken fast yet, alas!" quoth she. "For that I know a good remedy." She hastened into the town and fetched a pie all hot, and set it before the Pardoner. "Jenkin, I think? I know not, but is that your name, I pray you?"

"Yea surely, my own sister; so was I informed by them that fostered me. And what is yours?"

"Kit surely; so my mother called me."

"God's blessing on thee, Kit! enjoy thy name well!" And privily he
20 opened his eyelids and looked her full in the face amorously, and sighed a little too that she might hear it, and began to croon and say this song: "Now, love, do me right!"

"Eat and be merry," quoth she; "why don't ye break fast? To wait for more company would only waste time. Why make ye such dull cheer? For your love at home?"

"Nay forsooth, my own heart, it is for you alone!"

"For me? Alas, what say ye? That would be a foolish chase!"

"But truly," quoth the Pardoner, "it is as I say."

"Eat and be merry; we will speak thereof soon. 'Burned cat dreads fire.'
30 It is merry to be alone. For, by our Lady Mary, who bore Jesu on her arm, I never yet could love but it brought me hurt, for ever my manner hath been to love overmuch."

"Now Christ's blessing," quoth the Pardoner, "go with all such as ye are! Lo, how the skies work to make each man meet his match! For truly, gentle Christian, I have the same habit and have had many a year; I cannot refrain. For Nature will have its course though men swear the contrary."

Therewith he started up smartly and cast down a groat.

"What is this for, gentle sir? Nay, sir, I had rather lose my bodice than ye should pay a penny here and part so soon."
40 The Pardoner swore a greater oath that he would pay no less.

"Surely, sir, it's too much. But since it's your wish, I will put it in my purse, lest ye take it ill to refuse your courtesy." And therewith she bowed.

"Now truly," said the Pardoner, "your manners deserve praise; for if ye had counted strictly and left me no credit, I might well have thought that ye are unkind and untrue of heart and would sooner forget me. But since ye are pleased to be my treasurer, we shall meet the more often."

"Now surely ye interpret rightly," quoth the barmaid, "and would to God that ye could as well unravel my dream that I myself dreamed this past night, how I was in a church when mass was all said, and was at my devotions till the service was done, till the priest and the clerk rudely bade me begone, and put me out of church in an angry temper."

"Now may St. Daniel," quoth the Pardoner, "turn your dream to good! 10 I will tell you what it forecasts as best I can, and keep it in your mind; for commonly men find that these dreams turn out the contrary. Ye have been a lusty lover but had little joy. Now pluck up heart and be merry and glad; for ye shall have a husband that shall wed you to wife, and shall love you as heartily as his own life. The priest who put you out of church shall lead you back in, and help forward your marriage with all his might and main. This is the sum and substance of your dream. Kit, how doth it please thee?"

"By my troth, wondrous well. A blessing upon thee!"

Then he took leave for the time being until his return, and went back to the company . . . 20

When the Knight and all the company had been lodged, each according to his degree, as was proper and right, it was time to go to the church to make their offerings of silver brooches and rings, in accordance with their devotion. Then at the church door the question of precedence arose till the Knight, who knew well what to do, put first the clergymen, the Parson and his companion, the Monk, who took the holy water sprinkler in a manly fashion, and, as the custom is, moistened all pates, one after another, of the folk of good station. The Friar, who, for his cope, would not have missed that occupation in that holy place, sought cleverly to take the sprinkler to sprinkle the rest, his holy conscience so yearned to see the 30 Nun's face.

The Knight went with his compeers toward the holy shrine to do what they had come for before dinner. The Pardoner, the Miller, and the other rude fools entered the church like stupid goats, peered and pored up at the stained glass, imitating the gentry, to read the coats of arms, earnestly made out the painting, and studied the story, and interpreted it as rightly as would horned rams.

"He beareth a quarter-staff," said one, "or else a rake's end."

"Thou art wrong," quoth the Miller; "thou hast but little mind. It is a spear, if thou canst see, with a point before, to push down his enemy and 40 pierce him through the shoulder."

"Peace!" quoth the Host of Southwark, "let the glazed window be! Go up and make your offering! Ye seem half dazed! Since ye are in the company of honorable men and good, do as they do and for a time let your natural breeding pass. This is my best advice, for whoever followeth the example of his fellows may live in better quiet."

Then they passed on boisterously, turning their heads from side to side, kneeled down before the shrine, and heartily prayed to St. Thomas as well as they could. And then each man kissed the holy relics with his mouth, while a goodly monk named and described them. Then they approached the other holy places and were at their devotions till the services were all
10 done; and then they moved dinnerward as it drew toward noon. On their way, as the custom is, they bought tokens; . . . each man put his money into such things as he liked. Meanwhile the Miller filled his bosom with Canterbury brooches; Hugh the Pardoner and he privily put them afterward into their wallets so that no one perceived it, save that the Summoner spied something and said to them, privately whispering in their ear: "List! half share!"

"Hush, peace!" quoth the Miller, "seest thou not the Friar, how he lours under his hood with a doggish eye? It would be a secret thing that he couldn't spy. He knows something of every trick, Our Lady give him
20 sorrow!"

"Amen," quoth the Summoner, "both evening and morning! So cursed a tale he told of me, may the devil of hell aid him and myself too if I do not pay him out and give him his reward! If on the way homeward each man tells his tale as we did coming hither, even though we should be sitting in hall, I will not spare him all the malice I can, but will touch his tabard, somewhat to his grief!"

They fixed their tokens on their heads and some on their caps, and then started dinnerward. Every man in his order washed and took his seat as they were wont to do at supper and at meals, and were silent for a time
30 till their girdles began to swell. But then Nature demands, as wise old men know, that when veins are full, spirits will rise, and also sweet dishes stir up mirth, and besides it was no time for them to be sullen. Every man in his way made hearty cheer, telling his fellow of sports and jests that befell on the way, as is the custom of pilgrims, and hath been many a year. The Host, who was of Southwark as ye know, listened and thanked all the company, both high and low, for keeping so well the covenant made at Southwark, that every man on the way should gladden the whole company with a tale, to shorten the road. "And all is well performed. But now I announce that on our way homeward each man must tell another. Thus
40 we agreed, and I must be a rudder to guide your conduct by my fair judgment."

"Truly, Host," quoth the Friar, "that was assented to by all, and a little more besides which I shall add thereto. Ye granted of your courtesy that we should also, this whole company, sup with you at night. Thus it was, I believe; what say ye, sir Knight?"

"There is no need," quoth the Host, "to ask any witness. Your memory is good enough; and of your kindness I pray you again, for by St. Thomas' shrine, if ye will hold your bargain, I will hold mine."

"Now truly, Host," quoth the Knight, "ye have spoken right well, and, as for me, I am right well content, and so I think are we all. Sirs, what say ye?" The Monk and the Merchant and all said "Yea."

"Then all this afternoon," quoth the Host, "I hold it best that we disport ourselves, each man as he pleases, and go betimes to supper and then to bed. So we may rise early to begin our day's journey."

Therewithal the Knight arose and put on a fresher gown, and his son donned another, to walk in the town, and so did all the rest who had their changes with them. They made themselves fresh and gay and gathered in groups according to their tastes, as they were accustomed to do while traveling on their way. The Knight and his following went to see the wall and the defenses of the town, as befitted him, describing attentively the strong points around, and pointed out to his son the peril and danger to the fortifications of the town from shot of arbalest and bow and gun; and all the defenses against them he explained fully according to his understanding. His son perceived every point of his meaning, as he was well skilled in arms and in hardship and well suited in frame. He was naturally formed for any task. And as for his conduct, it seemed that his mind was much set on the lady whom he loved best and who made him oft sleepless when he should have been resting.

The Clerk of Oxford said to the Summoner: "Meseemeth that thou art innocent of learning, for thou chargest the Friar by way of reproof that he knoweth falsehood, vice, and theft. But I hold it virtuous and right commendable to have true knowledge of blameworthy things, for whoso hath knowledge thereof may eschew and avoid them, and otherwise he may fall into them suddenly and unaware. And though the Friar told a tale of a false summoner, thou oughtest not to take it for a dishonor, for in every occupation and rank not all are perfect, but some are right rude."

"Lo," said the Knight, "what a noble thing it is to be a scholar! To some among us this notion was nowise clear. I commend his wisdom and learning, for he hath preserved the honor of both parties."

The Monk took the Gray Friar and prayed him full courteously to go with him: "I have here an acquaintance who all these three years hath begged me in his letters that I would visit him. And ye are my brother in habit and in endowments. Now that I am here, methinketh it is right to put him to the test, what cheer he would make for me and for you, my friend, for my sake." They went forth together, talking of holy matters; but wot ye well they had no mind to drink water when they were met, for they had of the best that might be found and merry cheer besides, there is no doubt; for spices and wine went round, the Gascon and the Rhenish.

The Wife of Bath was so weary she had no will to walk. She took the Prioress by the hand. "Madam, will ye slip quietly into the garden to see the herbs grow, and afterwards rest with our host's wife in her parlor? I will give you wine, and ye shall do likewise for me, for till we go to sup-
10 per we have naught else to do."

The Prioress, like a well-bred woman of gentle blood, gave consent to her plan, and forth they went, passing softly into the herb-garden, where many an herb grew for soup and surgery; and all the alleys were fairly adorned and railed, the sage and the hyssop, protected and staked, and other beds in order, freshly set out, a pleasant sight for guests of the inn. The Merchant, the Manciple, the Miller, the Reeve, and the Clerk of Oxford and all the other company returned to the town and left none behind, save the Pardoner, who when they were all gone, stole secretly into the tap-room. For he would at all costs make sure of his bargain that he would
20 be lodged that same eve with the barmaid; that was his whole intent. But chance and fortune and the influence of the stars were clean against him, as ye shall afterwards hear, for he had better have been lodged all night in a lake than he was that same night ere the sun was risen. For, such was his luck, he drank without the cup! But of that he knew nothing as yet, and no man of us all may have that high wisdom to know what the future doth hold.

· 42 ·

Gesta Romanorum

(DEEDS OF THE ROMANS)

THE MAN AND THE HONEY IN THE TREE [1]

THERE was an Emperor reigning in the city of Rome, and among all other things he loved hunting well. And as he rode at a certain time in a forest, he saw a man run before him with all the might of his body, and a unicorn running after him, whereby the man was greatly afraid, so that for fear he fell into a great ditch. Nevertheless he took hold of a tree by which he won out. And then he looked down and he saw at the foot of the tree a hideous pit and a horrible dragon lying therein, undermining the tree and waiting with an open mouth when he should fall; and beside this dragon were two beasts, the one was white, the other was black; and they gnawed at the root of the tree with all their might, to throw it down, in so much 10 that the wretched man felt it wag; and about the sides of the ditch were four frogs moving about, which with their venomous breath envenomed all the ditch. He cast up his eyes and he saw a flow of honey falling from branch to branch; and he set his heart so much on this sweet sight of the honey, that he forgot that other peril. Now it happened that a friend of his went by the way, and because he saw him in such great peril, he fetched to him a ladder, that he might come safely down; but he gave himself so much to this sweetness that he would not thence, but ate the honey, and made him merry, and forgot the perils. Within a short time he fell down into the mouth of the dragon; and the dragon went down into the pit and de- 20 voured him.

MORALITY

Dear friends, this Emperor is to be understood as Jesu Christ, who loveth above all the hunting of souls; and in his hunting he beholdeth a man, *scil.*, secrets of the heart. The man that fleeth is a sinner; the unicorn is death,

---

[1] Derived from an ancient Buddhist parable, transmitted through Persian, Arabic, Georgian, and Greek into Latin, as part of the legend of Barlaam and Josaphat. See J. Jacobs, *Barlaam and Josaphat* (London, 1896), pp. lxx–lxxii; *Harvard Theological Review*, XXXII (1939), 131–9.

which ever followeth the man, to kill him; as it is said,[2] *Omnes morimur*, "All we die." This ditch is the world; the tree in the ditch is the life of man in the world, which life is the two beasts, black and white, *scil.*, two times, night and day, rocked and consumed the tree. The place where the four frogs come out is the body of man, from which come four qualities of humors, by which four, set together inordinately, the image of the body is dissolved. The dragon is the devil; the pit is hell; the sweetness is delight in sin, by which a man is blinded, so that he may not behold his high perils; the friend that reacheth down the ladder is Christ, or a preacher that 10 preacheth in the name of Christ: the ladder is penance. And when a man delayeth to take that ladder, for the delight ofttimes he hath in the world, he falleth suddenly into the mouth of the devil, *scil.*, that is to say, into his power in hell, where the devil devoureth him; of devouring there is no hope to escape, as it is said in the psalm, *Spes impiorum peribit*. This is to say, "The hope or trust of wicked men shall perish."

HOW A POOR MAN RACED WITH THE EMPEROR'S DAUGHTER [3]

Pompeius was a wise Emperor reigning in the city of Rome, who had a fair daughter named Aglaes, and she had two virtues over all other maidens. The first was, she was fair of face and pleasant to the eye of men; the second was, she was so nimble of foot that no man might run with her for a 20 great space but that she would come to the mark long before him. When the Emperor saw these two virtues in his daughter, he rejoiced and was glad in all his heart; and he made a proclamation in all that land, that whosoever would run with his daughter and come to the mark before her, he should wed her with infinite goods; and if there were any that would proffer himself to run with her and might not win over her, he should lose his head. Therefore lords of estate, dukes, barons, and knights came thick and offered to run with her, but there was no one who might hold foot with her; therefore each one for his failing lost his head, as the law was.

Now there was in the city a poor man, who thought to himself, "I am 30 poor, and come of low kindred; and a common cry is made that if any man might by skill or sleight pass in running the daughter of the Emperor, he should wed her, and be greatly advanced. And therefore, if such a poor fellow as I might overcome her by cunning, whereby I and all my kin might be raised and honored, truly it were a good turn."

Then went he forth and provided him with three cunning devices, *scil.*, a seemly garland of red roses, in royal array; the second device a silken

2 II Samuel, 14:14.
3 This is, of course, the famous classical story of Atalanta's race.

girdle, subtly made, for the damsel really loved such fantasies; the third a subtle purse made of silk, adorned with precious stones, and in this purse was a ball of three colors, and it had a superscription that said thus, *Qui mecum ludit, nunquam de meo ludo satiabitur*, which is to say, "He that playeth with me shall never have enough of my play." He put up in his bosom these three toys, and went to the gate of the palace, and cried and said, "Come, fair damsel, I am ready to run with thee and to fulfill the law in all points."

And when these words were carried to the Emperor, he commanded his daughter to run with him. The damsel looked out of the window, for 10 to see him; and when she had seen him, she defied him in her heart, and said to herself, "Alas! that I who have overcome so many noble men, should now run with such a churl's son as thou art; nevertheless I must fulfill the will of my father."

She went and made her ready to run with him, and she came to him and both stood together for to begin to run. And when they had run a while, the maid had run before him a great way. When the other saw that, he cast before her the fair garland; and as soon as she saw the fair garland before her, then she turned and took it up and set it on her head and made such great delight in it, that the other ran before her. When she saw that, 20 she wept bitterly and in great wrath cast away the garland, and ran and overtook him. And as soon as she was by him, she took up her hand and gave him a great buffet on the cheek and said, "Ignorant wretch, well beseemeth thy sire's son to wed me!" And she ran on far before.

And when he saw that, he took out the girdle and again in the same manner cast it in front of her; and as soon as she had a sight of it, she bowed down and took it up and girt her therewith; and she had such great pleasure therein that she stopped running, and by that time he was far before her. When she cast up her eyes and saw him, she made great lamentation, and took the girdle in anger and bit it with her teeth in three parts; and she ran 30 again with all the might that was in her and overtook him, and gave him a great buffet and ran from him and said, "What, rascal, thinkest thou to overcome me?"

That other one was wily and would not cast the purse until the time that he came near the mark; and then he cast the purse, as he did that other thing. And then she stopped again and took it up and opened it and took out the ball and read the superscription, *scil.*, "He that playeth with me, shall never have enough of my play." And then she began to play with the ball so long, that the trickster was before her at the mark. And then she made great lamentation; and he wedded her and had great riches, as the 40 law decreed.

Dear friends, this Emperor is our Lord Jesus Christ; the fair daughter is the soul of man, made like Himself, and cleansed from original sin by baptism; and it is swift in running, *scil.*, good works, while it is in its innocence, and is so swift that no deadly sins may overcome her; and so they [the suitors] lose their heads, *scil.*, their power, when they cannot overcome her. The poor man, who thought up these devices, is the devil, who studies night and day to overcome innocence; and therefore he provideth him with three devices, the first a garland. By the garland we may understand pride and for this reason, for a garland is not set on the arm, nor in any other 10 part of the body. It is set upon the head, because it should be seen. In the same wise will the proud man be seen and spread his fringes; and therefore saith Augustine, *Cum superbum videris, filium diaboli esse non dubites.* This is to say, "When thou seest a proud man, doubt not thou seest the son of the devil." Therefore when the devil casteth this garland of pride in thy eyes, weep, as did the damsel; and do off that garland of pride and cast it in the ditch of contrition, and so shalt thou give the devil a buffet and overcome him. Then when the devil seeth that he is overcome, he tempteth a man in another sin, and casteth before him a girdle of lechery; of which kind of girdle thus saith Gregory, *Cingite lumbos vestros in castitate.* This 20 is to say, or this is understood, "Gird your loins in chastity." For whosoever is girt with the girdle of lechery, certainly he leaveth the running of the good life and is overcome of the devil. As the Apostle saith, *Nullum opus bonum sine castitate.* This is to say, "There is no good work without chastity." And therefore do as she did; smite the girdle in three, *scil.*, in prayer, fasting, and almsdeed, and without doubt, then shalt thou overcome the devil. After this poor man, *scil.*, the devil, casteth forth a purse with a ball. What is that? Ye know well a purse is open above and shut beneath, and betokeneth the heart of man that should ever be open to heavenly things and shut to earthly things. The two cords that serve to open and to 30 shut the purse, signify the love of God and of thy neighbor; the ball that is round and colored so diversely betokeneth the vice of covetousness that moveth in the old as in the young; and therefore the saying that is written above is true, where it is said, *Qui mecum ludit, nunquam satiabitur;* for the covetous man can never be filled. And therefore let us beware that we play not with the ball of covetousness, as she did; for if we forsake God and give ourselves to transitory things and vanities, truly we shall never then come to the glory of everlasting life.

OF A YOUNG KNIGHT WHO HAD THREE FRIENDS [4]

Domician reigned, a wise Emperor in the city of Rome, and in his empire was a noble knight, who had only one son whom he greatly loved. On a time this son came to him and said, "Father, I am a young man; truly, if it be your will, I wish to go about to castles and kingdoms, and gain friends for myself, so that I may, when ye go hence out of this world, have knowledge."

"Yes," said the father, "well shall it please me, so that thou dost show me when thou comest again, what friends thou hast obtained."

Then said he, "Yes, father, thy will in that case shall be fulfilled."

The young man traveled through certain kingdoms, countries, and cities; 10 and at the end of three years he came home to his father. And the father was highly rejoiced by his presence and said, "Son, how sayest thou? Hast thou won any friends?"

"Yea, sir," he said, "I have found three friends since I went forth; and the first friend I love more than myself, and therefore would I for his love shed my blood, if need were; the second I love as much as myself; but the third I love little, in comparison with the others."

Then said the father, "Son, hast thou proved any of these three friends?"

"Nay, sir," quoth he.

Then quoth the father, "Do after my counsel and it shall please thee. Go, 20 and slay a swine and put it in a sack; and at midnight go to thy first friend and say to him, 'Dear friend, help me now in my great need, for through mischance I have slain a man, and he is here upon my back in a sack'; and then thou shalt see what thy friend will say to thee. After that, go to thy second friend, and so to the third; and write all their answers in thy heart."

The son went, as the father said to him; and at midnight he came to the gate of the first friend, whom he loved more than himself, and knocked at his gate. Anon as his friend heard him knock, he rose and let him in, and said, "Friend, thou art welcome."

"Ah, friend," quoth that other, "I am come to thee in my great need, for 30 I love thy body more than myself, and therefore succor me in this misfortune; for I have through mishap slain a man, and he is here upon my back in a sack; and therefore, I pray thee, that thou wilt hide him and conceal the body of this dead man in some secret place in thy house, for if the body be found with me, doubtless I must be hanged for him."

"Yea," quoth the other, "though thou wert my father, I would not do that for thee; for since thou hast slain the man, thou art worthy to be damned for him. Nevertheless, because of the great friendship that hath

---

[4] This also is based on a Buddhist parable from the same collection as that of "The Man and the Honey in the Tree." See Jacobs, *op. cit.*, pp. lxxvii–lxxix.

been between us heretofore for a long time, I shall give to thee two ells of linen cloth, for to wrap or to cover thy body, when thou art hanged."

Then the young man went to that other friend whom he loved as much as himself, and knocked at his gate. Anon when he heard the knocking, he rose and opened the door, and kissed him, and worshipfully received him. Then spake the young man, and said, "Ah! good friend, help me now in my greatest need that ever I had. I have through misfortune slain a man and he is here with me, and therefore, for all the friendship that is between thee and me, lay him in some secret place of thy house; for if he be found 10 with me, I am but dead."

"Nay," quoth that other, "that thou canst not make me do. Bear him hence, and make thee merry with him. Why didst thou slay him? But yet, friend, I shall tell thee, I will not have ado with him; but for the great love that hath been between us two, I will go with thee to the gibbet; and afterwards I will get me another friend."

The young man was heavy at these words; and he went to another friend, *scil.*, the one that he loved but little, and knocked at his gate. He rose up, as soon as he heard his voice, and let him in and kissed him and said, "Friend, who art half my soul, welcome be thou to me!"

20 Then said the other, "Truly, I am ashamed to speak with thee, for I have done little for thee, or else nothing, in all my life; and therefore with great shame I show thee mine errand."

"Yea, surely," said that other, "show me what thou wilt."

"Forsooth," quoth that other, "I have unhappily slain a man, and here I bear his body on my back, and therefore I pray thee, help me in this great need, and if ye will hide the body in your house, ye might not do me a better turn, for if it be found with me, I am but dead."

"Nay," quoth that other, "I will not hide the body, but I will die for thee tomorrow on the gibbet; and therefore, I pray thee, love thou never friend 30 so well as me after my death, but if he will die for thee, as I shall."

When the young man heard him say thus, he fell down on his knees, and prayed him that he would forgive him that he had loved the other two friends so much and him so little or not at all. "And therefore from henceforward I shall never love myself so much as thee."

The other took him by the neck and kissed him; and he went home, and told his father how it was with the three friends.

MORALITY

Good men, this Emperor is the Father of Heaven; by the knight understand prelates of Holy Church; by the son is understood every Christian man. And so do many of us get us friends, but they fail us in our need; and therefore saith the wise man, *Est amicus meus, et non permanebit in tempore necessitatis*. This is to say, "There is a friend at the table or at the meat board, the which will not or shall not abide in time of need." The first friend, that thou lovest more than thyself, is this world; for we see every day that men will for the world and worldly things to be had, put themselves in perils of the sea, in perils of battle, and of damnation. And therefore it is well proved that they love more the world than themselves, but in time of need, *scil.*, of death, when the soul shall pass from the body, after the will of God, and that the body be given to worms, then the world, that thou lovest so much, shall fail thee; in so much that if thou have two ells 10 of linen cloth, to wrap thy body in, it is a great thing. The second friend, that thou lovest as much as thyself, is thy wife and children, the which in time of death will go with thee to the sepulchre, and weep a little for thee, but when thou art in the earth, they go home and consider whom they may have in thy stead. The third friend, that thou lovest so little, is our Lord, Jesu Christ, for if thou come to Him with a clean heart, in time of thy need, He will not fail thee; and therefore is it said, *In quacumque hora peccator ingemuerit, salvus erit*. This is to say, "In what hour the sinner waileth, or is sorry for his sins, he shall be saved." And therefore when the sinner deserved by his wickedness everlasting death, then Christ, God's son, came 20 and took death for him on the gibbet of the cross. And therefore, sirs, let us bow our knees, and ask mercy of Him that we pleased these other two so much and Him so little, who is an unchangeable friend, a noble friend, and a mighty friend. Now pray we Him earnestly to be our friend, whose friendship never faileth, *Qui cum patre et spiritu sancto omnia regit secula.* Amen.

THE THREE CASKETS [5]

Ancelmus reigned Emperor in the city of Rome, and he wedded for wife the daughter of the King of Jerusalem, who was a fair woman, and long dwelt in his company. But she never conceived nor brought forth fruit, and therefore the lords were grieved and sorry. Haply on a certain evening, 30 as he walked after his supper in a fair green, and thought of all the world and especially that he had no heir, and thought how the King of Naples strongly annoyed him each year; so, when it was night, he went to bed and to sleep, and he dreamed this. He saw the firmament in the utmost clearness, and more clear than it was wont to be. And the moon was more pale, and on a part of the moon was a fair-colored bird, and beside her stood two beasts which nourished the bird with their heat and breath. After this

[5] This is a medley. The motif of the caskets was adapted from another Buddhist parable from the same collection. See Jacobs, *op. cit.*, pp. lxi–lxvii.

came divers beasts and birds flying, and they sang so sweetly that the Emperor was wakened with the song.

Then on the morrow the Emperor had great marvel about this dream, and he called to him diviners and lords of all the Empire and said to them, "Dear friends, tell me the what is the interpretation of my dream, and I will reward you; and unless you do so, ye shall be dead."

And then they said, "Lord, show us thy dream, and we will tell thee the interpretation of it."

And then the Emperor told them as is said before, from beginning to end.
10 And then they were glad, and with great gladness spoke to him and said, "Sir, this was a good dream. The firmament that thou sawest so clear is the Empire, which henceforth shall be in prosperity; the pale moon is the Empress, who hath conceived, and for her conceiving is the more discolored; the little bird is the fair son the Empress will bring forth when the time cometh; the two beasts are rich men and wise men, who will be obedient to thy child; the other beasts are other folk who never did homage, and now will be subject to thy son; the birds that sang so sweetly are the Empire of Rome that will rejoice of thy child's birth; and this, sir, is the interpretation of your dream."

20 When the Empress heard this, she was glad enough, and soon she bore a fair son, and thereof great joy was made. And when the King of Naples heard this, he thought to himself, "I have for a long time held war against the Emperor, and it may not be but that it will be told his son, when he cometh to his full age, how I have fought against his father all my life. Yea," thought he, "he is now a child, and it is good that I procure peace, that I may have rest from him when he is at his best and I at my worst."

So he wrote letters to the Emperor, for to have peace, and the Emperor, seeing that he did it more for cause of fear than of love, sent him word again and said that he would make with him surety of peace on condition that he 30 would be in his service and yield him homage all his life, each year. Then the King called his council and asked them what was best to do; and the lords of his kingdom said that it was good to follow the Emperor in his will. "At first, ask ye of him surety of peace. To that we say thus, 'Thou hast a daughter and he hath a son; let matrimony be made between them and so shall there be good security. Also it is good to do him homage and to yield him rents.' "

Then the King sent word to the Emperor and said that he would fulfill his will in all points, and give his daughter to his son for wife, if that were pleasing to him. This answer well pleased the Emperor, but he sent word 40 again that he would not assent to the matrimony unless his daughter had been a virgin from her birth. The King was herewith deeply glad, for his daughter was such a clean virgin. So letters were made of this covenant, and he made a ship to be ordained to take his daughter with certain knights and ladies to the Emperor, to be married to his son.

And when they were in the ship and had passed far from the land, there rose up a great horrible tempest and drowned all who were in the ship except the maid. Then the maid set all her hope strongly in God; and at the last, the tempest ceased, but there followed a great whale to devour this maid. And when she saw that, she greatly feared. And when the night came on, the maid, fearing that the whale would have swallowed the ship, smote fire from a stone and had great plenty of fire. And as long as the fire lasted, the whale durst come no nearer, but about cockcrow the maid, because of 10 the great trouble she had had with the tempest, fell asleep, and in her sleep the fire went out. And when it was out, the whale came near and swallowed both the ship and the maid.

And when the maid felt that she was in the belly of a whale, she smote, and made a great fire, and so grievously wounded the whale with a little knife that he drew to the land and died, for that is his nature, to draw to the land when he shall die. And at this time there was an Earl named Pirius, and he walked for pleasure by the sea, and before him he saw the whale come to the land. He gathered great strength and help of men; and with diverse instruments they smote the whale in every part of him. And when 20 the damsel heard the strokes, she cried with a loud voice and said, "Noble sirs, have pity on me, for I am the daughter of a king, and a maid have I been since I was born."

When the Earl heard this, he marveled greatly, and opened the whale and took out the damsel. Then by order the maid told how she was a king's daughter, and how she lost her goods in the sea, and how she should be married to the son of the Emperor. And when the Earl heard these words, he was glad, and kept the maid with him a great while, till the time that she was well comforted. And then he sent her to the Emperor in state. And when he saw her coming and heard that she had had tribulations on the 30 sea, he had great compassion for her in his heart and said to her, "Good damsel, thou hast suffered great woe for the sake of my son, nevertheless, if thou art worthy to have him, I shall soon prove."

The Emperor let make three vessels, and the first was of pure gold and full of precious stones on the outside and within full of dead bones; and it had a superscription in these words, *They that choose me shall find in me what they deserved.* The second vessel was all of pure silver and full of precious stones; and outside it had this superscription, *They that choose me shall find in me what their nature and kind desire.* And the third vessel was of lead, and within it was full of precious stones, and without was set this 40 writing, *They that choose me shall find in me what God hath disposed:* These three vessels the Emperor took and showed them to the maid, saying,

"Lo, dear damsel, here are three worthy vessels, and if thou dost choose the one of these wherein is value and ought to be chosen, then shalt thou have my son for husband; and if thou choose the one that is not of value to thee, nor to any other, truly then thou shalt not have him."

When the daughter heard this and saw the three vessels, she lifted up her eyes to God and said, "Thou, Lord, who knowest all things, grant me Thy grace now in the need of this time, *scil.*, that I may choose at this time in such way that I may enjoy the son of the Emperor, and have him for husband."

10   Then she beheld the first vessel that was so subtly made, and read the superscription. And then she thought, "What have I deserved to have so precious a vessel, and though it be never so gay without, I know not how foul it is within." So she told the Emperor that she would in no way choose that one. Then she looked at the second, that was of silver, and read the superscription, and then she said, "My nature and kind ask but delights of the flesh. Forsooth, sir," quoth she, "I refuse this." Then she looked at the third, which was of lead, and read the superscription, and then she said, "Truly, God never disposed evil. Forsooth, that which God hath disposed will I take and choose."

20   And when the Emperor saw that, he said, "Good damsel, open now that vessel and see what thou dost find." And when it was opened, it was full of gold and precious stones. And then the Emperor said to her again, "Damsel, thou hast wisely chosen and thou hast won my son for thy husband."

So the day was set for their bridal, and great joy was made; and the son reigned after the decease of his father, who made a fair end. *Ad quos nos perducat!* Amen.

LAURA HIBBARD LOOMIS

· 43 ·

I Sing of a Maiden

I sing of a Maiden
  Who no equal knows.
The King of all Kings
  For her Son she chose.
He came so still
  Where His Mother was
As April dew
  That falls on the grass.
He came so still
  To His Mother's bower   10

As April dew
  That falls on the flower.
He came so still
  Where His Mother lay
As April dew
  That falls on the spray.
Mother and maiden
  Was never none but she;
Well may such a lady
  God's Mother be!   20

· 44 ·

When Christ Was Born of Mary Free

Christo paremus canticam,
In excelsis gloria.[1]

When Christ was born of Mary free
In Bethlehem in that fair city,
Angels sang there with mirth and glee:
  In excelsis gloria.

Herdsmen beheld these angels bright,
To them appearèd with great light,
And said: "God's Son is born this night;
  In excelsis gloria.   10

[1] Let us prepare a canticle to Christ; glory in the highest!
[389]

This King is come to save mankind,
In the scripture as we find;
Therefore this song have we in mind:
   In excelsis gloria.

Then, Lord, for Thy great grace,
Grant us the bliss to see Thy face,
Where we may sing to thy solace:
   In excelsis gloria.

· 45 ·

The Boar's Head Carol

Caput apri refero,
Resonans laudes Domino.[1]

The Boar's head in hands I bring,
With garlands gay and birds singing.
I pray you all, help me to sing,
   Qui estis in convivio.[2]

The boar's head, I understand,
Is chief service in this land.
Wheresoever it may be found
   Servitur cum sinapio.[3]   10

The boar's head, I dare well say,
Anon after the twelfth day,
He taketh his leave and goeth away;
   Exivit tunc de patria.[4]

[1] I bear back the boar's head, sounding praises to the Lord.
[2] Who (antecedent "you") are at the banquet.
[3] It is served with mustard.   [4] He then departed from his native land.

· 46 ·

Here Have I Dwelt

Now have good day, now have good day!
I am Christmas, and now I go my way!

Here I have dwelt with more and less,
From Hallow-tide till Candlemas! [1]
And now must I from you hence pass,
  Now have good day!

I take my leave of King and Knight,
And Earl, Baron, and lady bright!
To wilderness I must me dight!
  Now have good day!   10

And at the good lord of this hall
I take my leave, and of guestes all!
Methinks I hear Lent doth call,
  Now have good day!

And at every worthy officer,
Marshal, panter, and butlér,
I take my leave as for this year,
  Now have good day!

Another year I trust I shall
Make merry in this hall!   20
If rest and peace in England may fall!
  Now have good day!

[1] From All Saints' Day, November 1, to the Presentation of Christ in the Temple, February 2.

· 47 ·

𝕳𝖊 𝕭𝖆𝖗𝖊 𝕳𝖎𝖒 𝖀𝖕, 𝕳𝖊 𝕭𝖆𝖗𝖊 𝕳𝖎𝖒 𝕯𝖔𝖜𝖓

Refrain:
Lully lullay, lully lullay,
The falcon hath borne my mate away.

He bare him up, he bare him down,
He bare him into an orchard brown.

In that orchard there was a hall,
That was behung with purple and pall.

And in that hall there was a bed;
It was behung with gold so red.

And in that bed there lies a knight,
His wounds a-bleeding day and night.   10

By that bed's side there kneels a may,[1]
And ever weeps both night and day.

By that bed's side there stands a stone,
"Corpus Christi" [2] writ thereon.

· 48 ·

𝕿𝖍𝖊 𝕯𝖎𝖛𝖎𝖓𝖊 𝕻𝖆𝖗𝖆𝖉𝖔𝖝

A God and yet a man?   A God, and can He die?
A Maid and yet a Mother?   A dead man, can He live?
Wit wonders what wit can   What wit can well reply?
Conceive this or the other. What reason Reason give?

God, truth itself, doth teach it.
Man's wit sinks too far under   10
By reason's power to reach it.
Believe, and leave [3] to wonder.

[1] Maiden.   [2] The body of Christ.   [3] Cease.

· 49 ·

𝕴 𝕳𝖆𝖚𝖊 𝖆 𝕹𝖔𝖇𝖑𝖊 𝕮𝖔𝖈𝖐

I have a noble cock
  Who croweth in the day.
He maketh me rise early,
  My matins for to say.

I have a noble cock,
  Whose breed is nothing low. 10
His comb is of red coral,
  His tail of indigo.

I have a noble cock,
  Descended from the great.
His comb is of red coral,
  His tail is all of jet.

His legs are like the azure,
  So slender and genteel.
His spurs are of white silver
  Up to the very heel.

His eyes are shining crystal,
  Rimmed all around with amber;
And every night he perches
  Within my lady's chamber. 20

St. Stephen and Herod

Saint Stephen was a clerk in King Herod's hall,
And served him with bread and cloth, as every king doth befall.

Stephen out of kitchen came with boar's head in hand;
He saw a star was fair and bright over Bethlehem stand.

He cast adown the boar's head and went into the hall.
"I forsake thee, King Herod, and thy workes all.

"I forsake thee, King Herod, and thy workes all;
There is a child born in Bethlehem is better than we all."

"What aileth thee, Stephen? what is thee befall?
Lacketh thee either meat or drink in King Herod's hall?"   10

"Lacketh me neither meat nor drink in King Herod's hall;
There is a child born in Bethlehem is better than we all."

"What aileth thee, Stephen? art thou mad or raving indeed?
Lacketh thee either gold or fee or any rich weed?"

"Lacketh me neither gold nor fee nor any rich weed;
There is a child born in Bethlehem shall help us in our need."

"That is as sooth, Stephen, all as sooth, ywis,[1]
As this capon shall crow that lieth here in my dish."

That word was no sooner said, that word in that hall,
The capon crew *"Christus natus est!"* [2] among the lords all.   20

"Rise up, my tormentors, by two and by one,
And lead Stephen out of this town and stone him with stone!"

Then took they Stephen and stoned him in the way,
And therefore is his eve on Christ's own day.[3]

[1] Surely.   [2] "Christ is born!"   [3] St. Stephen's day is celebrated on December 26.

Robin Hood and the Monk

In summer when the shaws be sheen,[1]
  And leaves be large and long,
It is full merry in fair forést
  To hear the fowles' song.

To see the deer draw to the dale,
  And leave the hilles high,
And shadow them in the leavès green,
  Under the greenwood tree.

It befell on Whitsuntide,
  Early in a May morníng,   10
The sun up fair gan shine,
  And the birds merry gan sing.

"This is a merry morning," said Little
    John,
  "By Him that died on tree;
A more merry man then I am one
  Lives not in Christiantee." [2]

"Pluck up thy heart, my dear mastér,"
  Little John gan say,
"And think it is a full fair time
  In a morning of May."   20

"Yea, one thing grieves me," said
    Robin,
  "And does my heart much woe,
That I may not on solemn day
  To mass nor matins go.

"It is a fortnight and more," said he,
  "Since I my Savior see;

To-day will I to Nottingham," said
    Robin,
  "With the might of mild Marý."

Then spake Much, the miller's son,—
  Evermore well him betide,—   30
"Take twelve of thy wight [3] yeomen
  Well weaponed by thy side.
Such one would thyself slon
  That twelve dare not abide." [4]

"Of all my merry men," said Robin,
  "By my faith I will none have;
But Little John shall bear my bow
  Till that me list to draw."

"Thou shall bear thine own," said
    Little John,
  "Master, and I will bear mine;   40
And we will shoot a penny," said Little
    John,
  "Under the greenwood line." [5]

"I will not shoot a penny," said Robin
    Hood,
  "In faith, Little John, with thee,
But ever for one as thou shoots," said
    Robin,
  "In faith I hold thee three."

Thus shot they forth, these yeomen
    two,
  Both at bush and broom,

---

[1] Bright.   [2] Christendom.   [3] Strong.
[4] Such a man as would slay thee alone would not dare to stand up against those twelve.
[5] Linden.

Till Little John won of his master
  Five shillings to hose and shoon.[6] 50

A ferly [7] strife fell them between,
  As they went by the way;
Little John said he had won five shill-
    ings,
  And Robin Hood said shortly nay.

With that Robin Hood lied [8] Little
    John,
  And smote him with his hand;
Little John waxed wroth therewith,
  And pulled out his bright brand.

"Wert thou not my master," said Lit-
    tle John,
  "Thou shouldest be hit full sore; 60
Get thee a man where thou wilt,
    Robin,
  For thou gets me no more."

Then Robin goes to Nottingham,
  Himself mourning alone,
And Little John to merry Sherwood;
  The paths he knew ilkone.[9]

When Robin came to Nottingham,
  Certainly withouten lain,[10]
He prayed to God and mild Mary
  To bring him out safe again. 70

He goes into Saint Mary church,
  And kneeled down before the rood;
All that ever were the church within
  Beheld well Robin Hood.

Beside him stood a great-headed
    monk,
  I pray to God woe he be;
Full soon he knew good Robin
  As soon as he him see.

Out at the door he ran
  Full soon and anon; 80
All the gates of Nottingham
  He made to be sparred every one.

"Rise up," he said, "thou proud sheriff,
  Busk [11] thee and make thee boun; [12]
I have spied the king's felon,
  Forsooth he is in this town.

"I have spied the false felon,
  As he stands at his mass;
It is long of thee," [13] said the monk,
  "An ever he fro us pass. 90

"This traitor's name is Robin Hood;
  Under the greenwood lind,[14]
He robbed me once of   hundred
    pound,
  It shall never out of my mind."

Up then rose this proud sheriff,
  And radly [15] made him yare; [16]
Many was the mother's son
  To the kirk with him gan fare.

In at the doors they throughly thrust,
  With staves full good wone.[17] 100
"Alas, alas," said Robin Hood,
  "Now miss I Little John."

But Robin took out a two-hand sword
  That hung down by his knee;
There as the sheriff and his men stood
    thickest,
  Thitherward would he.

Thrice throughout them he ran then,
  Forsooth as I you say,
And wounded many a mother's son,
  And twelve he slew that day. 110

6 For hose and shoes.   7 Strange.   8 Gave the lie to.
9 Each one.   10 Without reservation.   11 Prepare.
12 Ready.   13 Thy fault.   14 Linden.   15 Quickly.
16 Ready.   17 Number.

His sword upon the sheriff's head
  Certainly he brake in two;
"The smith that thee made," said
  Robin,
"I pray God work him woe!

"For now am I weaponless," said
  Robin,
"Alas, against my will;
But if [18] I may flee these traitors fro,
  I wot they will me kill."

Robin into the church ran,
Throughout them every one;   120

(*Gap in the manuscript. Robin was
captured, and the news was brought
to his band.*)

Some fell in swooning as they were
  dead,
  And lay still as any stone.
None of them were in their mind
  But only Little John.

"Let be your rule," [19] said Little John,
  "For His love that died on tree;
Ye that should be doughty men,
  It is great shame to see.

"Our master has been hard bestead,
  And yet escaped away;   130
Pluck up your hearts and leave this
  moan,
  And harken what I shall say.

"He has served Our Lady many a
  day,
  And yet will surely;
Therefore I trust in her specially
  No wicked death shall he die.

"Therefore be glad," said Little John,
  "And let this mourning be,

And I shall be the monk's guide,
  With the might of mild Marý.   140

"We will go but we two;
  An I meet him," said Little
  John, . . .

(*Another gap in the manuscript.*)

"Look that ye keep well our trysting
  tree
  Under the leavès small,
And spare none of this venison
  That goes in this vale."

Forth then went these yeomen two,
  Little John and Much infere,[20]
And looked on Much emy's house,[21]
  The highway lay full near.   150

Little John stood at a window in the
  morning,
  And looked forth at a stage; [22]
He was ware where the monk came
  riding,
  And with him a little page.

"By my faith," said Little John to
  Much,
  "I can thee tell tidings good;
I see where the monk comes riding,
  I know him by his wide hood."

They went into the way, these yeo-
  men both,
  As courteous men and hend [23]   160
They speered [24] tidings at the monk,
  As they had been his friend.

"Fro whence come ye?" said Little
  John;
  "Tell us tidings, I you pray,
Of a false outlaw called Robin Hood,
  Was taken yesterday.

[18] Unless.   [19] Behavior.   [20] Together.
[21] House of Much's uncle.   [22] From an upper story (?).
[23] Friendly.   [24] Asked.

"He robbed me and my fellows both
  Of twenty mark in certaín.
If that false outlaw be taken,
  Forsooth we would be fain." 170

"So did he me," said the monk,
  "Of a hundred pound and more;
I laid first hand him upon,
  Ye may thank me therefor."

"I pray God thank you," said Little
    John,
  "And we will when we may;
We will go with you, with your leave,
  And bring you on your way.

"For Robin Hood has many a wild fel-
    low,
  I tell you in certaín; 180
If they wist ye rode this way,
  In faith ye should be slain."

As they went talking by the way,
  The monk and Little John,
John took the monk's horse by the
    head
  Full soon and anon.

John took the monk's horse by the
    head,
  Forsooth as I you say,
So did Much the little page,
  For he should not stir away. 190

By the gullet [25] of the hood
  John pullèd the monk down;
John was nothing of him aghast,
  He let him fall on his crown.

Little John was sore aggrieved,
  And drew out his sword in hye; [26]
The monk saw he should be dead,
  Loud mercy gan he cry.

"He was my master," said Little John,
  "That thou hast brought in bale; [27]
Shall thou never come at our king 201
  For to tell him tale."

John smote off the monk's head,
  No longer would he dwell;
So did Much the little page,
  For fear lest he would tell.

There they buried them both
  In neither moss nor ling,
And Little John and Much infere
  Bare the letters to our king. 210

. . . . . .

He kneeled down upon his knee,
"God you save, my liege lord,
"Jesus you save and see. [28]

"God you save, my liege king!"
  To speak John was full bold;
He gave him the letters in his hand,
  The king did it unfold.

The king read the letters anon,
  And said, "So mot I thee, [29] 219
There was never yeoman in merry
    England
  I longed so sore to see.

"Where is the monk that these should
    have brought?"
  Our king gan say;
"By my troth," said Little John,
  "He died after the way."

The king gave Much and Little John
  Twenty pound in certaín,
And made them yeomen of the crown,
  And bade them go again. 230

He gave John the seal in hand,
  The sheriff for to bear,

[25] Throat.   [26] Haste.   [27] To harm.
[28] Look after.   [29] May I prosper.

[398]

To bring Robin him to,
  And no man do him dere.[30]

John took his leave at our king,
  The sooth as I you say;
The next way to Nottingham
  To take, he yede [31] the way.

When John came to Nottingham
  The gates were sparred each one;
John called up the porter,   241
  He answered soon anon.

"What is the cause," said Little John,
  "Thou sparrest the gates so fast?"
"Because of Robin Hood," said the
    porter,
  "In deep prison is cast.

"John and Much and Will Scathlock,
  For sooth as I you say,
They slew our men upon our walls,
  And saulten [32] us every day."   250

Little John speered after the sheriff
  And soon he him found;
He opened the king's privy seal,
  And gave him in his hand.

When the sheriff saw the king's seal,
  He did off his hood anon;
"Where is the monk that bare the let-
    ters?"
  He said to Little John.

"He is so fain of him," said Little John,
  "Forsooth as I you say,   260
He has made him abbot of West-
    minster,
  A lord of that abbéy."

The sheriff made John good cheer,
  And gave him wine of the best;

At night they went to their bed,
  And every man to his rest.

When the sheriff was on sleep
  Drunken of wine and ale,
Little John and Much forsooth
  Took the way into the jail.   270

Little John called up the jailer,
  And bade him rise anon;
He said Robin Hood had broken
    prison,
  And out of it was gone.

The porter rose anon certaín,
  As soon as he heard John call;
Little John was ready with a sword,
  And bare him to the wall.

"Now will I be porter," said Little
    John,
  "And take the keys in hand;"   280
He took the way to Robin Hood,
  And soon he him unbound.

He gave him a good sword in his hand,
  His head therewith for to keep,[33]
And there as the wall was lowest
  Anon down gan they leap.

By that the cock began to crow,
  The day began to spring,
The sheriff found the jailer dead,
  The common bell made he ring.   290

He made a cry throughout all the
    town,
  Whether he be yeoman or knave,
That could bring him Robin Hood,
  His warison [34] he should have.

"For I dare never," said the sheriff,
  "Come before our king,
For if I do, I wot certaín,
  Forsooth he will me hang."

[30] Harm.   [31] Went.   [32] Assault.   [33] Guard.   [34] Reward.

The sheriff made to seek Nottingham,
  Both by street and stye,[35]   300
And Robin was in merry Sherwood
  As light as leaf on lind.

Then bespake good Little John,
  To Robin Hood gan he say,
"I have done thee a good turn for an
    evil,
  Quit thee [36] when thou may.

"I have done thee a good turn," said
    Little John,
  "Forsooth as I you say;
I have brought thee under greenwood
    lind;
  Farewell, and have good day." 310

"Nay, by my troth," said Robin Hood,
  "So shall it never be;
I make thee master," said Robin Hood,
  "Of all my men and me."

"Nay, by my troth," said Little John,
  "So shall it never be,
But let me be a fellow," said Little
    John,
  "None other keep I be." [37]

Thus John got Robin Hood out of
    prison,
  Certain withouten lain;   320
When his men saw him whole and
    sound,
  Forsooth they were full fain.

They filled in wine, and made them
    glad,
  Under the leavès small,
And ate pasties of venison,
  That good was with ale.

Then word came to our king,
  How Robin Hood was gone,
And how the sheriff of Nottingham
  Durst never look him upon.   330

Then bespake our comely king,
  In an anger high,
"Little John has beguiled the sheriff,
  In faith so has he me.

"Little John has beguiled us both,
  And that full well I see,
Or else the sheriff of Nottingham
  High hangèd should he be.   338

"I made them yeomen of the crown,
  And gave them fee with my hand,
I gave them grith," [38] said our king,
  "Throughout all merry Englánd.

"I gave them grith," then said our
    king,
  "I say, so might I thee,
Forsooth such a yeoman as he is one
  In all England are not three.

"He is true to his master," said our
    king,
  "I say, by sweet Saint John;
He loves better Robin Hood,
  Then he does us each one.   350

"Robin Hood is ever bound to him,
  Both in street and stall;
Speak no more of this matter," said
    our king,
  "But John has beguiled us all."

Thus ends the talking [39] of the monk
  And Robin Hood ywis;
God, that is ever a crownèd king,
  Bring us all to His bliss.

[35] Lane.   [36] Repay.   [37] I care to be.   [38] Peace.   [39] Tale.

London Lickpenny [1]

To London once my steps I bent,
Where honesty should not be faint.
To Westminster I forthwith went,
To a man of law to make complaint. [2]
I said, "For Mary's love, that holy saint,
Pity the poor who would proceed!"
But for lack of money I could not speed. [3]

And as I thrust among the throng,
By froward chance my hood was gone;
Yet for all that I stayed not long,   10
Till to the King's Bench I was come.
Before the judge I kneeled anon,
Prayed him for God's sake to take heed;
But for lack of money I could not speed.

Beneath sat clerks in a great crowd,
Who fast did write by one assent:
There stood up one and cried aloud:
"Richard, Robert, and John of Kent!"
I knew not well what this man meant,
He called so confusedly indeed.   20
But he that lacked money could not speed.

Then to the Common Pleas I went,
Where sat one with a silken hood;
I made him a bow full reverent
And told my case as well as I could,
How I had been cheated of all my good.
I got not a mum of his mouth for my meed,
And for lack of money I could not speed.

[1] London was called "lickpenny" because of its expensiveness.
[2] The law courts were at Westminster, two miles from medieval London.
[3] Succeed.

Unto the Rolls I betook me thence,
Before the clerks of the Chancery,   30
Where many were busy earning pence,
But not one even looked at me.
I gave them my plaint upon my knee;
They liked it well when they had it read,
But, lacking money, I could not be sped.

In Westminster Hall I discovered one
Who went in a long gown of ray.[4]
I crouched and knelt before him anon,
And help for Mary's love did pray.
"I wot not thy meaning," he did say,   40
"And get thee hence, man, I thee bid."
For lack of money I could not speed.

Within this hall neither rich nor poor
Would do for me aught, though I should die.
Seeing this, I gat me out the door,
Where Flemings began at me to cry:
"Master, master, what will ye buy,
Fine felt hats or spectacles to read?
Lay down your silver and here ye may speed."

Then to Westminster Gate I presently went,   50
When the sun was standing at high prime.
Cooks on my patronage were intent,
And proffered me bread with ale and wine,
Ribs of beef both fat and fine;
A fair cloth they gan for to spread.
But, wanting money, I might not be sped.

Then unto London I did me hie;
Of all the land it beareth the prize.
"Hot peascods!" one began to cry;
"Strawberries ripe!" and "Cherries on the rise!" [5]   60
One bade me come near and buy some spice;
They offered me saffron and pepper indeed.
But for lack of money I might not speed.

Then unto Eastcheap I was drawn,
And there much people I saw stand.

---

[4] Striped cloth.   [5] Branch.

One offered me velvet, silk, and lawn;
Another took me by the hand:
"Here is Paris thread, the best in the land."
I never was used to such things indeed,
And, wanting money, I might not speed.   70

Then went I forth by London Stone,
And all the length of Canwick Street;
Drapers me offered much cloth anon.
I met one shouting "Hot sheep's feet!"
Others with "Mackerel!" and "Rushes green!" did me greet.
One bade me buy a hood to cover my head.
But for want of money I might not be sped.

I hied me then into East Cheap.
One cried "Ribs of beef!" and many a pie;
Pewter pots clattered in a heap;   80
There was harp, pipe, and minstrelsy.
"Yea, by cock!" "Nay, by cock!" some did cry.
Some sang of Jenkin and Julian for meed.[6]
But for lack of money I could not speed.

When to Cornhill my way I pursued,
To see stolen goods did not take me long;
For there I spied hanging the very same hood
That I had lost among the throng.
To buy my own hood back seemed wrong,
Though I knew it as well as I did my creed.   90
But for lack of money I could not speed.

The taverner took me by the sleeve;
"Sir," said he, "will you our wine essay?"
I answered: "That cannot much me grieve;
A penny can do no more than it may."
I drank a pint and for it did pay;
Yet I went thence hungry and craving bread,
For, wanting money, I could not be sped.

Then I hied me on to Billingsgate,
And one called out: "Ho, go we hence!"   100
I prayed a bargeman, for God's sake,

[6] Reward, pay.

That he would spare me my expense.
"Thou scap'st not," quoth he, "under two pence.
'Tis not yet my will to do an almsdeed!"
Thus, lacking money, I could not speed.

Into Kent I then myself conveyed,
For with the law I would meddle no more.
Since no man to me attention paid,
I went back to plow as I did before.
Now Jesus, whom Mary in Bethlehem bore,   110
Save London and send these lawyers their meed,
For whoso lacks money with them will not speed.

The Book of Margery Kempe

SECOND PREFACE

A SHORT treatise of a creature set in great pomp and pride of the world, who afterwards was drawn to our Lord by great poverty, sickness, shames, and great reproofs in many divers countries and places, of which tribulations some shall be shown hereafter, not in the order as they befell but as the creature could have mind of them when it was written; for it was twenty years and more from the time this creature had forsaken the world and busily cleaved to our Lord ere this book was written, notwithstanding this creature had great counsel for to have her tribulations and her feelings written, and a White Friar [1] proffered her to write freely if she would. And she was warned in her spirit that she should not write so soon. And 10 many years after she was bidden in her spirit to write. And yet it was then written first by a man who could write well neither English nor German, so it could not be read but only by special grace, for there was so much obloquy and slander about this creature that there would few men believe this creature. And so at the last a priest was sorely moved to write this treatise, and he could not well read it in four years together. And afterward at the request of this creature and the compelling of her own conscience, he essayed again for to read it, and it was much more easy than it was aforetime. And so he began to write in the year of Our Lord 1436 on the next day after Mary Magdalen, according to the information of this creature. 20

CHAPTER I

When this creature was twenty years of age or somewhat more, she was married to a worshipful burgess and, as nature would, was with child in a short time. And after she had conceived, she was afflicted with great illnesses till the child was born, and then, what for labor she had in childbirth and for the sickness going before, she despaired of her life, thinking she might not live. And then she sent for her spiritual father, for she had a thing on her conscience which she had never before shown in all her life. For she was ever hindered by her enemy, the Devil, evermore saying to her while she was in good health she needed no confession but to do penance

[1] Carmelite.

[405]

by herself alone, and all should be forgiven, for God is merciful enough. And therefore this creature often times did great penance in fasting on bread and water and other deeds of alms with devout prayers, save she would not show it in confession. And, when she was at any time sick or diseased, the Devil said in her mind that she should be damned, for she was not shriven of that fault.

Wherefore, after her child was born, she, not trusting her life, sent for her spiritual father, as I said before, in full will to be shriven of all her lifetime as nearly as she could. And when she came to the point for to say that 10 thing which she had so long concealed, her confessor was a little too hasty and began sharply to reprove her ere she had fully said her intent, and so she would say no more for nought he might do. And anon, for fear she had of damnation on the one side and his sharp reproving on that other side, this creature went out of her mind and was wondrously vexed and tormented with spirits half a year and eight weeks and odd days. And in this time she saw, as she thought, devils open their mouths all inflamed with burning flames of fire as though they would swallow her in, sometimes ramping at her, sometimes threatening her, sometimes pulling her and haling her both night and day during the aforesaid time. And also the devils 20 cried upon her with great threatenings, and commanded her she should forsake her Christian faith, and deny her God, His Mother, and all the saints in Heaven, her good works and all good virtues, her father, her mother, and all her friends. And so she did. She slandered her husband, her friends, and her own self; she spake many a reproving word and many a sharp word; she knew no virtue nor goodness; she desired all wickedness; just as the spirits tempted her to say and to do, so she said and did. She would have destroyed herself many a time at their stirrings and have been damned with them in hell, and in witness thereof she bit her own hand so violently that it was seen all her life thereafter. And also she tore her skin 30 on her body against her heart with her nails so despitously, for she had no other instruments, and worse she would have done except that she was bound and kept with strength both day and night, that she might not have her will.

And, when she had been long tormented in these and many other temptations so that men thought she never would have escaped or lived, then on a time, as she lay alone and her keepers were away from her, our merciful Lord Christ Jesu, ever to be trusted, worshiped be His name, never forsaking His servant in time of need, appeared to His creature which had forsaken Him, in the likeness of a man, most seemly, most beauteous, and 40 most amiable that might be seen with man's eye, clad in a mantle of purple silk, sitting upon her bedside, looking upon her with so blessed a countenance that she was strengthened in all her spirits, and said to her these words, "Daughter, why hast thou forsaken Me?"

And anon, as He said these words, she saw verily how the air opened as bright as any lightning, and He rose up into the air, not right hastily and quickly, but fair and easily that she might well behold Him in the air till it was closed again. And anon the creature was made stable in her wits and in her reason as much as ever she was before, and she prayed her husband as soon as he came to her that she might have the keys of the buttery to take her meat and drink as she had done before. Her maidens and her keepers counseled him he should deliver to her no keys, for they said she would but 10 give away such goods as there were, for, as they thought, she knew not what she said. Nevertheless, her husband, ever having tenderness and compassion of her, commanded they should deliver to her the keys. And she took her meat and drink as bodily strength would serve her and she knew her friends and her household and all others that came to her to see how Our Lord Jesu Christ had wrought His grace in her, so blessed may He be who ever is near in tribulation. When men think He is far from them, He is full near by His grace. Afterward this creature did all other occupations such as befell her to do, wisely and soberly enough, save that she knew not verily the call of Our Lord.   20

CHAPTER II

And, when this creature was thus graciously come again to her mind, she thought she was bound to God, and that she would be His servant. Nevertheless, she would not leave her pride nor her pompous array that she had used aforetime, neither for her husband nor for any other man's counsel. And yet she knew full well that men said of her much villany, for she wore gold pipes on her head and her hoods with the tippets were dagged.[2] Her cloaks also were dagged and laid with divers colors between the dags so that it should be the more striking to men's sight and herself be the more admired. And when her husband would speak to her to leave her pride, she answered sharply and shortly and said that she was come of worthy 30 kindred—he seemed never to have wedded her, for her father was sometime mayor of the town N.[3] and afterward he was alderman of the high Guild of the Trinity in N. And therefore she would have the honor of her kindred, whatsoever any man said. She had very great envy of her neighbors that they should be arrayed as well as she. All her desire was to

[2] Tippets were short capes covering the shoulders. Dags were pointed or scalloped projections.

[3] N. stands for Latin *nomen*, "name." In this case the name was King's Lynn in Norfolk.

[407]

be admired of the people. She would not heed any rebuke nor be content with the goods God had sent her, as her husband was, but ever desired more and more.

And then for very covetousness and for to maintain her pride, she began to brew and was one of the greatest brewers in the town N. for three years or four till she had lost much money, for she never had practice therein. For, though she had never such good servants and cunning in brewing, yet never would it be right with them. For, when the ale was standing as fair under barm as any man might see, suddenly the barm would fall down so
10 that all the ale was lost every brewing one after other, so that her servants were ashamed and would not stay with her. Then this creature thought how God had punished her aforetime and she would not be warned, and now again by losing of her goods, and then she stopped and brewed no more. And then she asked her husband mercy because she would not follow his counsel aforetime, and she said that her pride and sin was the cause of all her punishing and she would with good will amend what she had done wrongfully.

But yet she left not the world entirely, for now she bethought her of a new kind of housewifery. She had a horse mill. She got herself two good
20 horses and a man to grind men's corn and thus she trusted to get her living. This provision did not last long, for in a short time after on the eve of Corpus Christi befell this marvel. This man, being in good health of body and his two horses fat and in good condition, which aforetime had drawn well in the mill, when now he took one of these horses and put him in the mill as he had done before, this horse would draw no draft in the mill for anything the man could do. The man was sorry and tried with all his wits how he should make the horse to draw. Sometimes he led him by the head, sometimes he beat him, and sometimes he cherished him, and all availed not, for he would rather go backward than forward. Then this man set a
30 sharp pair of spurs on his heels and rode on the horse's back to make him pull, and it was never the better. When this man saw that it would in no way be, then he put up his horse in the stable and gave him food, and he ate well and freshly. And afterward he took the other horse and put him in the mill. And just as his fellow did so did he, for he would not pull for anything that the man might do. And then this man forsook his service and would no longer abide with the aforesaid creature. Anon as it was noised about the town of N. that neither man nor beast would do service for the creature, then some said she was accursed; some said God took vengeance upon her; some said one thing; and some said another. And some wise men,
40 whose mind was more grounded in the love of Our Lord, said it was the high mercy of Our Lord Jesu Christ called and summoned her from the pride and vanity of the wretched world. And then this creature, seeing

all these adversities coming on every side, thought they were the scourges of Our Lord that would chastise her for her sin. Then she asked God mercy and forsook her pride, her covetousness, and desire that she had of worldly honors, and she did great bodily penance, and entered the way of everlasting life, as shall be told hereafter.

CHAPTER V

Then on a Friday before Christmas day, as this creature, kneeling in a chapel of Saint John within a church of Saint Margaret in N.,[4] wept wondrous sore, asking mercy and forgiveness of her sins and trespass, our merciful Lord Christ Jesu, blessed may he be, ravished her spirit and said unto her: "Daughter, why weepest thou so sorely? I am come to thee, Jesu Christ, who died on the Cross, suffering bitter pains and passions for thee. I, the same God, forgive thee thy sins to the uttermost point. And thou shalt never come into hell nor into purgatory, but, when thou shalt pass out of this world, within the twinkling of an eye thou shalt have the bliss of Heaven, for I am the same God that brought thy sins to thy mind and made thee to be shriven thereof. And I grant thee contrition to thy life's end. Therefore I bid thee and command thee, boldly call Me Jesu, thy love, for I am thy love and will be thy love without end. And, daughter, thou hast a haircloth upon thy back. I will thee to put it away, and I will give thee a haircloth in thy heart that will please me much better than all the haircloths in the world. Also, my dear daughter, thou must forsake what thou lovest best in this world, and that is eating of flesh. And instead of that flesh thou shalt eat my flesh and my blood, which is the very body of Christ in the sacrament of the altar. This is my will, daughter, that thou receive my body every Sunday, and I will infuse so much grace into thee that all the world shall marvel thereof. Thou shalt be eaten and gnawed by the people of the world as any rat gnaweth the stockfish. Fear not, daughter, for Thou shalt have the victory over all thy enemies. I will give thee grace enough to answer every cleric in the love of God. I swear to thee by My majesty that I will never forsake thee in weal nor in woe. I will help thee and keep thee so that never shall devil in hell part thee from Me, nor angel in heaven, nor man on earth, for devils in hell may not, nor angels in heaven will not, nor man on earth shall not. And, daughter, I will thee to leave thy praying of many prayers and think such thoughts as I shall put in thy mind. I will give thee leave to pray till six of the clock to say what thou wouldst. Then shalt thou lie still and speak to Me by thought, and I will give to thee high meditation and true contemplation. And I bid thee to go to the anchorite at the Friar Preachers,[5] and show him My privities and My counsels

---

[4] See above note 3. [5] Dominicans.

which I show to thee, and do after his counsel, for My spirit shall speak in him to thee."

Then this creature went forth to the anchorite, as she was commanded, and showed him the revelations such as were shown to her. Then the anchorite with great reverence and weeping, thanking God, said, "Daughter, ye suck even on Christ's breast, and ye have a pledge-penny of Heaven. I charge you receive such thoughts when God will give them as meekly and as devoutly as ye can and come to me and tell me what they are, and I will, with the leave of Our Lord Jesu Christ, tell you whether they are
10 of the Holy Spirit or else of your enemy the Devil."

CHAPTER VI

Another day this creature would give herself to meditation, as she was commanded before, and she lay still, not knowing what she best might think. Then she said to Our Lord Jesu Christ, "Jesu, what shall I think?" Our Lord Jesu answered to her mind, "Daughter, think on my Mother, for she is cause of all the grace that thou hast."

And then anon she saw Saint Anne great with child, and then she prayed to be Saint Anne's maiden and servant. And anon Our Lady was born, and then she busied her to take the child to her and to keep it till it was twelve years of age with good food and drink, with fair white clothes and white
20 kerchiefs. And then she said to the blessed child, "Lady, ye shall be the Mother of God."

The blessed child answered and said, "I would I were worthy to be the handmaid of her that should conceive the Son of God."

The creature said, "I pray you, Lady, if that grace befall you, forsake not my service."

The blissful child passed away for a certain time, the creature being still in contemplation, and then came again and said, "Daughter, now am I become the Mother of God."

And then the creature fell down on her knees with great reverence and
30 great weeping and said, "I am not worthy, Lady, to do you service."

"Yes, daughter," she said, "follow thou me; thy service pleaseth me well."

Then went she forth with our Lady and with Joseph, bearing with her a pottle of wine and spices therein. Then went they forth to Elizabeth, mother of Saint John Baptist, and, when they met together, either of them honored the other, and so they dwelt together with great grace and gladness twelve weeks. And then Saint John was born, and Our Lady took him up from the earth with all manner of reverence and gave him to his mother, saying of him that he should be a holy man, and blessed him. Afterward they took their leave of each other with tender tears. And then the creature fell down on her knees to Saint Elizabeth and prayed her she would pray for her to Our Lady that she might do her service and pleasure. "Daughter," said Elizabeth, "meseemeth, thou dost right well thy duty."

And then went the creature forth with Our Lady to Bethlehem and procured her lodging every night with great reverence, and Our Lady was received with gladness. Also she begged Our Lady for fair white clothes and kerchiefs for to swathe her Son in when He should be born, and, when Jesu was born, she arranged bedding for Our Lady to lie in with her blessed Son. And then she begged food for Our Lady and her blessed Child. After- 10 ward with bitter tears of pity she swathed Him, having mind of the cruel death He should suffer for the love of sinful men, saying to Him, "Lord, I will deal gently with you. I will not bind you tightly. I pray you be not displeased with me."

CHAPTER XXVI

When the time came that this creature should visit the holy places where Our Lord was alive and dead, as she had done by revelation years before, she prayed the parish priest of the town where she was dwelling to say for her in the pulpit that, if any man or woman who claimed any debt of her husband or of her that they should come and speak with her before she went, and she, with the help of God, would make compensation to each of them so that they would be content. And so she did. Afterward she took 20 leave of her husband and of the holy anchorite, who had told her before the order of her going and of the great discomfort that she would suffer by the way, and, when all her fellowship forsook her, how a broken-backed man would lead her forth in safety through the help of our Lord. And so in fact it befell, as it shall be written afterward.

Then she took her leave of Master Robert and asked of him his blessing, and so of other friends. And then she went to Norwich and made offerings at the Trinity, and then she went to Yarmouth, and offered at an image of Our Lady, and there she took ship. And the next day they came to a great town called Zierikzee, where Our Lord of His goodness visited this creature 30 with abundant tears of contrition for her own sins and sometimes for other men's sins also. And specially she had tears of compassion in the memory of Our Lord's Passion. And she was houseled every Sunday where there was time and place convenient thereto, with great weepings and boisterous sobbings so that men marveled and wondered for the great grace that God wrought in His creature. This creature had eaten no flesh nor drunk any wine for four years before she went out of England. And as her spiritual father now charged her by virtue of obedience that she should both eat flesh and drink wine, so she did a little while. Then she prayed her con-

fessor he would hold her excused though she ate no flesh, and suffer her to do as she would for a time as it pleased him. And soon thereafter through influence of some of her company her confessor was displeased because she ate no flesh, and so were many of the company. And they were most displeased because she wept so much and spoke always of the love and goodness of Our Lord as well at the table as in other place. And therefore shamefully they reproved her and harshly chided her and said they would not suffer her as her husband did when she was at home and in England. And she said meekly again unto them, "Our Lord Almighty God is as great a
10 lord here as in England, and as great cause have I to love Him here as there, blessed may He be!"

For these words her fellowship was more wroth than they were before, whose wrath and unkindness to this creature was matter of great heaviness, for they were held right good men, and she desired greatly their love if she might have had it with the pleasure of God. And then she said to one of them specially, "Ye do me much shame and great grievance."

He answered again anon, "I pray that the Devil's death may overtake thee soon and quickly," and many more cruel words he said to her than she could repeat. And soon after some of the company in which she trusted
20 best and her own maiden also said she should no longer go in their fellowship, and they said they would take away her maiden from her so that she should not become a strumpet in her company. And then one of them who had her gold in keeping gave her a noble with great anger and wrath to go where she would and to help herself as much as she might, for with them, they said, she should no longer abide, and they forsook her that night. Then on the next morrow there came to her one of their company, a man who loved her well, praying her that she would go to his fellows and humble herself unto them and pray them that she might still go in their company till she came to Constance. And so she did, and went forth with them till
30 she came to Constance with great discomfort and great trouble, for they did her much shame and much reproof as they went in divers places. They cut her gown so short that it came but little below her knee and made her put on a white canvas like coarse sacking, so that she would be held a fool and the people should not make much of her nor hold her in repute. They made her sit at the table's end below all others so that she durst full ill speak a word. And, notwithstanding all their malice, she was held in more honor than they wherever they came. And the good man of the house where they were lodged, though she sat lowest at the table's end, would always cherish her before them all as he could and might and sent her of his own mess of
40 such serving as he had, and that grieved her fellowship very evilly. As they went by the way to Constance-ward, it was told them they should be harmed and have great discomfort unless they had great grace. Then this

creature came to a church and went in to make her prayer, and she prayed with all her heart, with great weeping and many tears, for help and succor against her enemies. Anon Our Lord said to her mind, "Fear not, daughter, thy fellowship shall have no harm while thou art in their company." And so, blessed may Our Lord be in all His works, they went forth in safety to Constance.

CHAPTER XXVIII

And so she had ever great tribulation till she came to Jerusalem. And, ere she came there, she said to them that she supposed they were grieved with her. "I pray you, sirs, be in charity with me, for I am in charity with you, and forgive me because I have grieved you by the way. And, if any 10 of you hath in any way trespassed against me, may God forgive it you, and I do."

And so they went forth into the Holy Land until they might see Jerusalem. And when this creature saw Jerusalem, she, riding on an ass, thanked God with all her heart, praying Him for His mercy that just as He had brought her to see this earthly city Jerusalem, He would grant her grace to see the blissful city Jerusalem above, the city of Heaven. Our Lord Jesu Christ, answering to her thought, granted her to have her desire. Then, for joy that she had and the sweetness that she felt in the converse of Our Lord, she was in point to have fallen off her ass, for she might not bear the 20 sweetness and grace that God wrought in her soul. Then two German pilgrims went to her and kept her from falling, of whom one was a priest. And he put spices in her mouth to comfort her, thinking she had been sick. And so they helped her forth to Jerusalem. And, when she came there, she said, "Sirs, I pray you be not displeased though I weep sorely in this holy place where Our Lord Jesu Christ was alive and dead."

Then they went to the Temple in Jerusalem, and they were let in on the one day at evensong-time and abode there till the next day at evensong-time. Then the friars lifted up a cross and led the pilgrims about from one place to another where Our Lord had suffered His pains and His passions, 30 every man and woman bearing a wax candle in hand. And the friars always, as they went about, told them what Our Lord suffered in every place. And the aforesaid creature wept and sobbed so plenteously as though she had seen Our Lord with her bodily eye suffering His Passion at that time. Before her in her soul she saw Him truly by contemplation, and that caused her to have compassion. And, when they came up on the Mount of Calvary, she fell down so that she might not stand or kneel but wallowed and twisted with her body, spreading her arms abroad, and cried with a loud voice as though her heart should have broken asunder, for in the city of her soul she saw verily and freshly how Our Lord was crucified. Before her face she heard and saw in her spiritual sight the mourning of Our Lady, of Saint John and Mary Magdalen, and of many others that loved Our Lord. And she had so great compassion and so great pain to see Our Lord's pain that she might not keep herself from crying and roaring though she should have died therefor.

And this was the first cry that ever she cried in any contemplation. And this manner of crying endured many years after this time for aught that any man might do, and therefore suffered she much despite and much re-
10 proof. The crying was so loud and wonderful that it made the people astonished unless they had heard it before or else that they knew the cause of the crying, and she had them so often that they made her very weak in her bodily mights, and especially if she heard of Our Lord's Passion. And sometime, when she saw the Crucifix, or if she saw a man or a beast (whichever it was) had a wound, or if a man beat a child before her or smote a horse or another beast with a whip, if she might see or hear it, she thought she saw Our Lord beaten or wounded, just as she saw in the man or in the beast, as much in the field as in the town, and by herself alone as much as among the people. First when she had her cryings in Jerusalem, she had
20 them often-times, and in Rome also. And, when she came home into England, first at her coming home it came but seldom as it were once a month, then once in the week, afterward daily, and once she had fourteen on one day, and at another she had seven, and even as God would visit her, sometimes in the church, sometimes in the street, sometimes in the chamber, sometimes in the field when God would send them, for she knew never time nor hour when they would come. And they came never without passing great sweetness of devotion and high contemplation. And, as soon as she perceived that she should cry, she would keep it in as much as she might so that the people should not have heard it to their annoyance. For
30 some said it was a wicked spirit vexed her; some said it was a sickness; some said she had drunk too much wine; some banned her; some wished she had been in the haven; some wished she had been in the sea in a bottomless boat; and so each man as he thought. Other holy men loved her and favored her the more. Some great clerics said Our Lady never cried so nor any saint in Heaven, but they knew full little what she felt, nor would they believe but that she might have abstained from crying if she had wished.

CHAPTER LII

There was a monk who preached in York who had heard much slander and much evil talk of the said creature. And, when he preached, there was a great multitude of people to hear him, and she was present with them.

And so, when he was in his sermon, he related many matters so openly that the people conceived well that it was because of her; wherefore her friends who loved her were full sorry and heavy thereof, and she was much the more merry, for she had matter to test her patience and her charity, whereby she trusted to please Our Lord Christ Jesu. When the sermon was done, a doctor of divinity who with many others also loved her well came to her and said, "Margery, how have ye done this day?"

"Sir," she said, "right well, blessed be God. I have cause to be merry and glad in my soul that I may suffer anything for His love, for He suffered much more for me." 10

Soon after came a man of good will who loved her right well with his wife and some others, and led her seven miles thence to the Archbishop of York, and brought her into a fair chamber, where came a good clerk, saying to the good man who had brought her thither, "Sir, why have ye and your wife brought this woman hither? She will steal away from you, and then will ye have a shame of her."

The good man said, "I dare well say she will abide and willingly submit to question."

On the next day she was brought into the Archbishop's Chapel, and there came many of the Archbishop's household, despising her, calling her 20 "Lollard" and "heretic," and they swore many a horrible oath that she should be burnt. And she, through the strength of Jesu, said to them again, "Sirs, I fear ye shall be burnt in hell without end unless ye amend you of your swearing of oaths, for ye keep not the commandment of God. I would not swear as ye do for all the good of this world."

Then they went away as though they had been shamed. She then, making her prayer in her mind, asked grace so to behave that day as was most pleasure to God and profit to her own soul and good example to her fellow-Christians. Our Lord, answering her, said it would be right well. At the last the said Archbishop came into the Chapel with his clergy, and sharply he 30 said to her, "Why goest thou in white? Art thou a maiden?"

She, kneeling on her knees before him, said, "Nay, sir, I am no maiden; I am a wife."

He commanded his men to fetch a pair of fetters and said she should be fettered, for she was a false heretic. And then she said, "I am no heretic, nor will ye prove me one."

The Archbishop went away and let her stand alone. Then she made her prayers to Our Lord God Almighty to help her and succor her against all her enemies, spiritual and bodily, a long while, and her flesh trembled and quaked wonderfully, so that she was fain to put her hands under her clothes 40 so that the quaking should not be espied. Then the Archbishop came again into the Chapel with many worthy clerics, amongst whom was the same doctor who had examined her before and the monk who had preached against her a short time before in York. Some of the people asked whether she were a Christian woman or a Jew; some said she was a good woman, and some said nay. Then the Archbishop took his seat, and his clerics also, each of them in his degree, many people being present. And in the time the people were gathering together and the Archbishop took his seat, the said creature stood all behind, making her prayers for help and succor against her enemies for so long and with such high devotion that she melted all into tears. At the last she cried loudly so that the Archbishop and his clerics

10 and many people had great wonder about her, for they had not heard such crying before. When her crying was passed, she came before the Archbishop and fell down on her knees, the Archbishop saying full roughly unto her, "Why weepest thou so, woman?"

She, answering, said, "Sir, ye shall wish some day that ye had wept as sorely as I."

And then shortly, after the Archbishop had put to her the articles of our faith, which God gave her grace to answer well and truly and readily without any great study so that he could not blame her, then he said to the clerics, "She knoweth her faith well enough. What shall I do with her?"

20 The clerics said, "We know well that she knoweth the articles of the faith, but we will not suffer her to dwell among us, for the people have great faith in her converse, and peradventure she might pervert some of them."

Then the Archbishop said unto her, "I have an evil report of thee; I hear say thou art a right wicked woman."

And she said again, "Sir, so do I hear say that ye are a wicked man. And, if ye are as wicked as men say, ye shall never come into Heaven unless ye amend you while ye are here."

Then said he full roughly, "Why, thou wretch, what do men say of me?"

30 She answered, "Other men, sir, can tell you well enough." Then said a great cleric with a furred hood, "Peace, speak of thyself and let him be."

Then said the Archbishop to her, "Lay thy hand on the book here before me and swear that thou shalt go out of my diocese as soon as thou may."

"Nay, sir," she said, "give me leave to go again into York to take leave of my friends."

Then he gave her leave for one day or two. She thought it was too short a time, wherefore she said again, "Sir, I may not go out of this diocese so hastily, for I must tarry and speak with good men ere I go, and I must, sir,

40 with your leave, go to Bridlington and speak with my confessor, a good man, who was the confessor of the good Prior who is now canonized."

Then said the Archbishop to her, "Thou shalt swear that thou shalt not teach or reprove the people of my diocese."

"Nay, sir, I will not swear," she said, "for I will speak of God and reprove them that swear great oaths wheresoever I go until the time that the Pope and Holy Church ordain that no man shall be so bold as to speak of God; for God Almighty forbiddeth not, sir, that we shall speak of Him. And also the Gospel maketh mention that when the woman had heard our Lord preach, she came before Him with a loud voice and said, 'Blessed be the womb that bore Thee and the teats that gave Thee suck.' Then Our Lord said in reply to her, 'Forsooth so are they blessed that hear the word of God 10 and keep it.' And therefore, sir, methinketh that the Gospel giveth me leave to speak of God."

"Sir," said the cleric, "here know we well that she hath a devil within her, for she speaketh of the Gospel." Quickly a great cleric brought forth a book and for his side cited St. Paul against her, that no woman should preach. She, answering thereto, said, "I preach not, sir; I come into no pulpit. I use but converse and good words, and that will I do while I live."

Then said a doctor who had examined her beforetime, "Sir, she told me the worst tale of priests that ever I heard."

The Bishop commanded her to tell that tale. "Sir, with your reverence, 20 I spoke of but one priest in the way of example, who went wandering in a wood through the sufferance of God for the profit of his soul until the night came upon him. He, destitute of lodging, found a fair arbor in which he rested that night, with a fair pear-tree in the midst all blooming and embellished with flowers and blossoms full delectable to his sight; and there came a bear, great and rough, ugly to behold, shaking the pear-tree and knocking down the flowers. Greedily this grievous beast ate and devoured the fair flowers. And, when he had eaten them, turning his tail-end in the priest's presence, voided them out again at the hinder part. The priest, having great abomination for that loathly sight, conceiving great sorrow 30 for doubt as to what it might mean, on the next day wandered forth on his way all heavy and pensive, and happened to meet with a seemly aged man like a palmer or a pilgrim, who inquired of the priest the cause of his heaviness. The priest, relating the matter before-written, said he conceived great fear and heaviness when he beheld that loathly beast defoul and devour such fair flowers and blossoms and afterward so horribly to void them before him at his tail's end, and he not understanding what this might mean. Then the palmer, showing himself the messenger of God, thus addressed him, 'Priest, thou thyself art the pear-tree, somewhat flourishing and flowering through thy service-saying and ministering of the sacraments, though thou 40 dost do it undevoutly, for thou takest full little heed how thou dost say thy matins and thy service, so it be babbled to an end. Then dost thou go to thy Mass without devotion, and for thy sin hast thou little contrition. Thou receivest there the fruit of everlasting life, the sacrament of the altar, in full feeble disposition. Then all the day after thou misspendest thy time, thou givest thyself to buying and selling, bartering and exchanging, like a man of the world. Thou sittest at the ale, giving thyself to gluttony and excess, to lust of thy body, through lechery and uncleanness. Thou breakest the commandments of God through swearing, lying, detraction, and backbiting, and using such other sins. Thus by thy misgovernance, like unto the 10 loathly bear, thou devourest and destroyest the flowers and blooms of virtuous living to thy endless damnation and the hindering of many men unless thou shouldst have grace of repentance and amending.' "

Then the Archbishop liked well the tale and commended it, saying it was a good tale. And the cleric who had examined her before-time in the absence of the Archbishop, said, "Sir, this tale smiteth me to the heart."

The aforesaid creature said to the cleric, "Ah, worshipful doctor, sir, in the place where my dwelling is there is a worthy cleric, a good preacher, who boldly speaketh against the misgovernance of the people and will flatter no man. He saith many times in the pulpit, 'If any man be ill pleased 20 with my preaching, note him well, for he is guilty.' And right so, sir," said she to the cleric, "fare ye by me, God forgive it you."

The cleric knew not well what he might say to her. Afterward the same cleric came to her and prayed her for forgiveness that he had been so against her. Also he prayed her especially to pray for him. And then awhile after the Archbishop said, "Where shall I get a man who will lead this woman away from me?"

Quickly there started up many young men, and every man of them said, "My Lord, I will go with her."

The Archbishop answered, "Ye are too young; I will not have you."

30 Then a good sober man of the Archbishop's household asked his Lord what he would give him an he should lead her away. The Archbishop offered him five shillings and the man asked a noble. The Archbishop answering, said, "I will not spend so much on her body."

"Yes, good sir," said the creature, "Our Lord shall right well reward you again."

Then the Archbishop said to the man, "See, here is five shillings, and lead her fast out of this country."

She, kneeling down on her knees, asked his blessing. He, praying her to pray for him, blessed her and let her go. Then she, going again to York, 40 was received by many people and by many worthy clerics who rejoiced that Our Lord had given her, unlettered, wit and wisdom to answer so many learned men without villany or blame, thanks be to God.

CHAPTER LVIII

On a time, as the aforesaid creature was in her contemplation, she hungered right sorely after God's word and said, "Alas, Lord, many as are the clerics Thou hast in this world, Thou wouldst not send me one of them who might fill my soul with Thy word and with reading of Holy Scripture, for all the clerics that preach may not fill it, for methinketh that my soul is always equally hungry. If I had gold enough, I would give every day a noble in order to have every day a sermon, for Thy word is worth more to me than all the goods in this world. And, therefore, blessed Lord, have pity on me, for Thou hast taken away the anchorite from me who was a singular solace and comfort to me and many times refreshed me with Thy holy word."

Then answered our Lord Jesu Christ in her soul, saying, "There shall come one from far away that shall fulfill thy desire."

So, many days after this answer, there came a priest newly to Lynn who had never known her before, and, when he saw her pass in the streets, he was greatly moved to speak to her and asked of other folk what kind of woman she was. They said they trusted to God that she was a right good woman. Afterward the priest sent for her, praying her to come and speak with him and with his mother, for he had hired a chamber for his mother and for him, and so they dwelt together. Then the said creature came to know his will and spoke with him and his mother and had right good cheer of them both. Then the priest took a book and read therein how Our Lord, seeing the city of Jerusalem, wept thereupon, relating the misfortunes and sorrows that should come thereto, for the city knew not the time of its visitation. When the said creature heard read how Our Lord wept, then wept she sorely and cried aloud, the priest and his mother knowing no cause for her weeping. When her crying and weeping ceased, they rejoiced and were right merry in Our Lord. Then she took her leave and parted from them at that time. When she was gone, the priest said to his mother, "Much it marveleth me of this woman, why she weepeth and crieth so. Nevertheless methinketh she is a good woman, and I desire greatly to speak more with her."

His mother was well pleased and counseled that he should do so. And afterwards the same priest loved her and trusted her greatly and blessed the time that ever he knew her, for he found great spiritual comfort in her and it caused him to examine much good writing and many a good doctor whom he would not have looked at at that time had she not been. He read to her many a good book of high contemplation and other books thereupon, such as the Bible with comments of doctors thereupon, Saint Bride's book, Hilton's book,[6] Bonaventura's *Stimulus Amoris, Incendium Amoris*,[7] and others like these. And then she knew that it was a spirit sent from God which said to her, as is written a little before, when she complained of lack of reading, these words, "There shall come one from far away that shall fulfill thy desire." And thus she knew by experience that it was a right true spirit.

CHAPTER LXXXIX

Also, while the aforesaid creature was occupied about the writing of this treatise, she had many holy tears and weepings, and oftentimes there came a flame of fire hot and delectable about her breast, and also he that was her
10 writer could not sometimes keep himself from weeping, and often in the meantime, when the creature was in church, Our Lord Jesu Christ with His glorious Mother and many saints also came into her soul and thanked her, saying that they were well pleased with the writing of this book. And also many times she heard a voice of a sweet bird singing in her ear, and oftentimes she heard sweet sounds and melodies that surpassed her wit to tell them. And many times she was sick while this treatise was in the writing, and, as soon as she would go about the writing of this treatise, she was suddenly in a way hale and whole. And often she was commanded in all haste to make her ready. And on a time, as she lay in her prayers in the church
20 during the time of Advent before Christmas, she thought in her heart she wished God of His goodness would make Master Aleyn to say a sermon as well as he could. And, as soon as she had thought thus, she heard Our Sovereign Lord Christ Jesu say in her soul, "Daughter, I know right well what thou thinkest now of Master Aleyn, and I tell thee truly that he will say a right holy sermon. And look that thou believe steadfastly the words he will preach as though I preached them Myself, for they shall be words of great solace and comfort to thee, for I will speak in him."

When she had heard this answer, she went and told it to her confessor and two other priests in whom she trusted greatly. And, when she had
30 told them her feeling, she was full sorry for fear whether he should say so well as she had felt or not, for revelations are hard sometimes to understand. And sometimes those that men think were revelations are deceits and delusions, and therefore it is not expedient to give readily credence to every stirring but soberly to wait and to prove if they are sent from God. Nevertheless as to the feeling of this creature, it was very truth showed in experience, and her fear and her sorrow turned into great spiritual comfort and gladness. Sometimes she was in great depression for her feelings,

[6] *The Ladder of Perfection*, a mystical work by Walter Hilton (d. 1396).
[7] A Latin work by Rolle.

because she knew not how they should be understood for many days together, for fear that she had of deceits and delusions, so that she thought she would rather have had her head smitten from her body till God of His goodness declared them to her mind. For sometimes what she understood bodily was to have been understood spiritually, and the fear that she had of her feelings was the greatest scourge that she had on earth and especially when she had her first feelings, and that fear made her meek, for she had no joy in the feeling till she knew by experience whether it was true or not. But ever blessed may God be, for He made her always more mighty and more strong in His love and in His fear and gave her increase of virtue 10 with perseverance. Here endeth this treatise, for God took him to His mercy who wrote the copy of this book, and, though he wrote not clearly nor openly in our way of speaking, he in his manner of writing and spelling made true meaning which, through the help of God and of herself who had all this treatise in feeling and working, is truly drawn out of the copy into this little book.

Laura Hibbard Loomis

The Examination of William Thorpe

Before the Archbishop of Canterbury [1]

William Thorpe

AND the Archbishop said unto me, "I will, shortly, that now thou swear here to me, that thou shalt forsake all the opinions which the Sect of Lollards hold, and is slandered [2] with; so that, after this time, neither privily nor apertly, thou hold any opinion which I shall, after that thou hast sworn, rehearse to thee here. Nor thou shalt favor no man nor woman, young nor old, that holdeth any of these foresaid opinions; but, after thy knowledge and power, thou shalt enforce thee to withstand all such distroublers of Holy Church in every diocese that thou comest in; and them that will not leave their false and damnable opinions, thou shalt put them up, publishing
10 them and their names; and make them known to the Bishop of the diocese that they are in, or to the Bishop's Ministers. And, over this, I will that thou preach no more, unto the time that I know, by good witness and true, that thy conversation be such that thy heart and thy mouth accord truly in one contrarying of all the lewd learning that thou hast taught here before."

And I, hearing these words, thought in my heart that this was an unlawful asking; and I deemed myself cursed of GOD, if I consented hereto; and I thought how SUSANNA said, "Anguish is to me on every side!"

ARCHBISHOP: And in that I stood still, and spake not; the Archbishop said to me, "Answer one wise or another!"

20 WILLIAM: And I said, "Sir, if I consented to you thus, as ye have rehearsed to me; I should become an Appealer, or every Bishop's Spy! Summoner of all England! For an I should thus put up and publish the names of men and women, I should herein deceive full many persons: yea, Sir, as it is likely, by the doom of my conscience, I should herein be cause of the death, both of men and women; yea, both bodily and ghostly.[3] For many

---

[1] From *Fifteenth Century Prose and Verse*, with an introduction by A. W. Pollard (1903). Reprinted by permission of Archibald Constable & Co. The examination took place in 1407 in Saltwood Castle, Kent, before Archbishop Arundell. Thorpe seems to have lived to 1460.

[2] Charged.   [3] Spiritual.

men and women that stand now in the Truth, and are in the way of salvation, if I should for the learning and reading of their Belief publish them or put them therefore up to Bishops or to their unpiteous Ministers, I know some deal by experience, that they should be so distroubled and dis-eased with persecution or otherwise, that many of them, I think, would rather choose to forsake the Way of Truth than to be travailed, scorned, and slandered or punished as Bishops and their Ministers now use [4] for to constrain men and women to consent to them.

"But I find in no place in Holy Scripture, that this office that ye would now enfeoff me with, accordeth to any priest of CHRIST's sect, nor to any 10 other Christian man. And therefore to do thus, were to me a full noyous bond to be bounden with, and over grievous charge. For I suppose that if I thus did, many men and women in the world, yea, Sir, might justly, unto my confusion say to me that I were a traitor to GOD and to them! since, as I think in mine heart, many men and women trust so mickle in me in this case, that I would not, for the saving of my life, do thus to them. For if I thus should do, full many men and women would, as they might full truly, say that I had falsely and cowardly forsaken the Truth, and slandered shamefully the Word of GOD! For if I consented to you, to do hereafter your will, for bonchief and mischief that may befall to me in this life, I 20 deem in my conscience that I were worthy herefore to be cursed of GOD, as also of all His Saints! From which inconvenience keep me and all Christian people, Almighty GOD! now and ever, for His holy name!"

ARCHBISHOP: And then the Archbishop said unto me, "O thine heart is full hard, endured [5] as was the heart of PHARAOH; and the Devil hath overcome thee, and perverted thee! and he hath so blinded thee in all thy wits, that thou hast no grace to know the truth, nor the measure of mercy that I have proffered to thee! Therefore, as I perceive now by thy foolish answer, thou hast no will to leave thine old errors. But I say to thee, lewd losel! [6] either thou quickly consent to mine ordinance, and submit thee 30 to stand to my decrees, or, by Saint Thomas! thou shalt be disgraded [7] and follow thy fellow in Smithfield!"

And at this saying, I stood still and spake not; but I thought in mine heart that GOD did to me a great grace, if He would, of His great mercy, bring me to such an end. And in mine heart, I was nothing afraid with this menacing of the Archbishop.

And I considered, there, two things in him. One, that he was not yet sorrowful, for that he had made WILLIAM SAUTRE wrongfully to be burnt.[8] And as I considered that the Archbishop thirsted yet after more shedding out of innocent blood. And fast therefore I was moved in all my wits, for 40

[4] Are accustomed.   [5] Hardened.   [6] Ignorant wretch.
[7] Degraded.   [8] In 1401 at Smithfield.

to hold the Archbishop neither for Prelate, nor for priest of GOD; and for that mine inward man was thus altogether departed from the Archbishop, methought I should not have any dread of him. But I was right heavy and sorrowful for that there was none audience of secular men [9] by: but in mine heart, I prayed the LORD GOD to comfort me and strengthen me against them that there were against the soothfastness. And I purposed to speak no more to the Archbishop and his Clerks [10] than me need behoved.

And all thus I prayed GOD, for His goodness, to give me then and always grace to speak with a meek and an easy spirit; and whatsoever thing that
10 I should speak, that I might thereto have true authorities of Scriptures and open reason.

* * * * *

ARCHBISHOP: And then, as if he had been wroth, he said to one of his Clerks, "Fetch hither quickly the Certification that came to me from Shrewsbury, under the Bailiff's seal, witnessing the errors and heresies which this losel hath venomously witnessed there!"

Then hastily the Clerk took out and laid forth on a cupboard divers rolls and writings; among which there was a little one, which the Clerk delivered to the Archbishop.

And by and by [11] the Archbishop read this roll containing this sentence.
20 "The third Sunday after Easter, the year of our Lord 1407, WILLIAM THORPE came unto the town of Shrewsbury, and, through leave granted to him to preach, he said openly in St. Chad's Church, in his sermon,

That the Sacrament of the Altar after the consecration was material bread.

And that images should in no wise be worshiped.

And that men should not go on any pilgrimages.

And that priests have no title to tithes.

And that it is not lawful to swear in any wise."

* * * * *

ARCHBISHOP: And the Archbishop took the Certification in his hand,
30 and looked thereon awhile; and then he said to me, "Lo, herein is certified against thee, by worthy men and faithful of Shrewsbury, that thou preachedst there openly in Saint Chad's Church, that the Sacrament of the Altar was material bread after the consecration. What sayest thou? Was this truly preached?"

WILLIAM: And I said, "Sir, I tell you truly that I touched nothing there of the Sacrament of the Altar, but in this wise, as I will, with GOD's grace, tell you here.

"As I stood there in the pulpit, busying me to teach the commandment

[9] Laymen.   [10] Clerics.   [11] Immediately.

of GOD, there knelled a sacring-bell; and therefore mickle people turned away hastily, and with great noise ran from towards me. And I seeing this, say to them thus, 'Good men! ye were better to stand here full still and to hear GOD's Word. For, certes, the virtue and the meed [12] of the most holy Sacrament of the Altar standeth much more in the Belief thereof that ye ought to have in your soul, than it doth in the outward Sight thereof. And therefore ye were better to stand quietly to hear GOD's Word, because that through the hearing thereof, men come to very true belief.' And otherwise, Sir, I am certain I spake not there, of the worthy Sacrament of the Altar." 10

ARCHBISHOP: And the Archbishop said to me, "I believe thee not! whatsoever thou sayest, since so worshipful men have witnessed against thee. But since thou deniest that thou saidest thus there what sayest thou now? Resteth there, after the consecration, in the host, material bread or no?"

WILLIAM: And I said, "Sir, I know of no place in Holy Scripture, where this term, *material bread*, is written: and therefore, Sir, when I speak of this matter, I use not [13] to speak of material bread."

ARCHBISHOP: Then the Archbishop said to me, "How teachest thou men to believe in this Sacrament?"

WILLIAM: And I said, "Sir, as I believe myself, so I teach other men." 20

ARCHBISHOP: He said, "Tell out plainly thy belief hereof!"

WILLIAM: And I said, with my Protestation, "Sir, I believe that the night before that CHRIST JESU would suffer wilfully Passion for mankind on the morn after, He took bread in His holy and most worshipful hands, lifting up His eyes, and giving thanks to GOD His Father, blessed this bread and brake it, and gave it to His disciples, saying to them, 'Take, and eat of this, all of you! This is My body!'

"And that this is, and ought to be all men's belief, MATTHEW, MARK, LUKE, and PAUL witnesseth.

"Other belief, Sir, have I none, nor will have, nor teach: for I believe 30 that this sufficeth in this matter. For in this belief, with GOD's grace, I purpose to live and die: acknowledging as I believe and teach other men to believe, that the worshipful Sacrament of the Altar is the Sacrament of CHRIST's flesh and his blood, in form of bread and wine."

ARCHBISHOP: And the Archbishop said to me, "It is sooth, that this Sacrament is very CHRIST's body in form of bread: but thou and thy sect teachest it to be the substance of bread! Think you this true teaching?"

WILLIAM: And I said, "Neither I nor any other of the sect that ye damn [14] teach any otherwise than I have told you, nor believe otherwise, to my knowing. 40

"Nevertheless, Sir, I ask of you, for charity! that will ye tell me plainly,

[12] Reward.   [13] Am not accustomed.   [14] Condemn.

how ye shall understand this text of Saint PAUL, where he saith thus, 'This thing feel you in yourselves, that is, in CHRIST JESU, while he was in the form of GOD.' Sir, calleth not PAUL here, the form of GOD, the substance or kind of GOD? Also, Sir, saith not the Church, in the *Hours* of the blessed Virgin, accordingly hereto, where it is written thus, 'Thou Author of Health! remember that some time thou took, of the undefiled Virgin, the form of our body!' Tell me, for charity! therefore, Whether the form of our body be called here, the kind of our body, or no?"

ARCHBISHOP: And the Archbishop said to me, "Wouldst thou make
10 me declare this text after thy purpose, since the Church hath now determined that 'there abideth no substance of bread after the consecration in the Sacrament of the Altar!' Believest thou not, on this Ordinance of the Church?"

*　　*　　*　　*　　*

WILLIAM: And I said, "Sir, as I understand, it is all one to grant or to believe that there dwelleth substance of bread, and to grant or to believe that this most worthy Sacrament of CHRIST's own body is one Accident without Subject. But, Sir, for as mickle as your asking passeth mine understanding, I dare neither deny it nor grant it, for it is a School matter,[15] about which I busied me never for to know it: and therefore I commit this term
20 *accidens sine subjecto*, to those Clerks [16] which delight them so in curious and subtle sophistry, because they determine oft so difficult and strange matters, and wade and wander so in them, from argument to argument, with *pro* and *contra*, till they wot not where they are! nor understand not themselves! But the shame that these proud sophisters have to yield them to men and before men, maketh them oft fools, and to be concluded shamefully before GOD."

ARCHBISHOP: And the Archbishop said to me, "I purpose not to oblige thee to the subtle arguments of Clerks, since thou art unable thereto! but I purpose to make thee obey to the determination of Holy Church."
30 WILLIAM: And I said, "Sir, by open evidence and great witness, a thousand years after the Incarnation of CHRIST, that determination which I have, here before you, rehearsed was accepted of Holy Church, as sufficient to the salvation of all them that would believe it faithfully, and work thereafter charitably. But, Sir, the determination of this matter, which was brought in since the Fiend was loosed by Friar THOMAS [17] again, specially calling the most worshipful Sacrament of CHRIST's own body, an Accident without Subject; which term, since I know not that GOD's law approveth it in this matter, I dare not grant: but utterly I deny to make this friar's

15 A subject for debate in the university schools.
16 Scholars.
17 The great theologian, Thomas Aquinas (d. 1274).

sentence [18] or any such other my belief; do with me, GOD! what Thou wilt!"

*　　*　　*　　*　　*

ARCHBISHOP: And then he said to me, "What sayest thou, to the third point that is certified against thee, preaching openly in Shrewsbury that Pilgrimage is not lawful? And, over this, thou saidest that those men and women that go on pilgrimages to Canterbury, to Beverley, to Carlington, to Walsingham, and to any such other places, are accursed; and made foolish, spending their goods in waste."

WILLIAM: And I said, "Sir, by this Certification, I am accused to you, that I should teach that no pilgrimage is lawful. But I never said thus. For 10 I know that there be true pilgrimages, and lawful and full pleasant to GOD; and therefore, Sir, howsoever mine enemies have certified you of me, I told at Shrewsbury of two manner of pilgrimages."

ARCHBISHOP: And the Archbishop said to me, "Whom callest thou true pilgrims?"

WILLIAM: And I said, "Sir, with my Protestation, I call them true pilgrims traveling towards the bliss of heaven, which (in the state, degree, or order that GOD calleth them) do busy them faithfully for to occupy all their wits bodily and ghostly, to know truly and keep faithfully the biddings of GOD, hating and fleeing all the seven deadly sins and every branch 20 of them, ruling them virtuously, as it is said before, with all their wits, doing discreetly, wilfully and gladly all the works of mercy, bodily and ghostly, after their cunning and power abling them to the gifts of the HOLY GHOST, disposing them to receive in their souls, and to hold therein the right blessings of CHRIST; busying them to know and to keep the seven principal virtues: and so then they shall obtain herethrough grace for to use thankfully to GOD all the conditions of charity; and then they shall be moved with the good Spirit of GOD for to examine oft and diligently their conscience, that neither wilfully nor wittingly they err in any Article of Belief, having continually (as frailty will suffer) all their business to 30 dread and to flee the offence of GOD, and to love over all things and to seek ever to do His pleasant will.

"Of these pilgrims, I said, 'Whatsoever good thought that they any time think, what virtuous word that they speak, and what fruitful work that they work; every such thought, word, and work is a step numbered of GOD towards Him into Heaven. These foresaid pilgrims of GOD delight sore, when they hear of saints or of virtuous men and women, how they forsook wilfully the prosperity of this life, how they withstood the suggestion of the Fiend, how they restrained their fleshly lusts, how discreet they

---

[18] Enunciation.

were in their penance doing, how patient they were in all their adversities, how prudent they were in counseling of men and women, moving them to hate all sin and to flee them and to shame ever greatly thereof, and to love all virtues and to draw to them, imagining how CHRIST and His followers (by example of Him) suffered scorns and slanders, and how patiently they abode and took the wrongful menacing of tyrants, how homely [19] they were and serviceable to poor men to relieve and comfort them bodily and ghostly after their power and cunning, and how devout they were in prayers, how fervent they were in heavenly desires, and how they absented

10 them from spectacles of vain seeings and hearings, and how stable they were to let [20] and to destroy all vices, and how laborious and joyful they were to sow and plant virtues. These heavenly conditions and such others, have the pilgrims, or endeavor them for to have, whose pilgrimage GOD accepteth.'

"And again I said, 'As their works show, the most part of men or women that go now on pilgrimages have not these foresaid conditions; nor loveth to busy them faithfully for to have. For (as I well know, since I have full oft assayed) examine, whosoever will, twenty of these pilgrims! and he shall not find three men or women that know surely a Commandment of

20 GOD,[21] nor can say their *Pater noster* and *Ave Maria!* nor their *Credo,* readily in any manner of language. And as I have learned, and also know somewhat by experience of these same pilgrims, telling the cause why that many men and women go hither and thither now on pilgrimages, it is more for the health of their bodies, than of their souls! more for to have richesse and prosperity of this world, than for to be enriched with virtues in their souls! more to have here worldly and fleshly friendship, than for to have friendship of GOD and of His saints in heaven. For whatsoever thing a man or woman doth, the friendship of GOD, nor of any other Saint, cannot be had without keeping of GOD's commandments.'

30 "For with my Protestation, I say now, as I said at Shrewsbury, 'though they that have fleshly wills, travel for their bodies, and spend mickle money to seek and to visit the bones or images, as they say they do, of this saint and of that: such pilgrimage-going is neither praisable nor thankful to GOD, nor to any Saint of GOD; since, in effect, all such pilgrims despise GOD and all His commandments and Saints. For the commandments of GOD they will neither know nor keep, nor conform them to live virtuously by example of CHRIST and of his Saints.'

"Wherefore, Sir, I have preached and taught openly, and so I purpose all my lifetime to do, with GOD's help, saying that 'such fond people waste

40 blamefully GOD's goods in their vain pilgrimages, spending their goods

---

[19] Unpretentious.   [20] Hinder.   [21] The ten commandments.

upon vicious hostelers,[22] which are oft unclean women of their bodies; and at the least, those goods with the which, they should do works of mercy, after GOD's bidding, to poor needy men and women.'

"These poor men's goods and their livelihood, these runners about offer to rich priests! which have mickle more livelihood than they need: and thus those goods, they waste wilfully, and spend them unjustly, against GOD's bidding, upon strangers; with which they should help and relieve, after GOD's will, their poor needy neighbors at home. Yea, and over this folly, ofttimes divers men and women of these runners thus madly hither and thither into pilgrimage, borrow hereto other men's goods (yea, and sometimes they steal men's goods hereto), and they pay them never again.

"Also, Sir, I know well, that when divers men and women will go thus after their own wills, and finding out one pilgrimage, they will ordain with them before to have with them both men and women that can well sing wanton songs; and some other pilgrims will have with them bagpipes: so that every town that they come through, what with the noise of their singing, and with the sound of their piping, and with the jangling of their Canterbury bells, and with the barking of dogs after them, they make more noise than if the King came there away, with all his clarions and many other minstrels. And if these men and women be a month out in their pilgrimage, many of them shall be, a half year after, great janglers, tale-tellers, and liars."

ARCHBISHOP: And the Archbishop said to me, "Lewd losel! thou seest not far enough in this matter! for thou considerest not the great travail of pilgrims; therefore thou blamest that thing that is praisable! I say to thee, that is right well done; that pilgrims have with them both singers and also pipers: that when one of them that goeth barefoot striketh his toe upon a stone and hurteth him sore and maketh him to bleed; it is well done, that he or his fellow begin then a song or else take out of his bosom a bagpipe for to drive away with such mirth, the hurt of his fellow. For with such solace, the travail and weariness of pilgrims is lightly and merrily brought forth."

ALFRED W. POLLARD

[22] Innkeepers.

The Paston Letters

To my right worshipful husband, John Paston, dwelling in the Inner Temple at London, in haste.

Right worshipful husband, I recommend me to you, desiring heartily to hear of your welfare, thanking God of your amending of the great disease that ye have had, and I thank you for the letter that ye sent me, for by my troth my mother and I were naught in heart's ease from the time that we wist of your sickness till we wist verily of your amending.

My mother behested [1] another image of wax of the weight of you, to Our Lady of Walsingham, and she sent four nobles to the four orders of
10 friars at Norwich to pray for you, and I have behested to go on pilgrimage to Walsingham and to St. Leonard's [2] for you; by my troth I had never so heavy a season as I had from the time that I wist of your sickness till I wist of your amending, and yet my heart is in no great ease, nor naught shall be till I wit that ye be very whole. Your father and mine was this day sennight [3] at Beccles, for a matter of the prior of Bromholm, and he lay at Gelderstone that night, and was there till it was nine of the clock and the other day. And I sent thither for a gown, and my mother said that I should none have till I had been there anon, and so they could none get.

My father Garneys [4] sent me word that he should have been here the
20 next week and my eme [5] also, and play them here with their hawks, and they should have me home with them; and so God help me, I shall excuse me of my going thither if I may, for I suppose I shall more readily have tidings from you here than I should have there. I shall send my mother a token that she brought me, for I suppose that the time is come that I should send it her, if I keep the behest that I have made; I suppose I have told you what it was. I pray you heartily that ye will vouchsafe to send me a letter as hastily as ye may, if writing be none disease to you, and that ye will vouchsafe to send me word how your sore does. If I might have had my will, I should have seen you ere this time; I would ye were at home if it were
30 your ease, and your sore might be as well looked to here as it is where ye be now, liefer than a new gown though it were of scarlet. I pray you if your sore be whole and so that ye may endure to ride when my father cometh to London, that he will ask leave and come home when the horse should

---

[1] Promised.   [2] At Norwich.   [3] A week ago today.
[4] Probably her godfather.   [5] Uncle.

be sent home again, for I hope ye shall be kept as tenderly here as ye be in London. I may no leisure have to do write [6] half a quarter as much as I should say to you if I might speak with you. I shall send you another letter as hastily as I may. I thank you that ye would vouchsafe to remember my girdle, and that ye would write to me at the time, for I suppose that writing was no ease to you. Almighty God have you in His keeping and send you health. Written at Oxnead, in right great haste, on St. Michael's eve.[7]

Yours, M. PASTON

My mother greeteth you well and sendeth you God's blessing and hers; and she prayeth you, and I pray you also, that ye be well dieted of meat 10 and drink, for that is the greatest help that ye may have now to your health-ward. Your son fareth well, blessed be God!

Errands to London of Agnes Paston, the 28th day of January, 1457, the year of King Henry VI the 36th.

To pray Greenfield to send me faithfully word by writing how Clement Paston hath done his endeavor in learning. And if he hath not done well nor will not amend, pray him that he will truly belash him till he will amend; and so did the last master and the best that ever he had at Cambridge. And say to Greenfield that if he will take upon him to bring him into good rule and learning so that I may verily know he doth his endeavor, I will give 20 him ten marks, for his labor, for I had liefer he were fairly buried than lost for default.

Item, to see how many gowns Clement hath, and they that be bare, let them be raised [8] . . .

Item, to do make [9] me six spoons of eight ounces of troy weight, well fashioned and double gilt.

And say to Elizabeth Paston that she must use [10] herself to work readily, as other gentlewomen do, and somewhat to help herself therewith.

Item, to pay the Lady Pole 26s. and 8d. for her board.

And if Greenfield have done well his devoir to Clement, or will do his 30 devoir, give him the noble.

AGNES PASTON

To Sir John Paston, Knight.[11]

Sir, pleaseth it to understand that I conceive, by your letter that ye sent me by Juddy, that ye have heard of Richard Calle's labor which he maketh by our ungracious sister's assent; but whereas they write that they have

[6] Dictate, cause to be written.   [7] Date 1443.
[8] Have a new nap.   [9] Have made.   [10] Accustom.
[11] Date 1469. From his brother concerning a contract of marriage, made without the family's approval, between their sister Margery and Richard Calle, a business agent of John Paston's.

my good will therein, saving your reverence, they falsely lie of it, for they never spake to me of that matter nor none other body in their name. Lovell asked me once a question whether I understood how it was betwixt Richard Calle and my sister; I can think that it was by Calle's means, for when I asked him whether Calle desired him to move me that question or not, he would have gotten it away by hems and haws, but I would not so be answered. Wherefore at the last he told me that his eldest son desired him to spere [12] whether Richard Calle were sure of her or not, for he said that he knew a good marriage for her, but I wot he [Lovell] lied, for he is

10 whole with Richard Calle in that matter. Wherefore to the intent that he nor they should pick no comfort of me, I answered him that, an my father (whom God assoil!) were alive and had consented thereto, and my mother and ye both, he [Calle] should never have my good will for to make my sister to sell candle and mustard in Framlingham; and thus, with more which were too long to write to you, we departed. . .

JOHN PASTON

To Mistress Margery Paston.

Mine own lady and mistress and, before God, very true wife, I with heart full sorrowful recommend me unto you, as he that cannot be merry, nor

20 naught shall be till it be otherwise with us than it is yet. For this life that we lead now is neither pleasure to God nor to the world, considering the great bond of matrimony that is made betwixt us and also the great love that hath been and as I trust yet is betwixt us, and as on my part never greater. Wherefore I beseech Almighty God comfort us as soon as it pleaseth Him, for we that ought of very right to be most together are most asunder. Meseemeth it is a thousand year ago since I spake with you. I had liefer than all the good in the world that I might be with you. Alas, alas! good lady, full little remember they what they do that keep us thus asunder; four times in the year are they accursed that let matrimony.[13] It causeth many

30 men to deem in them they have large [14] conscience in other matters as well as herein. But what, lady, suffer as ye have done, and make you as merry as ye can, for ywis,[15] lady, at the long way God will of His righteousness help His servants that mean truly and would live according to His laws, etc.

I understand, lady, ye have had as much sorrow for me as any gentlewoman hath had in the world, as would God all that sorrow that ye have had had rested upon me, and that ye had been discharged of it. For ywis, lady, it is to me a death to hear that ye be treated otherwise than ye ought

---

[12] Inquire.

[13] Excommunication was pronounced four times a year on all who offended against the Church, including those who broke up (let) marriages.

[14] Loose.   [15] Surely.

to be. This is a painful life that we lead. I cannot live thus without it be a great displeasure to God.

Also like you to wit [16] that I had sent you a letter by my lad from London, and he told me that he might not speak with you, there was made so great await upon him and upon you both. He told me John Thresher came to him in your name, and said that ye sent him to my lad for a letter or a token which I should have sent you; but he [the lad] trusted him not; he would not deliver him none. After that he [Thresher] brought him a ring, saying that ye sent it him that he should deliver the letter or token to him; which I conceive, since by [17] my lad it was not by your sending, it was by my [10] mistress' and Sir James' advice. Alas! what mean they? I suppose they deem we be not ensured together, and if they so do, I marvel, for then they are not well advised, remembering the plainness that I brake [18] to my mistress at the beginning, and I suppose by you, both, an ye did as ye ought to do of very right. And if ye have done the contrary, as I have been informed ye have done, ye did neither conscientiously nor to the pleasure of God, without [19] ye did it for fear and for the time, to please such as were at that time about you. And if ye did it for this cause, it was a reasonable cause, considering the great and importable calling upon [20] that ye had, and many an untrue tale was made to you of me, which, God know it, I was never [20] guilty of. . . .

Mistress, I am afraid to write to you, for I understand ye have showed my letters that I have sent you before this time. But I pray you let no creature see this letter; as soon as ye have read it, let it be burnt, for I would no man should see it in no wise. Ye had no writing from me this two year, nor will I send you no more; therefore I remit all this matter to your wisdom. Almighty Jesu preserve, keep, and give you your heart's desire, which I wot well should be to God's pleasure, etc.

This letter was written with as great pain as ever wrote I thing in my life, for in good faith I have been right sick, and yet am not verily at ease, [30] God amend it, etc.

RICHARD CALLE

To Sir John Paston, Knight.

I greet you well and send you God's blessing and mine, letting you wit that, on Thursday last was, my mother and I were with my lord [21] of Norwich, and desired him that he would no more do in the matter touching your sister till ye and my brother and others that were executors to your father might be here together, for they had the rule of her as well as I.

---

[16] May it please you to know.
[17] According to.
[18] The frankness with which I explained.
[19] Unless.
[20] Insupportable scolding.
[21] The bishop.

And he said plainly that he had been required so often to examine her that he might not nor would no longer delay it, and charged me on pain of cursing that she should not be deferred but that she should appear before him the next day. And I said plainly that I would neither bring her nor send her. And then he said that he would send for her himself, and charged that she should be at her liberty to come when he sent for her. And he said by his troth that he would be as sorry for her an she did not well as he would be an she were right near of his kin, both for my mother's sake and mine and other of her friends, for he wist well that her demeaning [22] had stuck
10 sore at our hearts.

My mother and I informed him that we could never understand by her saying, by no language that ever she had to him, that neither of them were bound to other, but that they might choose both. Then he said that he would say to her as well as he could before he examined her; and so it was told me by divers persons that he did as well and as plainly as she had been right near to him, which were too long to write at this time; hereafter ye shall wit and who were laborers therein. The chancellor was not so guilty therein as I weened he had been.

On Friday the bishop sent for her by Ashfield and others that are right
20 sorry of her demeaning, and the bishop said to her right plainly and put her in remembrance how she was born, what kin and friends she had, and should have more if she were ruled and guided after them; and if she did not, what rebuke and shame and loss should be to her if she were not guided by them, and cause of forsaking [23] of her for any good or help or comfort that she should have of them; and said that he had heard say that she loved such one that her friends were not pleased well with that she should have, and therefore he bade her be right well advised how she did; and said that he would understand the words that she had said to him, whether it made matrimony or not. And she rehearsed what she had said, and said if those
30 words made it not sure, she said boldly that she would make it surer ere she went thence; for she said she thought in her conscience she was bound whatsoever the words were. These lewd words grieve me and her grandam as much as all the remnant. And then the bishop and the chancellor both said that there was neither I nor no friend of hers would receive her.

And then Calle was examined apart by himself, that her words and his accorded, and the time and where it should have been done. And then the bishop said that he supposed that there should be found other things against him that might cause the letting [24] thereof; and therefore he said he would not be too hasty to give sentence thereupon, and said that he would
40 give over day till the Wednesday or Thursday after Michaelmas, and so

---

[22] Demeanor, conduct. [23] It would be the cause of their forsaking.
[24] Annulment.

it is delayed. They would have had her will performed in haste, but the bishop said he would none otherwise than he had said.

I was with my mother at her place when she was examined, and when I heard say what her demeaning was, I charged my servants that she should not be received in my house. I had given her warning; she might have been aware before if she had been gracious. . . As for the divorce that ye write to me of,[25] I suppose what ye meant, but I charge you upon my blessing that ye do not nor cause none other to do that should offend God and your conscience. For, an ye do or cause for to be done, God will take vengeance thereupon, and ye should put yourself and others in great jeopardy. For 10 wot it well she shall full sore repent her lewdness [26] hereafter, and I pray God she might so. I pray you for mine heart's ease be ye of a good comfort in all things; I trust God shall help right well, and I pray God so do in all our matters. I would ye took heed if there were any labor made in the court of Canterbury [27] for the lewd matter aforesaid.

[MARGARET PASTON] [28]

Unto my right worshipful cousin, John Paston, be this letter delivered, etc.

Right worshipful cousin, I recommend me unto you, etc. And I sent my husband a bill [29] of the matter that ye know of, and he wrote another bill to me again touching the same matter, and he would that ye should 20 go unto my mistress, your mother, and essay if ye might get the whole 20 pounds into your hands, and then he would be more glad to marry with you,[30] and will give you a 100 pounds; and, cousin, that day that she is married, my father will give her 50 marks. But, an we accord, I shall give you a great treasure, that is, a witty [31] gentlewoman, and if I say it, both good and virtuous; for, if I should take money for her, I would not give her for a 1000 pounds. But, cousin, I trust you so much that I would think her well beset [32] on you an ye were worth much more. And, cousin, a little after ye were gone, came a man from my cousin Derby and brought me word that such a change fell that he [Derby] might not come at the day 30 that was set, as I shall let you understand more plainly when I speak with you, etc. But, cousin, an it would please you to come again, what day that ye will set I dare undertake that they shall keep the same day; for I would be glad that, an my husband and ye might accord in this marriage, it might

---

[25] Apparently, if the bishop decided that the marriage contract was valid, Sir John had proposed divorcing the pair.
[26] Folly.   [27] The court of the archbishop.
[28] The letter is unsigned, but on the back is a note stating that it was written by Sir John's mother, and that Margery and Calle were afterwards formally married. The date is 1469.
[29] Letter.   [30] To marry his daughter to you.
[31] Intelligent.   [32] Bestowed.

be my fortune to make an end of this matter between my cousins and you,[33] that each of you might love other in friendly wise, etc. And, cousin, if this bill please not your intent, I pray you that it may be burnt, etc. No more unto you at this time, but Almighty Jesu preserve you, etc.

By your cousin,
DAME ELIZABETH BREWS

Unto my right well-beloved Valentine, John Paston, Esq., be this bill delivered, etc.

Right reverend and worshipful and my right well-beloved Valentine, I
10 recommend me unto you, full heartily desiring to hear of your welfare, which I beseech Almighty God long for to preserve unto His pleasure and your heart's desire. And if it please you to hear of my welfare, I am not in good health of body nor of heart, nor shall be till I hear from you.

> For there wotteth no creature what pain that I endure,
> And, for to be dead, I dare it not discure.[34]

And my lady, my mother, hath labored [35] the matter to my father full diligently, but she can no more get than ye know of,[36] for the which God knoweth I am full sorry. But if ye love me, as I trust verily that ye do, ye will not leave me therefor. For if ye had not half the livelihood [37] that ye
20 have, for to do the greatest labor that any woman alive might, I would not forsake you.

> And if ye command me to keep me true wherever I go,
> Ywis I will do all my might you to love, and never no mo.[38]
> And if my friends say that I do amiss,
> They shall not me let [39] so for to do.
> Mine heart me bids evermore to love you
> Truly over all earthly thing,
> And if they be never so wroth,
> I trust it shall be better in time coming.

30 No more to you at this time, but the Holy Trinity have you in keeping; and I beseech you that this bill be not seen of none earthly creature save only yourself, etc. And this letter was endited at Topcroft, with full heavy heart, etc.

By your own,
MARGERY BREWS

---

[33] Evidently there had been ill feeling between John Paston and Elizabeth Brews' relations.

[34] To save my life, I dare not reveal it.   [35] Urged.

[36] I.e. cannot get him to give a more liberal dowery.   [37] Income.

[38] Never any others.   [39] Prevent.

To my right well-beloved cousin, John Paston, Esq., be this letter delivered, etc.

Right worshipful and well-beloved Valentine, in my most humble wise I recommend me unto you, etc. And heartily I thank you for the letter which ye sent me by John Beckerton, whereby I understand and know that ye be purposed to come to Topcroft in short time, and without any errand or matter but only to have a conclusion of the matter betwixt my father and you. I would be most glad of any creature, so that the matter might grow to effect. And whereas ye say, an ye come and find the matter no more towards you than ye did aforetime, ye would no more put my 10 father and my lady, my mother, to no cost nor business for that cause a good while after, which causeth mine heart to be full heavy. And if ye come and the matter take to none effect, then should I be much more sorry and full of heaviness.

And, as for myself, I have done and understood [40] in the matter what I can or may, as God knoweth. And I let you plainly understand that my father will no more money part withal in that behalf but an 100 pounds and 50 marks, which is right far from the accomplishment of your desire. Wherefore, if ye could be content with that good and my poor person, I would be the merriest maiden on ground. And if ye think not yourself 20 so satisfied, or that ye might have much more good,[41] as I have understood by you before, good, true, and loving Valentine, take ye no such labor upon you as to come more for that matter, but let what is pass, and never more to be spoken of, as I may be your true lover and beadswoman during my life.

No more unto you at this time, but Almighty Jesu preserve you both body and soul, etc.

By your Valentine,
MARGERY BREWS

To his right reverend brother, Sir John Paston, at Caister Hall in Norfolk. 30

After all due reverence and recommendations, liketh it you to understand that I received a letter from my brother John, whereby I understood that my mother and you would know what the costs of my proceeding [42] should be. I sent a letter to my brother John certifying my costs and the causes why I would proceed, but, as I have sent word to my mother, I purpose to tarry now till it be Michaelmas, for if I tarry till then, some of my costs shall be paid. For I supposed, when I sent the letter to my brother John, that the Queen's brother should have proceeded at Midsummer, but he will tarry now till Michaelmas. But, as I sent word to my mother, I

---

[40] Undertaken (?).   [41] Get a larger dowery.
[42] Advancement to the degree of Bachelor of Arts.

would be inceptor [43] before Midsummer, and therefore I besought her to send me some money, for it will be some cost to me, but not much.

Sir, I beseech you to send me word what answer ye have of the Bishop of Winchester for that matter which ye spake to him of for me when I was with you at London. I thought for to have had word thereof ere this time. I would it would come, for our finding of [44] the Bishop of Norwich beginneth to be slack in payment. And if ye know not what this term meaneth, "inceptor," Master Edmund, that was my ruler at Oxford, bearer hereof, can tell you, or else any other graduate.

10   Also, I pray you send me word what is done with the horse I left at Tottenham, and whether the man be content that I had it of, or not. Jesu preserve you to His pleasure and to your most heart's desire. Written at Oxford the Saturday next after the Ascension of Our Lord.

WALTER PASTON [45]

[43] Graduate.   [44] Support from.   [45] The date is 1479.

𝕿𝖍𝖊 𝕾𝖊𝖈𝖔𝖓𝖉 𝕾𝖍𝖊𝖕𝖍𝖊𝖗𝖉𝖘' 𝕻𝖑𝖆𝖞 [1]

from the

Wakefield Mystery Cycle

DRAMATIS PERSONAE

FIRST SHEPHERD (Coll)
SECOND SHEPHERD (Gib)
THIRD SHEPHERD (Daw), a youth
MAK
JILL
ANGEL
MARY

SCENE I

[*Scene a moor. Enter* FIRST SHEPHERD, *stamping his feet and blowing on his nails.*]

FIRST SHEPHERD:

Lord, but it's cold and wretchedly I'm wrapped;
My wits are frozen, so long it is I've napped;
My legs are cramped, and every finger chapped.
All goes awry; in misery I'm trapped.
By storms and gales distressed,
Now in the east, now west,
Woe's him who gets no rest!
We simple shepherds walking on the moor,
We're like, in faith, to be put out of door,
And it's no wonder if we are so poor.   10
Our fields they lie as fallow as a floor;
We're driven till we're bowed;
We're taxed until we're cowed
By gentry, rich and proud.

---

[1] Reprinted from *Representative Medieval and Tudor Plays,* ed. by Roger S. Loomis and Henry W. Wells (Sheed and Ward, New York), by permission of the publishers.

They take our rest; them may our Lady blast!
For their own lords they make our plows stick fast.
Some say it's for the best, but at the last
We know that's false. We tenants are downcast,
And always we're kept under.
If we don't thrive, no wonder   20
When they so rob and plunder.
A man with broidered sleeve or brooch, these days,
Can ruin anyone who him gainsays.
There's not a soul believes one word he says,
Or dares rebuke him for his bumptious ways.
He makes his pride and boast,
He gets his very post
From those who have the most.
There comes a fellow, proud as a peacock, now,
He'd carry off my wagon and my plow.   30
Before he'd leave, I must seem glad and bow.
A wretched life we lead, you must allow.
Whatever he has willed
Must be at once fulfilled,
Or surely I'd be killed.
It does me good, when I walk round alone,
About this world to grumble and to groan.
Now to my sheep I'll slowly walk, and moan,
And rest awhile on some old balk or stone.
Some other men I'll see;   40
Before it's noon I'll be
In true men's company.

> [*Enter* SECOND SHEPHERD, *not noticing*
> FIRST SHEPHERD.]

SECOND SHEPHERD:
Good Lord, good Lord, what does this misery mean?
What ails the world? The like has seldom been.
The weather's spiteful cold and bitter keen;
My eyes they weep, such hideous frosts they've seen.
Now in the snow and sleet
My shoes freeze to my feet;
No easy life I meet.
So far as I can see, where'er I go,   50
The griefs of married men increase and grow.
We're always out of luck; I tell you so.
Capul, our hen, goes cackling to and fro,

But if she starts to croak,
Our cock suffers a stroke;
For him it is no joke.
These wedded men have never once their will;
When they're hard pressed, they sigh and just keep still,
Groan to themselves and take the bitter pill.
God knows they've got a nasty part to fill!   60
And as for me I've found—
I know the lesson's sound—
Woe to the man who's bound!
Late in my life it still amazes me,
And my heart stops such miracles to see;
But yet when destiny drives, such things can be:
Some men have two wives, some have even three!
But if his lot is sore
Who has one wife in store,
It's hell for him with more!   70
Young men who'd woo, before you're fairly caught,
Beware of wedding! Give the matter thought.
To moan, "Had I but known!" will help you nought.
Much misery has wedding often brought,
And many a stormy shower.
You catch in one short hour
A lifelong taste of sour.
I've one for mate, if ever I read the Epistle,
Who's rough as is a briar and sharp as thistle.
Her looks are sour; her eyebrows, like hog's bristle.   80
She'd sing "Our Father" if once she wet her whistle.
And like a whale she's fat,
Full of gall as a vat.
I don't know where I'm at.

FIRST SHEPHERD:
    Gib, look over the hedge! Are you deaf or no?

SECOND SHEPHERD:
    The devil take you! Was ever man so slow?
    Have you seen Daw?

FIRST SHEPHERD:
        Just now I heard him blow
    His horn. I see him on the lea below.
    Be quiet!

SECOND SHEPHERD:
        Tell me why.   90

FIRST SHEPHERD:

I think he's coming by.

SECOND SHEPHERD:

He'll trick us with some lie.

> [FIRST *and* SECOND SHEPHERDS *hide.*
> *Enter* THIRD SHEPHERD.]

THIRD SHEPHERD:

May Christ's cross help me, and St. Nicholas!
I've need of it; life's harder than it was.
Let men beware and let the false world pass.
It slips and slides, more brittle far than glass.
Never did it change so,
For now it's weal, now woe.
It's all a passing show.
Since Noah's flood, such floods were never seen,   100
Such dreadful winds and rains, and storms so keen.
Folk stammer or stand dumb with fear, I ween.
God turn it all to good! That's what I mean.
Just think how these floods drown
Us out in field and town;
No wonder that we're down.
We that walk at night, our herds to keep,
We see queer sights when others are asleep.

> [*He spies the other shepherds.*]

My heart jumps. There I see two fellows peep,
Tall rascals both. I'll turn back to my sheep.   110
It was a bad mistake
This lonely path to take;
My toes I'll stub and break.

> [FIRST *and* SECOND SHEPHERDS *come forward.*]

May God save you, and you, O master sweet!
I want a drink and then a bite to eat.

FIRST SHEPHERD:

Christ's curse, my boy, but you're a lazy cheat!

SECOND SHEPHERD:

Does the boy rave? Let him wait for his meat!
Bad luck now on your pate!
The wretch, though he comes late,
Would eat, so starved his state.   120

THIRD SHEPHERD:

Servants like me, who always sweat and swink,
We eat our bread too dry, that's what I think.

[442]

We're wet and weary while our masters blink.
It's late before we get to eat or drink.
Grand dame and noble sire
Delay and dock our hire,
Though we have run through mire.
But hear a truth, my master, for God's sake!
A fuss about my appetite you make!
But never supper gave me stomach-ache.   130
Henceforth I'll work as little as I take;
Or I can run away.
What one buys cheap, they say,
Won't in the long run pay.

FIRST SHEPHERD:
A fool you'd be if you yourself should bring
To serve a man who'd not spend anything.

SECOND SHEPHERD:
Peace, boy! I want no more rude chattering.
Or I will make you smart, by Heaven's King!
Our sheep are they left lorn?

THIRD SHEPHERD:
This very day at morn   140
I left them in the corn.
They have good pasture, so they can't go wrong.

FIRST SHEPHERD:
That's right. Oh, by the Rood, these nights are long!
Before we go, I wish we'd have a song.

SECOND SHEPHERD:
I thought myself 'twould cheer us all along.

THIRD SHEPHERD:
I'm set.

FIRST SHEPHERD:
         Tenor I'll try.

SECOND SHEPHERD:
And I the treble high.

THIRD SHEPHERD:
Then the middle am I.   150

> *Then* MAK *enters with a cloak drawn*
> *over his tunic.*

MAK:
Lord, of seven names, who made the moon that sails
And more stars than I know, Thy good will fails.
My brain is in a whirl; it's that which ails.

I wish I were in heaven where no child wails.

FIRST SHEPHERD:

Who is it pipes so poor?

MAK:

God knows what I endure,

A-walking on the moor!

SECOND SHEPHERD [*stepping forward*]:

Where do you come from, Mak? What news d'you bring?

THIRD SHEPHERD:

Is he come? Keep close watch on everything!

He snatches the cloak from him.

MAK [*with a southern accent*]:

I tell you I'm a yeoman of the King.   160

Make way for me! Lord's messages I bring.

Fie on you! Get ye hence!

This is no mere pretense.

I must have reverence!

FIRST SHEPHERD:

Why put on airs, Mak? It's no good to try.

SECOND SHEPHERD:

Or play the actor, for I know you lie.

THIRD SHEPHERD:

The scamp talks well, the Devil hang him high!

MAK:

I'll make complaint; I'll make you sizzle and fry!

I'll tell on you, in sooth.

FIRST SHEPHERD:

O Mak, ere you speak truth,   170

Take out your Southron tooth!

SECOND SHEPHERD:

The Devil's in your eye. You need a whack!

[*Strikes* MAK.]

THIRD SHEPHERD:

So you don't know me? I'll teach you better, Mak!

MAK [*changing his tune*]:

God keep all three! What I said I take back.

You're all good fellows.

FIRST SHEPHERD:

Now you've changed your tack.

SECOND SHEPHERD:

Why out so late, pray tell?

Everyone knows right well

You love roast-mutton smell. 180

MAK:

Ι'm true as steel, as anyone will say,
But I've a sickness takes my health away.
My belly's in a parlous state today.

THIRD SHEPHERD:

"The Devil seldom lies dead by the way."

MAK:

As still as stone I'll lie,
If this whole month have I
Eat even a needle's eye.

FIRST SHEPHERD:

How is your wife? how is she? tell us true.

MAK:

She's sprawling by the fire; that's nothing new.
The house is full of brats. She drinks ale, too. 190
Come good or ill, that she will always do.
She eats fast as she can,
And each year gives a man
A babe or two to scan.
Though I had much more money in my purse,
She'd eat and drink us to the Devil, sirs.
Just look at her near by, the ugly curse!
Will no one rid me of her?
I'd give all in my coffer
Mass for her soul to offer. 200

SECOND SHEPHERD:

I swear there's no one so tired in this shire.
I must get sleep though I take less for hire.

THIRD SHEPHERD:

I'm cold and nearly naked; I'd like a fire.

FIRST SHEPHERD:

And I'm worn out with running in the mire.
Keep watch.

        [Lies down.]

SECOND SHEPHERD:

      Not so, for I
Must sleep. I'll put me by.

        [Lies down.]

THIRD SHEPHERD:

Equal with you I'll lie.

        [Lies down.]

Here, Mak, come here! Between us you must be.

MAK:

You're sure you don't want to talk privately?

                             [Lies down, crosses himself and prays.]

And now from head to toe   210
Manus tuas commendo,
Pontio Pilato.

MAK, *while the* SHEPHERDS *sleep, rises and says:*

Now is the time for one who's short of gold
To enter stealthily into a fold
And nimbly work and yet be not too bold,
For he might rue the bargain if 'twere told.
He must be shrewd and wise
Who likes his victuals nice,
Yet hasn't got the price.

                                 [Pretends to be a magician.]

A circle round the moon I here fulfill.   220
Until it's noon or I have done my will,
You must each one lie there and be stone still.
To make it sure some good strong words I'll spill.
Over you my hands I lift;
Your eyes go out and drift
Till I make better shift.
Lord, but they're sleeping sound! All men can hear!
I never was a shepherd, but now I'll learn their gear,
And though the flock be scared, I'll creep right near.
This fat sheep with its fleece improves my cheer.   230
And now goodbye to sorrow!

                                 [Seizes sheep.]

Though I pay not tomorrow,
I'll in the meantime borrow.

                                 [Exit MAK.*]*

SCENE II

[Interior of MAK's *cottage.* JILL *sits spinning.]*

MAK *[outside]:*

Jill, are you in? Hello, get us some light!

JILL:

Who makes this racket at this time of night?
I'm busy spinning; I'll not stir a mite

To get a day's pay. Curses on you light!
It's thus a housewife fares.
She's always rushed with cares,
And all for nothing bears!

MAK [*outside*]:

Open the latch, good wife! See what I bring!

JILL:

I'll let you pull. ·

[*Opens door.* MAK *enters.*]

JILL:

Come in, my own sweet thing!

MAK:

Not much you care how long I stand and sing!   10

JILL:

By your bare neck, for this you're like to swing!

MAK:

I'm good for something yet;
For at a pinch I get
More than the fools who sweat.
I had a lucky lot and God's own grace.

JILL:

To hang for it would be a foul disgrace!

MAK:

I've dodged before, my Jill, as hard a case.

JILL:

Folk say that just so long a pot or vase
To water it can come,
Then broken it's brought home.   20

MAK:

On that old saw be dumb!
I wish that he were skinned; I want to eat.
For twelve months I've not hankered so for meat.

JILL:

Suppose they come here first and hear him bleat!

MAK:

They'd catch me then. That puts me in a heat.
Go bolt the door at back!
I'd get from that whole pack
The devil of a whack!

JILL:

A good trick I have spied since you have none:

We'll hide him in the crib till they have done.
I'll lie and groan and say that he's my son.
Let me alone to do what I've begun.

MAK:

And I will say, tonight
Of this boy you are light.

JILL:

It's luck I was born bright.
For cleverness this trick can't be surpassed.
A woman's wit helps always at the last.
Before they get suspicious, hurry fast.

MAK:

If I don't get there soon, they'll blow a blast!

[*Exit* MAK.]

SCENE III

[*The moor.* SHEPHERDS *sleeping. Enter* MAK.]

MAK:

These men are still asleep.
Their company I'll keep
As if I'd stolen no sheep.

[*Lies down between them.*]
[SHEPHERDS *wake one by one, and cross
themselves.*]

FIRST SHEPHERD:

Resurrex a mortruis! Here, take my hand!
Judas carnas Dominus! I can't well stand.
My foot's asleep and I'm as dry as sand.
I dreamt we lay down near the English land!

SECOND SHEPHERD:

I slept so well, I feel
As fresh as any eel,
And light upon my heel!

10

THIRD SHEPHERD:

Lord bless us all! My body's all a-quake!
My heart jumps from my skin, and that's no fake.
Who's making all this din and my head ache?
I'll teach him something! hear, you fellows, wake!
Where's Mak?

FIRST SHEPHERD:

I vow he's near.
He went nowhere, that's clear.

THIRD SHEPHERD:
    I dreamt he was dressed up in a wolf's skin.
FIRST SHEPHERD:
    That's what too many rogues are wrapped up in!
THIRD SHEPHERD:
    While we were snoozing, seemed he did begin
    To catch a sheep, without the slightest din.   20
SECOND SHEPHERD:
    Your dream has made you brood
    On phantoms, by the Rood.
    May God turn all to good!

                          [Shakes MAK.]

    Rise, Mak, for shame! You're sleeping far too long.
MAK:
    Now may Christ's holy name keep us from wrong!
    What's this? St. James! I can hardly move along.
    I'm just the same, and yet my neck's all wrong.

                   [SHEPHERDS *help him to his feet.*]

    Thank you! It's still uneven
    For I've been plagued since even
    With nightmares, by St. Stephen!   30
    I thought that Jill she groaned in travail bad;
    At the first cockcrow she had borne a lad
    To increase our flock. Guess whether I am glad!
    That's more wool on my distaff than I had!
    Woe's him who has no bread
    For young ones to be fed.
    The Devil crack each head!
    I must go home to Jill; she's in my thought.
    Just look into my sleeve that I steal nought.
    I wouldn't grieve you or take from you aught.   40
THIRD SHEPHERD:
    Go on, bad luck to you!

                          [Exit MAK.]

       I think we ought
    To count our sheep this morn.
FIRST SHEPHERD:
    I'll see if any's gone.
THIRD SHEPHERD:
    We'll meet at the Crooked Thorn.

                   [*Exeunt* SHEPHERDS.]

SCENE IV

[*Interior of* MAK's *cottage.* JILL *at work.*]

MAK [*outside*]:

Undo this door! How long shall I stand here?

JILL:

Go walk in the waning moon! Who's shouting there?

MAK [*outside*]:

It's me, your husband, Mak. Hey, Jill, what cheer?

JILL:

Now we shall see the Devil hanged, that's clear.
I seem to hear a sound
As if a rope were round
His throat, and tightly bound.

MAK [*outside*]:

Just hear the fuss she makes for an excuse;
She doesn't do a stroke but to amuse.

JILL:

Who sits up late? Who comes and goes? Who brews?   10
Who bakes? Whose hand knits stockings, tell me, whose?

[*Opens the door.* MAK *enters.*]

It's a pity to behold,
Whether in hot or cold,
A womanless household!
But tell me how you left the herdsmen, Mak.

MAK:

The last word that they said when I turned back
Was that they'd count the sheep, the cursed pack!
They'll not be pleased to find a sheep they lack!
And so, however it goes,
They surely will suppose   20
From me the trouble rose.
You'll keep your promise?

JILL:

Why, of course, I will.
I'll put him in the cradle, and with skill
I'll swaddle him. Trust in a pinch to Jill!

[*She wraps sheep and puts it in cradle.
Goes to bed.*]

Come tuck me up. I'll lie here very still.
It may be a narrow squeak.

[450]

MAK:

> Yes, if too close they peek,
> Or if the sheep should speak!

JILL:

> Hark, when they call, for they'll be here anon.
> Let everything be ready. Sing alone   30
> A lullaby, for I must lie and groan
> And cry out by the wall on Mary and John.
> You sing the lullaby,
> And never doubt that I
> Will pull wool over their eye.

SCENE V

[*The moor. Enter three* SHEPHERDS.]

THIRD SHEPHERD:

> Good morrow, Coll. What's wrong? Why not asleep?

FIRST SHEPHERD:

> Alas that I was born! For this we'll keep
> A villain's name. We've lost a good fat sheep!

SECOND SHEPHERD:

> God save us! Who on us such wrong would heap?

FIRST SHEPHERD:

> Some rascal. With my dogs
> I've searched through Horbury Shrogs,
> Found one ewe of fifteen hogs.[2]

THIRD SHEPHERD:

> Trust me, by Thomas, holy saint of Kent,
> 'Twas Mak or Jill who on that theft was bent.

FIRST SHEPHERD:

> Peace, man, be quiet. I saw when he went.   10
> You slander him unjustly and should repent.

SECOND SHEPHERD:

> Though I may never succeed,
> I'd say it though I bleed,
> 'Twas he who did the deed.

THIRD SHEPHERD:

> Then let's go thither at a running trot.
> I won't eat bread till at the truth I've got.

FIRST SHEPHERD:

> And I won't drink until I've solved the plot.

---

[2] Young sheep.

SECOND SHEPHERD:

>Until I find him, I won't rest one jot.
>I make this vow aright:
>Till I have him in sight   20
>I will not sleep one night
>In the same spot.

>   [*Exeunt.*]

SCENE VI

[MAK's *cottage. Within* MAK *sings,* JILL *groans.* SHEPHERDS *approach the door.*]

THIRD SHEPHERD:

>D'you hear them sing? Mak thinks that he can croon!

FIRST SHEPHERD:

>I never heard a voice so out of tune!

SECOND SHEPHERD:

>Hey, Mak, open your door, and do it soon.

MAK:

>Who is it shouts as if it were high noon?

THIRD SHEPHERD:

>Good men, if it were day—

MAK [*opening door*]:

>As much as ever you may,
>Speak very soft, I pray.
>Here is a woman sick and ill at ease;
>I'd rather die than she had more misease.

JILL:

>Go to some other place, I beg you, please, 10
>Each footfall knocks my nose and makes me sneeze.

FIRST SHEPHERD:

>How are you, Mak, I say?

MAK:

>And how are you today,
>And what brings you this way?
>You're wet all through; you've run so in the mire.
>If you'll sit down, I'll light you here a fire.
>I've got what's coming to me. I'm no liar;
>My dream's come true; a nurse I've got to hire.
>I've more babes than you knew.
>Surely the saying's true: 20
>"We must drink what we brew."

Stay eat before you go; I see you sweat.

SECOND SHEPHERD:

Nothing will cheer us, neither drink nor meat.

MAK:

What ails you, sir?

THIRD SHEPHERD:

We've had a loss that's great;

We found a sheep was stolen, when we met.

MAK:

Alas! Had I been there,

Someone had paid full dear.

FIRST SHEPHERD:

Marry, some think you were!

SECOND SHEPHERD:

Yes, Mak, just tell us who else could it be?

THIRD SHEPHERD:

'Twas either you or else your wife, say we.   30

MAK:

If you suspect us, either Jill or me,

Come rip our house apart, and then you'll see

That here within this spot

No sheep or cow I've got;

And Jill's not stirred a jot.

As I am true and leal, to God I pray,

This is the first meal that I've had today.

FIRST SHEPHERD:

Upon my soul, Mak, have a care, I say;

He's early learned to steal who can't say nay.

[SHEPHERDS *begin to search.*]

JILL:

Out, thieves, get out from here!   40

MAK:

When her great groans you hear,

Your hearts should melt for fear.

JILL:

Out, thieves; don't touch my child! Get out the door!

MAK:

Knew you her pangs, your conscience would be sore.

You're wrong, I warn you, thus to come before

A woman in her pain. I say no more.

JILL:

O God, who art so mild,

[453]

If you I e'er beguiled,
Let me eat up this child!

MAK:

Peace, woman, for God's passion, speak more low!   50
You spoil your brains and terrify me so.

SECOND SHEPHERD:

I think our sheep is slain. Think you not so?

THIRD SHEPHERD:

We search here all in vain. We may well go.
There's nothing I can find,
No bone or scrap or rind,
But empty plates behind.
Here's no tame cattle, and no wild there is
That smells like our old ram, I'll swear to this.

JILL:

You're right; and of this child God give me bliss!

FIRST SHEPHERD:

I think we've failed and that we've done amiss.   60

SECOND SHEPHERD:

Dame, is't a boy you have?
Him may Our Lady save!

MAK:

A son a lord might crave.
He grabs so when he wakes, it's a joy to see.

THIRD SHEPHERD:

Luck on his buttocks! Happy may they be!
But who god-fathered him so hurriedly?

MAK [*hesitating*]:

Blest be their lips!

FIRST SHEPHERD:

                    A lie it's going to be!

MAK:

Gibbon Waller was one,
And Perkin's mother's son;
John Horn supplied the fun.   70

SECOND SHEPHERD:

Mak, let us all be friends again, I say.

MAK [*haughtily*]:

It's little friendship you've shown me today.
Goodbye, I'm glad to see you go away.

[454]

THIRD SHEPHERD:

    Fair words, no warmth—that's just as plain as day.

                         [SHEPHERDS *turn to go out.*]

FIRST SHEPHERD:

    Gave you the child a thing?

SECOND SHEPHERD:

    Not even one farthing!

THIRD SHEPHERD:

    Wait here; fast back I'll fling.

                 [THIRD SHEPHERD *returns.* SECOND *and*

                        FIRST SHEPHERDS *follow.*]

THIRD SHEPHERD:

    To see your baby, Mak, I ask your leave.

MAK:

    No. Only insults from you I receive.

THIRD SHEPHERD:

    Well, it won't make that little daystar grieve   80

    If you let me give sixpence, I believe.

                          [*Approaches cradle.*]

MAK:

    Go way; I say he sleeps.

THIRD SHEPHERD:

    I think instead he peeps.

MAK:

    When he wakes up, he weeps.

THIRD SHEPHERD:

    Just let me kiss him once and lift the clout.

    What in the devil! What a monstrous snout!

FIRST SHEPHERD:

    He's birth-marked maybe. Let's not wait about!

    The ill-spun cloth in truth comes foully out.

    He looks like our own sheep!

THIRD SHEPHERD:

    What, Gib! give me a peep.   90

FIRST SHEPHERD:

    Where Truth can't walk 'twill creep.

SECOND SHEPHERD:

    That was a clever trick, a shabby fraud!

    The bare-faced swindle should be noised abroad.

THIRD SHEPHERD:

    Yes, sirs, let's bind her fast and burn the bawd.

If she should hang, everyone would applaud.
Tucked in a cradle so,
I never saw, I vow,
A boy with horns till now!

MAK:

Peace, peace I ask! You'll give the child a scare.
For I'm his father and that's his mother there.   100

FIRST SHEPHERD:

What devil is he named for? Look, Mak's heir!

SECOND SHEPHERD:

Let be all that! I say, God give him care!

JILL:

A pretty child is he
To sit on woman's knee,
And make his father glee!

THIRD SHEPHERD:

I know him by his earmark, a good token.

MAK:

I tell you, sirs, his nose in truth was broken.
He was bewitched; so has a wise clerk spoken.

FIRST SHEPHERD:

Liar! you deserve to have your noddle broken!

JILL:

An elf took him away;   110
I saw him changed for aye
At stroke of twelve today.

SECOND SHEPHERD:

You two are fit to lie in the same bed!

THIRD SHEPHERD:

Since they maintain their theft, let's leave them dead.

MAK:

If I do wrong again, cut off my head!
I'm at your will.

THIRD SHEPHERD:

        Men, take my plan instead.
We'll neither curse nor fight,
But here in canvas tight
We'll toss him good and right.

> [SHEPHERDS *exeunt, carrying* MAK
> *in a blanket.*]

SCENE VII

[*Moor. Enter* SHEPHERDS.]

FIRST SHEPHERD:

Lord, I'm about to burst, I am so sore!

Until I rest, in faith I can't do more.

SECOND SHEPHERD:

He's heavy as a sheep of seven score.

And now I'll lay me down to snooze and snore.

THIRD SHEPHERD:

Let's lie down on this green.

FIRST SHEPHERD:

These thieves are rascals mean!

THIRD SHEPHERD:

We'd best forget what's been.

[SHEPHERDS *lie down.*]

An ANGEL *sings "Gloria in excelsis"; then*

let him say:

ANGEL:

Rise, herdsmen, rise, for now the Child is born

Who frees mankind, for Adam's sin forlorn.

To thwart the wicked fiend this night He's born.   10

High God is made your friend. This very morn,

To Bethlehem go ye;

The new-born Deity

In manger laid ye'll see.

[*The* ANGEL *withdraws.*]

FIRST SHEPHERD:

That was as queer a voice as ever I heard;

Wonder enough to make a man be scared.

SECOND SHEPHERD:

To speak of God's own Son of Heaven he dared,

And all the wood I thought with lightning glared.

THIRD SHEPHERD:

He said the Baby lay

In Bethlehem today.   20

THIRD SHEPHERD:

That star points out the way.

[*Points to star.*]

Let's seek Him there!

SECOND SHEPHERD:

Did you hear how he cracked it?

Three breves, one long.

[457]

THIRD SHEPHERD:
               Yes, and he surely smacked it.
  There was no crotchet wrong, and nothing lacked it.
FIRST SHEPHERD:
  I'd like us three to sing, just as he knacked it.
SECOND SHEPHERD:
  Let's harken how you croon.
  Can you bark at the moon?
THIRD SHEPHERD:
  Shut up and hark, you loon!

                        [SHEPHERDS *sing off tune.*]

SECOND SHEPHERD:
  To Bethlehem he ordered us to go.
  I'm much afraid that we have been too slow.   30
THIRD SHEPHERD:
  Be merry, fellow, and don't croak like a crow.
  This news means endless joy to men below.
FIRST SHEPHERD:
  Though we are tired and wet,
  We'll hurry now and get
  Where Mother and Child are set.

                        [*They start to walk.*]

SECOND SHEPHERD:
  We find by ancient prophets—stop your din!—
  David, Isaiah, others of their kin,
  That God's own Son would someday light within
  A virgin's womb, to cleanse away our sin.
  Isaiah, don't forget,   40
  Foretold that one day yet
  "*Virgo concipiet.*"
THIRD SHEPHERD:
  Right merry should we be that now's the day
  The lovely Lord is come who rules for aye.
  I'd be the happiest man if I could say
  That I had knelt before that Child to pray.
  But still the angel said
  The Babe was poorly arrayed
  And in a manger laid!
FIRST SHEPHERD:
  Prophets and patriarchs of old were torn   50
  With yearning to behold this Child now born.
  Without that sight they never ceased to mourn.

But we shall see Him, now this very morn.
When I see Him, I'll know
The prophets' words were so.
No liars were they, no!
To men as poor as we He will appear.
We'll find Him first, His messenger said clear.

SECOND SHEPHERD:

Then let us hurry, for the place is near.

THIRD SHEPHERD:

Ready am I and glad; let's go with cheer.   60
Lord, if Thy will it be,
Allow poor yokels three
This happy sight to see.

SCENE VIII

[*Bethlehem, a stable. The* VIRGIN *seated, the* CHILD *on her knee. The* SHEP-
HERDS *enter and kneel.*]

FIRST SHEPHERD:

Hail, pure and sweet one; hail, thou holy Child!
Maker of all, born of a Maiden mild.
Thou hast o'ercome the Devil, fierce and wild.
That wily Trickster now has been beguiled.
Look, how He laughs, sweet thing!
As my poor offering
A cherry bunch I bring.

SECOND SHEPHERD:

Hail, Savior King, our ransom Thou hast bought!
Hail, mighty Babe, Thou madest all of naught.
Hail, God of mercy, Thou the Fiend hast fought.   10
I kneel and bow before Thee. Look, I've brought
A bird, my tiny one!
Other faith we have none,
Our day-star and God's Son.

THIRD SHEPHERD:

Hail, pretty darling, Thou art God indeed.
I pray to Thee, be near when I have need.
Sweet is Thy look, although my heart does bleed
To see Thee here, and dressed in such poor weed.
Hail, Babe, on Thee I call.
I bring a tennis ball.   20
Take it and play withal.

[459]

MARY:

> The Lord of Heaven, God omnipotent,
> Who made all things aright, His Son has sent.
> My name He named and blessed me ere He went.
> Him I conceived through grace, as God had meant.
> And now I pray Him so
> To keep you from all woe!
> Tell this where'er you go.

FIRST SHEPHERD:

> Farewell, Lady, thou fairest to behold,
> With Christ-child on thy knee!

SECOND SHEPHERD:

>   He lies full cold,   30
> But well it is for me that Him you hold.

THIRD SHEPHERD:

> Already this does seem a thing oft told.

FIRST SHEPHERD:

> Let's spread the tidings round!

SECOND SHEPHERD:

> Come; our salvation's found!

THIRD SHEPHERD:

> To sing it we are bound!

>   [*Exeunt* SHEPHERDS *singing.*]
>   *Here ends the Pageant of the* SHEPHERDS.

The Testament of Cresseid[1]

Robert Henryson

A dreary season to a tragic tale
Should correspond and be equivalent;
In truth, wild winter weather did prevail
As I began to write this *Testament;*
When Aries set free in midst of Lent
Showers of hail that from the North descend,
Scarce from the cold could I myself defend.

Yet in my oratory none the less
I stood, when Titan had his beams of light
Withdrawn below and cloaked in cloudiness,   10
And Venus fair, the beauty of the night,
Arose and set unto the west full right
Her golden face, in opposition bound
To Phoebus the divine, descending down.

And through the pane her beams now burst so fair
That I could see on every side of me,
The northern wind had purified the air,
And swept the misty clouds from heaven free;
The white frosts froze, the night blasts bitterly
From Arctic Pole came whistling loud and shrill,   20
And caused me to withdraw against my will.

For I had hoped that Venus, Love's great Queen,
To whom I once had vowed obedience,
My withered heart with love would now make green,
And thereupon, with humble reverence,

[1] Reprinted from *Indiana Univ. Publications, Humanities Series*, No. 13 (1945), by permission of Professor M. W. Stearns.

I thought of praying to her Excellence,
But as the cold prevented my desire,
I stepped within my chamber to the fire.

Though love be hot, yet in a man of age
It kindles not so fast as in the young,   30
Whose blood flows swiftly in their passion's rage;
An outward fire is the best cure among
The old from whom all vigor has been wrung:
When Nature's forces fail, seek Physic's aid;
I am expert for both I have essayed.

I stirred the fire, and basking turned about,
Then took a drink my spirits to comfórt,
And armed myself against the cold without.
To cut the winter night and make it short,
I took a book and left all other sport,   40
Written by worthy Chaucer glorious,
Of fair Cresseid and worthy Troilus.

And there I found that after Diomede
Had thus received that lady bright of hue,
Troilus was near maddened by the deed,
And sorely wept with visage pale of hue;
For which Despair aroused his tears anew
Till Esperance did gladden him again;
Thus now in joy he lived, and now in pain.

But in her vow he found great comforting,   50
Trusting to Troy that she would homeward turn,
Which he desired o'er every earthly thing—
She was his only love and dear concern;
But when both day and hour for her return
Had passed, then sorrow did oppress
His woeful heart with care and heaviness.

Of his distress I do not need to tell,
For worthy Chaucer in that very book,
In goodly terms and lively verse as well,
Concluded has his cares, for all who look.   60
To break my sleep another work I took,

In which I found the fatal destiny
Of fair Cresseid, that ended wretchedly.

Who knows if all that Chaucer wrote were true?
Nor know I not if this tale actually
Is authorized or falsified anew
By some inventive poet, whose phantasy
Made him report the end in misery   70
And sad lament of amorous Cresseid,
And what distress and death upon her preyed.

When Diomede had all his appetite
And more fulfilled by her, then shamelessly
Upon another he set his whole delight,
Sent to Cresseid his own divorce decree
And thus he banned her from his company;
Then desolate, she wandered up and down,
And some men say turned woman of the town.

O fair Cresseid, the flower and paragon
Of Troy and Greece, compelled by evil fate
To drop thy virtue and such filth to don,   80
And be with fleshly lust so maculate,
And go among the Greeks from dawn till late,
So strumpet-like taking thy foul delight!
I grieve that thou shouldst suffer such a plight.

Yet nevertheless, whatever men deem or say
In scornful language of thy wantonness,
I shall defend as ably as I may,
Thy wisdom, womanhood, and loveliness,
Which Fortune since has put to such distress
As pleased her, ruining with Rumor's whine,   90
And not indeed through any guilt of thine.

This lady fair, deprived then in this wise
Of comfort and consoling sympathy,
Companionless, on foot, and in disguise,
From town a mile or two fled secretly
Unto a manse enriched with tracery
In which her father Calchas dwelt in peace
During this time among the knights of Greece.

When he saw her, the cause he did inquire
Of her return; she said, with sighs full sore: 100
"When Diomede had gotten his desire
He waxed weary and would of me no more."
Quoth Calchas, "Daughter, weep thou not therefor;
Perchance all this has happened for the best:
Welcome to me, thou art full dear a guest."

As priest,—such was the law of long ago,—
Old Calchas of the temple bore the care,
Where Venus and her son Dan Cupido
Were worshiped; thus Cresseid in her despair
Was wont to go unto his chamber there 110
So that in sacred silence she might pray.
Until at last upon a Sabbath day,

As custom was, the people far and wide
Devout in manner to the temple went
With sacrifice before the high noon-tide.
But still Cresseid, oppressed with thought and spent,
Within the church would not herself present,
For fear it would set people whispering
Of her divorce from Diomede the King.

She to a secret chapel passed, heart-sore, 120
Where she might mourn her woeful destiny,
Behind her back she bolted fast the door,
And fell upon her bare knees hastily;
On Venus and on Cupid angrily
She then cried out, and said in this same wise,
"Alas! that ever I made you sacrifice.

"Ye gave me once a sacrosanct reply
That I should be the flower of love in Troy.
An outcast now, in misery I lie,
And into care translated is my joy. 130
Who shall me guide? Who shall me now convoy,
Since I from Diomede and noble Troilus
Am banished clean, cast-off and odious?

"O Cupid false, none is to blame but thou,
And thy blind mother, goddess of wantonness!

Ye caused me always to believe and trow
That seed of love was sown within my face
And aye grew green through your support and grace.
But now, alas, that seed with frost is slain,
And I, by lovers left, forlorn with pain." 140

When this was said, down in an ecstasy,
Ravished in soul, into a dream she fell.
From where she lay, she heard apparently
Cupid the King ringing a silver bell,
Which men might hear from heaven unto hell,
And at whose sound a lustrous throng appears,—
The planets seven, descending from their spheres,

Which have the power o'er all things generable
To rule and move by their great influence,
Weather and wind, and courses variable. 150
Now Saturn, first to state his sentiments,
For Cupid had but little reverence,
But like a surly churl came crabbedly
With looks and mien of cold austerity,

With shriveled face, with livid skin like lead,
With teeth that chinked and chattered with his chin;
His sunken eyes were hollows in his head,
While from his nose streamed drops of crystaline;
His lips were pale, his cheeks were lean and thin;
The icicles that from his hair hung sheer, 160
Were wondrous great and long as any spear.

About his belt in silvery disarray,
His locks fell matted, flecked with twinkling frost;
His garments and his hood were pearly gray;
His tattered ashen rags were tempest tossed;
He bore in hand a sturdy bow, embossed;
A sheaf of arrows, by his girdle gripped,
Feathered with ice, by stones of hail were tipped.

Then Jupiter, so fair and amiable,
God of the stars within the firmament, 170
And mighty nurse to all things generable,
From his father Saturn far different,

[465]

With pleasant face and brows benevolent,
Upon his head a garland wondrous gay,
Of flowers fair, as if it were in May.

His voice was clear, his eyes were crystal keen,
Like golden wires his hair all glittering o'er;
His garment and his hood were gaily green,
With golden borders gilt on every gore;
A sturdy sword about his waist he wore;   180
In his right hand he had a sharpened spear,
His father's wrath away from us to veer.

Next after him came Mars, the god of ire,
Who ever strife, dispute, and discord made,
To chide and fight as fierce as any fire,
In armor, helm, and coat of mail arrayed,
And on his haunch a dreadful bronzy blade,
And in his hand he had a rust-red sword.
Twisting his face with many an angry word,

Shaking his sword, past Cupid he did come   190
With glowering eyes and face incarnadine,
While at his mouth a bubble stood of foam,
Thus like a boar whetting his tushes keen,
Cantankerous, without restraint of spleen;
A horn he blew with many a boisterous blast
Which shook this world with horror unsurpassed.

Then Phoebus fair, lantern and lamp of light
Of man and beast, both fruit and flowering,
The tender nurse, and banisher of night;
His moving and his influence can bring   200
Life in this world to every earthly thing,
Without whose comfort, all must come to naught
Perforce that ever on this earth was wrought.

His chariot, which Phaeton once dared
To guide, he rode, a royal king by right;
The brightness of his face when it was bared,
None might behold for dazzling of his sight.
This golden car with beams of flaming light,

[466]

His four yoked steeds each of a different hue,
Tirelessly through the spheres forever drew.   210

The sorrel first, with mane as red as rose,
Is called Eoye in the Orient;
The second steed, whose name is Ethios,
Whitish and pale, was somewhat ascendent;
The third Peros, aflame and candescént;
The fourth was black and callèd Phlegonie,
Which rolls fair Phoebus down into the sea.

Venus was present there, that goddess gay,
Her son's case to uphold, nor did she lack
Her own complaint, clad in her fine array,   220
The one half green, the other sable black;
Fair hair like gold, combed and parted in back;
But in her face great variance could be,
Now perfect truth, and now inconstancy.

A cold deceit lies coiled beneath her smiles;
Provocative, with glances amorous,
She swiftly changes and everything reviles,
Angry as any serpent venomous,
Ready to sting with words now odious;
Beware of her; from mood to mood she sweeps,   230
With one eye laughs, and with the other weeps.

Betokening that carnal love in men,
O'er which she has both rule and governance,
Is sometimes sweet and sometimes sour again,
Mercurial and full of variance,
With cheerless joy and false beneficence;
Now hot, now cold, now blithe, now full of woe,
Now green as leaf, now withered long ago.

All eloquent and full of rhetoric,
With book in hand, there hastened Mercury,   240
His terms delicious and most politic,
Prepared with pen and ink the clerk to be,
Composing songs and singing merrily;
His scalloped hood, wound in a scarlet pile,
Was like a poet's of old-fashioned style.

[467]

Boxes he bore with fine electuaries,
All sugared syrups for digestion known,
Spices belonging to apothecaries,
With wholesome sweet confections of renown;
Doctor of Physic, clad in scarlet gown,   250
Well trimmed with fur, befitting one so high,
Honest and good, he could not tell a lie.

Next Lady Cynthia came after him,
The last of all and swiftest in her sphere,
Adorned with horns, of color black and grim,
And in the night she best likes to appear,
Livid as lead, of color nothing clear;
For all her light she borrows from her brother,
Titan, for by herself she has no other.

Her guise was gray, bespattered o'er with black,   260
And on her breast a churl was painted even,
Bearing a bunch of thorns upon his back,
Who for his theft might climb no nearer heaven.
Thus when the gods were gathered there, all seven,
Mercurius they chose with one assent,
To be chief speaker in the parliament.

Whoever had been there and wished to hear
His facile tongue and terms so exquisite,
Rhetoric's art might learn and well revere,
To brief discourse a pregnant thought might fit.   270
Confronting Cupid he doffed his cap a bit
And asked the cause of convocation there;
So Cupid then his purpose did declare.

"Lo!" said he, "whoever blasphemes the name
Of his own god, either in word or deed,
Unto all gods he brings both blame and shame,
And should have bitter anguish as his meed.
I speak of yonder wretch Cresseid, take heed!
Though once the flower of love by my decree,
She strongly has reproved my mother and me;   280

"Saying that her great infelicity
Was brought upon her by the two of us.

She said my mother was blind and could not see,
With slander and with lies injurious;
Thus her behavior foul and lecherous
She now would blame on me and on my mother,
To whom I show my grace above all other.

"And since ye seven all are deified,
All sharing in the sacred sapience,
Ye then should punish her who vilified   290
Our high estate for her great insolence,
For never Gods were done such violence.
As well for you as for myself I say;
So help me to obtain revenge I pray."

To Cupid, Mercury replied with cheer
And said, "Sir King, my counsel is that ye
Refer thy case unto the highest here,
And take with him the lowest of degree,
As Saturn and the Goddess Cynthia be,
That they may well decide her punishment."   300
"To take these two," he said, "I am content."

Thus Saturn and the Moon proceeded there,
When they the case had pondered to their best,
For wronging Cupid and his mother fair,
A crime so open and so manifest,
To sentence her with pain to be oppressed,
And torment sore, with ills incurable,
And to all lovers be abominable.

This sentence Saturn took in their behalf,
And glided down where cheerless Cresseid lay,   310
And laid upon her head his frosty staff;
Then in this wise he lawfully did say:
"Thy great fairness and all thy beauty gay,
Thy wanton blood, and e'en thy golden hair,
Are banished evermore, I now declare.

"I change thy mirth to sombre melancholy,
Which is the mother of all pensiveness;
Thy heat and moisture, cold and dry be wholly;
Thy insolence, thy play and wantonness

Be great disease; thy pomp and thy richéss 320
Be mortal need; and thou shalt poverty
Endure, and meet thy death in beggary."

O cruel Saturn! angry and adverse,
Hard is thy doom and too invidious;
Why didst thou cast on fair Cresseid this curse,
Who was so gentle, sweet, and amorous?
Withdraw thy sentence and be generous
As thou hast never been nor e'er could be,
In sentencing Cresseid so ruthlessly.

Then Cynthia, when Saturn passed away, 330
Down from her seat descended instantly,
And read a bill o'er Cresseid where she lay,
Containing this definitive decree:
"I now divorce thy body's heat from thee,
And for thy sickness there shall be no cure,
But in distress thy days thou shalt endure.

"Thy crystal eyes with blood shall mingled be,
Thy voice so clear, be rough and hoarse apace,
Thy skin with blotches black spread loathsomely,
With livid lumps appearing on thy face. 340
Where goest thou, each man shall flee the place;
Thus begging shalt thou go from door to door,
With cup and clapper, leper evermore."

This ugly dream, this vision of despair
Brought to an end, Cresseid her sleep forsook,
And all that court of gods assembled there
Vanished away. Then she arose and took
A polished glass from which her image looked,
And when she saw her face so changed, her throes
Of grief were terrible enough, God knows. 350

Weeping with woe, "Look what it is," quoth she,
"To anger so our crabbed gods who hear
Our froward words; this may be seen in me!
Now have I bought my blasphemy full dear,
My earthly joy and mirth lie in arrear.

Alas this day, alas this woeful tide,
When I my gods began to taunt and chide."

When this was said, a child came from the hall
To warn Cresseid that supper time drew nigh,
First knocked upon the door and then did call: 360
"Madame, your father bids you to him fly,
Your groveling so long does mystify
Him greatly, for he says that you can dwell
In prayer too long; your thoughts the gods know well."

Quoth she: "Fair child, go to my father dear,
And beg him come to speak with me anon."
And so he did and said: "Daughter, what cheer?"
"Alas," quoth she, "Father, my mirth is gone."
"How so?" quoth he; and then, as I have done,
She told him all, how Cupid ruthlessly   370
Had punished her for her iniquity.

He looked upon her ugly leper face,
Which once had been as white as lily flower;
Wringing his hands, he mourned her vanished grace,
And wept that he had lived to see that hour;
For he knew well there was no earthly power
Could cure her now, and that increased his pain;
Thus was there woe enough between the twain.

When they for long had mourned together so,   380
Said Cresseid, "Father, I would not be kenned,
So therefore secretly now let me go
Unto the hospital which stands at end
Of town, and there for charity please send
Me meat to live upon, for all my mirth,
Pursued by wicked weird,[2] has fled this earth."

Then in a mantle and a beaver hat
She took her cup and clapper; privily
He opened a secret gate and out through that
Conducted her, by way that none could spy,   390
Unto a village half a mile near by

[2] The Anglo-Saxon Wyrd, Fate.

Where stood the hospital, and daily sent
His alms unto her for her nourishment.

Some knew her well and some no knowledge had
Of her, who was deformed beyond belief,
With blackish boils over her visage spread,
And her fair color faded like a leaf;
Yet they assumed because of her proud grief
And quiet tears, she was of noble kin:
With better will therefore they took her in.

The day passed by and Phoebus went to rest,   400
The blackest clouds o'erwhelmed the evening sky:
God knows if Cresseid was a sorry guest
On seeing that strange fare and shelter nigh!
She touched no meat nor drink but went to lie
In a dark corner of the house alone;
And in this wise, weeping, she made her moan.

The Complaint of Cresseid

O sop of sorrow, dipped in deep despair!
O cheerless Cresseid, joy and mirth will ne'er
Return again, for grief is thy estate;
Of all thy blithesomeness thou art stripped bare;   410
No salve may save thee from thy sickness rare.
Fell is thy fortune, wicked is thy fate;
Thy bliss is banned, thy woes accumulate;
God grant that I may find a grave somewhere
That none of Greece or Troy may desecrate.

Where is thy chamber decked in luxury,
Thy bed with its embroidered tapestry,
Spices and wines that were thy banquet's crown,
Thy cups of gold and silver brilliancy,
Thy saffron sauces seasoned perfectly,   420
Savoury meats in platters clean, passed round,
Thy garments gay, with many a goodly gown,
Clipped with a golden pin for all to see?
Vanished has all thy royal great renown.

Where is thy garden with those grasses gay
And flowers fresh which Flora in her play

Had painted pleasantly in every bed;
Where thou wast wont so merrily in May
To walk and take the dew when it was day,
To hear the merle and thrush sing overhead,   430
To carol with thy ladies garlanded,
And see the royal folk in their array,
With every hue their gay garb garnishèd?

Thy great triumphant fame, the honored hour
When thou wast called of mortal men the flower,—
All has decayed, so changed thy weird, that saw
Thy high estate turn into darkness dour.
This leper's lodge take for thy goodly bower,
And for thy bed take now a bunch of straw;
Lay thy choice wine and meat aside to gnaw   440
This mouldy bread and sip this cider sour;
Take cup and clapper ordered by the law. . . .

O ladies fair of Greece and Troy, attend   452
My misery that none may comprehend,
My fickle fate, my infelicity,
My great distress, that no man can amend.
Beware in time, when I such woes portend,
And in your mind a mirror make of me.
As I am now, perchance it may be ye
Who shall, for all your might, find this same end,
Or else much worse, if any worse there be. . . .   460

———————

Thus chiding with her dreary destiny,   470
With wails she waked all night from dusk to dawn.
In vain, her weeping was no remedy
For woe, nor cure for sorrow undergone.
A leper lady went to her anon
To say, "Why dash thyself against the wall,
To slay thyself, and mend no thing at all?

"Since weeping only multiplies thy woe,
Then make a virtue of necessity,
And learn to shake thy clapper to and fro,
And live after the laws of leprosy."   480
There was no help, and so it was that she

Went forth with them to beg from place to place,
By cold and hunger forced to this disgrace.

At that same time the garrison of Troy,
Which had as chieftain worthy Troilus,
Through chance of war was able to destroy
The knights of Greece in numbers marvelous:
With triumph great and songs victorious,
Again to Troy right royally they rode,
Past Cresseid's and the leper folk's abode.   490

Seeing that troop, the lepers came them towards;
They gave a cry and shook their cups with speed;
And said, "For love of heaven, worthy lords,
Give alms unto us leper folk in need."
Then to their cry Sir Troilus paid heed,
And paused with pity for their misery
Near fair Cresseid, not knowing it was she.

Upon him then she raised her eyes apace,
And with a glance it came into his thought
That he sometime before had seen her face;   500
Yet she was in such plight he knew her not;
But still her look into his mind had brought
The winsome visage and the amorous gaze
Of fair Cresseid, his love in former days.

No wonder was, if in his mind thus he
Recalled her features hastily. And why?
The image of a thing perhaps may be
So deep imprinted in the phantasy,
That it deludes the reason outwardly,
And so appears in form and like estate   510
Within the mind as it was imaged late.

A spark of love unto his heart did spring,
And kindled all his body in a fire.
With fever's heat, a sweat and shivering
O'ertook him, till he felt he would expire.
To bear his shield, his breast began to tire.
Within a while, he changed full many a hue,
And, nevertheless, not one the other knew.

For knightly pity and sweet memory
Of fair Cresseid, a girdle he purveyed,   520
A purse of gold and gayest gems which he
Flung down into the skirt of sad Cresseid:
Then rode away, and not a word he said,
Pensive in heart, until he reached the town,
And for great grief, he ofttimes near fell down.

The leper folk to Cresseid near did draw,
So they might see the alms were equally
Distributed, but when the gold they saw,
Each whispered to the other secretly,
And said, "Yon lord, however it may be,   530
Has more affection for this leper maid
Than for us all, we know this by his aid."

"What lord is yon," quoth she, "can ye not tell,
Who showed for us such great humanity?"
"Yes," quoth a leper man, "I know him well;
Noble and kind Sir Troilus you see."
When Cresseid understood that it was he,
Stronger than steel up sprang a bitter pain
Within her heart and she fell, all but slain.

When she revived, with sighing sad and sore,   540
With many cheerless cries she called, "Ochone!
Now is my breast with savage sorrow scored,
Wrapped in such woe, a wretch whose hope has flown.
Then swooned she oft, ere she could cease her moan,
And ever in her swooning cried she thus:
"O, false Cresseid! And true knight Troilus!

"Thy love, thy loyalty and gentleness,
I held as naught in my prosperity,
So swept away was I in wantonness,
And climbed on Fortune's wheel so high and free: 550
All faith and love that I once promised thee,
Were in themselves fickle and frivolous;
O false Cresseid! and true knight Troilus!

"For love of me thou kept good continence,
In conversation ever true and chaste,

Of all women protector and defense,
Defending their good name, while I disgraced
Thy love; my mind, with fleshly filth debased,
Was e'er inclined to lusts so lecherous.
Fie, false Cresseid! O, true knight Troilus!   560

"Lovers, beware, and take good heed of those
Whom ye do love, for whom ye suffer pain,
For there exist but few, I will disclose,
From whom ye ever may true love obtain.
Try when ye will, your labor is in vain.
So take them as they come, and bear in mind,
Steadfast they are as weather cocks in wind.

"Because I know this great unstableness,
Brittle as glass, unto myself I say,
Expect in others as great unfaithfulness,   570
As false and as inconstant in its way;
Though some be true, I know right few are they;
Who finds the truth, let him his lady praise;
None but myself shall I accuse these days."

With paper she sat down, with speaking done,
And in this manner made her testament:
"Here I bequeath my corpse and carrion
To worms and toads to be their nourishment;
My cup and clapper and my ornament
And all my gold, the leper folk's shall be   580
When I am dead, if they will bury me.

"This royal ring, set with this ruby red,
Which Troilus in token once did send,
I leave again to him when I am dead,
That he my doleful death may apprehend:
Thus I conclude shortly and make an end;
My soul I leave to Diane, where she dwells,
To walk with her in woodland wastes and wells.

"Thou hast both brooch and belt, O Diomede!
Which Troilus gave me betokening   590
His own true love"—and with that word she died.
With haste a leper man took off the ring,

Dispatched without delay her burying,
And soon the ring to Troilus conveyed,
Declaring there the death of fair Cresseid.

When he had heard of her infirmity,
Her legacy and sorrowful lament,
And how she ended in such poverty,
He swooned for woe and to the ground fell spent;
Ready to burst, his heart with grief was rent: 600
Sighing he said: "Now I can do no more;
She was untrue, and woe is me therefor!"

Some said he made a tomb of marble gray
And wrote her name and an inscription there,
And laid it on the grave in which she lay,
In golden letters voicing his despair:
"Lo, fair ladies, Cresseid of Troy, who ere
Was held the flower of love, now quieted
Under this stone, a leper late, lies dead."

Now, worthy women, in this ballad short   610
For your high honor and instruction penned,
From charity I caution and exhort,
Mix not your love with false deceit, amend
Your ways and bear in mind the bitter end
Of fair Cresseid, as I have said before.
Since she is dead, I speak of her no more.

MARSHALL W. STEARNS
(revised by R. S. L.)

The Golden Legend

Translated and Expanded by

William Caxton

SAINT AGNES

(JANUARY 21)

THE interpretation of her name.

Agnes is said of *agna*,[1] "a lamb," for she was humble and debonair [2] as a lamb, or *agna* [3] in Greek, which is to say "debonair and piteous," for she was debonair and merciful. Or *Agnes* of *agnoscendo*,[4] for she knew the ways of truth, and after this St. Austin [5] saith, "Truth is opposed against vanity, falsehood, and doubleness," for these three things were taken from her for the truth that she had.

The blessed virgin St. Agnes was much wise, and well taught, as St. Ambrose [6] witnesseth, and wrote her passion.[7] She was of fair visage, but much 10 fairer in the Christian faith; she was young of age, and aged in wit, for in the thirteenth year of her age she lost the death that the world giveth, and found life in Jesu Christ. When she came from school the son of the prefect of Rome, for the emperor, loved her. And when his father and mother knew it, they offered to give much riches with him if he might have her in marriage, and offered St. Agnes precious jewels, which she refused to take; whereof it happed that the young man was ardently esprised [8] in the love of St. Agnes, and came and took with him more precious and richer adornments, with all manner of precious stones, and as well as by his parents as by himself offered to St. Agnes rich gifts and possessions, and all the de-20 lights and deduits [9] of the world, and all to the end to have her in marriage. But St. Agnes answered him in this matter:

"Go from me, thou fardel [10] of sin, nourishing of evils, and morsel [11] of death; and depart and know thou I am prevented [12] and am loved of another lover, which hath given to me many better jewels, which hath fianced [13]

---

[1] Latin *agna*, "ewe lamb."   [2] Gracious, kind.
[3] Greek *agnā*, fem. of *agnos*, "pure, chaste."   [4] Latin *agnoscere*, "to know well."
[5] Augustine, bishop of Hippo, d. 430.   [6] Bishop of Milan, d. 397.
[7] Martyrdom.   [8] Inflamed.   [9] Pleasures.   [10] Bundle.
[11] Food for death.   [12] Anticipated.   [13] Taken as one's betrothed.

me by His faith, and is much more noble of lineage than thou art, and of estate. He hath clad me with precious stones and with jewels of gold. He hath set in my visage a sign that I receive none other spouse but Him, and hath showed me over-great treasures which He must give me if I abode with Him. I will have none other spouse but Him, I will seek none other; in no manner may I leave Him; with Him am I firm and fastened in love, which is more noble, more puissant,[14] and fairer than any other, whose love is much [15] sweet and gracious; of whom the chamber is now for to receive me where the virgins sing merrily. I am now embraced of Him of whom the mother is a virgin, and His father knew never woman, whom 10 the angels serve. The sun and the moon marvel them of His beauty, whose works never fail, whose riches never minish,[16] by whose odor dead men are raised again to life, by whose touching the sick men be comforted, whose love is chastity. To Him I have given my faith, to Him I have commended my heart. When I love Him, then am I chaste, and when I touch Him, then am I pure and clean, and when I take Him, then am I a virgin: this is the love of my God."

When the young man had heard all this, he was despaired, as he that was taken in blind love, and was over-sore tormented, in so much that he lay down sick in his bed for the great sorrow that he had. Then came the 20 physicians and anon knew his malady, and said to his father that he languished of carnal love that he had to some woman. Then the father enquired and knew that it was this woman, and did do speak to St. Agnes for his son, and said to her how his son languished for her love. St. Agnes answered that in no wise she would break the faith of her first husband. Upon that the provost demanded who was her first husband, of whom she so much avaunted, and in his power so much trusted. Then one of her servants said she was a Christian, and that she was so enchanted that she said Jesu Christ was her spouse.

And when the provost heard that she was a Christian, the provost was 30 much glad because to have power on her, for then the Christian people were in the will of the lord; and if they would not reny [17] their God and their belief, all their goods should be forfeited. Wherefore then the provost made St. Agnes to come in justice,[18] and he examined her sweetly, and after cruelly by menaces. St. Agnes, well comforted,[19] said to him, "Do what thou wilt, for my purpose shalt thou never change." And when she saw him now flattering and now terribly angry, she scorned him. And the provost said to her, being all angry, "One of two things thou shalt choose, either do sacrifice to our gods with the virgins of the goddess Vesta, or go to the brothel to be abandoned to all that thither come, to the great shame 40

---

[14] Powerful. [15] Very. [16] Diminish. [17] Renounce.
[18] Before the court, in trial. [19] Strengthened.

and blame of thy lineage." St. Agnes answered, "If thou knewest who is my God, thou wouldst not say to me such words, for as much as I know the virtue [20] of my God, I set nothing by thy menaces, for I have His angel which is keeper of my body."

Then the judge, all araged,[21] made to take off her clothes, and all naked to be led to the brothel. And thus St. Agnes, that refused to do sacrifice to the idols, was delivered naked to go to the brothel, but anon as she was unclothed God gave to her such grace that the hairs of her head became so long that they covered all her body to her feet, so that her body was not 10 seen. And when St. Agnes entered into the brothel, anon she found the angel of God ready for to defend her, and environed St. Agnes with a bright clearness [22] in such wise that no man might see her nor come to her. Then she made of the brothel her oratory, and in making her prayers to God she saw tofore her a white vesture, and anon therewith she clad her and said, "I thank thee Jesu Christ which accountest me with thy virgins and hast sent me this vesture." All they that entered made honor and reverence to the great clearness that they saw about St. Agnes, and came out more devout and clean than they entered.

At last came the son of the provost with a great company for to accom-20 plish his foul desires and lusts. And when he saw his fellows come out and issue all abashed, he mocked them and called them cowards. And then he, all araged, entered for to accomplish his evil will. And when he came to the clearness, he advanced him for to take the virgin, and anon the devil took him by the throat and strangled him that he fell down dead.

And when the provost heard these things of his son, he ran weeping to the brothel, and began crying, to say to St. Agnes, "O thou cruel woman, why hast thou showed thy enchantment on my son?" and demanded of her how his son was dead, and by what cause. To whom St. Agnes answered, "He took him into his power to whom he had abandoned his will." 30 "Why be not all they dead," said he, "that entered here before him?" "For his fellows saw the miracle of the great clearness and were afeard and went their way unhurt, for they did honor to my God which hath clad me with this vesture and hath kept my body, but your villainous son, as soon as he entered into this house began to bray and cry, and when he would have laid hand upon me, anon the devil slew him as thou seest." "If thou mayst raise him," said he, "it may well appear that thou hast not put him to death." And St. Agnes answered, "How well [23] that thy creance [24] is not worthy to impetre [25] ne get that of our Lord, nevertheless because it is time that the virtue of God be showed, go ye all out that I may make my prayer to God." 40 And when she was in her prayers the angel came and raised him to life,

[20] Power.   [21] Enraged.   [22] Radiance.   [23] Although.
[24] Faith, belief.   [25] Obtain, but perhaps, ask.

and anon he went out and began to cry with a loud voice, that the God of Christian men was very God in heaven, and in earth, and in the sea, and that the idols were vain that they worshiped, which might not help them nor none other.

Then the bishops of the idols made a great discord among the people, so that all they cried, "Take away this sorceress and witch which that turned men's minds and alieneth [26] their wits." When the provost saw these marvels he would gladly have delivered St. Agnes because she had raised his son, but he doubted [27] to be banished, and set in his place a lieutenant named Aspasius, for to satisfy the people, and because he could not deliver her, he departed sorrowfully. This Aspasius did do make a great fire among all the people and did do cast St. Agnes therein. Anon as this was done the flame desparted [28] in two parts, and burnt them that made the discords, and she abode all whole without feeling the fire. The people weened that she had done all by enchantment. Then made St. Agnes her orison to God, thanking him that she was escaped from the peril to lose her virginity, and also from the burning of the flame. And when she had made her orison the fire lost all his heat, and quenched it. Aspasius, for the doutance [29] of the people, commanded to put a sword [30] to her body, and so she was martyred. Anon came the Christian men and the parents of St. Agnes and buried the body, but the heathen defended [31] it, and cast so stones at them that unnethe [32] they escaped. She suffered martyrdom in the time of Constantine the Great, which began to reign the year of our Lord three hundred and nine.

Among them that buried her body was one Emerenciana, which had been fellow to St. Agnes, howbeit she was not yet christened, but an holy virgin. She came also to the sepulchre of St. Agnes, which [33] constantly reproved the gentiles, and of them she was stoned to death and slain. Anon there came an earthquaver, lightning and thunder, that many of the paynims perished, so that forthon [34] the Christian people might surely come to the sepulchre unhurt, and the body of Emerenciana was buried by the body of St. Agnes. It happed that when the friends of St. Agnes watched at her sepulchre on a night, they saw a great multitude of virgins [35] clad in vestments of gold and silver, and a great light shone tofore them, and on the right side was a lamb more white than snow, and saw also St. Agnes among the virgins, which said to her parents, "Take heed, and see that ye bewail me no more as dead, but be ye joyful with me, for with all these virgins Jesu Christ hath given me most brightest habitation and dwelling, and am with Him joined in

[26] Troubles, makes strange.   [27] Feared.   [28] Separated.   [29] Fear.
[30] She belongs to a group of saints who could be martyred by the sword alone, an aristocratic death.
[31] Prevented.   [32] With difficulty.   [33] Who (Emerenciana).
[34] For this reason.   [35] Cf. Revelation 14:4.

heaven whom in earth I loved with my thought." And this was the eighth day after her passion. And because of this vision Holy Church maketh memory of her the eight days of the feast after, which is called *Agnetis secundo.*[36]

Of her we read an example that in the church of St. Agnes was a priest which was named Paulus, and always served in that church, and had right great temptation of his flesh, but because he doubted [37] to anger our Lord he kept him from sin, and prayed to the pope that he would give him leave to marry. The pope considered his simpleness, and for his bounty he gave
10 him a ring in which was an emerald,[38] and commanded that he should go to the image of St. Agnes which was in his church, and pray her that she would be his wife. The simple man did so, and the image put forth her finger and he set the ring thereon, and then she drew her finger again, and kept the ring fast. And then anon all his temptation carnal was quenched and taken away from him, and yet,[39] as it is said, the ring is on the finger of the image.

THE ASSUMPTION OF THE VIRGIN

(AUGUST 15)

We find in the book sent to St. John the Evangelist, or else the book which is said to be *apocryphum* [1] is ascribed to him, in what manner the assumption of the blessed Virgin Mary was made.
20   The apostles were departed and gone into divers countries of the world for the cause of preaching, and the blessed Lady and Virgin was in a house by the Mount of Sion, and as long as she lived, she visited all the places of her Son with great devotion, that is to say, the place of His baptism, of His fasting, of His passion, of His sepulture, of His resurrection, and of His ascension. And after that Epiphanius [2] saith, she lived four and twenty years after the ascension of her Son; and he saith also; "When our Lady had conceived Jesu Christ, she was of the age of fourteen years, and she was delivered in the fifteenth year, and lived and abode with Him three and thirty years. And after His death she lived four and twenty years, and
30 by this account when she departed out of this world she was seventy-two years old; but it is more probable that which is read in another place, that she lived after the ascension of her Son twelve years, and so then she was sixty years old."

And on a day, when all the apostles were spread through the world in preaching, the glorious Virgin was greatly esprised [3] and embraced with

---

[36] Actually, the octave of her feast.   [37] Was afraid.
[38] The emerald was a protection against lust.   [39] Still.
[1] Non-canonical, spurious.   [2] Bishop of Salamis, d. 403.   [3] Kindled.

desire to be with her Son Jesu Christ, and her courage [4] was eschafed [5] and moved, and great abundance of tears ran withoutforth,[6] and because she had not equally the comforts of her Son, which were withdrawn from her for the time. And an angel came tofore her, with great light, and saluted her honorably as the mother of his Lord, saying, "All hail, blessed Mary, receiving the blessing of Him that sent His blessing to Jacob, lo! here a bough of palm [7] of Paradise, Lady, which I have brought to thee, which thou shalt command to be borne tofore thy bier. For thy soul shall be taken from thy body the third day next following, and thy Son abideth [8] thee, His honorable mother."

To whom she answered, "If I have found grace tofore thine eyes, I pray thee that thou vouchsafe to show me thy name, and yet I pray thee more heartily that my sons and brethren the apostles may be assembled with me, so that tofore I die I may see them with my bodily eyes, and after, to be buried of them, and they being here, I may yield up my ghost to God. And also yet I pray and require that my spirit, issuing out of the body, see not the horrible and wicked spirit and fiend,[9] and that no might of the devil come against me."

And then the angel said, "Lady, wherefore desirest thou to know my name? which is great and marvelous. All the apostles shall assemble this day to thee, and shall make to thee noble exequies [10] at thy passing, and in the presence of them thou shalt give up thy spirit. For He that brought the prophet by the hair [11] from Judea to Babylon, may without doubt suddenly in an hour bring the apostles to thee. And wherefore doubtest thou to see the wicked spirit, sith thou has broken utterly his head,[12] and hast despoiled [13] him from the empire of his power? Nevertheless thy will be done, that thou see not the fiend." And this said, the angel mounted into heaven with great light, and the palm shone by right great clearness, and was like to a green rod whose leaves shone like the morning star.

And it happed as St. John the Evangelist preached in Ephesus, the heaven suddenly thundered, and a white cloud took him up and brought him tofore the gate of the blessed Virgin Mary. And he knocked at the door and entered, and saluted the Virgin honorably. Whom the blessed Virgin beheld, and was greatly abashed for joy, and might not abstain her from weeping, and said to him, "John, my son, remember thee of the word of thy Master, by which He made me mother unto thee, and thee a son unto me.[14] Lo! I am called of thy master and my God. I pay now the debt of condition human,[15] and commend my body unto thy busy care. I have heard say that

4 Heart. 5 Stirred, excited. 6 Outwardly.
7 The palm is a symbol of death as well as of victory. 8 Awaits.
9 Originally Death, or the angel of death. 10 Funeral rites.
11 Bel and the Dragon 37. 12 Cf. Genesis 3:15. 13 Deprived him of.
14 John 19:26-27. 15 Human nature.

the Jews have made a council, and said, 'Let us abide, brethren, unto the time that she that bare Jesu be dead, and then incontinent [16] we shall take her body, and shall cast it into the fire to burn it.' Thou therefore take this palm, and bear it tofore the bier when ye shall bear my body to the sepulchre." Then said John, "O, would God that all my brethren the apostles were here, that we might make thine exequies convenably [17] as it behoveth and is digne [18] and worthy."

And as he said that, all the apostles were ravished [19] with clouds from the places where they preached, and were brought tofore the door of the
10 blessed Virgin Mary. And when they saw them assembled, they marveled, and said, "For what cause hath our Lord assembled us here?" Then St. John went out and said to them that our Lady should pass and depart out of this world, and added more thereto, saying, "Brethren, beware and keep you from weeping when she shall depart, because [20] that the people that shall see it be not troubled, and say, 'Lo, these, how they dread the death which preach to others the resurrection!' "

And Denis,[21] disciple of Paul, affirmeth this same in the *Book of Divine Names*, that is to wit that all the apostles were assembled at the assumption and death of our Lady Mary, and were together there, and that each of
20 them made a sermon unto the praising and laud of Jesu Christ and the blessed Virgin His mother. And he said thus, speaking to Timothy, "Thus we and thou, as thou well knowest, and many of our holy brethren, did assemble at the vision of the mother that received God. And James, brother of God, was there, and Peter the apostle, most noble and sovereign of the theologians. And after that me seemed that all the Hierarchies [22] lifted her up, after and according to her virtue without end." This saith St. Denis.

And when the blessed Virgin Mary saw all the apostles assembled, she blessed Our Lord, and sat in the midst of them where the lamps, tapers and lights burned. And about the third hour of the night Jesu Christ came with
30 sweet melody and song, with the orders of angels, the companies of patriarchs, the assemblies of martyrs, the convents of confessors, the carols of virgins. And tofore the bed of our blessed Lady the companies of all these saints were set in order and made sweet song and melody. And what exequies [23] were done of our blessed Lady, and there hallowed, it is all said and enseigned [24] in the foresaid book which is attributed to St. John.

For first, Jesu Christ began to say, "Come, My chosen, and I shall set thee in My seat,[25] for I have coveted the beauty of thee." And Our Lady answered, "Sire, my heart is ready," and all they that were come with Jesu

---

[16] Forthwith.   [17] Suitably.   [18] Right, proper.   [19] Taken up.
[20] In order that.
[21] Dionysius the Areopagite (cf. Acts 17:34), to whom were attributed a number of works of the sixth century and later.
[22] Orders of angels.   [23] Rites.   [24] Set forth, explained.   [25] Throne.

Christ entuned sweetly, saying, "This is she that never touched the bed of marriage in delight, and she shall have fruit in refection of holy souls." Then she sang of herself, saying, "All generations shall say that I am blessed, for He that is mighty hath done great things to me, and the name of Him is holy." And the Chanter of Chanters [26] entuned more excellently above all others, saying, "Come from Lebanon, my spouse, come from Lebanon, come, thou shalt be crowned." And she said, "I come, for in the beginning of the book it is written of me that I should do Thy will, for my spirit hath joyed in Thee God, my health." And thus in the morning the soul issued out of the body, and fled into the arms of her Son. And she was as far estranged from the pain of the flesh as she was from corruption of her body.

Then said Our Lord to the apostles, "Bear ye the body of this virgin, My mother, unto the Vale of Josephat,[27] and lay ye her in a new sepulchre that ye shall find there, and abide me there three days till I return to you." And anon she was environed with flowers of roses, that was the company of martyrs, and with lilies of the valley, that was the company of angels, of confessors and virgins. And the apostles cried after her saying, "Right wise virgin, whither goest thou? Lady, remember thee of us." And then the company of saints that were abidden [28] there, were awaked with the sound of the song of them that mounted, and came against her, and saw their King bear in His proper arms the soul of a woman, and saw that this soul was joined to Him, and were abashed, and began to cry, saying, "Who is this that ascendeth from the desert, full of delights, joined to her friend?" And they that accompanied her said, "This is the right fair among the daughters of Jerusalem, and like as ye have seen her full of charity and delection, so is she joyously received, and set in the seat of glory on the right side of her Son." And the apostles saw the soul of her being so white that no mortal tongue might express it.

And then three maidens that were there took off their clothes from the body for to wash it. The body anon shone by so great clearness that they might well feel it in touching and washing, but they might not see it. And the light shone as long as they were about the washing of it. And then the apostles took the body honorably and laid it on the bier, and John said to Peter, "Bear this palm tofore the bier, for our Lord hath ordained thee above us, and hath made thee pastor and prince of His sheep." To whom Peter said, "It appertaineth better to thee to bear it, for thou art chosen virgin of our Lord, and thou oughtest to bear this palm of light at the exequies of chastity and holiness, thou that drankest of the fountain of per-

[26] Christ, referred to as author of the *Song of Solomon*, from which the following verse is taken, 4:8.   [27] The valley of the Kedron, east of Jerusalem.
[28] Summoned; they were overpowered by sleep at the advent of Jesus.

durable [29] clearness. And I shall bear the holy body with the bier, and these other apostles our brethren shall go round about the body, yielding thankings to God." And then St. Paul said to him, "I, that am the least of the apostles and of you all, shall bear with thee." And then Peter and Paul lifted up the bier, and Peter began to sing and say, "Israel issued out of Egypt," and the other apostles followed him in the same song, And our Lord covered the bier and the apostles with a cloud, so that they were not seen, but the voice of them was heard only. And the angels were with the apostles singing, and replenished [30] all the land with marvelous sweetness.

10 And then all the people was moved with that sweet melody, and issued hastily out of the city and enquired what it was, and then there were some that said to them that Mary, such a woman, is dead, and the disciples of her son Jesu bear her and make such melody as ye hear about her. And then ran they to arms, and they warned each other saying, "Come let us slay all the disciples, and let us burn the body of her that bare this traitor." And when the prince of the priests saw that, he was all abashed [31] and full of anger, and said, "Lo, here the tabernacle [32] of him that troubled us and our lineage; behold what glory she now receiveth," and in saying so, he laid his hands on the bier, willing to turn it, and overthrow it to the ground.

20 Then suddenly both his hands waxed dry and cleaved to the bier, so that he hung by the hands on the bier, and was sore tormented and wept and brayed.[33] And all the angels that were in the clouds blinded all the other people, that they saw nothing. And the prince of the priests said, "St. Peter, despise me not in this tribulation, and I pray thee to pray for me to our Lord. Thou oughtest to remember when the chamberer, that was usher, accused thee, and I excused thee." [34] And St. Peter said to him, "We be now empeached [35] in the service of our Lady, and may not now entend [36] to heal thee, but, and if thou believest in our Lord Jesu Christ, and in this that bare him, I ween and hope that thou shalt soon have health and be all whole."

30 And he answered, "I believe our Lord Jesu Christ to be the Son of God, and that this is His right holy mother." And anon his hands were loosed from the bier, and yet the dryness and the pain ceased not in him. And then St. Peter said to him, "Kiss the bier and say, 'I believe in God Jesu Christ that this woman bare in her belly, and remained virgin after childing.' " And when he had so said, he was anon all whole perfectly. And then said Peter to him, "Take that palm of the hand of our brother John, and lay it on the people that be blind, and who that will believe shall receive his sight again. And they that will not believe shall never see."

And then the apostles bare Mary unto the monument, and sat by it, like

[29] Eternal.　　　　[30] Filled.　　　　[31] Astonished (at their presumption).
[32] Dwelling place.　　　　[33] Cried out.
[34] An apocryphal amplification of Matthew 26:69-73.
[35] Occupied, hindered.　　　　[36] Attend, give attention.

as our Lord had commanded. And at the third day Jesu Christ came with a great multitude of angels and saluted them, and said, "Peace be with you." And they answered, "God, glory be to Thee which only makest the great miracles and marvels." And our Lord said to the apostles, "What is now your advice that I ought now to do to My mother of honor and of grace?" "Sire, it seemeth to us Thy servants that like as Thou hast vanquished the death and reignest world without end, that Thou raise also the body of Thy mother, and set her on Thy right side in perdurability." [37] And He granted it. And then Michael the angel came and presented the soul of Mary to our Lord.   10

And the Savior spake and said, "Arise up, haste thee, My culver, or dove, tabernacle of glory, vessel of life, temple celestial, and like as thou never feltest [38] conceiving by none atouchment,[39] thou shalt not suffer in the sepulchre any corruption of body." And anon the soul came again to the body of Mary, and issued gloriously out of the tomb, and thus was received in the heavenly chamber, and a great company of angels with her.

And St. Thomas was not there, and when he came he would not believe this. And anon the girdle with which her body was girt came to him from the air, which he received, and thereby he understood that she was assumpt [40] into heaven.   20

And all this heretofore is said and called *apocryphum*. Whereof St. Jerome saith in a sermon to Paula and Eustochia her daughter, "That book is said to be *apocryphum*, save that some words be worthy of faith and be approved of saints as touching nine things: that is, to wit, that the comfort of the apostles was promised and given to the Virgin, and that all the saints assembled there, and that she died without pain, and was buried in the Vale of Josephat. And there were made ready the obsequies and the devotion of Jesu Christ, and the coming of the celestial company, and the persecution of the Jews, and the shining of the miracles, and that she was assumpt into heaven, body and soul. But many other things be put there 30 more at fantasy and simulation [41] than at truth. As that, that St. Thomas was not there, and when he came he doubted, and other things semblable, which be better not to believe them than not to believe her clothes and vestments were left in the tomb, to the comfort of good Christian men."

SAINT THOMAS OF CANTERBURY

(DECEMBER 29)

Here followeth the life of St. Thomas, martyr, of Canterbury, and first the exposition of his name.

---

[37] Eternity.   [38] Experience.   [39] Bodily contact.
[40] Taken up.   [41] Fiction.

Thomas [1] is as much to say as [2] "abysm" or "double," or "trenched and hewn": he was an abysm profound in humility, as it appeared in the hair [3] that he wore, and in washing of the feet of poor people; double in prelation,[4] that is in word and ensample, and hewn and trenched in his passion.[5]

St. Thomas the Martyr was son to Gilbert Becket, a burgess of the city of London, and was born in the place where as now standeth the church called St. Thomas of Acre. And this Gilbert was a good devout man, and took the cross upon him, and went on pilgrimage into the Holy Land, and had a servant with him. And when he had accomplished his pilgrimage, he was taken homeward by the heathen men and brought into the prison of a prince named Amarant, where long time he and his fellowship suffered much pain and sorrow. And the prince had great affection towards this Gilbert, and had often communication with him of the Christian faith, and of the realm of England, by which conversation it fortuned that the daughter of this prince had especial love unto this Gilbert, and was familiar with him.[6] And on a time she disclosed her love to him, saying if he would promise to wed her she should forsake friends, heritage and country for his love and become Christian; and after long communication between them he promised to wed her if she would become Christian, and told her the place of his dwelling in England. And after, by the purveyance of God, this same Gilbert escaped and came home.

And after this it fortuned so that this prince's daughter stole privily away, and passed many a wild place and great adventure, and by God's purveyance at last came to London, demanding and crying "Becket! Becket!", for the more English could she not; [7] wherefore the people drew about her, what for the strange array of her, as for that they understood her not, and many a shrewd [8] boy. So long she went till she came tofore Gilbert's door, and as she there stood, the servant that had been with Gilbert in prison, which was named Richard, saw her and knew that it was she, and went in to his master, and told him how that this maid stood at his door; and anon he went out to see her. And as soon as she saw him she fell in a swoon for joy, and Gilbert took her up, and comforted her, and brought her into his house, and sith [9] went to the bishops, which then were six at St. Paul's, and rehearsed all the matter, and after they christened her, and forthwith wedded her unto Gilbert Becket, and within time reasonable and accustomed, was brought forth between them a fair son named

---

[1] The name originally Aramaic, and meaning "twin," was translated into Greek as Didymus, hence the "doubled" of this passage; but it was also transliterated as Thomas (John 20:24 shows both forms). Thomas interpreted as from Greek *tomos*, from a root "to cut," would give rise to the explanations "hewn" and "trenched."

[2] Means.   [3] Hair shirt.   [4] Two-fold in his life as a prelate.

[5] Martyrdom.   [6] Frequently in his company.

[7] That was all the English she knew.   [8] Bad, rowdy.   [9] Then.

Thomas.[10] And after this yet the said Gilbert went again to the Holy Land and was there three years ere he came again.

And this child grew forth till he was sent to school, and learned well and became virtuous,[11] and when he was twenty-four years old his mother passed out of this world. And after this he served a merchant of London a while keeping his charge and accounts, and from him he went to Stigand,[12] archbishop of Canterbury, and he was in so great favor with him that he made him archdeacon and chief of his council; and well executed he his office in punishing the culpable and cherishing the good people, and divers times went to Rome for to support and help holy church. 10

And after this Henry II, that was the Empress's[13] son, was made king of England, and he ordained Thomas his chancellor, and had great rule, and the land stood in prosperity. And St. Thomas stood so greatly in the king's favor that the king was content with all that he did, and when the king went into Normandy, he betook[14] the governance of his son and the realm into the rule of St. Thomas, which he wisely governed till his return again.

And anon after died Theobald, the archbishop of Canterbury,[15] and then the king gave his nomination to St. Thomas, and by the chapter was elected the year of his age forty-four, and was full loath to take that great charge[16] 20 on him. And so at last, his bulls had,[17] he was sacred and stalled[18] and became a holy man, suddenly changed into a new man, doing great penance, as in wearing hair with knots,[19] and a breech of the same down to his knees. And on a Trinity Sunday received he his dignity, and there was at that time the king with many a great lord and sixteen bishops. And from thence was sent the abbot of Evesham to the pope with other clerks for the pall which he got and brought to him, and he full meekly received it. And under his habit he wore the habit of a monk, and so was he under within forth[20] a monk, and outward a clerk,[21] and did great abstinence, making his body lean and his soul fat. And he used to be well served at his 30 table, and took little refection thereof, and lived holily in giving good example.

[10] 1117 or 1119. The story of St. Thomas' parentage is pure romance, and was added by Caxton.   [11] Able, competent.

[12] This is an error: Stigand died in 1072. It was actually Theobald's family that Thomas entered.

[13] Henry II, born 1133, king 1154–1189, was the son of Geoffrey, Count of Anjou, and Matilda, daughter of Henry I. Matilda's first husband had been the emperor Henry V, who died in 1125.

[14] Committed.   [15] 1139–1161.   [16] Responsibility.

[17] Enabling documents from the pope being received.

[18] Consecrated (as priest) and installed (as archbishop).

[19] Haircloth woven with knots to make the wearing more painful.

[20] Thereafter in his private life he observed the life of a monk.

[21] A clergyman, perhaps with the notion of an official.

After this, many times the king went over into Normandy, and in his absence always St. Thomas had the rule of his son and of the realm, which was governed so well that the king could [22] him great thanks, and then abode long in this realm. And when so was that the king did anything against the franchise and liberties of Holy Church, St. Thomas would ever withstand it to his power. And on a time when the Sees of London and of Winchester were vacant and void, the king kept them both long in his hand for to have the profit of them; [23] wherefore St. Thomas was heavy,[24] and came to the king and desired him to give those two bishoprics to some virtuous man. And anon the king granted him his desire and ordained one master Roger bishop of Winchester, and the Earl of Gloucester's son, bishop of London, named Sir Robert. And soon after St. Thomas hallowed the abbey of Reading, which the first Henry founded. And that same year he translated [25] St. Edward, king and confessor, at Westminster, where he was laid in a full rich shrine.

And in short time after, by the enticement of the devil, fell great debate, variance, and strife, between the king and St. Thomas, and the king sent for all the bishops to appear tofore him at Westminster at a certain day, at which day they assembled tofore him, whom he welcomed, and after said to them how that the archbishop would destroy his law, and not suffer him to enjoy such things as his predecessors had used tofore him. Whereto St. Thomas answered that he never intended to do thing that should displease the king as far as it touched not the franchise and liberties of Holy Church. Then the king rehearsed how he would not suffer clerks [26] that were thieves to have execution of the law; to which St. Thomas said, that he ought not to execute them,[27] but they belong to the correction of Holy Church, and other divers points, to the which St. Thomas would not agree. To the which the king said: "Now I see well that thou wouldst fordo [28] the laws of this land which have been used in the days of my predecessors, but it shall not lie in thy power," and so the king being wroth departed. Then the bishops all counseled St. Thomas to follow the king's intent, or else the land should be in great trouble; and in like wise the lords temporal [29] that were his friends counseled him to the same; and St. Thomas said: "I take God to record, it was never mine intent to displease the king, or to take any thing that longeth to his right or honor." And then the lords were glad and brought him to the king to Oxford, and the king deigned not to speak to him. And then the king called all the lords spiritual and temporal tofore him, and said he would have all the laws of his forefathers

---

[22] Gave him great thanks.
[24] Worried, troubled.
[26] Thomas opposed the trying of clerks, the clergy, in secular courts.
[27] Take action against them.
[29] The nobles; the bishops are lords spiritual.

[23] The revenue from them.
[25] Moved the body, in 1163.

[28] Set aside.

there new confirmed, and there they were confirmed by all the lords spiritual and temporal.

And after this the king charged them to come to him to Clarendon to his parliament at a certain day assigned, on pain to run in [30] his indignation, and at that time so departed. And this parliament was holden at Clarendon, the eleventh year of the king's reign, and the year of our Lord eleven hundred and sixty-four. At this parliament were many lords which all were against St. Thomas. And then the king sitting in his parliament, in the presence of all his lords, demanded them if they would abide and keep the laws which had been used in his forefathers' days. Then St. Thomas spoke for 10 the part of Holy Church, and said: "All old laws that be good and rightful, and not against our mother Holy Church, I grant with good will to keep them." And then the king said he would not leave [31] one point of his law, and waxed wroth with St. Thomas. And then certain bishops required St. Thomas to obey the king's desire and will, and St. Thomas desired respite to know the laws, and then to give him an answer. And when he understood them all, to some he consented, but many he denied and would never be agreeable to them, wherefore the king was wroth and said he would hold and keep them like as his predecessors had done before him, and would not minish one point of them. Then St. Thomas said to the king 20 with full great sorrow and heavy cheer, "Now, my most dear lord and gracious king, have pity on us of Holy Church, your bedemen,[32] and give to us respite for a certain time." And thus departed each man.

And St. Thomas went to Winchester, and there prayed our Lord devoutly for Holy Church, and to give him aid and strength for to defend it, for utterly he determined to abide by ne liberties and franchise, and fell down on his knees and said, full sore weeping, "O good Lord, I acknowledge that I have offended, and for mine offence and trespass this trouble cometh to Holy Church. I purpose, good Lord, to go to Rome for to be assoiled of mine offences," and departed towards Canterbury. And anon 30 the king sent his officers to his manors and despoiled [33] them, because he would not obey the king's statutes. And the king commanded to seize all his lands and goods into his hands. And then his servants departed from him, and he went to the seaside for to have gone over sea, but the wind was against him. And so thrice he took ship and might not pass. And then he knew that it was not Our Lord's will that he should yet depart, and returned secretly to Canterbury, of whose coming his meiny [34] made great joy. And on the morn came the king's officers, for to seize all his goods, for the noise was that St. Thomas had fled the land; wherefore they had despoiled all his manors and seized them into the king's hand. And when 40

[30] Incur.   [31] Yield.   [32] Petitioners.   [33] Confiscated.
[34] Staff, household.

they came they found him at Canterbury, whereof they were sore abashed, and returned to the king informing him that he was yet at Canterbury.

And anon after St. Thomas came to the king at Woodstock for to pray him to be better disposed towards Holy Church. And then said the king to him in scorn, "May not we two dwell both in this land? Art thou so sturdy and hard of heart?" To whom St. Thomas answered, "Sire, that was never my thought, but I would fain please, and do all that ye desire so that ye hurt not the liberties of Holy Church, for them will I maintain while I live, ever to my power." With which words the king was sore moved,
10 and swore that he would have them kept, and especial if a clerk were a thief, he should be judged and executed by the king's law, and by no spiritual law; and said he would never suffer a clerk to be his master in his own land, and charged St. Thomas to appear tofore him at Northampton, and to bring all the bishops of this land with him, and so departed. St. Thomas besought God of help and succor, for the bishops which ought to be with him were most against him.

After this St. Thomas went to Northampton where the king held then his great council in the castle with all his lords; and when he came tofore the king he said, "I am come to obey your commandment, but before this
20 time was never bishop of Canterbury thus entreated, for I am the head of the Church of England, and am to you, Sir King, your ghostly father, and it was never God's law that the son should destroy his father which hath the charge of his soul. And by your striving have you made all the bishops that should abide by the right of the church to be against Holy Church and me, and ye know well that I may not fight, but am ready to suffer death rather than I should consent to lose the right of Holy Church." Then said the king, "Thou speakest as a proud clerk! [35] But I shall abate thy pride ere I leave thee, for I must reckon with thee. Thou understandest well that thou wert my chancellor many years, and once I lent to thee £500, which thou
30 never hast yet repaid, which I will that thou pay me again or else incontinent [36] that thou shalt go to prison." And then St. Thomas answered, "Ye gave me the five hundred pounds, and it is not fitting to demand that which ye have given." Notwithstanding he found surety for the said £500 and departed for that day. And after this, the next day the king demanded £30,000 that he had surmised [37] on him to have stolen, he being chancellor, whereupon he desired day to answer; at which time he said that when he was archbishop [38] he [39] set him free therein without any claim or debt before good record,[40] wherefore he ought not to answer unto that demand. And the bishops desired St. Thomas to obey the king, but in no wise would

---

[35] Churchman.   [36] Immediately.
[37] Charged him with having stolen.   [38] When he became archbishop.
[39] The king.   [40] Because of his good record.

he not agree to such things as should touch against the liberties of the church. And they came to the king, and forsook St. Thomas, and agreed to all the king's desires, and the proper [41] servants of St. Thomas fled from him, and then the poor people came and accompanied him. And on the night came to him two lords and told to him that the king's meiny had emprised [42] to slay him. And the next night after he departed in the habit of a brother of Sempringham, and so chevissed [43] that he went over sea.

And in the meanwhile certain bishops went to Rome to complain on him to the pope, and the King sent letters to the king of France not to receive him. And the king of France said that, though a man were banished and committed there [44] trespasses, yet should he be free in France. And so after when this holy St. Thomas came, he received him well, and gave him licence to abide there, and do what he would.

In this mean while the king of England sent certain lords unto the pope complaining on the Archbishop Thomas, which made grievous complaints, which when the pope had heard said, he would give none answer till that he had heard the Archbishop Thomas speak, which would hastily come thither. But they would not abide his coming, but departed without speeding their intents,[45] and came into England again.

And anon after, St. Thomas came to Rome on St. Mark's [46] day at after noon, and when his caterer should have bought fish for his dinner, because it was a fasting day,[47] he could get none for no money, and came and told to his lord St. Thomas so; and he bade him buy such as he could get, and then he bought flesh and made it ready for their dinner. And St. Thomas was served with a capon roasted, and his meiny with boiled meat. And so it was that the pope heard that he was come, and sent a cardinal to welcome him, and he found him at his dinner eating flesh, which anon returned and told the pope how he was not so perfect a man as he had supposed, for contrary to the rule of the church he eateth this day flesh. The pope would not believe him, but sent another cardinal which for more evidence took the leg of the capon in his kerchief and affirmed [48] the same, and opened his kerchief tofore the pope, and he found the leg turned into a fish called a carp. And when the pope saw it, he said, "They are not true men to say such things of this good bishop." They said faithfully that it was flesh that he ate. After this St. Thomas came to the pope and did his reverence and obedience, whom the pope welcomed; and after communication he demanded him what meat [49] he had eaten, and he said, "Flesh, as ye have heard tofore," because he could find no fish and very need compelled him thereto.

---

[41] His own servants. [42] Undertaken. [43] Managed.
[44] In English territory. [45] Succeeding in their intentions.
[46] April 25.
[47] The feast happened to fall on a fast day, presumably a Friday.
[48] Perhaps, made the same charge. [49] Food.

Then the pope understood of the miracle that the capon's leg was turned into a carp, and of his goodness granted to him and to all them of the diocese of Canterbury licence to eat flesh ever after on St. Mark's day when it falleth on a fish day, and pardon withal, which is kept and accustomed unto this day.

And then St. Thomas informed the pope how the king of England would have him consent to divers articles against the liberties of Holy Church, and what wrongs he did to the same, and for to die [50] he would never consent to them. And when the pope heard that he wept for pity, and thanked
10 God that he had such a bishop under him that had so well defended the liberties of Holy Church, and anon wrote out letters and bulls commanding all the bishops of Christendom to keep and observe the same. And then St. Thomas offered to the pope his bishopric up into the pope's hand, and his mitre with the cross and ring, and the pope commanded him to keep them still, and said he knew no man more able than he was. And after [51] St. Thomas said mass tofore the pope in a white chasuble; and after mass he said to the pope that he knew by revelation that he should suffer death for the right of Holy Church, and when it should fall that chasuble should be turned from white into red.[52] And after he departed from the pope and
20 came down into France unto the abbey of Pontigny, and there he had knowledge that when the lords spiritual and temporal which had been at Rome were come home and had told the king that they might in no wise have their intent, that the king was greatly wroth, and anon banished all the kinsmen that were longing [53] unto St. Thomas that they should incontinent avoid [54] his land, and made them swear that they should go to him [55] and tell him that for his sake they were exiled, and so they went over sea to him at Pontigny, and he being there was full sorry for them. And after there was a great chapter in England of the monks of Citeaux, and there the king desired them to write to Pontigny that they should no longer keep
30 nor sustain Thomas the Archbishop, for if they did, he would destroy them of that order being in England. And for fear thereof they wrote so over to Pontigny that he must depart from thence with his kinsmen, and so he did, and was then full heavy, and remitted his cause to God. And anon after, the king of France sent to him that he should abide where it pleased him, and dwell in his realm, and he would pay for the costs of him and of his kinsmen. And he departed and went to Sens, and the abbot brought him on the way. And St. Thomas told him how he knew by a vision that he should suffer death and martyrdom for the right of the church, and prayed him to keep it secret during his life. And after this the king of England
40 came into France, and then there told how he [55] would fordo such laws

[50] Though he were to die.   [51] Afterwards.
[52] The liturgical color signifying a martyr.   [53] Belonging.
[54] Leave, go out of.   [55] St. Thomas.

as his elders had used tofore him, wherefore St. Thomas was sent for, and they were brought together. And the king of France labored sore for to set them at accord, but it would not be, for that the one would not minish his laws and customs, and St. Thomas would not grant that he should do contrary [56] the liberties of holy church. And then the king of France held with the king of England against St. Thomas, and was wroth with him and commanded him to void his realm with all his kinsmen. And then St. Thomas wist not whither to go; but comforted his kinsmen was well as he might, and purposed to have gone into Provence for to have begged his bread. And as he was going, the king of France sent for him again, and 10 when he came he cried him mercy and said he had offended God and him, and bade him abide in his realm where he would, and he would pay for the dispenses of him and of his kin.

And in the mean while the king of England ordained his son [57] king, and made him to be crowned by the archbishop of York, and other bishops, which was against the statutes of the land, for the archbishop of Canterbury should have consented and also have crowned him, wherefore St. Thomas got him a bull for to do curse [58] them that so did against him, and also on them that occupied the goods belonging to him.

And yet after this the king [59] labored so much that he accorded the king 20 of England and St. Thomas, which accord endured not long, for the king varied from it afterward. But St. Thomas, upon this accord, came home to Canterbury, where he was received worshipfully, and sent for them that had trespassed against him, and by the authority of the pope's bull openly denounced them accursed [60] unto the time they come to amendment. And when they knew this they came to him and would have made him to assoil [61] them by force; and sent word over to the king how he had done, whereof the king was much wroth, and said, "If he had men in his land that loved him they would not suffer such a traitor in his land to live."

And forthwith four knights took their counsel together and thought 30 they would do to the king a pleasure, and emprised [62] to slay St. Thomas, and suddenly departed and took their shipping towards England. And when the king knew of their departure, he was sorry and sent after them, but they were on the sea and departed ere the messengers came, wherefore the king was heavy and sorry. These be the names of the four knights: Sir Reginald Bereson,[63] Sir Hugh Morville, Sir William Tracy, Sir Richard the Breton. On Christmas Day St. Thomas made a sermon at Canterbury in his own church, and weeping, prayed the people to pray for him, for

---

[56] Would not permit him to act contrary to.
[57] Henry, the second son of Henry II, was in 1170 crowned king, but died in 1183, six years before his father.   [58] Excommunicate.
[59] The king of France.   [60] Declared them excommunicated.
[61] Absolve.   [62] Undertook.   [63] Fitzurse.

he knew well his time was nigh, and there executed the sentence on them that were against the right of Holy Church. And that same day as the king sat at meat all the bread that he handled waxed anon mouldy and hoar, that no man might eat of it, and the bread that they [64] touched not was fair and good for to eat.

And these four knights aforesaid came to Canterbury on the Tuesday [65] in Christmas week about evensong time, and came to St. Thomas and said that the king commanded him to make amends for the wrongs that he had done, also that he should assoil all them that he had accursed anon, or else 10 they should slay him. Then said St. Thomas, "All that I ought to do by right, that will I with a good will do; but as to the sentence that is executed I may not undo, but [66] that they will submit them to the correction of Holy Church, for it was done by our holy father the pope and not by me." Then said Sir Reginald, "But [66] if thou assoil the king and all other standing in the curse, it shall cost thee thy life." And St. Thomas said, "Thou knowest well enough that king and I were accorded on Mary Magdalene [67] day, and that this curse should go forth on them that had offended the church."

Then one of the knights smote him as he kneeled before the altar on the head. And one Sir Edward Grim, that was his crozier,[68] put forth his arm 20 with the cross to bear off the stroke, and the stroke smote the cross asunder and his arm almost off, wherefore he fled for fear, and so did all the monks, that were at that time at compline. And then smote each at him, that his brain fell on the pavement. And so they slew and martyred him, and were so cruel that one of them brake the point of his sword against the pavement. And thus this holy and blessed Archbishop St. Thomas suffered death in his own church for the right of all Holy Church.

And when he was dead they stirred his brain, and after went into his chamber and took away his goods, and his horse out of the stable, and took away his bulls and writings, and delivered them to Sir Robert Broke to 30 bear into France to the king. And as they searched his chamber they found in a chest two shirts of hair made full of great knots, and then they said, "Certainly he was a good man," and coming down into the churchyard they began to dread and fear that the ground would not have borne them, and were marvellously aghast, but they supposed that the earth would have swallowed them all quick.[69] And then they knew that they had done amiss. And anon it was known all about, how that he was martyred, and anon after took his holy body, and unclothed him, and found bishop's clothing above, and the habit of a monk under. And next his flesh he wore hard hair, full of knots, which was his shirt. And his breech was of the same, 40 and the knots sticked fast within the skin, and all his body was full of

---

[64] The king's hands.   [65] St. Thomas was killed on December 29.
[66] Unless.   [67] July 22.   [68] Cross-bearer.   [69] Alive.

worms; he suffered great pain. And he was thus martyred the year of our Lord one thousand one hundred and seventy one, and was fifty-three years old. And soon after tidings came to the king how he was slain, wherefore the king took great sorrow and sent to Rome for his absolution.

Now after that St. Thomas departed from the pope, the pope would daily look upon the white chasuble that St. Thomas had said mass in, and the same day that he was martyred he saw it turn into red, whereby he knew well that that same day he suffered martyrdom for the right of Holy Church, and commanded a mass of requiem solemnly to be sung for his soul. And when the choir began to sing requiem, an angel on high began 10 the office of a martyr: *Letabitur justus*,[70] and then all the choir followed singing forth the mass of the office of a martyr. And the pope thanked God that it pleased him to show such miracles for his holy martyr, at whose tomb by the merits and prayers of this holy martyr our blessed Lord hath showed such miracles. The blind have recovered their sight, the dumb their speech, the deaf their hearing, the lame their limbs, and the dead their life. If I should here express all the miracles that it hath pleased God to show for this holy saint it should contain a whole volume, therefore at this time I pass over unto the feast of his translation,[71] where I purpose with the grace of God to recite some of them. Then let us pray to this glorious 20 martyr to be our advocate, that by his petition we may come to everlasting bliss. Amen.

THE TRANSLATION[1] OF ST. THOMAS OF CANTERBURY

(JULY 7)

The reverend father in God, Stephen, Archbishop of Canterbury, Richard, bishop of Salisbury, Walter, the prior of the same place, with the convent, with spiritual songs and devout hymns, when it was night, went to the sepulchre of this holy martyr, and all that night and day of his translation, they persevered in prayers and fastings. And after midnight four priests, elected and thereto chosen, approaching to his body, took up the holy head with great devotion and reverence, and unto them all offered it for to kiss it. Then the archbishops and all the others made great honor to it, and 30 took all the relics of the precious body and laid them in a chest, and shut it fast with iron locks, and set it in a place for to be kept unto the day that the translation should be solemnized.

The day, then, of this holy translation being come, there were present a great innumerable multitude of people, as well of rich as of poor. There

---

[70] Ps. 64:10 (Vulg. 63:11), one of the introits for a mass for a martyr.
[71] July 7.
[1] Transference of the relics from one spot to another.

was Pandulphus, a legate of our holy father the pope, and two archbishops of France, of Rheims and Arles, with many other bishops and abbots, and also King Harry the Third with earls and barons; which king himself took the chest upon his shoulders, and with other prelates and lords, brought it with great joy and honor into the place where it is now worshiped, and was laid in a fair and much rich shrine. At whose holy translation were showed, by the merits of this holy martyr, St. Thomas, many miracles. To blind men was given their sight, to deaf men their hearing, to dumb men their speech, and to dead men was restored life.

10   Among all others there was a man, because of great devotion that he had to be at this holy translation and visit the holy martyr, which came to the bridge at Brentford by London; and when he was in the middle of the bridge, meeting there one,[2] was cast into the water. This man, not forgetting himself, called St. Thomas unto his help, and besought him not to suffer his pilgrim to perish, ne [3] to be there drowned. And five times he sank down to the ground,[4] and five times arose above the water, and then he was cast to the dry ground. Then he affirmed that he received no water into his mouth, ne into his ears that did him grievance ne hurt that he felt, save in his falling he felt in his mouth a little salt water; and added more

20 thereto, saying that, when he sank, a bishop held him up that he might not sink.

This holy translation was done and accomplished the year of Our Lord twelve hundred and twenty, in the nones of July, at three o'clock, in the fiftieth year after his passion. For this glorious saint Our Lord hath showed many great miracles, as well by his life as after his death and martyrdom. For a little tofore his death a young man died and was raised again by miracle. And he said that he was led to see the holy order of saints in heaven, and there he saw a seat void, and he asked for whom it was, and it was answered to him that it was kept for the great bishop of England, St. Thomas

30 of Canterbury.

There was also a simple priest that daily sang no other mass but of Our Lady, whereof he was put to St. Thomas, his ordinary; [5] whom accused he apposed and found him full simple of cunning,[6] wherefore he suspended him and inhibited him his mass. Wherefore this priest was full sorry and prayed humbly to Our Blessed Lady that he might be restored again to say his mass. And then Our Blessed Lady appeared to this priest, and bade him go to St. Thomas, and bid him "by the token that the Lady whom thou servest hath sewed his shirt of hair with red silk, which he shall find there as he laid it, that he give thee leave to sing mass, and assoil thee of his sus-

---

[2] Meeting a person there.   [3] Nor.   [4] Bottom.
[5] Ecclesiastical superior.
[6] He (Thomas) interrogated the accused and found him very ignorant.

pending and thine inhibiting, and restore thee again to thy service." And when St. Thomas heard this he was greatly abashed, and went and found like as the priest had said, and then assoiled [7] him to say mass as he did before, commanding him to keep this thing secret as long as he lived . . .

There was a tame bird kept in a cage which was learned [8] to speak. And on a time he fled out of the cage and flew into the field; and there came a sparrowhawk and would have taken this bird and pursued after. And the bird, being in great dread, cried: "St. Thomas! help!" like as he had heard others speak, and the sparrowhawk fell down dead, and the bird escaped harmless.   10

Also there was a man that St. Thomas loved much in his days, and he fell in a grievous sickness, wherefore he went to the tomb of St. Thomas to pray for his health, and anon he had his desire and was whole. And as he turned homeward, being all whole, then he began to dread lest this health should not be most profitable for his soul. Then he returned again to the tomb of St. Thomas, and prayed if his health were not profitable to his soul, that his old sickness might come again to him. And it came anon again to him, and endured unto his life's end . . .

Who should tell all the miracles that Our Blessed Lord hath showed for this holy martyr, it should overmuch endure,[9] for ever sith his passion unto 20 this day God hath showed continually for him many great miracles. Then let us pray this holy saint to be a special advocate for us wretched sinners unto Our Lord God, who bring us into His everlasting bliss in heaven!

[7] Absolved.   [8] Taught.   [9] Would last too long.

Preface to Malory's
Book of Arthur and His Knights

William Caxton

AFTER that I had accomplished and finished divers histories, as well of contemplation as of other historical and worldly acts of great conquerors and princes, and also certain books of ensamples and doctrine, many noble and divers gentlemen of this realm of England came and demanded me, many and ofttimes, wherefore that I have not do made and imprinted the noble history of the Saint Greal, and of the most renowned Christian king, first and chief of the three best Christian and worthy, King Arthur, which ought most to be remembered among us English men tofore all other Christian kings.

10   For it is notoriously known through the universal world that there be nine worthy and the best that ever were.[1] That is to wit three paynims, three Jews, and three Christian men. As for the paynims they were tofore the Incarnation of Christ, which were named, the first, Hector of Troy, of whom the history is come both in ballad and in prose; the second, Alexander the Great; and the third, Julius Caesar, Emperor of Rome, of whom the histories be well-known and had. And as for the three Jews which also were tofore the Incarnation of Our Lord, of whom the first was Duke Joshua, which brought the children of Israel into the land of behest; the second David, King of Jerusalem; and the third Judas Maccabaeus: of these three 20 the Bible rehearseth all their noble histories and acts. And since the said Incarnation have been three noble Christian men stalled and admitted through the universal world into the number of the nine best and worthy, of whom was first the noble Arthur, whose noble acts I purpose to write in this present book here following. The second was Charlemagne or Charles the Great, of whom the history is had in many places both in French and English; and the third and last was Godfrey of Bouillon, of whose acts and life I made a book unto the excellent prince and king of noble memory, King Edward the Fourth.

   [1] The list of the Nine Worthies (Valiant Men) was invented by Jacques de Longuyon and included by him in his *Voeux du Paon* (ca. 1312). See the *Alliterative Morte Arthur*. Tapestries representing them (woven about 1400) are in the Cloisters Museum, New York City.

The said noble gentlemen instantly required me to imprint the history of the said noble king and conqueror, King Arthur, and of his knights, with the history of the Saint Greal, and of the death and ending of the said Arthur; affirming that I ought rather to imprint his acts and noble feats, than of Godfrey of Bouillon, or any of the other eight, considering that he was a man born within this realm, and king and emperor of the same; and that there be in French divers and many noble volumes of his acts, and also of his knights. To whom I answered, that divers men hold opinion that there was no such Arthur, and that all such books as be made of him be but feigned and fables, by cause that some chronicles make of him no men- 10 tion nor remember him no thing, nor of his knights. Whereto they answered and one in special said, that in him that should say or think that there was never such a king called Arthur, might well be credited great folly and blindness; for he said that there were many evidences of the contrary: first ye may see his sepulture in the Monastery of Glastonbury. And also in *Polichronicon*,[2] in the fifth book the sixth chapter, and in the seventh book the twenty-third chapter, where his body was buried and after found and translated into the said monastery. Ye shall see also in the history of Boccaccio, in his book *De Casu Principum*, part of his noble acts, and also of his fall. Also Galfridus [3] in his British book recounteth his life; and 20 in the divers places of England many remembrances be yet of him and shall remain perpetually, and also of his knights. First, in the Abbey of Westminster, at Saint Edward's shrine, remaineth the print of his seal in red wax closed in beryl, in which is written *Patricius Arthurus, Britannie, Gallie, Germanie, Dacie Imperator.*[4] Item, in the castle of Dover ye may see Gawain's skull and Craddock's mantle: at Winchester the Round Table: at other places Launcelot's sword and many other things. Then all these things considered, there can no man reasonably gainsay but there was a king of this land named Arthur. For in all places, Christian and heathen, he is reputed and taken for one of the nine worthy, and the first of the three 30 Christian men. And also he is more spoken of beyond the sea, more books made of his noble acts than there be in England, as well in Dutch, Italian, Spanish, and Greek, as in French. And yet of record remain in witness of him in Wales, in the town of Camelot,[5] the great stones and marvelous works of iron, lying under the ground, and royal vaults, which divers now living hath seen. Wherefore it is a marvel why he is no more renowned in his own

[2] By Ranulph Higden (ca. 1350).

[3] Geoffrey of Monmouth, who wrote his *History of the Kings of Britain* about 1136, was a brazen fabricator, but his account of Arthur was long accepted as authoritative.

[4] "Nobly-born Arthur, Emperor of Britain, Gaul, Germany and Denmark."

[5] The Camelot of the French and English romances is probably a name due to the corruption of Carlion (Caerleon on Usk). What specific place Caxton had in mind is uncertain, but very likely he had in mind the Roman remains of Caerleon, and so by happy chance was right.

country, save only it accordeth to the Word of God, which saith that no man is accept for a prophet in his own country.

Then all these things foresaid alleged, I could not well deny but that there was such a noble king named Arthur, and reputed one of the nine worthy, and first and chief of the Christian men; and many noble volumes be made of him and of his noble knights in French, which I have seen and read beyond the sea, which be not had in our maternal tongue, but in Welsh be many and also in French, and some in English, but no where nigh all. Wherefore, such as have late been drawn out briefly into English I have, 10 after the simple cunning that God hath sent to me, under the favor and correction of all noble lords and gentlemen, emprised to imprint a book of the noble histories of the said King Arthur, and of certain of his knights, after a copy unto me delivered, which copy Sir Thomas Malory did take out of certain books of French, and reduced it into English. And I, according to my copy, have done set it in imprint, to the intent that noble men may see and learn the noble acts of chivalry, the gentle and virtuous deeds that some knights used in those days, by which they came to honor; and how they that were vicious were punished and oft put to shame and rebuke; humbly beseeching all noble lords and ladies, with all other estates, 20 of what estate or degree they be of, that shall see and read in this said book and work, that they take the good and honest acts in their remembrance, and to follow the same. Wherein they shall find many joyous and pleasant histories, and noble and renowned acts of humanity, gentleness, and chivalries. For herein may be seen noble chivalry, courtesy, humanity, friendliness, hardiness, love, friendship, cowardice, murder, hate, virtue, and sin. Do after the good and leave the evil, and it shall bring you to good fame and renown. And for to pass the time this book shall be pleasant to read in; but for to give faith and believe that all is true that is contained herein, ye be at your liberty; but all is written for our doctrine, and for to beware 30 that we fall not to vice nor sin; but to exercise and follow virtue; by which we may come and attain to good fame and renown in this life, and after this short and transitory life, to come unto everlasting bliss in heaven, the which He grant us that reigneth in heaven, the blessed Trinity. Amen.

The Book of Arthur and His Knights

Sir Thomas Malory

MERLIN, KING PELLINORE, AND THE LADY OF THE LAKE

(BK. I, CHAP. XXIII–XXVII)

AND so Arthur rode a soft pace till it was day, and then was he ware of three churls chasing Merlin, and would have slain him. Then the king rode unto them, and bade them: "Flee, churls!" then were they afeard when they saw a knight, and fled.

"O Merlin," said Arthur, "here hadst thou been slain for all thy crafts, had I not been."

"Nay," said Merlin, "not so, for I could save myself an I would; and thou art more near thy death than I am, for thou goest to the deathward, an God be not thy friend."

So as they went thus talking they came to the fountain, and the rich 10 pavilion there by it. Then King Arthur was ware where sat a knight armed in a chair. "Sir knight," said Arthur, "for what cause abidest thou here, that there may no knight ride this way but if he joust with thee?" said the king. "I rede [1] thee leave that custom," said Arthur.

"This custom," said the knight, "have I used and will use maugre [2] who saith nay; and who is grieved with my custom let him amend it that will."

"I will amend it," said Arthur.

"I shall defend thee," said the knight. Anon he took his horse and dressed his shield and took a spear, and they met so hard either in other's shields, that all to-shivered their spears. Therewith anon Arthur pulled out his 20 sword.

"Nay, not so," said the knight; "it is fairer," said the knight, "that we twain run more together with sharp spears."

"I will well," said Arthur, "an I had any more spears."

"I have enow," said the knight; so there came a squire and brought two good spears, and Arthur chose one and he another; so they spurred their horses and came together with all their mights, that either brake their spears to their hands. Then Arthur set hand on his sword.

[1] Advise.   [2] In spite of.

"Nay," said the knight, "ye shall do better; ye are a passing good jouster as ever I met withal, and once for the love of the high order of knighthood let us joust once again."

"I assent me," said Arthur.

Anon there were brought two great spears, and every knight gat a spear, and therewith they ran together that Arthur's spear all to-shivered. But the other knight hit him so hard in midst of the shield, that horse and man fell to the earth, and therewith Arthur was eager, and pulled out his sword, and said, "I will assay thee, sir knight, on foot, for I have lost the honor on 10 horseback."

"I will be on horseback," said the knight.

Then was Arthur wroth, and dressed his shield toward him with his sword drawn. When the knight saw that, he alit, for him thought no worship [3] to have a knight at such avail, he to be on horseback and he on foot, and so he alit and dressed his shield unto Arthur. And there began a strong battle with many great strokes, and so hewed with their swords that the cantels flew in the fields, and much blood they bled both, that all the place thereas they fought was overbled with blood, and thus they fought long and rested them, and then they went to the battle again, and so hurtled 20 together like two rams, that either fell to the earth. So at the last they smote together that both their swords met even together. But the sword of the knight smote King Arthur's sword in two pieces, wherefore he was heavy.

Then said the knight unto Arthur, "Thou art in my daunger,[4] whether me list to save thee or slay thee, and but thou yield thee as overcome and recreant, thou shalt die."

"As for death," said King Arthur, "welcome be it when it cometh, but to yield me unto thee as recreant, I had liefer die than to be so shamed." And therewithal the king leapt unto Pellinore, and took him by the middle and threw him down, and rased [5] off his helm. When the knight felt that, 30 he was adread, for he was a passing big man of might, and anon he brought Arthur under him, and rased off his helm and would have smitten off his head.

Therewithal came Merlin and said, "Knight, hold thy hand, for, an thou slay that knight, thou puttest this realm in the greatest damage that ever was realm: for this knight is a man of more worship than thou wotest of."

"Why, who is he?" said the knight.

"It is King Arthur."

Then would he have slain him for dread of his wrath, and heaved up his sword, and therewith Merlin cast an enchantment to the knight, that 40 he fell to the earth in a great sleep. Then Merlin took up King Arthur, and rode forth on the knight's horse.

---

[3] It seemed to him no honor.　　　　[4] Power.　　　　[5] Cut.

"Alas!" said Arthur, "what hast thou done, Merlin? liveth not so worshipful a knight as he was; I had liefer than the stint [6] of my land a year that he were alive."

"Care ye not," said Merlin, "for he is wholer than ye; for he is but asleep, and will awake within three hours. I told you," said Merlin, "what a knight he was; here had ye been slain had I not been. Also there liveth not a bigger knight than he is one, and he shall hereafter do you right good service; and his name is Pellinore, and he shall have two sons that shall be passing good men; save one they shall have no fellow of prowess and of good living, and their names shall be Percival of Wales and Lamorak of Wales, and he shall tell you the name of your own son begotten of your sister that shall be the destruction of all this realm."

Right so the king and he departed, and went unto an hermit that was a good man and a great leech. So the hermit searched all his wounds and gave him good salves; so the king was there three days, and then were his wounds well amended that he might ride and go, and so departed. And as they rode, Arthur said, "I have no sword."

"No force," [7] said Merlin; "hereby is a sword that shall be yours, an I may."

So they rode till they came to a lake, the which was a fair water and broad, and in the midst of the lake Arthur was ware of an arm clothed in white samite, that held a fair sword in that hand.

"Lo!" said Merlin, "yonder is that sword that I spake of."

With that they saw a damosel going upon the lake. "What damosel is that?" said Arthur.

"That is the Lady of the Lake," said Merlin; "and within that lake is a rock, and therein is as fair a place as any on earth, and richly beseen; and this damosel will come to you anon, and then speak ye fair to her that she will give you that sword."

Anon withal came the damosel unto Arthur, and saluted him, and he her again. "Damosel," said Arthur, "what sword is that, that yonder the arm holdeth above the water? I would it were mine, for I have no sword."

"Sir Arthur, king," said the damosel, "that sword is mine, and if ye will give me a gift when I ask it you, ye shall have it."

"By my faith," said Arthur, "I will give you what gift ye will ask."

"Well!" said the damosel, "go ye into yonder barge, and row yourself to the sword, and take it and the scabbard with you, and I will ask my gift when I see my time."

So Sir Arthur and Merlin alit and tied their horses to two trees, and so they went into the ship, and when they came to the sword that the hand held, Sir Arthur took it up by the handles, and took it with him, and the

---

[6] Loss. [7] No matter.

arm and the hand went under the water. And so they came unto the land and rode forth, and then Sir Arthur saw a rich pavilion.

"What signifieth yonder pavilion?"

"It is the knight's pavilion," said Merlin, "that ye fought with last, Sir Pellinore; but he is out, he is not there. He hath ado with a knight of yours that hight Egglame, and they have foughten together, but at the last Egglame fled, and else he had been dead, and he hath chased him even to Caerleon, and we shall meet with him anon in the highway."

"That is well said," said Arthur, "now have I a sword, now will I wage
10 battle with him, and be avenged on him."

"Sir, you shall not so," said Merlin, "for the knight is weary of fighting and chasing, so that ye shall have no worship to have ado with him; also he will not be lightly matched of one knight living, and therefore it is my counsel, let him pass, for he shall do you good service in short time, and his sons after his days. Also ye shall see that day in short space, you shall be right glad to give him your sister to wed."

"When I see him, I will do as ye advise me," said Arthur. Then Sir Arthur looked on the sword, and liked it passing well.

"Whether liketh you better," said Merlin, "the sword or the scabbard?"
20 "Me liketh better the sword," said Arthur.

"Ye are more unwise," said Merlin, "for the scabbard is worth ten of the swords, for whiles ye have the scabbard upon you, ye shall never lose no blood, be ye never so sore wounded; therefore keep well the scabbard always with you."

So they rode unto Caerleon, and by the way they met with Sir Pellinore; but Merlin had done such a craft, that Pellinore saw not Arthur, and he passed by without any words. "I marvel," said Arthur, "that the knight would not speak."

"Sir," said Merlin, "he saw you not, for an he had seen you, ye had not
30 lightly departed."

So they came unto Caerleon, whereof his knights were passing glad. And when they heard of his adventures, they marveled that he would jeopard his person so, alone. But all men of worship said it was merry to be under such a chieftain, that would put his person in adventure as other poor knights did.

*   *   *   *   *

Then King Arthur let send for all the children born on Mayday, begotten of lords and born of ladies; for Merlin told King Arthur that he that should destroy him should be born on Mayday, wherefore he sent for them all, upon pain of death; and so there were found many lords' sons, and all
40 were sent unto the king, and so was Mordred sent by King Lot's wife, and

all were put in a ship to the sea, and some were four weeks old, and some less. And so by fortune the ship drove unto a castle and was all to-riven [8] and destroyed the most part, save that Mordred was cast up, and a good man found him and nourished him till he was fourteen year old, and then he brought him to the court, as it rehearseth afterward and toward the end of the *Morte Arthur*.[9]

THE MARVELS OF THE HOLY GRAIL

(BK. XVII, CHAP. XIX–XXII)

So departed he [Galahad] from thence, and commended the brethren to God; and so he rode five days till that he came to the Maimed King. And ever followed Percivale the five days, asking where he had been; and so one told him how the adventures of Logris [10] were achieved. So on a day it befell that they came out of a great forest, and there they met at traverse with Sir Bors, the which rode alone. It is none need to tell if they were glad; and them he saluted, and they yielded him honor and good adventure, and every each told other.

Then said Bors: "It is more than a year and an half that I ne lay ten times where men dwelled, but in wild forests and in mountains, but God was ever my comfort."

Then rode they a great while till that they came to the castle of Carbonek.[11] And when they were entered within the castle, King Pelles knew them; then there was great joy, for they wist well by their coming that they had fulfilled the quest of the Saint Greal.[12] Then Eliazar, King Pelles' son, brought tofore them the broken sword wherewith Joseph [13] was stricken through the thigh. Then Bors set his hand thereto, if that he might have soldered it again; but it would not be. Then he took it to Percivale, but he had no more power thereto than he.

"Now have ye it again," said Percivale to Galahad, "for an it be ever achieved by any bodily man, ye must do it."

And then he took the pieces and set them together, and they seemed that they had never been broken, and as well as it had been first forged. And

---

[8] Split asunder.

[9] This refers to the last book of Malory's collection, not the collection as a whole.

[10] England.

[11] An imaginary castle, called in Malory's French source "Corbenic," a corruption of *Cor beneit*, meaning "Blessed Horn." The castle was so called because in the original tradition it contained, not only the Grail, but also a miraculous drinking horn. The French words *cors beneiz* were misunderstood as "blessed body," and so instead of the horn we have the eucharistic wafer.

[12] *Greal*, strictly speaking, is a French word meaning a "rather deep platter," not a chalice.

[13] Joseph of Arimathea, who took down Christ's body from the cross.

when they within espied that the adventure of the sword was achieved, then they gave the sword to Bors, for it might not be better set; for he was a good knight and a worthy man.

And a little afore even the sword arose great and marvelous, and was full of great heat that many men fell for dread. And anon alit a voice among them and said: "They that ought not to sit at the table of Jesu Christ arise, for now shall very knights be fed."

So they went thence, all save King Pelles and Eliazar, his son, the which were holy men, and a maid which was his niece; and so these three fellows 10 and they three were there, no more. Anon they saw knights all armed come in at the hall door, and did off their helms and their arms, and said unto Galahad: "Sir, we have hied right much for to be with you at this table where the holy meat shall be departed." [14]

Then said he: "Ye be welcome, but of whence be ye?"

So three of them said they were of Gaul, and other three said they were of Ireland, and the other three said they were of Denmark. So as they sat thus there came out a bed of tree, of a chamber, the which four gentlewomen brought; and in the bed lay a good man sick, and a crown of gold upon his head; and there in the middes of the place they set him down, and 20 went again their way. Then he lift up his head, and said: "Galahad, Knight, ye be welcome, for much have I desired your coming, for in such anguish I have been long. But now I trust to God the term is come that my pain shall be allayed, that I shall pass out of this world, so as it was promised me long ago."

Therewith a voice said: "There be two among you that be not in the quest of the Saint Greal, and therefore depart ye."

Then King Pelles and his son departed. And therewithal beseemed them that there came a man, and four angels from heaven, clothed in likeness of a bishop, and had a cross in his hand; and these four angels bare him in a 30 chair, and set him down before the table of silver whereupon the Saint Greal was; and it seemed that he had in middes of his forehead letters the which said: "See ye here Josephes,[15] the first bishop of Christendom, the same which Our Lord sacred [16] in the city of Sarras in the spiritual palace."

Then the knights marveled, for that bishop was dead more than three hundred year tofore. "O knights," said he, "marvel not, for I was sometime an earthly man."

With that they heard the chamber door open, and there they saw angels; and two bare candles of wax, and the third a towel, and the fourth a spear which bled marvelously, that three drops fell within a box which he held 40 with his other hand. And they set the candles upon the table, and the third the towel upon the vessel, and the fourth the holy spear even upright upon

[14] Divided.   [15] Son of Joseph of Arimathea.   [16] Consecrated.

the vessel. And then the bishop made semblant as though he would have gone to the sacring [17] of the mass. And then he took an ubblye [18] which was made in likeness of bread. And at the lifting up there came a figure in likeness of a child, and the visage was as red and as bright as any fire, and smote himself into the bread, so that they all saw it that the bread was formed of a fleshly man; and then he put it into the holy vessel again, and then he did that longed [19] to a priest to do to a mass. And then he went to Galahad and kissed him, and bade him go and kiss his fellows: and so he did anon.

"Now," said he, "servants of Jesu Christ, ye shall be fed afore this table 10 with sweetmeats that never knights tasted."

And when he had said, he vanished away. And they set them at the table in great dread, and made their prayers. Then looked they and saw a man come out of the holy vessel, that had all the signs of the passion of Jesu Christ, bleeding all openly, and said: "My knights, and my servants, and my true children, which be come out of deadly life into spiritual life, I will now no longer hide me from you, but ye shall see now a part of my secrets and of my hidden things: now hold and receive the high meat which ye have so much desired."

Then took He himself the holy vessel and came to Galahad; and he 20 kneeled down, and there he received his Savior, and after him so received all his fellows; and they thought it so sweet that it was marvelous to tell. Then said He to Galahad: "Son, wotest thou what I hold betwixt my hands?"

"Nay," said he, "but if ye will tell me."

"This is," said He, "the holy dish wherein I ate the lamb on Sher-Thursday. And now hast thou seen that thou most desired to see, but yet hast thou not seen it so openly as thou shalt see it in the city of Sarras in the spiritual palace. Therefore thou must go hence and bear with thee this holy vessel; for this night it shall depart from the realm of Logris, that it 30 shall never be seen more here. And wotest thou wherefore? For he is not served nor worshiped to his right by them of this land, for they be turned to evil living; therefore I shall disherit them of the honor which I have done them. And therefore go ye three to-morrow unto the sea, where ye shall find your ship ready, and with you take the sword with the strange girdles, and no more with you but Sir Percivale and Sir Bors. Also I will that ye take with you of the blood of this spear for to anoint the Maimed King, both his legs and all his body, and he shall have his health."

"Sir," said Galahad, "why shall not these other fellows go with us?"

"For this cause: for right as I departed my apostles one here and another 40 there, so I will that ye depart; and two of you shall die in my service, but

---

[17] Consecration. [18] Wafer. [19] Pertained.

one of you shall come again and tell tidings." Then gave He them His blessing and vanished away.

And Galahad went anon to the spear which lay upon the table, and touched the blood with his fingers, and came after to the Maimed King and anointed his legs. And therewith he clothed him anon, and start upon his feet out of his bed as an whole man, and thanked Our Lord that He had healed him. And that was not to the world-ward, for anon he yielded him to a place of religion of white monks, and was a full holy man.

The same night about midnight came a voice among them which said:
10 "My sons and not my chief sons, my friends and not my warriors, go ye hence where ye hope best to do and as I bade you."

"Ah, thanked be Thou, Lord, that Thou wilt vouchsafe to call us, Thy sinners. Now may we well prove that we have not lost our pains."

And anon in all haste they took their harness and departed. But the three knights of Gaul, one of them hight Claudine, King Claudas' son, and the other two were great gentlemen. Then prayed Galahad to every each of them, that if they come to King Arthur's court that they should salute my lord, Sir Launcelot, my father, and of them of the Round Table; and prayed them if they came on that part that they should not forget it.

20 Right so departed Galahad, Percivale, and Bors with him; and so they rode three days, and then they came to a rivage, and found the ship whereof the tale speaketh of tofore. And when they came to the board they found in the middes the table of silver which they had left with the Maimed King, and the Saint Greal which was covered with red samite. Then were they glad to have such things in their fellowship; and so they entered and made great reverence thereto; and Galahad fell in his prayer long time to Our Lord, that at what time he asked, that he should pass out of this world. So much he prayed till a voice said to him: "Galahad, thou shalt have thy request; and when thou askest the death of thy body thou shalt have it,
30 and then shalt thou find the life of the soul."

Percivale heard this, and prayed him, of fellowship that was between them, to tell him wherefore he asked such things. "That shall I tell you," said Galahad; "the other day when we saw a part of the adventures of the Saint Greal I was in such a joy of heart, that I trow never man was that was earthly. And therefore I wot well, when my body is dead my soul shall be in great joy to see the blessed Trinity every day, and the Majesty of Our Lord, Jesu Christ."

So long were they in the ship that they said to Galahad: "Sir, in this bed ought ye to lie, for so saith the scripture."
40 And so he laid him down and slept a great while; and when he awaked he looked afore him and saw the city of Sarras. And as they would have landed they saw the ship wherein Percivale had put his sister in.

"Truly," said Percivale, "in the name of God, well hath my sister holden us covenant."

Then took they out of the ship the table of silver, and he took it to Percivale and to Bors, to go tofore, and Galahad came behind. And right so they went to the city, and at the gate of the city they saw an old man crooked. Then Galahad called him and bade him help to bear this heavy thing.

"Truly," said the old man, "it is ten year ago that I might not go but with crutches."

"Care thou not," said Galahad, "and arise up and show thy good will." And so he essayed, and found himself as whole as ever he was. Then ran 10 he to the table, and took one part against Galahad.

And anon arose there great noise in the city, that a cripple was made whole by knights marvelous that entered into the city. Then anon after, the three knights went to the water, and brought up into the palace Percivale's sister, and buried her as richly as a king's daughter ought to be. And when the king of the city, which was cleped Estorause, saw the fellowship, he asked them of whence they were, and what thing it was that they had brought upon the table of silver. And they told him the truth of the Saint Greal, and the power which that God had set there. Then the king was a tyrant, and was come of the line of paynims, and took them and put them 20 in prison in a deep hole.

But as soon as they were there Our Lord sent them the Saint Greal, through whose grace they were alway fulfilled while that they were in prison. So at the year's end it befell that this King Estorause lay sick, and felt that he should die. Then he sent for the three knights, and they came afore him; and he cried them mercy of that he had done to them, and they forgave it him goodly; and he died anon. When the king was dead all the city was dismayed, and wist not who might be their king. Right so as they were in counsel there came a voice among them, and bade them choose the youngest knight of them three to be their king: "For he shall 30 well maintain you and all yours."

So they made Galahad king by all the assent of the holy city, and else they would have slain him. And when he was come to behold the land, he let make above the table of silver a chest of gold and of precious stones, that hylled [20] the holy vessel. And every day early the three fellows would come afore it, and make their prayers.

Now at the year's end, and the self day after Galahad had borne the crown of gold, he arose up early and his fellows, and came to the palace, and saw tofore them the holy vessel, and a man kneeling on his knees in likeness of a bishop, that had about him a great fellowship of angels as it 40 had been Jesu Christ himself; and then he arose and began a mass of Our

[20] Covered.

Lady. And when he came to the sacrament of the mass, and had done, anon he called Galahad, and said to him: "Come forth, the servant of Jesu Christ, and thou shalt see that thou hast much desired to see."

And then he began to tremble right hard when the deadly flesh began to behold the spiritual things. Then he held up his hands toward heaven and said: "Lord, I thank thee, for now I see that that hath been my desire many a day. Now, blessed Lord, would I not longer live if it might please thee, Lord."

And therewith the good man took Our Lord's body betwixt his hands, 10 and proffered it to Galahad, and he received it right gladly and meekly. "Now wotest thou what I am?" said the good man.

"Nay," said Galahad.

"I am [Josephes, the son of] Joseph of Aramathie, the which Our Lord hath sent here to thee to bear thee fellowship; and wotest thou wherefore that He hath sent me more than any other? For thou hast resembled me in two things; in that thou hast seen the marvels of the Saint Greal, in that thou hast been a clean maiden, as I have been and am."

And when he had said these words Galahad went to Percivale and kissed him, and commended him to God; and so he went to Sir Bors and kissed 20 him, and commended him to God, and said: "Fair lord, salute me to my lord, Sir Launcelot, my father, and as soon as ye see him, bid him remember of this unstable world."

And therewith he kneeled down tofore the table and made his prayers, and then suddenly his soul departed to Jesu Christ, and a great multitude of angels bare his soul up to heaven, that the two fellows might well behold it. Also the two fellows saw come from heaven an hand, but they saw not the body. And then it came right to the Vessel, and took it and the spear, and so bare it up to heaven. Sithen [21] was there never man so hardy to say that he had seen the Saint Greal.

THE PASSING OF ARTHUR

(BK. XXI, CHAP. III–VII)

30 Then Sir Mordred araised much people about London, for they of Kent, Sussex, and Surrey, Essex, and of Suffolk, and of Norfolk, held the most part with Sir Mordred; and many a full noble knight drew unto Sir Mordred and to the king: but they that loved Sir Launcelot drew unto Sir Mordred. So upon Trinity Sunday at night, King Arthur dreamed a wonderful dream, and that was this: that him seemed he sat upon a chaflet [22] in a chair,

[21] Thereafter.   [22] Scaffold.

and the chair was fast to a wheel, and thereupon sat King Arthur in the richest cloth of gold that might be made; and the king thought there was under him, far from him, an hideous deep black water, and therein were all manner of serpents, and worms, and wild beasts, foul and horrible; and suddenly the king thought the wheel turned up so down, and he fell among the serpents, and every beast took him by a limb; and then the king cried as he lay in his bed and slept: "Help!" And then knights, squires, and yeomen, awaked the king; and then he was so amazed that he wist not where he was; and then he fell on slumbering again, not sleeping nor thoroughly waking. 10

So the king seemed verily that there came Sir Gawain unto him with a number of fair ladies with him. And when King Arthur saw him, then he said: "Welcome, my sister's son; I ween thou hadst been dead, and now I see thee on live, much am I beholding unto almighty Jesu. O fair nephew and my sister's son, what be these ladies that hither be come with you?"

"Sir," said Sir Gawain, "all these be ladies for whom I have foughten when I was man living, and all these are those that I did battle for in righteous quarrel; and God hath given them that grace at their great prayer, because I did battle for them, that they should bring me hither unto you: thus much hath God given me leave, for to warn you of your death; for 20 an ye fight as tomorn with Sir Mordred, as ye both have assigned, doubt ye not ye must be slain, and the most part of your people on both parties. And for the great grace and goodness that almighty Jesu hath unto you, and for pity of you, and many more other good men there shall be slain, God hath sent me to you of his special grace, to give you warning that in no wise ye do battle as tomorn, but that ye take a treaty for a month day; and proffer you largely, so as tomorn to be put in a delay. For within a month shall come Sir Launcelot with all his noble knights, and rescue you worshipfully, and slay Sir Mordred, and all that ever will hold with him."

Then Sir Gawain and all the ladies vanished. And anon the king called 30 upon his knights, squires, and yeomen, and charged them wightly to fetch his noble lords and wise bishops unto him. And when they were come, the king told them his avision, what Sir Gawain had told him, and warned him that if he fought on the morn he should be slain. Then the king commanded Sir Lucan the Butler, and his brother Sir Bedivere, with two bishops with them, and charged them in any wise, an they might, "Take a treaty for a month day with Sir Mordred, and spare not, proffer him lands and goods as much as ye think best." So then they departed, and came to Sir Mordred, where he had a grim host of an hundred thousand men. And there they entreated Sir Mordred long time; and at the last Sir Mordred 40 was agreed for to have Cornwall and Kent, by Arthur's days: after, all England, after the days of King Arthur.

Then were they condescended [23] that King Arthur and Sir Mordred should meet betwixt both their hosts, and every each of them should bring fourteen persons; and they came with this word unto Arthur. Then said he: "I am glad that this is done:" and so he went into the field. And when Arthur should depart, he warned all his host that an they see any sword drawn: "Look ye come on fiercely, and slay that traitor, Sir Mordred, for I in no wise trust him."

In likewise Sir Mordred warned his host that: "An ye see any sword drawn, look that ye come on fiercely, and so slay all that ever before you
10 standeth; for in no wise I will not trust for this treaty, for I know well my father will be avenged on me."

And so they met as their appointment was, and so they were agreed and accorded thoroughly; and wine was fetched, and they drank. Right soon came an adder out of a little heath bush, and it stung a knight on the foot. And when the knight felt him stung, he looked down and saw the adder, and then he drew his sword to slay the adder, and thought of none other harm. And when the host on both parties saw that sword drawn, then they blew beams,[24] trumpets, and horns, and shouted grimly. And so both hosts dressed them together. And King Arthur took his horse, and said: "Alas
20 this unhappy day!" and so rode to his party. And Sir Mordred in likewise. And never was there seen a more dolefuler battle in no Christian land; for there was but rushing and riding, foining and striking, and many a grim word was there spoken either to other, and many a deadly stroke. But ever King Arthur rode throughout the battle of Sir Mordred many times, and did full nobly as a noble king should, and at all times he fainted never; and Sir Mordred that day put him in devoir, and in great peril.

And thus they fought all the long day, and never stinted till the noble knights were laid to the cold earth; and ever they fought still till it was near night, and by that time was there an hundred thousand laid dead upon
30 the down. Then was Arthur wood wroth out of measure, when he saw his people so slain from him. Then the king looked about him, and then was he ware, of all his host and of all his good knights, were left no more on live but two knights; that one was Sir Lucan the Butler, and his brother Sir Bedivere, and they were full sore wounded.

"Jesu mercy," said the king, "where are all my noble knights become? Alas that ever I should see this doleful day, for now," said Arthur, "I am come to mine end. But would to God that I wist where were that traitor Sir Mordred, that hath caused all this mischief." Then was King Arthur ware where Sir Mordred leaned upon his sword among a great heap of dead
40 men. "Now give me my spear," said Arthur unto Sir Lucan, "for yonder I have espied the traitor that all this woe hath wrought."

[23] Agreed.   [24] Trumpets.

"Sir, let him be," said Sir Lucan, "for he is unhappy; and if ye pass this unhappy day ye shall be right well revenged upon him. Good lord, remember ye of your night's dream, and what the spirit of Sir Gawain told you this night, yet God of his great goodness hath preserved you hitherto. Therefore, for God's sake, my lord, leave off by this, for blessed be God ye have won the field, for here we be three on live, and with Sir Mordred is none on live; and if ye leave off now this wicked day of destiny is past."

"Tide me death, betide me life," said the king, "now I see him yonder alone, he shall never escape mine hands, for at a better avail shall I never have him." 10

"God speed you well," said Sir Bedivere.

Then the king gat his spear in both his hands, and ran toward Sir Mordred, crying: "Traitor, now is thy death day come." And when Sir Mordred heard Sir Arthur, he ran until him with his sword drawn in his hand. And there King Arthur smote Sir Mordred under the shield, with a foin of his spear, throughout the body, more than a fathom. And when Sir Mordred felt that he had his death wound, he thrust himself with the might that he had up to the bur of King Arthur's spear. And right so he smote his father Arthur, with his sword holden in both his hands, on the side of the head, that the sword pierced the helmet and the brain pan, and therewithal Sir 20 Mordred fell stark dead to the earth; and the noble Arthur fell in a swoon to the earth, and there he swooned ofttimes.

And Sir Lucan the Butler and Sir Bedivere ofttimes heaved him up. And so weakly they led him betwixt them both, to a little chapel not far from the seaside. And when the king was there he thought him well eased. Then heard they people cry in the field. "Now go thou, Sir Lucan," said the king, "and do me to wit what betokens that noise in the field."

So Sir Lucan departed, for he was grievously wounded in many places. And so he as yede, he saw and hearkened by the moonlight, how that pillers and robbers were come into the field, to pill and to rob many a full noble 30 knight of brooches, and beas,[25] of many a good ring, and of many a rich jewel; and who that were not dead all out, there they slew them for their harness and their riches. When Sir Lucan understood this work, he came to the king as soon as he might, and told him all what he had heard and seen. "Therefore by my rede," said Sir Lucan, "it is best that we bring you to some town."

"I would it were so," said the king. "But I may not stand, mine head works so. Ah Sir Launcelot," said King Arthur, "this day have I sore missed thee: alas, that ever I was against thee, for now have I my death, whereof Sir Gawain me warned in my dream." 40

Then Sir Lucan took up the king the one part, and Sir Bedivere the other

[25] Rings.

[515]

part, and in the lifting the king swooned; and Sir Lucan fell in a swoon with the lift, that the part of his guts fell out of his body, and therewith the noble knight's heart brast. And when the king awoke, he beheld Sir Lucan, how he lay foaming at the mouth, and part of his guts lay at his feet.

"Alas," said the king, "this is to me a full heavy sight, to see this noble duke so die for my sake, for he would have holpen me, that had more need of help than I. Alas, he would not complain him, his heart was so set to help me: now Jesu have mercy upon his soul!" Then Sir Bedivere wept for the
10 death of his brother.

"Leave this mourning and weeping," said the king, "for all this will not avail me, for wit thou well an I might live myself, the death of Sir Lucan would grieve me evermore; but my time hieth fast," said the king. "Therefore," said Arthur unto Sir Bedivere, "take thou Excalibur, my good sword, and go with it to yonder water side, and when thou comest there I charge thee throw my sword in that water, and come again and tell me what thou there seest."

"My lord," said Bedivere, "your commandment shall be done, and lightly bring you word again." So Sir Bedivere departed, and by the way he beheld
20 that noble sword, that the pommel and the haft was all of precious stones; and then he said to himself: "If I throw this rich sword in the water, thereof shall never come good, but harm and loss."

And then Sir Bedivere hid Excalibur under a tree. And so, as soon as he might, he came again unto the king, and said he had been at the water, and had thrown the sword in the water.

"What saw thou there?" said the king.

"Sir," he said, "I saw nothing but waves and winds."

"That is untruly said of thee," said the king, "therefore go thou lightly again, and do my commandment; as thou art to me lief and dear, spare not,
30 but throw it in."

Then Sir Bedivere returned again, and took the sword in his hand; and then him thought sin and shame to throw away that noble sword, and so eft he hid the sword, and returned again, and told to the king that he had been at the water, and done his commandment.

"What saw thou there?" said the king.

"Sir," he said, "I saw nothing but the waters wap and waves wan." [26]

"Ah, traitor untrue," said King Arthur, "now hast thou betrayed me twice. Who would have weened that, thou that hast been to me so lief and dear? and thou art named a noble knight, and would betray me for the
40 richness of the sword. But now go again lightly, for thy long tarrying putteth me in great jeopardy of my life, for I have taken cold. And but if thou

[26] Waters lap and waves turn dark.

do now as I bid thee, if ever I may see thee, I shall slay thee with mine own hands; for thou wouldst for my rich sword see me dead."

Then Sir Bedivere departed, and went to the sword, and lightly took it up, and went to the water side; and there he bound the girdle about the hilts, and then he threw the sword as far into the water as he might; and there came an arm and an hand above the water and met it, and caught it, and so shook it thrice and brandished, and then vanished away the hand with the sword in the water. So Sir Bedivere came again to the king, and told him what he saw.

"Alas," said the king, "help me hence, for I dread me I have tarried over 10 long."

Then Sir Bedivere took the king upon his back, and so went with him to that water side. And when they were at the water side, even fast by the bank hoved a little barge with many fair ladies in it, and among them all was a queen, and all they had black hoods, and all they wept and shrieked when they saw King Arthur.

"Now put me into the barge," said the king. And so he did softly; and there received him three queens with great mourning; and so they set them down, and in one of their laps King Arthur laid his head.

And then that queen said: "Ah, dear brother, why have ye tarried so long 20 from me? alas, this wound on your head hath caught over-much cold." And so then they rowed from the land, and Sir Bedivere beheld all those ladies go from him.

Then Sir Bedivere cried: "Ah my lord Arthur, what shall become of me, now ye go from me and leave me here alone among mine enemies?"

"Comfort thyself," said the king, "and do as well as thou mayest, for in me is no trust for to trust in; for I will into the vale of Avilion to heal me of my grievous wound: and if thou hear never more of me, pray for my soul."

But ever the queens and ladies wept and shrieked, that it was pity to 30 hear. And as soon as Sir Bedivere had lost the sight of the barge, he wept and wailed, and so took the forest; and so he went all that night, and in the morning he was ware betwixt two holts hoar, of a chapel and an hermitage.

Then was Sir Bedivere glad, and thither he went; and when he came into the chapel, he saw where lay an hermit groveling on all four, there fast by a tomb was new graven. When the hermit saw Sir Bedivere he knew him well, for he was but little tofore Bishop of Canterbury, that Sir Mordred flemed.[27]

"Sir," said Bedivere, "what man is there interred that ye pray so fast for?"

"Fair son," said the hermit, "I wot not verily, but by deeming. But this 40 night, at midnight, here came a number of ladies, and brought hither a dead

[27] Put to flight.

corpse, and prayed me to bury him; and here they offered an hundred tapers, and they gave me an hundred besants."

"Alas," said Sir Bedivere, "that was my lord King Arthur, that here lieth buried in this chapel." Then Sir Bedivere swooned; and when he awoke he prayed the hermit he might abide with him still there, to live with fasting and prayers. "For from hence will I never go," said Sir Bedivere, "by my will, but all the days of my life here to pray for my lord Arthur."

"Ye are welcome to me," said the hermit, "for I know you better than ye ween that I do. Ye are the bold Bedivere, and the full noble duke, Sir Lucan
10 the Butler, was your brother." Then Sir Bedivere told the hermit all as ye have heard tofore. So there bode Sir Bedivere with the hermit that was tofore Bishop of Canterbury, and there Sir Bedivere put upon him poor clothes, and served the hermit full lowly in fasting and in prayers.

Thus of Arthur I find never more written in books that be authorised, nor more of the very certainty of his death heard I never read, but thus was he led away in a ship wherein were three queens; that one was King Arthur's sister, Queen Morgan le Fay; the other was the Queen of Northgalis; the third was the Queen of the Waste Lands. Also there was Nimue, the chief lady of the lake, that had wedded Pelleas the good knight; and this lady
20 had done much for King Arthur. And this dame Nimue would never suffer Sir Pelleas to be in no place where he should be in danger of his life; and so he lived to the uttermost of his days with her in great rest. More of the death of King Arthur could I never find, but that ladies brought him to his burials; and such one was buried there, that the hermit bare witness that sometime was Bishop of Canterbury, but yet the hermit knew not in certain that he was verily the body of King Arthur: for this tale Sir Bedivere, knight of the Table Round, made it to be written.

Yet some men say in many parts of England that King Arthur is not dead, but had by the will of our Lord Jesu into another place; and men say
30 that he shall come again, and he shall win the holy cross. I will not say it shall be so, but rather I will say, here in this world he changed his life. But many men say that there is written upon his tomb this verse: HIC JACET ARTHURUS, REX QUONDAM REXQUE FUTURUS.[28] Thus leave I here Sir Bedivere with the hermit, that dwelled that time in a chapel beside Glastonbury, and there was his hermitage. And so they lived in their prayers, and fastings, and great abstinence.

And when Queen Guenever understood that King Arthur was slain, and all the noble knights, Sir Mordred and all the remnant, then the queen stole away, and five ladies with her, and so she went to Amesbury; and
40 there she let make herself a nun, and ware white clothes and black, and great penance she took, as ever did sinful lady in this land, and never crea-

[28] "Here lies Arthur, a king of old and a king to be."

ture could make her merry; but lived in fasting, prayers, and almsdeeds, that all manner of people marveled how virtuously she was changed.

THE PARTING OF LAUNCELOT AND GUENEVER

(BK. XXI, CHAP. IX–X)

Then came Sir Bors de Ganis, and said: "My lord Sir Launcelot, what think ye for to do, now to ride in this realm? wit ye well ye shall find few friends."

"Be as be may," said Sir Launcelot, "keep you still here, for I will forth on my journey, and no man nor child shall go with me."

So it was no boot to strive, but he departed and rode westerly, and there he sought a seven or eight days; and at the last he came to a nunnery, and then was Queen Guenever ware of Sir Launcelot as he walked in the 10 cloister. And when she saw him there she swooned thrice, that all the ladies and gentlewomen had work enough to hold the queen up.

So when she might speak, she called ladies and gentlewomen to her, and said: "Ye marvel, fair ladies, why I make this fare. Truly," she said, "it is for the sight of yonder knight that yonder standeth; wherefore I pray you all call him to me."

When Sir Launcelot was brought to her, then she said to all the ladies: "Through this man and me hath all this war been wrought, and the death of the most noblest knights of the world; for through our love that we have loved together is my most noble lord slain. Therefore, Sir Launcelot, wit 20 thou well I am set in such a plight to get my soul heal; and yet I trust through God's grace that after my death to have a sight of the blessed face of Christ, and at Doomsday to sit on his right side, for as sinful as every I was are saints in heaven. Therefore, Sir Launcelot, I require thee and beseech thee heartily, for all the love that ever was betwixt us, that thou never see me more in the visage; and I command thee, on God's behalf, that thou forsake my company, and to thy kingdom thou turn again, and keep well thy realm from war and wrack; for as well as I have loved thee, mine heart will not serve me to see thee, for through thee and me is the flower of kings and knights destroyed; therefore, Sir Launcelot, go to thy realm, and there 30 take thee a wife, and live with her with joy and bliss; and I pray thee heartily, pray for me to our Lord that I may amend my misliving."

"Now, sweet madam," said Sir Launcelot, "would ye that I should now return again unto my country, and there to wed a lady? Nay, madam, wit you well that shall I never do, for I shall never be so false to you of that I have promised; but the same destiny that ye have taken you to, I will take me unto, for to please Jesu, and ever for you I cast me specially to pray."

"If thou wilt do so," said the queen, "hold thy promise, but I may never believe but that thou wilt turn to the world again."

"Well, madam," said he, "ye say as pleaseth you, yet wist you me never false of my promise, and God defend [29] but I should forsake the world as ye have done. For in the quest of the Saint Greal I had forsaken the vanities of the world had not your lord been. And if I had done so at that time, with my heart, will, and thought, I had passed all the knights that were in the Saint Greal except Sir Galahad, my son. And therefore, lady, sithen ye have taken you to perfection, I must needs take me to perfection, of right.
10 For I take record of God, in you I have had mine earthly joy; and if I had found you now so disposed, I had cast to have had you into mine own realm. But since I find you thus disposed, I ensure you faithfully, I will ever take me to penance, and pray while my life lasteth, if I may find any hermit, either gray or white, that will receive me. Wherefore, madam, I pray you kiss me and never no more."

"Nay," said the queen, "that shall I never do, but abstain you from such works:" and they departed. But there was never so hard an hearted man but he would have wept to see the dolour that they made; for there was lamentation as they had been stung with spears; and many times they
20 swooned, and the ladies bare the queen to her chamber.

And Sir Launcelot awoke, and went and took his horse, and rode all that day and all night in a forest, weeping. And at the last he was ware of an hermitage and a chapel stood betwixt two cliffs; and then he heard a little bell ring to mass, and thither he rode and alit, and tied his horse to the gate, and heard mass. And he that sang mass was the Bishop of Canterbury. Both the Bishop and Sir Bedivere knew Sir Launcelot, and they spake together after mass. But when Sir Bedivere had told his tale all whole, Sir Launcelot's heart almost brast for sorrow, and Sir Launcelot threw his arms abroad, and said: "Alas, who may trust this world?" And when he kneeled down
30 on his knee, and prayed the Bishop to shrive him and assoil [30] him. And then he besought the Bishop that he might be his brother. Then the Bishop said: "I will gladly;" and there he put an habit upon Sir Launcelot, and there he served God day and night with prayers and fastings.

[29] Forbid.   [30] Absolve.

The Nut-Brown Maid

Be it right or wrong, these men among [1]
  On women do complain:
Affirming this, how that it is
  A labor spent in vain
To love them well; for never a dele [2]
  They love a man again;
For let a man do what he can
  Their favor to attain,
Yet if a new do them pursue,
  Their first true lover then   10
Laboreth for naught, for from her thought
  He is a banished man.

I say not nay, but that all day
  It is both writ and said
That woman's faith is, as who saith,
  All utterly decayed;
But nevertheless right good witnéss
  In this case might be laid,
That they love true and continue:
  Record the Nut-brown Maid,   20
Which, when her love came her to prove,
  To her to make his moan,
Would not depart, for in her heart
  She loved but him alone.

Then between us let us discuss
  What was all the mannére
Between them two; we will also
  Tell all the pain and fear
That she is in. Now I begin
  So that ye me answére;   30

[1] Often.   [2] Bit.

Wherefore all ye that present be
   I pray you give an ear.
I am the knight; I come by night,
   As secret as I can,
Saying, "Alas! thus stands the case:
   I am a banished man."

SHE

And I your will for to fulfill
   In this will not refuse,
Trusting to show in wordes few
   That men have an ill use   40
(To their own shame) women to blame,
   And causeless them accuse.
Therefore to you I answer now,
   All women to excuse.
"Mine own heart dear, with you what cheer?
   I pray you, tell anon.
For in my mind, of all mankind
   I love but you alone."

HE

"It standeth so, a deed is do
   Whereof much harm shall grow.   50
My destiny is for to die
   A shameful death, I trow,
Or else to flee; the one must be.
   None other way I know
But to withdraw as an outlaw
   And take me to my bow.
Wherefore adieu, my own heart true!
   None other rede I can,[3]
For I must to the greenwood go,
   Alone, a banished man."   60

SHE

"O Lord, what is this worldes bliss,
   That changeth as the moon?

[3] Plan I know.

My summer's day in lusty May
  Is darked before the noon.
I hear you say farewell. Nay, nay,
  We depart not so soon.
Why say ye so? whither will ye go?
  Alas! what have ye done?
All my welfare to sorrow and care
  Should change if ye were gone,   70
For in my mind, of all mankind
  I love but you alone."

HE

"I can believe, it shall you grieve
  And somewhat you distrain;
But afterward your paines hard
  Within a day or twain
Shall soon aslake, and ye shall take
  Comfort to you again.
Why should ye not? for to take thought
  Your labor were in vain.   80
And thus I do, and pray you too
  As heartily as I can,
For I must to the greenwood go,
  Alone, a banished man."

SHE

"Now since that ye have showed to me
  The secret of your mind,
I shall be plain to you again
  Like as ye shall me find.
Since it is so that ye will go,
  I will not leave behind;   90
Shall never be said the Nut-brown Maid
  Was to her love unkind.
Make you ready, for so am I,
  Although it were anon,
For in my mind, of all mankind
  I love but you alone."

He

"Yet I you rede [4] to take good heed
  What men will think and say;
Of young and old it shall be told
  That ye be gone away   100
Your wanton will for to fulfill,
  In greenwood you to play,
And that ye might from your delight
  No longer make delay.
Rather than ye should thus for me
  Be called an ill womán,
Yet would I to the greenwood go,
  Alone, a banished man."

She

"Though it be sung of old and young
  That I should be to blame,
Theirs be the charge that speak so large   110
  In hurting of my name;
For I will prove that faithful love
  It is devoid of shame,—
In your distress and heaviness
  To share with you the same.
And sure all tho [5] that do not so
  True lovers are they none;
But in my mind, of all mankind
  I love but you alone."   120

He

"I counsel you, remember how
  It is no maiden's law
Nothing to doubt but to run out
  To wood with an outlaw.
For ye must there in your hand bear
  A bow, ready to draw;
And as a thief thus must ye live
  Ever in dread and awe,
By which to you great harm might grow.
  Yet had I liefer then   130

[4] Advise.   [5] Those.

That I had to the greenwood gone,
  Alone, a banished man."

SHE

"I think not nay, but, as ye say,
  It is no maiden's lore;
But love may make me for your sake,
  As I have said before,
To come on foot, to hunt and shoot,
  To get us meat and store;
For so that I your company
  May have, I ask no more.   140
For which to part it makes my heart
  As cold as any stone,
For in my mind, of all mankind
  I love but you alone."

HE

"For an outlaw this is the law
  That men him take and bind,
Without pitée hanged to be
  And waver with the wind.
If I had need, as God forbid!
  What rescues could ye find?   150
Forsooth I trow ye and your bow
  For fear would draw behind.
And no marvail, for little avail
  Were in your counsel then.
Wherefore I will to the greenwood go,
  Alone, a banished man."

SHE

"Right well know ye that women be
  But feeble for to fight;
No womanhead it is indeed
  To be bold as a knight.   160
Yet in such fear if that ye were
  With enemies day or night,
I would withstand, with bow in hand,
  To grieve them as I might,

[525]

And you to save, as women have
From death many a one;
For in my mind, of all mankind
I love but you alone."

He

"Yet take good heed, for ever I dread
That ye could not sustain   170
The thorny ways, the deep valléys,
The snow, the frost, the rain,
The cold, the heat; for, dry or wet,
We must lodge on the plain,
And us above no other roof
But a brake bush or twain;
Which soon should grieve you, I believe,
And ye would gladly then
That I had to the greenwood gone,
Alone, a banished man."   180

She

"Since I have here been partinere
With you of joy and bliss,
I must also part of your woe
Endure, as reason is.
Yet I am sure of one pleasúre,
And, shortly, it is this:
That where ye be, meseems, pardee,
I could not fare amiss.
Without more speech, I you beseech
That we were soon agone,   190
For in my mind, of all mankind
I love but you alone."

He

"If ye go thither, ye must consider,
When ye have lust to dine,
There shall no meat be for to get,
Nor drink, beer, ale, nor wine;
Nor sheetes clean to lie between
Made of thread and twine;

[526]

None other house but leaves and boughs
  To cover your bed and mine.   200
O my heart sweet, this ill diét
  Should make you pale and wan;
Wherefore I will to the greenwood go,
  Alone, a banished man."

SHE

"Among the wild deer, such an archere
  As men say that ye be,
He may not fail of good vitail
  Where is so great plentee;
And water clear of the rivere
  Shall be full sweet to me,   210
With which in health I shall right well
  Endure as ye shall see.
And, ere we go, a bed or two
  I can provide anon,
For in my mind, of all mankind
  I love but you alone."

HE

"Lo, yet before ye must do more
  If ye will go with me,
As cut your hair up by your ear,
  Your kirtle by the knee,
With bow in hand, for to withstand   220
  Your enemies if need be.
And this same night before daylight
  To woodward will I flee.
If that ye will all this fulfill,
  Do it shortly as ye can;
Else will I to the greenwood go,
  Alone, a banished man."

SHE

"I shall as now do more for you
  Than longs to womanhead,   230
To short my hair, a bow to bear,
  To shoot in time of need.

[527]

O my sweet mother, before all other
  For you I have most dread.
But now adieu! I must ensue [6]
  Where fortune doth me lead.
All this make ye. Now let us flee;
  The day comes fast upon;
For in my mind, of all mankind
  I love but you alone."   240

HE

"Nay, nay, not so. Ye shall not go,
  And I shall tell you why.
Your appetite is to be light
  Of love, I well espy.
For right as ye have said to me,
  In like wise hardily
Ye would answere whosoe'er it were
  In way of company.
It is said of old, 'Soon hot, soon cold';
  And so is a woman.
Wherefore I to the wood will go,   250
  Alone, a banished man."

SHE

"If ye take heed, it is no need
  Such words to say by me;
For oft ye prayed and long essayed
  Ere I you loved, pardee.
And though that I of ancestry
  A baron's daughter be,
Yet have I proved how I you loved,
  A squire of low degree,
And ever shall, whatso befall,   260
  To die therefor anon;
For in my mind, of all mankind
  I love but you alone."

HE

"A baron's child to be beguiled,
  It were a cursed deed!

[6] Follow.

[528]

To be fellow with an outlaw,
  Almighty God forbid!
Yet better were the poor squiere
  Alone to forest yede [7]
Than ye should say another day
  That by my wicked deed
Ye were betrayed. Wherefore, good maid,
  The best rede that I can
Is that I to the greenwood go,
  Alone, a banished man."

SHE

"Whate'er befall, I never shall
  Of this thing you upbraid;
But if ye go and leave me so,
  Then have ye me betrayed.   280
Remember well how that ye deal,[8]
  For if ye, as ye said,
Be so unkind to leave behind
  Your love, the Nut-brown Maid,
Trust me truly that I shall die
  Soon after ye be gone;
For in my mind, of all mankind
  I love but you alone."

HE

"If that ye went, ye should repent,
  For in the forest now   290
I have purveyed me of a maid
  Whom I love more than you.
Another more fair than ever ye were,
  I dare it well avow.
And of you both each should be wroth
  With other, as I trow.
It were mine ease to live in peace;
  So will I, if I can.
Wherefore I to the wood will go,
  Alone, a banished man."   300

[7] Should go.   [8] Act.

SHE

"Though in the wood I understood
   Ye had a paramour,
All this may not remove my thought
   But that I will be your.
And she shall find me soft and kind
   And courteous every hour,
Glad to fulfill all that she will
   Command me, to my power.[9]
For had ye, lo, an hundred mo,[10]
   Of them I would be one,   310
For in my mind, of all mankind
   I love but you alone."

HE

"Mine own dear love, I see the proof
   That ye be kind and true,
Of maid and wife, in all my life
   The best that ever I knew.
Be merry and glad, be no more sad!
   The case is changed new.
For it were ruth that for your truth
   Ye should have cause to rue.   320
Be not dismayed! Whatsoe'er I said
   To you when I began,
I will not to the greenwood go,
   Alone, a banished man."

SHE

"These tidings be more glad to me
   Than to be made a queen
If I were sure they would endure;
   But it is often seen,
When men will break promise, they speak
   The wordes on the spleen.   330
Ye shape some wile me to beguile
   And steal from me, I ween.
Then were the case worse than it was,
   And I more woe-begone.

[9] As far as I am able.   [10] More.

For in my mind, of all mankind
    I love but you alone."

HE

"Ye shall not need further to dread.
    I will not disparage
You, God defend! [11] since you descend
    Of so great lineage.   340
Now understand; to Westmoreland,
    Which is my heritage,
I will you bring, and with a ring
    By way of marriage
I will you take and lady make
    As shortly as I can.
Thus ye have won an earle's son
    And not a banished man."

BOTH

Here may ye see that women be
    In love meek, kind, and stable.   350
Let never man reprove them then
    Or call them variable,
But rather pray God that we may
    To them be comfortable,
Who sometimes proveth such as He loveth
    If they be charitable.
For since men would that women should
    Be meek to them each one,
Much more ought they to God obey
    And serve but Him alone.   360

[11] Forbid.

Everyman

[*Enter Messenger as Prolog.*]

MESSENGER: I pray you all give your audience [1]
And hear this matter with reverence,
By figure a moral play.
The Summoning of Everyman called it is,
That of our lives and ending shows
How transitory we be all day.
This matter is wondrous precious,
But the intent of it is more gracious
And sweet to bear away.
The story saith: Man, in the beginning,   10
Look well and take good heed to the ending,
Be you never so gay!
Ye think sin in the beginning full sweet,
Which in the end causeth the soul to weep,
When the body lieth in clay.
Here shall you see how Fellowship and Jollity,
Both Strength, Pleasure, and Beauty
Will fade from thee as flower in May.
For ye shall hear how our Heaven King
Calleth Everyman to a general reckoning.   20
Give audience and hear what He doth say.   [*Exit.*]
God speaketh [from above].

GOD: I perceive here in My majesty
How that all creatures be to Me unkind,
Living without dread in worldly prosperity.
Of ghostly [2] sight the people be so blind,
Drowned in sin, they know Me not for their God.
In worldly riches is all their mind. . . .
I see, the more that I them forbear,   42
The worse they be from year to year;
All that liveth appaireth [3] fast.

---

[1] Attention.   [2] Spiritual.   [3] Deteriorates.

Therefore I will in all haste
Have a reckoning of every man's person. . . .
They be so cumbered with worldly riches   60
That needs on them I must do justice,
On every man living without fear.
Where art thou, Death, thou mighty messenger?

[*Enter Death.*]

DEATH: Almighty God, I am here at your will,
Your commandment to fulfill.

GOD: Go thou to Everyman,
And show him in my name
A pilgrimage he must on him take
Which he in no wise may escape,
And that he bring with him a sure reckoning   70
Without delay or any tarrying.   [*God withdraws.*]

DEATH: Lord, I will in the world go run over all
And cruelly outsearch both great and small.
Every man will I beset that liveth beastly
Out of God's laws and dreadeth no folly.
He that loveth riches I will strike with my dart,
His sight to blind and from heaven to depart,[4]
(Except that alms be his good friend)
In hell for to dwell, world without end.

[*Enter Everyman at a distance.*]

Lo, yonder I see Everyman walking.   80
Full little he thinketh on my coming!
His mind is on fleshly lusts and his treasure;
And great pain it shall cause him to endure
Before the Lord, Heaven King.

Everyman, stand still. Whither art thou going
Thus gaily? Hast thou thy Maker forgot?

EVERYMAN: Why askest thou?
Wouldst thou wit?

DEATH: Yea, sir, I will show you:
In great haste I am sent to thee   90
From God out of His majesty.

EVERYMAN: What! sent to me?

DEATH: Yea, certainly.
Though thou have forgot Him here,

---

[4] Separate.

He thinketh on thee in the heavenly sphere,
As, ere we depart, thou shalt know.

EVERYMAN: What desireth God of me?

DEATH: That shall I show thee:
A reckoning he will needs have
Without any longer respite. 100

EVERYMAN: To give a reckoning longer leisure I crave.
This blind matter troubleth my wit.

DEATH: On thee thou must take a long journey;
Therefore thy book of count with thee thou bring,
For turn again thou cannot by no way.
And look thou be sure of thy reckoning,
For before God thou shalt answer and show
Thy many bad deeds and good but a few,
How thou hast spent thy life and in what wise,
Before the Chief Lord of Paradise. 110
Have ado that we were in that way,
For wit thou well thou shalt make none attorney.

EVERYMAN: Full unready am I such reckoning to give.
I know thee not. What messenger art thou?

DEATH: I am Death, that no man dreadeth;
For every man I arrest and no man spareth;
For it is God's commandment
That all to me should be obedient.

EVERYMAN: O Death, thou comest when I had thee least in mind!
In thy power it lieth me to save; 120
Yet of my good will I give thee, if thou wilt be kind.
Yea, a thousand pound shalt thou have
An thou defer this matter till another day.

DEATH: Everyman, it may not be by no way.
I set not by gold, silver, nor riches,
Nor by pope, emperor, king, duke, nor princes,
For, an I would receive gifts great,
All the world I might get.
But my custom is clean contrary.
I give thee no respite; come hence and not tarry. 130

EVERYMAN: Alas! shall I have no longer respite?
I may say that Death giveth no warning!
To think on thee it maketh my heart sick,
For all unready is my book of reckoning.

[534]

But, twelve year an I might have abiding,[5]
My counting book I would make so clear
That my reckoning I should not need to fear.
Wherefore, Death, I pray thee, for God's mercy,
Spare me till I be provided of remedy!

DEATH: Thee availeth not to cry, weep, and pray,   140
But haste thee lightly that thou wert gone the journey! [6]
And prove thy friends, if thou can;
For wit thou well, the tide abideth no man,
And in the world each living creature
For Adam's sin must die of nature.

EVERYMAN: Death, if I should this pilgrimage take,
And my reckoning surely make,
Show me, for Saint Charity,
Should I not come again shortly?

DEATH: No, Everyman, an thou be once there,   150
Thou mayst never more come here,
Trust me verily.

EVERYMAN: O gracious God, in the high seat celestial,
Have mercy on me in this most need.
Shall I have no company from this vale terrestrial
Of mine acquaintance, that way me to lead?

DEATH: Yea, if any be so hardy
That would go with thee and bear thee company.
Hie thee, that thou wert gone to God's magnificence,
Thy reckoning to give before His presence.   160
What! weenest thou thy life is given thee
And thy worldly goods also?

EVERYMAN: I had weened so verily.

DEATH: Nay, nay, it was but lent thee,
For as soon as thou art go,
Another a while shall have it and then go therefro,
Even as thou hast done.
Everyman, thou art mad! Thou hast thy wits five,
And here on earth wilt not amend thy life;
For suddenly I do come.   170

EVERYMAN: O wretched caitiff, whither shall I flee,
That I might scape this endless sorrow?
Now, gentle Death, spare me till tomorrow,

[5] If I might have a delay of twelve years.
[6] Hasten quickly to make ready for the journey.

That I may amend me
With good advisement.

DEATH: Nay, thereto I will not consent,
Nor no man will I respite,
But to the heart suddenly I shall smite
Without any advisement.
And now out of thy sight I will me hie. 180
See that thou make thee ready shortly,
For thou mayst say this is the day
That no man living may scape away. [*Exit Death.*]

EVERYMAN: Alas, I may well weep with sighs deep!
Now have I no manner of company
To help me in my journey and me to keep;
And also my writing is full unready.
How shall I do now for to excuse me?
I would to God I had never been get! [7]
To my soul a full great profit it had been, 190
For now I fear pains huge and great.
The time passeth. Lord, help, that all wrought!
For though I mourn, it availeth naught.
The day passeth and is almost ago. [8]
I wot not well what for to do.
To whom were I best my complaint to make?
What an I to Fellowship thereof spake
And showed him of this sudden chance?
For in him is all my affiance, [9]
We have in the world so many a day 200
Been good friends in sport and play.

[*Enter Fellowship.*]

I see him yonder certainly;
I trust that he will bear me company,
Therefore to him will I speak to ease my sorrow.
Well met, good Fellowship, and good morrow!

Fellowship speaketh.

FELLOWSHIP: Everyman, good morrow, by this day!
Sir, why lookest thou so piteously?
If anything be amiss, I pray thee me say,
That I may help to remedy.

EVERYMAN: Yea, good Fellowship, yea, 210
I am in great jeopardy.

[7] Begotten.   [8] Gone.   [9] Trust.

FELLOWSHIP: My true friend, show to me your mind.
I will not forsake thee to thy life's end,
In the way of good company.

EVERYMAN: That was well spoken and lovingly.

FELLOWSHIP: Sir, I must needs know your heaviness;
I have pity to see you in any distress.
If any have you wronged,[10] ye shall revenged be;
Though I on the ground be slain for thee,
Though that I know before that I should die.   220

EVERYMAN: Verily, Fellowship, gramercy.

FELLOWSHIP: Tush, by thy thanks I set not a straw!
Show me your grief and say no more.

EVERYMAN: If I my heart should to you break,
And then you to turn your mind from me,
And would not me comfort when ye hear me speak,
Then should I ten times sorrier be.

FELLOWSHIP: Sir, I say as I will do in deed.

EVERYMAN: Then be you a good friend at need.
I have found you true herebefore.   230

FELLOWSHIP: And so ye shall evermore,
For, in faith, an thou go to hell,
I will not forsake thee by the way.

EVERYMAN: Ye speak like a good friend; I believe you well.
I shall deserve it an I may.

FELLOWSHIP: I speak of no deserving, by this day!
For he that will say and nothing do
Is not worthy with good company to go.
Therefore show me the grief of your mind,
As to your friend most loving and kind.   240

EVERYMAN: I shall show you how it is:
Commanded I am to go a journey,
A long way, hard and dangerous,
And give a strict count,[11] without delay,
Before the high Judge, Adonai.[12]
Wherefore I pray you, bear me company,
As ye have promised, in this journey.

FELLOWSHIP: That is matter indeed! Promise is duty;

---

[10] If any have wronged you.   [11] Accounting.
[12] A Hebrew name for God.

But, an I should take such voyage on me,
I know it well, it should be to my pain.   250
Also it maketh me afeard, certain.
But let us take counsel here, as well as we can,
For your words would fear [13] a strong man.

EVERYMAN: Why, ye said if I had need,
Ye would me never forsake, quick nor dead,
Though it were to hell, truly.

FELLOWSHIP: So I said certainly,
But such pleasures be set aside, sooth to say;
And also, if ye would take such a journey,
When should we come again?   260

EVERYMAN: Nay, never again till the day of doom.

FELLOWSHIP: In faith, then will not I come there.
Who hath you these tidings brought?

EVERYMAN: Indeed, Death was with me here.

FELLOWSHIP: Now, by God, that all hath bought, [14]
If Death were the messenger,
For no man that is living today
I will not go that loath journey,
Not for the father that begat me!

EVERYMAN: Ye promised otherwise, pardee!   270

FELLOWSHIP: I wot well I said so, truly.
And yet if thou wilt eat and drink and make good cheer,
Or haunt to women the lusty company, [15]
I would not forsake you while the day is clear,
Trust me verily.

EVERYMAN: Yea, thereto ye would be ready!
To go to mirth, solace, and play
Your mind will sooner apply
Than to bear me company in my long journey.

FELLOWSHIP: Now, in good faith, I will not that way.   280
But an thou wilt murder or any man kill,
In that I will help thee with a good will.

EVERYMAN: Oh that is a simple [16] advice indeed!
Gentle fellow, help me in my necessity.
We have loved long and now I need;
And now, gentle Fellowship, remember me.

[13] Frighten.   [14] Redeemed.   [15] Frequent the lively company of women.
[16] Foolish.

FELLOWSHIP: Whether ye have loved me or no,
By St. John, I will not with thee go!

EVERYMAN: Yet I pray thee, take the labor and do so much for me
To bring me forward, for Saint Charity,   290
And comfort me till I come without the town.

FELLOWSHIP: Nay, an thou would give me a new gown,
I will not a foot with thee go.
But, an thou had tarried, I would not have left thee so.
And, as now,[17] God speed thee in thy journey,
For from thee I will depart as fast as I may.

EVERYMAN: Whither away, Fellowship? will thou forsake me?

FELLOWSHIP: Yea, by my fay![18] To God I betake[19] thee.

EVERYMAN: Farewell, good Fellowship. For thee my heart is sore!
Adieu forever; I shall see thee no more.   300

FELLOWSHIP: In faith, Everyman, farewell now at the end!
For you I will remember that parting is mourning.   [*Exit Fellowship.*]

* * *

[*Everyman then appeals in succession to Kindred and Cousin, and to Goods
to accompany him, but is rejected with scorn.*]

EVERYMAN: Oh, to whom shall I make my moan,   463
For to go with me in that heavy journey?
First Fellowship said he would with me go;
His words were very pleasant and gay,
But afterwards he left me alone.
Then spake I to my kinsmen all in despair,
And also they gave me words fair.
They lacked no fair speaking,   470
But all forsook me in the ending.
Then went I to my Goods, that I loved best,
In hope to have comfort, but there had I least;
For my Goods sharply did me tell
That he bringeth many into hell.
Then of myself I was ashamed,
And so I am worthy to be blamed.
Thus may I well myself hate.
Of whom shall I now counsel take?
I think that I shall never speed[20]   480
Till that I go to my Good Deed.
But, alas, she is so weak
That she can neither go nor speak.

[17] For the present.   [18] Faith.   [19] Entrust.   [20] Succeed.

Yet will I venture on her now.
My Good Deeds, where be you?

[*Good Deeds answers from the ground.*]

GOOD DEEDS: Here I lie, cold in the ground.
Thy sins have me sore bound
That I cannot stir.

EVERYMAN: O Good Deeds, I stand in great fear.
I must pray you of counsel, 490
For help now should come right well.

GOOD DEEDS: Everyman, I have understanding
That ye be summoned a count to make
Before Messiah, of Jerusalem King;
An you do by me,[21] the journey with you will I take.

EVERYMAN: Therefore I come to you my moan to make.
I pray you that ye will go with me.

GOOD DEEDS: I would full fain, but I cannot stand verily.

EVERYMAN: Why, is there anything on you fall? [22]

GOOD DEEDS: Yea, sir, I may thank you of all! 500
If ye had perfectly cheered me,
Your book of count now full ready had be.
Look, the book of your works and deeds eke!
Ah see how they lie under the feet,
To your soul's heaviness! [23]

EVERYMAN: Our Lord Jesu help me!
For one letter here I cannot see.

GOOD DEEDS: There is a blind reckoning in time of distress!

EVERYMAN: Good Deeds, I pray you help me in this need,
Or else I am forever damned indeed. 510
Therefore help me to make my reckoning
Before the Redeemer of all thing,
That King is and was and ever shall.

GOOD DEEDS: Everyman, I am sorry of your fall,
And fain would I help you, an I were able.

EVERYMAN: Good Deeds, your counsel I pray you give me.

GOOD DEEDS: That shall I do verily,
Though that on my feet I may not go.
I have a sister that shall with you also,
Called Knowledge, which shall with you abide, 520

---

[21] Act by my advice.   [22] Has anything happened to you?   [23] Sorrow.

To help you to make that dreadful reckoning.

[*Enter Knowledge.*]

KNOWLEDGE: Everyman, I will go with thee and be thy guide,
In thy most need to go by thy side.

EVERYMAN: In good condition I am now in every thing,
And am wholly content with this good thing,
Thanked be God, my Creator!

*　　*　　*

[*Everyman is taken to Confession and does penance for his sins, whipping himself with a knotted scourge. Good Deeds rises from the floor.*]

GOOD DEEDS: Everyman, pilgrim, my special friend,　　　　629
Blessed be thou without end!
For thee is prepared the eternal glory.
Ye have made me whole and sound;
Therefore I will bide by thee in every stound.

EVERYMAN: Welcome, my Good Deeds! Now I hear thy voice,
I weep for very sweetness of love.

KNOWLEDGE: Be no more sad, but ever rejoice;
God seeth thy living in His throne above.
Put on this garment to thy behoof,[24]
Which is wet with your tears,
Or else before God you may it miss,　　　　640
When ye to your journey's end come shall.

EVERYMAN: Gentle Knowledge, what do you it call?

KNOWLEDGE: It is called the garment of sorrow;
From pain it will you borrow.[25]
Contrition it is,
That getteth forgiveness.
It pleaseth God passing well.

GOOD DEEDS: Everyman, will you wear it for your heal?[26]

EVERYMAN: Now blessed be Jesu, Mary's Son,
For now have I on true contrition.　　　　650
And let us go now without tarrying.
Good Deeds, have we clear our reckoning?

GOOD DEEDS: Yea, indeed, I have it here.

EVERYMAN: Then I trust we need not fear.
Now, friends, let us not part in twain.

KNOWLEDGE: Nay, Everyman, that will we not, certaín.

[24] Advantage.　　　　[25] Release.　　　　[26] Health.

GOOD DEEDS: Yet must thou lead with thee
Three person of great might.

EVERYMAN: Who should they be?

GOOD DEEDS: Discretion and Strength they hight,[27]   660
And thy Beauty may not abide behind.

KNOWLEDGE: Also ye must call to mind
Your Five Wits,[28] as for your counselors.

GOOD DEEDS: You must have them ready at all hours.

EVERYMAN: How shall I get them hither?

KNOWLEDGE: You must call them all together,
And they will hear you incontinent.[29]

EVERYMAN: My friends, come hither and be present,
Discretion, Strength, my Five Wits, and Beauty!

[*Enter Discretion, Strength, Five Wits, and Beauty.*]

BEAUTY: Here at your will we be all ready   670
What will ye that we should do?

GOOD DEEDS: That ye should with Everyman go,
And help him in his pilgrimage.
Advise you, will ye with him or not in that voyage?

STRENGTH: We will bring him all thither
To his help and comfort, ye may believe me.

DISCRETION: So will we go with him all together.

*　　*　　*

[*Everyman goes off stage to receive from a priest the sacrament and extreme unction. Knowledge denounces evil priests.*]

FIVE WITS: I trust to God no such may we find.   764
Therefore let us priesthood honor,
And follow their doctrine for our souls' succor.
We be their sheep, and they shepherds be,
By whom we all be kept in surety.
Peace! for yonder I see Everyman come,
Which hath made true satisfaction.   770

GOOD DEEDS: Methinks it is he indeed.

[*Re-enter Everyman.*]

EVERYMAN: Now Jesu be our alder speed! [30]
I have received the sacrament for my redemption,
And then my extreme unction.
Blessed be all they that counseled me to take it!

---

[27] Are called.   [28] Senses.   [29] At once.   [30] Be help of us all.

And now, friends, let us go without longer respite.
I thank God that ye have tarried so long.
Now set, each of you, on this rod his hand,
And shortly follow me.
I go before there I would be. God be our guide!   780

STRENGTH: Everyman, we will not from you go
Till ye have gone this voyage long.

DISCRETION: I, Discretion, will bide by you also.

KNOWLEDGE: And though this pilgrimage be never so strong,
I will never part you fro.

STRENGTH: Everyman, I will be as sure by thee
As ever I was by Judas Maccabee.

[*All proceed to the grave.*]

EVERYMAN: Alas, I am so faint I may not stand!
My limbs under me do fold!
Friends, let us not turn again to this land,   790
Not for all the world's gold.
For into this cave must I creep,
And turn to the earth and there sleep.

BEAUTY: What, into this grave, alas!

EVERYMAN: Yea, there shall ye consume, more and less.

BEAUTY: And what, should I smother here?

EVERYMAN: Yea, by my faith, and never more appear.
In this world live no more we shall,
But in heaven before the highest Lord of all.

BEAUTY: I cross out all this! Adieu, by Saint John!   800
I take my tap in my lap [31] and am gone.

EVERYMAN: What, Beauty, whither will ye?

BEAUTY: Peace! I am deaf. I look not behind me,
Not an thou wouldst give me all the gold in thy chest.   [*Exit Beauty.*]

EVERYMAN: Alas, whereto may I trust?
Beauty goeth fast away from me.
She promised with me to live and die.

STRENGTH: Everyman, I will thee also forsake and deny.
Thy game liketh [32] me not at all.

EVERYMAN: Why then, ye will forsake me all?   810
Sweet strength, tarry a little space.

STRENGTH: Nay, sir, by the Rood of grace!

---

[31] Idiomatic expression meaning "make a hasty departure."   [32] Pleases.

I will hie me from thee fast,
Though thou weep till thy heart tobrast! [33]

EVERYMAN: Ye would ever bide by me, ye said.

STRENGTH: Yea, I have you far enough conveyed.[34]
Ye be old enough, I understand,
Your pilgrimage to take on hand.
I repent me that I hither came.

EVERYMAN: Strength, you to displease I am to blame.   820
Yet promise is debt, this ye well wot.

STRENGTH: In faith, as for that I care not!
Thou art but a fool to complain.
You spend your speech and waste your brain.
Go, thrust thee into the ground!   [*Exit Strength.*]

EVERYMAN: I had weened surer I should you have found,
But I see well he that trusteth in his strength,
She him deceiveth at the length,
For Strength and Beauty forsaketh me.
Yet they promised me fair and lovingly.   830

DISCRETION: Everyman, I will after Strength be gone.
As for me, I will leave you alone.

EVERYMAN: Why, Discretion, will ye forsake me?

DISCRETION: Yea, in good faith, I will go from thee,
For when Strength goeth before,
I follow after evermore.

EVERYMAN: Yet I pray thee, for love of the Trinity,
Look in my grave once piteously.

DISCRETION: Nay, so nigh will I not come.
Now farewell, fellows, every one.   [*Exit Discretion.*]   840

EVERYMAN: Oh, all thing faileth save God alone,
Beauty, Strength, and Discretion.
For when Death bloweth his blast,
They all run from me full fast.

FIVE WITS: Everyman, my leave now of thee I take.
I will follow the other, for here I thee forsake.

EVERYMAN: Alas, then may I wail and weep,
For I took you for my best friend.

FIVE WITS: I will no longer thee keep.
Now farewell, and there an end!   [*Exit Five Wits.*]   850

[33] Breaks in pieces.   [34] Escorted.

EVERYMAN: O Jesu, help! All hath forsaken me!

GOOD DEEDS: Nay, Everyman, I will bide with thee.
I will not forsake thee indeed.
Thou shalt find me a good friend at need.

EVERYMAN: Gramercy, Good Deeds, now may I true friends see;
They have forsaken me, every one.
I loved them better than Good Deeds alone.
Knowledge, will ye forsake me also?

KNOWLEDGE: Yea, Everyman, when ye to death shall go;
But not yet, for no manner of danger.   860

EVERYMAN: Gramercy, Knowledge, with all my heart.

KNOWLEDGE: Nay, yet I will not from hence depart
Till I see where ye shall be come.

EVERYMAN: Methinks, alas, that I must be gone
To make my reckoning and my debts pay,
For I see my time is nigh spent away.
Take example, all ye that this do hear or see,
How they that I love best do forsake me,
Except my Good Deeds, that bideth truly.

GOOD DEEDS: All earthly things is but vanity.   870
Beauty, Strength, and Discretion do man forsake,
Foolish friends and kinsmen, that fair spake.
All fleeth save Good Deeds, and that am I.

EVERYMAN: Have mercy on me, God most mighty,
And stand by me, thou Mother and Maid, Holy Mary!

GOOD DEEDS: Fear not, I will speak for thee.

EVERYMAN: Here I cry God mercy!

GOOD DEEDS: Short [35] our end and minish [36] our pain.
Let us go and never come again.

EVERYMAN: Into Thy hands, Lord, my soul I commend.   880
Receive it, Lord, that it be not lost.
As Thou me boughtest, so me defend,
And save me from the fiend's boast,
That I may appear with that blessed host
That shall be saved at the day of doom.
In manus tuas, of mights most,
For ever *commendo spiritum meum*.[37]

[Everyman and Good Deeds descend into the grave.]

[35] Shorten.   [36] Diminish.
[37] "Into Thy hands, O greatest in might, I commend my spirit forever."

KNOWLEDGE: Now hath he suffered that we all shall endure.
The Good Deeds shall make all sure.
Now hath he made ending   890
Methinketh that I hear angels sing
And make great joy and melody
Where Everyman's soul received shall be.
ANGEL [*within*]: Come, excellent elect spouse to Jesu!
Here above thou shalt go
Because of thy singular virtue.
Now the soul is taken the body fro,
Thy reckoning is crystal clear.
Now shalt thou into the heavenly sphere,
Unto the which ye all shall come   900
That liveth well before the day of doom.   [*Exit Knowledge.*]

[*Enter Doctor of Divinity as Epilog.*]
DOCTOR: This moral men may have in mind.
Ye hearers, take it of worth, old and young,
And forsake Pride, for he deceiveth you in the end.
And remember Beauty, Five Wits, Strength, and Discretion,
They all at the last do Everyman forsake,
Save his Good Deeds there doth he take.
But beware; an they be small,
Before God he hath no help at all.
None excuse may be there for Everyman!   910
Alas, how shall he do then?
For after death amends may no man make.
For then mercy and pity doth him forsake.
If his reckoning be not clear when he doth come,
God will say: "*Ite, maledicti, in ignem eternum!*" [38]
And he that hath his account whole and sound,
High in heaven he shall be crowned.
Unto which place God bring us all thither
That we may live, body and soul together!
Thereto help the Trinity! [39]   920
Amen, say ye, for Saint Charity!

[38] "Depart, ye accursed, into eternal fire."
[39] May the Trinity help toward this end!

Bibliography and Notes

ABBREVIATIONS

Baugh. *A Literary History of England,* ed. by Albert C. Baugh (1948).

Bennett, *Chaucer.* H. S. Bennett, *Chaucer and the Fifteenth Century* (1957).

CBEL. *Cambridge Bibliography of English Literature,* ed. by F. W. Bateson (1941). *Supplement* ed. by G. Watson (1957).

Chambers. *English Literature at the Close of the Middle Ages* (1945).

CHEL. *Cambridge History of English Literature,* ed. by A. W. Ward and A. R. Waller.

Cook. A. S. Cook, *Literary Middle English Reader* (1915).

EETS. Early English Text Society, Original Series.

EETSES. Early English Text Society, Extra Series.

Everett. Dorothy Everett, *Essays on Middle English Literature* (1955).

JEGP. *Journal of English and Germanic Philology.*

Kane. George Kane, *Middle English Literature* (1951).

MLN. *Modern Language Notes.*

MP. *Modern Philology.*

PMLA. *Publications of the Modern Language Association of America.*

Wells. J. E. Wells, *Manual of Writings in Middle English, 1050–1400* (1916). Nine supplements covering publications through 1945.

Wilson. R. M. Wilson, *Early Middle English Literature* (1939).

GENERAL REFERENCES ON MIDDLE ENGLISH LITERATURE

Besides Baugh, Bennett, Chambers, Everett, Kane, and Wilson consult:

G. G. Coulton, *Medieval Panorama* (1938).

W. P. Ker, *English Literature, Medieval.* Home University Library of Modern Knowledge.

W. H. Schofield, *English Literature from the Norman Conquest to Chaucer* (1906).

NOTES

1. Layamon, *The Brut*. Ed. F. Madden (1847). This poem was written by a Worcestershire priest (whose name is properly spelled Laȝamon) between 1189 and 1207, and consists of over 16,000 lines, in which the Anglo-Saxon principle of alliteration is combined with assonance and rime. The main source is Wace's Norman French *Brut* (1155), which in turn renders freely the pseudo-historical Latin work, *Historia Regum Britanniae* (ca. 1136). The other sources mentioned by Layamon he did not use, but he elaborated somewhat from his own imagination and added scenes (such as the fairy gifts to Arthur, the founding of the Round Table, and the passing of Arthur) from the tales circulated by Breton reciters. On Layamon cf. *CBEL*, I, 163–5; V, 117; Wells, ch. I, 19; ch. III, 3; Baugh, pp. 170–72; Wilson, pp. 205–13; *Arthurian Literature in the Middle Ages*, ed. R. S. Loomis (1959), pp. 72–111; J. S. P. Tatlock, *Legendary History of Britain* (1950), pp. 483–531; Everett, pp. 28–45; H. C. Wyld, "Laȝamon as an English Poet," *Review of English Studies*, VI (1930), 1–30; F. L. Gillespy, "Layamon's *Brut*," *Univ. of Calif. Publications in Mod. Phil.*, III (1916), 361–510. The Arthurian parts of Wace and Layamon are translated (not very accurately) in *Arthurian Chronicles Represented by Wace and Layamon*, Everyman's Library.

2. *The Vision of Paul*. Text from *Old English Homilies*, ed. R. Morris, EETS 29 (1868), pp. 41–7. This sermon is a greatly condensed vernacular form of one of the many Latin redactions of the long Latin version of the *Vision of Paul*, with emphasis on the Sabbath-day rest in hell. This apocryphal narrative originated in the Near East, spread westward, and was well known in Anglo-Saxon and medieval England. Cf. *CBEL*, I, 176 f.; A. B. van Os, *Religious Visions* (1932), p. 137; T. Silverstein, *Visio Sancti Pauli* (1935), pp. 6–12, 79–81. On *Lambeth Homilies* cf. *CBEL*, I, 170; Wells, ch. V, 12.

3. *The Owl and the Nightingale*. Ed. J. W. H. Atkins (1922). The poem was written about 1200, perhaps by Nicholas of Guildford himself. Cf. *CBEL*, I, 181 f.; V, 122; Wells, ch. IX, 8; Wilson, pp. 149–67; Baugh, pp. 154–7; F. Tupper, "The Date and Historical Background of *The Owl and the Nightingale*," *PMLA*, XLIX (1934), 406–27; Atkins' edition; J. W. H. Atkins, *English Literary Criticism: The Medieval Phase* (1943), pp. 143–5. There is a complete translation by G. Eggers (1955), with preface by P. Baum.

4. *The Rule of Anchoresses* (*Ancrene Riwle*). Ed. M. Day, J. A. Herbert, EETS (1952). Written by an unknown cleric for the guidance of three women who had chosen to withdraw from the world, not as nuns in a convent, but as recluses in cells near a church. The date is early thirteenth century, and the dialect of the original was probably West Midland. Cf. *CBEL*, I, 179 f.; V, 121; Wells, ch. VI, 40; Wilson, pp. 128–48; Baugh, pp. 127–34; R. W. Cham-

bers, *On the Continuity of English Prose*, EETS (1932), pp. xciv–c. Complete translations: J. Morton, *The Nun's Rule* (King's Classics, 1905; Medieval Library, 1924); M. B. Salu, *The Ancrene Riwle* (1957).

5. Thomas of Hales, *A Love-Song*. Text in Carleton Brown, *English Lyrics of the XIIIth Century*, pp. 68–74. Composed at the request of a nun between 1240 and 1272 by a learned Franciscan friar, a friend of the theologian Adam Marsh. Cf. Wells, ch. XIII, 173; *Dictionary of National Biography*, VIII, 920; C. Brown, *op. cit.*, pp. 198 f.; R. H. Robbins, "The authors of the Middle English Religious Lyrics," *JEGP*, XXXIX (1940), 230–8; Kane, pp. 116 f.

6–11. *Six Thirteenth-Century Lyrics*. Texts in C. Brown, *op. cit.*, pp. 19, 32, 42, 54, 119, 138. Cf. Brown's notes on these. On the early English lyric cf. *CBEL*, I, 267–71; Baugh, pp. 212 f.; E. K. Chambers, F. Sidgwick, *Early English Lyrics* (1907), pp. 257–96 (reprinted in Chambers, *Sir Thomas Wyatt*, 1933, pp. 46–97); Robbins, *loc. cit.*; *Harley Lyrics*, ed. G. L. Brook (1948), introd.

12. *The Bestiary*. Text in J. Hall, *Selections from Early Middle English* (1920), I, 176–96. The *Bestiary* is a series of thirteen short poems in varying metres, employing alliteration, assonance, and rime, all but one translated about 1240 from a Latin source. This unnatural natural history was concocted in the monasteries of Egypt some time before 500. It can be comprehended only when one perceives that its authors were men of books, removed from life, who, assuming that the world was created by God expressly for the sake of man, concluded that the animal creation must exist to reveal God's purposes to man. In one form or another the *Bestiary* was translated into most of the languages of Christendom and exerted an enormous influence on the art and literature of Europe down to Shakespeare's time. Cf. Wells, ch. II, 24; Wilson, pp. 187–9; E. Mâle, *Religious Art in France in the Thirteenth Century* (1913), pp. 31–46; T. H. White, *The Book of Beasts* (1954), pp. 7–11, 105–7, 187, 196–8, 231–63; P. A. Robin, *Animal Lore in English Literature* (1932); G. Cronin, "The Bestiary and the Mediaeval Mind," *Modern Language Quarterly*, II (1941), 191–8.

13. *Havelok*. Ed. W. W. Skeat, rev. K. Sisam (1915). Composed in four-stress rimed couplets in Lincolnshire dialect about 1285. It seems to be the work of a minstrel, appealing to an audience in a tavern or manor house. The hero is probably to be identified with a historic Anlaf, who ruled for short periods in the middle of the tenth century over the Danish settlements in the North and East of England, but the romance consists wholly of fictions which grew up about him. Cf. *CBEL*, I, 148 f.; V, 115; Wells, ch. I, 5; Wilson, pp. 216–8, 221–5; H. L. S. Creek, "The Author of *Havelok*," *Englische Studien*, XLVIII (1915), 193–212; L. A. Hibbard, *Medieval Romance in England* (1924), pp. 103–14. A complete translation, with introduction, is in R. S. and L. H. Loomis, *Medieval Romances*, Modern Library, pp. 284–310.

14. *The Debate of the Body and the Soul.* Text in O. F. Emerson, *Middle English Reader*, pp. 47–64. Written in stanzas of eight, four-stress lines, riming *abababab*. The dialect is Midland and the date in the second half of the thirteenth century. There are *Addresses of the Soul to the Body* in Anglo-Saxon, and versions of the debate between the two are extant in Latin and other languages. Cf. *CBEL*, I, 177 f.; Wells, ch. IX, 1; Baugh, pp. 162–4; R. Willard, "The Address of the Soul to the Body," *PMLA*, L (1935), 957–83; E. K. Heningham, *An Early Latin Debate of the Body and Soul* (1939).

15. *The Land of Cockayne.* Text in *Bonner Beiträge zur Anglistik*, XIV (1904), 145–50; selection in Cook, pp. 368–72. Consists of 95 rimed couplets, composed in Ireland in the second half of the thirteenth century. It is a Rabelaisian satire on Cistercian monks, probably by an English Franciscan friar. Suggestions for the satire came from a French poem, *Li Fabliaux de Coquaigne*, and possibly from the Irish *Vision of Mac Conglinne* (T. P. Cross, *Ancient Irish Tales*, pp. 562 f., 572–83). Cf. Wells, ch. IV, 29; *JEGP*, XXXIX (1940), 235.

16. *Sir Orfeo.* Ed. A. J. Bliss (1954). Composed in four-stress rimed couplets in the South-Western dialect early in the fourteenth century. It is a redaction of a lost French or Anglo-French poem by a Breton minstrel, in which the classical story of Orpheus and Eurydice was gracefully blended with Celtic legends of the abduction of a queen by a faery king. Cf. *CBEL*, I, 151 f.; V, 116; Wells, ch. I, 89; L. A. Hibbard, *Mediaeval Romance in England*, pp. 195–99; L. H. Loomis, "Chaucer and the Breton Lays of the Auchinleck MS," *Studies in Philology*, XXXVIII (1941), 14–33; Kane, pp. 80–4; R. S. Loomis, "*Sir Orfeo* and Map's *De Nugis*," *MLN*, LI (1936), 28–30; R. S. and L. H. Loomis, *Medieval Romances*, pp. 311–4.

17. Robert Mannyng, *Handling Sin.* Ed. F. J. Furnivall, EETS, 119, 123 (1901–02). A poem of over 12,600 lines in couplets, treating the Ten Commandments, the Deadly Sins, the Sacraments, and Confession. The author was a canon of Sempringham Priory in southern Lincolnshire, began the poem in 1303, wrote the Prologue after 1317, and completed a translation of two chronicles from the French in 1338. His main source for *Handling Sin* was an Anglo-French *Manuel des Péchés*, to which he added thirteen stories. Cf. *CBEL*, I, 183 f.; V, 122; Wells, ch. VI, 2; R. Crosby, "Robert Mannyng of Brunne: A New Biography," *PMLA*, LVII (1942), 15–28; D. W. Robertson, "The Cultural Tradition of *Handlyng Synne*," *Speculum*, XXII (1947), 162–85.

18–20. Richard Rolle, *The Bee and the Stork; Meditations on the Passion; The Form of Living.* Texts in *English Writings of Richard Rolle*, ed. H. E. Allen (1931). Except for the *Meditations*, which is of doubtful authorship, these prose works were written in the Yorkshire dialect by Rolle, who was born at Thornton Dale, studied at Oxford, became a hermit near his home, and died at Hampole in 1349, probably of the Black Death. He was read more than any other English writer of the Middle Ages; 400 manuscripts containing his work have survived. Cf. *CBEL*, I, 191–4; V, 124 f.; Wells, ch. XI, 1–3, 5–9; Baugh, pp. 227–9; *English Writings of Rolle*, ed. H. E. Allen; F. M. M. Comper, *Life of Richard Rolle* (1928, 1933); R. W. Chambers, *Continuity of English Prose* (1932), pp. ci–ciii.

21. Dame Julian of Norwich, *Revelations of Divine Love*. Modernized text ed. G. Warrack (1901, 1923). Written in 83 short chapters of prose about the year 1387. The author was an anchoress, who was born in 1342, received her revelations in 1373, and was still living in 1413. Cf. *CBEL*, I, 195; V, 125; Wells, ch. XI, 65, 66; *Book of Margery Kempe*, ed. S. B. Meech, and H. E. Allen, I, EETS 212 (1940), pp. 42 f.

22. *The Alliterative Morte Arthur*. Ed. E. Björkman (1915). Composed in 4346 lines in the Northwest Midland dialect about 1360. Based ultimately on Geoffrey of Monmouth but freely elaborated, this poem is one of the most vigorous works of the alliterative revival. Malory condensed a large part of it in his fifth book. Cf. *CBEL*, I, 136 f.; V, 113; Wells, ch. I, 21; Baugh, p. 191; Kane, pp. 69–73; *Arthurian Literature in the Middle Ages*, ed. R. S. Loomis, pp. 521–6; Everett, pp. 46–67. A complete translation may be found in *Morte Arthur, Two Early English Romances*, Everyman's Library, pp. 1–93.

23. *Sir Gawain and the Green Knight*. Ed. J. R. R. Tolkien and E. V. Gordon (1936). Probably composed in southern Lancashire or a neighboring district about 1375 by the author of *The Pearl, Purity*, and *Patience*. He may well have been an aristocratic layman or a cleric in minor orders (though not a priest), was well read in French and Latin literature, and was certainly a genius. Though opinions differ, the plot was probably borrowed from a lost French romance, which combined skillfully materials from Irish and Welsh sagas. Cf. *CBEL*, I, 135 f.; V, 111–3; Baugh, pp. 236–8; *Arthurian Literature in the Middle Ages*, ed. R. S. Loomis, pp. 528–40; H. L. Savage, *The Gawain-Poet* (1956), 3–30; A. Buchanan, "The Irish Framework of *Gawain and the Green Knight*," *PMLA*, XLVII (1932), 315–38; R. S. Loomis, *Wales and the Arthurian Legend* (1956), 77–90.

24. *The Pearl*. Ed. E. V. Gordon (1953). Composed by the author of *Gawain and the Green Knight*. An exquisite elegy for a baby girl, possibly the poet's daughter. Note the rime scheme, the linking of stanzas, and the organization in stanza groups. Cf. *CBEL*, I, 201 f.; V, 128 f.; Wells, ch. XV, 2; Baugh, pp. 233–5; *Pearl*, ed. Gordon, introd.; Everett, pp. 85–96.

25. *Saint Erkenwald*. Ed. H. L. Savage (1926). Written in the Northwest Midland dialect, possibly about 1386 and possibly by the author of *The Pearl*. The poem deals with the question which vexed Dante and Langland, whether the

righteous heathen can be saved. Cf. *CBEL*, I, 203; Wells, ch. V, 41; Baugh, p. 238; *Saint Erkenwald*, ed. Savage, introd.; R. W. Chambers, "Long Will, Dante, and the Righteous Heathen," *Essays and Studies of the English Association*, IX (1923), 50 ff.

26. *Abraham and Isaac*. Text in J. Q. Adams, *Chief Pre-Shakespearean Dramas* (1924), pp. 117–24. The play consists of 465 lines in rimed stanzas and was composed, probably in Suffolk, late in the fourteenth century on the basis of the Chester play on the same subject. It was probably acted on a "pageant," or movable stage, as was common in England, and is notable for its naturalness and pathos. On medieval drama see *CBEL*, I, 274–9; V, 156–8; Wells, ch. XIV; Baugh, pp. 276–83; Chambers, pp. 1–65, 207–18; H. W. Wells and R. S. Loomis, *Representative Medieval and Tudor Plays* (1942), introd.; H. Craig, *English Religious Drama of the Middle Ages* (1955). On *Abraham and Isaac* cf. *ibid.*, pp. 305–10; Wells, ch. IV, 10.

27. John Barbour, *The Bruce*. Ed. W. M. Mackenzie (1909). Consists of over 13,500 lines in couplets. It was written in 1375 by John Barbour, archdeacon of Aberdeen, who was born about 1320, studied at Oxford, was royal auditor of Scotland, and died in 1395. The poem is a somewhat romantic chronicle of the Scottish king, Robert Bruce, the victor of the battle of Bannockburn (1314), which inspired Burns to write his well known "Bruce's Address to His Army." Cf. *CBEL*, I, 168; V, 118; Wells, ch. III, 8; *CHEL*, II, ch. V; F. Brie, *Die nationale Literatur Schottlands* (1937), pp. 33–122.

28. *Thomas of Erceldoune*. Text in Cook, pp. 70–80. This romance, composed 1388–1400, served as an introduction to political prophecies credited to a certain Thomas Rymer, who lived at Earlston in the Scottish Border country in the thirteenth century, and was still venerated throughout Scotland in the nineteenth. The story told to account for Thomas's prophetic powers is similar to an anecdote related of a Welsh visionary and to traditions about Morgan le Fay. It was a great favorite with Walter Scott. Cf. *CBEL*, I, 168; Wells, ch. IV, 25; *PMLA*, XXIII (1908), 375–420; *Thomas of Erceldoune*, ed. J. A. H. Murray, EETS 61 (1875), introd.; H. M. Flasdieck, *Tom der Reimer: Von keltischen Fee und politischen Propheten* (1934); F. J. Child, *English and Scottish Popular Ballads* (1956), I, 317–23.

29. *The Travels of Sir John Mandeville*. Ed. P. Hamelius, EETS 153 (1919). Except for occasional mistakes and the addition of the papal confirmation, the book is a faithful rendering into Southeast Midland prose, late in the fourteenth century, of an Anglo-French original composed about 1356 by an unidentified Englishman. A slightly later French version, doctored by a notary of Liège in Belgium, has caused much confusion. Of course, the book was a hoax; almost every sentence was derived from a romance of Alexander, a pilgrim's guide to the Holy Land, an encyclopedia, or some authentic account of travels in Asia. By his zest for marvels, confidential manner, and somewhat liberal opinions,

the author achieved a sensation, and his book was translated into almost every European language, and was one of those which inspired Columbus to sail west to India. Cf. *CBEL*, I, 191; Wells, ch. X, 31; Baugh, p. 267. All previous discussions of the original text and its author have been rendered obsolete by Josephine W. Bennett, *The Rediscovery of Sir John Mandeville* (1954).

30, 31. John Purvey, *The General Prolog to the Translation of the Old Testament; Translation of the Bible.* Texts in Wyclif, *Select English Writings*, ed. H. E. Winn (1929), pp. 26–9, and *Wycliffite Versions of the Holy Bible*, ed. J. Forshall and F. Madden (1850). Purvey was a secular clerk of Oxford, an outstanding scholar, and a disciple of Wyclif. He was, in all probability, the author of the second Wyclifite translation of the Bible, which was completed by 1395. Within the next year or two he wrote the *General Prolog*, a long tract in defense of such translations. He was imprisoned, recanted in 1401, and died some time after 1410. Cf. Wells, ch. VIII, 41; G. P. Krapp, *The Rise of English Literary Prose* (1915), pp. 220–32; G. G. Coulton, *Medieval Panorama* (1938), pp. 485–92, 681–8; M. Deanesly, *The Lollard Bible* (1920), pp. 225–85.

32. *A Treatise against Miracle-Plays.* Text in E. Mätzner, *Altenglische Sprach-proben*, pt. II (1900), 222 ff.; selections in Cook, pp. 278–86. Written in prose of the late fourteenth century by a Wyclifite, whose attitude was shared by some orthodox churchmen. Cf. Wells, ch. XII, 77; G. R. Owst, *Literature and Pulpit in Medieval England* (1933), pp. 479–85.

33. William Langland, *The Vision concerning Piers Plowman.* Ed. W. W. Skeat (1886). Three versions are preserved, which used to be assigned roughly to the years 1362, 1377, and 1393, but the first seems to fit better the situation after 1373, the second may have taken two or three years to complete, and the third should probably be moved back to about 1387 or earlier. The general trend of opinion now is that the author was named William Langland, was born about 1332 near the Malvern Hills on the Welsh border, perhaps the illegitimate son of a landed gentleman and a peasant woman, was schooled in a monastery, came to London, and made a meager living by singing psalms and repeating the paternoster. In its pungent and sometimes lofty phrasing, its fierce intensity, the poem is one of the great medieval masterpieces. Cf. *CBEL*, I, 197–200; V, 126–8; Wells, ch. IV, 51; Baugh, pp. 241–7; M. W. Bloomfield, "Present Status of Piers Plowman Studies," *Speculum*, XIV (1939), 215–32; Kane, pp. 182–248; R. W. Chambers, *Man's Unconquerable Mind* (1939), pp. 97–169. A modern rendering of the whole poem, combining readings from all three versions, was made by H. W. Wells (1935), with introduction by N. Coghill. See also D. and R. Attwater, *The Book concerning Piers the Plowman*, Everyman's Library.

34. *Piers the Plowman's Creed.* Ed. W. W. Skeat, EETS 30 (1867). A Wyclifite attack on the friars, written in 1394. Cf. *CBEL*, I, 200; Wells, ch. IV, 53; Baugh, p. 247.

35. John Gower, *Confessio Amantis*. Ed. G. C. Macaulay, *Complete Works of Gower*, vols. II, III (1901). The author, a landed gentleman of Kent, was born about 1330, married in 1398, shortly after became blind, died in 1408, and was buried in what is now Southwark cathedral, then a priory. Besides some minor pieces, Gower wrote a long didactic poem in French, a satire on the times in Latin elegiacs, and a poem in English, *Confessio Amantis*, of over 33,000 lines in couplets (three versions, 1390–1393). He was a trusted friend of Chaucer and a skillful metrist. Cf. *CBEL*, I, 205–8; V, 129 f.; Baugh, pp. 164–6; W. P. Ker, *Essays in Medieval Literature* (1905), pp. 101–34; G. R. Coffman, "John Gower in His Most Significant Role," *Univ. of Colorado Studies*, ser. B, v. II, No. 4 (1945), 52–61. On source of tale of Florent cf. S. Eisner, *A Tale of Wonder* (1958).

36. Thomas Clanvowe, *The Cuckoo and the Nightingale*. Text in *Chaucerian and Other Pieces*, ed. W. W. Skeat (1897), pp. 347–58. Sir Thomas Clanvowe was a kinsman of Sir John Clanvowe, Chaucer's friend, and was a member of the court circle. The poem (also called *The Book of Cupid*) was written, perhaps, in 1392. It was modernized by Wordsworth in 1801. Cf. Baugh, p. 293; *Chaucerian Pieces*, ed. Skeat, pp. lvii–lxi; C. E. Ward, "The Authorship of the *Cuckoo and the Nightingale*," *MLN*, XLIV (1929), 217–26.

37, 38. Thomas Hoccleve, *La Male Regle; The Regement of Princes*. Works, ed. F. J. Furnivall, EETS 61, 72 (1892, 1897). Hoccleve was born about 1368, became a government clerk at Westminster when about twenty years old, was befriended by Chaucer, whose portrait he caused to be painted in the margin of *The Regement of Princes*, married about 1410, and died in retirement at the priory of Southwick, Hampshire, about 1437. Government salaries were irregularly paid, and several of Hoccleve's poems were appeals for financial help. *La Male Regle* was written in 1406; *The Regement of Princes* (5463 lines) was written in 1411–12 and was addressed to Prince Hal. Cf. *CBEL*, I, 252 f.; Baugh, pp. 297 f.; E. P. Hammond, *English Verse between Chaucer and Surrey* (1927), pp. 53–76; H. S. Bennett, *Six Medieval Men and Women* (Cambridge, 1955), pp. 69–92.

39. John Lydgate, *The Temple of Glass*. Ed. J. Schick, EETSES 60 (1891). Born about 1375 a few miles from Bury St. Edmunds, Suffolk, the poet spent most of his life as a monk in the famous monastery of the place, and died in 1449. But he seems to have seen a good deal of the world, and wrote for noble and royal patrons, as well as for the citizens of London. He has left over 140,000 lines of verse, in various metres and of many types—religious and secular allegory, romances of Troy and Thebes, lives of the saints and of the Virgin, begging poems, verses for tapestry, etc. His prosody is awkward, and his other defects of style, as well as his echoing of Chaucer, are illustrated in *The Temple of Glass*, composed in heroic couplets and rime royal in 1410. Cf. *CBEL*, I, 250–2; V, 146; Baugh, pp. 295–7; Bennett, *Chaucer*, pp. 110 f., 138–46,

289–92; Hammond, *English Verse*, pp. 77–187; C. S. Lewis, *The Allegory of Love* (1936), pp. 239–43; *The Temple of Glass*, ed. Schick, introd.; W. F. Schirmer, *Lydgate, ein Kulturbild aus dem fünfzehnten Jahrhundert* (1952).

40. King James I of Scotland, *The King's Quair*. Ed. W. M. Mackenzie (1939). King James was born in 1394, was captured on a voyage to France by the English in 1406, and held prisoner for eighteen years. In 1424 he married Chaucer's grand-niece, the Lady Joan Beaufort, was released from prison and crowned king. After a vigorous rule he was murdered in 1437. *The King's Quair* is generally regarded as an allegorized account of his suit for the Lady Joan, composed about 1423, and as one of the most charming imitations of Chaucer's romantic manner. Cf. *CBEL*, I, 256; V, 147; Baugh, pp. 293 f.; Bennett, *Chaucer*, pp. 170–3, 287; E. M. W. Balfour-Melville, *James I, King of Scots* (1936).

41. *The Pilgrims at Canterbury* (from *The Tale of Beryn*). Text in *The Tale of Beryn*, ed. F. J. Furnivall (1887), pp. 1–24; also EETSES 105 (1909). Composed between 1400 and 1450, perhaps by a Canterbury monk, as an introduction to a second tale by the Merchant. Cf. Baugh, p. 292; *Text of the Canterbury Tales*, ed. J. M. Manly and E. Rickert (1940), I, 391 f.

42. *Gesta Romanorum*. Ed. S. J. Herrtage, EETSES 33 (1879). A translation in the Midland dialect, made in the first half of the fifteenth century. The original was a Latin collection of *exempla* (illustrative tales), compiled in England by a Franciscan friar about 1340. It was the most famous of such compilations made for the use of preachers, and illustrates the tendency toward sensationalism and strained applications. Cf. *CBEL*, I, 266, 301; Bennett, *Chaucer*, pp. 186 f., 305 f.; J. T. Welter, *L'Exemplum dans la littérature religieuse et didactique du moyen âge* (1927), pp. 369–74. For influence on Shakespeare cf. W. W. Lawrence, *Shakespeare's Problem Comedies* (1931), pp. 19–22.

43–46. *Four Christmas Carols*. Texts in Cook, pp. 464, 466; A. W. Pollard, *Fifteenth-Century Prose and Verse*, pp. 89 f., 92. On Christmas carols cf. Chambers, pp. 82–104. On No. 43 cf. Kane, pp. 161–5; *MP*, VII (1909–10), 165–7. On carols in general cf. R. L. Greene, *Early English Carols* (1935).

47. *He Bare Him Up, He Bare Him Down*. Text in Cook, pp. 440 f. Late fifteenth century. The deposition of Christ's body from the cross has been strangely blended with the concept of the Maimed King in the hall of the Grail castle. Cf. Greene, *Early English Carols*, pp. liv–lvi, 221 f., 411 f.; Kane, pp. 174 f.

48. *The Divine Paradox*. Text in Carleton Brown, *Religious Lyrics of the XVth Century* (1939), p. 187. Cf. *ibid.*, pp. 330 f.; Kane, p. 153.

Bibliography and Notes

49. *I Have a Noble Cock.* Text in Cook, p. 429. Composed about 1450.

50. *St. Stephen and Herod.* Text in *English and Scottish Popular Ballads*, ed. H. C. Sargent and G. L. Kittredge (1904), pp. 282–6. An amusing ballad of the mid-fifteenth century, showing popular distortion of the biblical account of Stephen's martyrdom. Cf. F. J. Child, *English and Scottish Popular Ballads*, I, 233–41.

51. *Robin Hood and the Monk.* Text in *English and Scottish Popular Ballads*, ed. Sargent and Kittredge, pp. 282–6. A spirited ballad written down about 1400, but recited or sung earlier among the country folk of Nottinghamshire. Ballads on the outlaw and his band were familiar in the fourteenth century, and a Robin Hood's Stone in Yorkshire was mentioned in 1322. Who Robin Hood was and when he lived is unknown, but the ballads about him seem to express the economic and antimonastic sentiments which became pronounced in the fourteenth century. Three other ballads of this group survive from the fifteenth century and many from the sixteenth. On all these cf. Baugh, p. 311; Chambers, pp. 129–37, 228; W. E. Simeone, "The Historic Robin Hood," *Journal of American Folklore*, LXVI (1953), pp. 303–8. On ballads in general cf. *CBEL*, I, 272 f.; V, 155; Baugh, pp. 308–12; W. J. Entwistle, *European Balladry* (1951); M. J. C. Hodgart, *The Ballads* (1950). On ballad tunes and American survivals of British ballads cf. Evelyn Wells, *The Ballad Tree* (1950).

52. *London Lickpenny.* Text in A. R. Benham, *English Literature from Widsith to the Death of Chaucer* (1916), pp. 351–4. A popular satire, wrongly attributed to Lydgate, describing the experiences of a plowman in the Westminster law-courts and among the tradesmen of London. Cf. Hammond, *English Verse*, pp. 237–9, 476–8.

53. *The Book of Margery Kempe.* Ed. S. B. Meech and H. E. Allen, EETS 212 (1940). This remarkable autobiography was dictated by a well-to-do but illiterate woman of King's Lynn, Norfolk, and was revised in 1436. It displays the effect of the mystical writings of England and Germany on a hysterical temperament. Margery was born about 1373 and died in or after 1438. Cf. Baugh, 230 f.; H. S. Bennett, *Six Medieval Men and Women*, pp. 124–50; H. Thurston, "Margery the Astonishing," *The Month*, Nov. 1936, pp. 446–56.

54. *The Examination of William Thorpe.* Modernized version in A. W. Pollard, *Fifteenth-Century Prose and Verse* (1903), pp. 97–174. Thorpe studied at Oxford, took priest's orders, was tried for heresy in 1397 and imprisoned. On his release he continued to preach even after the first burnings of the Lollards, was examined by Arundell, Archbishop of Canterbury in 1407, and wrote an account of the dialogue. Cf. Bennett, *Chaucer*, pp. 182–4, 298. On Arundell cf. H. B. Workman, *John Wyclif* (1926), II, 341–59.

55. *The Paston Letters.* Ed. J. Gairdner (1904). The Pastons were landed gentry of Norfolk, and some 1100 letters, written by or addressed to them, survive and give a most strikingly intimate picture of the period between 1422 and 1509. A selection from them is given in Everyman's Library. Cf. H. S. Bennett, *The Pastons and Their England* (1922).

56. *The Second Shepherds' Play.* Text in Cook, pp. 524–54. The mystery play cycle to which this play belongs was composed for performance by the craft gilds of Wakefield in the West Riding of Yorkshire. Five of them (including two on the Nativity) are attributed to the so-called Wakefield Master, who wrote between 1420 and 1450. The second of the Nativity plays, with its rugged realism combined with reverence, is the supreme example of English comedy before the Elizabethans. Cf. *CBEL*, I, 277 f. (Towneley Plays); V, 158; Wells, ch. XIV, 7; Baugh, p. 281; Chambers, *English Literature*, pp. 34–41, 214 f.; H. A. Watt, "The Dramatic Unity of the *Secunda Pastorum*," in *Essays and Studies in Honor of Carleton Brown* (1940), pp. 158–66. M. Carey, *The Wakefield Group in the Towneley Cycle* (1929); R. C. Cosbey, "The Mak Story," *Speculum*, XX (1945), 310–7; H. Craig, *English Religious Drama of the Middle Ages*, pp. 151–8, 199–234.

57. Robert Henryson, *The Testament of Cresseid.* Text in *Chief British Poets of the 14th and 15th Centuries*, ed. W. A. Neilson and K. G. T. Webster (1916), pp. 367–75. Henryson was a schoolmaster at Dunfermline, Scotland, may have studied law at Glasgow University in 1462, and practised as notary in 1477. He composed a sprightly pastoral, some animal fables in the Aesopic tradition, and *The Testament of Cresseid* in the Chaucerian tradition. He is distinguished for his social feeling, keen observation, and dramatic power. Cf. *CBEL*, I, 257 f.; V, 147; Baugh, p. 294; Bennett, *Chaucer*, pp. 173–6; M. W. Stearns, *A Study of Robert Henryson* (1948).

58, 59. William Caxton, *The Golden Legend;* Preface to Malory's *Book of Arthur and His Knights. The Golden Legend* (modernized) ed. F. S. Ellis. Caxton was born in Kent about 1421, and after becoming a prosperous merchant in Flanders, took up the art of printing, published his first translation from a French romance of Troy in 1472, and in 1476 set up the first English printing press at Westminster. Here he published nearly 100 books, of which twenty-four were his own translations. Some of the hundred were service books or merely utilitarian, but the rest represent fairly the whole range of English literary taste on the eve of the Renaissance. Caxton published in 1483 *The Golden Legend*, which he had redacted, with the aid of an earlier English and a French translation, from the most famous collection of readings (*legenda*) for the ecclesiastical year, that made by Jacopo da Varagine, Archbishop of Genoa, about 1260. Cf. *CBEL*, I, 261–3; V, 148; Baugh, pp. 301–7; Bennett, *Chaucer*, pp. 203–13, 267–70; N. S. Aurner, *Caxton* (1926). On Preface to Malory cf. *Works of Sir Thomas Malory*, ed. E. Vinaver (1947), I, pp. xxix–xxxv, cxi–cxv.

60. Sir Thomas Malory, *The Book of Arthur and His Knights*. Ed. E. Vinaver (1947). Malory came of a Warwickshire family, served in the garrison of Calais, probably in 1436, and saw service again in Northumberland in 1462–3. He sat as a member of Parliament in 1445, but between 1450 and 1460 he was accused of all sorts of violent crimes, from horse-thieving to attempted murder, but was never convicted. He spent much of this decade in prison, and was again in prison when he made his abridgement of French prose romances and of two English poems, which he completed in 1469 and called *The Book of Arthur and His Knights*. He died in 1471. Caxton edited and published it in 1485 with the mistaken title of *Le Morte d'Arthur*. Cf. Chambers, pp. 185–205, 229–31; *Arthurian Literature in the Middle Ages,* ed. R. S. Loomis, pp. 541–52; W. H. Schofield, *Chivalry in English Literature* (1912), pp. 87–110; R. D. Altick, *The Scholar Adventurers* (1951), pp. 65–85; Baugh, pp. 305–7. On the Grail legend see R. S. Loomis, *Wales and the Arthurian Legend* (1956), 19–41; A. Pauphilet, *Etudes sur la Queste del Saint Graal* (1921).

61. *The Nut-Brown Maid.* Text in *Early English Lyrics*, ed. Chambers and Sidgwick, pp. 34–48. This moving dialogue was written about 1500 and seems intended for dramatic recital by two impersonators. It belongs to the long-drawn-out controversy over the question whether women were essentially vicious or virtuous. Cf. A. K. Moore, "The Form and Content of the *Notbrowne Mayde*," MLN, LXV (1950), 11–16; F. L. Utley, *The Crooked Rib* (1944).

62. *Everyman.* Text in J. Q. Adams, *Chief Pre-Shakespearean Dramas* (1924), pp. 288–303. A morality play, translated from the Dutch *Elckerlijc* about 1500. The basic idea is derived from the parable of the man and his three friends, which is found in *The Golden Legend* and the *Gesta Romanorum* (see above, pp. 383 f.) and goes back to a lost Buddhist source. The play also shows the influence of the Dance of Death. Its power has been proved by many successful performances in modern times. Cf. CBEL, I, 515; V, 247; Baugh, p. 286; *Everyman,* ed. K. Goedeke (1865); J. M. Manly, "*Elkerlijc-Everyman*: the Question of Priority," MP, VIII (1910), 269–77. On morality plays cf. E. N. S. Thompson, *English Moral Plays* (1910); W. R. Mackenzie, *English Moralities from the Point of View of Allegory* (1914); W. Farnham, *The Medieval Heritage of Elizabethan Tragedy* (1936), pp. 173–212.